BEITRÄGE ZUR REGIONALEN GEOLOGIE DER ERDE BAND 12

# BEITRÄGE ZUR REGIONALEN GEOLOGIE DER ERDE

Herausgegeben von Prof. Dr. F. Bender, Hannover,
Prof. Dr. V. Jacobshagen, Berlin, Prof. Dr. J. D. de Jong,
Heemstede/Niederlande, und Prof. Dr. G. Lüttig, Hannover
Band 12

Raoul C. Mitchell-Thomé

# GEOLOGY OF THE MIDDLE ATLANTIC ISLANDS

1976

GEBRÜDER BORNTRAEGER · BERLIN · STUTTGART

# GEOLOGY OF THE
# MIDDLE ATLANTIC ISLANDS

*by*

### Dr. Raoul C. Mitchell-Thomé

*Consulting Geologist-Geophysicist*
*Mamer, Gr. D. de Luxembourg*

*With 102 figures and 68 tables*
*in the text and on 5 folders*

1976

GEBRÜDER BORNTRAEGER · BERLIN · STUTTGART

«Le chef de toutes les sciences est sans contredit le point d'interrogation; nous devons la plupart des grandes découvertes
au COMMENT? et la sagesse dans la vie consiste peut-être à
se demander à tout propos: ‹Pourquoi?›. Mais aussi cette factice
prescience détruit-elle nos illusions.»

HONORÉ DE BALZAC

Alle Rechte, auch die der Übersetzung, des auszugsweisen Nachdrucks, der Herstellung
von Mikrofilmen und der photomechanischen Wiedergabe, vorbehalten
© 1976 by Gebrüder Borntraeger, Berlin · Stuttgart
Papier: Papierfabrik Scheufelen KG, Oberlenningen
Druck: Maisch + Queck, Gerlingen
Printed in Germany

ISBN 3 443 11012 6

# Preface

The authors of that incomparable funny book "1066 and All That", began with a page entitled "Compulsory Preface (This Means You)". The public demand a preamble, a clearing of the throat, as it were, so herewith a preface, which by rights should state the subject, scope, character, purpose, the problems and views expressed.

This work then treats of those islands long known before the age of tourism has made many almost household words. Of all the islands spread out across the immensity of the Atlantic Ocean, none are so well known to the world at large, none have captivated adventurer, scholar, traveller to the same extent. The motives propelling such people to these islands have differed, yet all who have known them have been unanimous in their enthusiasms, whether for material gain, scholarly acquisition or relaxation, that these Atlantic archipelagoes have an attraction, from many points of view, which can scarce be met anywhere else in the world. Travel brochures should rightly be scanned with a jaundiced eye, but as regards natural attractions, of climate, seascape and landscape, for once such blurbs come very near the truth.

Since the publications of GAGEL in 1910 and VON WOLFF in 1931, no book has appeared treating of the geology of these Middle Atlantic islands. In the past 45 odd years, a great amount of new knowledge has come into our hands, as perusal of the bibliography will show. Further, the pace of geological and geophysical interest is quickening, at this time several projects are under way by institutions and scientific groups, the tempo of new publications increases.

It is with the intention of providing an appreciation of geological studies ranging over a period of 170 years, condensing into the limits of a convenient-sized volume, that the writing of this book has been undertaken.

As these are all volcanic islands, the importance of the volcanics and all aspects of such must obviously take a prominent place in what follows. But because the petrography, petrochemistry, petrogenesis of igneous rocks looms so large in the literature, the writer intentionally has tried to give a fair coverage of other geological considerations, in order to present a more balanced account. Slowly a start is being made in geophysical and geochronological studies, the new global tectonic approach no less is paying attention to the general region, though at times, some schemes proposed often seem rather akin to special pleadings.

For most of these archipelagoes, sterling reconnaissance studies date back a hundred years and more, and for some island groups, only recently have more detailed investigations been made. It is right then that due recognition be taken of these early works, to indicate the foundations and historic continuity upon which those who came after have built upon.

Two of the oldest points at issue are those related to the connexions if any, by what means, to what degree, of these Atlantic archipelagoes with the mainlands of Africa and/or Europe, and the origin of those imposing calderas – a word whose origin stems from the Canary Islands. In both instances, we still cannot be dogmatic one way or the other about such topics.

Macaronesia lies in a region of strategic global tectonic concern. The temptation to engage in discussions involving the Mid-Atlantic Ridge, plate tectonics, ocean-floor spreading, Wegenerian drift, has been strong, but it had to be realized that this is not a tectonic presentation, it is not concerned with the origin of the Atlantic, movements of continents and ocean floors; the topic is the geology of the Middle Atlantic Islands. Hence for this reason and to keep within space limits, such matters are given only passing reference.

From what follows it will be clear that much remains to be done in these islands, there is ample choice for the geologist, whatever his speciality, Earth scientists have a delightful happy hunting ground awaiting them.

Due to circumstances beyond the control of both the publisher and the author, the final printing of the book has undergone a long delay, the MS being received by the publisher in mid-1974. Publisher and author would trust that the reader, being thus made aware of delays, would excuse them, as for reasons stated above, publications and references to works which have appeared in print since mid-1974 could not be incorporated in the original MS.

The secret of oratory lies in having the opening and the closing of the speech as conveniently close as possible. Following upon such sound advice, let this suffice by way of a foreward.

> "Here are we for the last time face to face,
> Thou and I, Book, before I bid thee speed
> Upon thy perilous journey".

Mamer, Gr. D. de Luxembourg

RAOUL C. MITCHELL-THOMÉ

# Table of Contents

CHAPTER 1

## Introduction

Relatively close to the coasts of Iberia and N.Africa lie several archipelagoes. As far back as some 4,500 years, in the protohistoric period of the Bronze Age and before the Iron civilizations arose, peoples from Mediterranean and/or African regions ventured out into the boisterous waters of the Atlantic, some to settle in the Canary Islands, forming the aboriginal population of the Guanches.

Not till the 14th and 15th centuries, however, were these archipelagoes discovered – or then re-discovered – by Spanish and Portuguese adventurers. Since then, increasingly have the islands become better known to the world at large, and today the annual influx of one or two million tourists speak well for the great attraction which many islands afford, and no less speak ill for the pristine charm, quiet and beauty which once reigned here.

These entrancing Middle Atlantic Islands have been collectively termed Macaronesia, patterned after Polynesia, Melanesia and Micronesia of the Western Pacific. It seems probable that the English naturalist P. BARKER WEBB was the first to use the name in a publication of J. HOOKER (1849), although the popularizing of the name originates with CHEVALIER (1935). The succinctness of ›Macaronesia‹ in contrast to the more cumbersome ›Middle Atlantic Islands‹ is apparent, though for the title of this volume the writer uses the latter in keeping with his earlier work on the South Atlantic Islands.

Since the earliest days of European discovery and settlement, these archipelagoes have remained firmly in the hands of the Spaniards and Portuguese. All, except the Cape Verde Islands, are administratively integral parts of Spain and Portugal, respectively. The Cape Verde Islands were Overseas Territories (Provincia Ultramarina), though one might be forgiven showing surprise at the large notice »Portugal« which once greeted the visitor on arriving at the international airport at Sal, some 2,600 km distant from metropolitan Portugal.

The archipelagoes are scattered over 2,700 km km in latitude, 1,800 km in longitude, have a total area of ca. 15,000 km². Inter-archipelago communications are poor other than via small, crowded coastal vessels with irregular schedules and itineries. Hence the easiest, and certainly the most comfortable way to engage in inter-archipelago journeys is to take regular liners and planes originating from Lisbon, Madrid and major Spanish

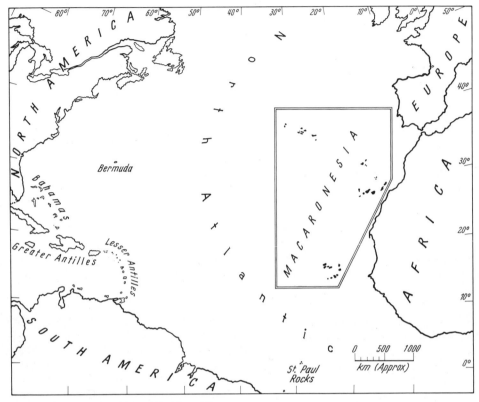

Fig. 1. Macaronesia and its Atlantic setting.

ports, much lesser so from Dakar, Gibralter. On the other hand, movement within the archipelagoes is much better, except perhaps the general infrequency of scheduled trips.

It is interesting to note that earlier scholars, in more distant leisurely times, travelled more from one to the other archipelago than is done today by those bent on scientific studies. VON HUMBOLDT, SAINT-CLAIRE DEVILLE, WOLLASTON, HARTUNG, GAGEL, FRIEDLÄNDER all visited more than one archipelago making observations. In later days scholars no doubt found there was quite enough to engage their interests in one archipelago, in one island, indeed in one particular district. The advantages of travel via luxurious liners and jet planes conform to the modern trend of haste, the need to hurry up and finish the thesis, complete the field and laboratory studies before the grants expire.

Such officers as ZBYSZEWSKI, C. A. and O. V. FERREIRA of the Serviços Geologicos de Portugal, have covered the Azores and Madeira, but in only two instances have single individuals attempted investigations on an archipelago basis. BEBIANO carried out reconnaissance studies in the Cape Verde Islands prior to his important contribution of 1932. The Finnish geologist HAUSEN carried out extensive investigations in the Canary Islands between 1947 and 1972, publishing monographs on each island. These one-man studies of Prof. HAUSEN represent a truly herculean effort and all interested in the geology of these islands owe him a very great debt.

The writer is best acquaint with the Cape Verde Islands, but with the exception of the Selvagens archipelago, all have been visited on several occasions during the past 35 years.

Only the Cape Verde archipelago lies beyond the reaches of tourism – but propaganda is on the way, big plans are ahead, alas. For at least five to six months annually, the Azores, Madeira, the Canaries are inundated with tourists, vast building projects of hotels, roads, super-highways, airports, harbour extensions are marring all that is lovely, serene, idyllic. Property developers, tourist agents are forever on the prowl: one had better hurry and see these beautiful islands ere it is too late, and already large coastal sections have become sheer horrors, roaring jets disturb the quiet of mountains and beaches alike, garish behemoths of hotels ruin the pleasing aspect of hill and strand alike.

For some 170 years geological interest has been shown of these Atlantic outposts. Yet from what follows, it is obvious that a host of geological problems remain, much mapping is still needed, the geophysicist and geochronologist no less have plenty at their disposal, the quest goes on, there is so much to captivate the earth scientist.

## Acknowledgements

It is with pleasure and gratitude that acknowledgements are made to many who have proven loyal and generous with their assistance in many ways, and the writer would express his indebtedness to: Dr. E. AGUIRRE, Eng. M. F. ALEXANDRE, Dr. F. M. ALMEIDA, Exmo. Senh. J. M. ALMEIDA, Prof. I. AMARAL, Dr. F. A. APARICIO, Srta. C. ARRIBAS, Prof. C. F. T. ASSUNÇAO, Dr. J. M. AYMÉ, Dr. L. A. BARROS, Dr. W. A. BERGGREN, Prof. L. BERTHOIS, Dr. B. BOOTH, Dr. G. BORLEY, Prof. A. CENDRERO, Prof. Dr. G. COLOM, Dr. S. CORON, Prof. M. E. DENAEYER, Dr. R. DINGMAN, Dr. O. V. FERREIRA, Prof. R. FURON, Prof. H. HAUSEN, Dr. A. HERNANDEZ-PACHECO, Dr. E. IBARROLA, Dr. J. KLERKX, Prof. H. KLUG, Prof. K. KREJCI-GRAF, Dr. X. LE PICHON, Dr. J. LIETZ, Dr. F. MACHADO, Dr. J. M. MARTINS, Prof. R. G. MASON, Prof. J. MATZNETTER, Mr. G. E. MAUL, Mr. J. MECO, Dr. L. A. MENDES-VICTOR, Dr. E. MIDDLEMOST, Exmo. Senh. R. B. MOITA, Dr. L. MONTAGGIONI, Prof. O. RIBEIRO, Dr. W. I. RIDLEY, Dr. P. RONA, Dr. P. ROTHE, Eng. L. SALDANHA, Prof. H-U. SCHMINCKE, Dr. A. SERRALHEIRO, Prof. K. SMULIKOWSKI, Dr. J. M. P. SOARES, Dr. K. STAESCHE, Dr. H. TAZIEFF, Prof. M. VUAGNAT, Dr. N. D. WATKINS, Dr. G. ZBYSZEWSKI.

Further thanks are extended to: Departmento de Petrologia, Universidad de Madrid; Instituto Geografico y Catastral, Madrid; Instituto Geologico y Minero de Espana; Instituto »Lucas Mallada«, Madrid; Instituto »Juan Sebastian Elcano«, Madrid; Instituto de Estudios Africanos, Madrid; Oficina de Informacion de Turismo, Madrid; Instituto Geografico e Cadastral, Lisbon; Serviços Geologicos de Portugal, Lisbon; Sociedade de Geografia de Lisboa; Junta de Investigaçoes do Ultramar, Lisbon; Agencia-Geral do Ultramar, Lisbon; Museu e Laboratorio Mineralogico e Geologico, Universidade de Coimbra; National Statistical Institute, Lisbon; Dirrecçao-Geral do Turismo, Lisbon; Museu Municipal do Funchal, Madeira; El Museo Canario, Las Palmas, Gran Canaria;

Laboratoire de Géologie du Muséum National d'Histoire Naturelle, Paris; Institut Océanographique, Monaco; Institut royal des Sciences naturelles de Belgique, Bruxelles; Tourist Information Bureaux in the various archipelagoes.

To all the above the author would express his profound thanks, but whatever the shortcomings, he alone must assume responsibility. Finally to Dr. E. NÄGELE, of Gebrüder Borntraeger Verlagsbuchhandlung and E. Schweizerbart'sche Verlagsbuchhandlung, a special word of thanks for his unfailing kindness, consideration and helpfulness at all stages, whereby publisher and author have established a rare working relationship.

CHAPTER 2

# The Geography of Macaronesia

## Macaronesia

Macaronesia includes the archipelagoes in the lower latitudes on the eastern side of the North Atlantic. The area in question extends between latitudes 39°45' N and 14°49' N, between longitudes 31°17' W and 13°20' W of Greenwich.

The total area of these Middle Atlantic Islands is approx. 14,700 km², comprised as follows: Canary Islands, 7,500 km², Cape Verde Islands, 4,033 km²; Azores, 2,344 km²; Madeira, 810 km² and Selvagens, ca. 4 km². Corvo, northernmost island in the Azores, is some 2,700 km distant from Brava, southernmost island in the Cape Verde archipelago, whilst the E-W extent, between Flores (Azores) and Fuerteventura (Canary Islands) is ca. 1,800 km. Flores, the most westerly island in Macaronesia, lies some 1,900 km distant from the Portuguese mainland, whilst Fuerteventura lies ca. 100 km off the African coast.

W of the coasts of Iberia and Northern Africa, the Atlantic descends to depths in excess of 5,000 m, Madeira, Selvagens, Canary and Cape Verde Islands lying between the 5,000 m isobath and the mainlands of Europe and Africa. To the W of these archipelagoes a broad stretch of water runs N-S greater than 5,000 m in depth, but to the W of this deeper zone the sea bed rises to form the Mid-Atlantic Ridge, near which stands the Azores. In a bathymetric sense, therefore, the Azores are quite separate from the other archipelagoes.

The highest summit in Macaronesia, and indeed of all the N and S Atlantic Islands, is Pico de Teide, 3,718 m, in Tenerife, Canary Islands. Three other high peaks include Pico, 2,829 m, in Fogo, Cape Verde Islands, Roque de los Muchachos, 2,423 m, La Palma, Canary Islands, and Ponta do Pico, 2,351 m, in Pico, Azores Islands. In contrast to such maximum elevations, highest peaks are only 395 m in Sta. Luzia (Cape Verde), 402 m in Graciosa (Azores), 406 m in Sal and 436 m in Maio, (Cape Verde). No less is there a great difference in the relief of the respective islands, ranging from extremely strong in Sto. Antao (Cape Verde) and La Palma (Canaries), to extremely mild in Sal and Maio (Cape Verde).

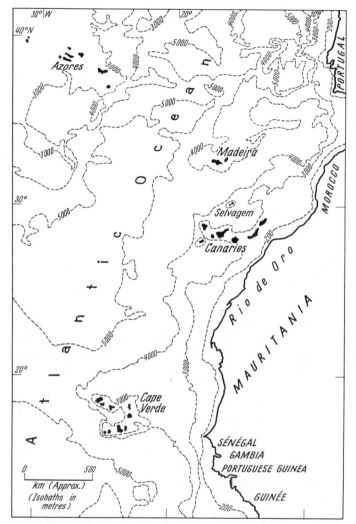

Fig. 2. Geographical location and bathymetry of Macaronesia. (Modified after Carte Gén. Bathy, des Océans, Bur. Hydro. Intern., Monaco, 1968).

Climatically the Middle Atlantic Islands range from warm, temperate (Csa and Csb climates of KÖPPEN) to dry (BWh climate of KÖPPEN). In the western islands of the Azores, for much of the year the climate is quite similar to that of NW Spain, whereas in the eastern Cape Verde islands, climatic conditions parallel those of the neighbouring African mainland.

The primitive vegetation on all islands is sparse in the extreme, this having been drastically depleted by the inhabitants for firewood, construction, some woods exported, as well as domestic animals, especially goats, the animals causing grievous harm not only in consuming the native plants but in promoting soil erosion no less.

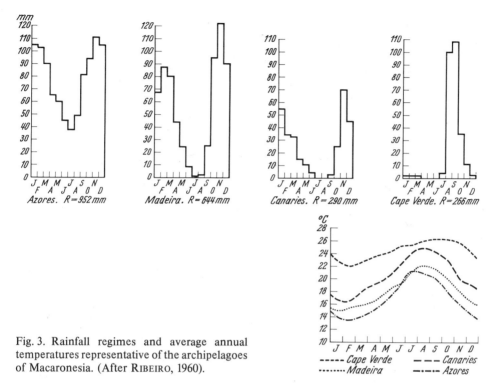

Fig. 3. Rainfall regimes and average annual temperatures representative of the archipelagoes of Macaronesia. (After RIBEIRO, 1960).

On many of the islands, small local industries have been established, largely concerned with products of the lands and seas, construction materials, handicrafts. The only major industry is that of oil refining, centred mostly at Sta. Cruz de Tenerife.

Agriculture and fishing are of prime importance on all islands, and nearly all depend to some extent on the exports of crops, fruits, wine, fish and fish products.

More and more the impact of tourism is felt, and in the Canaries, Madeira and the Azores such is of great significance as a source of revenue. One can understand how the islanders in general are enthusiastic about this new-found source of livelihood, but it is undeniable that much of the natural beauty of the islands has been sadly spoiled – thousands upon thousands of tourists in seminude attire littering the lovely beaches, glaring, cheaply constructed towering hotels dotting the coastal landscapes.

As per the 1970 census figures, the population of Macaronesia is some 1,990,000, with only the Selvagens having no settled inhabitants. In the last decade the Azores and Madeira populations have declined, those of the Canaries and Cape Verde have steadily increased during the past odd 30 years, and in the case of the Cape Verde Islands, pressure of population increase presents grave problems.

The Canary Islands are an integral part of Spain, as are the Azores, Madeira and Selvagens integral parts of Portugal. The Cape Verde Islands formerly constituted part of the Overseas Territories of Portugal. Chief Government representatives are and were the Governors, appointed by the respective mother countries.

Pertinent geographic data for Macaronesia are shown in Table 1.

The Geography of Macaronesia

Table 1         Geographic data regarding the principal islands of the Middle Atlantic Archipelagoes

| Arch. | Island | Mid-N. lat. | Mid-W. long. | Area km$^2$ | Max. elev. m | Name of max. alt. |
|---|---|---|---|---|---|---|
| CAPE VERDE | Sto. Antao | 17° 04' | 25° 10' | 779 | 1979 | Tope de Coroa |
| | S. Vicente | 16° 51' | 24° 59' | 227 | 774 | Mte. Verde |
| | Sta. Luzia | 16° 46' | 24° 45' | 35 | 395 | Toponha |
| | S. Nicolau | 16° 36' | 24° 15' | 343 | 1304 | Mte. Gordo |
| | Sal | 16° 43' | 22° 56' | 216 | 406 | Mte. Grande |
| | Boa Vista | 16° 05' | 22° 50' | 620 | 390 | Estancia |
| | Maio | 15° 13' | 23° 10' | 269 | 436 | Penoso |
| | S. Tiago | 15° 05' | 23° 29' | 991 | 1392 | Pico Antonia |
| | Fogo | 14° 56' | 24° 24' | 476 | 2829 | Pico |
| | Brava | 14° 51' | 24° 43' | 64 | 976 | Fontainhas |
| | Il. Razo | 16° 37' | 24° 36' | 7 | 164 | Mte. Rib. Ladrao |
| | Il. Branco | 16° 39' | 24° 41' | 3 | 327 | Tope de Berca |
| | Il. Grande | 14° 58' | 24° 42' | 2 | 96 | Mte. Grande |
| | Il. Cima | 14° 58' | 24° 39' | 1.2 | 77 | Mte. Ilheu |
| CANARIES | Hierro | 27° 45' | 18° 00' | 278 | 1501 | Malpaso |
| | La Palma | 28° 38' | 17° 52' | 730 | 2423 | Roq. Muchachos |
| | Gomera | 28° 06' | 17° 12' | 380 | 1482 | Garajonay |
| | Tenerife | 28° 30' | 16° 30' | 2058 | 3718 | Pico Teide |
| | Gran Canaria | 27° 56' | 15° 32' | 1532 | 1950 | Pozo Nieves |
| | Fuerteventura | 28° 28' | 14° 45' | 1725 | 807 | Pico Zarza |
| | Lanzarote | 29° 08' | 13° 39' | 796 | 671 | Penas Chache |
| | Graciosa | 29° 14' | 13° 30' | 27 | 266 | Pedro Barba |
| | Alegranza | 29° 23' | 13° 30' | 12 | 289 | La Caldera |
| | Lobos | 28° 45' | 13° 49' | 6 | 122 | La Caldera |
| SELV-AGENS | Selv. Grande | 30° 08' | 16° 51' | ca. 3.5 | 153 | Pico Atalaia |
| | Selv. Pequena | 30° 01' | 16° 01' | ca. 0.5 | 49 | Pico Veado |
| MADEIRA | Madeira | 32° 44' | 16° 58' | 728 | 1862 | Pico Ruivo |
| | Porto Santo | 33° 04' | 16° 20' | 69 | 517 | Pico Facho |
| | Des. Grande | 32° 31' | 16° 30' | ca.10.3 | 478 | . . . . . . . . . . . . . . |
| | Bugio | 32° 25' | 16° 29' | ca. 4 | 384 | . . . . . . . . . . . . . . |
| | Il. Chao | 32° 35' | 16° 32' | ca. 0.5 | 99 | Il. Chao |
| AZORES | Corvo | 39° 42' | 31° 06' | 17 | 718 | Morro Homens |
| | Flores | 39° 27' | 31° 11' | 143 | 914 | Morro Alto |
| | Faial | 38° 35' | 28° 43' | 173 | 1043 | Carego Gordo |
| | Pico | 38° 29' | 28° 17' | 446 | 2351 | Ponta Pico |
| | S. Jorge | 38° 38' | 28° 01' | 246 | 1053 | Pico Esperança |
| | Graciosa | 39° 03' | 28° 02' | 61 | 402 | Caldeira |
| | Terceira | 38° 43' | 27° 12' | 401 | 1021 | Sta. Barbara |
| | S. Miguel | 37° 47' | 25° 29' | 757 | 1103 | Pico Vara |
| | Sta. Maria | 36° 58' | 25° 07' | 97 | 587 | Pico Alto |

## The Azores Archipelago

The islands of the archipelago, including the Formigas Banks, total 10 in number, and lie between latitudes 36°55' and 39°43' N, longitudes 25° and 31°17' W They are thus the farthest N and W of the Macaronesian islands, Flores, the most westerly island of the

| Max. extents km | | Av. ann. temp. °C | Av. ann. rain mm | 1970 Census | Chief town |
|---|---|---|---|---|---|
| 42.7 E–W | 23.9 N–S | 22.6 | 475 | 44,916 | Rib. Grande |
| 24.2 E–W | 16.2 N–S | 23.6 | 175 | 31,462 | Mindelo |
| 12.4 E–W | 5.3 N–S | ? | ? | Uninhab. | . . . . . . . . . . . . |
| 44.4 E–W | 22.0 N–S | 23.9 | 200 | 16.280 | Rib. Brava |
| 11.8 E–W | 29.7 N–S | 23.5 | 95 | 5,622 | Sta. Maria |
| 30.8 E–W | 28.9 N–S | 24.0 | 275 | 3,527 | Sal Rei |
| 16.3 E–W | 24.1 N–S | ? | 373 | 3,466 | Vila de Maio |
| 28.8 E–W | 54.9 N–S | 21.6 | 455 | 129,358 | Praia |
| 23.9 E–W | 26.3 N–S | 22.1 | 665 | 29,592 | S. Felipe |
| 9.3 E–W | 10.5 N–S | 21.5 | 400 | 7,848 | Nova Cintra |
| 3.6 E–W | 2.8 N–S | ? | ? | Uninhab. | . . . . . . . . . . . . |
| 4.0 NW–SE | 1.3 NE–SW | ? | ? | Uninhab. | . . . . . . . . . . . . |
| 1.9 E–W | 2.4 N–S | ? | ? | Uninhab. | . . . . . . . . . . . . |
| 2.4 E–W | 0.7 N–S | ? | ? | Uninhab. | . . . . . . . . . . . . |
| 29.5 NE–SW | 24.5 N–S | ? | 280 | 5,503 | Valverde |
| 27.3 E–W | 45.6 N–S | 19.0 | 450 | 65,291 | Sta. Cruz |
| 24.6 E–W | 22.3 N–S | 19.3 | ? | 19,339 | S. Sebastian |
| 78.0 NE–SW | 44.5 N–S | 21.1 | 430 | 500,381 | Sta. Cruz |
| 45.2 E–W | 46.0 N–S | 19.6 | 400 | 519,606 | Las Palmas |
| 32.8 E–W | 104.8 NE–SW | 21.0 | 130 | 18,192 | Puerto Rosario |
| 38.0 E–W | 64.0 NE–SW | 20.5 | 175 | 41,912 | Arrecife |
| 4.6 E–W | 8.3 NE–SW | ? | ? | ? | Calheta |
| 4.0 E–W | 3.5 N–S | ? | ? | ? | Alegranza |
| 2.3 E–W | 3.2 N–S | ? | ? | ? | El Puertilo |
| 1.9 E–W | 1.8 N–S | ? | ? | Uninhab. | . . . . . . . . . . . . |
| 0.8 E–W | 0.5 N–S | ? | ? | Uninhab. | . . . . . . . . . . . . |
| 57.6 E–W | 23.0 N–S | 18.8 | 602 | 253,220 | Funchal |
| 11.7 NE–SW | 6.7 NW–SE | 19.0 | 355 | 3,927 | Porto Santo |
| 1.9 E–W | 10.5 N–S | ? | ? | Uninhab. | . . . . . . . . . . . . |
| 0.9 E–W | 7.5 N–S | ? | ? | Uninhab. | . . . . . . . . . . . . |
| 0.6 E–W | 1.8 N–S | ? | ? | Uninhab. | . . . . . . . . . . . . |
| 4.0 E–W | 6.4 N–S | 17.6 | 1047 | 469 | Corvo |
| 12.4 E–W | 16.9 N–S | 17.4 | 1430 | 5,302 | Sta. Cruz |
| 21.5 E–W | 14.7 N–S | 17.3 | 1240 | 17,464 | Horta |
| 45.1 E–W | 16.0 N–S | 17.3 | 1195 | 18,014 | Roque do Pico |
| 53.3 NW–SE | 6.8 NE–SW | 17.4 | 1045 | 12,853 | Velas |
| 12.4 NW–SE | 7.1 NE–SW | 17.2 | 991 | 7,188 | Sta. Cruz |
| 29.3 E–W | 18.0 N–S | 17.2 | 1130 | 70,368 | Angra do Heroismo |
| 62.3 E–W | 16.0 N–S | 17.3 | 968 | 149,873 | Ponta Delgada |
| 15.5 E–W | 10.0 N–S | 17.3 | 652 | 9,487 | Vila Porto |

archipelago being some 1,900 km from the Portuguese mainland. The area of the archipelago totals 2,344 km².

Portuguese seafarers in the employ of Prince Henry the Navigator discovered the islands ca. 1427, Santa Maria being the first sighted. By 1452 when Flores and Corvo had been discovered, all the archipelago was known. The first settlements were in Santa

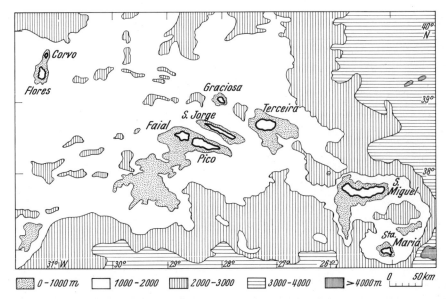

Fig. 4. Geographical situation and bathymetry, Azores Archipelago. (Modified after unpublished map, Inst. Hidrografico, Lisbon).

Maria in 1439, under the supervision of FREI CONÇALO WELHO CABRAL, who later became the first Governor. In the 16th century, many Flemish families settled in the central islands, but these were gradually assimilated by the Portuguese as time went on. Today in all islands the population is dominantly white and Portuguese.

Because of its geographical location within the Atlantic, the Azores in the past were of paramount importance as a port of call for ships bound to and from the New World, as well as those to and from India. It is not surprising therefore that the archipelago

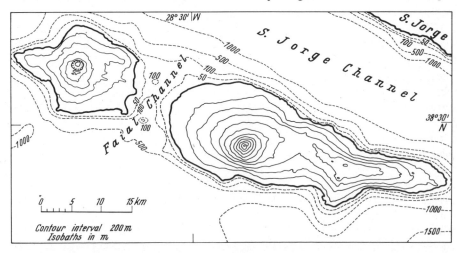

Fig. 5. Contour and bathymetric map of Faial-Pico, Azores.

was often raided by Moorish, French and British pirates. In both World Wars, the Azores were used by the Allies as naval and air bases, and Portugal, being a member of NATO, the island bases are still of considerable strategic importance.

The Azores lie on the Mid-Atlantic Ridge, rising from depths of 2,000 m. The 1,000 m isobath surrounds all islands, with a broad extent of water between 1,000–2,000 m and here and there, e. g. between S. Miguel and Terceira and between the central and western island groups, depths exceed 2,000 m, even 3,000 m some  30 km NW of S. Miguel. The 100 m isobath usually lies within 3 km km of the island coasts, and the 20 m isobath, usually within a kilometre. Offshore slopes are greatest off the coasts of Faial, Pico and S. Jorge, the 1,000 m isobath lying as close as 3 km km along parts of the S coast of S. Jorge. The submarine slope is thus here ca. 18°15', whilst off the NW coast of S. Miguel, the slope is ca. 5°45' down to the 3,000 m submarine contour.

The islands vary in area from 17 km² for Corvo to 757 km² for S. Miguel. Highest peaks vary from 402 m in Graciosa to 2,351 m in Pico. In some islands, e. g. Faial, Pico, Corvo, one commanding summit dominates the scene; in others, e. g. Flores, Terceira, Graciosa and S. Miguel several prominent summits characterize the landscape; in the remaining islands of S. Jorge and Sta. Maria rather than individual peaks it is the mountain range which dominates. Carego Gorda, 1,043 m, and Ponta do Pico, 2,351 m, highest summits in Faial and Pico, respectively, have well developed symmetrical slopes as typified by Fujiyama, and although Ponta do Pico is considerably lower than Pico de Teide, 3,718 m, in Tenerife, the former rises steeply up from the coasts with unimpeded views, thus enhancing its grandeur. Other high peaks are to be found along the walls of the calderas, e. g. in Corvo, Graciosa and Terceira.

The numerous rounded depressions, either of crater or caldera size, are most striking features within most of the islands. Calderas with high, steeply-inclined inner walls are superbly developed in Corvo, Graciosa, Faial, Terceira and S. Miguel. The best known, to scientist and tourist alike, are found in S. Miguel, and of these the outstanding one is Caldeira das Sete Cidades (of which several legends exist regarding the ›Seven Cities‹). From wall-to-wall, this measures 5 km in diameter, and within the great depression lie four lakes, Lagoa Azul, 2,6 km long and 2,4 km broad, largest lake in the archipelago, Lagoa Verde, Lagoa Santiago and Lagoa Rasa. The striking difference between the blue and green waters of the first two lakes presents a truly glorious scene, surrounded by steep wooded slopes, lush meadows, pretty clean houses, white sandy beaches. (Several secondary volcanic centres with dry craters also occur within the large caldera.) In central and eastern S. Miguel occur two equally interesting calderas, those represented by Lagoas Fogo and Furnas. All three calderas are the sites of many mineral springs. In central Terceira is Caldeira de Guilherme Moniz with its semicircular rim of Serra do Moriao on the S. The rim rises to 682 m, with very steep slopes down to the caldera floor lying at an elevation of 460 m. This floor is remarkably flat, some 4 km long, up to 2 km broad. There is no lake here, but a stream drains eastwards along the N edge of this depression down to the NE coast. Though less massive, less imposing, of lesser altitude, the many adventitious cones which dot the islands give a distinct irregularity to the topograhy. In some regions, e. g. the volcanic complex of Lagoa do Fogo in S. Miguel, the landscape takes on an appearance similar to the famous Puys de Auverge area of France, a chaotic accumulation of cratered and

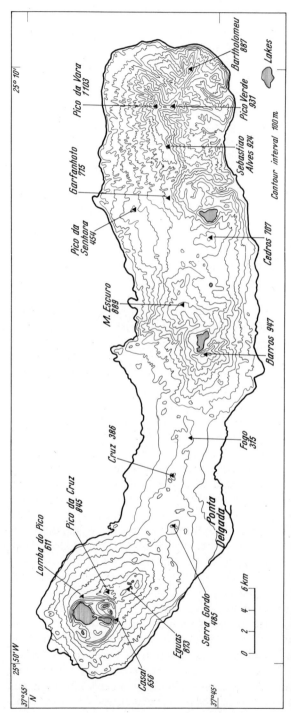

Fig. 6.  Contour map of S. Miguel, Azores.

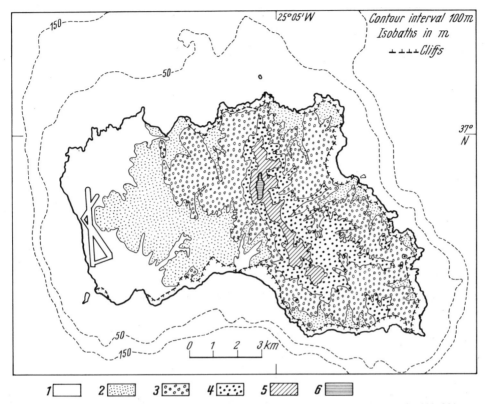

Fig. 7. Hypsometric-bathymetric map of Santa Maria, Azores. 1: 0–100 m. 2: 100–200 m. 3: 200–300 m. 4: 300–400 m. 5: 400–500 m. 6: > 500 m.

uncratered cones all showing smooth profiles, usually symmetrical. A notable feature here and there in the islands is the presence of either peninsular or insular cones. The former are represented by the strombolian cones of Monte da Guia – Monte Queimado of Horta, Faial, and by Monte Brasil at Angra do Heroismo, Terceira. These adventitious cones formed beneath sea level close to the main islands and became attached – volcanic tombolos – to the islands by a combination of their ejected materials and sediments brought by long-shore currents. An excellent example of an insular cratered cone is the islet of Vila Franca do Campo, ca. one km off the S coast of S. Miguel, and of much more recent date and interest, Capelhinos volcano, off the extreme western point of Faial, which was in eruption in 1957 and 1958. In the case of Guia-Queimado and Vila Franca do Campo, the well-formed craters have been breached by the sea so as to create circular embayments.

In all islands there are parts where the relief is strong. This is most noticeable along the inner walls of craters and calderas where, e. g. in the case of Sete Cidades, there is a very sudden drop from elevations of 700 m to 250 m, or in the case of Caldeira, Faial, a drop from 900 m to 600 m, also very steep. In eastern S. Miguel occurs the strongest relief in the archipelago, and it is here that the highest peaks in the island are found.

From the highland known as Planalto dos Graminhais, the land descends abruptly in all directions, the radially patterned streams carving out gorges and narrow V-shaped valleys, everywhere slopes are very steep, the topography has a massive, chaotic appearance. Extents of flatter, lower land in the archipelago are few. The three outstanding examples are in western Sta. Maria, the topographic ›saddle‹ extending from Ponta Delgada to the N coast in western S. Miguel and in NE Terceira. It is not surprising therefore that here occur the three largest airports of the archipelago.

Characteristic of the islands and throughout much of each island is the steep decent down to coastal areas. Cliffing of the coasts is typical, in some instances rising to 400 – 500 m as almost vertical walls. Even where coastal cliffs are not outstanding, steep slopes lead down from the interior of the islands to littoral regions. In Corvo, e. g. with the exception of the extreme S of the island, spectacular cliffs and very abrupt slopes lead up into the interior, slopes too steep to allow agriculture, villages, even houses.

In S. Jorge and Sta. Maria occur distinct mountain ranges. In the former, the range parallels the NW-SE trend of the island, with peaks reaching 700–1,000 m. From the higher interior slopes downward are relatively gentle to elevations varying between 400 m and 800 m, and thereafter sharp drops down to the coasts, especially on the N coast.

The land-submarine slope southwards from Pico da Esperança, 1,053 m, to the 1,000 m isobath, 6,200 m distant, measures ca. 18°20', land slopes and submarine slopes here being almost identical. The highland axis in Sta. Maria trends NNW-SSE across the central part of the island, with low, flat land to the W, more rugged terrain varying between 250 m and 587 m, to the E.

Scenically, the Azores and Madeira have much in common. Here the landscape is more gentle, subdued, slopes are covered in vegetation, contrasting with that of the Canary and Cape Verde Islands where the landscape is more harsh, relief much stronger, often bare, rocky slopes, and, in the case of the Cape Verde Islands, the pronounced barrenness of the landscape.

The more northerly and westerly position of the archipelago results in a climatic regime somewhat different from the rest of Macaronesia, latitude and insularity being of paramount significance. The chief factor regulating the climate is the high pressure zone named after the archipelago, the Azores anticyclone, whose position, orientation and evolution varies throughout the year. Maximum intensity occurs in summer, minimum in spring and autumn. The high is centred generally to the S or SW of the Azores in December-January; to the SE for much of the rest of the year. As a rule, it evolves to a maximum in its northerly and westerly part in summer; its southerly or easterly part in winter. The archipelago, and especially the eastern part, experiences the Trade Winds in summer, but all islands nearly always have much wind coming from the west. Daily the intensity and direction of the winds change. When the Azores anticyclone exercises its influence well N of the archipelago, depressions related to the polar front circulate in latitudes N of the archipelago. In summer there is a shifting of air masses so that the high centres itself over the archipelago, when warm, maritime tropical air masses are felt, giving ideal weather from June to September. The rest of the year, the polar front and the anticyclone move S so that the archipelago comes under the influence of westerly lows, when long periods of bad weather may pertain.

If these centre themselves SW of the archipelago, strong winds, gales and distinctly uncomfortable weather affects the islands, especially the western and central groups. Throughout some 8 months of the year, weather is unstable and wet. Though by and large the archipelago experiences relatively pleasant climatic conditions, this are not quite as perfect as tourist brochures would have us believe, the islands experiencing cooler, wetter, more unstable climatic conditions than the other archipelagoes of Macaronesia.

Temperatures never exceed 30°C nor go as low as freezing point. The average for the archipelago is 14.3°C during February, the coldest month, and 22.3°C for August, the hottest month. Mildness typifies the climate, and even winters can be compared, as regards temperature, with spring-like conditions in much of Europe and North America.

Of all the elements of the climate, rainfall varies the most within the archipelago. October-January is the period of greatest rainfall and July invariably the driest month. Naturally elevation and relief influence the precipitation, no less other elements, and in the many caldera depressions, distinct microclimatic regimes are experienced. There is an overall decrease in rainfall from W to E through the archipelago. This, for example, is evident in noting the average rainfall (in mm) for the wettest and driest months at stations in the respective islands from W to E, thus: Santa Cruz (Flores), 200, 57; Corvo (Corvo), 108, 31; Horta (Faial), 119, 46; Lages (Pico), 169, 65; Calheta (S. Jorge) 161, 49; Santa Cruz (Graciosa), 122, 37; Angra (Terceira), 116, 35; Ponta Delgada (S. Miguel) 85, 19; Vila do Porto (Sta. Maria), 83, 18. This feature is equally evident in considering average annual totals of rainfall, where Flores, the most westerly but neither the highest nor the most rugged, has the heaviest rainfall, and Sta. Maria, the easternmost inhabited island, is the driest.

Cloudiness is more prevalent than in any other of the Macaronesian archipelagoes, but thick fogs on land are very rare.

The prevailing winds in the western and central islands are from the N, NW and SW, whereas in the eastern group, these are the NE Trade Winds, except when SW show a strong dominance in winter. It is especially the SW winds which bring inclement weather to the Azores.

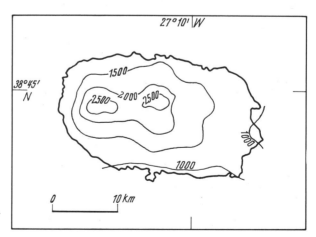

Fig. 8. Isohyetal map of Terceira, Azores. Isohyets in mm.

Table 2                                              Climatic data for the Azores Islands

| Groups | Western | Central | | Eastern |
|---|---|---|---|---|
| Islands | Corvo | Graciosa | Terceira | S. Miguel – Sta. Maria |
| **Temperature ($^{\circ}$C)** | | | | |
| Av. maximum | 22.7 | 22.0 | 24.9 | 20.5 |
| Av. minimum | 14.1 | 13.9 | 11.5 | 14.1 |
| Annual average | 17.6 | 17.2 | 17.2 | 17.3 |
| **Rainfall (mm)** | | | | |
| Av. annual | 1047 | 991 | 1130 | 802 |
| **Rel. humidity (%)** | | | | |
| Av. lowest | 77 | 77 | | 76 |
| Av. highest | 82 | 83 | | 83 |
| Annual average | 79 | 80 | 80 | 79 |
| **Insolation** | | | | |
| Av. lowest (hrs/mth) | | | | 92.1 |
| Av. highest (hrs/mth) | | | | 208.7 |
| Av. annual (hrs/year) | 1622 | 1576 | 1650 | 1764 |
| **Wind vel. (km/hr)** | | | | |
| Average annual | 18.8 | 14.4 | 12.6 | 11.7 |
| **De Martonne index of aridity** | 37 | 43 | 35 | 24 |

Insolation increases from W to E through the archipelago, with Sta. Maria experiencing most hours of sunshine, Flores the least.

Table 2 illustrates the chief climatic features for the various island groups.

As in other Macaronesian archipelagoes, the natural vegetation has been drastically reduced by Man. Peoples foraged for woods to burn and for various construction purposes: domestic animals, and especially goats, devoured the primitive vegetal covering. In the 16th century, reports comment upon extensive woodlands which no longer exist, woodlands which in earlier years represented a significant economic asset, being exported to Europe. Today there are ca. 700 species, sub-species and varieties of vascular plants, or some 400 individual species. Of these, 75% were introduced into the islands by Man, and of the remaining 25%, 38% are exclusive to Macaronesia, 30% are endemic. Amongst the vascular flora, those having the best facilities for dispersal, chiefly by winds, are the cryptogams, whose spores are so very small. For this reason, the ratio of cryptogams to other vascular plants becomes higher the further removed the Macaronesian archipelagoes are from the mainlands, so that the proportions are 32 per 1,000 in the Canary Islands, 53 per 1,000 in Madeira and 73 per 1,000 in the Azores. In the eastern Azores islands the vegetation is more varied, with 390 species, whereas in the central group of islands, it is 376 species and in the western islands, 241 species. The most important plants of the primitive vegetal covering include: *Myrica faya* AIT., *Juniperus brevifolia* HOCHST., *Erica azorica* HOCHST., *Persea azorica* SEUB. and *Taxus baccata* LINNÉ. In an interesting discussion on the distribution and significance of *Persea* within the archipelago, AGOSTINHO (1950) concluded that air temperature was a more important factor than rainfall to account for its distribution, and that at least in the central-western islands many centuries ago the climate was considerably cooler and wetter than at present.

With a generally mild-to-warm climate, adequate rainfall throughout the year, relatively rapid development of soils which in character are neutral or a slight tendency towards acidity, a somewhat subdued topography, less spectacular relief, agriculture within the archipelago is a less hazardous, more prosperous undertaking than in other archipelagoes. This is obvious in even a casual view of the islands, best appreciated from the air, where one notes wide vistas of neatly tended fields, lush meadows, the general rich character of the land, the intensely developed many small hortas, the terraced slopes of vineyards, all presenting a clothed, ›warm‹ appearance. In all islands a relatively large proportion of the land is given over to agriculture in some form or another, varying from ca. 60% to 80%. Climatic conditions allow of the growing of a wide range of products, from temperate to semi-tropical crops, fruits, vegetables and flowers. Wheat, corn, barley, sweet and ordinary potatoes, beans of different varieties, vines, citrus fruits, pears, plums, apples, pineapples, tea, not to mention a wide range of vegetables and a glorious variety of flowers, of which azaleas, rhododendrons, camellias and hydrangeas are the commonest, all such testify to the agricultural richness of these islands. In many localities conditions are such that two plantings can be made on the same land within the year, e. g. corn from March-October and wheat from October to March. Yet in spite of such favourable aspects, such staples as corn and wheat are not enough to feed the islands and further supplies must be imported.

Domestic animals such as beef and milk cattle, oxen, sheep, pigs, donkeys and the ubiquitous goats are raised as sources of food, nourishment and beasts of burden.

As with all island peoples, fishing enters into their daily living. Of such activities, whaling is worth noting. The hunting of whales dates back to the 16th century, and in the course of the centuries the Azoreans have become most efficient whalers. Fourteen different kinds of cetaceans are found in the neighbouring seas. There are many whaling companies in the Azores, several whaling societies, more than a hundred small boats and over a thousand men are engaged in the actual hunting of whales in the vicinal waters, not to mention office staff and workers in the whaling factories. As distinct from whalers of other countries, e. g. the Norwegians and Japanese, the Azoreans restrict their hunting activities to the waters around the islands.

Industrialization refers only to smaller activities, such as preserving and canning of fish, fruits, cheese making, wine making, sugar refining, tobacco and tea processing, whale oil, manufacture of tiles and ceramics, etc. The Portuguese Government has made studies of developing geothermal energy within the archipelago (ZBYSZEWSKI, 1970), concentrating on hot springs, fumarolian activities and gas eruptions at high temperatures. In these respects, the islands of S. Miguel, Terceira, Graciosa, Pico, Faial and Flores offer the best prospects. Nowhere are mineral resources of economic significance other than for various construction purposes. On the other hand, the many mineral springs, especially those of Furnas, S. Miguel, have distinct commercial interest. As a source of revenue for the islands, we must note the increasing importance of tourism, building of hotels, bathing resorts, etc. etc.

For administrative purposes, the archipelago is divided into three districts. Ponta Delgada on S. Miguel is the most important town (35,000 inhabitants) and also district capital, comprising the islands of S. Miguel and Sta. Maria. Angra do Heroismo district includes the islands of Terceira, Graciosa and S. Jorge, whilst Horta district includes the islands of Faial, Pico, Flores and Corvo. In population, Ponta Delgada district is the largest, Horta the smallest.

The 1970 census for the archipelago showed a population of 291,028. For the respective islands it was: S. Miguel, 149,873; Terceira 70,368; Pico, 18,014; Faial, 17,474; S. Jorge, 12,853; Sta. Maria, 9,487; Graciosa, 7,188; Flores, 5,302; Corvo, 469. S. Miguel has the greatest density – 198 inhabitants per km², and Corvo the least, 27 persons per km². From 1864 to 1960 the archipelago population increased 32%, but from 1960 to 1970 there was a decrease of 11%.

## The Madeira Archipelago

The principal islands are Madeira (by far the largest), Porto Santo and the group known as Ilhas Desertas-Chao, Deserta Grande and Bugio. Madeira itself lies some 700 km from the African coast, about 900 km from Lisbon. The archipelago lies between 33°10' and 33° 20' N.

The first island to be discovered was Porto Santo by JOAO GONÇALVES ZARCO and TRISTAO VAZ TEIXEIRA in the year 1418. The next year these two brothers-in-arms and equiries of Prince Henry the Navigator landed on Madeira. It is believed that the Madeira archipelago was the first of these Portuguese Middle Atlantic archipelagoes to be discovered. Whether or not the archipelago was known to antiquity or even by the Portuguese in earlier years is uncertain.

The first discoverers were impressed by the abundance of wild woods and shrubs on the major island and so named it ›Madeira‹-Portuguese for wood. The name of the capital, Funchal, was similarly taken from the abundance of the yellow-flowered, frangrant funcho or fennel (*Faeniculum vulgare*).

Madeira has an area of 728 km², 58 km long by 23 km broad; Porto Santo, 45 km to the NE, has an area of 69 km². The entire archipelago comprises some 810 km². Pico Ruivo, 1,862 m, in Madeira, is the highest summit; Pico de Faco, 517 m, highest point in Porto Santo.

In Madeira the topographic axis runs approx. W-E, with highest altitudes in the longitude of Funchal. The relief is remarkably strong, with very precipitous slopes, deep, ravine-like valleys. About 1/3 of the area lies above 1,000 m. High cliffs comprise some 80% of the coastline. At Cabo Girao occur breathtaking cliffs rising 580 m almost sheer from the shore. The submarine basement extends the island topography below sea level, so that if the sea sank 100 m, the relief would be almost the same. The 200 m isobath links Ilhas Desertas to the main island. The submarine descent is steep down to 1,000 m everywhere around Madeira-Desertas, whilst depths in excess of 2,500 m separate Madeira from Porto Santo. The Madeira archipelago thus represents the culmination above a large submarine plateau, forming a small massif rising 5,000 m above this level, of which ca. 3/5 is at present submerged.

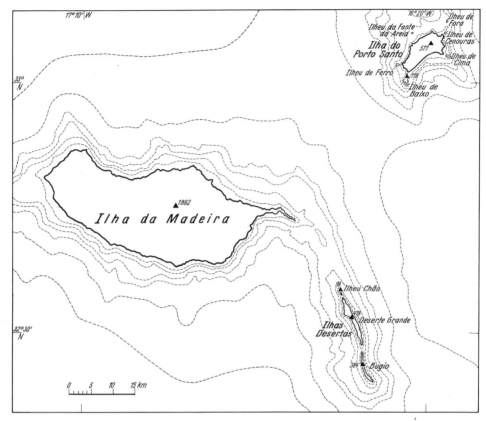

Fig. 9. General situation and bathymetry, Madeira Archipelago. Isobaths at 20, 50, 100, 500, 1000, 2000, 3000 and 4000 m. (After Topog. Map, Inst. Geogr. e Cad., Lisboa, 1972).

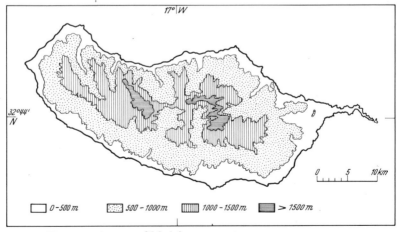

Fig. 10. Hypsometric map of Madeira.

In all islands the relief is of volcanic origin, and from what can be gleaned from the geology, the topography and relief of Madeira back in Miocene times was rather similar to the present. Most volcanic forms have been severely eroded, for vulcanism appears to have died out a long time ago. However, one or two well-preserved evidences of more recent vulcanism are seen in the half-demolished craters of Arco de S. Jorge and Arco da Calheta, also the crater of Santo da Serra. On the basis of state of preservation, younger volcanic forms occur peripherally around the older, more central eruptive centres. In the latter area are thick pyroclastic accumulations cut by resistant dykes. The contrast between less resistant pyroclastics and harder dyke rocks is well brought out by erosive action, with dykes forming thin crests and prominent peaks, tuffs, cinders weathering into very deep valleys. Yet it is in the higher central part where the most extensive level areas occur, the largest, Paul da Serra, being a structural platform slightly inclined to the SW. Recent uplift has taken place in Madeira, with river terraces occurring up to 100 m. The entire river network shows evidences of this uplift, hence the cycle of erosion is in a very youthful stage – no broad meandering belts, no river ›captures‹, no smoothing-out of longitudinal profiles, powerful vertical corrasion everywhere, complete absence of finegrained alluvials. Only two rivers, the Brava and Socorridos, show marked reception basins of funnel-shape, exiting via gorges, and here walls rising sheer for 500–600 m above the gorge base are found, the basins enclosed by walls rising a further 1,000 m, such as, e. g. in the Curral das Freiras.

It has often been remarked that Madeira has no littoral, cliffs dominant almost everywhere. Common throughout the island are great scree slopes which temporarily preserve the ›toes‹ of the cliffs, but on the other hand promote great rockfalls, landslides, etc. The fact that nowhere are there sandy beaches, only gravels and pebbles, is witness of constant replenishment of rock-fall material to the strand, and further evidence of the recency of marine geomorphologic phenomena. In a sense, Porto Santo is a somewhat subdued replica of Madeira: heights are less, relief less strong, cliffs less high, the island is more asymmetric than Madeira, more longer, gentler slopes – to the SE. But the most significant difference refers to the long SE sandy beach, studied by D'ORCHYMONT (1936). The more arid character of Porto Santo, especially on the leeward side of the island, is no less reflected in the topography. Lastly we would note the greater extent of level land in this island, on which has been built the international airport serving the archipelago.

The islands of Desertas have odd worm-like shapes, strung out in a general N-S direction. All three islands are surrounded by cliffs, elevations rise to a maximum height of 478 m. As the name indicates, there are no inhabitants on these islands. The isobaths show clearly that these islands were once united to Madeira.

The contention of the tourist brochures that »Madeira has the best climate in the world« may at first sight be taken as typical advertising propaganda, and yet, on closer inspection, there is a grain of truth here, if by »best« we mean salubrious, balmy, warm, sunny skies, freshness. The late Admiral CASTELO BRANCO's monograph (1938) goes into much detail regarding the Madeira climate, treats of its medicinal values, shows what an excellent health resort it is.

The archipelago lies within the NE Trade Wind belt during all the year. In both the major islands there are marked differences between the N and S coasts because of this.

N and NE winds occur from 67–80% of the time during summer, when the winds incorporate air masses of the Azores anticyclonic belt. But in spite of their journey over the ocean, there is a long, dry summer. Thermal regularity results from oceanic location. The cold, deep Canaries current sweeps round the archipelago, giving moderate climates, and it is only as one rises into the higher interiors that noticeable temperature changes occur. Other than during summer, the archipelago lies within the belt of Westerlies winds and cyclones, causing abundant rains, at which time winds from the SW and W are very common, often of violent nature. The closeness of the archipelago to Africa is felt by the E winds which can suddenly raise temperatures and cause alarming drops in the relative humidity. Fortunately these dry, parching winds last only a few days, are not regular annual events. However, it must be noted that extreme eastern Madeira, Porto Santo and Ilhas Desertas do experience at least semi-arid conditions, where water, in the case of inhabited Porto Santo, is a serious problem.

At Funchal the average annual temperature is 18.3°C. Southern slopes tend to be warmer. Naturally altitude affects temperature and at Arieira (1,610 m), the average winter temperature is 5.2°C, in summer not warmer than 14.5°C. The average annual rainfall at Funchal is 640 mm, concentrated largely into 65 days annually, with October – December the wettest period. Since the 18th century several disastrous floods have occurred in Madeira. No less do altitude and location affect rainfall quantities: Santana (425 m, NE coastal area) 1,340 mm; Ponta do Pargo (640 m, W coast) 847 mm; Encumeada (950 m, central) 2,340 mm; Caramujo (1,260 m, N slope) 2,898 mm; Arieiro (1,610 m S-central) 2,281 mm. The N coast is distinctly wetter than the S coast. In the Funchal area, average annual evaporation is 1,382 mm, with extremely small daily variations. September is the sunniest month everywhere. Snow occurs only on the very highest summits; fogs are infrequent, short duration.

The natural vegetation has been profoundly affected by Man. On the S slopes of Madeira none occurs below 600–700 m, where agriculture is carried out. Above this elevation, laurels (native), maritime pines and many shrubs grow, but the highest altitudes are bare or then in pasture.

Regarding Madeira proper, in spite of the rugged terrain, some 25% is cultivated. Most cultivated land is given over to non-irrigated crops. Cultivated land is of two major types, plantations and crop rotation. The best soils are given over to sugar cane and bananas, which also receive most irrigated water. These two, plus vines, constitute the ›rich cultures‹, important in the export trade but of very little significance as regards local needs. Crops, fruits, vegetables and nuts of tropical, Mediterranean and Western-Central European type are all found growing here. Of both aesthetic and export value is the wondrous riot of many gayly-coloured flowers, presenting a wondrous kaleidoscope all year through.

Vicinal waters are not rich in fish life, hence fish foods enter little into the diets of the people.

There are no metallics or non-metallics of any significance in all the archipelago, no fossil fuels, no hydroelectric developments, hence no real industries. Of significance, however, is artisan work, notably embroidery and wickerwork, for which Madeira is justly famous.

The 1970 census showed 257,147 inhabitants, with densities of 344 per km² for

Madeira, 93 per km² for Porto Santo. Much more telling is the density with respect to cultivated land, and in this Madeira attains 1,500 persons per km². In 1949 RIBEIRO, on the basis of 1940 figures, was lamenting the alarming pressure of population, when Madeira had 1,100 persons per km² of cultivated land. During the last decade 1960–70 the population showed a decrease of 11,770. As would be expected, most people dwell at lower elevations, especially along the S coasts. Funchal, capital of the archipelago, has more than 100,000 people, and including the environs, 125,000 people, making it, population-wise, one of the most important Portuguese cities. Porto Santo, capital of the island of the same name, has ca. 1,800 people.

Road building in Madeira especially is a most difficult, often a most dangerous task. There are some 700 km of paved roads on the main island, completely circling it. In Porto Santo roads are restricted to the SE slopes.

Undeniably Madeira is a hauntingly beautiful island, as every tourist will confess. The writer CLAUDE DERVENN summed up the impression: »It happens that God remembers Eden, whence He drove out mankind and that His pity gave back a fragment of the lost garden. Thus five centuries ago the Portuguese found in mid-ocean the divine gift of Madeira«.

## The Selvagens Archipelago

This, the smallest of the archipelgoes discussed here, centrally located at Lat. 30°06' N, Long. 15°58' W. W, lies some 160 km N of Pta. de Anaga, Tenerife, 250 km SSE of Pta. S. Lourenço, Madeira. The archipelago comprises Selvagem Grande (largest islet), Selvagem Pequena, Ilheu de Fora, Ilheu Alto, Ilheu Comprido, Ilheu Baixo, Ponta do Sul, Ponta do Oeste and Ilheus do Norte, plus many small rocks, banks and reefs. The total area is perhaps of the order of 4 km². km². The maximum elevation, Pico da Atalaia, 153 m, lies near the W coast of the largest islet; highest point in Selvagem Pequena is Pico do Veado, 49 m, and on Fora, 18 m. Some tiny islets are merely emergent at high tide.

Selvagem Grande has a somewhat table-shaped profile, with steep cliffs, 50–100 m high, particularly well developed along the NW, N, E and SE coasts. Though cliffs are high in the S, they have a gentler slope seaward, in places giving a terraced profile. The upland plateau is interrupted by volcanic cones, e. g. Pico do Atalaia, Pico das Tormorellas, some half dozen unnamed hills. The topography is crudely basin-shaped, open towards the SW. Three intermittent streams flow eastward. Two of these valleys, each ca. 1,250 m in length, penetrate well inland, rising on the eastern slopes of the highest peak.

In Selvagem Pequena also the coasts are lined by steep cliffs. Both here and in the larger islet, access from the sea is difficult, and in Selvagem Grande the only landing place is a small cove on the SW coast, Enseada das Cagarras, protected from the NE winds. The other islets are actually reefs and banks, and these, plus the many exposed and slightly submerged rocks, reefs and banks make navigation close in-shore a hazardous matter.

Many sea birds, especially gulls, crowd the islets. Rabbits, brought there by Man,

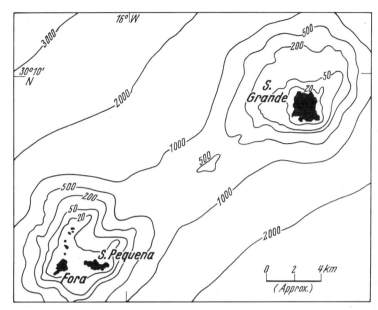

Fig. 11. Geographic situation and bathymetry, Selvagens Archipelago. Depths in m. (Adapted from 1 : 50,000 Topog. Map, Inst. Geogr. e Cad., Lisboa, 1970).

devour the scant vegetation, thus promoting wastage of soil and erosion. Other animals include lizards, also black geckos, as well as many insects, especially spiders. The marine life in the vicinal waters includes sharks, tuna, dogfish, conger eels, also a great profusion of large barnacles (*Patella candei*). The native flora includes the tobacco plant and many saltworts (*Mesembriantenum crystallinum* and *M. nodiflorum*), with Ciana trees on higher slopes. The saltworts, which form bush vegatation, form the chief food of the rabbits, which former were once collected for the extraction of soda. A lichen (*Roccella tinctoria* D. C.) was also collected as a source of carmine dye.

It appears that at no time have there been permanent settlements in the archipelago. On the other hand, hunters and fishermen regularly use the islets – the former going after the rabbits. Seasonally fishermen stay for odd periods, may build temporary crude dwellings for themselves – or live in artificial caves – as well as huts used for the salting of fish. Two cisterns have been built to provide fresh water for these itinerants. An astronomical marker also stands on a prominent hill. All such indications of human life are concentrated in the SW part of the chief islet.

Climatic data are lacking, but conditions are similar to those experienced in MadeiraCentral Canaries, likely somewhat drier than both but similar temperatures, the same dominance of the NE Trade Winds.

The 1,000 m isobath, trending NE-SW, links all the archipelago; the 500 m isobath forms three separate areas – around Selvagem Grande, the other islets and a small area in between. The 100 m isobath also has a NE-SW direction, this depth representing the limit of present marine destruction. If we adopt the 10 m isobath as the limit of

isletgroups, then we have: (a) a western group – Fora, Comprido, Alto, Norte; (b) an
eastern group – Selvagem Pequena, Oeste, Baixo, Sul; (c) Selvagem Grande itself.

The dominant winds being from the N and NE sectors, the waves coming mostly
from the NW, means that the SE coastal ares of Selvagem Grande, Selvagem Pequena
and Fora are the quietest, here there is more beach sand development. Above a depth
of some 70 m there occurs a marine abrasion platform which was later upraised to a
depth of 20 m and slightly tilted.

## The Canaries Archipelago

Seven principal islands comprise the archipelago, having a total area of 7,500 km²,
largest of the groups here discussed. Of all the archipelagoes, the Canaries lie closest
to the mainland, Fuerteventura being some 100 km WNW of Cape Juby, Morocco.

The islands are located between the latitudes of 27°40' and 29°20' N, extending about
450 km E-W.

It is of special interest that the Canaries alone, of all the Atlantic islands, had an
aboriginal population, known as the Guanches. These people had a well developed
Neolithic culture, a quite astonishing knowledge of mummification, and the earliest of
these peoples must have mastered the arts of navigation, as doubtless they originated
from the Mediterranean or neighbouring African regions. Just when these aboriginals
arrived is far from certain, but it is thought that this was some time between 2,500 and
2,000 years B. C., that 3,000 B. C. the islands were uninhabited.

The archipelago was known in ancient days to various Mediterranean peoples,
Phoenicians and perhaps earlier peoples having visited the islands, but concrete
evidence is lacking. Having no mineral wealth to attract these early voyagers, the only
feature likely to appeal to them was the delightful climate. To the Phoenicians and

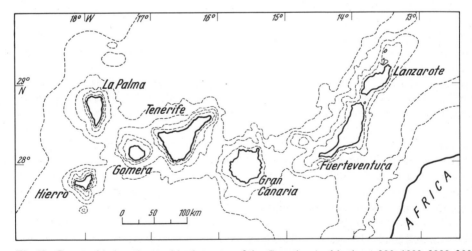

Fig. 12. Geographic location and bathymetry of the Canaries Archipelago. 200, 1000, 2000, 3000
and 4000 m isobaths shown. (Modified after KLUG, 1968).

Greeks, the islands were known as Hesperis, whence the legend of the Garden of Hesperides, fabled western isles beyond the evening star. Cartheginians and Romans also knew of these islands, the latter naming them Insulae fortunatae, the Fortunate or Blessed Islands. During the Moorish invasion of Spain, Arabs are known to have visited here, naming the archipelago Kaledad-al Yezair al Jalidad, i. e. »The New Islands«.

In the 14th century, the archipelago was ›re-discovered‹, with Catalans, Mallorcans, Castillians and Genoese voyaging thither for plunder and the capture of the aborigines as slaves. A papal bull of 1344 by Pope Clement VI placed the Canaries as a dependency of the Holy See, then located at Avignon in France. The pope awarded the islands to the Infante Don Luis de la Cerda, great-grandson of both French and Spanish kings, with the title Principe de Fortuna. King Alfonso XI of Castile then made known that the Canaries and vicinal African coasts belonged to him. In 1393, with his approval, some Andalusians and Vizcayans surveyed the prospects of the archipelago, sending back a rich harvest of slaves to Seville from Lanzarote. The official conquest of the islands began in 1402 when King Henry III of Castile granted right of conquest to the Breton JUAN DE BÉTHENCOURT and the Norman GADIFER DE LA SALLE. Lanzarote fell in 1404, and by 1496 total conquest and occupation of the archipelago had been completed. It was at this date when there ended the long, often bitter struggles with Portugal for their possession, since when the islands have remained Spanish possessions. In 1589 the first Captain-General was appointed, at which time the city of La Laguna, Tenerife, was founded, today the chief cultural and religious centre of the Canaries. During the 16th, 17th and 18th centuries the islands were often attacked by pirates, and during Spain's foreign wars, British, French and Dutch invasions took place. Wishing to curry favour with the islanders under Napoleonic threats, Spain granted some autonomy in 1808, and after NAPOLEON's defeat in 1815 the islands were given the status of an insular province of Spain. Since 1927 the Canaries have been divided into two provinces, Sta. Cruz de Tenerife (Tenerife, La Palma, Gomera, Hierro), capital Sta. Cruz de Tenerife; and Las Palmas province (Gran Canaria, Fuerteventura, Lanzarote), capital Las Palmas, Gran Canaria. These provinces rank in importance with those of Spain. The Canaries, like the Balearics, are treated as part of metropolitan Spain.

In passing, it might be mentioned that the name Canarias is thought to have first been used by King Juba of Mauritania about 40 B. C. because of the »mulitudes of dogs of great size« (*L. canis*, a dog.) These half-wild dogs still roam the islands. Admittedly the name ›canaria‹ means female Canary bird (*Serinus canarius*) in Spanish. This species, endemic in the Canaries, Azores and Madeira, has become known worldwide as a delightful songster.

The 200 m isobath hugs five of the islands, being closest inshore off La Palma, and in these islands in general, this isobath lies no more than a few kilometres offshore. Fuerteventura and Lanzarote have much broader submarine shelves, especially off the W coast of the former, the N coast of the latter, and further, these two islands are enclosed by this submarine contour. In spite of the relative closeness of Fuerteventura to the African mainland, depths of almost 1,500 m intervene.

In Pico de Teide (Tenerife), 3,718 m, we have not only the highest summit in the Canaries, in all Spanish lands, but also in the entire islands of the Atlantic, a peak high enough to be snow covered for much of the year. Apart from Tenerife, La Palma rises

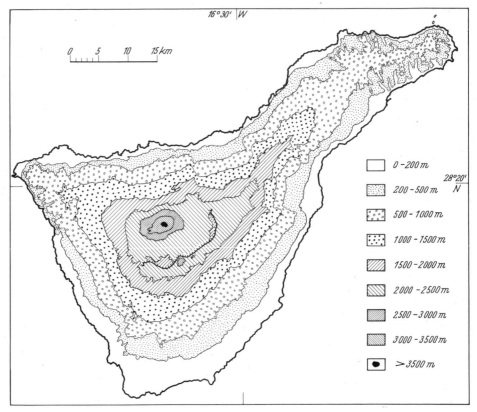

Fig. 13. Hypsometric map of Tenerife, Canary Islands.

over 2,000 m, Gran Canaria almost as high, Gomera and Hierro to ca. 1,500 m, Fuerteventura and Lanzarote less than 1,000 m. Even islets can be high, e. g. tiny Montana Clara, N of Lanzarote, with an area of 1 km², rises to 258 m. Gran Canaria and Gomera are of rounded shape, but in the other elongated islands the highlands trend generally NE-SW. In five of the islands highest land is centrally located, but in Fuerteventura and Lanzarote such occurs in the extreme NE and SW regions. Further, in these two islands – collectively named Purpuras, after the gastropod genus *Murex* whose shells yielded a purple dye – topography and relief is more subdued, few peaks have a commanding aspect, there is more low and level land. In other islands, the radial drainage network, short, steep descents, has carved most imposing ravines, gorges, awesome destruction of the land has taken place. Calderas have been deeply scooped out, rimmed by walls rising almost sheer for 700–900 m, the most striking examples being Caldera de Taburiente, La Palma, Caldera de Las Canadas, Tenerife, Caldera de Tirajana, Gran Canaria. (It is to be noted that within the archipelago there might occur explosion, erosion and collapse calderas, sometimes combinations of these, but whatever their origin, the powerful effects of fluvial erosion are evident.) Precipitous slopes both along coasts and in valleys, combined with copious and deep infiltration of

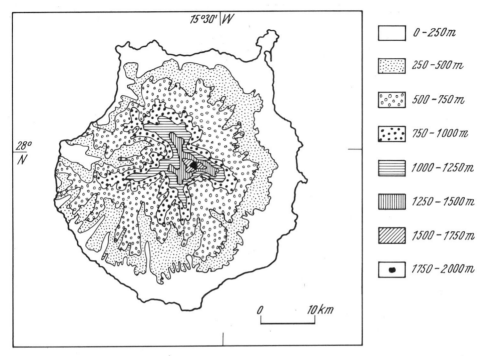

Fig. 14. Hypsometric map of Gran Canaria, Canary Islands.

meteoric waters in higher areas, results in promoting many rockfalls, landslides, rockcreep, as has been pointed out by HAUSEN (1971). The interior of many islands presents a wild, rugged, often even lunar aspect, island slopes gashed by ravines often too steep for any form of plant life except perhaps pines, which manage to grow to hights as great as 60 m in the case of the well known species *Pinus canariensis*, a truly remarkable feat when one ralizes that their roots are dug-in to slopes often as great as 50°! The higher islands, receiving more rainfall, are more deeply carved out by roaring torrents during the rainy season. But as these torrents dry out in the dry season, transportaion of material is brought to a standstill till the next period of rains. This results in valleys being choked with coarse rock débris, from fluvial erosion, rockfalls, etc., so that transportation is always lagging behind deposition by a large margin. Estuaries form at the mouths of longer, more powerful streams where the more abrupt decrease in longitudinal profile near the coast causes them to drop their loads. Such action also forms alluvial fans, well seen, e. g. in S and SE Gran Canaria. Valleys in the archipelago lack typical continental features; they are short, steep, narrow, flood plains and meanders absent, especially in the leeward sides of islands they are not favoured either for agriculture or settlements. Common to all islands is the prevalence of bold, steep coasts on the N and W sides. In La Palma, these attain 400 m, 600 m in Lanzarote, 750 m in Fuerteventura and Tenerife, 800 m in Gomera, 700–1,000 m in Gran Canaria, Hierro. In general the coasts are not highly indented, as so frequently massive lava flows have advanced downwards radially from higher central vents as smooth walls

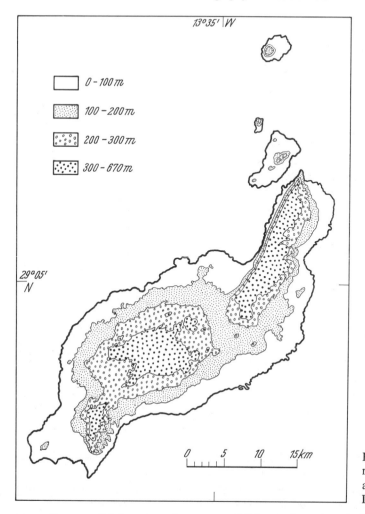

Fig. 15. Hypsometric
map of Lanzarote
and Las Isletas, Canary
Islands.

presenting a solid front to the waves. Offshore there is relatively deep water, no
protecting biologic reefs to cushion the effect of waves, particularly strong during
winter months (350–400 waves per hour), such ›reefs‹ (Nautical) as do occur being flows
which have penetrated below sea level and become disintegrated into lava blocks,
admittedly forming some protection. Notable is the scarcity of offshore islands around
the major islands, and actually more pronounced coastal indentation and offshore
islands are commonest in N Lanzarote. N and NE coasts usually experience more
violent seas, S and SE coasts are to leeward, with the result that estuaries, incipient
deltas, sandy or pebbly beaches are developed here and invariably the major ports seek
the more sheltered coasts. Undeniably there exist topographic, relief and
geomorphologic differences between Fuerteventura-Lanzarote and the other islands,
the former being more subdued, relief less striking, the landscapes have a more mature
aspect. Such characteristics betoken greater geological age, as usually interpreted.

The belt of subtropical variable winds and calms, the so-called ›horse latitudes‹, which oscillates N-S seasonally, influences the climate of the archipelago. Within this belt are cells of high pressure, strongest in summer, giving fair, clear weather with a tendency to dryness. To the E and SE of this belt lies the zone of the NE Trade Winds, fresh, humid winds with a ceiling reaching up to 2,000–2,500 m. These life-giving winds ameliorate the climate, bring warmer air, are humid but are not the cause of heavy rainfalls. The higher parts of the islands block the passage of these winds, so causing orographic rainfalls on NW, N and NE slopes, whereas S and SE slopes experience higher temperatures but are somewhat drier. The eastern islands do not benefit to the same extent from such winds because of lower elevations, are more under Saharan influences, hence are distincly drier, often of arid aspect, Lanzarote in particular. Higher than the NE Trades are the Counter-Trades, blowing northwards from equatorial regions. These drier winds bring clear skies, brilliant sunshine to the highest zones of the islands. In between the NE Trades and the Counter-Trades lies a zone often covered with heavy cloud, blanketing lower slopes, higher peaks projecting therefrom like islands in the sea. These clouds are usually brought by NW winds. When anticyclones develop over the Sahara, then the archipelago experiences the dry, seering Harmattan winds blowing out from the desert, but such are seldom felt above 1,800 m. S and SE slopes, especially on the higher islands, frequently have winds of foehn type, dry and warm, but not so devastating to plant life as the eastern winds. When the subtropical belt moves S of the Canaries and cold fronts invade the Sahara, especially in late autumn and winter, then winds from the W and SW blow over the islands. These rain-bearing winds, when gentle, are of great value to the drier southern slopes, but when strong they bring heavy, often disastrous rainfalls, wild seas pound the islands. The role of the Canaries Current has a significant influence on the archipelago. This Current, an offshoot of the Gulf Stream, swings E towards Eur-Africa, follows the trend of the African coast to the S then SW. Colder water here upwells to the surface, thus moderating the climate of the Canaries.

Gran Canaria, a high, centrally located island, can be taken as typical of climatic regimes pertaining within the archipelago, it being remembered that islands to the W tend to be cooler, more humid, the lower eastern islands somewhat warmer, drier. BENITEZ (1959) has furnished pertinent data for Gran Canaria thus:

Mean annual temperatures vary between 18° and 25° at Gando (20 m, E coast), 17° and 24° at Las Palmas (10 m, NE coast), 14° and 21° at Sta. Brigida (500 m, NE), 8° and 19° at Valleseco (1,000 m, NE), figures representing minimums and maximums. Southern exposures, especially at low elevations, experience considerably higher temperatures.

Average annual rainfalls are: Gando, 125 mm; Galdar, (100 m, NW), 215 mm; Tafira (350 m, NE) 402 mm; San Mateo (800 m, NE) 528 mm; Valleseco, 1,021 mm. The rainfall at Gando is typical of the southern, eastern sides of the island.

Relative humidity varies between 69% and 73% in the northern parts, considerably less in southern sectors.

The DE MARTONNE Index of Aridity varies thus: Gando, 4; Galdar, 7; Sta. Brigida, 14; San Mateo, 21; Valleseco, 43. The value for Gando typifies the southern half of the island.

43% of the winds experienced come from the N, 20% from the NE, 17% from the

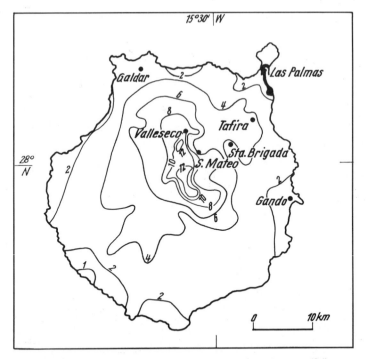

Fig. 16. Isohyetal map of Gran Canaria, Canary Islands. Isohyets in hundreds of mm. (After BENITEZ, 1959).

NW, so that for some 300 days annually winds emanate from northern sectors. Taking this into account, plus the fact that it is these northern winds which nourish the islands with rainfalls, allow of crop growth, make the land verdant, it is understandable how, to the islanders, there are but two points of the compass, N and S. An overall, generalized appreciation of the climate of the archipelago can be gained from the following Table 3.

Table 3                                                                  Climatic data for the Canary Archipelago

|  | J | F | M | A | M | J | J | A | S | O | N | D | Average monthly/Y |
|---|---|---|---|---|---|---|---|---|---|---|---|---|---|
| Average month. T, °C | 17.8 | 18.1 | 18.6 | 19.2 | 20.4 | 21.9 | 23.6 | 24.4 | 23.9 | 23.1 | 21.1 | 18.9 | 20.9 |
| Av. monthly rain, mm | 83 | 48 | 28 | 31 | 16 | 6 | 3 | 6 | 19 | 29 | 85 | 75 | 35.6 |
| Rel. humidity % | 67 | 67 | 66 | 64 | 63 | 62 | 59 | 60 | 65 | 66 | 69 | 67 | 65 |
| Cloudy days | 2 | 1 | 0 | 0 | 1 | 0 | 0 | 0 | 0 | 0 | 1 | 2 | 7 tot. ann. |
| Clear days | 6 | 6 | 6 | 8 | 7 | 8 | 11 | 12 | 9 | 6 | 3 | 4 | 86 tot. ann. |
| Sunny days | 18 | 16 | 20 | 18 | 18 | 16 | 13 | 12 | 17 | 18 | 17 | 16 | 199 tot. ann. |
| Rainy days | 7 | 6 | 5 | 4 | 2 | 1 | 1 | 1 | 2 | 6 | 10 | 9 | 54 tot. ann. |

The vegetal zonation closely parallels that of the climate, thus: (1) Maritime zone, xerophytic in lower areas, well developed in the eastern islands. Commonest here are the saltworts *Mesembryantenum crystallium* and *M. modiflorum*, formerly cultivated for their yield of sodium carbonate ash used in the manufacture of glass and soap. (2) Above some 600–800 m lies the zone of laurisilva and fayal heaths. Here the vegetation presents a selva aspect, lush, dense growths, of which laurel trees are outstanding. This is the region known as ›monte verde‹ to the islanders – green highlands. (3) Usually between 800 and 1,500 m lies the zone of pine trees, of which the most majestic is the Canary pine, but absent in Gomera, Fuerteventura and Lanzarote. This species of pine (*Pinus canariensis*) is found growing as high as 2,500 m on Pico Viejo, Tenerife. Broom also is found in this zone, yielding dense, tangled undergrowth, much prized as a source of firewood. (4) The hairy *Cytisus* is common between elevations of 1,600–2,000 m, also forming dense underbrush. On Teide-Viejo, Tenerife, this plant occurs as high as 3,000 m in local spots. Yellow-flowered dyewoods (*Genista*) are best developed in the central high mountains, e. g. in Tenerife they grow within the snow zone, causing the piling up of this into deep snow-drifts, whereas in La Palma they are found on the highest summits of some 2,400 m, up to 2,000 m in Gran Canaria. (5) The sub-Alpine zone is the highest, best observed in Tenerife. Few plants can withstand the climatic rigours here, but the outstanding exception is the Teide violet (*Viola cheirantifolia*) found a mere 20 m below the summit of this peak. This charming pale-blue plant, of fragrant scent, lends a rare colour against the snow background of winter, the earthy landscape of summer. Of fossil plants in the archipelago, the commonest by far is the Dragon tree (*Dracaena*) still flourishing today in the islands, some old, gnarled specimens said to be several thousand years old.

The economic life of the archipelago depends upon agriculture, and this in turn depends mostly upon European markets. Today of first importance is the banana (400,000 tons annual export), first introduced in the Canaries from the Caribbean island of Santo Domingo (Hispaniola) shortly after its discovery by Christopher Columbus – though the plant is said to be a native of SE Asia. Tomatoes (130,000 tons annual export) are next in importance, but new potatoes, sweet potatoes, onions, Mediterranean-type fruits and nuts, sugar cane, vegetables, cereals, flowers are representative products. Not all the above enter into the export trade, e. g. cereal production is not enough to meet local needs, imports are required. With several of these items there have been serious crises in the past, chiefly in the form of competition, e. g. bananas and sugar cane of the West Indies. Further the production of saltworts and cochineal (obtained from parasitic insects feeding on cacti which yield carmine dye) have decreased greatly in the face of chemicals competition. It is also to be noted that the raising of Mediterranean-type fruits competes with the same raised in continental Europe. However, refrigeration, fast cargo steamers, air transport have all aided in maintaining a healthy export market for agricultural products.

The islands are quite lacking in mineral wealth, fossil fuels, hydroelectric energy, and hence industrialization refers to the lighter ones, results in small factories. The fact that all the main harbours are free ports eases the financial strain in importing raw materials. Breweries, tobacco, glass, wool, paints, fish, building materials, pharmaceuticals, clothes and cheeses for the local market are representative of industrial activity. But the largest industry is that of oil refining, chiefly centred at Sta. Cruz de Tenerife, where oil tankers are the principal types of ships entering and leaving the port. The major part of the refined oil products are destined for the bunkering of ships and aircraft.

The commercial activities of the archipelago are related to agricultural and refined oil products. Fruits and oil derivatives are the chief items of export; crude oil, cereals, chemicals, machinery the major imports.

The population of the Canary Islands represents ca. 50% of that of Macaronesia. As per the 1970 census, there were 1,170,224 people inhabiting the seven islands. Of these islands, Tenerife and Gran Canaria account for some 87% of the archipelago population. These two islands have population densities of 243 and 340 inhabitants per km² – high indeed when one considers the topography, relief, possibilities for agriculture. Again, in the case of these two islands, the fact that some million people are concentrated into an area of some 3,600 km² indicates the pressure of population. As could be expected, the smallest island, Hierro, has also the smallest population, ca. 5,500.

### The Cape Verde Archipelago

The Cape Verde Islands, totalling 15 in number, have a total area of 4,033 km². Cape Verde in Sénégal, from which the islands take their name, lies some 460 km ESE of the

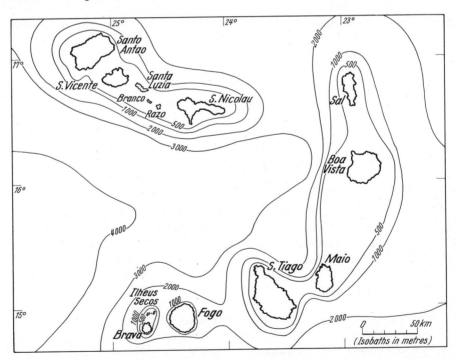

Fig. 17. Geographic situation and bathymetry of the Cape Verde Archipelago. (Modified after TORRES & SOARES, 1946).

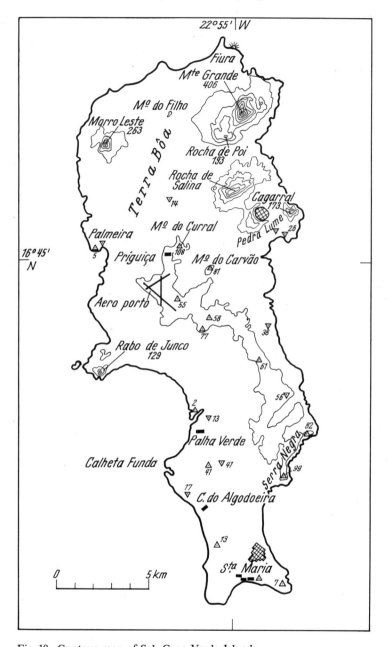

Fig. 18.  Contour map of Sal, Cape Verde Islands.

nearest island. The archipelago is the most southerly of those studied here, lying between 15° and 17° N latitude.

There still lingers some doubt as to when and by whom these islands were first discovered. The major contenders are: VICENTE DIAS, in the employ of Prince Henry the Navigator, 1445; ALVISE DE CADAMOSTO, 1456; DIOGO GOMES, 1460; ANTONIO DE NOLA, also in the employ of the Prince, 1460. What does seem certain is that under the incentive and patronage of the great Portuguese Prince, the discovery was made in the 15th century, and since then the islands have remained firmly in Portuguese hands. (General opinion seems to favour either DIAS or GOMES as worthy of the honour.) The oldest document relating to the islands is a map, dated December 3, 1460, by which King Dom Alfonso V bequeathed to his brother, Dom Fernando, the five islands of Fogo, S. Tiago, Maio, Boa Vista and Sal, in which it is stated that these were discovered jointly by GOMES and NOLA whilst in the employ of Prince Henry.

On the basis of topography, relief, geomorphological evolution and age, the archipelago comprises two distinct groupings: islands which are not so high, slopes more gentle, deposition more evident than erosion, where relatively extensive areas of level land occur – Sal, Boa Vista, Maio, Sta. Luzia; islands of considerable elevation, pronounced relief, erosion dominant, relatively little level land – Sto. Antao, S. Nicolau, S. Tiago, Fogo, Brava. The island of S. Vicente occupies a somewhat intermediate position, in age tending towards the former group but in general aspect more like the latter group. (In the present status of our knowledge of matters stratigraphical, the age aspect applied to the above islands is in considerable doubt, but the other attributes hold.)

On the volcanic island of Fogo, Pico rises to an elevation of 2,829 m, highest in the archipelago and second highest in the Middle Atlantic Islands. On this circular-shaped island, slopes descend steeply in all directions from the caldera. Pronounced cliffing is only noteworthy in certain islands and certain parts thereof, e. g. NE coast of Sto. Antao, much of Brava, and in general the terrain rises gradually from the coasts.

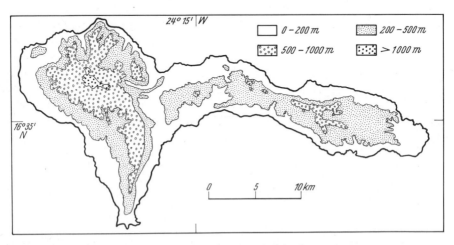

Fig. 19. Hypsometric map of S. Nicolau, Cape Verde Islands.

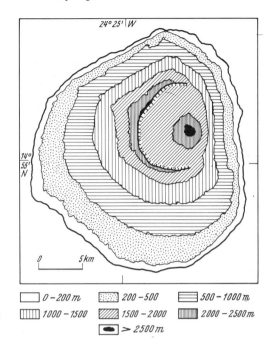

Fig. 20. Hypsometric map of Fogo, Cape Verde Islands.

0 – 200 m    200 – 500    500 – 1000 m

1000 – 1500    1500 – 2000    2000 – 2500 m

> 2500 m

In the higher, more rugged islands, the scenery can be most impressive with great cliffs sweeping down to agitated seas, narrow defiles, imposing basins enclosed in steepwalled mountains, one or two outstanding caldera level floors and their commanding perpendicular rims. Contrasting with such are extensive rolling, at times level terrain, the tawny landscape scarce relieved by a single prominence, rock or plant. Again, in some islands, e. g. Boa Vista, on occasion one might imagine one's self in a hot desert, sand dunes and palms shimmering under a cloudless sky.

The relatively small areas of all islands means that nowhere are valleys or drainage basins large. Streams are entirely of ephemeral type, and only in NE Sto. Antao are there two very small permanent streams. In general, streams adopt a rather direct route from source to the sea, which further explains their short courses. The longest stream and largest drainage basin is that of the Ribeira Rabil in Boa Vista, 24 km in length, area of 140 km². Its length is accounted for by its circuitous route, its source being a mere 8 km from the SE coast, but the stream is directed first to the SW, then W and finally NW to enter the sea in the NW section of the island. In islands having stronger relief, streams in their upper courses tend to have narrow valleys, cascades and waterfalls are present, whereas when they debouch on to lower, more level terrain, many become widely anastomosed, broad, slightly incised valleys choked with rubble.

Nowhere in the archipelago are there any lakes or reservoirs.

The archipelago lies within KÖPPEN's Dry Zone (BWh), classed as experiencing a hot, desert-type of climate. The temperature regime is of equatorial type, with small annual ranges, never excessively hot or cold, with maximum and minimum temperatures in the northern summer and winter. Average annual temperatures vary from 22.6°C (Sto.

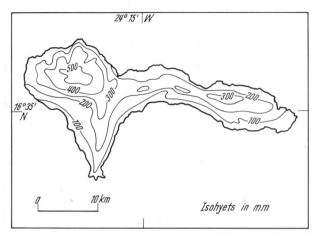

Fig. 21. Isohyetal map of S. Nicolau, Cape Verde Islands.

Antao) to 24°C (Boa Vista). Altitude naturally affects the temperatures as also location
with respect to the on-shore maritime winds. High locations with a NE exposure have
the lowest temperatures and there is every reason to think that freezing occurs high
on Pico (Fogo) during winter. Rainfall deficiency is the greatest natural problem of the
islands and droughts result in catastrophic economic aftermaths – the archipelago at
present is experiencing its eighth year of drought, the worst in 50 years. Average annual

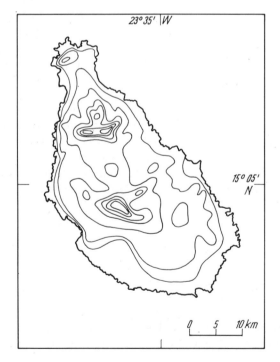

Fig. 22. Isohyetal map of S. Tiago, Cape
Verde Islands. Isohyets of 250, 300, 500,
700, 800, 900, 1000 and > 1000 mm.

Table 4

Some climatic data for the Cape Verde Islands

| Island | S. Vicente | Sto. Antao | S. Nicolau | Sal | Boa Vista | Maio | S. Tiago | Fogo | Brava |
|---|---|---|---|---|---|---|---|---|---|
| Station | Mindelo | Pta. do Sol | Preguiça | Sta. Maria | Sal Rei | Vila de Maio | Serra Mala-gueta | S. Felipe | Nova Cintra |
| Location | Coastal N coast | Coastal NE coast | Coastal S coast | Coastal S coast | Coastal NW coast | Coastal SW coast | 850 m N-Central | Coastal SW coast | 507 m NE |
| Temp. °C Av. coldest month Av. warmest month | 21 26 | 21 26.5 | 21.5 27 | 21.5 27 | 21.5 27.3 | | 13.5 20 | 20 26 | 18.5 22 |
| Av. annual rainfall (mm) | 133 | 465 | 129 | 102 | 383 | 371 | 1055 | 202 | 549 |
| Av. total evaporation (mm) | 1614 | 1580 | 1283 | 2179 | 1146 | | 493 | 1394 | 490 |
| Dominant winds | NE | NE, E | NE, E | N, NE, E | N, NE, E | | NE | NE | NE |
| de Martonne aridity index | 4.0 | 6.5 | 3.8 | 3.6 | 2.6 | | 17.8 | 5.8 | 13.5 |

rainfall varies from 95 mm (Sal) to 665 mm (Fogo). Again location with respect to both altitude and windward directions cause great variations. In the mountains of NE Sto. Antao, average annual rainfall may total 4,000 mm, whereas 20 km away on the low, leeward coastal area, 200 mm may be received in the same year. Not only in quantity is the rainfall deficient, but the temporal distribution and nature of the rains are unfavourable. An entire year's rainfall may occur in a few weeks, a few days, even a few hours, as in Sal. Further the rains are violent, a large quotient comprises run-off, thus denying benefit to soils and plants, causing erstwhile dry river beds to become fast, full rivers. However, flash-floods, in the meaning of causing actual flooding seem to be very rare, perhaps because the steep, short valley profiles manage to hasten the water quickly to the sea.

The average relative humidity stays around 70–72% for most of the year. It is only at the time of the Harmattan (vide sub) that relative humidites reach low values.

Winds tend to be strong throughout the year. The NE Trade Winds are dominant, and these, along with winds from the N and E, are greatly in excess. It is the constancy of such winds blowing over the ocean and reaching the islands which maintains a relative evenness in temperature, so that very seldom is it uncomfortably warm. The hot, parching Harmattan winds blowing out from the Sahara in summer are felt as far off as the Cape Verde islands. These winds have a devastating effect upon vegetation, make people and animals alike nervous, fidgety, bad-tempered.

The total annual evaporation runs high for the islands, varying from average values of 500 mm to 2,180 mm. The latter figure refers to Sal, where average annual rainfall is only 95 mm, and hence why Sal is quite the most barren, drought-ridden of all the islands.

Only in selected localities is there any greenness. Throughout most of the islands, it is a barren, tawny land, no water in valleys, bare rock and bare disintegration products constitute much of the landscape. Only in higher and windward sites is there vegetation. Forests are very few, some of the best stands being in the highlands of S. Tiago and Sto. Antao. Here delightful cool tropical forests are found, even complete with chattering red monkeys. The low, eastern islands present wide vistas of stony, level land with scarce a single tree breaking the monotony.

CHEVALIER (1935) classified the soils of the archipelago into: Saline soils, aeolian soils, arid soils with calcareous crusts and terra rossa. (A pedological survey of the islands has been underway for several years, but so far only three memoirs are available.) Of these groups, only the chernozens, mountain soils and laterite soils hold out good agricultural prospects.

Agriculture is the economic mainstay of the archipelago. Recurring droughts have caused many economic crises in the past, invariably requiring substantial financial assistance from the Portuguese Government. The main field crops are corn, beans, manioc and sweet potatoes. The major export crops are coffee and bananas. Citrus fruits, oils derived from oleagious plant products, tobacco, sugar cane, vegetables are more for local consumption. Of domestic animals, goats are most numerous, these ubiquitous, scavenging animals being a very mixed blessing indeed.

The economy depends principally upon the export of coffee, bananas, tunafish and salted fish products, salt. Mindelo, chief port of the islands, is a stopping place for many ships, mostly cargo-tanker vessels, where the ships bunker, take on board fresh fruits and vegetables and even fresh water – brought over from western Sto. Antao in small local vessels to Mindelo. The standard of living is low indeed, and economic survival is only maintained through heavy subsidies. Villages strike one as being impoverished, good roads are lacking everywhere, inter-island communication is poor. Yet though undeniably the archipelago is to be classed as under-developed, the innate sense of cleanliness, neatness of the people is most impressive, and nowhere is there sordid poverty, vile slums. No less is one impressed by the cheery, friendly, kindly attitude of the native Cabo Verdians, all of distinctly negroid ancestry.

At the last 1970 census, the archipelago population was 272,071. S. Tiago has most people (129,358), and Maio least (3,466). During the past two decades, the population has increased almost 71%. This demographic increase over the years has placed an increasing strain upon the administrations of all islands – in 100 years the population has increased from 76,053 to its present 1970 figure. Each island has its own administrative capital, the capital of the archipelago being Praia, S. Tiago. Mindelo is the commercial capital. The international airport in Sal links the islands with the outside **world – Europe and South America. Portuguese vessels (passenger) en route to Africa call at Praia and/or Mindelo.**

The archipelago rises from depths exceeding 5,000 m to the W, N and S; to the E depths descend to 4,000 m before rising gradually towards the African coast. The 500 m isobath divides the archipelago into four groups of islands: (i) Sto. Antao, S. Vicente, Sta. Luzia, S. Nicolau; (ii) Sal, Boa Vista, Maio, S. Tiago; (iii) Fogo; (iv) Brava. A tongue of deeper water intervenes between the northern and southern groups of islands. Likewise deeper water separates Sal and S. Nicolau, with, however, a small shallow of ca. 80 m depth almost midway between. Steepest submarine slopes lie to the NW of Brava, where the 5,000 m isobath lies some 60 km distant, an average slope of 5°. Islands which are geographically close to one another may have relatively deep water intervening. In the Canal de S. Vicente, between S. Vicente and Sto. Antao, at the narrowest point (11.5 km) the maximum depth is 351 m, and between Fogo and Brava (16.5 km) depths exceed 1,000 m. In general, off-shore rocks and other navigational hazards are relatively rare in the vicinity of the islands. Such are most prevalent around the coasts of Boa Vista and Maio, and, as might be expected, these coasts have witnessed more shipwrecks than elsewhere. At all seasons of the year, seas around the islands are usually quite agitated – either swells or then locally-created waves. Waves approach the archipelago mostly from the NE and SW, and certainly in the case of the latter, there is a very long ›fetch‹. Rough seas can usually be expected in the Canal de S. Vicente and off the SE coasts of Fogo. These unquiet seas take a fearsome toll in marine erosion. Along the N coast of Sal, immense boulders can be seen resting some 200 m from the sea's edge, some 8 m above high tide, which have been hurled into their present position by storms.

CHAPTER 3

# The Geology of Macaronesia

## General

Geological interest in the Middle Atlantic Islands dates back to the early 19th century. During the second decade there appeared papers dealing with Madeira, in the third decade, on the Canaries and Azores and in the 1840's on Cape Verde. During the period from about 1850 to 1880, for all archipelagoes except the Selvagens, appeared the first really significant publications. This was followed in the period from about 1905 to 1915 by more detailed investigations and in essence we may say throughout the archipelagoes the contributions made during this latter period have formed the foundations of all subsequent studies.

A remarkably large band of international scholars have focussed their interests on these archipelagoes, and especially in the Canary Islands. Throughout Macaronesia one is impressed by the relatively large number of German scholars who have done work here, the roll-call conjuring up many respected names of former days – VON HUMBOLDT, VON BUCH, VON FRITZ, HARTUNG, REISS, MÜGGE, DOELTER, ROTHPLETZ, SAPPER, GAGEL, FINCKH, FRIEDLÄNDER, VON WOLF and such German interest extends down to modern times with the names of ROTHE, SCHMINCKE, LIETZ, KLUG, MATZNETTER.

A glance at a map or atlas of the North Atlantic and neighbouring mainlands shows these archipelagoes lying relatively close to the shores of Europe and Africa, giving the appearance of detached pieces of terra firma protruding above the ocean waves. The legendary concepts of a lost ›Atlantis‹, the Garden of Hesperides, the Fortunate Islands, etc. finds an echo in geological thinking too, for some would see continental geological associations; structures built on African marginal shelves, extensions of Alpine orogeny in Iberia and Marocco, stratigraphic correlations with the African mainland, etc.

Macaronesia is of prime interest to the vulcanologist and specialist in igneous matters. Vulcanism, igneous rocks dominate the scene in all islands, and thus it is understandable that such studies should captivate scholars, past and present. But alas the sedimentaries, their stratigraphy, palaeontology, geomorphologic and structural studies have been given far less attention, we are still very vague about much that refers to these disciplines.

With the advent in more recent times of geophysical and geochronological studies, developing hypotheses along the lines of global and plate tectonics, ocean floor spreading, a new emphasis and interest has been added. It might be that even already too much emphasis is given to such, too dogmatic assertions are made, too little attention is given to other geological aspects, there is an unseemly haste to be à la mode and follow the fashion, that the new tectonics is the ›open sesame‹ to geological secrets long perplexing. In truth, however, we should welcome new approaches, new concepts, new tools, new means of probing these secrets, recognizing imperfections here no less than in other geological approaches, but also aware that all go together to advance our knowledge of Geology, »the Science which treats of the Earth«.

## Geomorphology

Small islands, not immediately contiguously to a mainland, can be grouped into three major types: (a) worn down stumps of crystallines-metamorphics, old geologically and geomorphologically, e. g. the Outer Hebrides of Scotland; (b) low islands of very mild relief, essentially of coral and/or sand constitution, young geologically, in a young or early mature stage geomorphologically, such as the Bahamas; (c) high islands of strong relief, young in age and geomorphological development such as the Lesser Antilles. Volcanic islands, whether in the Antilles, Pacific or in Macaronesia are notable for their relative great heights in comparison to their small areas, ruggedness of the terrain, lack of more extensive low, level areas.

The Middle Atlantic Islands, with few exceptions, show steep descents down to peripheral seas. Sheetflood waters and streams take the direct shortest courses downward, the latter developing a radial pattern. When rains fall, dry valleys are turned into torrents, slopes are covered with thin sheets of water moving downward seeking channels. Vertical corrasion is dominant, valleys are narrow, steep both transversely and longitudinally. Sedimentaries and pyroclastics are particularly subject to denudation, the common interlayering of such with lava flows creating somewhat irregular profiles, the latter being more resistant to erosion, forming ledges, waterfalls, etc. The role of gravitational mass movements of materials is particularly strong causing landslides, rockfalls, mudflows, creep, etc., creating massive talus slopes, backtilting and bending of strata, leaving great scars on mountain and valley sides.

In general, deep waters lie well in-shore. The exposed position of the islands, lacking protecting off-shore islets, reefs, dominant NE Trade Winds blowing constantly, storms originating westward where there is a long fetch, all such means that marine erosion is a most powerful agent of destruction and modification. In many islands the W, NW and N coasts show magnificent cliff development whereas S and SE coastal regions are more subdued, beaches, etc. Wind is significant as an agent of transport and deposition, with extensive dune developments in certain islands.

Landscapes of the world today date usually not much older than Neogene at the outside. Within such a time framework, geomorphologic youth accentuates juvenility.

In view of repeated rejuvenations within Macaronesia, created by fresh vulcanism, uplift of islands, withdrawals of the sea, it follows that the youthful stage of landscape development has known repeated interruptions, streams re-invigorated, new base-levels formed, terrains inundated with lava flows, covered by pyroclastics, new coastal regions developed. Hence geomorphologic youth characterizes the archipelagoes, with strong relief, deep, narrow valleys, vertical corrasion active, lack of meandering streams, flood plains all but non-existent, sharp crests, relatively few areas where fluvial or marine deposition has been prominent. Only in the eastern parts of the archipelagoes, in Maio, Boa Vista and Sal (Cape Verde), Fuerteventura and Lanzarote (Canary Islands), Porto Santo (Madeira), Sta. Maria (Azores) are valleys more open, meandering occurs, narrow flood plains, more subdued inland topography, etc. testify to a more advanced geomorphologic stage more consistent perhaps with maturity. It is worth noting also that with the possible exception of Porto Santo, the other islands either are or then are suggestive, of greater geological age.

## Igneous Rocks

Lava flows and volcanic ejectamenta constitute the building blocks of all islands, and the repeated interlayering of such indicate the persistent role of explosive phenomena. In most cases it appears that the islands stemmed from submarine outpourings on the ocean bed, and when built up to sea level, the edifices grew by subaerial vulcanism. Earlier workers spoke of ›Tiefengesteine‹ as forming basement material, but though plutonics in general have low stratigraphic positions and are of older age, it is doubtful if such actually constitute island foundations; volcanics, even sedimentaries, seem rather to play this role. Yet in some islands, e. g. in the Canaries, plutonic ›basal‹ complexes are of real significance, their occurrence as enclaves in volcanics and sedimentaries are of distinct interest. Dyke swarms are common in several islands, e. g. in the Canary and Cape Verde Islands. On occasion dykes may represent as much as some 90% of the host rocks, and the proliferation and complexity of such in Fuerteventura, Gran Canaria, Gomera and La Palma are considered by some as representing perhaps the finest dyke swarm complexes anywhere in the world.

The whole gamut of volcanic forms and structures are superbly displayed in these archipelagoes, none of which are more impressive that the great calderas, plugs and spines, dykes, lava and columnar structures, the great volcanic edifices of a Pico (Fogo), Pico de Teide (Tenerife), Montanha do Pico (Pico), etc. etc.

Petrochemically the igneous rocks belong to the alkalic magma series, with low alkalilime indices resulting in undersaturated residua. The ›Atlantic‹ suite can be subdivided into strongly-, moderately- and weakly-alkaline, depending upon the degree of silica deficiency, development of feldspathoids and titaniferous minerals. The ›Pacific‹ or calcalkaline series is not lacking, and to a lesser degree, the potassic or ›Mediterranean‹ suite. Representing extremes are the strongly alkaline or Na-alkaline occurrences of the Canary and Cape Verde Islands, and the tendency towards weakly alkaline to acidic character of the Azores. Such a variation in degree of alkalinity is no less obvious in other S. Atlantic Islands, e. g. strongly alkaline in Fernando de Noronha and St. Helena to strongly acidic in Ascension.

Table 5                                             Isofal values for Macaronesia and other Atlantic Islands

| I.  | *Macaronesian Islands* | | II. | *Macaronesian Archiperlagoes* | |
|---|---|---|---|---|---|
| | Azores: | | | Azores | 158 |
| | Flores ⎫ | | | Cape Verde | 130 |
| | Corvo ⎭ | 160 | | Canaries | 133 |
| | S. Miguel ⎫ | | | Madeira | 143 |
| | Sta. Maria ⎭ | 161 | III. | *Other Atlantic Islands* | |
| | Pico ⎫ | | | | |
| | Graciosa ⎬ | 142 | | Fernando Noronha | 124 |
| | S. Jorge ⎭ | | | Trindade | 119 |
| | Terceira | 240 | | S. Tomé-Principe | 127 |
| | | | | Fernando Poo | 150 |
| | Cape Verde: | | | St. Helena | 158 |
| | Fogo | 120 | | Ascension | 192 |
| | Maio | 120 | | Tristan da Cunha | 144 |
| | S. Vicente | 132 | | Gough | 158 |
| | | | | | |
| | Canaries: | | | | |
| | Tenerife | 135 | | | |
| | Gomera | 140 | | | |
| | Gran Canaria | 142 | | | |
| | La Palma | 130 | | | |
| | Fuerteventura | 150 | | | |
| | Hierro | 142 | | | |
| | | | | | |
| | Madeira: | | | | |
| | Madeira | 142 | | | |
| | Porto Santo | 145 | | | |

We refrain from entering into a detailed discussion of the petrochemistry of Macaronesian rocks, and of the various approaches that can be made we would mention only that of isofal values as determined from NIGGLI variation diagrams. In Tables 5, 6 we show such for Macaronesia with comparisons with other Atlantic islands. The strongly rhyolitic character of Ascension, with its late differentiates of quartztrachytes and rhyolites and yielding an isofal point value of 192 has frequently been referred to in the literature, and indeed this island has been thought to represent an isofal extreme for these islands. However, more recent study shows that Terceira in the Azores is even more extreme, 240, an exceptionally high value, which at this time has not been satisfactorily explained.

The view has been expressed more than once that there might be some compositional relationship with respect to distance of Atlantic islands from the MidAtlantic Ridge. The Azores approximately straddle the Ridge and show moderate-weak alkalinity and acidic characteristics; Ascension and Bouvet, close to or about on the Ridge are strongly rhyolitic; Gough and Tristan, further removed show moderate alkalinity with trachytic late differentiates of slight phonolitic tendencies; St. Helena, more removed still, is strongly alkaline with phonolitic late differentiates; yet further removed still are the more strongly phonolitic and alkaline nature of the Canary and

# The Geology of Macaronesia

Table 6    Petrochemical comparisons and isofalia of some Atlantic petrographic provinces (ESENWEIN 1929)

|        | Si  | Azores | Madeira | Canaries | Ascension | St. Helena |
|--------|-----|--------|---------|----------|-----------|------------|
|        | 80  | 13     | 15      | 15       |           |            |
|        | 100 | 17     | 20      | 21       | 20        | 17         |
| al     | 120 | 22     | 26      | 27       | 23        | 27         |
|        | 150 | 30     | 32      | 34       | 26        | 31         |
|        | 200 | 37     | 37      | 40       | 30        | 34         |
|        | 250 | 43     | 40      | 41       | 37        | 40         |
|        | 80  | 60     | 58      | 53       |           |            |
|        | 100 | 50     | 46      | 43       | 50        | 52         |
| fm     | 120 | 41     | 37      | 34       | 43        | 48         |
|        | 150 | 32     | 28      | 23       | 36        | 34         |
|        | 200 | 21     | 21      | 16       | 29        | 21         |
|        | 250 | 14     | 15      | 16       | 19        | 15         |
|        | 80  | 22     | 22      | 25       |           |            |
|        | 100 | 25     | 25      | 26       | 25        | 23         |
| c      | 120 | 26     | 24      | 23       | 23        | 20         |
|        | 150 | 20     | 21      | 15       | 20        | 18         |
|        | 200 | 13     | 13      | 5        | 14        | 11         |
|        | 250 | 4      | 11      | 5        | 7         | 5          |
|        | 80  | 5      | 5       | 7        |           |            |
|        | 100 | 8      | 9       | 10       | 5         | 8          |
| alk    | 120 | 11     | 13      | 16       | 11        | 15         |
|        | 150 | 18     | 19      | 28       | 18        | 17         |
|        | 200 | 29     | 29      | 39       | 27        | 34         |
|        | 250 | 39     | 34      | 39       | 37        | 40         |
|        | 80  | −40    | −40     | −48      |           |            |
|        | 100 | −32    | −36     | −40      | −20       | −32        |
| qz     | 120 | −24    | −32     | −44      | −24       | −40        |
|        | 150 | −22    | −26     | −62      | −22       | −18        |
|        | 200 | −16    | −16     | −56      | − 8       | −36        |
|        | 250 | − 6    | +14     | − 8      | + 2       | −10        |
|        | 80  | 8      | 10      | 8        |           |            |
|        | 100 | 9      | 11      | 11       | 15        | 9          |
| al-    | 120 | 11     | 13      | 12       | 12        | 12         |
| alk    | 150 | 12     | 13      | 6        | 8         | 14         |
|        | 200 | 8      | 8       | 1        | 3         | 0          |
|        | 250 | 4      | 6       | 3        | 0         | 0          |
|        | 80  | 14     | 12      | 17       |           |            |
|        | 100 | 14     | 16      | 15       | 10        | 14         |
| c-     | 120 | 15     | 11      | 12       | 11        | 8          |
| (al-   | 150 | 8      | 8       | 9        | 12        | 4          |
| alk)   | 200 | 5      | 5       | 4        | 11        | 11         |
|        | 250 | 0      | 5       | 2        | 7         | 5          |
| al=fm  |     | 31     | 30      | 30       | 29.5      | 31         |
| c      |     | 17.5   | 18      | 20       | 15        | 17         |
| alk    |     | 20.5   | 22      | 20       | 26        | 21         |
| qz     |     | −24    | −45     | −50      | −12       | −26        |
| si     |     | 158    | 143     | 130      | 192       | 158        |

Cape Verde Islands, Fernando de Noronha, Trindade. It thus seems as if the strongly alkaline character develops at a distance of some 700–800 km from the Ridge, becoming more rhyolitic as one approaches the Ridge, alkaline-acidic in the case of the Azores lying stride this major tectonic feature. In Macaronesia there is a strong likelihood that the respective islands increase in age from W to E, and adopting oceanfloor spreading concepts, the petrochemistry of the archipelagoes and other islands may indeed indicate both temporal sequences and spatial sequences in relation to the Rift.

## Sedimentary Rocks

Sedimentaries occupy a very minor place, yet in the past fossiliferous strata in ascertaining ages of volcanic events have proven of value.

Calcareaous material, in the form of various types of limestones, dolomites, calcareous sands and sandstones represent the dominant lithology – perhaps to the extent of some 90%. Sands, sandstones, clays, shales marls are much less important, but here and there conglomerates and breccias assume importance. Lignites and subbituminous coals are negligible, but in the past proved of some economic significance.

Table 7      Highest reported occurrences of Pre-Quaternary
             marine sediments in Macaronesia

| Island | Archipelago | Elev. (in m) | |
|---|---|---|---|
| Hierro | Canary Is. | ca. | 500 ? |
| Sta. Maria | Azores | | 400 |
| Madeira | Madeira | | 400 |
| Porto Santo | Madeira | | 350 |
| La Palma | Canary Is. | | 350 |
| Gran Canaria | Canary Is. | ca. | 300 |
| Fuerteventura | Canary Is. | ca. | 275 ? |
| Maio | Cape Verde | | 265 |
| S. Nicolau | Cape Verde | | 250 |
| Brava | Cape Verde | | 235 |
| Gomera | Canary Is. | | 200 ? |
| Lanzarote | Canary Is. | ca. | 200 ? |
| S. Tiago | Cape Verde | | 168 |
| Boa Vista | Cape Verde | ca. | 150 |
| Fogo | Cape Verde | | 114 |
| Sal | Cape Verde | | 105 |
| Sel. Grande | Selvagens | | 98 |
| S. Vicente | Cape Verde | | 70 |
| Tenerife | Canary Is. | | 65 |
| Il. Baixo | Madeira | | 61 |
| Il. Secos | Cape Verde | | 52 |
| Sta. Luzia | Cape Verde | | 50 |
| Il. Cima | Madeira | | 20 |
| Sel. Pequena | Selvagens | | 20 |
| Il. Razo | Cape Verde | | 18 |
| Sto. Antao | Cape Verde | | 4 |
| Formigas | Azores | | 1.5 ? |

Table 8      Chemical analyses of Macaronesian duricrusts (KREJCI–GRAF 1960)

|  | 1 | 2 | 3 | 4 | 5 | 6 | 7 | 8 | 9 | 10 | 11 | 12 |
|---|---|---|---|---|---|---|---|---|---|---|---|---|
| $H_2O$ | } 43.52a | } 43.05a | } 43.6a | } 43.70a | 0.27 | 0.52 | } 43.05 | 2.25 | 1.18 | 1.91 | 1.21 | 0.70 |
| Heat Loss |  |  |  |  | 44.2 | 44.37 |  | 36.85 | 21.28 | 43.86 | 42.41 | 38.95 |
| $MgCO_3$ | 0.1 | 1.96 | 1.27 | 3.30 | 3.57 | 2.50 | 6.67 | 9.48 | 9.40 | 3.26 | 5.13 | 1.18 |
| $CaCO_3$ | 98.88 | 95.60 | 98.5 | 94.21 | 94.7 | 94.0 | 86.21 | 70.1 | 45.6 | 85.7 | 85.1 | 94.7 |
| $Al_2O_3$ |  |  | } 0.008 |  | 0.17 | 0.09 | 1.28 | 0.38 | 0.59 | 0.38 | 0.26 | 0.60 |
| $Fe_2O_3$ | 0.11 | 0.19 |  | 0.17 | 0.60 | 0.10 | 0.84 | 2.32 | 0.25 | 0.30 | 0.97 | 0.54 |
| $SiO_2$ | 0.80 | 1.1 | 0.018 | 0.69 | 0.078 | 0.71 | 2.80 | 10.67 | 20.61 | 1.91 | 3.61 | 4.52 |
| Na |  |  |  |  | 0.016 | 0.024 | } 0.07b | 0.43 | 0.97 | 0.32 | 0.22 | 0.050 |
| K |  |  |  |  |  | 0.011 |  | 0.16 | 0.28 | 0.10 | 0.065 | 0.013 |
| Mg | 0.03 | 0.57 | 0.45 | 1.25 | 1.03 | 0.72 | 1.93 | 2.72 | 2.71 | 0.94 | 1.48 | 0.34 |
| Ca | 39.5 | 38.2 | 39.4 | 37.7 | 37.9 | 37.7 | 35.2 | 28.10 | 18.27 | 34.35 | 34.10 | 37.95 |
| Sr |  |  |  |  | 0.12 | 0.037 |  | 0.057 | 0.057 | 0.182 | 0.098 | 0.021 |
| $SO_4$ |  |  | <0.05 |  | 0.27 | 0.42 | 0.67 | 0.04 | 0.12 | 0.58 | 0.42 | <0.01 |
| Cl |  |  | <0.05 |  | <0.05 | <0.01 |  | 0.09 | <0.01 | 0.90 | <0.01 | 0.08 |
| Insol. in HCl | 0.1 | 0.9 |  | 0.47 |  | 0.09 |  | 3.10 | 18.81 | 0.51 | 2.12 | 0.15 |

(a)   $CO_2$ plus traces of $H_2O$ plus organic substances

(b)   $Na_2O + K_2O = 0.10\%$

1. Rib. Morro, Maio.
2. Vila de Maio, Maio.
3. Vila de Maio, Maio.
4. Cascabulho, Maio.
5. Cascabulho, Maio.
6. Casas Velhas, Maio.
7. Fuerteventura.
8. Caniçal, Madeira.
9. Caniçal, Madeira.
10. Fonte da Areia, Porto Santo.
11. Cabeço da Cruz, Porto Santo.
12. Ilheu da Cima, Porto Santo.

Maximum thickness is supposed to occur in West-Central Fuerteventura where some 900–1,300 m have been suggested. Little work has been done here, however, but the 435 m thickness of Mesozoics in Maio are well established. In the former island distinct folding occurs; and in the latter island very high dips, even vertical, are found, but in general throughout the archipelagoes dips of 25–30° are considered high. Occurrences extend from sea level up to some 400 m in the Azores and Madeira (Table 7).

Structures imposed upon the rocks are due essentially to volcano-tectonic disturbances or emplacements or then acquired through exogenic processes – bendings, bucklings, puckerings etc. brought about by mass gravitational movements. Only in Fuerteventura and Maio are there any significant foldings, with anticlines and synclines, strong tilting of strata, only here is one more certain of postulating faultings.

The repeated and often violent vulcanism throughout the history of these islands involves intercalations of lava flows, pyroclastics with sediments as the common form of occurrence of the latter, which in turn means that extensive, massive sedimentary outcrops are lacking except in Fuerteventura and Maio.

The above applies to pre-Quaternary sediments. Largely unconsolidated Quaternary and Recent sedimentary accumulations are to be found occurring along littoral areas and in flatter, lower inland areas, of terrestrial and marine origin. So frequently these represent drifting material, moved by winds, waves, steams, here and there forming quite large extents and thicknesses.

The climatic regimes pertaining favour strongly in some islands the development of duricrusts, the precipitation-out as evaporates of groundwaters. Such hardpans are usually thin – less than ca. 3 cm – but on occasion up to nearly 2 m. They are of pronounced calcareous nature – vd. Table 8. Their chief significance is of a negative nature in that they impede infiltrating waters, a most critical matter in the arid eastern Cape Verde Islands.

## Stratigraphy

Only in Maio, Cape Verde, have Mesozoics been substantially dated palaeontologically. Here the Neocomian occurs, but the question of Malm is a debatable one, long discussed, but even today no dogmatic stand can be taken. In West-Central Fuerteventura the Mesozoic has also been postulated, but here we are on much more doubtful ground. That Cenomanian-Turonian occurs is indeed quite probable, but suggestions of Dogger and Lias are highly questionable at this stage of our knowledge. Senonian in Cape Verde is not proven but is probable – in S. Nicolau at least. Further work in Fuerteventura, Maio and S. Nicolau are of cardinal importance as regards the Mesozoic in the broader implications of the geological history not only of the archipelagoes but also the N. Atlantic, palaeogeography, tectonics, continental linkages, oceanic evolution, etc. etc.

Palaeogene is not well established in any of the archipelagoes, but its presence in Cape Verde seems more likely.

With the Miocene, and especially the Vindobonian (Table 9) the stratigraphic sequence can be established throughout. Burdigalian is probable in Cape Verde and the

Table 9                    Sedimentary stratigraphic correlation chart, Macaronesia

| Eras | Systems | Series | Stages | Cape Verde | | | | | | | | | | | |
|---|---|---|---|---|---|---|---|---|---|---|---|---|---|---|---|
| | | | | Sto. Antão | S. Vicente | Sta. Luzia | Razo | S. Nicolau | Sal | Boa Vista | Maio | S. Tiago | Fogo | Brava | Ilheus Secos |
| Kainozoic | Neogene | Pliocene | Astian | ● | ● | | | x | ● | ● | ● | x | | ● | |
| | | | Plaisancian | | | | | | | | | | | | |
| | | Miocene | Pontian | | | | | | ● | | ● | | | | |
| | | | Vindobonian | ● | ● | x | x | x | ● | ● | ● | x | x | | ● |
| | | | Burdigalian | | | | | | ● | | ● | | | | |
| | Palaeogene | Oligocene | Aquitanian | | | | | | | | | | | | |
| | | | Stampian | | | | | | | ○ | ○ | | | | |
| | | | Sannoisian | | | | | | | | | | | | |
| | | Eocene | Ludian | | | | | | | | | | | | |
| | | | Bartonian | | | | | | | | | | | | |
| | | | Ledian | | | | | | | | | | | | |
| | | | Lutetian | | | | | ● | | ○ | ● | | | | |
| | | | Ypresian | | | | | | | | | | | | |
| | | | Landenian | | | | | | | | | | | | |
| | | | Montian | | | | | | | | | | | | |
| Mesozoic | Cretaceous | Upper (Senonian) | Danian | | | | | | | | | | | | |
| | | | Maestrichtian | | | | | | | | | | | | |
| | | | Campanian | | | | | ● | | | ○ | | | | |
| | | | Santonian | | | | | | | ○ | | | | | |
| | | | Coniacian | | | | | | | | | | | | |
| | | Upper | Turonian | | | | | | | | | | | | |
| | | | Cenomanian | | | | | | | | ● | | | | |
| | | Lower | Albian | | | | | | | | ● | | | | |
| | | | Aptian | | | | | | | | x | | | | |
| | | Lower (Neocomian) | Barremian | | | | | | | | x | | | | |
| | | | Hauterivian | | | | | | ○ | ○ | x | | | | |
| | | | Valanginian | | | | | | | | x | | | | |
| | Jurassic | Malm | Portlandian | | | | | | | ○ | ● | | | | |
| | | | Kimmeridgian | | | | | ● | | | | | | | |
| | | | Lusitanian | | | | | | | | | | | | |
| | | | Oxfordian | | | | | | | | | | | | |
| | | | Callovian | | | | | | | | | | | | |
| | | Dogger | | | | | | | | | | | | | |
| | | Lias | | | | | | | | | | | | | |

x : Recognized          ● : Probable or Possible          ○ : Conjectural

| Eras | Systems | Series | Stages | Hierro | La Palma | Gomera | Tenerife | Gran Canaria | Fuerteventura | Lanzarote | Selvagem Grande | Selvagem Pequena | Madeira | Porto Santo | Sta. Maria | Formigas |
|---|---|---|---|---|---|---|---|---|---|---|---|---|---|---|---|---|
| | | | | | | | | | | | Selvagens | | Madeira | | Azores | |
| | | | | | | | | Canaries | | | | | | | | |
| Kainozoic | Neogene | Pliocene | Astian | O | | | O | ● | O | | | | | ● | | |
| | | | Plaisancian | | | | | | | | | | | | ● | |
| | | Miocene | Pontian | | | | | ● | | | | | | ● | | |
| | | | Vindobonian | | ● | ● | | x | | ● | x | ● | x | x | x | x |
| | | | Burdigalian | | | | | ● | O | ● | | | | | | |
| | Palaeogene | Oligocene | Aquitanian | | | | | ● | | ● | | | | | | |
| | | | Stampian | | | | | | | | ● | | | | | |
| | | | Sannoisian | | | | | | | | | | | | | |
| | | Eocene | Ludian | | | | | | | | | | | | | |
| | | | Bartonian | | | | | | | | | | | | | |
| | | | Ledian | | | | | | | | | | | | | |
| | | | Lutetian | | | | | | | | | | | | | |
| | | | Ypresian | | | | | | | | | | | | | |
| | | | Landenian | | | | | | | | | | | | | |
| | | | Montian | | | | | | | | | | | | | |
| Mesozoic | Cretaceous | Upper (Senonian) | Danian | | | | | | | | | | | | | |
| | | | Maestrichtian | | | | | | | | | | | | | |
| | | | Campanian | | | | | | | | | | | | | |
| | | | Santonian | | | | | | | | | | | | | |
| | | | Coniacian | | | | | | | | | | | | | |
| | | Upper | Turonian | | | | | | | | | | | | | |
| | | | Cenomanian | | | | | | O | | | | | | | |
| | | Lower | Albian | | | | | | ● | | | | | | | |
| | | | Aptian | | | | | | | | | | | | | |
| | | Lower (Neocomian) | Barremian | | | | | | | | | | | | | |
| | | | Hauterivian | | | | | | O | | | | | | | |
| | | | Valanginian | | | | | | | | | | | | | |
| | Jurassic | Malm | Portlandian | | | | | | | | | | | | | |
| | | | Kimmeridgian | | | | | | | | | | | | | |
| | | | Lusitanian | | | | | | O | | | | | | | |
| | | | Oxfordian | | | | | | | | | | | | | |
| | | | Callovian | | | | | | | | | | | | | |
| | | Dogger | | | | | | | O | | | | | | | |
| | | Lias | | | | | | | O | | | | | | | |

4  Mitchell-Thomé, Middle Atlantic Islands

Canaries, perhaps Aquitanian in the latter. The Vindobonian is either established or then highly probable in all islands except Brava, Hierro and Tenerife. In the firstmentioned Vindobonian has been postulated, but evidence is equivocal; general poverty in pre-Quaternary sediments in Tenerife has so far militated against pronouncements whilst Hierro is a product of the Pliocene. Pliocene is present or probable in the majority of the Cape Verde Islands, less certain elsewhere.

Thus we can accept that parts of Macaronesia, as per stratigraphic studies, date back to lowermost Cretaceous, perhaps Upper Jurassic, maybe even earlier. For some archipelagoes suggestions were made in former years that Palaeozoic occurs, e. g. Cape Verde and Canary Islands. At the time such suggestions were proposed, they represented a minority view, and with increasing investigations the overwhelming opinion is that nowhere within Macaronesia is Palaeozoic present. The archipelagoes are products of Mesozoic times at the earliest for some islands, Pliocene at the latest. Isotopic datings for the Canaries (the only archipelago having any significant radiometric investigations) indicate that the volcanics date back no further than the Upper Palaeogene, and it would be in order to assume such for the other archipelagoes. We can say then that parts of Macaronesia date back to Mesozoic times, some 140 my ago or so, that most islands date from the Palaeogene, perhaps some 40 my ago, that probably Hierro, some 3 my old, is likely the youngest island in Macaronesia.

The stratigraphic correlation chart herewith presented must be viewed with all caution, it is far from being definitive, revisions, perhaps drastic at times, are to be expected, but may be of interest in summarizing our present stratigraphic knowledge of these islands.

## Palaeontology

Within the archipelagoes, fossil collections show great unevenness both spatially and temporally, and the same applies to studies made of the palaeontology. Certain islands and certain strata, e. g. the Mesozoic of Maio, the Miocene of Las Palmas, Gran Canaria, have been much studied and discussed by various workers as regards the palaeontology and stratigraphy, contrasting, e. g. with Gomera where in essence no studies whatsoever along these lines have been carried out. The reporting by scholars of large numbers of species from certain areas of certain islands, the mentioning of one or two species here and there, the absence of any palaeontological information from yet other regions and islands tends therefore to give a very distorted view, giving an unfounded impression that some areas, some islands, show rich faunal collections whilst other areas, other islands, are lacking in such.

We would also note that in many instances collections have been given only preliminary study or then that collections have only been investigated by one person, that evidently there are stacked away in various places valuable collections which scholars hope one day to have the time to study.

Then there are the usual topics of taxonomic debate and stratigraphic age or range, character of the marine environment, endemic and migrant, continental affinities and with which continent, etc. etc. No less has criticism been voiced upon the undue emphasis and unnecessarily long and involved debates over one particular feature of animals, e. g. the aptychi of the Maio Mesozoic Ammonoids, to the detriment not only of other characteristics of these animals but to a general study of the Ammonoids as a whole.

Lastly we might mention the disproportionate studies made on the macrofauna with respect to the microfauna, the latter having received much less attention.

All the phyla and classes consistent with the time scale of the archipelagoes are to be found, terrestrial and marine organisms, littoral, neritic environments in general, nektonic and planktonic forms dominant for the macrofauna, benthonic for the microfauna. Many scholars have commented upon the great diversity of forms of the Helicidae family of terrestrial gastropods which all show strong European affinities, and indeed in general, the faunal associations of all archipelagoes are close to those of Western Europe and N. Africa - a fact obviously seized upon by palaeontologists in advocating continental linkages in some way.

The history of the islands has not been conducive to the preservation of plants but such do have occurrences, e. g. in Gran Canaria, Madeira, Sta. Maria, Sto. Antao. The literature quite frequently refers to fossil floral finds, but no further information is given - exactly where, geological environment, species, etc.

Without question, for the sedimentologist, stratigrapher, palaeontologist Macaronesia represents a future happy hunting ground.

## Vulcanicity and Seismicity of Historic Times

That not all the islands are volcanically ›dead‹ is witnessed by the eruptions of historic times (Table 10). Vulcanism within the past 550 odd years has occurred in the Azores, Canaries and Cape Verde Islands, with at least some 57 volcanic events, about one event every 9 years. Fogo in Cape Verde and S. Miguel in the Azores have shown the liveliest activity, Lanzarote (Canaries), Faial and S. Jorge (Azores) the least. Since Europeans discovered Fogo, vulcanism has taken place each century, a regularity unknown in other islands. Contrasting with this, in Pico (Azores) no activity has been recorded for some 250 years. This century alone has seen five occasions of eruptivity, and the most recent of all, that in La Palma, occurred in 1971.

As vulcanism in Macaronesia dates back to Palaeogene times, with many many occasions of quiet and explosive emissions, submarine and subaerial, it is obvious that this part of the earth has shown a persistence in vulcanism spanning a period of some 40 odd my. Taking a proper perspective of geological time, and with the future unknown, it is hazardous to speculate whether or not vulcanism is quietening down.

Along with the historic vulcanism in the above islands, tremors, preceding, during and following after such outbursts have been experienced, but earthquakes of tectonic origin within historic times are restricted to the Azores. This archipelago lies on the Atlantic extension of the Gibralter-Mediterranean seismic belt. In the Azores tremors have been neither particularly violent nor frequent and not all islands have been equally affected. S. Miguel more than any other Azorean island has experienced earthquakes in historic times, whilst such have been unknown in Corvo and Flores. The Azores are

# The Geology of Macaronesia

Table 10          Recorded vulcanism within historic times in Macaronesia

| | Cape Verde | Canaries | | | Azores | | | | |
|---|---|---|---|---|---|---|---|---|---|
| | Fogo | Tenerife | La Palma | Lanzarote | S. Miguel | Terceira | Faial | Pico | S. Jorge |
| 1427–1432 ? | | x | | | x? | | | | |
| 1432–1444 ? | | x | | | x? | | | | |
| 1500 | x | | | | x | | | x | |
| 1562–1564 | x | | | | x | | | x | |
| 1580–1585 | x | | x | | | | | | x |
| 1596 | x | | | | | | | | |
| 1604 | x | | | | | | | | |
| 1630 | | | | | x | | | | |
| 1638 | | | | | x | | | | |
| 1646 | | | x | | | | | | |
| 1652 | | | | | x | | | | |
| 1662–1663 | x | | | | | | | | |
| 1664 | x | | | | | | | | |
| 1672–1673 | x | | | | | | x | | |
| 1675 | x | | | | | | | | |
| 1677–1678 | | | x | | | | | | |
| 1680 | x | | | | | | | | |
| 1682 | | | | | x | | | | |
| 1689 | x | | | | | | | | |
| 1693 | x | | | | | | | | |
| 1695 | x | | | | | | | | |
| 1699 | x | | | | | | | | |
| 1704–1706 | | x | | | | | | | |
| 1712 | x | | x | | | | | | |
| 1713 | x | | | | | | | | |
| 1718–1720 | | | | | | x | | x | |
| 1721–1725 | x | | | | | | | | |
| 1730–1736 | | | | x | | | | | |
| 1761 | x | | | | | x | | | |
| 1774 | x | | | | | | | | |
| 1785 | x | | | | | | | | |
| 1799 | x | | | | | | | | |
| 1808 | | | | | | | | | x |
| 1811 | | | | | x | | | | |
| 1816–1817 | x | | | | | | | | |
| 1824 | | | | x | | | | | |
| 1847 | x | | | | | | | | |
| 1852 | x | | | | | | | | |
| 1857 | x | | | | | | | | |
| 1867 | | | | | | x | | | |
| 1909 | | x | | | | | | | |
| 1949 | | | x | | | | | | |
| 1951 | x | | | | | | | | |
| 1957–1958 | | | | | | | x | | |
| 1971 | | | x | | | | | | |

closest of all Macaronesian archipelagoes to the tectonically significant Mid-Atlantic Ridge which suggests a causal relationship, and yet we must notice that the Azorean islands closest of all to this feature (the presumed axis thereof anyway) namely, Corvo and Flores, have been seismically inactive these past 500 odd years. whilst the S. Miguel-Sta. Maria region, furthest removed from said axis, has been seismically the most active within this same period.

## Structure-Tectonics

Structures of purely tectonic origin seem singularly lacking in the archipelagoes: Macaronesia is not a region where orogenies have held sway. Folding and proven faulting, other than on a small and local scale is absent. Only in West-Central Fuerteventura and in Maio is significant folding, steep tilting of strata, faulting to be observed, and even here it is more likely that such are due to the emplacements of igneous rocks or at least of volcano-tectonic origin. It is further to be noted that in the above islands it is the Mesozoics which are thus disturbed and here and elsewhere younger rocks show much less deformation. This is not to say that such younger rocks are devoid of all evidences of disturbance – indeed the minor puckerings, wrinklings, bendings, breaks are notable features, but such are superficial, local in nature, very frequently due to mass gravitational movements, deformations due to more localized volcanic events, structures imposed by wind, waves and running waters. Other than in the Fuerteventura and Maio Mesozoics, one is impressed rather by the gentle dips, the horizontality or quasi-horizontality of volcanics and sediments alike. This is particularly so with the great sequences of lava flows which so frequently present the appearance of tableland forms, so excellently displayed in many cliffed coastal sections and within the steep, narrow valleys.

In most islands one can recognize or then surmise centres of greater volcanic activity of higher elevation, flows and pyroclastics being spread out radially so that in general in each island strata are inclined towards the respective peripheries.

The literature makes copious references to that conveniently nebulous term ›fractures‹, not only in the islands themselves but in the vicinal seas also. A veritable plethora of ›fractures‹, ›zones of disturbance‹, ›deep fissures‹ etc. have been suggested and delineated in maps, but the evidence for all these is flimsy in the extreme – trends of bathymetric contours, island outlines, coastal trends, alignments of volcanoes, trends of valleys, orientation of scarps, and, in a few cases, geophysical proposals for such. Protagonists of lineament tectonics have ample room here to use their imaginations, sweeping straight or gently curved lines can be extended for hundreds, even some thousands of kilometres, in the subjective approach so characteristic of lineament delineations, it just seems so obvious that such and such must be connected by some kind of alignment. Frequently one cannot help but suspect that the Almighty is being dictated to.

That fissuring in the crust, perhaps down to the Upper Mantle, has provided the means of egress of magmas to higher levels we do not doubt but to assume therefrom that such have provided the means for great transform, transcurrent faulting, gravity

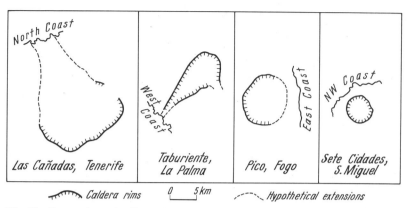

Fig. 23. Comparisons in dimensions of major calderas of Macaronesia.

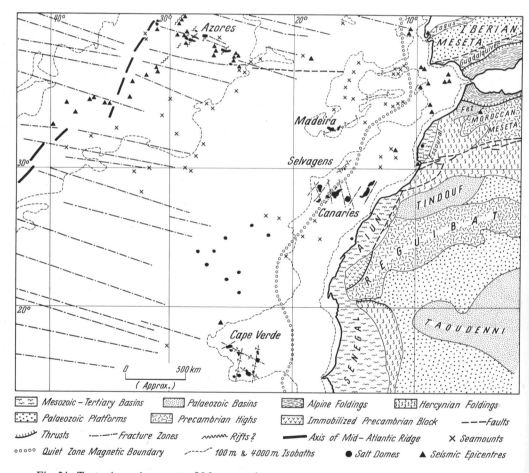

Fig. 24. Tectonic environment of Macaronesia.

faulting with hundred of metres of vertical displacement, subsidences and uplifts experienced, snapping of continental linkages, etc. is surely unwarranted. Continental linkages of some islands, inter-island linkages are matters of pure speculation at this time, the role of isostatic readjustments tends to be overplayed, and certainly on an island (i. e. terra firma) basis, more and more are scholars impressed by the role of exogenic processes in the outlining of several features once thought to be of tectonic origin. Even the great calderas (vd. Fig. 23) seem to owe their present appearance as much to exogenic processes as to volcano-tectonic subsidence.

Eustatism and uplift of islands must certainly be recognized, no less must one have some regard for the contentions of biologists and palaeontologists who would postulate continental linkages – via landbridges or shallow intervening seas, and the same also for some inter-island and inter-archipelago linkages. Geologists are as fashion-conscious as the next man, marine geophysics, palaeomagnetism, ocean-floor spreading, the ›new global tectonics‹ are all the rage of the moment, that these have stimulated new interests, enthusiasms is but natural, but one has an uncomfortable feeling that such disciplines as stratigraphy, palaeontology, petrological considerations are being pushed too much in the background, and the time-worn adage »Things are not always what they seem« gives extra food for thought.

Fig. 24 shows the tectonic environment of these Middle Atlantic Islands. The many seamounts, seismic epicentres, ›fractures‹, presumed ›riftings‹ other than that of the central Ridge, unevenness of the ocean floor, the faulted and folded character of the neighbouring mainlands of Iberia and Africa, the prolonged, extensive and often violent vulcanism experienced in Macaronesia, seismicity in the Azores, all this is indicative how unstable is this part of the earth, critically located near Alpine orogenic belts, the stable craton of Africa, the immense Central Atlantic fracture, near to where the Eurasian, African and American plates meet. In this eastern part of the Atlantic this ocean originated, a tectonic event of the first magnitude, and Macaronesia lying between continental margins and the Mid-Atlantic Rift, occupies a focal area in global tectonics.

## Economic Geology

Macaronesia is singularly lacking in mineral resources of economic significance. Metallics are quite negligible, only very rarely might these warrant prospecting, e. g. the black sands of southern Hierro, said to be rich in magnetite and/or Ti-magnetite. The non-metallics have slightly more importance and of these sodium chloride, evaporated from sea waters in coastal pans in several islands thus provides local sources of salt, important especially in the fishing industry. At one time the carbonaceous deposits of Madeira were of local value, not any more, but seemingly no investigations have been made here as regards potentialities. For various local building purposes, the volcanics and pyroclastics are noteworthy, but largescale developments, quarries, crushing centres, etc. are only of minor concern. Clays, pumice and pozzuolane deposits enter locally into the manufacture of pottery, tiles; local sands in the cement industry. As one might expect, mineral and thermal springs are quite plentiful, of local significance, the bottling of waters forms local industries. Discussions on developing geothermal energy from thermal springs, especially in the Azores, have been made, but to date nothing further has been done.

Lacking all fuels and the basic ingredients of light and heavy industries, imports must therefore be made. Such lacks are not critical for the islands, where agriculture and tourism form the chief sources of revenue.

Water, that common, ordinary, unexciting commodity, is seldom given its proper place as an economic asset. As a generalization, fresh water for all needs is a problem in all archipelagoes, none more so than in the arid to semi-arid Cape Verde Islands. All archipelagoes experience long, dry warm spells, all islands have their wetter and drier regions, all islands know what torrential rains are, swollen rivers, long parched periods, in the majority of islands more plentiful water supplies are available not in the flatter, lower areas where the major populations and agriculture are to be found. In some cases, e. g. Cape Verde, pressure of population aggravates the water situation, in other cases, e. g. the Canary Islands, the enormous influx of tourists, especially in summer when it is driest, places heavy strains on water supplies. The surrounding seas offer the obvious solution via desalinization methods, but technological feasibilities are not always to be equated with economic feasibilities. In only relatively few cases would the establishment of desalinization plants offer much respite or be justified on economic grounds. In all islands, agriculture has the greatest need of water, either direct or then via irrigation, and certainly for the foreseeable future there is no question of irrigation using desalinized waters on a cost basis. Yearly the situation worsens in all archipelagoes, yet one sees the tremendous propaganda to encourage tourists, building of great hotels and other prestige structures, emphasis is placed on increasing crop yields, use of fertilizers, etc., but plans to study, develop the water resources are meagre in comparison. The obvious solution everywhere in the world to water shortage problems is to make water more expensive, for the true worth of cheap items is never apprecciated.

## Geologic Evolution

In Fuerteventura and Maio, thick, highly disturbed Mesozoic rocks outcrop, the oldest known in Macaronesia. Further, Lanzarote, Sal and Boa Vista are thought to be old, possibly dating from the same period. These five islands are the nearest of all Macaronesian islands to the African mainland, some 100–450 km distant. These islands show continental affinities, in crustal type, sedimentary lithologies, stratigraphy and palaeontology, perhaps also in structural characteristics. On the other hand, it appears that the volcanics date no older than the Upper Palaeogene, and hence the origins of Macaronesia began with the formation of thick deposits, largely of limestones mixed with detritals, that is, of marine deposition with incursions of material from a continental source upon a continental margin. After the formation of these Mesozoics deformations took place, resulting in pronounced folding, faulting also in Fuerteventura, up-ending of the strata as far as the vertical in Maio. The formation and disturbance of these older rocks predates vulcanism. The cause(s) of the diastrophism are not certain: in the case of Fuerteventura, much nearer to the mainland, deformations experienced might represent more distant echoes of Alpine orogeny in Iberia and the Atlas region; in Maio disturbances may have resulted from diapiric-type intrusions, piercing, thrusting aside, jostling of loosened Mesozoic blocks. The birth of Macaronesia then began with sedimentation in a marine environment, followed by strong deformation.

Elsewhere in the Middle Atlantic Islands, events began with submarine outpourings on the sea bed which appear to date from the Upper Palaeogene. Deep crustal fissures, perhaps penetrating down to the Upper Mantle, allowed means of egress for magmas to attain higher levels, spewing forth on the sea floor, building up to sea level, continuing as subaerial emissions, a process which has continued down to the present. In some islands vulcanism likely began rather in Lower Miocene times, and in the case of Hierro, youngest of the islands, this dates from the Pliocene, so that vulcanism is a feature of Tertiary times. Various interruptions occurred during this relatively long period of vulcanicity – cessations of volcanic activity, uplifts of islands, subsidences, marine depositions over volcanics, burying of landscapes under fresh outpourings of lava and inundations of pyroclastics. That vertical movements have been significant is seen in the occurrence of pillow lavas at elevations of ca. 600 m in La Palma, marine limestones at 400 m in Sta. Maria and Madeira, old beach deposits at 150 m in Flores (vd. Table 11), river terraces at 250 m in S. Nicolau. Along with positive and negative movements of terra firma there was also eustatic fluctuations of sea level. No geological process has been allowed to pursue its course uninterruptedly for any great length of time, some event has taken place to break the rhythm so that geomorphologic youth is typical.

The opening of the N. Atlantic is postulated to have been initiated some 190 my ago, but some 70% of the total drift took place during the last 70 odd my. This places the active phase of drift as beginning in Albian-Aptian times, the time when the Mesozoic succession on Maio becomes more interrupted, when transgressions began, when emergences took place. The more active phase of drifting occurred at the beginning of the Palaeogene, and as we have noted, by Upper Palaeogene it is believed that the majority of the islands had begun their volcanic evolution. The slowest rate of ocean floor spreading for this part of the Atlantic occurred during the period 38 to 9 my ago, the time within which almost all the islands established themselves volcanically. Whilst speculation on the matter is perhaps premature, at this time one is inclined to associate vulcanism and the construction of the islands, which are all essentially volcanic edifices, with the development of the Atlantic Ocean, with the evolution of ocean floor spreading, drifting, such have acted as ›triggers‹: in more than one sense, most islands here are the offspring of the parent ocean.

The Geology of Macaronesia

Table 11     Correlation of marine terraces (heights in m) in Macaronesia and neighbouring mainlands

| Archipelago | Azores | | | | | | | | |
|---|---|---|---|---|---|---|---|---|---|
| Island | Flores | Corvo | Faial | Pico | S. Jorge | Gracio-sa | Tercei-ra | S. Miguel | Sta. Maria |
| Flandrian | | | 0.5−2 | 3−5 | | | | 4 | 2−4.5 |
| Neo-Tyrrhenian (Tyrr. III) | 8−15 | | | 6 | 8? | 5−9 | 7−10 | | 6−12 |
| Eu-Tyrrhenian (Tyrr. II) | 12−20 | | 15 | | | | | | 12−15 |
| Palaeo-Tyrrhenian (Tyrr. I) | 30 | 30 | | | | | | | |
| Milazzian (Neo−Sicilian II) | − | | | | | | | | 50−60 |
| Palaeo-Sicilian (I) | 150 | | | | | | 100 | 90 | 80−100 |
| Calabrian | | | | | | | | | |
| Pliocene ? | | | | | | | | | |

| Archipelago | Canaries | | | | | | |
|---|---|---|---|---|---|---|---|
| Island | Hierro | La Palma | Gomera | Tenerife | Gran Canaria | Fuerte-ventura | Lanzar-ote |
| Flandrian | 4 | 4 | 3.5−4 | 3.5−4.8 | 3.5−4.8 | 4 | 3−4 |
| Neo-Tyrrhenian (Tyrr. III) | | 6−13 | | 7.6−8.2 | 6−13 | 7 | 4.9−7 |
| Eu-Tyrrhenian (Tyrr. II) | ca. 18 | ca. 25 | 18 | ca. 15 | 15−22 35− | 15−18 | 15−18 |
| Palaeo-Tyrrhenian (Tyrr. I) | 30? | | | | ca.100 | 25−35 | 25−45 |
| Milazzian (Neo-Sicilian II) | | | | | 55 | 55 | 55 |
| Palaeo-Sicilian (I) | | | | | 100? | 60 | 60 |
| Calabrian | | | | | | | |
| Pliocene ? | | | | 60 | | | |

Table 11      (continued)

| Archipelago | Cape   Verde | | | | | | | | |
|---|---|---|---|---|---|---|---|---|---|
| Island | S. Antao | S. Vicente | S. Nico-lau | Ilheus Secos | Fogo | S. Tiago | Maio | Sal | Boa Vista |
| Flandrian | 3–6 | 2–6 | 3–4 | | | 2–6 | 2–6 | 2–6 | 3 |
| Neo-Tyrrhenian (Tyrr. III) | | | | ca. 10 | | 8–12 | 8–12 | 7–8 | 10? |
| Eu-Tyrrhenian (Tyrr. II) | ca. 17 | | | | | 15–20 | 15–20 | 13 | |
| Palaeo-Tyrrhenian (Tyrr. I) | | | | | | 30–45 | 30–40 | 55 | |
| Milazzian (Neo-Sicilian II) | | | | | 50 | 50–60 | 50–60 | | |
| Palaeo-Sicilian (I) | | | 70–90 | | 100 | | 80–100 | | |
| Calabrian | | | | | | | | | |
| Pliocene ? | | | | | | | | | |

| Archipelago | Madeira | | Selvagens | | Mauri-tania | Moroc-co | Gibral-ter | Portugal |
|---|---|---|---|---|---|---|---|---|
| Island | Madeira | Porto Santo | S. Grande | S. Pequema | | | | |
| Flandrian | 4.5? | 1.5 / 4–6 | 2 | | | 2 | 5 | ± 2 |
| Neo-Tyrrhenian (Tyrr. III) | 8–10 | | 7–11 | 10? | 2–7 | 6–8 | 8.5 | 5–8 |
| Eu-Tyrrhenian (Tyrr. II) | 15 | 12–15 | | | 12–20 | 15–20 | 15 | 12–20 |
| Palaeo-Tyrrhenian (Tyrr. I) | 30? | ± 25 | | | 30–40 | 25–30 | 33 | 30–45 |
| Milazzian (Neo-Sicilian II) | 50 | | | | 55 | 55–60 | 62 | 50–60 |
| Palaeo-Sicilian (I) | 100 | 100 | | | | 100 | 99 | 80–90? |
| Calabrian | | | | | | + 100 | 180–210 | 150–160? |
| Pliocene ? | | | | | | | | 180–190 |

# CHAPTER 4

# Geology of the Azores Archipelago

## General

Probably the earliest publication to mention geological matters is that of ALBUQUERQUE (1826). A landmark in the literature was the appearance of HARTUNG's book in 1860, a real geological contribution. BRONN (1860) was the first to report on fossils in Sta. Maria, whilst REISS (1862) was the first to describe the Tertiary beds here.

FOUQUÉ between 1867 and 1873 wrote several papers dealing mostly with various aspects of vulcanism and the petrography of some rocks. From about 1880 to 1890, CANTO in a series of papers described earlier historic eruptivities as well as some mineral and petrographic studies.

In 1883 appeared the first detailed publication devoted solely to igneous petrography, that of MÜGGE, and in 1888 OSANN described sanidinites from S. Miguel.

Two Azorean scholars, AGOSTINHO and CHAVES have written on the geology of the islands, the former being especially interested in vulcanicity, seismicity and tectonics.

ESENWEIN (1929), FRIEDLÄNDER (1929) and BERTHOIS (1953b) treat of the whole archipelago, the first two restricting themselves to igneous matters whilst BERTHOIS discusses the physical and chemical character of both igneous and sedimentary rocks. Of more recent times, ZBYSZEWSKI in particular, O. V. Ferreira, C. R. Ferreira, Almeida, Medeiros, Machado and ASSUNÇAO have contributed many papers.

An excellent series of geological maps is available for all islands on scales of 1:25,000 and 1:50,000. These sheets, along with their accompanying descriptive accounts (›Noticias explicativas‹) have appeared at intervals from 1961 to 1973. Even the allbut-submerged (at high tide) Formigas Banks have been visited and geologically reported upon.

As is so frequently the case with these larger archipelagoes, the status of our knowledge and number of publications vary considerably amongst the islands. The outermost islands of Corvo and Flores, also Graciosa and S. Jorge have received less attention than others, whilst S. Miguel seems to have attracted most scholars, has a more copious bibliography.

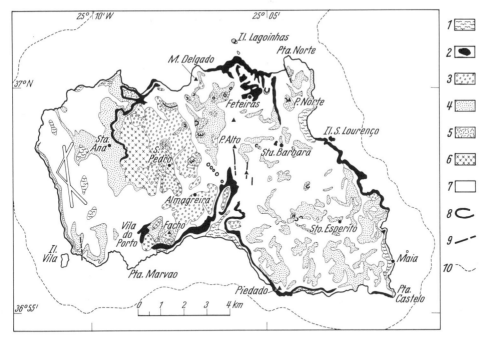

Fig. 27. Geological map of Ilha de Santa Maria, Azores. 1: Alluvium, scree deposits, old Quaternary beaches. 2: Tuffs, sandstones, conglomerates, limestones; Vindobonian. 3: Almagreira and S. Pedro red tuffs. 4: Pyroclastics. 5: Scoria cones. 6: S. Pedro and Facho basalts. 7: Undifferentiated basalts. 8: Chief preserved craters. 9: Faults. 10: 100 m isobath. (Modified after Carta Geol. de Portugal, Serv. Geol., 1960).

After the Canary Islands, the Azores have been better surveyed than any other archipelago mentioned here.

## Geomorphology

In general the Azores are lacking in more spectacular landscapes. The relief is less pronounced, slopes less steep down to coasts, high cliffs less prominent, valleys more winding and open, level terrains in island interiors and low coastal areas more common than in other archipelagoes. This is the only archipelago to have crater- and calderalakes and ponds. The islands tend to display a more subdued, rolling aspect, yet the islands do possess landforms of distinct interest.

The literature gives little more than passing reference to topographic and geomorphologic features and only the islands of Corvo (MEDEIROS, 1967) (Fig. 35), Graciosa (FERREIRA, 1968) (Fig. 36) and Terceira (MOTTET, 1972) (Figs. 31, 34, 37) have been given somewhat more morphological study. Terceira, a centrally located island, can be taken as representative of the archipelago, which we shall discuss.

The island comprises four volcanic massifs with calderas as follows:

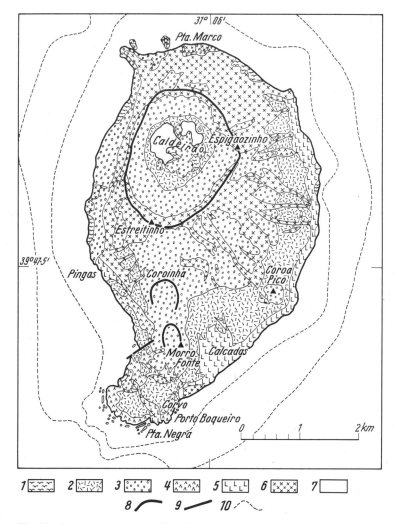

Fig. 29. Geological map of Ilha do Corvo, Azores. 1: Alluvium. 2: Pyroclastics. 3: Scoria accumulations. 4: Andesites and peridotitic andesites. 5: Doleritic basalts, olivine-basalts, etc. with andesitic tendencies. 6: Basalts with plagioclase and olivine, ankaramites, etc. 7: Craters. 8: Faults. 9: Crater lakes. 10: 50 and 100 m isobaths. (Modified after Carta Geol. de Portugal, Serv. Geol., 1967).

Fig. 30. Geological map of Ilha das Flores, Azores. 1: Alluvium, beach pebbles, talus deposits. 2: Old beach deposits. 3: Pyroclastics. 4: Breccia and scoria cones. 5: Trachytes. 6: Trachyte-andesite complex. 7: Peridotitic andesites. 8: Andesite complex. 9: Basalt complex. 10: Volcanic craters. 11: Crater lakes. 12: Faults. 13: 20 and 50 m isobaths. (Modified after Carta Geol. de Portugal, Serv. Geol., 1968).

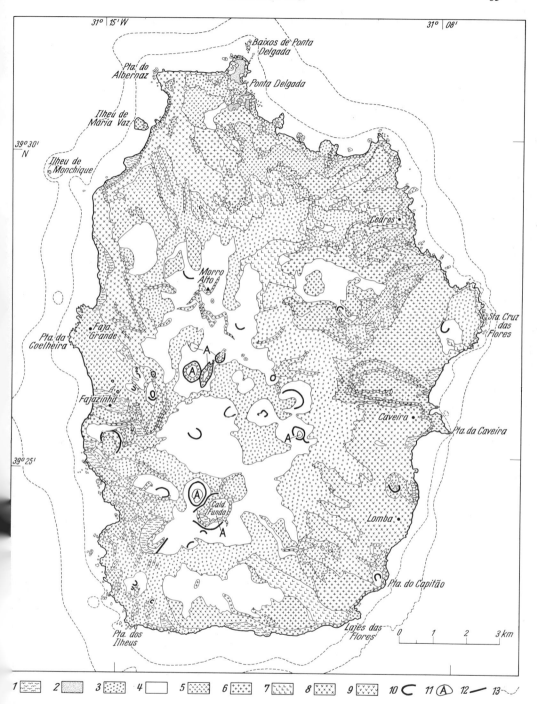

31° 15' W

Baixos de Ponta Delgada

Pta. do Albernaz

Ponta Delgada

31° 08'

Ilheu de Maria Vaz

39° 30' N

Ilheu de Monchique

Cedros

Morro Alto

Sta. Cruz das Flores

Faja Grande

Pta. da Coelheira

Fajazinha

Caveira

Pta. da Caveira

39° 25'

Cald. Funda

Lomba

Pta. do Capitão

Pta. dos Ilheus

Lajes das Flores

0    1    2    3 km

1    2    3    4    5    6    7    8    9    10    11 Ⓐ    12    13

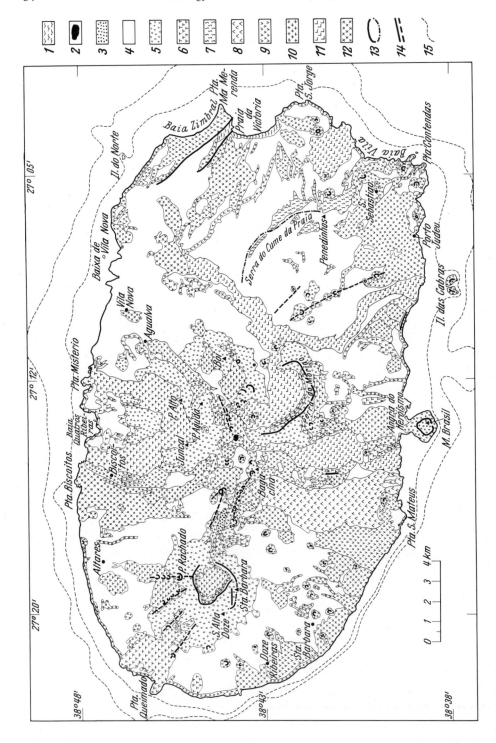

(A) **Serra do Cume.** The range rises to a height of 545 m, gentle external slopes showing radial drainage well incised. To the W is a more abrupt slope down to an altitude of ca. 300 m, extending for 6 km to the SW. The Cume scarp has evolved from the faulted caldera rim, it being a fault-line scarp. Within the caldera strombolian cones rise up to 482 m, a small barrier-type lake has developed by volcanic blockage. To the

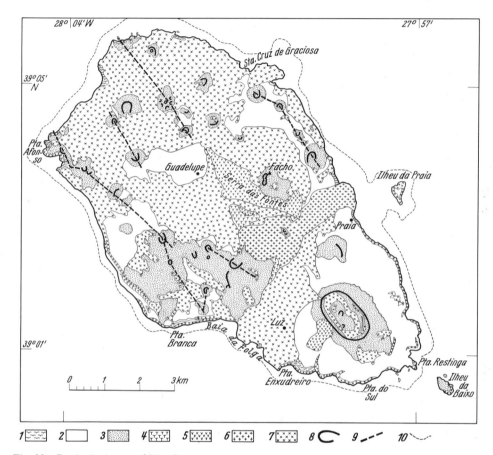

Fig. 33. Geological map of Ilha Graciosa, Azores. 1: Alluvium – beach sands and pebbles, old Quaternary beaches. 2: Pyroclastics. 3: Scoria cones. 4: Trachytes. 5: Andesites. 6: Praia basalts. 7: Basalt complex. 8: Volcanic craters. 9: Faults. 10: 20 m isobath. (Modified after Carta Geol. de Portugal, Serv. Geol., 1971).

Fig. 31. Geological map of Ilha Terceira, Azores. 1: Alluvium, beach sands, dunes. 2: Fumarolic deposits of "Furnas do Euxofre". 3: Pyroclastics of "Misterio dos Negros" (1761 eruption). 4: Pyroclastics. 5: Scoria cones. 6: Trachytes and trachy-andesites. 7: Trachytic-andesitic complex of Serra do Cume. 8: Andesitic outpourings of S. Mateus. 9: Andesitic complex. 10: Basalts of the 1761 eruption. 11: Basalt flows of Caldeira do G. Moniz, Terra Cha, Porto Martins and Pico das Contendas. 12: Basalt complex. 13: Volcanic craters. 14: Faults. 15: 50 and 100 m isobaths. (Modified after Carta Geol. de Portugal, Serv. Geol., 1970).

5  Mitchell-Thomé, Middle Atlantic Islands

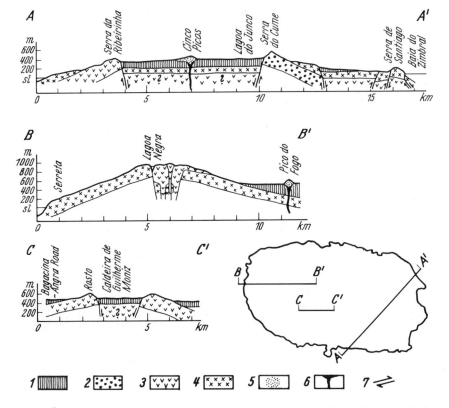

Fig. 34. Geological cross-sections, Ilha Terceira, Azores. 1: Basalts. 2: Trachy-andesites. 3: Trachytes. 4: Andesites. 5: Scoria. 6: Chimney of Strombolian cone. 7: Faults. (Modified after MOTTET, 1972).

SW the caldera is enclosed by another asymmetric chain rising to 410 m, the Serra da Ribeirinha, again with steeper interior slopes, outer slopes descending gently towards the island capital. The NE part of the island, an outer extremity of this volcanic complex, on the basis of stage of morphologic development, appears to be the oldest part of the island. Tectonism has occured here, earth-tremors are not unknown, and the resulting landscape owes more to diastrophism than vulcanism. A graben trends NW-SE, 8 km in length and 3.5 km in breadth, bounded by a fault scarp of the NE side and an abrupt break in slope (fault-linc scarp?) on the SW side. The floor of the graben is gently tilted towards the NW, meeting the coast in 40 m high cliffs, but also declining towards the SE. A smaller secondary graben occurs where the township of Praia de Vitoria lies, and in this SE part of the graben(s) sandy beaches and swampy areas are to be found, the former being the only extensive sandy beach in the island. The Serra de Santiago NE of the graben, rising to 124 m and with a scarp, probably fault-scarp, some 5 km in length, rises above the graben in the nature of a horst. The intervening graben has separated the two Serras, Santiago once forming the outer slopes of Cume. However,

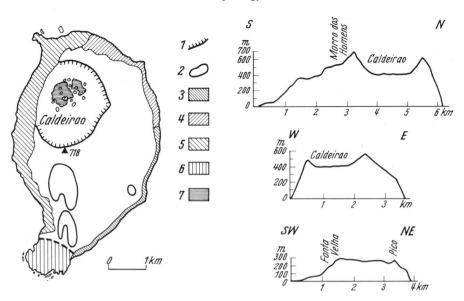

Fig. 35. Morphologic map and topographic profiles of Corvo, Azores. 1: Caldera. 2: Secondary
cones. 3: Abrupt slopes < 200 m. 4: Abrupt slopes 200–400 m. 5: Abrupt slopes to > 400 m.
6: Upraised marine platform 10–60 m altitude. 7: Lakes. (Modified after MEDEIROS, 1967).

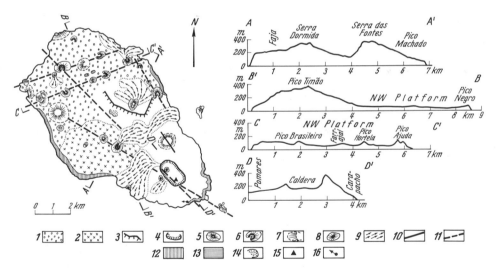

Fig. 36. Morphologic map and topographic profiles of Ilha Graciosa, Azores. 1: Basaltic platform. 2: Eroded trachytic massif. 3: Fault scarp. 4: Caldera. 5: Well-preserved cone of circular
crater. 6: Well preserved cone of clearly-defined craters. 7: Eroded volcanic form. 8: Cupula.
9: Recent lava flows. 10: Observed fracture. 11: Probable fracture. 12: Steep slopes of 150–300 m.
13: Steep slopes of 50–150 m. 14: Talus. 15: Fumarole. 16: Thermal spring. (Modified after
A. B. FERREIRA, 1968).

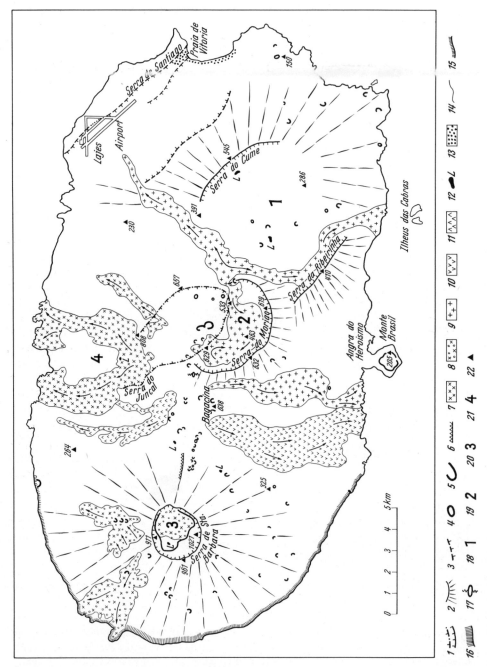

Fig. 37. Generalized morphologic map of Terceira, Azores. 1: Caldera scarps. 2: External slopes of caldera massifs. 3: Fault-scarp of the NE. 4: Adventive Strombolian cones. 5: Breaches Strombolian cones. 6: Mushroom-domes of 1761 eruption. 7: Trachytic northern lava flows.

upraise of Santiago also occurred as is shown by Quaternary beach deposits 15 m above present sea level. Thus this NE part of the island has undergone faulting, creating grabens and horst, both of these have undergone tilting, and here tectonism rather than vulcanism has been the controlling factor. The caldera itself was initiated by foundering though erosive processes and later vulcanism have combined to create the present appearance of steep inner slopes adventive strombolian cones, flows, talus deposits, etc.

(B) **Serra do Moriao.**     This range, rising to 632 m, forms some 2/3 of the southern rim of the Guilherme Moniz caldera, both features being smaller than the Cume complex. The caldera floor is remarkably flat, lying some 160 m below the rim, and dotted over its surface are many small ponds so shallow that they often are dry in summer. The Serra is offset here and there by radial faulting, and such fractures control the paths of several streams flowing down the gentler exterior slopes. On the outer flanks occur secondary cones whose alignments again suggest fissure control. Like Cume, later volcanic infilling has occurred in the caldera, basaltic flows pouring in from the E and trachytic flows from the N.

(C) **Serra de Sta. Barbara.**     Here occur the maximum elevations on the island, reaching to 1,021 m. This volcanic complex is the largest, though its caldera is much smaller. This strato-volcano, froming ca. 1/3 of the island, shows regular western slopes of 5-8°, with the densest stream network of the island, narrow valleys deeply incised separated by long, narrow relatively flat interfleuve regions. Many adventive cones, trachytic domes and lava flows have controlled the courses of the streams so that the latter are more winding than would appear necessary from a topographic map. These western slopes receive the highest rainfalls in Terceira, there is often much cloud, humid conditions prevail most of the year, hence agriculture and vegetation is well developed here. The eastern slopes, lesser so those to the N and NW, are much less regular, due to interruptions of eruptive centres. To the NW six major emission centres are aligned in a NW-SE direction, with trachytic domes and flows extending down to the coast. Slightly E of here, further trachytic domes, flows head N towards the coast. The eastern part shows a succession of overlapping thick basaltic, trachytic and andesitic flows with many scoria cones and domes, including the Misterio dos Negros mushroom-domes of the 1761 eruption. These secondary volcanic eruptive centres on the flanks of the major massif seem to be largely radially controlled by fissures and throughout all the flanks, radial fracturing is characteristic. The caldera floor lies some 150 m below the surrounding walls, with some half dozen trachytic effusions aligned ENE-WSW rising above the floor. The walls show two levels of trachytic and andesitic flows, and on the W side of the wall a convex circular surface rises some dozens of metres above a marshy area. It is possible that here we have evidences of an older

---

8: Trachytic flows of Sta. Barbara. 9: Aa basaltic flows contributing to infilling of calderas 1 and 2. 10: Andesite flows of S. Mateus. 11: Basaltic flows of 1761 eruption. 12: Lakes. 13: Low sandy coast of Praia da Vitoria. 14: Rock coasts < 50 m altitude. 15: Rocky coasts 50–100 m altitude. 16: Rocky coasts > 100 m altitude. 17: Solfatare of Furnas do Enxofre. 18: Serra do Cume caldera. 19: Guilherme Moniz cadera. 20: Sta. Barbara caldera. 21: Trachytic massif of North-centre (Pico Alto). 22: Heights in m. (Modified after MOTTET, 1972).

subsidence followed by a younger one, the latter more likely having more profound subsidence, which resulted in the ›capturing‹ of headwater streams, blocking their exit and creating marshy conditions and also the small lake. There thus are differences between the Cume and Sta. Barbara massifs. In the former, the caldera represents about one half of the massif, whilst with Sta. Barbara this represents only ca. 1/30. Infilling of the caldera has been more complete in Sta. Barbara than in Cume though the summit of the former has been better preserved, and further there are evidences of subsidence or collapse in two stages at Sta. Barbara.

**(D) Pico Alto massif.** This is later than the other three massifs and its caldera has been obliterated and infilled by later materials. In this N-Central part of the island, a complex of trachytic domes, flows, adventive cones, was probably initiated by a pretrachytic massif which underwent subsidence, suggested by the abrupt NE slopes of Serra do Juncal, followed by the outpouring of vast volumes of trachytic lavas either as domes or domes-flows. Perhaps subsidence was not too great so that this earlier massif maintained its altitude to cause flows to flow around it to E and to W down to the coast. Possibly circular fracturing allowed magmas to pour forth on to the surface. Juncal and such strombolian edifices as Pico Alto, 808 m; Pico de Areeiro, 533 m and Algar do Carvao, 629 m very possibly mark the outer edges of the destroyed caldera. At the last-mentioned peak the central vent was not completely plugged-up, and from the NW side an entrance leads down to the ›throat‹ of the volcano, and 80 m below the surface is a subterranean lake formed on the lower plugged vent. Here also there occur ›rooms‹ such as one finds in limestone caves. It is also in this general area that the only evidences of present volcanicity in the island are to be found. At Furnas do Enxofre, sulphurous vapours emanate from a smaller cone with a crater, vapours hot enough to heat the surrounding rocks to almost $100°$ C.

Also later than the three major volcanic massifs are many cones and flows. From the general area of the peak Bagacina, basaltic flows of the 1761 eruption flow northwards, andesitic flows of S. Mateus trend southward as also blocky basaltic flows to coalesce near the coast. In the SE of the island, many adventive cones show a NW-SE fissurecontrolled orientation.

The NE coasts developed through faulting with graben-horst structures, coastlines smooth and rectilinear or curved. Elsewhere in the island, coastal development stems from tectonic-volcanic-exogenic processes. In the W occur the highest cliffs – up to 150 m – and here access from the sea to the island is most difficult, no settlements by the sea edge but rather on higher inland slopes. Coasts where lavas reach the sea edge are inclined to be more strenuously cliffed and at the base, especially where lava flows meet the sea, the strand presents a wild, chaotic appearance of jagged blocks, some of enormous size, many of which have tumbled into the sea, been moved outward by waves and currents and present hazardous areas for coastal navigation. Trachytic headlands no less are prominent features, especially in the N and NW. Where less resistant pyroclastics reach the coast, embayments frequently occur, but where lavas and pyroclastics are interbedded, lavas protrude more seaward, pyroclastics are more eaten into, providing often stepped coastal profiles. In the Monte Brasil, on the outskirts of the capital, we have a superb example of a peninsula cone. Rising to 205 m, 1.5 km diameter, bounded by cliffs on three sides and attached to the mainland by a volcanic isthmus, with a breached crater, this feature seems to have resulted from the combined action of faulting, vulcanism plus marine erosion. Formed entirely of tuffs (though the basement is ankaramitic, enclaves of which occur in the tuffs), this is the largest tuff structure in the Azores. Off-shore are the two insular cones of Ilheus das Cabras, submarine structures now but presumably formed subaerially on the backward slopes of Serra da Ribeirinha. The structure has been split into two islets, probably an initial fracture which marine erosion took advantage of to widen, split apart the structure.

The landscape, landforms of Terceira are volcanic, here the role of vulcanism in landscape development is paramount. But tectonism and exogenic processes no less have been important in moulding the surface to its present appearance. Uplift, subsidence, outpouring of lava flows, erecting of adventitious cones have all tended to maintain a stage of geomorphologic late youth or even early maturity.

Terceira geomorphologically is typical of the archipelago, but in comparison with other archipelagoes it is likely that tectonism plays a greater role here, likely a consequence of its nearer location to the great Central Atlantic tectonic feature of the Ridge.

## Igneous Rocks

Earlier studies of the volcanics of these islands include the works of HARTUNG (1860), FOUQUÉ (1873e), MÜGGE (1883), CANTO (1887b, 1888) whilst later investigations are those of ESENWEIN (1929), FRIEDLÄNDER (1929), BERTHOIS (1953b), JÉRÉMINE (1957), CASTELO BRANCO et al. (1957), ASSUNÇAO (1961), ASSUNÇAO & CANELHAS (1971) and the many papers of ZBYSZEWSKI and ZBYSZEWSKI et al., to many of which ASSUNÇAO added sections dealing with the volcanics.

The publications of HARTUNG and MÜGGE were the first to give detailed petrographic information. The former recognized an older and a younger group of volcanics, believing such to be younger than the volcanics of Madeira and the Canary Islands. MÜGGE carried out petrographic examinations of HARTUNG's and earlier collections, from which he recognized the following types of rocks:

I.   Trachytic rocks
    1. Typical Trachytes
      a) Granular – sanidinites, domites
      b) Porphyritic – similar rocks
      c) Vitreous – trachy-pitchstones
    2. Andesitic Trachytes
    3. Acmite-Trachytes
II.  Andesitic rocks
    1. Amphibole- and Mica-Andesites
      a) Both coarse and fine granular – andesites, some with dioritic structure
      b) Porphyritic and vitreous varieties of same rocks
    2. Augite-Andesites
III. Basaltic rocks
    1. Andesitic-basalts
    2. Normal basalts of granular, porphyritic and vitreous types
    3. Anorthite-basalts

ESENWEIN's detailed account on the petrography of the Azorean volcanics was the most complete up to that date and still represents the best and broadest discussion of

Geology of the Azores Archipelago

Table 12    Chemical analyses of Azores rock (ESENWEIN, 1929; ASSUNÇAO, 1961; ASSUNÇAO & CANELHAS 1971)

|  | 1 | 2 | 3 | 4 | 5 | 6 | 7 | 8 | 9 | 10 |
|---|---|---|---|---|---|---|---|---|---|---|
| $SiO_2$ | 65.17 | 64.20 | 63.02 | 52.96 | 56.27 | 52.72 | 50.42 | 49.08 | 49.92 | 51.60 |
| $Al_2O_3$ | 10.66 | 10.26 | 13.28 | 17.32 | 17.27 | 17.46 | 15.25 | 16.78 | 16.93 | 16.16 |
| $Fe_2O_3$ | 2.43 | 4.32 | 4.64 | 6.67 | 2.98 | 2.30 | 4.91 | 5.62 | 2.64 | 3.68 |
| $FeO$ | 5.04 | 3.85 | 2.70 | 2.70 | 5.45 | 6.57 | 6.61 | 6.19 | 7.63 | 6.25 |
| $M_nO$ | 0.19 | 0.12 | 0.82 | 0.24 | 0.22 | 0.17 | 0.19 | 0.20 | 0.24 | 0.22 |
| $MgO$ | 0.24 | 0.36 | 0.68 | 2.98 | 3.02 | 4.03 | 4.59 | 4.18 | 3.69 | 3.73 |
| $CaO$ | 1.20 | 1.09 | 1.29 | 4.26 | 4.91 | 9.11 | 8.33 | 7.65 | 8.74 | 6.73 |
| $Na_2O$ | 7.14 | 6.79 | 6.85 | 4.42 | 4.95 | 3.58 | 3.55 | 4.28 | 3.64 | 4.79 |
| $K_2O$ | 5.74 | 6.40 | 4.69 | 2.60 | 2.14 | 1.38 | 1.54 | 1.78 | 2.31 | 2.04 |
| $TiO_2$ | 0.84 | 0.60 | 0.59 | 2.29 | 1.63 | 2.62 | 3.35 | 3.49 | 3.18 | 2.57 |
| $P_2O_5$ | 0.12 | 0.34 | 0.06 | 0.82 | 0.48 | 0.67 | 0.70 | 0.70 | 0.74 | 0.98 |
| $H_2O+$ | 1.08 | 1.48 | 0.89 | 1.91 | 0.25 | 0.01 |  | 0.42 | 0.78 | 0.64 |
| $H_2O-$ |  |  | 1.71 | 0.96 | 0.50 |  | 0.31 | 0.37 |  | 0.34 |
| Total | 99.85 | 99.81 | 100.68 | 100.13 | 100.07 | 100.62 | 99.75 | 100.74 | 100.44 | 99.73 |

|  | 11 | 12 | 13 | 14 | 15 | 16 | 17 | 18 | 19 | 20 |
|---|---|---|---|---|---|---|---|---|---|---|
| $SiO_2$ | 48.56 | 46.28 | 45.11 | 44.57 | 46.96 | 45.66 | 46.38 | 50.52 | 62.72 | 44.06 |
| $Al_2O_3$ | 15.88 | 14.48 | 15.40 | 15.11 | 14.09 | 16.02 | 13.64 | 17.25 | 16.50 | 15.10 |
| $Fe_2O_3$ | 3.83 | 3.36 | 3.88 | 4.43 | 4.36 | 3.93 | 3.42 | 6.21 | 3.20 | 5.23 |
| $FeO$ | 8.35 | 8.01 | 9.79 | 9.51 | 8.33 | 9.84 | 8.49 | 4.03 | 2.74 | 7.93 |
| $M_nO$ | 0.28 | 0.19 | 0.22 | 0.19 | 0.21 | 0.17 | 0.15 | 0.20 | 0.18 | 0.36 |
| $MgO$ | 4.17 | 6.17 | 5.50 | 5.00 | 6.76 | 5.41 | 7.90 | 3.21 | 0.20 | 9.84 |
| $CaO$ | 8.31 | 10.49 | 9.03 | 8.47 | 10.37 | 9.42 | 11.16 | 9.14 | 2.33 | 12.56 |
| $Na_2O$ | 3.52 | 4.03 | 2.90 | 2.84 | 3.13 | 3.09 | 3.02 | 3.54 | 6.03 | 2.20 |
| $K_2O$ | 2.34 | 2.09 | 1.12 | 1.35 | 1.13 | 1.29 | 1.07 | 1.65 | 4.27 | 0.93 |
| $TiO_2$ | 3.39 | 3.75 | 4.18 | 4.28 | 3.81 | 4.30 | 3.37 | 2.97 | 1.04 | 1.80 |
| $P_2O_5$ | 1.00 | 0.45 | 0.70 | 0.68 | 1.08 | 0.53 | 1.04 | 0.64 | Tr | 0.53 |
| $H_2O+$ | 0.73 | 1.08 | 0.87 | 1.80 | 0.03 | 0.12 | 0.01 | 0.48 | 0.64 | 0.30 |
| $H_2O-$ |  |  | 1.52 | 2.04 |  | 0.89 | 0.24 | 0.12 | 0.03 |  |
| Total | 100.36 | 100.38 | 100.22 | 100.27 | 100.26 | 100.67 | 99.89 | 99.96 | 99.98 | 100.84 |

|  | 21 | 22 | 23 | 24 | 25 | 26 | 27 | 28 | 29 |
|---|---|---|---|---|---|---|---|---|---|
| $SiO_2$ | 44.38 | 45.30 | 45.48 | 45.68 | 46.20 | 46.24 | 46.39 | 53.32 | 53.78 |
| $Al_2O_3$ | 6.21 | 13.40 | 17.99 | 8.90 | 13.40 | 15.98 | 16.46 | 17.32 | 13.98 |
| $Fe_2O_3$ | 4.19 | 7.25 | 3.20 | 4.80 | 4.00 | 4.10 | 4.38 | 2.60 | 3.07 |
| $FeO$ | 6.29 | 6.26 | 4.25 | 7.84 | 8.56 | 8.17 | 8.62 | 6.10 | 4.98 |
| $M_nO$ | 0.19 | 0.34 | 0.20 | 0.17 | 0.28 | 0.32 | 0.40 | 0.09 |  |
| $MgO$ | 22.59 | 11.53 | 4.14 | 13.92 | 18.92 | 5.23 | 4.09 | 3.15 | 6.49 |
| $CaO$ | 10.05 | 10.34 | 11.18 | 12.63 | 12.24 | 8.77 | 8.70 | 6.30 | 6.06 |
| $Na_2O$ | 1.40 | 2.17 | 3.48 | 1.69 | 2.82 | 4.68 | 4.74 | 3.52 | 3.92 |
| $K_2O$ | 1.28 | 0.23 | 2.40 | 2.07 | 0.48 | 2.66 | 2.43 | 4.06 | 4.55 |
| $TiO_2$ | 2.22 | 2.50 | 3.40 | 1.77 | 2.18 | 4.74 | 2.30 | 2.33 | 2.55 |
| $P_2O_5$ | 0.60 | 0.39 | 1.36 | 0.47 | 0.53 | 2.49 | 0.96 | 1.26 | 0.58 |
| $H_2O+$ | 0.53 | 0.18 | 1.74 | 0.35 | 0.18 | 0.02 | 0.35 |  | 0.06 |
| $H_2O-$ | 0.56 |  | 1.53 | 0.18 |  | 0.06 | 0.20 | 0.39 |  |
| Total | 100.49 | 99.89 | 100.35 | 100.47 | 101.79 | 100.48 | 100.02 | 100.44 | 99.95 |

Table 12 (continued)

| | 30 | 31 | 32 | 33 | 34 | 35 | 36 | 37 | 38 |
|---|---|---|---|---|---|---|---|---|---|
| $SiO_2$ | 55.37 | 59.06 | 61.99 | 62.80 | 63.36 | 63.44 | 63.86 | 65.50 | 44.88 |
| $Al_2O_3$ | 18.02 | 16.62 | 20.14 | 15.22 | 16.57 | 17.85 | 18.90 | 16.00 | 16.06 |
| $Fe_2O_3$ | 4.71 | 4.89 | 1.25 | 2.85 | 2.46 | 2.82 | 1.40 | 2.50 | 5.91 |
| FeO | 2.41 | 1.04 | 2.87 | 1.34 | 1.15 | 1.79 | 1.26 | 2.14 | 6.47 |
| $M_nO$ | 0.04 | 0.06 | | 0.11 | 0.03 | | 0.22 | 0.20 | 0.23 |
| MgO | 1.21 | 1.32 | 0.38 | 0.67 | 0.36 | 0.37 | 0.46 | 0.22 | 3.48 |
| CaO | 3.97 | 3.44 | 1.35 | 1.14 | 1.68 | 0.69 | 0.81 | 0.91 | 7.90 |
| $Na_2O$ | 5.38 | 5.49 | 6.02 | 7.86 | 6.71 | 7.36 | 6.90 | 5.91 | 4.00 |
| $K_2O$ | 5.41 | 5.56 | 4.87 | 5.56 | 6.40 | 5.48 | 5.08 | 5.55 | 2.72 |
| $TiO_2$ | 1.48 | 1.03 | | 0.48 | 0.45 | | 0.74 | 0.57 | 3.71 |
| $P_2O_5$ | 0.41 | 0.49 | | 0.93 | 0.38 | | Tr | 0.31 | 1.29 |
| $H_2O_+$ | 0.58 | 0.59 | 0.98 | 0.69 | 0.54 | 0.76 | 0.20 | 0.38 | 3.59 |
| $H_2O_-$ | 1.29 | 0.62 | | 0.64 | 0.53 | | 0.09 | 0.09 | |
| Total | 99.98 | 100.21 | 99.85 | 100.29 | 100.65 | 99.56 | 99.92 | 100.28 | 100.24 |

| | 39 | 40 | 41 | 42 | 43 | 44 | 45 | 46 | 47 |
|---|---|---|---|---|---|---|---|---|---|
| $SiO_2$ | 45.38 | 53.28 | 45.87 | 48.01 | 46.78 | 47.56 | 59.60 | 45.58 | 42.53 |
| $Al_2O_3$ | 16.25 | 17.96 | 17.66 | 14.45 | 14.84 | 20.36 | 18.66 | 13.89 | 13.65 |
| $Fe_2O_3$ | 4.62 | 3.63 | 3.87 | 6.27 | 6.23 | 3.33 | 2.20 | 2.55 | 5.64 |
| FeO | 6.83 | 4.17 | 7.15 | 5.62 | 7.38 | 5.79 | 2.53 | 6.60 | 6.43 |
| $M_nO$ | 0.12 | 0.24 | 0.16 | 0.19 | 0.18 | 0.14 | 0.10 | 0.17 | 0.24 |
| MgO | 3.55 | 2.75 | 5.05 | 6.35 | 5.61 | 3.18 | 1.08 | 10.53 | 7.96 |
| CaO | 8.18 | 5.57 | 11.09 | 11.35 | 9.66 | 12.09 | 3.34 | 14.03 | 10.82 |
| $Na_2O$ | 4.03 | 4.88 | 3.47 | 2.58 | 3.24 | 2.76 | 6.07 | 2.35 | 4.17 |
| $K_2O$ | 2.71 | 3.63 | 1.47 | 0.86 | 1.56 | 1.07 | 4.15 | 0.77 | 1.37 |
| $TiO_2$ | 3.35 | 2.31 | 4.02 | 3.28 | 3.93 | 3.25 | 1.26 | 2.67 | 2.96 |
| $P_2O_5$ | 0.68 | 0.80 | 0.25 | 0.51 | 0.40 | 0.41 | 0.19 | 0.11 | 0.82 |
| $H_2O_+$ | 4.20 | 0.88 | 0.22 | 0.30 | 0.13 | 0.35 | 0.46 | 0.06 | 1.90 |
| $H_2O_-$ | | 0.14 | 0.15 | 0.06 | | 0.19 | 0.23 | 0.04 | 1.56 |
| Total | 99.90 | 100.24 | 100.43 | 99.81 | 99.89 | 100.48 | 99.87 | 99.35 | 100.05 |

*Rock analyses from the Azores* (to Tables 12, 13, 14)

1. Rhyolitic Trachyte, Terceira.
2. Rhyolitic Trachyte, Terceira.
3. Trachyte, Terceira.
4. Trachyandesite, Terceira.
5. Oligoclase-Andesite, Terceira.
6. Porphyritic-Andesite, Terceira.
7. Labradorite-Andesite, Terceira.
8. Labradorite-Andesite, Terceira.
9. Slightly Peridotitic-Andesite, Terceira.
10. Andesine-Andesite, Terceira.
11. Peridotitic-Andesite, Terceira.
12. Basanitoid-Basalt, Terceira.
13. Slightly Peridotitic-Basalt, Terceira.
14. Andesinitic-Basalt, Terceira.
15. Olivine-Basalt, Terceira.
16. Aphyric-Basalt, Terceira.
17. Olivine-Basalt, Terceira.
18. Plagioclase-Basalt, Sta. Barbara, Terceira.
19. Hornblende-Aegerine-Sanidinite, Calderao, Terceira.
20. Basalt, Pta. Delgada, S. Miguel.
21. Ankaramite, 1 km NNW of Matas, S. Miguel.
22. Basalt, Pta. Delgada, S. Miguel.
23. Andesite, 250 m N of Pir. Bodes, S. Miguel.
24. Olivine-Dorite, Fayal d'Agua, S. Miguel.
25. Anamesite, Pta. Delgada, S. Miguel.
26. Basanitoid, Faja de Baixo, S. Miguel.

27.   Peridotitic-Andesite, W of Pico de Pedra,
      S. Miguel.
28.   Shoshonite, 800 m W of Pico Verde,
      S. Miguel.
29.   Alk-Feldspar-Olivine-Basalt, Porto Formoso,
      S. Miguel.
30.   Latite, 700 m E of Pir. Bodes, S. Miguel.
31.   Trachyte, 500 m SSE of Pir. Bodes,
      S. Miguel.
32.   Trachyte-Obsidian, Furnas, S. Miguel.
33.   Alkali-Trachyte, 250 m N of Pir. Bodes,
      S. Miguel.
34.   Phonolitic-Trachyte, Rib. Quente. S. Miguel.
35.   Kalaphorite-Trachyte, Lagoa Sete Cidades,
      S. Miguel.

36.   Aegerine-Trachyte, Grutta Enferno,
      S. Miguel.
37.   Soda-Sanidinite, Lagoa do Fogo, S. Miguel.
38.   Peridotitic-Andesite, Flores.
39.   Oligoclase-Andesite, Flores.
40.   Biotite-Hornblende-Essexite, Queb. da Muda,
      Flores.
41.   Miarolitic Essexite-Gabbro, Pico, Pico.
42.   Plagioclase-Basalt, Bandeiras, Pico.
43.   Plagioclase-Basalt, S. Antonio, S. Jorge.
44.   Plagioclase-Basalt, Faja S. Joao, S. Jorge.
45.   Plagioclase-Trachyte, Caldeira, Faial.
46.   Olivine-Basalt, Pesqueiro, Corvo.
47.   Olivine-Basalt, Figueiral, Sta. Maria.

the archipelago volcanics. He devised three major groupings: trachytic, basaltic and a very minor group of other types. Under trachytic he included: (a) Normal plagioclase-poor trachytes – vd. nos. 19, 32, 35, 36, 37, Tables 12, 13, 14. – (b) plagioclase-trachytes, no. 45. The second group includes: (a) plagioclase-basalts – nos. 41, 42, and (b) olivine-basalts – nos. 20, 22, 24, 25, 46, 47. As regards his third group, ESENWEIN refers to MÜGGE who noted rocks from S. Miguel and Faial of trachytic, andesitic and basaltic character, either olivine-free or olivine-bearing. ESENWEIN recognized these as transitional between his normal and plagioclase-trachytes on the one hand and his plagioclase- and olivine-rich basalts on the other. Such transitional rocks were much scarcer than his other two groups, the general charcter of said rocks of this minor group being intermediate between plagioclase-basalts and plagioclase-trachytes, thus recognizing ›trachy-dolerites‹, biotite-hornblende essexites (no. 40), alkali-feldspar olivine-basalts (no. 29) and orthoclase-basalts.

ESENWEIN summarized the characteristics of his major rock groups thus:

(a) Plagioclase-poor or Normal Trachytes.   Poor in calcium and rich in soda, consisting mostly of Na-sanidine with dark ingredients of alkali-amphibole, aegerine-augite, rarely diopsidic augite, commonest accessories apatite, zircon, magnetite, ilmenite and hematite. Textures may be holocrystalline porphyritic or hemi-crystalline porphyritic, trachytic, glassy trachytic, rarely pumaceous trachytic. Mineral constituents include little quartz, Na-sanidine, barkevitite, aegerine-augite. Miarolitic cavities are common.

(b) Plagioclase-Trachytes.   Rich in plagioclase, especially andesine, with disseminated Na-sanidine. Rocks show strong reabsorption of basaltic hornblende and biotite. Texture dominantly trachytic or then shows an interstitial base of hyalolitic texture. The matrix comprises Na-sanidine, albite-rich plagioclase, small amounts of colourless diopsidic augite, biotite, basaltic hornblende. Accessories include apatite, zircon, magnetite, more rarely olivine.

(c) Plagioclase-Basalts.   Relatively leucocratic, very rich in disseminated basic plagioclases and basaltic augites, sparsely scattered olivine in very subordinate amounts. Texture is ophitic, holocrystalline or then with interstitial glass. Major ingredients of the groundmass are lath-shaped plagioclase (chiefly andesine), much basaltic augite, subordinate olivine, with Ti-rich magnetite and apatite as the chief

Table 13    Molecular norms of Azores rocks (ESENWEIN, 1929; ASSUNÇAO 1961; ASSUNÇAO & CANELHAS, 1971)

|       | 1     | 2     | 3     | 4     | 5     | 6     | 7     | 8     | 9     | 10    |
|-------|-------|-------|-------|-------|-------|-------|-------|-------|-------|-------|
| Q     | 15.21 | 14.33 | 4.62  | 6.03  | 3.79  | 3.03  | 3.22  |       |       |       |
| Or    | 33.92 | 37.82 | 27.53 | 15.34 | 12.63 | 8.10  | 9.12  | 10.44 | 13.59 | 12.08 |
| Ab    | 22.88 | 17.14 | 41.91 | 37.34 | 41.85 | 30.10 | 30.10 | 35.94 | 30.65 | 40.62 |
| An    |       |       |       | 15.75 | 18.57 | 27.32 | 21.17 | 21.15 | 22.92 | 16.61 |
| Ne    |       |       |       |       |       |       |       |       |       |       |
| Aeg   |       |       |       |       |       |       |       |       |       |       |
| Ac    | 7.03  | 12.50 | 13.33 |       |       |       |       |       |       |       |
| Wo    |       |       |       |       |       |       |       |       |       |       |
| En    |       |       |       |       |       |       |       |       |       |       |
| Fesil |       |       |       |       |       |       |       |       |       |       |
| Fs    |       |       |       |       |       |       |       |       |       |       |
| Fa    |       |       |       |       |       |       |       |       |       |       |
| Ns    | 6.88  | 6.08  | 0.12  |       |       |       |       |       |       |       |
| Di    | 4.56  | 2.78  | 5.10  |       | 2.16  | 10.78 | 12.48 | 9.44  | 12.64 | 8.45  |
| Hy    | 6.42  | 5.74  | 3.55  | 7.41  | 11.72 | 10.83 | 8.43  | 2.85  | 2.18  | 5.71  |
| Ol    |       |       |       |       |       |       |       | 3.09  | 5.67  | 2.99  |
| Mt    |       |       |       | 2.84  | 4.32  | 3.31  | 3.31  | 8.09  | 3.81  | 5.35  |
| Hm    |       |       |       | 4.70  |       |       |       |       |       |       |
| Il    | 1.60  | 1.14  | 1.11  | 4.34  | 3.09  | 4.94  | 6.38  | 6.58  | 6.01  | 4.89  |
| Ru    |       |       |       |       |       |       |       |       |       |       |
| Ap    | 0.28  | 0.81  | 0.14  | 1.94  | 1.14  |       | 1.66  | 1.65  | 1.74  | 2.33  |

|       | 11    | 12    | 13    | 14    | 15    | 16    | 17    | 18    | 19    | 20    |
|-------|-------|-------|-------|-------|-------|-------|-------|-------|-------|-------|
| Q     |       |       |       |       |       |       |       |       | 6.06  |       |
| Or    | 13.83 | 12.30 | 6.60  | 7.95  | 6.66  | 7.57  | 6.33  | 9.42  | 25.02 | 5.56  |
| Ab    | 29.79 | 15.05 | 24.48 | 23.96 | 26.40 | 25.97 | 23.77 | 30.12 | 51.35 | 5.24  |
| An    | 20.62 | 15.19 | 25.63 | 24.42 | 20.99 | 25.85 | 20.51 | 26.42 | 5.35  | 28.63 |
| Ne    |       | 10.24 |       |       |       |       |       |       |       | 7.10  |
| Aeg   |       |       |       |       |       |       |       |       |       |       |
| Ac    |       |       |       |       |       |       |       |       |       |       |
| Wo    |       |       |       |       |       |       |       |       |       |       |
| En    |       |       |       |       |       |       |       |       |       |       |
| Fesil |       |       |       |       |       |       |       |       |       |       |
| Fs    |       |       |       |       |       |       |       |       |       |       |
| Fa    |       |       |       |       |       |       |       |       |       |       |
| Ns    |       |       |       |       |       |       |       |       |       |       |
| Di    | 11.50 | 27.13 | 11.80 | 10.60 | 18.65 | 13.93 | 22.58 | 12.39 | 5.58  | 28.90 |
| Hy    | 3.48  |       | 7.92  | 9.93  | 5.02  | 0.21  |       | 4.70  | 0.23  |       |
| Ol    | 6.11  | 6.00  | 6.00  | 3.19  | 6.18  | 10.46 | 11.76 | 2.43  |       | 15.60 |
| Mt    | 5.55  | 4.85  | 5.61  | 6.40  | 6.30  | 5.66  | 4.96  | 9.10  | 4.64  | 7.42  |
| Hm    |       |       |       |       |       |       |       |       |       |       |
| Il    | 6.44  | 7.09  | 7.92  | 8.10  | 7.21  | 8.11  | 6.40  |       |       |       |
| Ru    |       |       |       |       |       |       |       | 2.97  | 1.04  | 1.86  |
| Ap    | 2.37  | 1.06  | 1.65  | 1.61  | 2.55  | 1.25  | 2.46  | 1.24  |       | 1.34  |

Table 13 (continued)

|       | 21    | 22    | 23    | 24    | 25 | 26    | 27    | 28    | 29    |
|-------|-------|-------|-------|-------|----|-------|-------|-------|-------|
| Q     |       |       |       |       |    |       |       | 0.96  |       |
| Or    | 7.78  | 1.11  | 13.90 | 11.23 |    | 16.12 | 14.46 | 24.46 | 26.69 |
| Ab    | 6.29  | 19.39 | 18.34 | 3.36  |    | 20.70 | 19.91 | 29.36 | 21.96 |
| An    | 6.67  | 25.58 | 26.41 | 10.78 |    | 14.46 | 16.68 | 19.46 | 17.24 |
| Ne    | 3.12  |       | 5.96  | 5.96  |    | 10.36 | 10.79 |       | 3.96  |
| Aeg   |       |       |       |       |    |       |       |       |       |
| Ac    |       |       |       |       |    |       |       |       |       |
| Wo    | 16.47 |       | 8.35  |       |    | 6.26  | 8.35  | 1.51  |       |
| En    | 13.30 |       | 7.00  |       |    | 3.50  | 4.30  | 7.90  |       |
| Fesil | 1.19  |       | 0.26  |       |    | 2.51  | 3.83  | 5.41  |       |
| Fs    | 30.24 |       | 2.80  |       |    | 6.72  | 4.13  |       |       |
| Fa    | 2.86  |       | 0.10  |       |    | 5.61  | 3.98  |       |       |
| Ns    |       |       |       |       |    |       |       |       |       |
| Di    |       | 18.31 |       | 39.65 |    |       |       |       | 7.60  |
| Hy    |       | 7.09  |       |       |    |       |       |       |       |
| Ol    |       | 13.71 |       | 20.50 |    |       |       |       | 13.80 |
| Mt    | 6.03  | 10.44 | 4.64  | 6.96  |    | 6.03  | 6.50  | 3.71  | 4.41  |
| Hm    |       |       |       |       |    |       |       |       |       |
| Il    | 4.26  |       | 5.93  |       |    | 3.34  | 4.41  | 4.41  |       |
| Ru    |       | 2.48  |       | 1.96  |    |       |       |       | 2.56  |
| Ap    | 1.34  | 1.10  | 3.36  | 1.39  |    | 5.04  | 2.35  | 3.02  | 1.34  |

|       | 30    | 31    | 32    | 33    | 34    | 35    | 36    | 37    | 38    |
|-------|-------|-------|-------|-------|-------|-------|-------|-------|-------|
| Q     |       | 0.12  | 1.50  | 1.86  |       | 1.80  | 1.14  | 7.98  |       |
| Or    | 31.69 | 32.80 | 28.91 | 32.80 | 37.81 | 32.00 | 30.03 | 32.80 | 16.07 |
| Ab    | 37.20 | 46.11 | 50.83 | 47.16 | 47.29 | 60.78 | 58.16 | 49.78 | 26.04 |
| An    | 8.90  | 4.45  | 6.67  |       |       |       | 3.89  | 0.83  | 17.83 |
| Ne    | 4.54  |       |       |       | 1.04  |       |       |       | 4.23  |
| Aeg   |       |       |       | 8.32  | 6.93  |       |       |       |       |
| Ac    |       |       |       |       |       |       |       |       |       |
| Wo    | 3.36  | 4.06  |       |       | 2.32  |       |       |       |       |
| En    | 2.90  | 3.30  |       | 4.70  | 0.90  |       |       |       |       |
| Fesil |       |       |       | 4.85  | 1.32  |       |       |       |       |
| Fs    | 0.07  |       |       |       |       |       |       |       |       |
| Fa    |       |       |       |       |       |       |       |       |       |
| Ns    |       |       |       |       |       |       |       |       |       |
| Di    |       |       |       |       |       | 1.52  |       | 1.76  | 10.22 |
| Hy    |       |       | 5.22  |       |       | 0.70  | 2.68  | 1.88  |       |
| Ol    |       |       |       |       |       |       |       |       | 3.66  |
| Mt    | 2.32  | 0.46  |       |       |       | 2.32  | 2.09  | 3.71  | 8.57  |
| Hm    |       | 4.64  | 1.86  |       |       |       |       |       |       |
| Il    | 2.89  | 1.98  |       | 0.91  | 0.91  |       |       |       | 7.05  |
| Ru    |       |       |       |       |       |       | 0.64  | 0.56  |       |
| Ap    | 1.01  | 1.01  |       | 2.02  | 1.01  |       |       | 0.67  | 3.06  |

Table 13  (continued)

|       | 39    | 40    | 41    | 42    | 43    | 44    | 45    | 46    | 47    |
|-------|-------|-------|-------|-------|-------|-------|-------|-------|-------|
| Q     |       |       |       |       |       |       |       |       |       |
| Or    | 16.03 | 21.30 | 8.90  | 5.00  | 8.90  | 6.12  | 24.46 | 4.45  | 7.78  |
| Ab    | 22.03 | 36.16 | 15.72 | 22.01 | 25.68 | 23.06 | 51.35 | 7.34  | 27.75 |
| An    | 18.26 | 16.41 | 28.08 | 26.30 | 21.13 | 40.31 | 11.40 | 25.02 | 14.45 |
| Ne    |       | 2.84  | 7.38  |       | 0.85  |       |       | 6.82  | 3.13  |
| Aeg   |       |       |       |       |       |       |       |       |       |
| Ac    |       |       |       |       |       |       |       |       |       |
| Wo    |       |       |       |       |       |       |       |       |       |
| En    |       |       |       |       |       |       |       |       |       |
| Fesil |       |       |       |       |       |       |       |       |       |
| Fs    |       |       |       |       |       |       |       |       |       |
| Fa    |       |       |       |       |       |       |       |       |       |
| Ns    |       |       |       |       |       |       |       |       |       |
| Di    | 14.40 | 6.28  | 20.23 | 22.60 | 19.65 | 14.94 | 4.39  | 35.68 | 15.82 |
| Hy    |       |       |       |       |       | 0.56  | 3.55  |       |       |
| Ol    | 3.85  | 6.45  | 9.20  | 10.00 | 9.27  | 5.86  |       | 13.88 | 14.11 |
| Mt    | 6.70  | 5.34  | 5.57  | 9.05  | 9.10  | 4.87  | 3.25  | 5.71  | 7.34  |
| Hm    |       |       |       |       |       |       |       |       |       |
| Il    | 6.37  |       |       |       |       |       |       |       |       |
| Ru    |       | 2.31  | 4.00  | 3.30  | 3.92  | 3.28  | 1.28  | 2.64  | 2.96  |
| Ap    | 1.61  | 1.86  | 0.67  | 1.10  | 1.06  | 1.01  |       | 0.34  | 1.83  |

accessories. Rocks are granular, holocrystalline, phenocrysts may or may not be present, many miarolitic cavities or then clear ophitic appearance. Minerals include lath-shaped plagioclase, highly Ti-rich augite, some olivine, and as accessories, Ti-rich magnetite, some apatite.

(d) Olivine-Basalts.   Dark, porphyritic rocks, with much disseminated olivine and basaltic augite. Groundmass is largely granular, ophitic, rich in dark hyalopilitic glass, chief components being lath-shaped plagioclase – chiefly andesine – much basaltic augite and olivine, with magnetite and apatite as accessories.

(e) Biotite-hornblende essexites may be equigranular or porphyritic. Mineral constitution includes Na-sanidine (perthite), albite-rich plagioclase, basaltic hornblende, biotite, sometimes colourless diopside. Accessories are Ti-rich magnetite, zircon, apatite.

The plagioclase-poor trachytes conform to nordmarkitic-pulaskitic magma types of NIGGLI; plagioclase-trachytes of normal larvikitic magma type. Plagioclase-basalts are associated with normal essexite-gabbroidal magma type, and olivine-basalts with normal hornblenditic type. Other rocks of the third group belong to yogoitic and essexitic-magma types. Tables 15 and 16 indicate ESENWEIN's scheme of differentiation of the various Azores magmas. Throughout his publication, ESENWEIN makes much reference to the NIGGLI magma types, invariably trying to pigeon-hole his rocks within appropriate magma type slots. Regarding the proliferation of NIGGLI's magma types – 183 in number – we quite agree with SHAND (1950) that: »we learn nothing definite about

Table 14                                          Niggli parameters of Azores rocks (ESENWEIN, 1929)

|     | 37 | 19 | 36 | 35 | 32 | 45 | 41 | 18 | 44 | 43 |
|-----|----|----|----|----|----|----|----|----|----|----|
| si  | 270 | 242 | 256 | 245 | 238 | 208 | 107 | 133 | 117 | 111 |
| al  | 40 | 37 | 44.5 | 40 | 45.5 | 38.5 | 24 | 27 | 29.5 | 20.5 |
| fm  | 17 | 20 | 12 | 16 | 15 | 19 | 39 | 35 | 20 | 45.5 |
| c   | 4 | 10 | 3.5 | 3 | 5.5 | 12.5 | 27 | 26 | 32 | 24 |
| alk | 39 | 33 | 40 | 41 | 34 | 30 | 10 | 12 | 8.5 | 10 |
| k   | 0.36 | 0.31 | 0.30 | 0.30 | 0.35 | 0.31 | 0.22 | 0.22 | 0.20 | 0.2 |
| mg  | 0.07 | 0.06 | 0.22 | 0.13 | 0.15 | 0.81 | 0.46 | 0.34 | 0.39 | 0.4 |
| ti  | 2 | 3 | 2 |  |  | 3 | 7 | 6 | 6 | 7 |
| p   | 0.5 |  |  |  |  | 0.2 | 0.3 | 0.7 | 0.3 | 0.4 |
| Ls  | 0.89 | 0.85 | 0.98 | 1.00 | 0.95 | 0.95 | 0.82 | 0.77 | 0.79 | 0.7 |
| Fs  | 0.07 | 0.11 | 0.04 | 0.06 | 0.04 | 0.11 | 0.48 | 0.34 | 0.34 | 0.5 |
| Qs  | + 0.06 | + 0.04 | − 0.02 | − 0.06 | + 0.01 | − 0.06 | − 0.30 | − 0.12 | − 0.13 | − 0.2 |

|     | 42 | 46 | 47 | 20 | 24 | 25 | 40 | 29 | 22 |
|-----|----|----|----|----|----|----|----|----|----|
| si  | 112 | 90 | 93 | 87 | 86.5 | 76 | 158 | 141 | 91.5 |
| al  | 20 | 16 | 17.5 | 17.5 | 10 | 12.5 | 31 | 21.5 | 16 |
| fm  | 45 | 48 | 47.5 | 50.5 | 59 | 61.5 | 31 | 44 | 57 |
| c   | 28 | 30 | 25.5 | 26.5 | 25.5 | 21 | 17.5 | 17 | 22.5 |
| alk | 7 | 6 | 9.5 | 5.5 | 5.5 | 5 | 20.5 | 17.5 | 4.5 |
| k   | 0.18 | 0.16 | 0.20 | 0.22 | 0.45 | 0.16 | 0.32 | 0.43 | 0.05 |
| mg  | 0.50 | 0.64 | 0.55 | 0.58 | 0.67 | 0.74 | 0.40 | 0.58 | 0.61 |
| ti  | 6 | 4 | 5 | 3 | 2.5 | 2.7 | 5 | 5 | 8.5 |
| p   | 0.4 | 0.1 | 1 | 0.5 | 0.3 | 0.4 | 1 | 0.4 |  |
| Ls  | 0.61 | 0.62 | 0.78 | 0.62 | 0.51 |  | 0.91 |  | 0.56 |
| Fs  | 0.53 | 0.76 | 0.70 | 0.71 | 0.92 |  | 0.24 |  | 0.73 |
| Qs  | − 0.14 | − 0.38 | − 0.48 | − 0.33 | − 0.43 |  | − 0.15 |  | − 0.29 |

the composition of the magma, anything about its cooling history or anything about the actual mineralogical composition of the rock that is being classified«.

ESENWEIN made interesting comments on the relation of the Azores petrographic province with other Atlantic ones, treating specifically of those of Madeira, Canary Islands, St. Helena and Ascension, presenting petrochemical comparisons – vd. Table 6. (Vide MITCHELL-THOMÉ, 1970, for more recent data on the last two islands.)

BERTHOIS (1953b) mentioned volcanics reported by others – mostly those by ESENWEIN – as also determinations he himself made. His own studies showed the presence of: labradorite-basalts and analcime-basanites (Sta. Maria); oligoclase-andesites, doleritic-basalts, labradoritic-basalts, analcime-basalts, sölvsbergites, trachytes, sanidinites (S. Miguel); aegerine-trachytes, pyroxene-amphibole-trachytes, barkevitic-andesites, oligoclase-andesites, biotite-augite-basalts, pyroxene-amphibolebasalts, pyroxene-basalts, peridotitic-basalts and olivine-basalts (Terceira); sölvsbergites, amphibole-basalts, pyroxene-basalts, peridotitic-basalts, nepheline-basanites, micro-gabbros and troctolites (Graciosa); feldspathic-olivine-basalts bytownite-basalts, labradorite-basalts, andesitic-hornblende-basalts (S. Jorge); labradorite-basalts, basanites (Pico); labradorite-basalts and basalts (Faial);

Table 15        Probable vertical differentiation development of Azores magmas (ESENWEIN, 1929)

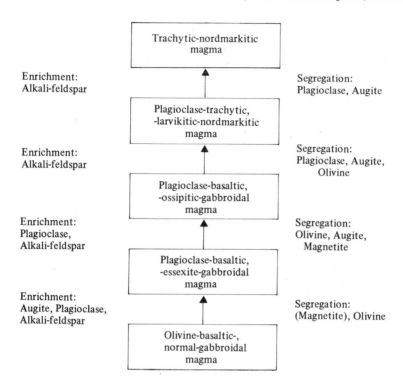

|  |  |  |
|---|---|---|
|  | Trachytic-nordmarkitic magma |  |
| Enrichment: Alkali-feldspar | ↑ | Segregation: Plagioclase, Augite |
|  | Plagioclase-trachytic, -larvikitic-nordmarkitic magma |  |
| Enrichment: Alkali-feldspar | ↑ | Segregation: Plagioclase, Augite, Olivine |
|  | Plagioclase-basaltic, -ossipitic-gabbroidal magma |  |
| Enrichment: Plagioclase, Alkali-feldspar | ↑ | Segregation: Olivine, Augite, Magnetite |
|  | Plagioclase-basaltic, -essexite-gabbroidal magma |  |
| Enrichment: Augite, Plagioclase, Alkali-feldspar | ↑ | Segregation: (Magnetite), Olivine |
|  | Olivine-basaltic-, normal-gabbroidal magma |  |

sölvsbergites, pumaceous trachytes, labradorite-basalts and andesites (Flores). BERTHOIS re-calculated ESENWEIN's analyses, made petrochemical computations on his own collected samples and also on samples housed in the Muséum national d'Histoire naturelle in Paris. (It should be noted that ESENWEIN never visited the Azores, his studies being made on the collections of HARTUNG, MÜGGE and FRIEDLÄNDER-) BERTHOIS's mg-k and Fs-Qs-Ls diagrams show very close similarity, with a somewhat greater spread of basalts in BERTHOIS' triangle compared to that of ESENWEIN, andesites being squeezed into a small locus between the basalts and trachytes, the latter being bunched in a narrow zone. BERTHOIS, on the basis of a re-study of all ESENWEIN's analyses, plus his studies of his own collections and those from the Muséum confirmed in general the opinions of ESENWEIN regarding the petrography of the Azores volcanics.

In the »Noticias Explicativas« (ZBYSZEWSKI et al., 1958–1973) accompanying the geological sheets of the individual islands prepared by the Serviços Geologicos de Portugal, ASSUNÇAO gives descriptions of rocks as shown in Table 17. A much greater variety is shown than in previous works, largely a result of the perpetual confusion and ambiguity forever associated with igneous nomenclature. This, for example, partially explains the addition of five extra rock types to the list for S. Miguel as given by ASSUNÇAO (1961), viz. augitic-andesites, hornblende-andesites, ankaramites, diorites and mafraites. No doubt for chiefly the same reason, ZBYSZEWSKI et al. (1962c) add the

Table 16                              Differentiation scheme for Azores magmas (ESENWEIN, 1929)

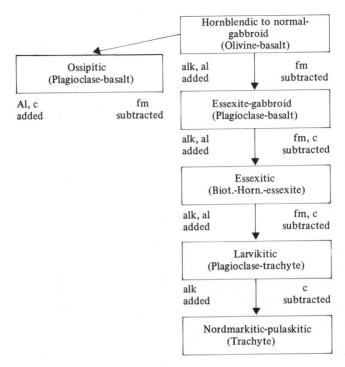

following rock types to the list presented in Table 17: olivine-basalts, plagioclase-basalts, andesitic-plagioclase-basalts, olivine-augite-basalts, doleritic-peridotitic-basalts, peridotitic-andesites, basaltic-andesites for the island of Pico.

To date, plutonics, almost invariably in the form of xenoliths, have been reported in S. Miguel, Terceira, Graciosa, Pico, Corvo and Flores by MÜGGE, LACROIX (1893), ESENWEIN, BERTHOIS and ASSUNÇAO. In S. Miguel sanidinites (vd. No. 37) occur at Agua do Pau, Lagoa de Fogo, Pico Alto and Ribeira Grande, mafraites at Ponta da Ferreira and Furnas, and the literature makes mention of gabbros, diorites and pyroxenites in the island. The sanidinites have a miarolitic structure, formed essentially of alkali-feldspars – orthoclase and anorthoclase, often in micro-perthitic association –, scarce sodic amphibole (arfedsonite?), augite marginally altered to aegerine, and biotite. Zircon, pyrites, and such rare species as lavenite and astrophyllite occur as accessories or then accidentally. Secondary quartz and aegerine sometimes are present in miarolitic vesicles. Mineralogically there is a close relation between the sanidinites and aegerine-trachytes of the island, with which latter they are mostly associated. ESENWEIN gives analyses of a hornblende-aegerine-sanidinite from Calderao, Terceira (No. 19), alkali-feldspar and black hornblende prominent, witb accessories quartz, biotite, titanite and zircon in the miarolitic cavities. In Graciosa occur micro-gabbros on the western slopes of Serra de Caldeira, troctolites just S of (500 m) Sta. Cruz. The former occur as large blocks, and comprise 65% labradorite, albite, abundant augite,

Table 17

Igneous rocks reported by the Serviços Geológicos de Portugal in the Azores

| | Flores | Corvo | Faial | Pico | S. Jorge* | Graciosa | Terceira | S. Miguel | Sta. Maria | Formigas |
|---|---|---|---|---|---|---|---|---|---|---|
| Basalts | x | x | x | x | x | x | x | x | x | x |
| Olivine-Basalts | x | | x | | x | x | x | x | x | |
| Basanitoids | x | x | x | | | x | | x | x | x |
| Mugearites | x | | | | | | | | | |
| Hawaiites | x | | | | | | | | | |
| Peridotitic-Basalts | | | x | x | x | x | x | x | x | |
| Doleritic-Basalts | | | x | x | x | | | | x | |
| Limburgitic-Basalts | | | | | | | x | | x | |
| Ankaramites | | x | | x | x | x | | | | |
| Ankaramitic-Basalts | x | | | x | | | | | x | |
| Tephritoids | | | x | | | | | x | | |
| Limburgites | | | | | | | | | x | |
| Trachytes | | | x | | | x | x | x | | |
| Alkali-Trachytes | x | | x | | x | x | x | x | | |
| Cal-Alk.-Trachytes | x | | x | | x | x | | x | | |
| Akeritic-Trachytes | | | x | | | | | | | |
| Hyperalk.-Trachytes | | | | | | | x | x | x | |
| Latites | | | x | | | | | x | | |
| Monzonitic-Trachytes | | | x | | | | | | | |
| Rhyolitic-Trachytes | | | | | | | x | | | |
| Tautirites | | | x | | | | | | | |
| Andesites | x | x | x | x | | x | x | x | x | |
| Trachy-Andesites | x | x | x | x | x | x | x | x | | |
| Peridotitic-Andesites | x | x | | | x | x | x | x | x | |
| Dolerites | | | x | | x | | | x | | |
| Camptonites | | | x | | | | | x | | |
| Gabbros | | | | | | | | x | | |
| Olivinitic-Gabbros | x | x | | | | | | | | |
| Akali-Syenites | | x | | | x | | | | | |
| Sanidinites | | | | | | | | x | | |
| Pyroxenites | | | | | | | | x | | |

\* Author's observations

little biotite, apatite is scarce. The groundmass is constituted of 50% An, augite and magnetite, the last-mentioned being scarce and present only as tiny grains. The troctolites occur in pyroxene- and olivine-basalts, mineralogically contain up to 75% bytownite, abundant olivine, scarce augite, and magnetite is present as acicular crystals within the augite cleavage zones. In Pico, miarolitic essexite-gabbros are found on Pico mountain (No. 41). In Corvo olivinitic-gabbros are present at Ribeira Poço de Agua, and alkali-syenites at Baia. The former have, as essential constituents, 62% labradorite, brown augite and olivine, the last-mentioned with a partial rim of pyroxene and of magnetite. The syenite comprises chiefly alkali-feldspar of anorthoclase character and green sodic augite, along with oligoclase, magnetite and sphene. Gabbro-dioritic xenoliths occur in the same general area. As previously noted, biotite-hornblende essexites occur in Flores, alkali-microsyenites NNW of Francisçao. The latter are composed essentially of potassic feldspar, albite and aegerine-augite, with prominent calcite as an accessory, also metallic oxides. The parameters of these rocks are identical with sölvsbergites. N of Alto da Cova is a rock of similar mineralogical composition, named by ASSUNÇAO as an alkali-syenite with sodic pyroxene. These syenitic rocks of Flores are the equivalents of the alkali-trachytes of the island.

MÜGGE, LACROIX and ASSUNÇAO considered the xenoliths in trachytes, basalts and basanitoids as the deeper equivalents of these extrusives and in no way representatives of a crystalline basement. But BERTHOIS mentions in Graciosa blocks, one of which was ›plusiers mètres cubes‹ but was unable to find any in situ outcrops nor does he mention any gabbro enclaves within lavas in this region. This exception to the general xenolithic nature of these plutonics is of interest and requires more detailed field studies.

As per SCHMINCKE & WEIBEL (1972) and SCHMINCKE (1973) the rocks of S. Miguel and Terceira are of potassic character. Peralkaline rocks – comenditic trachytes in S. Miguel and comendites and pantellerites in Terceira – show the presence of rhyolitic affinities in late differentiates in these islands at least. The potassic nature of Azores rocks thus places them along with other potassic provinces of the Atlantic such as Gough, Tristan and Jan Mayen. It appears that Terceira is younger than S. Miguel, is more silica oversaturated, less alkalic and potassic. Faial rocks are definitely more alkalic than those from Terceira.

The Azores volcanics are of alkaline character, having undergone various modifications. From published data and personal work, the following can be said by way of petrochemical summary.

From QLM diagrams, analyses are strung out along the M-F axis, with greater concentration towards the L corner, hence indicating saturation-supersaturation.

Silicity-acidity degree diagrams ($Si°-Az°$), types fall in the range $Si°$ 60–100, $Az°$ 40–70. In Terceira there is a microscopically trachytic facies, the lavas with excess silica being considered rhyolitoids containing glass.

In the silica-total alkalis diagrams, $SiO_2$ ranges from 40 to 65, $Na_2O + K_2O$ from 2 to 14, illustrating the alkaline character, with a tholeiitic tendency. Such diagrams also demonstrate the petrochemical groupings of the islands into Corvo-Flores, Faial-Pico-S. Jorge-Terceira-Graciosa and S. Miguel-Sta. Maria. The last-mentioned show a tholeiitic tendency whilst the first-mentioned is more clearly alkaline.

This feature is confirmed by the MURATA diagrams, $MgO-Al_2O_3/SiO_2$. In Corvo-Flores, many andesitic samples fall within the hawaiite-mugearite class, basalts being relatively rare. These andesites are typical oceanic, not continental, andesites. In the central group of islands the tholeiitic character is more dominant, basalts much commoner, particularly in Faial, Pico and Terceira, whilst trachytes are lacking in Pico, Graciosa and S. Jorge. The eastern group of islands are dominantly alkaline, where we have tholeiitic and alkaline basalts. In these latter two islands we also have ›accumulative rocks‹ close to oceanites and ankaramites.

The $SiO_2$-(FeO + $Fe_2O_3$/FeO + $Fe_2O_3$ + MgO) SIGVALDASON diagrams show almost a total absence of intermediate rocks of $SiO_2$ 50-55%, clearly evident in Corvo, Flores and Faial, whereas in Terceira-S. Miguel-Sta. Maria this gap has limits of approximately 53-60% $SiO_2$. This hiatus corresponds to the ‹DALY gap‹, observed in various oceanic islands, marking the absence or then scarcity of true andesites. In these Fe-$SiO_2$ diagrams one notices that for Terceira, throughout the $SiO_2$ range, the Fe range fluctuates much less than for other islands, in support of the tholeiitic trend.

The MgO-(FeO + $Fe_2O_3$) diagrams for Corvo, Flores, Faial and Terceira define a trachytic group, as also the presence of less well-defined ›accumulative rocks‹. Again the near total absence of trachytes is noted for Pico-S. Jorge-Graciosa. (It should be noted, however, that petrographically trachytes are recognized in Graciosa, but petrochemical analyses of such are wanting.)

As regards the si-fm, alk, c, al diagrams and isofalic values, these show four groupings of the islands: Pico-S. Jorge-Graciosa, 142; Corvo-Flores, 160; S. Miguel-Sta. Maria, 161; Terceira, 240. The low value of 142 is somewhat questionable, for considerably fewer analyses were available than for the other islands, and as regards Faial, acceptable analyses have not been obtained. The exceptionally high value for Terceira cannot be ascribed to the presence of rocks with excess silica, and here we frankly do not know the cause of such at this time.


### Sedimentary Rocks

As distinct from the Canaries, Madeira and Cape Verde archipelagoes, the Azores show a very restricted development of pre-Recent sedimentaries, and in fact such are only known in Sta. Maria and the miniature islets of Rocas Formigas.

The Sta. Maria occurrences have long been known, being first reported by MORELET and also HARTUNG in 1860. The latter's book, the first more or less systematic account of the geology of the archipelago, gives fuller details of these rocks, and since then the lithology, stratigraphy, palaeontology of these occurrences have often been described.

Reference to the geological map (Fig. 27) shows these rocks are chiefly exposed along coastal sections and up valleys, there being large areas in the interior and in the W where no such rocks are exposed. AGOSTINHO (1937b) claimed that these Miocene sediments did not occur above elevations of some 120-130 m, but the 1960 geological map of the island shows them occurring as high as 400 m on the S slopes of Pico Alto in the headwaters of a valley running S to Prainha, and, as per the same map, there are many localities where the rocks lie above 130 m.

Principal constituents are limestones, breccias, sandstones, conglomerates and tuffs.

Table 18      Chemical analyses and probable mineral composition of Miocene limestones, Sta. Maria (BERTHOIS, 1953)

|  |  | 1 | 2 | 3 | 4 |
|---|---|---|---|---|---|
| Fraction soluble in HCl | $SiO_2$ | 0.42 | 0.42 | 0.15 | 0.58 |
| | $Al_2O_3$ | 2.50 | 2.66 | 2.24 | 1.55 |
| | $Fe_2O_3$ | 1.25 | 2.15 | 1.39 | 0.75 |
| | MgO | 0.20 | 0.91 | 1.19 | 0.04 |
| | CaO | 39.90 | 42.30 | 46.97 | 49.51 |
| | $CO_2$ | 31.57 | 34.36 | 38.26 | 38.93 |
| | $H_2O+$ | 2.77 | 4.93 | 3.63 | 3.51 |
| | $H_2O-$ | 4.46 | 0.33 | 0.71 | 0.46 |
| Insoluble | $SiO_2$ | 10.96 | 7.72 | 2.96 | 2.21 |
| | $Al_2O_3$ | 3.21 | 2.50 | 0.63 | 1.20 |
| | $Fe_2O_3$ | 1.20 | 0.82 | 0.35 | 0.80 |
| | MgO | 0.06 | Tr | 0.09 | Tr |
| | CaO | 0.30 | 0.74 | 0.43 | 0.25 |
| | $Na_2O$ | 0.60 | 0.70 | 0.52 | -- |
| | $K_2O$ | Tr | Tr | Tr | -- |
| | | 99.40 | 100.54 | 99.52 | 99.79 |
| Soluble | Giobertite | 3.70 | 5.35 | 2.52 | 1.64 |
| | Calcite | 71.20 | 75.80 | 84.00 | 88.40 |
| | Göthite | 1.72 | 2.77 | 1.92 | 1.07 |
| | Kaolinite | 1.03 | 1.03 | 1.03 | 1.29 |
| | Gibbsite | -- | -- | 3.12 | -- |
| | $H_2O+$ | 1.19 | 2.90 | 1.63 | 2.01 |
| | $H_2O-$ | 4.46 | 0.33 | 0.71 | 0.46 |
| Insoluble | $SiO_2$ | 4.70 | 2.22 | -- | 0.66 |
| | Anorthite | 1.39 | 3.62 | -- | 1.11 |
| | Albite | 5.24 | 5.77 | 3.70 | -- |
| | $CaSiO_3$ | -- | -- | 0.93 | -- |
| | $SiO_2Al_2O_3$ | 2.75 | -- | -- | 1.29 |
| | $MgSiO_3$ | 0.10 | -- | 0.20 | -- |
| | $FeSiO_3$ | 2.12 | -- | 0.53 | 1.32 |
| | Hematite | -- | 0.80 | -- | -- |
| | | 99.60 | 100.59 | 100.29 | 99.25 |

1.     Limestone with few organisms.
2, 3.   Limestone with abundant organisms.
4.     Limestone exclusively organogenic (with *Amphisteginae*).

In general thicknesses are not great – 3–4 m though 10–12 m occurrences are known. There occur also detached blocks within volcanic formations.

BERTHOIS (1953) classed the sedimentaries, on the basis of microscopic study, into three major lithologic groups: (1) Limestones having calcareous cement, which are subdivided into: (a) Limestones having rare organisms. These show fish scales; echinoid spines, débris of Brachiopoda, Gastropoda, *Lithothamnium*, Bryozoa, Rotalidae. (b) Limestones having abundant organisms, showing plates and spines of Echinoidea, spicules of Holothuriae and Alcyonareae, pieces of Bryozoa, Brachiopoda and such

Foraminifera as Globigerinidae, Rotalidae, Miliodae, Texturalidae and rarely Bulminidae and Amphisteginidae. (2) Limestones exclusively organic. These limestones are formed essentially of masses of Amphisteginidae and only rarely are fragments of *Lithothamnium* and some enigmatic tubular structures entirely filled with clear grains of calcite encountered. (3) Limestones with isotropic cementation. The cement is of yellowish vitreous character in which occur coccoliths and sporangia of Dasycladaceae. Such structures, as well as the ooliths accompanying them, rarely show their initial structures, as recrystallinization has been the rule. There also occur calcareous grains seemingly of detrital origin, and more or less rounded fragments of Bivalvia.

The presence of calcareous algae and Bryozoa in most samples indicate a littoral deposit in waters not exceeding some 40 m in depth, but the limestones with Amphisteginidae alone were likely formed at somewhat greater depths in a zone of strong currents. The alternation of limestones and volcanics is corroborated in petrographic studies, where the latter occur as pebbles, etc. - chiefly analcime-basalts similar to the older basalts of the island, but also labradorite-basalts which occur as numerous dykes especially in the Vila do Porto area. BERTHOIS believed that the old basalts were not yet formed when the limestones were deposited, but that at this time active subaerial and submarine volcanic activity was taking place, during which newer basalts poured out over older ones, which former furnished the pebbles, etc. in the calcareous sediments. It was his opinion that limestones were formed in varying depths and that the present various elevations of such are partly original.

ZBYSZEWSKI et al. (1961c) mention various successions in the island:

1. E of Ponta dos Frades.   (Top to base): Breccia and scoria; Miocene limestones; compact basalt; sandy limestones; slightly inclined volcanic breccias; alternation of volcanic breccias and tuffs, dipping S.

2. Scarp at Pinheiros.   Altered basalts covered by tuffs; 0.3 m basalts; 0.10 m tuffs; 0.60 m coarse conglomerate; sands and shelly tuffs with whale bones, Miocene; 3–4 m basaltic lavas; shelly tuffs; 0.60 m conglomerate with calcareous cement; thick tuffs; 3 m coarse, shelly conglomerate; 9 m yellowish tuffs; scoria cut by many dykes.

3. New road from Almagreira to Praia.   Reddish tuffs; 10–12 m basalts tending to prismatic jointing; yellow horizontally-bedded tuffs, 1.5–2 m; basalts; 4 m conglomerate; 10–12 m red, well-stratified tuff with some coarsely agglomeratic layers; 2 m volcanic breccia cut by dykes and alternating with thin shelly tuffs; 15 m conglomerate; grey-yellow tuffs with *Janthina typica*, small molluscs and bone fragments; hard, greenish tuffs; 1 m yellowish and brownish tuffs; 1.5 m volcanic breccia passing into conglomerate; 2 m yellow conglomerates; volcanic breccia; 2.5 m yellow tuffs with pebbles; 8–10 m greyish coarse conglomerate; 2 m yellowish tuffs with pebbles; 1.5 m conglomerate with large boulders; 5–6 m greyish volcanic breccia with yellowish stripes; pre-Vindobonian ankaramitic basalt.

The view is held that such Miocene sediments extend at depth under all the island, and indeed AGOSTINHO (1937a) believed that at greater depths such rocks were present in all the archipelago, Sta. Maria being considered likely the oldest island and also the only one where there are no indications of recent vulcanism. Formigas Bank (also often known as Rocas Formigas) comprises a group of reefs some 35 km NE of Sta. Maria,

Table 19     Elevations (m) of abrasion platforms (A) and marine terraces (B) of the Azores Archipelago

| | | | | | | | | | |
|---|---|---|---|---|---|---|---|---|---|
| Flores | | | 8–15 B | 12–20 B | | | | 30–150 B | |
| Corvo | | | | | 30 B | | | | |
| Faial | 0.5 B | 2 B | | 15 B | | | | | |
| Pico | 1 B | 3–5 B | 6 B | | | | | | |
| S. Jorge | | | 8 ? B | | | | | | |
| Graciosa | | | 5–9 B | | | 60 A | | | |
| Terceira | | | 7–10 B | | | | 100 B | | |
| S. Miguel | | 4 B | | | 15–30 A | 50–75 A | 90 B | 80–120 A | |
| Sta. Maria | 1 B | 2–5 B | 6–12 B | 12–15 B | | 50–60 B | 80–100 AB | 120 A | 200 A |
| Azores | 0.5–1 | 2–5 | 5–12 | 12–15 | 15–30 | 50–75 | 80–100 | 150 | 200 |

strung out in a N-S direction for ca. 1,000 m, some of which are only emergent at low tide. ZBYSZEWSKI (1962b) remarked that on the largest islet with the lighthouse there occur Miocene limestones intercalated with volcanics, the former sometimes having the appearance of compact, shelly masses of fossil fragments from which various genera of fossils have been recognized.

On all the major islands of the archipelago, alluvium, beach sands, scree, dunes, old beaches and Quaternary terraces are to be found, many of which have been studied petrographically, chemically and granulometrically by BERTHOIS (op. cit.) (vide Table 20 for granulometric characteristics). On many islands there also occur fumarole and hotspring deposits.

On all islands allochthonous rocks are encountered in the littoral zones; HARTUNG (1860) and BARROIS (1898). These are chiefly granites, mica-schists, quartzites, sandstones and limestones, which obviously take on importance in studying the mineralogic content of littoral sands. To HARTUNG the importance of such exotic rocks mixed with local material testified to vestiges of glacial times, these rocks being floated by glaciers which became stranded along the coasts. CHAVES, on the other hand (in a letter to BARROIS) thought they represented discarded ballast of merchant ships, seemingly chiefly by ships plying back and forth to England. (On the island of S. Jorge, at the abandoned lime-kiln near the port of Calheta, the writer picked up a 15 cm subrounded block of limestone extraordinarily like the ›blues‹ Purbeckian limestones of Sussex, England). The limestones amongst the exotic rocks, even in Sta. Maria, differ from the Miocene calcareous rocks, as the former limestones were imported for the lime-kilns of the islands. It is noticeable that exotics are found largely near abandoned

---

Legend to Table 20

| x | Present marine sands | ○ | Present fluviatile sands |
|---|---|---|---|
| + | Old marine sands | y | Old fluviatile sands |
| ● | Marine terrace sands | k | Present dune sands |

[1]/ As Azores samples show a much lower selectivity in sorting than general, BERTHOIS used a module of 2 instead of $\sqrt{2}$ as proposed by BIETLOT.

Table 20                    Granulometric features of Quaternary sands of Azores (BERTHOIS, 1953)

| Sample No. | Type | Mean diam. (Qm) in mm | Sorting index ($^1/$) | Asymmetry index | Depth (m) or beach slope(°) | Locality and island |
|---|---|---|---|---|---|---|
| a | x | 0.240 | 0.975 | + 0.011 | 27 | S. Miguel |
| b | x | 0.270 | 0.948 | + 0.008 | 33 | S. Miguel |
| c | x | 0.290 | 0.970 | + 0.004 | 20 | S. Miguel  dredged sands |
| d | x | 0.430 | 0.945 | + 0.005 | 21 | S. Miguel |
| e | x | 0.380 | 0.730 | + 0.070 | – | S. Miguel |
| 11 | x | 0.300 | 0.973 | + 0.013 | 10 | Caetanos beach, S. Miguel |
| 12 | x | 0.440 | 0.875 | + 0.075 | | Caetanos beach, S. Miguel |
| 13 | x | 0.405 | 0.962 | – 0.002 | | Caetanos beach, S. Miguel |
| 14 | + | 0.280 | 0.982 | – 0.002 | | Caetanos beach, S. Miguel |
| 25 | x | 0.415 | 0.977 | + 0.007 | 7 | Rib. Grande beach, S. Miguel |
| 26 | x | 1.100 | 0.600 | + 0.100 | | Rib. Grande beach, S. Miguel |
| 27 | + | 0.370 | 0.997 | – 0.001 | | Rib. Grande beach, S. Miguel |
| 45 | + | 0.480 | 0.750 | – 0.070 | | Baia de Prainha, Sta. Maria |
| 46 | + | 1.350 | 0.740 | – 0.260 | | Baia de Prainha, Sta. Maria |
| 51 | x | 0.227 | 0.993 | + 0.003 | | Baia de S. Lourenço, Sta. Maria |
| 52 | + | 0.440 | 0.830 | – 0.090 | | Baia de S. Lourenço, Sta. Maria |
| 60 | + | 0.729 | 0.600 | 0.000 | | Betw. Angra and S. Mateus, Terceira |
| 64 | + | 0.190 | 0.987 | + 0.007 | | Praia da Victoria, Terceira |
| 68 | x | 0.350 | 0.835 | + 0.115 | | Praia da Victoria, Terceira |
| 69 | + | 0.350 | 0.989 | + 0.005 | | Praia da Victoria, Terceira |
| 71 | + | 0.340 | 0.960 | + 0.020 | | Praia da Victoria, Terceira |
| 73 | + | 0.375 | 0.970 | – 0.010 | | Praia da Victoria, Terceira |
| 91 | + | 1.150 | 0.600 | + 0.110 | | 1 km W of S. Mateus, Terceira |
| 92 | + | 0.275 | 0.948 | + 0.028 | | Angra do Heroismo, Terceira |
| 101 | ● | 2.120 | 0.720 | + 0.020 | | Sta. Cruz, Graciosa |
| 105 | x | 0.930 | 0.790 | + 0.090 | | Baia da Barra, Graciosa |
| 111 | ○ | 0.590 | 0.630 | – 0.110 | | Afonso do Porto, Graciosa |
| 116 | x | 0.315 | 0.921 | + 0.071 | 5 | Praia, Graciosa |
| 121 | x | 1.750 | 0.315 | + 0.035 | | South coast, S. Jorge |
| 126 | x | 3.250 | 0.520 | 0.000 | | South coast, S. Jorge |
| 135 | x | 0.490 | 0.820 | + 0.110 | | W of Ribeiras, Pico |
| 136 | x | 0.310 | 0.860 | + 0.060 | | W of Ribeiras, Pico |
| 142 | ○ | 1.300 | 0.840 | – 0.140 | | W of Ribeiras, Pico |
| 145 | x | 1.060 | 0.986 | + 0.106 | 4 | Areia Larga, Pico |
| 146 | ● | 0.075 | 0.650 | – 0.010 | | Areia Larga, Pico |
| 148 | ● | 0.385 | 0.500 | 0.000 | | Areia Larga, Pico |
| 149 | x | 0.385 | 0.805 | + 0.045 | | Areia Larga, Pico |
| 152 | x | 0.900 | 0.905 | + 0.025 | 16 | 1.5 km N of Madalena, Pico |
| 153 | x | 0.560 | 0.880 | – 0.040 | | 1.5 km N of Madalena, Pico |
| 157 | x | 0.210 | 0.959 | + 0.039 | 3 | Porto Pim, Faial |
| 160 | ○ | 0.729 | 0.800 | – 0.020 | | Rib. dos Flamengos, Faial |
| 162 | x | 0.365 | 0.830 | + 0.130 | 1 | N of Rib. dos Flamengos, Faial |
| 167 | y | 1.025 | 0.688 | + 0.012 | | Pasteleiro, Faial |
| 170 | x | 0.305 | 0.905 | + 0.055 | 8 | Almoxarife, Faial |
| 171 | k | 0.325 | 0.995 | – 0.003 | | Rocha Vermelha, Faial |
| 173 | x | 0.295 | 0.961 | + 0.031 | 3 | Rocha Vermelha, Faial |
| 178 | x | 0.500 | 0.660 | + 0.060 | | Rocha Vermelha, Faial |
| 301 | x | 0.600 | 0.550 | + 0.050 | | Sta. Cruz, Flores |
| 302 | x | 1.800 | 0.575 | + 0.175 | | Rib. da Silva Lomba, Flores |
| 303 | x | 0.960 | 0.710 | + 0.130 | | Sta. Cruz, Flores |
| 304 | x | 5.000 | 0.670 | – 0.190 | | Ferrao Jorge, Flores |
| 305 | x | 0.790 | 0.910 | + 0.010 | | Palha Grande, Flores |
| 306 | x | 0.750 | 0.840 | – 0.060 | | Faja Grande, Flores |
| 307 | x | 0.729 | 0.780 | + 0.080 | | Porto d' Areia, Corvo |

lime-kilns, within ports or then near ports, and none are known inland or at high locations. Such facts led Berthois to agree with Chaves which undoubtedly is the correct interpretation.

## Stratigraphy

For more than a hundred years, the Sta. Maria limestones have been recognized as Miocene. The earlier tendency was to regard the strata as Helvetian, but more recent work, e. g. Zbyszewski & Almeida (1950), Ferreira (1955), Colom (in Krejci-Graf et al., 1958) would broaden somewhat the time-range, certainly up into the Tortonian, for certain determined species of fauna up to the Pontian and down to the Aquitanian.

In Formigas, on the basis of well-preserved specimens of *Clypeaster altus* Klein, Chaves (1924) determined a Helvetian age for the rocks, and seemingly Zbyszewski (1962b) would agree.

Of 59 species of various marine fauna studied by Ferreira (1955), 33 were known in the Miocene (i. e. Burdigalian-Tortonian) of the Tejo Basin, Portugal.

In essence then we can say that these Santa Maria calcareous deposits are of Vindobonian age, with, as per Zbyszewski & Ferreira (1962d) a slight tendency towards the Tortonian.

(Berthois (1953) remarked that all earlier workers had classed the rocks as Upper Miocene (étage Mayencien), i. e. Pontian or Sahelian. French stratigraphers prefer to recognize only Upper Miocene (Vindobonian and Pontian) and Lower Miocene (Aquitanian and Burdigalian), but more generally the Vindobonian is placed in the Middle Miocene. The problematic matter of the stratigraphic position of the Pontian is of course recognized).

## Palaeontology

From Santa Maria a rich faunal collection has been made and reported on by Morelet (1860), Bronn (in Hartung 1860: in Reiss 1862), Mayer (in Hartung 1864). Cotter (1892), Berthois (1950b), Ferreira (1952, 1955, 1961), Zbyszewski & Ferreira (1961d, 1962d), Zbyszewski (1962), Krejci-Graf & Colom (in Krejci-Graf et al., 1958).

Localities from where fossils have been gathered include: Pinheiros, Feiteirinha, Furna da Cré, Boca da Cré, Figueiral, Raposo, Ponta dos Matos, Praia, Prainha, Meio Moio, Monte Gordo, Feteira, Alfares, Pico do Facho, Vila do Porto (at bridge). This represents a rather widespread occurrence around coastal areas, except in the west where Miocene exposures are lacking.

The microfauna comprises both planktonic and benthonic species. Colom pointed out that the prevalence of Textulariidae and *Cibicides*, along with the scarcity in Miliolidae suggested an environment with waters less than 100 m in depth. Several littoral species, such as *Planorbulina mediterranensis, Discorbis subrotundata, Quinqueloculina bicarinata* and *Cibicides lobatulus* today inhabit sandy depths shallower than 30 m in the Mediterranean. Forms such as *Robulus* and *Marginulina*, though rare, would testify to colder waters and hence greater depths.

The macrofauna includes Coelenterata, Echinoidea, Annelida, Bryozoa, Brachiopoda, Bivalvia, Gastropoda, Crustacea and Fish, the greatest number of identified fossils being Bivalvia and Gastropoda.

ZBYSZEWSKI & FERREIRA (1962), on the basis of a study of 126 species claimed that 38 were restricted to the Azores and Madeira. They listed the following table, based on the above forms:

| | |
|---|---|
| Species known in the Aquitanian | 32 |
| Species known in the Burdigalian | 56 |
| Species known in the Helvetian | 76 |
| Species known in the Tortonian | 78 |
| Species known in the Pliocene | 61 |
| Species known in the Quaternary | 44 |

In the reefs forming the islets of Formigas, fragments of Bivalvia, Gastropoda, Bryozoa, Echinoidea and Foraminifera occur, several genera also being present in the Miocene of Santa Maria.

Between Praia and Prainha, on the S coast of Santa Maria, on a low marine terrace, Bivalvia and Gastropoda have been studied by ZBYSZEWSKI & FERREIRA (1961). Of 36 species described, 15 are known in the Miocene, 24 in the Pliocene and 35 in the Quaternary, with 11 restricted to the Quaternary. Only *Cerithiopsis nana* MAYER, a Quaternary form, is limited to Sta. Maria.

It remains to add that AGOSTINHO (1950b) mentioned that in excavations made in the younger tuffs on which Angra do Heroismo, Terceira, is built, fossilized plant remains have been found of *Persea azorica* and *Hedera canariensis*. Also KREJCI-GRAF (KREJCIGRAF et al., 1958) mentioned receiving some photographs from a friend in Faial of fossilized leaves from Monte Guia, the peninsula S of Horta formed of scoria cones, which Prof. R. KRÄUSEL thought might belong to *Ilex hartungi* HEER.

The Miocene fauna of Sta. Maria includes the following: *Orbulina universa* D'ORBIGNY, *Globigerinoides elongatus* (D'ORBIGNY), *G. trilobatus* (REUSS), and var. *irregularis* LE ROY, *Pullenia bulloides* D'ORBIGNY, *Globigerina bulloides* D'ORBIGNY, *G. diplostoma* REUSS, *Globorotalia puncticulata* (D'ORBIGNY), *G. hirsuta* (D'ORBIGNY), *Sphaeroidina bulloides* D'ORBIGNY, *Textularia transversaria* BRADY, *T. conica* D'ORBIGNY, *T.* cf. *rugosa* REUSS, *T. sagittula* cf. var. *atrata* CUSHMAN, *T.* cf. *gramen* D'ORBIGNY, *Cibicides haidingeri* (D'ORBIGNY), *C. lobatulus* (WALKER & JACOB), *C. pseudo-ungerianus* CUSHMAN, *Discorbis* cf. *subrotundata* (D'ORBIGNY), *Planorbulina mediterranensis* D'ORBIGNY, *Angulogerina fornasinii* SELLI, *Quinqueloculina bicarinata* D'ORBIGNY, *Marginulina* sp., *Robulus orbicularis* (D'ORBIGNY), *Entosolenia* cf. *marginata* (WALKER & BOYS), *Cassidulina subglosa* BRADY, *Ehrenbergina* cf. *compressa* CUSHMAN, *Biloculina* sp., *Carriophyllia clavus* (SCACCHI), *Parasmilia radicula* MAY., *Ditrupa cornra* LINNÉ, *Spirorbis concamerata* MAY., *Cyathocidaris avenionensis* DESM., *Eucidaris tribuloides* LAMARCK; *Echinocyamus pusillus* MÜLLER, *Clypeaster altus* LAMARCK, *Eschara lamellosa* MICH., *Escharnia celleporacea* MUNST., *Cupularia intermedia* MICH., *Polytrema lyncurium*? LAMARCK, *P. simplex* MICH., *Terebratula caput-serpentis* LINNÉ, *Arca noe* LINNÉ, *A. tetragona* POLI, *A. (Anadara) crassissima* BRONN, *A. (Anadara) fichteli* DESHAYES, *A. (Anadara)* aff. *okeni* MAY., *A. (Fossularca) lactea* LINNÉ, *Pinna pectinata* LINNÉ, *Pycnodonta* cf. *navicularis* BROCCHI, *P. squarrosa* M. DE SERRES, *Ostrea lacerata* GOLDFUSS, *Lopha (Alectryonia) plicatuloides* (MAY.), *Pecten dunkeri* (MAY.),

*Flabellipecten burdigalenis* LAMARCK, *Chlamys reissi* (BRONN), *C. latissima* BROCCHI, *C. sardoa* UGOLINI, *C. inaequicostalis* LAMARCK, *C. macrotis* SOWERBY, *C. opercularis* (LINNÉ), *C. blumi* MAY., *C. varia* LINNÉ, *C. multistriata* POLI, *C. pes-felis* LINNÉ, *C. fasciculata* MILLET, *C. hartungi* MAY., *Plicatula bronnina* MAY., *P. striata* DEFRANCE, *Spondylus gaederopus* LINNÉ var. *deshayesi* MICHT, *S. concentricus* BRONN var. *imbricata* MICHT, *Lima (Mantellum) inflata* CHEMNITZ, *Anomia ephippium* LINNÉ, *Mytilus aquitanicus* MAY., *Lithophagus* sp., *Septifer domengensis* (LAMARCK), *Verticordia granulata* SEGU, *Cardita calyculata* LINNÉ, *C. mariae* MAY., *Chama gryphina* LAMARCK, *C. gryphoides* LINNÉ, *Lucina pagenstecheri* MAY., *L. (Divaricella) divaricata* LINNÉ, *L. (Jagonia) reticulata* POLI, *Diplodonta rotundata* MONTAGU, *Cardium (Nemocardium) comatulum* BRONN, *C. (Pavicardium) papillosum* POLI, *C. (Discors) spondyloides* V. HAUER, *C. (Discors) hartungi* BRONN, *Venus (Ventricola) libellus* DE RAYN., *V. (Ventricola) multilamella* LAMARCK var. *boryi* SACCO, *V. (Chamelea) confusa* MAY., *V. (Timoclea) ovata* PENNANT, *Meretrix (Callista) chione* LINNÉ, *M. heeri* (MAY.), *M. (Pitar) rudis* POLI, *Tapes vetula* BASTEROT, *Tellina incarnata* LINNÉ, *T. (Moerella) donacina* LINNÉ, *T. (Macoma) elliptica* BROCCHI, *Psammobia (Psammocola) aequilateris* BRONN, *Mactra (Pseudoxyperas) emporitense* ALMERA & BOFFIL, *Lutraria lutraria* LINNÉ, *Ervillia castanea* MONTAGU, var. *pusilla* PHILIPPI, *E. elongata* MAY., *Solenocurtus basteroti* DESMOULINS, *Ensis magnus* SCHUM., *Solarium simplex* BROCCHI, *Capulus hungaricus* LINNÉ, *Hipponyx sulcatus* BORSON, *Mitrularia semicanalis* BRONN, *Nerita plutonis* BASTEROT, *Natica atlantica* MAY., *Rissoa (Alvania) cancellata* DA COSTA, *Rissoina bronni* MAY., *R. pusilla* (BROCCHI), *Turbo hartungi* BRONN, *T. mariae* MAY., *Danilia pterostomus* (BRONN), *Janthina typica* (BRONN), *Pleurotomaria atlantica* COTTER, *Vermetus (Serpulorbis) arenarius* LINNÉ, *V. (Petaloconchus) intortus* (LAMARCK), *Cerithium crenulosum* BRONN, *C. hartungi* MAY., *C. incultum* MAY., *Trigonostoma (Ventrilia)* cf. *acutangula* (FAUJ.), *Bitium reticulatum* (DA COSTA), *B. spina* (PARTSCH), *Cerithiopsis (Dizoniopsis) bilineata* (HOERNES), *Trivia parcicosta* BRONN, *Cypraea (Adusta)* cf. *physis* BROCCHI, *C. (Zonaria)* cf. *sanguinolenta* GMEL., *C. stenostoma* MAY., *Erato laevis* (DONOVAN), with var. *elongata* SEGU and *dertincrassata* SACCO, *Ranella (Bursa) bicoronata* BRONN, *R. (Bursa) marginata* MARTINI, *Cymathium secans* (BRONN), *Murex (Tritonalia) vindobonensis* HOERNES, *Pyrene (Anachis) bellardi* (HOERNES), *Euthria* aff. *magna* BELLARDI, *Cantharus (Pollia) exsculpta* DUJ., *Nassa atlantica* MAY., *N. doderleini* MAY., *N. vetulum* MAY., *Fusus longiroster* BROCCHI, *Euthriofusus virgineus* GRAT., *Fasciollaria (Pleuroploca) tarbelliana* GRAT., *Mitra hoernesi* MAY., *M. peregrinula* MAY., *M. volvaria* BRONN, *Tenagodes anguinus* LINNÉ, *Plertotoma perturrita* BRONN, *P. (Mangelia) vauquelini* PEYRAUDEAU, *Conus* cf. *mercati sharpeanus* P. DA COSTA, *C.* cf. *antiquus* LAMARCK, *C. (Conospira) dujardini* DESHAYES, *C.* cf. *pelagicus* BROCCHI, *C. puschi* MICHT., *C. eschwegi* P. DA COSTA, *Acteon semistriatus* FERUSSAC, *Cylichna brocchii* (MICHT.), *Scaphander lignarius* LINNÉ mut. *grateloupi* MICHT., *Sabatia (Roxania) utricula* BROCHI, *Bulla micromphalus* MAY., *Hyala (Diacria) marginata* BRONN, *Cuvieria (Cleodora) columella* RANG, *Balanus laevis* BRUG., *B. pullus* MAY., *Neptunus granulatus* EDWARDS, *Cavolinia mariae* n. sp., *Diplodus jomnitanus* (VALENC.). *Hexanchus (Notidanus) primigenius* (AGASSIZ), *Isurus (Oxyrhina) benedeni* (LE HON), *Carcharhinus (Prionodon) egertoni* (AGASSIZ), *Isurus (Oxyrhina) hastalis* (AGASSIZ), *Isurus oxyrhynchus* (RAFINESQUE), *Sparus cinctus* (AGASSIZ), *Labrodon pavimentatum* GERVAIS.

## Historic Vulcanicity

Within historic times (vide Table 10) S. Miguel, Terceira, S. Jorge, Pico and Faial have all shown vulcanism, sometimes effusive, sometimes exclusively explosive, at times mixed, in all cases yielding basic material, giving a total of perhaps 19 volcanic episodes in the last 550 odd years (AGOSTINHO, 1932, 1936, 1937a, c, 1960; FRIEDLÄNDER, 1929). The earliest suggestion of historic vulcanism dates from the very beginnings of European discovery when activity is thought to have been in progress between 1427 and 1432 in S. Miguel with pumice falls at Sete Cidades. As there is considerable doubt about this event the eruptivity in 1444 at Agua de Pau in central S. Miguel is usually listed as the first authenic eruption of historic times. The first event to be described in detail was that by FRUTUOSO (1591) regarding the 1563-1564 occurrence at Agua de Pau. After three days of earth rumblings, on June 28, 1563 a 2,000 m thick plinian cloud with abundant trachytic pumice falls heralded the volcanic onset, pumice being widely scattered over the island and in the sea, forming 5 m thick pumice beds on land. At the same time the central part of the caldera foundered, though FRIEDLÄNDER is no doubt right in stating that this complex feature resulted from several eruptions at varying times. On July 2nd basaltic flows welled forth from a parasitic cone on the N side, one flow reaching the coast. By the end of the month vulcanism seemed to have ceased, but on Feb. 10th, 1564 a small explosion took place within the caldera, which in time became filled with water, becoming the present Fogo lake. Fumarolic activity on the slopes of the volcano, as well as gushing forth of mineral springs in this region today bear witness to this former activity.

MACHADO (1962a) has spoken of the Faial-Pico-S. Jorge volcanic ›system‹ of historic times. In these islands, vulcanicity occured in 1562-1564, 1580, 1672-1673, 1718, 1720, 1808 and 1957-1958, but in no instance was vulcanism simultaneous in any of these three islands. From a study of seismic intensity anomalies (1954) he believed that the magmatic chambers of Faial and Pico, separated by only a 7 km wide channel, lay at a depth of some 3-5 km, said chambers likely being connected. For Pico and S. Jorge, MACHADO (1959c) envisaged these two islands as representing the borders of a tectonic valley, prolonged towards S. Miguel, with present depths of more than 1,000 m and forming a rather level submarine valley some 2.5 km broad, with steep slopes up to the respective islands. This valley he thought was probably related to the magmatic chambers of these islands. Because of such possible magmatic chamber relations between the three islands, he believed one could speak of a single volcanic ›system‹. The submarine valley or ›rift‹ is believed also to be related to the vulcanism in S. Miguel, where vulcanism occurred in 1563-1564, 1652 and 1811. MACHADO remarked that on occasion vulcanism is provoked by horizontal stresses in the crust on which are superimposed the control of terrestrial tides, citing the fact that as regards the latter, the initiation of eruptivity at times near the equinoxes corresponds to the influence of the solar semiannual component of terrestrial tides. (Vide section on Cape Verde Vulcanology.)

The volcanic event of Capelhinos, Faial, has been well documented by TAZIEFF (1958), MACHADO (1958a, 1962c, 1967a), ZBYSZEWSKI (1960, 1962a). This spectacular event, drawing worldwide attention in 1957, was preceded by some 200 earth tremors up to

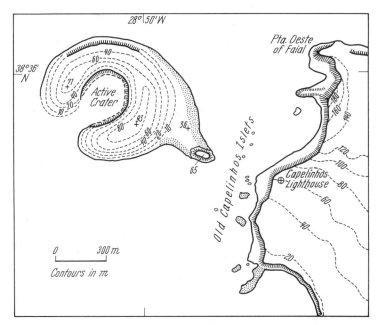

Fig. 38. Embryo Cinder Island, on October 10, 1957, Capelinhos, Faial, Azores. (Modified after MACHADO, 1965).

intensity V on the MERCALLI scale during the period Sept. 16–27, this continuous quaking having an epicentre near the Capelhinos lighthouse (Fig. 38). At 7.00 hrs approximately, Sept. 27th vapours could be seen gushing up through the sea off the western point of Faial, some 1,000 m offshore, where depths reached some 90 m. Gradually the white plumes became more dense, accompanied by ejections of scoria, and before long four vents were active simultaneously throughout a length of 250 m trending WSW-ENE. By the next day these four centres had coalesced and by the 29th had formed an embryo islet with a crater 500 m in diameter, total height 80 m, a length of ca. 1 km, all within 48 hours. This intense explosive activity hurled bombs, scoria, lapilli and cinders to great heights, the volcanic clouds reaching a height of 6 km.

Three successive stages in the eruptivity can be recognized:

(1) Sept. 27–Nov. 5, 1957. During this time the islet – Ilha Nova – was formed, and by Oct. 30 the structure had built up to some 170 m above its submarine base, the crater diameter was 300 m, the circular talus forming a horse-shoe shape with a 100 m wide breach on the SW side whereby sea water flooded in to the active crater. Maximal paroxysms occurred on Oct. 26 followed by an abrupt calming of activity, after which foundering of the structure occurred and in a few days this islet had disappeared out of sight. During this first phase, as indeed during the others, the eruptivity displayed explosive, fragmentary, effusive, electric, solfataric, seismic and degradation episodes as defined by PERRET (1914), or, as per TAZIEFF, pseudovulcanian phases and vesuvian or plinian phases.

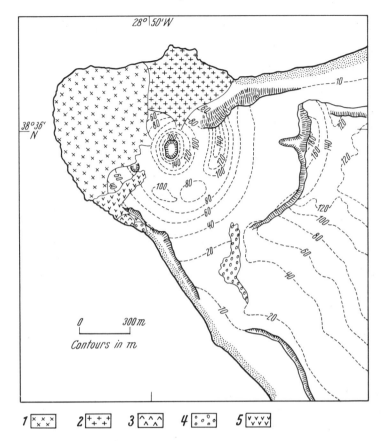

Fig. 39. Capelinhos cone, November 4, 1958 till period of repose, Capelinhos, Faial, Azores.
1: Lava of May–October. 2: Flow of July 31 st. 3: Lava of June–October. 4: Flows of August
23 rd. 5: Flow of October 21 st. (Modified after MACHADO, 1965).

(2) Nov. 6, 1957–May 12, 1958.    Activity was resumed and a new islet formed,
gradually enlarging towards the Faial coast. Eruptivity became greatly increased and
a quite astonishing building-up continued till May 12 (Fig. 39). By March 19, tremendous
explosions were hurling ejectamenta almost 2 km into the air, but thereafter explosive
activity became more moderate and regular until May 12.

(3) May 12–Oct. 25, 1958.    At 18.00 hrs May 12, brady-seismism started with shocks
about every 30 seconds. The intensity of the tremors increased from I to VII, MERCALLI,
during the night, and a value of IX was felt at Ribeira Funda and Praia do Norte, 8 and
6 km respectively from the centre of eruptivity, with total destruction of the rather frail
buildings, etc. Accompanying this powerful seismism, from May 12–14 numerous
fissures opened, lava fountains spewed as high as 600 m, then a marked change in the
regime of vulcanicity, becoming less intense but more regular, lava emissions
continuing until Oct. 25. The volcanic structure underwent some foundering, maximum

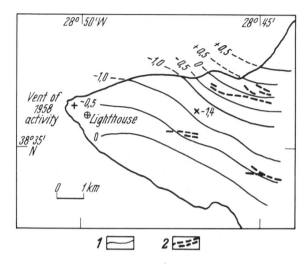

Fig. 40. Ground movement in western extreme of Faial, consequent upon 1957–58 Capelinhos eruptivity, Azores. 1: Lines of equal variation in level, in m. 2: Fractures. (Modified after MACHADO, 1965).

of ca. 2 m, whilst in two zones to the N and S of here uprise attained 0.6 m, depression 1.4 m (Fig. 40). Vulcanism ended very suddenly on Oct. 25, but from then until Nov. 30, 1958, fumarolic activity was intense and pronounced weathering occurred around the crater edges.

TAZIEFF attempted to estimate the eruptive energy of Capelhinos, this authority considering Capelhinos one of the most significant volcanic events of the last several years prior to his publication. He estimated the volume of lavas formed to be 778 m³, weighing 1,945 tonnes, the volume of gases as 107,223 m³. The energy would thus be represented as $10^{17}$ ergs per second, compared with $10^{20}$ ergs per second for Asama Yama, Sept. 23, 1950, 6 x $10^{19}$ ergs per second for Vesuvius, March 23, 1944, $10^{16}$ ergs per second for Etna, May, 1957, 8.5 x $10^{15}$ ergs per second for Izalco (El Salvador), Nov. 1956, 1.5 x $10^{15}$ ergs per second, Stromboli, Aug. 1957, etc. (It should be noted that TAZIEFF wrote his paper when Capelhinos vulcanism had been operative for only 19 weeks, i. e. about Feb. 1st, 1958, and although post-script notes were added in July, 1958, no further mention is made regarding energy matters.)

The vesicular lavas expelled during the vulcanism have the character of basanitoids, showing the following order of consolidation: (a) large phenocrysts of olivine and augite, (b) small phenocrysts of olivine with some reabsorption of the former, (c) microlites of dispersed labradorite along with grains of olivine, (d) essentially vitreous groundmass with aggregates of augite and metallic oxides. The long duration of the plinian and strombolian types of violence emitting basic material would seem unusual to those who hold the view of the simplified scheme of parallelism between the acidity degree of a magma and its explosive degree, but we must realize that the viscosity of a magma depends not only upon its silica and alumina content but also upon such factors as temperature, proportion of water vapour present, velocity and mass of expelled material, gas content, and in this case of a submarine eruption, the thousands of tonnes of sea water blocking the mouth(s) of the underwater channels. (Cf. the basic explosive phenomena, also submarine, at Myojin Reef, Indonesia.)

TAZIEFF pointed out rightly that it is incorrect to consider Capelhinos as a new volcanic outburst comparable to Paricutin, as the former is rather a resuscitation of a pre-existing volcanic feature.

It may finally be remarked that in view of the violence of both the vulcanicity and seismicity associated with Capelhinos, it is remarkable that no human lives were lost, evacuations having been ordered in time.

## Seismicity

None of the other archipelagoes discussed here have shown such seismic disturbances within historic times as the Azores.

From the Mediterranean two seismic zones diverge westwards into the Atlantic: one trends WNW from Gibralter towards the Azores and includes the epicentral location of the famous 1755 Lisbon earthquake; the other branch trends SW through the Atlas towards Agadir – 1960 earthquake – and on towards the Canary Islands.

AGOSTINHO (1937a) gave an appraisal of seismicity in the Azores up to that time, commenting that not all islands were equally affected, that violent tremors were neither frequent nor particularly dangerous. The westernmost islands of Corvo and Flores appear exempt from earthquakes within historic times, in spite of the fracturing and rifting(?) characteristic of the region – vide Fig. 45. Since the 15th century Sta. Maria has experienced none centred within the island, and only very mild tremors have been noted in Graciosa. However, the other islands of Terceira, Pico, Faial, S. Jorge and S. Miguel, especially the last-mentioned, have known their share of earthquakes.

For Sta. Maria there are three epicentral areas: (a) submarine deeps SW of the island, e. g. 1937, 1952; (b) between Sta. Maria and S. Miguel, e. g. 1932, 1935, 1952; (c) E and SE of the island, e. g. 1930, 1939. In Terceira centres are located at: (a) NW part of the island, e. g. 1547; (b) in the western part, e. g. 1841; (c) in the eastern part, e. g. 1614, whilst overall tremors were experienced in 1591, 1720 and 1933. In Faial are four epicentral areas: (a) NW and WNW of the island, e. g. 1926, 1947; (b) SW of the island; e. g. 1926; (c) W part of the island, e. g. 1958; (d) in the channel between Faial and Pico, e. g. 1926. In S. Jorge the most devastating tremor had its epicentre in the eastern part of the S coast. Undoubtedly S. Miguel has experienced more powerful quakes than any other Azorean island, with three chief epicentral areas: (a) submarine depression running NE-SW between this island and Sta. Maria; (b) along the S coast; (c) W part of island.

The oldest recorded earthquake was that of 1522 in S. Miguel, claiming 5,000 victims. The quake of July 9, 1757, epicentre along the eastern part of the S coast in S. Jorge, is claimed to have been the strongest tremor ever to affect the archipelago. This had a magnitude of 7.4 on the RICHTER scale (Lisbon 1755 tremor, 9.0, Messina quake 1908, 7.6) and caused 1,000 deaths out of the then island population of 5,000. The extreme seismic instability of the archipelago is witnessed, for example, by the fact that no less than 400 significant tremors were experienced during February, 1964, in S. Jorge.

The most important Azorean tremors were: 1522, S. Miguel; 1547, Terceira; 1591, S. Miguel; 1614, Terceira; 1713, S. Miguel; 1757, S. Jorge; 1841, Terceira; 1848, S. Miguel;

1852, S. Miguel; 1926, Faial; 1932, S. Miguel; 1933, between S. Miguel and Terceira; 1935, S. Miguel; 1939, E of Sta. Maria; 1958, Faial; 1964, S. Jorge. By far the greater majority of these seismic disturbances were of tectonic origin, it being realized that almost invariably tremors are associated with volcanic outbursts.

AGOSTINHO (op. cit.) believed that seismic and volcanic phenomena in the Azores of significant proportions are related to older volcanic activity, evident in the geomorphological aspect of the islands. Evidences of recent vulcanism represent areas of rejuvenation of volcanic activity, the magma being maintained in a lively condition at depth which could readily be reactivated under favourable circumstances. Tectonically destructive tremors would not be expected in such regions, and even when such occur within a radius of action of such tremors, damage would not likely be great. For example, the 1926 quake in Faial caused very little destruction in the eastern part of the island where recent vulcanism is evident, but at Horta, the oldest area of the island, destruction was great. He believed that in those zones where volcanic activity was decadent but where real equilibrium had not been attained, such zones were periodically subjected to shocks until such time as a degree of quiescence reigned. MACHADO (1970), noting that in the years 1935–1970 there were, on an average, 50 tremors per annum, claimed that such seismic crises appeared to show a periodicity of ca. 11 years, but the maximas do not occur simultaneously in all islands.

## Geophysical Aspects

QUINTINO (1962) carried out some geomagnetic studies in three islands and MACHADO, QUINTINO & MONTEIRO (1972) have given more information.

In S. Miguel (Fig. 41) there are two distinct regions, in the E and W, where negative magnetic anomalies occur. The central BRUNHES normal magnetic polarity zone is paralleled on either side by MATUYAMA reverse magnetic polarity zones, followed by GAUSS normal magnetic polarity zones at extreme E and W of the island. The time range then is from the present to some 3.35 my. The BRUNHES epoch is presumed to correlate with the many dykes here with polarity of the present. The GILBERT reverse zone, older than 3.35 my, is not present in S. Miguel.

In Terceira BRUNHES positive magnetic anomalies show a NE-SW orientation, bounded by negative MATUYAMA polarity on either side, probably as far as SE coastal regions where positive anomalies approach zero.

In Faial positive BRUNHES values occupy some 90% of the island, with MATUYAMA negative values in a small area in the E.

On the basis of such geomagnetic studies, MACHADO, QUINTINO & MONTEIRO (1972) supposed rifting to have occurred and computed rates of ocean floor spreading. For S. Miguel, a rate of spreading, to both E and W, of 1 cm/year is claimed, slightly less for Terceira and not less than this for Faial, which agree well enough for values in these latitudes of the Atlantic of 1.1 to 1.2-cm/year of LE PICHON (1968). These authors surmised that the chief Atlantic rift is offset eastwards so that it traverses every Azorean island where there has been active vulcanism (Vd. Fig. 45).

COELHO (1968) carried out some gravity studies throughout the archipelago (Figs. 42,

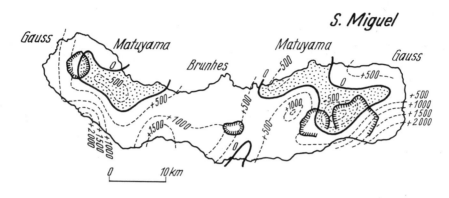

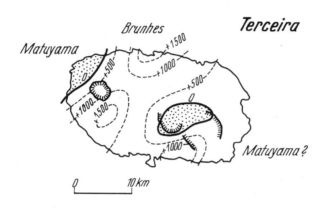

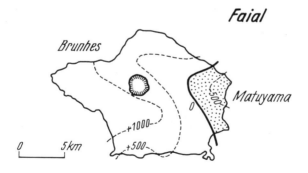

Fig. 41. Magnetic anomalies over S. Miguel, Terceira and Faial, Azores. (Modified after
MACHADO, QUINTINO & MONTEIRO, 1972).

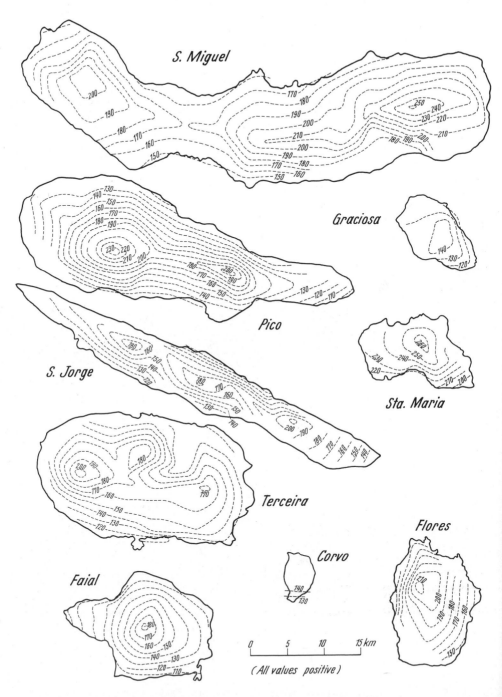

Fig. 42. Free-air (Faye) anomalies, Azores Archipelago. (COELHO, 1968).

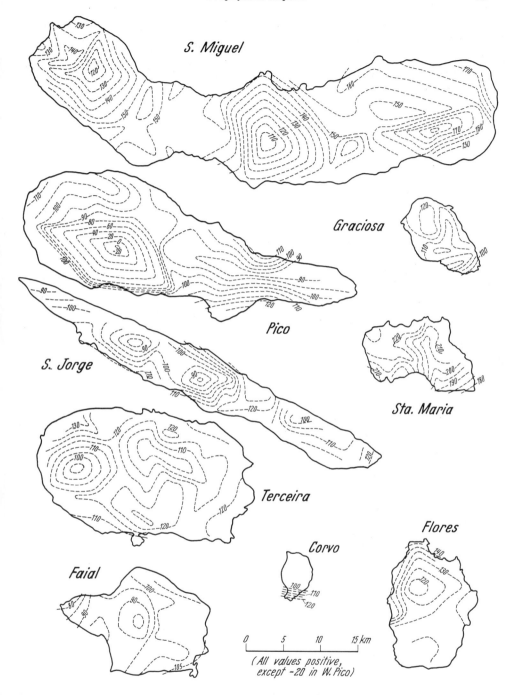

Fig. 43. Bouguer anomalies, Azores Archipelago. (COELHO, 1968).

43). In general, eruptive centres and calderas are well outlined by the FAYE and BOUGUER anomalies. As would be expected of these corrections which are intimately related to elevation, there is broad correlation with the topography and relief in each island. Major topographic forms, the chief eruptive centres are characterized by FAYE maxima and BOUGUER minima. Larger areas of lower, more level topography, e. g. western Sta. Maria and W-central S. Miguel, the FAYE values more closely indicate the degree of isostatic equilibrium attained, the higher values for the former island a lesser degree of compensation than in S. Miguel. It is to be noted that it is in western Sta. Maria that AGOSTINHO postulated greater uplift of the ›basement‹ older basaltics than elsewhere in the archipelago, and here also BOUGUER anomalies reach almost the double of those known elsewhere within the islands.

Lacking both subsurface data and further gravity computations, one cannot translate the FAYE and BOUGUER anomalies into terms which allow of worthwhile estimates of the structure. Here in the Azores we have an area neither continental nor shelf seas, so that BOUGUER values are less valid in interpreting local and regional gravity anomalies in terms of subsurface mass distributions, whilst as regards the FAYE anomalies, which are more valuable in interpreting gravity anomalies across oceans and continents, these are not the best of even rough tests of isostasy. Hence too much can not be read into these FAYE and BOUGUER portrayals as regards isostatic conditions, mass distributions at depth or geological structure.

## Structure-Tectonics

The literature mentions plentiful ›fracturas‹, ›accidents‹, ›verrenkungs‹ but seems somewhat shy of specifying more definitely what these might be, though the naming of faults, dyke patterns are not entirely lacking. Further, in these volcanic islands, it is far from clear in many instances whether fractures are of purely tectonic or of volcanotectonic origin. Undeniably in all islands centres of eruptivity, whether major or minor, can be aligned in various directions, the supposition being that such have a fissural origin. The available literature makes almost no reference to structural details – kinds of faults, length, type and degree of movement, charcteristics of folding, jointing, etc. – the inference being that structural features are but minor concomitants of eruptivity in the archipelago, and in no case have structural studies been made of the islands. Here, as elsewhere in Macaronesia, the great emphasis in geological studies has been on vulcanism; petrography, petrochemistry, petrogeneses of igneous rocks.

The geological maps herewith presented of the islands do show what the Serviços Geologicos sheets more boldly claim to be faults. From these, plus the literature, one observes that faults and dykes no less tend rather to have diagonal patterns, NW-SE and WNW-ESE being most charcteristic, SW-NE and WSW-ENE lesser so, and those trending N-S are fewest. In several islands, e. g. Corvo, Pico, Terceira, more localized fractures and dykes have a radial pattern around major eruptive centres. On other island, e. g. S. Jorge, Pico, Graciosa, the general trend of the islands and their dorsal spines are coincident with major structural trends. Active faults occur in western Faial and are suspected along the southern coasts of S. Miguel. Many coastal cliff sections

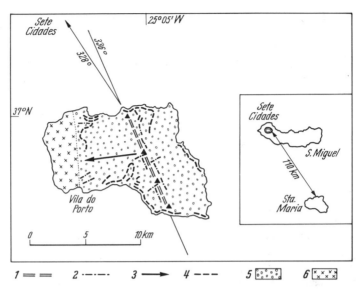

Fig. 44. Tectonics of Sta. Maria, Azores. 1: Volcanic dorsal. 2: Major dykes. 3: Direction of tilting. 4: Miocene sediments. 5: Vindobonian and post-Vindobonian volcanics. 6: Pre-Vindobonian volcanics. (Based on concepts of AGOSTINHO, 1937 b).

give plentiful evidence of dykes and at least smaller disturbances. In the Furnas and Sete Cidades regions of S. Miguel faults are marked by springs and natural gas emanations, lesser so in Flores.

AGOSTINHO (1937b) appeared to treat of Sta. Maria as a special case in the Azores. A NNW-SSE orientated chain of volcanoes runs across the eastern part of the island, forming the topographic axis (Fig. 44). He claimed there were three distinct geological formations: (a) older basaltics, (b) limestones of Miocene age, (c) younger basaltics, represented by the above volcanic chain. (The Serviços Geologicos indicate three major episodes of vulcanicity; pre-Vindobonian, Vindobonian and post-Vindobonian.) AGOSTINHO agreed in principle with HARTUNG (1860) that here positive vertical movements had occurred in conjunction with similar movements in the European mainland during the Miocene. AGOSTINHO mentioned that the sedimentaries – and this would also include the Vindobonian volcanics – and part of the older volcanics were subjected to powerful abrasional planation in the western part of the island and were gradually removed from here by marine attack, likely aided by positive movements which accelerated events, so that today only vestiges of Miocene limestones are found in the W. (This corresponds to the pre-Vindobonian tectonic phase of the Serviços Geologicos.) On the other hand a dense network of dykes, of general E-W orientation, were intruded in pre-Vindobonian times into the so-called older volcanics. The younger volcanics (post-Vindobonian) are also transected by many dykes but rather of more longitudinal orientations, with many smaller faults and dykes normal to the volcanic chain. It was AGOSTINHO's belief that perhaps Sta. Maria indicated the general tectonic evolution of the rest of the archipelago, claiming that the volcanics of these other islands were to be correlated with his younger volcanics and not with the older ones, i.e. post-Vindobonian. He contended that were Sta. Maria to be lowered some dozens of metres, the entire island would then show a pattern similar to the other islands, formed by a great chain of volcanic centres trending towards Sete Cidades in western S. Miguel, which latter he considered the chief centre of eruptivity in the archipelago. As per this scheme then, under the volcanics in the other islands there should be present Miocene sedimentaries which underwent the same positive movements as in Sta. Maria but did not reach the surface, i. e. uplift was less with only vestiges of the younger volcanics in these other islands, which would place the age of the eruptives as largely pre-Vindobonian, perhaps also Vindobonian. (In Sta. Maria lavas are in intimate association with the Vindobonian limestones, thus indicating contemporaneity.) In support of his thesis, AGOSTINHO pointed to the dredging from vicinal seas off the other islands of rocks similar to those in Sta. Maria, specifically mentioning calcareous sands (disintegrated Miocene limestones?) at Praia de Vitoria, Terceira, and also the fact that the younger volcanic dorsal of Sta. Maria trends towards Sete Cidades in S. Miguel, the chief volcanic centre of the archipelago, the Sta. Maria dorsal lying on a volcanic radius from this major centre. The small thickness of the Miocene beds in Sta. Maria – 3-4 m in general – were taken by AGOSTINHO to represent an interval of the order of some dozens of centuries (though known thickness of 10-12 m for limestones would likely argue for a considerable lengthening of the time-span) indicating a cessation of vulcanicity for a much longer period than has occurred during later times, but this opinion is upset by the recognition of vulcanicity contemporaneous with the development of the Miocene sedimentaries. Finally he points to the greater degree of

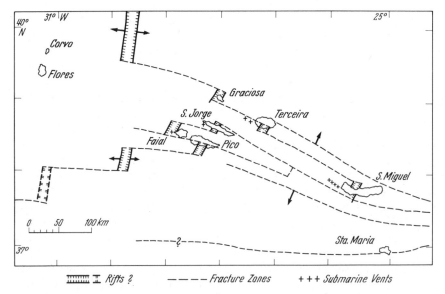

Fig. 45. Fracture patterns, Azores Archipelago (cf. with Fig. 24). (Modified after MACHADO, QUINTINHO & MONTEIRO, 1972).

weathering and alteration of the Sta. Maria younger volcanics as compared with those
of other islands, taken to indicate an older age for this island.

We would note that the major calderas of the archipelago, e. g. Sete Cidades and
Agua de Pau, S. Miguel, Guilherme-Moniz and Cinco Picos, Terceira, Pico da Se, Flores,
Caldeira, Faial, etc. are bordered by abrupt fault scarps, subsidence being achieved by
single-block stoping as at Glen Coe, Scotland (MACHADO 1955a).

As regards folding, the only contribution on this topic is that of KREJCI-GRAF (1956a)
who discusses, along with excellent photographs, examples of slump-folds
(Rutschfaltung) in S. Miguel and Faial.

Various marine geophysical studies in the overall vicinity of the Azores have
delineated the outlines of numerous ›fracture zones‹ (Vd. Figs. 24, 45). AGOSTINHO
(1937a) had commented upon three major tectonic trends passing through the
archipelago: a northern one linking S. Miguel, Terceira, Graciosa and Corvo; a middle
one through S. Jorge and a southern one through Faial-Pico. Deeps (between
2,000–3,000 m) within the island distributions align themselves closely with these zones
(Fig. 44). MACHADO et al. (1972) added a fourth trend of general E-W direction through
Sta. Maria. These four trends (subscribing to the vincula of the writer –
MITCHELLTHOMÉ, 1961) appear to converge eastwards beyond S. Miguel-Sta. Maria. In
this connexion it is of interest to note the mapping of a large submarine feature to the
E of Sta. Maria by LAUGHTON et al. (1972). This feature, along the Azores-Gibralter
Ridge, can be clearly traced for some 400 km, has a S-facing escarpment with relative
uplift of ca. 1,000 m on the N side, forming a pronounced V-shaped valley varying in
width from 2–6 km, and was named the Gloria Fault, of transcurrent type. The
AzoresGibralter Ridge, initially outlined rather by seismic epicentres than bathymetric
topography (the Fault was determined by long-range side-scan sonar methods) extends
for a distance of some 1,100 km, and the valley-floor part of the Fault has every
indication of relative youth. AGOSTINHO interpreted his fracture trends marked the
boundary between a more resistant, stable northern Atlantic sector and a less stable
southern sector, with Sete Cidades, S. Miguel, the principal volcanic centre of the
archipelago according to him, lying where these trends focused.

As per plate-tectonics concepts of later times, the Azores-Gibralter Ridge which, as
we have seen, seems to extend this fracture zone well to the E of the Azores, is taken
as the boundary between a Eurasian plate and an African plate, with anti-clockwise
rotation, of the latter with respect to the former.

The Azores abut against the Mid-Atlantic Ridge. As per modern views of global
tectonics (e. g. MORGAN, 1968; DEWEY & BIRD, 1970) the Azores represent the locus of
an important triple junction, where the Eurasian, African and American plates meet,
with the two former undergoing differential rotational movements relative to the
American plate. The rate of spread of the Mid-Atlantic Ridge S of the Azores is less
than that to the N, suggesting a dextral transcurrent motion of 0.23 cm yr[1], as per
KRAUSE & WATKINS (1970).

MACHADO et al. (1972) in their small geological maps of the islands show meridionally
directed ›rifts?‹ through all islands except Sta. Maria, Corvo and Flores. Such were
postulated on the basis of geomagnetic studies of QUINTINO (1962), the magnetic
anomalies showing positive and negative meridional stripes. Such ›rifts‹ were also

postulated for the marine area between Flores-Corvo and the other islands to the E. These authors believed that the Mid-Atlantic Ridge is displaced by transcurrent faulting such that it strikes through all islands from Faial to S. Miguel, i. e. those which have experienced more recent volcanic activity. In earlier times, when Sta. Maria, Corvo and Flores experienced eruptivity, the ›rifting‹ pattern was somewhat different to that of now. There is no doubt that the Azores occupy a critical position in the elucidation of Atlantic and global tectonics.

## Economic Geology

The development of natural mineral resources is all but non-existant. No metallics have been exploited, and only clays (for tiles), building stones, sands and formerly limestones for lime-kilns are or were worked.

Clays associated with pyroclastics are developed in some islands, e. g. Graciosa, S. Miguel for the manufacture of tiles. These are of indifferent quality, only for insular use.

Construction material includes chiefly scoria, tuffs, trachytes, andesites, basalts, for road surfacing, building of walls, bridges, etc. As we have seen the only significant limestones occur in Sta. Maria. At one time there were many lime-kilns in the archipelago, many getting the limestone from this island. Today, a great many kilns are abandoned, those larger ones remaining using limestone arriving as ship ballast from Portugal.

Sands are used throughout in cement manufacture. Pozzualanes and pumice occur in various islands, but no significant exploitation so far.

Natural gases are found, e. g. Montanha do Pico, Pico, Furnas do Enxofre, Terceira, calderas at Furnas and Reibeira Grande, S. Miguel, etc. In Pico a lighted cigarette held near these emanating gases will cause dense fumes to form.

In such volcanic islands, it is natural that fumaroles, mineral waters, hot springs should be present. Such are mentioned by almost all writers on the various islands, four of the best being LEPIERRE (1917), MORAIS (1953), QUINTINO (1966) and ZBYSZEWSKI (1970). The chemical features of waters (and accompanying muds) are shown in Tables 21, 22. These mineralized waters, especially those of S. Miguel, have been shown to possess distinct therapeutic qualities. Several commissions have been appointed to enquire into possibilities of commercially developing the mineral waters as well as.exploiting the geothermal energy of thermal springs, after the fashion of New Zealand, Japan, Italy, etc. (ZBYSZEWSKI, 1970b) but to date no further progress along these lines have been made.

In essence then, with the possible exception of the mineral and thermal springs, economic exploitation is only of very minor concern.

Table 21    Analyses of mineral waters in S. Miguel and Pico (ŽBYSZEWSKI, 1970; LEPIER-
RE 1931, unpubl.)

1. Waters of S. Miguel Caldeiras

|  | Caldeira das Furnas | Cald. Lagoa Furnas | Cald. Rib. Grande |
|---|---|---|---|
| Silica | Abundant | Notable quantity | Very little |
| Sulphates |  | Abundant |  |
| Chlorates |  | Abundant |  |
| Mg salts |  | Scarce |  |
| Ca salts |  | Min. vestiges |  |
| Fe salts |  | Absent |  |
| Boric acid | Slight | Notable quantity | Abundant |
| Al salts |  | Vestiges |  |
| Arsenic |  | Vestiges |  |
| Ammonia |  | Vestiges |  |

2. Muds of S. Miguel Caldeiras

| | | | |
|---|---|---|---|
| $H_2O$ | 20.30–22.07 | 19.12–45.74 | 10.42 |
| $SiO_2$ | 40.06–51.70 | 30.64–45.74 | 60.41 |
| $TiO_2$ | 0.02–29.07 | 0.02 | ––– |
| $Al_2O_3$ | 22.01–29.07 | 17.04–26.31 | 21.02 |
| $Fe_2O_3$ | 1.74– 2.27 | 1.12– 2.10 | 0.02 |
| MgO | 0.05– 0.07 | 0.02– 0.10 | ––– |
| CaO | 0.34– 0.41 | 0.47– 0.61 | 0.32 |
| $Na_2O$ | 2.21– 3.02 | 1.67– 2.11 | 0.81 |
| $K_2O$ | 0.50– 1.42 | 0.87– 1.74 | 0.32 |
| $SO_4$ | 0.39– 0.40 | 0.51– 0.62 | 0.12 |
| S | 1.12– 1.27 | 5.81–27.60 | 6.96 |

N.B. All samples show vestiges of $H_2Bo$.

3. Quantitative determinations (per litre) of mineral waters W of Silveira, Pico

| | gr. |
|---|---|
| Dry residue at 180° | 1.040 |
| Chlorides (in chlorine) | 0.390 |
| Chlorides (in sodium chloride) | 0.643 |
| Nitrates (in potassium nitrate) | 0.001 |
| Nitrates (in $N_2O_3$) | Nil |
| Ammonium salts (in $NH_3$) | Nil |
| Organic matter (in consumed oxygen) | 0.0001 |
| Organic matter (in crystoxalic oxide) | 0.0008 |
| Alkalinity (in calcium carbonate) | 0.300 |
| Alkalinity (in sodium carbonate) | 0.318 |
| Sulphuric acid ($SO_4$) | 0.053 |
| Carbonic acid ($CO_3$) of carbonates | 0.180 |
| Calcium | 0.024 |
| Magnesium | 0.002 |
| Silica | 0.048 |
| Oxides of Fe and Al | 0.253 |
| Potassium | 0.006 |

Table 22    Chemical features of some thermal waters in S. Miguel (ZBYSZEWSKI, 1970)
(Samplings done between 5.8.53 and 12.8.53)

| | Quenturas | Agua Prata | Agua Santa | Caldeira do Esguicho (Muddy water) | Caldeira do Esguicho (Clear water) | Caldeira do Esguicho |
|---|---|---|---|---|---|---|
| Temp. of local water (°C) | 60 | 33 | 37 | 84 | 89 | 97 |
| Temp. surrounding water | 27 | 28.5 | 28 | 28 | 28 | 28 |
| Atm. Pressure (mm/Hg) | 753 | 754 | 753.5 | 754 | 754 | 753.5 |
| Volumetric comp. referred to 0°C, 760 mm/Hg: | | | | | | |
| % Carbonate anhydride | 99.5 | 97.5 | 98.0 | 99.2 | 99.1 | 99.1 |
| % Sulphuric acid | 0.00 | 0.07 | -- | 0.28 | 0.37 | 0.38 |
| % Oxygen | -- | 0.4 | 0.2 | -- | -- | -- |
| % Hydrogen | -- | -- | -- | -- | -- | -- |
| % Nitrogen | -- | -- | -- | -- | -- | -- |
| % Residual gas | 0.50 | 2.03 | 1.8 | 0.52 | 0.53 | 0.52 |

| | Caldeira dos Vimes | Caldeira do Asmodeu | Caldeira Grande | Cald. da Lagoa Furnas (S side) | Cald. da Lagoa Furnas (E side) | Caldeira Velha | Caldeira Grande da Rib. Grande |
|---|---|---|---|---|---|---|---|
| Temp. of local water (°C) | 89 | 98.5 | 97 | 92 | 62 | 92 | 55 |
| Temp. surrounding water | 27.5 | 27 | 26 | 28 | 28 | 24 | 24 |
| Atm. Pressure (mm/Hg) | 753.5 | 753 | 754 | 753.5 | 753.5 | 742 | 750 |
| Volumetric comp. referred to 0°C, 760 mm/Hg: | | | | | | | |
| % Carbonate anhydride | 99.3 | 99.1 | 99.1 | 97.6 | 96.9 | 98.3 | 98.4 |
| % Sulphuric acid | 0.25 | 0.42 | 0.44 | 0.29 | 0.06 | 0.06 | 0.04 |
| % Oxygen | -- | -- | 0.09 | 0.4 | 0.41 | 0.41 | 0.26 |
| % Hydrogen | -- | -- | 0.03 | -- | 0.15 | 0.09 | 0.23 |
| % Nitrogen | -- | -- | 0.34 | -- | 2.48 | 1.14 | 1.07 |
| % Residual gas | 0.45 | 0.48 | -- | 1.71 | -- | -- | -- |

## Geological Evolution

Only in Sta. Maria are there stratigraphically dated sedimentaries. For the NE Complex of S. Miguel, ABDEL-MONEM et al. (1968) determined a minimum isotopic age of 1-2 my for the basalts. Other than these accounts, the literature is singularly lacking in treating of the geological evolution. Under these circumstances, we shall pay attention to Sta. Maria in enabling us to envisage archipelagic events. We have noted earlier that AGOSTINHO recognized in Sta. Maria three distinct units, older basaltics, Miocene limestones, younger basaltics, which obviously allows us to distinguish pre- from postMiocene vulcanism. This can be refined somewhat more and adjusted by recognizing pre-Vindobonian vulcanicity, Vindobonian vulcanicity and Post-Vindobonian vulcanicity. BERTHOIS has elaborated upon the sequence in this island thus:

(a) Older basaltics and basaltic tuffs, at least partially submarine.
(b) Aphanitic basaltic dykes intruded into the above.
(c) Development of abrasion platform at depth of 100 m around the island, on which were formed Miocene limestones admixed with pebbles, etc. of old basalts-tuffs and dyke basalts. Vulcanism, at least part submarine, taking place concurrently – the Vindobonian period of eruptivity.
(d) Uplift of the island with the carving out of valleys on the upraised platform. The upraised limestones acquired dips, were dislocated. As the limestones were formed in various marine depths of less than 100 m, their occurrence at various altitudes in the island can be correlated perhaps with said depths in a crude fashion, i. e. higher occurrences of limestones formed in shallower depths.
(e) Renewed basaltic vulcanism, laid on top of the Miocene beds, and forming the NWSE dorsal of the island. These effusions likely occurred shortly after the formation of the sedimentaries. Further no significant modifications of these later volcanics can be noted, implying formation over a short period of time.
(f) Immersion of the W and NW parts of the island, formation of the + 90 to + 100 m marine terrace in Western Sta. Maria.
(g) Emergence of short duration as valleys only slightly entrenched.
(h) Renewed vertical movement with development of + 3 to + 5 m marine terrace, accompanied by infilling of valleys to heights of + 10 m.
(j) Lowering of sea level – emerged period of the present.

AGOSTINHO was of the view that the other islands show essentially a similar history, only in Sta. Maria uplift has been greater – Miocene limestones as high as 400 m – whereas these rocks are to be expected at depth in other islands, where uplift has been less. It was his view that the volcanics outcropping on other islands were postVindobonian (perhaps Vindobonian also) but not pre-Vindobonian, that such older rocks occurred only at greater depths here and one gets the impression that he visualized a gradual increment of degree of uplift from W to E across the archipelago.

The established sequences of vulcanism in other islands show, as in Sta. Maria, an initial basaltic phase, and from petrographic description of such, it is not easy to say whether they represent the older or younger basaltic phases of Sta. Maria, a case in point where isotopic analyses would surely be decisive. Apart from AGOSTINHO, the tendency of others is to see vulcanism in all (or most) islands dating back to preMiocene or Early Miocene times, frequently represented by submarine outpourings.

Volcanic sequences, whether of older or younger type, show variations within the archipelago. In S. Miguel, e. g. this is: basalts, trachytes, andesites, trachytes-andesites, trachytes-andesites-basalts; in Faial: basalts, andesites, basalts; in Graciosa: trachytes, andesites, andesites-basalts, basalts; in Flores trachytes-andesites-basalts, basalts, trachytes-andesites, andesites, etc.

For the archipelago then we can postulate an origin dating back to pre-Miocene or Early Miocene, initial vulcanism being largely submarine and when the islands had been built up above sea level, then subaerial, of charcteristic basaltic type. Positive and negative movements allowed of the deposition of limestones and the raising of them to present elevations. Post-Miocene vulcanism has continued into historic times with a marked reduction in frequency and activity since the Tyrrhenian. Since the Grimaldian the archipelago has also experienced greater stability even although seismicity is active today, vulcanism no less. As of now we cannot postulate with any degree of precision when positive-negative pronounced movements were taking place, nor are we sure what the respective roles of eustatism, isostasy or volcano-tectonic events may have been. All things are relative, and it is true to say that the Azores today are more ›lively‹ than any other archipelago mentioned here, possibly the youngest also.

CHAPTER 5

# Geology of the Madeira Archipelago

## General

Geological interest dates back to the early days of last century with the appearance of short reports by BENNET (1811) and DRUMONDO (1818). By about the middle of the century appeared works by ALBUQUERQUE (1837) SMITH (1840), MACAULAY (1840) and LYELL (1854) on general geology, fossil flora by HEER (1857) and BUNBURY (1858), fossil fauna by LOWE (1851, 1854) and ALBERS (1854). A landmark in the literature of the archipelago is the publication by HARTUNG (1864), and this, plus the later publications of JOKSIMOWITSCH (1911), FINCKH (1913) and GAGEL (1913, 1915) have formed the basis of all later studies.

For a relatively longer period thereafter few publications appeared until MORAIS contributed several papers (1939, 1943, 1945, 1948) followed over a decade later by several palaeontological papers by SILVA (1956, 1957, 1959).

In more recent times appeared the publications of MONTAGGIONI (1968, 1969) dealing with marine-littoral geology, LIETZ & SCHWARZBACH (1970, 1971) dealing with Tertiary-Quaternary sediments, FERREIRA (1969) BARROS & OLIVEIRA (1969), HUGHES & BROWN (1972), SCHMINCKE & WEIBEL (1972) dealing with igneous petrology.

For long there have been no satisfactory maps of the archipelago, but in 1969 a Missao dos Serviços Geologicos was established to map the islands (ZBYSZEWSKI, 1971, 1972) and now excellent geological maps are available.

Like the Mesozoics of Maio (Cape Verde), the prevalence of calcareous sands in Madeira and Porto Santo have drawn special attention, e. g. D'ORCHYMONT (1936), PUREZA (1961), MOURA (1961) plus other papers, e. g. MORAIS (1943, 1945).

In this archipelago, of extraordinary beauty, delightful climate, sparkling greenness, freshness, cleanliness, there is still ample work, problems enough to engage for long the geologist. No less is there need for geophysical and geochronological studies to elucidate and unravel the geological past.

## Geomorphology

Though at first glance it might seem that one volcanic mass dominates the main island, Madeira actually comprises two distinct structural-geomorphologic units – the Pico Ruivo and Paul da Serra massifs – and four volcanic series or complexes. The vulcanism giving rise to these massifs dates from the Lower (perhaps earlier) Miocene and the Middle Miocene, and such later vulcanicity as the island has experienced plays a minor role although giving rise to better preserved volcanic forms. It follows then that as distinct from some archipelagoes and some islands, Madeira proper has not gone through repeated volcanic rejuvenations of the landscape. On the other hand, pronounced positive vertical movements, lowering of base level, have occurred, so that in this sense rejuvenations have taken place, with the result that geomorphic youth characterizes the island. Exogenic processes – stream and marine erosion, wind transportation and deposition, gravitational mass movements – have all been most active, so that the relief is strong, slopes very abrupt, average elevation is high, valleys and depressions deeply incised into the land.

The Ruivo-Areeiro basal volcanic complex is the oldest, occupying the centraleastern part of Madeira, forming a central topographic spine extending E-W for some 12 km, containing the two supreme summits of the island, Pico Ruivo, 1,862 m and Pico das Torres, 1,851 m, with many peaks over 1,700 m. The outstanding feature of this massif is the two calderas of Curral das Freiras and Serra de Agua, both open towards the S. The former is a centre of attraction to tourist and scientist alike, variously

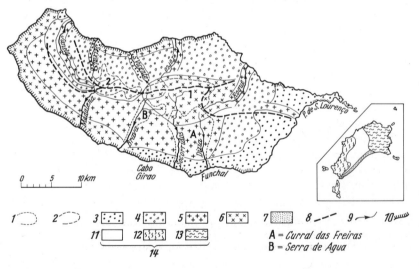

Fig. 46. Morpho-volcanic maps of Madeira and Porto Santo. 1: Calderas–Curral (A), Serra de Agua (B). 2: Structural-morphologic units of Pico Ruivo (1) and Paul da Serra (2). 3: Modern volcanic complex. 4: Paul da Serra post-Vindobonian volcanic complex. 5: Vindobonian volcanic complex. 6: Pico Ruivo pre-Vindobonian volcanic complex. 7: Sandy beaches. 8: Topographic axis. 9: Streams. 10: Cliffs 100– > 500 m. 11: Low level terrain. 12: Hill country. 13: High hill country. 14: Porto Santo.

described as »a scene conjured up by Walt Disney« and »an earthly representation of Dante's Inferno«. 1,000 m walls rise precipitously up to the rim enclosing the amphitheatre on the N, dominated by Areeiro, 1,818 m high, and within this great depression, sharp crests, pyramidal peaks, gorges, bare precipitous slopes, the chaotic appearance of natural features all present a truly breath-taking panorama. The smaller caldera of Serra de Agua on the other hand is, by comparison, a more smiling landscape, with terraced agriculture, abundant trees, many neat white red-tiled villas clambering up the slopes. From both of these calderas streams exit, the Ribeira Brava from Serra da Agua, the Rib. das Socorridos from Curral. Both are deep narrow valleys flowing direct down to the sea, presumably controlled by volcanic fissuring. These calderas owe more of their present appearance to erosion, though no doubt originally magma withdrawals allowed of initial collapse, but such has been emphasized, enlarged by stream work, landslides, etc.

Paul da Serra is a volcanic horst or a structural platform, forming a plateau (planalto), average elevation ca. 1,400 m, with very abrupt slopes leading down to the N coast, valleys to E and W, somewhat gentler southern slopes. Rising above the even surface are smaller cones, volcanic peaks, craters, etc. The Janela stream which drains the western slopes of Paul da Serra NW towards the coast is an unusual feature. Transversely from crest to crest the valley is ca. 4.5 km broad, paradoxically broad for a valley only some 17 km in length. This ›misfit‹ stream owes its origin to a path taken by lava flows of Paul da Serra eruptive centre, and upon this surface the stream established itself, incising itself deeply into easily eroded volcanics, the stream itself being quite insignificant in size compared with the broad valley. Several other occurrences of ›misfit‹ streams which have utilized paths taken by lava flows occur in the island.

The eastern peninsula, narrowing into the oddly-shaped Ponta de S. Lourenço constitutes the volcanically youngest part of the island. Elevations decline to the E and to the S. The Ponta itself is highly asymmetrical longitudinally, mostly with steeper slopes northward. As will be mentioned below, this peninsula, curving to the SE, is extended further in the Ilhas Desertas, and geologically the peninsula and the Ilhas are of the same age and constitution. Here the landscape is subdued, slopes more gentle, relief much less marked, more akin to what we find in Porto Santo.

The drainage pattern is distinctly radial, all streams taking direct routs down to the coasts. Slopes to N and S are steep (especially the former), corrosion is intense, headward eating back of the streams most active. It results that in several instances valleys almost transect the island in a N-S direction, e.g. the valleys of the Madalena-Seixal, Brava-S. Vicente, Socorridos-Porco, Roque-Dizia. Barring rejuvenation, in the near geological future one would expect some significant river ›capturing‹ to take place, N-flowing streams having the greater slopes being the potential ›capturers‹. The dense network of streams, all with remarkably straight courses, are very probably in by far the greater majority of cases pure erosional features, fractures, volcanic fissuring only very rarely playing a role.

Extending out to maximum depths of some 200 m but nearer to 70 m in general are marine abrasion platforms forming distinct insular platforms (Fig. 47). These are broadest off western Madeira and northern Porto Santo but are not developed around

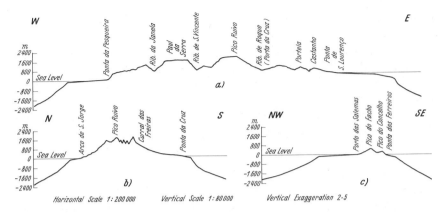

Fig. 47. Topographic-bathymetric profiles of Madeira (A, B) and Porto Santo (C) illustrating submarine platform character of the islands.

Ilhas Desertas, though the latter are but prolongations of Madeira. The fashioning of cliffs and abrasion platforms is not conditioned only by lithology, jointing, direction and degree of dip, etc. but also by mass gravitational movements and wave attack. Heterogeneity of rock constitution greatly aids the process of cliff-abrasion platform development – here the porous volcanics and the more friable pyroclastics. The rolling back and forth by waves-currents of loosened debris from terra firma has worn out the platforms of weak relief with slopes of 2-5°. Beyond with average slopes of 40° lies submarine talus slopes.

Rock constitution, volcanic sequences and bathymetric trends all indicate that the Ilhas Desertas are but prolongations of the main island to the SE. These islands, remarkably narrow for their lengths, rise steeply from the coasts but all, to varying degrees, show regular upper level or gently sloping surfaces, and to some, e. g. MONTAGGIONI (1968) these are thought to represent structural rather than terrestrial or marine surfaces. These islands rise more immediately from ocean depths than do Madeira and Porto Santo, the orientation of the islands as that of the many dykes, fissures, smaller faults follow the same trend, giving the impression of a building up of fissure eruptions along a narrow crest.

Porto Santo is separated from Madeira by depths in excess of 2,500 m in the intervening distance of some 45 km. Stronger relief is restricted to the NE where maximum elevations reach 517 m in Pico do Facho. The topography is much more subdued in this island, relatively speaking there are wide extents of low, smooth terrain. In general there is a topographic tilt of the island to the SE, longer, gentler slopes in this direction. Of significant contrast is the deeply indented, high-cliffed NW coast and the even, low sandy SE coast – the largest area of sandy beach development within the archipelago. Along this coast are many sand dunes and extending almost to the NW coast are extents of sand sheets. In the western half of the island there occurs a relatively large low region of very gentle slopes covered by massive white calcareous material (›salao‹) of subhorizontal disposition above which rise several isolated volcanic peaks – scoria cones. This region, on which the airport has been built, of 50 m average elevation, may represent an uplifted marine abrasion platform. In this island we find marine limestones at hights of 350 m compared to 400 m in Madeira, older complexes of Madeira are not exposed here, suggesting that Porto Santo experienced lesser positive movement. Perhaps this or then less frequent uplifts accounts for the more advanced geomorphologic stage characteristic of the island more akin with maturity. Depth of marine waters between here and Madeira and geomorphologic differences have led some to postulate that Port Santo never had any connexion with the main island, and certainly in many geological features the two differ.

## Igneous Rocks

Of the earlier studies made of igneous rocks, those of COCHIUS (1864), HARTUNG (1864), STÜBEL (1865), FINCKH (1913) and GAGEL (1913, 1915) are most important, especially those of the last two mentioned authors, and it can truly be said that FINCKH and GAGEL laid the groundwork of our geological knowledge of the archipelago.

GAGEL's lengthy papers are in two parts. Part I goes into great detail regarding the igneous rocks especially of Madeira proper, but mention is also made of Porto Santo. He recognized plutonics, hypabyssals and volcanics. In the first group he placed essexites, theralitic-essexites, nephelenitic-syenites, also basic and ultrabasic differentiation products (»Randfacies«) present in the region of Porto da Cruz and within the large caldera of Curral. He considered that the largest plutonic outcrop occurred in the Ribeira de Massapez forming a 60 m high, 40–50 m broad stock or laccolith, with a great well-smoothed wall, the essexites being well exposed in the streambed under the wall. Here also is found a trachydolerite layer which has undergone contact metamorphism, the essexites occurring like ›klippen‹. Similar essexite ›klippen‹ are to be seen in the bed of the Rib. das Voltas. Chemical analyses of these plutonics are shown in Table 23, Nos. 1–6. GAGEL compared these analyses with essexites from the Caldera of La Palma, S. Vicente, Cape Verde Islands, Germany, Czechoslovakia and Tahiti. The extreme ultrabasic differentiation products of these essexites magmas are to be seen, e. g. within the tuffs at Porto Moniz where there occur large and small volcanic bombs of holocrystalline, miarolitic olivine-rock, mostly with only olivine cores. No. 30 shows an analysis of an olivine-rock bomb. These olivine-rocks interested GAGEL in that they were the only known rocks in Madeira showing rhombic pyroxenes – diallagic diopside – at that time no rhombic pyroxenes being known in the Middle Atlantic Islands, other than examples reported by DOELTER (1882a) from the Cape Verde Islands – aluminous augite in a calc-rich, alkali-poor rock, and enstatite crystals in basalts and limburgites reported by FINCKH (1911) from Selvagem Grande. To some dark green, macrocrystalline rocks, formed chiefly of black augite and greenish olivine, which were more basic than diabases, GAGEL coined the name madeirite, placing such with the peridotites.

Hypabyssals (Ganggesteine), Nos. 7 and 8, are represented by trachoidal trachydolerites and basaltic rocks with prominent olivine.

Typical melanocratic rocks, e. g. the camptonites of the Caldera in La Palma, are not abundant in Madeira. GAGEL compared No. 7 with alkali-trachytes typical of the

Geology of the Madeira Archipelago

Table 23 Chemical analyses, norms and trace elements, Madeira rocks (COCHIUS, 1864; FINCKH, 1913; GAGEL, 1913, 1915; FERREIRA, M.R. 1969; SCHMINCKE & WEIBEL 1972; HUGHES & BROWN, 1972)

|  | 1 | 2 | 3 | 4 | 5 | 6 | 7 | 8 | 9 |
|---|---|---|---|---|---|---|---|---|---|
| $SiO_2$ | 52.47 | 49.87 | 49.15 | 45.04 | 45.69 | 40.07 | 65.43 | 57.67 | 55.54 |
| $Al_2O_3$ | 15.84 | 14.98 | 17.86 | 16.41 | 17.02 | 8.95 | 17.20 | 19.17 | 18.20 |
| $Fe_2O_3$ | 3.30 | 6.17 | 1.07 | 6.02 | 4.59 | 4.82 | 1.57 | 4.55 | 5.92 |
| $FeO$ | 8.42 | 4.40 | 10.77 | 7.30 | 8.52 | 7.81 | 1.06 | 0.99 | 1.14 |
| $MnO$ | –– | –– | 0.75 | –– | –– | –– | Tr | –– | –– |
| $MgO$ | 1.52 | 1.77 | 3.24 | 3.93 | 5.62 | 13.86 | 0.36 | 1.22 | 1.32 |
| $CaO$ | 5.05 | 6.34 | 6.57 | 11.40 | 11.31 | 13.83 | 2.14 | 3.94 | 5.64 |
| $Na_2O$ | 7.03 | 5.08 | 5.49 | 3.09 | 3.21 | 1.34 | 6.14 | 6.84 | 6.44 |
| $K_2O$ | 2.52 | 2.04 | 2.29 | 0.93 | 1.07 | 0.56 | 3.78 | 3.35 | 2.30 |
| $TiO_2$ | 1.57 | 2.60 | 0.83 | 3.67 | 1.30 | 2.35 | 0.19 | 0.40 | 0.71 |
| $P_2O_5$ | 0.14 | 0.74 | 0.99 | 0.47 | 0.57 | 0.35 | 0.16 | 0.34 | 0.56 |
| $CO_2$ | –– | 3.22 | Tr | 0.36 | –– | 3.78 | –– | –– | –– |
| $S$ | 0.09 | 0.76 | –– | 0.13 | 0.08 | 0.04 | 0.04 | 0.06 | 0.06 |
| $H_2O$ | 1.94 | 1.66 | 1.21 | 1.41 | 0.76 | 2.45 | 1.82 | 1.77 | 2.35 |
| Total | 99.89 | 99.88ab | 100.22c | 100.18 | 99.78d | 100.21 | 99.89 | 100.30 | 100.18 |
| S.G. | 2.766 | 2.772 | 2.790 | 3.003 |  | 3.096 | 2.504 | 2.607 | 2.628 |

|  | 10 | 11 | 12 | 13 | 14 | 15 | 16 | 17 | 18 |
|---|---|---|---|---|---|---|---|---|---|
| $SiO_2$ | 52.75 | 52.40 | 51.78 | 47.70 | 46.44 | 46.08 | 44.86 | 44.40 | 43.85 |
| $Al_2O_3$ | 18.29 | 19.27 | 18.68 | 17.32 | 16.30 | 17.39 | 16.18 | 15.40 | 12.94 |
| $Fe_2O_3$ | 4.68 | 4.56 | 6.42 | 5.43 | 4.82 | 10.95 | 7.22 | 5.20 | 2.70 |
| $FeO$ | 4.33 | 3.57 | 2.77 | 4.71 | 7.07 | 2.56 | 7.10 | 7.81 | 10.51 |
| $MnO$ | –– | Tr | –– | –– | –– | –– | –– | –– | –– |
| $MgO$ | 2.15 | 2.03 | 1.86 | 3.62 | 4.92 | 2.66 | 5.34 | 7.23 | 11.90 |
| $CaO$ | 7.39 | 6.68 | 6.04 | 7.98 | 10.03 | 8.87 | 9.95 | 9.92 | 9.49 |
| $Na_2O$ | 5.66 | 5.50 | 5.53 | 4.21 | 3.82 | 3.72 | 3.78 | 2.83 | 2.42 |
| $K_2O$ | 2.29 | 2.03 | 2.34 | 2.45 | 1.44 | 1.38 | 1.39 | 1.19 | 1.06 |
| $TiO_2$ | 0.94 | 1.60 | 1.05 | 2.54 | 2.90 | 2.73 | 2.52 | 2.77 | 2.53 |
| $P_2O_5$ | 0.71 | 0.52 | 0.71 | 0.99 | 0.82 | 1.11 | 0.92 | 0.77 | 0.61 |
| $CO_2$ | –– | –– | –– | –– | –– | –– | –– | –– | –– |
| $S$ | 0.05 | 0.10 | 0.04 | 0.04 | 0.08 | 0.02 | 0.06 | 0.04 | 0.05 |
| $H_2O$ | 0.75 | 1.82 | 2.78 | 3.08 | 1.40 | 2.37 | 0.55 | 2.15 | 1.69 |
| Total | 99.98 | 100.12 | 100.00 | 100.07 | 100.04 | 99.84 | 100.17 | 99.71 | 99.75 |
| S.G. | 2.770 | 2.798 | 2.698 | 2.673 | 2.906 | 2.809 | 2.939 | 2.931 | 3.006 |

(a) Incl. 0.25 $SO_3$      (b) Incl. Tr. Cl.      (c) Incl. Tr. Cl.      (d) Incl. 0.04 Cl.

*Rocks and localities*

1. Analcime-syenite. (F), Soca, near Porto da Cruz.
2. Hornblende-akerite. (F), Rib. das Voltas.
3. Essexite. (F), Rib. de Massapez.
4. Essexite-diabase. (F), Rib. das Voltas.
5. Essexite-diabase. (F), Rib. de Massapez.
6. Pyroxenitic Essexite-diabase. (F), Rib. de Massapez.

7. Trachyte (F), Alkali-trachyte (G) Gran Curral.
8. Trachyandesite (F), Gauteite (G) Gran Curral.
9. Trachydolerite (F), Sodalite-tephrite (G) Pico Serrado.
10. Trachydolerite (F), Sodalite-tephrite (G) Rib. de Massapez.

Table 23  (continued)

| | 19 | 20 | 21 | 22 | 23 | 24 | 25 | 26 | 27 |
|---|---|---|---|---|---|---|---|---|---|
| $SiO_2$ | 42.71 | 42.40 | 42.39 | 41.96 | 43.30 | 43.79 | 44.50 | 42.19 | 42.27 |
| $Al_2O_3$ | 14.62 | 14.19 | 15.77 | 15.85 | 14.07 | 13.73 | 13.85 | 13.80 | 13.29 |
| $Fe_2O_3$ | 3.12 | 6.14 | 5.89 | 7.64 | 5.53 | 3.37 | 3.47 | 5.52 | 3.79 |
| $FeO$ | 9.34 | 7.69 | 8.66 | 7.24 | 7.17 | 10.20 | 9.02 | 8.87 | 10.24 |
| $MnO$ | -- | -- | -- | -- | -- | -- | -- | -- | -- |
| $MgO$ | 8.91 | 9.02 | 7.44 | 8.45 | 9.62 | 9.46 | 11.00 | 8.55 | 10.79 |
| $CaO$ | 10.68 | 11.08 | 9.40 | 9.54 | 10.87 | 10.54 | 10.06 | 11.39 | 11.17 |
| $Na_2O$ | 3.11 | 2.50 | 2.05 | 2.05 | 2.41 | 2.71 | 2.70 | 2.50 | 2.94 |
| $K_2O$ | 1.55 | 1.43 | 1.24 | 1.17 | 1.12 | 1.25 | 0.92 | 1.21 | 1.17 |
| $TiO_2$ | 3.38 | 3.68 | 2.61 | 2.16 | 2.83 | 2.82 | 2.61 | 3.15 | 3.21 |
| $P_2O_5$ | 0.74 | 0.67 | 0.78 | 0.88 | 0.65 | 0.67 | 0.84 | 0.72 | 0.57 |
| $CO_2$ | -- | -- | -- | -- | -- | -- | -- | -- | -- |
| S. | 0.09 | 0.06 | Tr | 0.02 | 0.10 | 0.04 | 0.07 | 0.12 | 0.09 |
| $H_2O$ | 1.55 | 1.37 | 3.55 | 3.07 | 2.52 | 1.66 | 0.71 | 1.91 | 0.56 |
| Total | 99.90 | 100.23 | 99.78 | 100.03 | 100.19 | 100.24 | 99.75 | 99.85 | 100.16 |
| S.G. | 3.027 | 3.033 | 2.967 | 2.902 | 2.997 | 3.022 | 3.034 | 3.010 | 3.098 |

| | 28 | 29 | 30 | 31 | 32 | 33 | 34 | 35 | 36 |
|---|---|---|---|---|---|---|---|---|---|
| $SiO_2$ | 41.43 | 41.72 | 42.42 | 47.70 | 40.22 | 39.82 | 68.79 | 66.99 | 43.03 |
| $Al_2O_3$ | 13.18 | 11.47 | 1.32 | 17.32 | 13.68 | 12.55 | 16.83 | 16.20 | 12.80 |
| $Fe_2O_3$ | 6.95 | 4.04 | 4.27 | 5.43 | 6.39 | 5.52 | 1.54 | 3.95 | 5.73 |
| $FeO$ | 7.31 | 10.58 | 6.96 | 4.71 | 6.59 | 8.19 | 0.61 | | 8.34 |
| $MnO$ | -- | -- | -- | -- | -- | -- | -- | -- | -- |
| $MgO$ | 11.91 | 12.55 | 40.80 | 3.62 | 7.24 | 12.14 | 0.24 | 1.91 | 10.76 |
| $CaO$ | 10.74 | 10.82 | 1.19 | 7.98 | 12.95 | 10.71 | 0.51 | 0.77 | 9.87 |
| $Na_2O$ | 1.60 | 2.28 | 0.72 | 4.21 | 2.25 | 1.45 | 6.65 | 7.40 | 2.27 |
| $K_2O$ | 0.93 | 1.22 | 0.65 | 2.45 | 0.97 | 0.92 | 3.71 | 2.78 | 1.22 |
| $TiO_2$ | 2.67 | 3.41 | 0.30 | 2.54 | 2.73 | 2.73 | -- | -- | 1.60 |
| $P_2O_5$ | 0.66 | 0.66 | 0.10 | 0.99 | 0.49 | 0.59 | 0.10 | -- | 0.65 |
| $CO_2$ | -- | -- | -- | -- | -- | -- | -- | -- | -- |
| S | 0.05 | 0.04 | 0.04 | 0.04 | 0.07 | 0.07 | 0.05 | -- | 0.07 |
| $H_2O$ | 2.15 | 1.11 | 0.70 | 3.08 | 4.03 | 4.90 | 0.99 | 2.60 | 3.84 |
| Total | 99.65 | 99.60 | 99.67c | 100.12 | 100.19 | 99.78 | 100.02 | 102.60 | 99.98 |
| S.G. | 3.043 | 3.079 | 3.255 | 2.673 | 2.842 | 2.944 | 2.558 | 2.890 | 2.899 |

(e) Incl. 0.40 $Cr_2O_3$

11.  Trachydolerite (F), Sodalite-tephrite (G) Porto da Cruz.
12.  Trachydolerite (F), Sodalite-tephrite (G), Islet off P. da Cruz.
13.  Trachydolerite (F), Amph.-aug.-monchiquite (G), Rib. Frio.
14.  Trachydolerite (F), Hauyne-tephrite (G), Ponta do Sol.
15.  Trachydolerite (F), Pico Serrado.
16.  Trachydolerite (F), Pico Serrado.
17.  Trachydolerite (F), Lombo Grande.
18.  Trachydolerite (F), Essexite porphyry (G), Hornblende-basalt (G), Rib. de Massapez.

19.  Feldspar-basalt (F), Alkali-basalt (G) Bocca dos Corregos.
20.  Feldspar-basalt (F), Alkali-basalt (G) Gran Curral.
21.  Feldspar-basalt (F), Alkali-basalt (G) Chaparina, NW of Funchal.
22.  Feldspar-basalt (F), Alkali-basalt (G) Pico Serrado.
23.  Feldspar-basalt (F), Alkali-basalt (G) Rib. Frio.
24.  Feldspar-basalt (F), Alkali-basalt (G) Rabaçal.
25.  Feldspar-basalt (F), Alkali-basalt (G) Ponta Delgado.

Table 23 (continued)

| | 37 | 38 | 39 | 40 | 41 | 42 | 43 | 44 | 45 | 46 |
|---|---|---|---|---|---|---|---|---|---|---|
| $SiO_2$ | 69.30 | 64.65 | 61.57 | 56.49 | 56.40 | 54.07 | 53.88 | 46.26 | 44.01 | 34.56 |
| $Al_2O_3$ | 18.19 | 19.24 | 16.96 | 22.08 | 21.47 | 13.65 | 19.83 | 20.40 | 21.81 | 12.10 |
| $Fe_2O_3$ | 4.00 | 5.18 | 9.65 | 5.11 | 12.46 | 17.17 | 9.42 | 12.83 | 14.60 | 6.68 |
| FeO | | | | | | | | | | 2.56 |
| $M_nO$ | -- | -- | -- | -- | -- | -- | -- | -- | -- | 0.18 |
| MgO | 0.52 | 0.90 | 0.80 | 3.00 | 1.82 | 0.26 | 3.55 | 6.09 | 5.12 | 4.49 |
| CaO | 2.01 | 4.22 | 4.05 | 5.49 | 2.39 | 4.99 | 5.13 | 9.89 | 9.93 | 18.76 |
| $Na_2O$ | 5.98 | 3.28 | 3.65 | 5.77 | 5.46 | 5.59 | 8.19 | 4.53 | 3.96 | 3.09 |
| $K_2O$ | Tr | 2.53 | 3.32 | 2.06 | Tr | 4.27 | Tr | Tr | 0.57 | 0.49 |
| $TiO_2$ | -- | -- | -- | -- | -- | -- | -- | -- | -- | 2.71 |
| $P_2O_5$ | -- | -- | -- | -- | -- | -- | -- | -- | -- | 2.12 |
| $CO_2$ | -- | -- | -- | -- | -- | -- | -- | -- | -- | 7.57 |
| S | -- | -- | -- | -- | -- | -- | -- | -- | -- | -- |
| $H_2O$ | 0.52 | 0.90 | 2.79 | 1.89 | 3.35 | 1.17 | 0.66 | 0.96 | 3.00 | + 1.89 |
| | | | | | | | | | | − 3.40 |
| Total | 100.52 | 100.90 | 102.79 | 101.89 | 103.35 | 101.17 | 100.66 | 100.96 | 103.00 | 99.89 |
| S.G. | 2.62 | 2.51 | 2.57 | 2.43 | 2.92 | 2.57 | 2.88 | 2.97 | 3.04 | ---- |

| | 47 | 48 | 49 | 50 | 51 | 52 | 53 | 54 | 55 |
|---|---|---|---|---|---|---|---|---|---|
| $SiO_2$ | 46.42 | 43.0 | 44.1 | 44.1 | 44.9 | 45.2 | 46.8 | 47.9 | 48.2 |
| $Al_2O_3$ | 18.31 | 14.6 | 12.4 | 14.6 | 14.2 | 15.4 | 18.0 | 13.5 | 18.0 |
| $Fe_2O_3$ | 6.29 | 3.0 | 3.2 | 2.6 | 2.5 | 4.9 | 5.1 | 2.8 | 5.7 |
| FeO | 4.52 | 10.0 | 8.3 | 9.85 | 10.15 | 9.0 | 6.2 | 9.8 | 4.6 |
| $M_nO$ | 0.18 | .20 | .20 | .22 | .20 | .22 | .23 | .10 | .22 |
| MgO | 2.91 | 8.8 | 14.6 | 9.9 | 10.2 | 6.6 | 4.3 | 7.4 | 3.4 |
| CaO | 10.54 | 10.5 | 11.7 | 11.0 | 10.3 | 9.2 | 9.8 | 10.1 | 9.2 |
| $Na_2O$ | 4.19 | 3.1 | 2.4 | 3.0 | 2.9 | 3.7 | 3.3 | 3.1 | 3.9 |
| $K_2O$ | 0.91 | 1.0 | .8 | .9 | .9 | 1.1 | 1.2 | .8 | 1.4 |
| $TiO_2$ | 3.14 | 4.4 | 2.0 | 2.3 | 2.4 | 3.2 | 2.4 | 3.4 | 2.3 |
| $P_2O_5$ | 1.08 | .47 | .43 | .68 | .49 | .74 | .70 | 43 | 1.0 |
| $CO_2$ | 0.40 | -- | -- | -- | -- | -- | -- | -- | -- |
| S | -- | -- | -- | -- | -- | -- | -- | -- | -- |
| $H_2O$ | + 0.74 | .8 | .2 | .7 | .6 | .8 | 1.6 | .6 | 1.8 |
| | − 0.53 | | | | | | | | |
| Total | 100.11 | 99.9 | 100.33 | 99.5 | 99.74 | 100.06 | 99.63 | 100.0 | 99.7 |
| S.G. | -- | | | | | | | | |

| | 48 | 49 | 50 | 51 | 52 | 53 | 54 | 55 |
|---|---|---|---|---|---|---|---|---|
| Q | | | | | | | | .56 |
| C | | | | | | | | |
| Or | 5.97 | 4.72 | 5.36 | 5.36 | 6.55 | 7.23 | 4.76 | 8.45 |
| Ab | 13.65 | 6.92 | 12.77 | 16.00 | 25.40 | 28.49 | 26.38 | 33.70 |
| An | 23.18 | 20.67 | 23.92 | 23.27 | 22.33 | 31.38 | 20.68 | 28.06 |
| Ne | 6.95 | 7.24 | 6.95 | 4.74 | 3.33 | | | |
| Di | 21.18 | 27.51 | 21.58 | 20.29 | 15.18 | 10.87 | 21.85 | 9.28 |
| Hy | | | | | | 5.05 | 5.05 | 4.68 |
| Ol | 15.15 | 23.52 | 19.62 | 20.94 | 12.22 | 3.15 | 9.71 | |
| Il | 8.44 | 3.79 | 4.41 | 4.60 | 6.12 | 4.65 | 6.49 | 4.46 |
| Mt | 4.39 | 4.63 | 3.80 | 3.66 | 7.16 | 7.54 | 4.08 | 8.44 |
| Ap | 1.12 | 1.02 | 1.62 | 1.17 | 1.77 | 1.69 | 1.02 | 2.42 |
| D.I. | 26.56 | 18.89 | 25.09 | 26.10 | 35.28 | 35.72 | 31.14 | 42.71 |

Table 23 (continued)

| | 56 | 57 | 58 | 59 | 60 | 61 | 62 | 63 | 64 |
|---|---|---|---|---|---|---|---|---|---|
| $SiO_2$ | 54.0 | 54.0 | 45.78 | 47.04 | 45.18 | 48.54 | 49.18 | 54.88 | 51.96 |
| $Al_2O_3$ | 18.5 | 18.6 | 15.19 | 14.22 | 14.53 | 16.14 | 15.86 | 20.54 | 16.89 |
| $Fe_2O_3$ | 3.0 | 3.3 | 1.48 | 3.54 | 2.42 | 4.90 | 3.98 | 2.75 | 1.42 |
| FeO | 3.7 | 3.7 | 10.19 | 8.52 | 8.64 | 6.21 | 5.71 | 3.17 | 9.03 |
| MnO | .23 | .23 | 0.19 | 0.21 | 0.20 | 0.22 | 0.19 | 0.21 | 0.21 |
| MgO | 2.0 | 2.0 | 8.76 | 8.01 | 8.91 | 4.95 | 5.83 | 1.84 | 2.44 |
| CaO | 7.3 | 7.2 | 9.89 | 10.30 | 10.74 | 9.86 | 8.98 | 6.51 | 5.75 |
| $Na_2O$ | 5.6 | 5.5 | 3.79 | 3.77 | 4.73 | 4.23 | 5.39 | 6.02 | 6.85 |
| $K_2O$ | 2.0 | 2.0 | 0.99 | 0.96 | 1.07 | 1.27 | 1.39 | 2.02 | 2.18 |
| $TiO_2$ | 1.8 | 1.7 | 3.19 | 2.91 | 2.63 | 2.96 | 2.90 | 1.58 | 2.23 |
| $P_2O_5$ | .50 | .50 | 0.55 | 0.53 | 0.94 | 0.72 | 0.59 | 0.48 | 1.03 |
| $CO_2$ | -- | -- | -- | -- | -- | -- | -- | -- | -- |
| S | -- | -- | -- | -- | -- | -- | -- | -- | -- |
| $H_2O$ | .9 | .9 | -- | -- | -- | -- | -- | -- | -- |
| Total | 99.9 | 99.6 | 31.4x | 33.7x | 34.1x | 41.4x | 46.6x | 61.4x | 62.0x |

x = THORNTON-TUTTLE Index

| | | | | | | | | | |
|---|---|---|---|---|---|---|---|---|---|
| Q | | | | | | | | | |
| C | | | | | | | | | |
| Or | 11.93 | 11.97 | 5.85 | 5.67 | 6.32 | 7.51 | 8.21 | 11.94 | 12.88 |
| Ab | 46.05 | 46.67 | 17.89 | 23.37 | 13.32 | 31.67 | 29.75 | 47.72 | 38.70 |
| An | 19.63 | 20.42 | 21.51 | 19.04 | 15.25 | 21.30 | 14.98 | 23.06 | 8.90 |
| Ne | .98 | .25 | 7.68 | 4.62 | 14.47 | 2.24 | 8.59 | 1.75 | 10.43 |
| Di | 10.90 | 9.98 | 19.48 | 23.04 | 25.74 | 18.23 | 20.39 | 4.88 | 10.92 |
| Hy | | | | | | | | | |
| Ol | .92 | 1.42 | 18.11 | 12.38 | 14.21 | 4.68 | 5.44 | 2.57 | 9.47 |
| Il | 3.45 | 3.27 | 6.06 | 5.53 | 5.00 | 5.62 | 5.51 | 3.00 | 4.24 |
| Mt | 4.98 | 4.85 | 2.15 | 5.13 | 3.51 | 7.11 | 5.77 | 3.99 | 2.06 |
| Ap | 1.20 | 1.20 | 1.27 | 1.22 | 2.18 | 1.67 | 1.36 | 1.11 | 2.39 |
| D.I. | 58.96 | 58.90 | | | | | | | |

| | | | | | | | | | |
|---|---|---|---|---|---|---|---|---|---|
| Rb | | | 23 | 24 | 23 | 27 | 37 | 45 | 51 |
| Sr | | | 625 | 569 | 863 | 918 | 941 | 1179 | 590 |
| Zr | | | 219 | 262 | 262 | 310 | 419 | 567 | 541 |
| Ni | | | 120 | 151 | 181 | 47 | 39 | 24 | 25 |
| Y | | | 24 | 29 | 29 | 31 | 36 | 42 | 55 |
| Ce | | | 86 | 51 | 162 | 203 | 142 | 460 | 353 |
| Nd | | | 30 | 40 | 64 | 84 | 46 | 127 | 98 |
| K/Rb | | | 357 | 325 | 382 | 351 | 309 | 372 | 351 |

Trace Elements in ppm.

26. Feldspar-basalt (F), Alkali-basalt (G) Carriçal.
27. Feldspar-basalt (F), Alkali-basalt (G) Carriçal.
28. Feldspar-basalt (F), Hornblende-basalt (G) Calheta.
29. Feldspar-basalt (F), Hornblende-basalt (G) Pico Serrado.

30. Olivine-rich bomb (G), Porto Moniz.
31. Amphibole-augite-monchiquite (G) Rib. Frio.
32. Amphibole-augite-monchiquite (G) Lombo Grande.
33. Amphibole-augite-monchiquite (G) Lombo Grande.

Legend to Table 23 (continued)

34. Quartz-bostonite (G) Serra do Feteira, Porto Santo.
35. Quartz-bostonite (G) Pico do Baixo, Porto Santo.
36. Hornblende-basalt (G), Trachyte (C), Rib. Frio.
37. Trachyte (C) Pico do Facho, Porto Santo.
38. Trachyte (C) Pico do Castelo, Porto Santo.
39. Trachyte (C) Abelheira.
40. Trachydolerite (C) Western Porto Santo.
41. Trachydolerite (C) Rabaçal.
42. Trachydolerite (C) Abelheira.
43. Basalt (C) Arrebentao.
44. Basalt (C) New road?
45. Basalt (C) Rib. S. Jorge.
46. Diorite (M) Eastern Porto Santo.
47. Diorite (M) Western Porto Santo.
48. Alkali-olivine-basalt, route Pico Areeira to Pico de Ruivo. (W)
49. Alkali-olivine-basalt, 1 km N of S. Vicente bridge. (W)
50. Alkali-olivine-basalt, route Pico Areeira to Pico de Ruivo. (W)
51. Al-ol.-basalt and Hy-normative basalt, dyke, route Pico Areeira to Pico de Ruivo. (W)
52. Alkali-basalt, mouth of Rib. da Brava. (W)
53. Transitional basalt, road cut between Arco da Calheta and Madalena do Mar. (W)
54. Al-ol.-basalt and Hy-normative basalt, dyke, route Pico Areeira to Pico de Ruivo. (W)
55. Hawaiite, top of Pico de Ruivo. (W)
56. Mugearite, route Pico Areeira to Pico de Ruivo. (W)
57. Mugearite, coast 200 m E of Puerto de la Cruz. (W)
58. Basalt dyke, summit of Pico do Areeiro. (H)
59. Basalt dyke, SW cliff of Deserta Grande. (H)
60. Hawaiite flow, 1.5 km S of Cruzinhas. (H)
61. Hawaiite dyke, 2 km E of S. Vicente. (H)
62. Advanced Hawaiite dyke, elev. 500 m, Pta. de S. Lourenço. (H)
63. Mugearite flow, elev. 50 m, SE of Porto da Cruz. (H)
64. Essexite intrusion, elev. 150 m, 1 km SW of Porto da Cruz. (H)

*Note:* Determinations as made by COCHIUS (C); FINCKH (F); GAGEL (G); FERREIRA (M); SCHMINCKE & WEIBEL (W); HUGHES & BROWN (H).

---

Drachenfels, Germany, and domites of the Puy de Dome region of France. No. 8 was termed gauteite by GAGEL corresponding closely chemically to those of the Oslo region, Norway and the Bohemian Massif. GAGEL also included within his hypabyssals trachydolerites, e. g. at Pico de Gatos.

Of volcanic rocks of overwhelming significance in the archipelago, GAGEL recognized nepheline-basanites, sodalite-tephrites, hauyne-tephrites, hornblende-basalts, trachy-dolerites, trachytes, basalts, essexitic porphyries and essexitic melaphyres. In the Table, Nos. 9–36, taken from GAGEL and FINCKH and Nos. 37–45 from COCHIUS, are illustrative of such rocks. (We are well aware of the caution needed in presenting old chemical analyses – RITTMANN (1960) remarking on the remarkably high percentage which are useless, the gross errors contained so frequently therein – but in the case of Madeira there is little else to fall back upon.)

FINCKH (1913) made major groupings as per GAGEL. Amongst plutonics, he recognized sodalite-syenites, akerites, foyaites, essexites, essexite-diabases and pyroxenitic-essexite-diabases – Nos. 1–6. His hypabyssals included camptonitic or monchiquitic melanocratic rocks, also leucocratic Ca-bostonites and gauteites. Trachytes, trachy-andesites, trachy-dolerites – grouped into trachoidal trachy-dolerites, basaltic trachy-dolerites and hornblende-basalts – were included in FINCKH's volcanics. In Table 23, Nos. 9–13 are termed trachoidal trachy-dolerites by FINCKH, Nos. 14–18, basaltic trachy-dolerites, whilst his hornblende-basalt shows relations to nepheline-basanite and the essexitic melaphyres of GAGEL; FINCKH also recognized dolerites, feldspar-basalts (Nos. 19–29).

In GAGEL's Part II paper (1915) he made use of a study of FINCKH's paper and also upon an examination of 60 more thin-sections of Madeira rocks. The varieties of plutonics mentioned by FINCKH, GAGEL would prefer to treat rather as small facies differentiates of essexites. Of the hypabyssals, he enters into more detail than in his earlier paper. No. 13, the trachoidal trachy-dolerite or nepheline-basanite (?) of FINCKH, upon consultation with HIBSCH regarding the Bohemian Massif monchiquites, GAGEL re-defined as an amphibole-augite-monchiquite, also for Nos. 31–33, and at Pico de Gatos he recognized hornblende-monchiquites, monchiquites at Pico Furao. Further study of the vein fissures in volcanics at Pico de Gatos and Pico Sidrao led GAGEL to recognize hauyne-tephrites and sodalite-tephrites, and at Rib. de Massapez, picrite-basalts with serpentinized olivines. Nos. 18, 28, 29 and 36 GAGEL now classified as hornblende-basalts, Nos. 9–12 are named sodalite-tephrites and No. 14, hauyne-tephrite. GAGEL also recognized what he termed ›basaltoide Gesteine‹, the feldspar-basalts being now termed alkali-basalts, as per the opinion of HIBSCH, as they were comparable to those of the Bohemian Massif – Nos. 19–29. The terms essexite-porphyry and essexite-melaphyre used in his 1913 paper were so coined for what GAGEL considered unusual rock types, these names being thought of only as general type names and related to certain types of the Oslo region by BROGGER. But GAGEL did n o t want to suggest a similar Palaeozoic age connotation for such would be contrary to the recognized Tertiary age of the Madeira rocks. It might have been more to the point to have used inverted commas around these names in order to obviate confusion, for, as he pointed out, these rocks could not easily nor without considerable more information be termed trachy-dolerites, feldspar-basalts or alkali-basalts, as their character and rock environment is not typical of trachy-dolerites, etc.

MORAIS (1945) made some geological studies of Madeira, treating of the general geology as well as the petrology of the igneous rocks, the latter relying much on the work of GAGEL and FINCKH. The Porto de Cruz rocks, MORAIS, like FINCKH, termed essexites, seemingly in a sensu stricto sense. In these rocks he noted 70% oligoclase and orthoclase, 15% augite, 15% biotite, barkevikite, magnetite, ilmenite, olivine, serpentine, appatite and analcime. These were the rocks FINCKH said showed analcime and nepheline and GAGEL noted the presence of sodalite. To FINCKH the diabasic essexites were those rocks which were more basic, lacking orthoclase, plagioclase and richer in calcium. Near here, MORAIS recognized a basaltic-type dyke rock entirely pulverized and having undergone contact metamorphism. The same type of metamorphosed basaltic rock occurred in the Rib. das Voltas as an 80 m thick dyke, which he termed trachy-basalt. These trachy-basalts of MORAIS were named trachy-dolerites by GAGEL. GAGEL showed that all the above-mentioned rocks were not, as had once been thought, the socle of the island, corresponding to ancient continental granitic rocks, but were rather much younger intrusions in the form of laccoliths into the volcanics, a view shared entirely by MORAIS. MORAIS also appears to share the view of GAGEL that the various kinds of syenites – foyaites, akerites, etc. of FINCKH – were rather small differentiation masses of essexites. GAGEL's madeirite MORAIS thought did not show the ophitic texture of diabase and should be considered rather as a marginal facies of such, madeirite then being actually a transition rock between pyroxene-essexite (or the essexitic-gabbro of LACROIX) and peridotite.

Amongst his 53 igneous samples, Morais recognized many melabasalts, using the term in the sense of Johannsen for dark, calc-alkali rocks. The Madeira specimens all have the minerals of normal basalts but could not always be separated into calc-alkali and alkali varieties. Of 18 melabasalt specimens microscopically examined, labradorite ranged from 20–40%, augite from 30–60%, olivine from 5–35%, magnetite from 5–20%, some specimens showing glass and some possibly feldspathoids.

Finally Morais described some limburgitic trachy-basalts from Camara dos Lobos and the small peninsula at Porto da Cruz, both showing abundant cloudy glass. That from the latter locality was described as a limburgitic trachy-basalt by Gagel. A specimen of pyroxenite (Rosenbusch) or peridotite (Johannsen) was described, also volcanic bombs and pumice. Unfortunately Morais only occasionally gives precise details as to where his specimens were collected, in many instances no locality whatsoever is mentioned.

Grabham (1948) criticized the determinations by Gagel of essexites, claiming that the original essexites of Essex County, Massachusetts, are characterized by phenocrysts of easily visible titanaugites. We now know, however, that the type essexites are hybrids, mixtures of gabbro and nepheline-syenite, and even today this rock is one of the least satisfactorily defined of basic rocks, the name being applied to widely varying mineral assemblages. Grabham preferred to associate such rocks rather with teschenites because they showed no titanaugite phenocrysts. As the essexites and diabases of Gagel and Finckh do on occasion include analcime as an essential constituent, a characteristic of teschenites, Grabham has a point here. He stated that basalts are the commonest rocks of Madeira proper, with the same composition as diabases but, due to more rapid cooling, have a finer grain, sometimes with visible phenocrysts of olivine and/or augite.

In connexion with the recent geological survey of the archipelago (Zbyszewski, 1971, 1972) it has been appropriately expressed that the terminologies for igneous rocks as used in these islands in the past are in need of revision, for contradictions, overlappings, etc. are all too frequent in earlier publications. The survey recognized trachytes, trachy-andesites, trachy-basalts, trachy-dolerites, andesites, basalts, essexites, teschenites and madeirites as the principal rock types. The major volcanic complexes and their sequences in Madeira are given below – vd. also Fig. 46.

| Western Madeira | Eastern Madeira |
|---|---|
| 4. Modern Volcanic Complex | 4. Modern Volcanic Structures |
| 3. Paul da Serra Post-Vindobonian Volcanic Complex. | 3. Post-Vind. Vol. Complex II<br>Post-Vind. Vol. Complex I |
| 2. Vindobonian Volcanic Complex. | 2. ? |
| 1. Pre-Vindobonian Volcanic Complex – perhaps pre-Miocene. | 1. Pre-Vindobonian Complex of Picos Ruivo and Areeiro. |

SCHMINCKE & WEIBEL (1972) claimed that the only rocks in Madeira which can be termed trachytes and quartz-trachytes (taking such to mean rocks with a scarcity in Fe-Mg minerals and silica polymorphs present in the matrix) are to be found as dykes and intrusives within the S. Vicente valley. (It should be noted that theirs was only a reconnaissance study.) They failed to detect any systematic differences in rocks of the various stratigraphic units. The rocks of both Madeira and Porto Santo show a distinct sodic nature, due rather to low $K_2O$ rather than unusually high $Na_2O$ content. In comparison with rocks studied from Porto Santo, those of Madeira are slightly undersaturated and mildly alkalic.

HUGHES & BROWN (1972) studied some Neogene Madeira suite minor intrusives and lavas of unusually soda-rich alkali-olivine-basalts, along with hawaiite, mugearite and essexitic derivatives. These basalts with their fractional crystallization products represent the sole igneous rocks of Madeira and also Deserta Grande, the sequence being alkali-olivine-basalt – hawaiite – mugearite, essexites being intrusive associates of mugearites. Nodular inclusions in the basalts include dunites, pyroxenites and wehrlites, there being no important chemical difference between these nodules and the host rock phenocryst phases. In the evolution of the Madeira lavas, two stages can be postulated: (a) partial melting and fractional crystallization at depth produced the alkali-olivine-basalt mother magma, possibly at pressures exceeding 25 kb outside the hornblende stability field. (b) later crystal fractionation of this material at low pressures in shallow levels, generated advanced fractionated liquids, leading to the hawaiite trend, which was completed by the separating out of extrusive mugearite and intrusive essexite by means of feldspar floatation within a high-level magma chamber which contained the highly fractionated liquid.

COCHIUS (1864) first studied the volcanics of Porto Santo and subjected 35 samples to analysis – a number not equalled till 80 years later. Already he noted that the rocks were considerably more acidic than those of Madeira. FINCKH (1913) considered that some quartz-bostonites and trachytes (Nos. 35 and 37, Table 23) had counterparts in the Curral das Freiras of Madeira and could be compared to the Drachenfels-type rocks of Germany. GAGEL (1915) remarked upon the uncommonly strongly miarolitic character of some essexite pebbles in the Ribeira de Cimbral. MORAIS (1943) from a collection of 89 rocks studied 38 microscopically, of which 24 were trachytes, trachy-andesites and trachy-dolerites (one), 11 were basaltic rocks and one possibly bostonite – the other two samples were limestones. The first group show feldspars dominant, much feldspathoids and quartz only rarely; the basalts showed olivine varying between 10–40%, augite 20–50%, magnetite up to 20% with labradorite ranging from 20–55%. FERREIRA (1969) mentioned the occurrence of plutonic xenoliths within the volcanics at three localities, 800 m NW of Pico do Concelho, 150 m E of Pico Castelo and 1,000 m N of Pico Ana Ferreira. Chemical analyses of these are given in Nos. 46 and 47, the rocks being diorites, chemically similar to diorites and gabbros occurring at Sintra, Portugal. BARROS & OLIVEIRA (1969) noted the sodic alkaline character of the Porto Santo lavas – akeritic rhyolites and trachytes – as also basic lavas tending towards undersaturation – basanitic basalts and basanitic ankaramites. As regards NIGGLI parameters, the isofalic point is si = 145 (143 in Madeira), showing the saturated tendency in magmatic differentiation. The k-mg diagram illustrates the sodic

Geology of the Madeira Archipelago

Table 24  Chemical analyses, norms and NIGGLI parameters of some Porto Santo rocks (BARROS & OLIVEIRA, 1969; SCHMINCKE & WEIBEL, 1972)

| | 1 | 2 | 3 | 4 | 5 | 6 | 7 | 8 | 9 |
|---|---|---|---|---|---|---|---|---|---|
| $SiO_2$ | 63.97 | 64.38 | 56.27 | 61.06 | 59.19 | 43.14 | 43.71 | 46.8 | 47.0 |
| $Al_2O_3$ | 18.57 | 18.43 | 19.57 | 19.51 | 19.89 | 15.65 | 13.45 | 17.1 | 15.2 |
| $Fe_2O_3$ | 3.17 | 2.86 | 6.38 | 2.58 | 2.75 | 4.90 | 8.09 | 3.5 | 3.8 |
| FeO | 0.14 | 0.10 | 0.32 | 0.55 | 0.72 | 9.29 | 5.44 | 8.45 | 7.4 |
| MnO | 0.10 | 0.17 | 0.20 | 0.16 | 0.28 | 0.24 | 0.21 | .21 | .17 |
| MgO | 0.61 | 0.67 | 1.98 | 0.91 | 1.11 | 6.39 | 10.08 | 5.2 | 7.7 |
| CaO | 3.08 | 1.85 | 4.63 | 3.36 | 3.22 | 10.23 | 10.80 | 9.8 | 10.5 |
| $Na_2O$ | 5.46 | 6.70 | 5.59 | 5.87 | 7.52 | 3.36 | 2.81 | 3.2 | 2.8 |
| $K_2O$ | 2.18 | 2.13 | 1.96 | 2.58 | 2.38 | 1.05 | 0.88 | .8 | .8 |
| $TiO_2$ | 0.45 | 0.47 | 1.24 | 0.58 | 0.62 | 3.48 | 2.47 | 2.3 | 2.4 |
| $P_2O_5$ | 0.15 | 0.17 | 0.68 | 0.37 | 0.20 | 1.00 | 0.69 | .63 | .50 |
| $H_2O+$ | 0.92 | 1.12 | 0.52 | 1.07 | 1.53 | 0.56 | 0.60 | } 1.8 | } 1.6 |
| $H_2O-$ | 0.96 | 0.72 | 0.43 | 1.19 | 0.35 | 0.37 | 0.58 | | |
| Total | 99.76 | 99.77 | 99.72 | 99.79 | 99.76 | 99.66 | 99.81 | 99.79 | 99.9 |

| | 1 | 2 | 3 | 4 | 5 | 6 | 7 | 8 | 9 |
|---|---|---|---|---|---|---|---|---|---|
| Q | 16.92 | 12.54 | 5.16 | 9.24 | | | | | |
| C | 2.04 | 2.02 | 1.43 | 1.73 | | | | | |
| Or | 12.78 | 12.78 | 11.68 | 15.57 | 13.90 | 6.12 | 5.00 | 4.80 | 4.81 |
| Ab | 46.11 | 56.59 | 47.16 | 49.78 | 60.78 | 19.45 | 9.96 | 27.63 | 24.11 |
| An | 14.18 | 8.34 | 18.63 | 14.18 | 13.62 | 24.46 | 21.68 | 30.55 | 27.01 |
| Ne | | | | | 1.42 | 4.79 | 7.38 | | |
| Di | 1.50 | 1.70 | 5.00 | 2.30 | 3.28 | 16.61 | 36.80 | 12.17 | 18.20 |
| Mt | | | | 0.70 | 1.39 | 7.19 | 10.90 | 5.18 | 5.61 |
| Il | 0.30 | 0.46 | 1.06 | 1.06 | 1.22 | 6.54 | 4.71 | 4.46 | 4.64 |
| Hm | 3.20 | 2.88 | 6.40 | 2.08 | 1.76 | | 0.64 | | |
| Ru | 0.24 | 0.24 | 0.64 | | | | | Hy 5.69 | 6.10 |
| Fo | | | | | | 7.58 | | Ol 8.02 | 8.35 |
| Ap | 0.34 | 0.34 | 1.68 | 1.01 | 0.33 | 2.35 | 1.68 | Ap 1.52 | 1.21 |
| $H_2O$ | 1.88 | 1.84 | 0.95 | 2.26 | 1.88 | 0.93 | 1.18 | + 32.46 | 28.92 |
| Total | 99.49 | 99.75 | 99.79 | 99.91 | 99.58 | 99.91 | 99.93 | | |

| | 1 | 2 | 3 | 4 | 5 | 6 | 7 | | |
|---|---|---|---|---|---|---|---|---|---|
| si | 263.6 | 267.3 | 197.3 | 231.7 | 208.5 | 95.4 | 89.8 | | |
| al | 45.0 | 45.1 | 36.8 | 43.5 | 41.2 | 20.3 | 16.3 | | |
| fm | 14.1 | 14.0 | 26.2 | 14.8 | 15.9 | 46.9 | 53.3 | | |
| c | 13.4 | 8.2 | 15.7 | 13.7 | 12.0 | 24.2 | 23.8 | | |
| alk | 27.5 | 32.7 | 21.3 | 28.0 | 30.9 | 8.6 | 6.6 | | |
| k | 0.21 | 0.17 | 0.19 | 0.23 | 0.17 | 0.16 | 0.17 | | |
| mg | 0.26 | 0.30 | 0.36 | 0.35 | 0.36 | 0.45 | 0.58 | | |
| qz | 53.6 | 36.5 | − 5.9 | 19.7 | −15.1 | −39.0 | −36.6 | | |
| ti | 1.2 | 1.5 | 2.9 | 1.6 | 1.7 | 5.7 | 3.8 | | |
| p | 0.2 | 0.3 | 1.0 | 0.7 | 0.2 | 0.9 | 0.6 | | |
| Q | 46.6 | 44.1 | 36.5 | 41.9 | 36.1 | 21.0 | 21.0 | | |
| L | 46.5 | 48.9 | 50.9 | 49.9 | 56.5 | 38.0 | 31.6 | | |
| M | 6.9 | 7.0 | 12.6 | 8.2 | 7.4 | 41.0 | 48.3 | | |

Table 24 (continued)

| | 10 | 11 | 12 | 13 | 14 | 15 | 16 | 17 | 18 |
|---|---|---|---|---|---|---|---|---|---|
| $SiO_2$ | 54.0 | 60.0 | 60.5 | 60.5 | 62.5 | 65.0 | 68.5 | 70.0 | 70.6 |
| $Al_2O_3$ | 17.8 | 19.6 | 19.0 | 18.6 | 19.2 | 17.7 | 16.7 | 16.3 | 16.0 |
| $Fe_2O_3$ | 5.1 | 3.0 | 2.7 | 4.0 | 3.0 | 2.5 | 1.8 | 1.0 | .9 |
| FeO | 3.1 | .8 | .8 | 1.0 | .4 | .7 | .5 | .4 | .4 |
| MnO | .20 | .22 | .26 | .15 | .07 | .18 | .08 | .11 | .09 |
| MgO | 2.1 | .88 | .7 | .9 | .3 | .5 | .1 | .2 | .2 |
| CaO | 8.0 | 3.1 | 2.9 | 4.1 | 2.8 | 2.1 | 2.1 | .9 | 1.0 |
| $Na_2O$ | 4.5 | 6.3 | 7.7 | 5.6 | 6.8 | 6.8 | 5.4 | 6.4 | 6.6 |
| $K_2O$ | 1.2 | 2.4 | 2.6 | 2.0 | 2.4 | 2.7 | 2.7 | 2.2 | 3.3 |
| $TiO_2$ | 1.7 | .8 | .7 | .9 | .7 | .8 | .4 | .3 | .2 |
| $P_2O_5$ | .60 | .22 | .14 | .30 | .15 | .10 | .06 | .03 | .04 |
| $H_2O+$ / $H_2O-$ | } 1.6 | } 2.7 | } 1.8 | } 1.6 | } 1.2 | } .8 | } 1.4 | } 1.0 | } .3 |
| Total | 99.9 | 99.9 | 99.8 | 99.7 | 99.8 | 99.9 | 99.7 | 99.8 | 99.6 |

| | 10 | 11 | 12 | 13 | 14 | 15 | 16 | 17 | 18 |
|---|---|---|---|---|---|---|---|---|---|
| Q | 6.51 | 7.15 | | 11.21 | 7.85 | 10.25 | 22.65 | 18.60 | 17.46 |
| C | | 1.57 | | .50 | .69 | .01 | 1.24 | .75 | |
| Or | 7.33 | 14.59 | 15.68 | 12.05 | 14.38 | 16.10 | 16.22 | 19.13 | 19.63 |
| Ab | 39.35 | 54.82 | 66.13 | 48.33 | 58.35 | 58.07 | 46.47 | 54.79 | 56.22 |
| An | 25.65 | 14.34 | 9.80 | 18.75 | 13.09 | 9.86 | 10.20 | 4.32 | 4.32 |
| Ne | | | .19 | | | | | | |
| Di | 9.04 | | 3.08 | | | | | | .32 |
| Mt | 7.64 | 1.01 | 1.43 | 1.13 | | .53 | .73 | .79 | 1.01 |
| Il | .33 | 1.56 | 1.36 | 1.74 | 1.01 | 1.53 | .77 | .58 | .38 |
| Hm | | 2.39 | 1.77 | 3.30 | 3.35 | 2.16 | 1.33 | .47 | .21 |
| Hy | 2.71 | 2.05 | | 2.29 | .76 | 1.26 | .25 | .50 | .35 |
| Ol | | | .25 | | | | | | |
| Ap | 1.47 | .54 | .34 | .73 | .36 | .24 | .15 | .07 | .10 |
| + | 53.19 | 76.56 | 82.00 | 71.59 | 80.57 | 84.42 | 85.34 | 92.52 | 93.32 |
| § | | .66 | | .61 | .72 | .80 | .71 | | .90 |

+ THORNTON-TUTTLE differentiation index.  § Agpaicity index.

1. Rhyolite, Penedo.
2. Rhyolite, Serra de Nossha Senhora.
3. Trachyte, Penedo.
4. Trachyte, Pico do Facho.
5. Trachyte, Pico do Castelo.
6. Olivine-basalt, Pedregal de Dentro.
7. Basanitic Ankaramites, Rib. Cabeço do Meio.
8. Transitional basalt, centre of dyke, Pico Espigao.
9. Transitional alkali-basalt, dyke, 500m E of Pico Juliana.
10. Mugearite instrusion; Quarry, N end of Pico A. Ferreira ridge.
11. Trachyte, sill centre, 100 m E of quarry, Pico Castelo.
12. Trachyte, sill centre, quarry at top of Pico Castelo.
13. Trachyte instrusion, road cut, S. Portella, W of Terra de Maria.
14. Trachyte intrusion, top of Pico Baixo.
15. Trachyte intrusion, 500 m E of Pico Juliana.
16. Rhyolite dyke, 200 m E of Pico Juliana.
17. Rhyolite, dyke centre, 200 m NE of Pico Castelo.
18. Rhyolite, dyke border, 200 m NE of Pico Castelo.

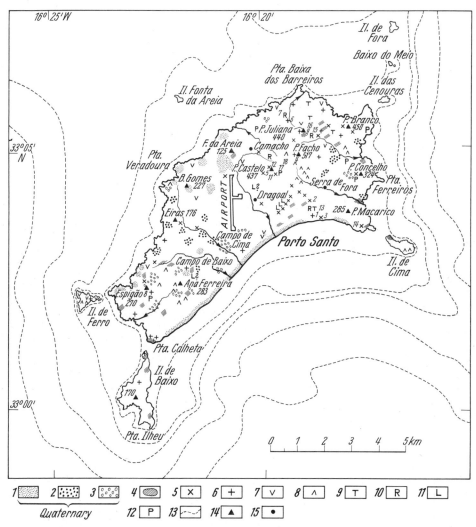

Numbers refer to approx. locations of samples in Table 24.

Fig. 49. Geological map of Porto Santo. 1: Calcareous sands. 2: Calcareous arenites. 3: Calcareous concretions. 4: Vindobonian limestones. 5: Trachytes, trachyandesites. 6: Basalts and kindred rocks. 7: Volcanic breccias, agglomerates. 8: Basaltic tuffs, ashes. 9: Bostonites. 10: Rhyolites. 11: Essexites. 12: Plutonic xenoliths. 13: Isobaths of 20, 50, 100, 500, 1000 and 2000 m. 14: Peaks, heights in m. 15: Villages. (Based on available literature citings, sketch map of MORAIS, 1943, and personal observations).

Fig. 50. Geological map of Ilhas Desertas, Madeira. 1: Scree deposits. 2: Breccias and scoria. 3: Hawaiitic-type lavas and tuffs. 4: Upper basaltic complex. 5: Lower basaltic complex. 6: Pyroclastics predominant in basalts. 7: Crater. 8: Faults. 9: Elevations, in m. 10: Isobaths, in m. (Modified after Serv. Geol. de Portugal map, 1972).

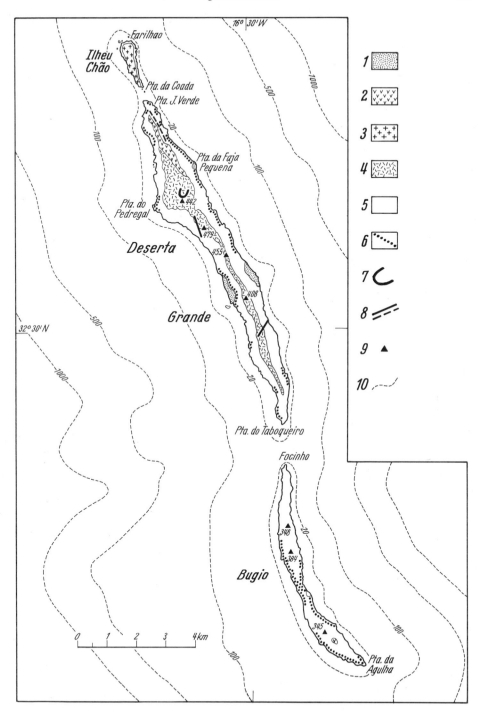

alkaline nature, whilst the QLM diagram suggests magmatic evolution near the o = 0 line, both these diagrams showing similar features for Madeira. SCHMINCKE & WEIBEL (1972) remark upon the silica content of Nos. 16, 17, 18, Table 24, which they term rhyolites due to their high normative quartz content. This confirms the earlier belief of GAGEL (1913) that ›high silica‹ rocks were present in the island. Studies of their samples from Madeira and Porto Santo (their ›Madeira suite‹) show high $Al_2O_3$ content, high CaO content (much plagioclase and sphene) and extremely high $Na_2O/K_2O$ ratios.

Of the Ilhas Desertas, Ilheu Chao comprises lavas of hawaiitic tendency, along with pyroclastics, all quasi-horizontal. The basaltic complex of Deserta Grande comprises four units: (a) brownish and reddish scoria overlying greyish basaltic lavas, cut by many basaltic dykes; (b) mostly reddish basaltic lavas; (c) horizontal lavas forming the crest of the island; (d) black scoria cones in the N part. The first two units comprise the Lower Basaltic Complex and the other two, the Upper Basaltic Comples. The dominant rocks are basalts rich in olivine, often highly porphyritic, but aphyric types also occur. Ankaramites, andesitic basalts, andesites and peridotitic andesites are likewise present. NNW-SSE and N-S oriented dykes of hawaiitic tendency are extremely plentiful. Ilheu do Bugio is formed of rocks belonging to the Lower Basaltic Complex of Deserta Grande. Again there are many hawaiitic-type dykes trending parallel to the island outline. Tuffs, scoria and cinders are common throughout the islands, both superficially and interlayered with the lavas. Deserta Grande and Bugio are the older islands, and all three show geological similarities to eastern Madeira, and are to be considered as an SE extension of the main island.

Azores rocks are of potassic character whilst those of Madeira are of sodic nature, as also seems to apply to rocks from the Selvagens.

From the partial studies of HUGHES & BROWN, SCHMINCKE & WEIBEL, some petrochemical features of Madeira rocks can be noted. An average of 3.95% sodium in $Na_2O$ in basalts shows a special enrichment when compared to alkali basalts of other oceanic islands. Variation diagrams of MgO, CaO, $Fe_2O_3$ + FeO, Sr, Ni, Y and Zr plotted against the THORNTON-TUTTLE index indicates that with fractionation there is a pronounced reduction in magnesium, calcium and nickel, the iron content remains quite steady until the late stage where irregular depletion occurs. During fractionation there is a steady increase in Sr, Zr and Y. Of note is the variation in content of Fe and Sr in the mugearites and essexites, the former showing marked reduction in Fe and enrichment in Sr, whereas the latter show the converse, though in other respects the rocks are chemically similar. Chondrite normalized rare-earth abundance patterns (taking Ce, Nd and Y as representative members) showing the degree of rare-earth enrichment also demonstrates the alkali character of the rocks, whereas the abundance pattern in later fractionates displays relative enrichment of light, large rare-earth elements to heavy, small rare-earth elements characterisitc of the basalt fractionation series.

Analyses of the more aphyric samples show them to be somewhat Ne-normative and can be labelled as alkali-basalt. Intermediate rocks are just undersaturated, those more evolved are all oversaturated. The basaltic rocks are not related to olivine control lines, for the CaO does not increase with corresponding decrease in MgO.

Differentiation here would seem to be influenced by olivine, probably also spinel, as well as Ca-rich clinopyroxenes and later, plagioclases. The Madeira rocks are slightly alkalic and undersaturated, ranging from basanites-saturated basalts via slightly undersaturated intermediate rocks to subalkalic rhyolites. Trachytes and rhyolites are distinct from the usual peralkaline end members of other Atlantic islands on both a chemical and mineralogic basis. Madeira (along with Iceland) with their low alkalic suites, show the least total alkalis weight percentage (less than 10%) of any Atlantic islands removed from the Mid-Atlantic Ridge, as per available analyses.

In this part of the Atlantic at least there would appear to be no simple relationship as regards chemical composition and distance from the Mid-Atlantic Ridge, Madeira rocks, e. g. being even less alkalic than those of the Azores.

It must be stressed, however, that the above petrochemical conclusions are based on limited sampling and analyses, especially as regards Madeira proper.

## Sedimentary Rocks

Sedimentary rocks, other than Holocene material, occur in Madeira, Porto Santo and the islets of Baixo, Cima and Ferro.

The best known occurrences are in the Ribeira S. Vicente, Madeire, close to the N coast. Yellowish, coralliferous, saccharoidal limestones, marmorized in appearance, predominate, sandwiched between lavas below and tuffs above. These limestones outcrop at elevations of 360–400 m. Actual exposures are not large in area, usually but a few metres, but sections 2–3 m thick can be observed in quarries and cliffs. However, these occurrences are of scientific interest because of their contained fossils and once were also of economic importance as a source of lime, not only here but in Ilheu de Baixo whose other name is Ilheu da Cal (Lime Islet).

The only other place where better known sediments occur in Madeira itself is at Ponta de S. Lourenço, the odd-shaped peninsula in the extreme E, where Quaternary calcareous arenites and sands are found.

Limestones similar to those of the Ribeira S. Vincente are also exposed in Porto Santo and the islets of Baixo, Ferro and Cima. Older publications make reference to scattered occurrences of Miocene limestones throughout the SE sloping side of Porto Santo, but such are singularly lacking in specific details. The rather short paper by LIETZ & SCHWARZBACH (1970) gives adequate information on 14 new fossil occurrences in these limestones. The literature would indicate that the limestones of Porto Santo and the islets are, in essence, similar to those at Ribeira S. Vicente, Madeira, again intimately associated with lavas and tuffs, pyroclastics and agglomerates. LIETZ & SCHWARZBACH, e. g. give the following profile description of an occurrence in the upper Ribeira da Serra de Dentro:

| | | |
|---|---|---|
| Top | 2 m | Chalky-white band within argillaceous rocks with oblong siliceous nodules in lowest zone. |
| | 20–30 m | Light-greenish, coarse sand in dense, compact limestone and other partially darkish rock débris, several mm thick, slightly banded. In upper part occur spines of sea urchins. |
| | 2–3 m | Partially hard-baked, banded limestone detritus with marine fossils, and layers, mostly 3–4 cm thick, of whitish or reddish-brown, more or less rounded calcareous algae nodules. |
| Bottom | | At least 10 m greenish, tightly packed, lithic tuffs. |

The beds dip at 20° to the SE. A thin, sometimes only a cm thick basaltic vein cuts the profile. This exposure lies between 280–300 m above sea level.

On Ilheu de Baixo are similar type limestones on eastern side, occurring as high as 90 m above sea level. The beds attain thicknesses of 5 m, and as before, are intimately associated with tuffaceous, conglomeratic and basaltic material. SILVA (1959) quotes the following section behind Portinho:

| | |
|---|---|
| 65–66 m | Calcareous fossilized breccia, very coarse. |
| 61–65 m | Basalt |
| 58–61 m | Calcareous, fossilized, very coarse breccia. Cut by fault striking N2OE, downthrow of approx. 2 m. |
| 50.4–58 m | Pyroclastics |
| 50–50.4 m | Fossilized calcareous breccia |
| 45.6–50 m | Pyroclastics |
| 45–45.6 m | Fossilized calcareous breccia |
| 0–45 m | Pyroclastics |

These breccias contain Miocene fossils.

On Ilheu de Cima, at Porto do Cais, occurs a marmorized limestone between a half and one metre thick, and at Cabeço das Laranjas, at elevations between 25 and 40 m there are breccioidal limestones with fossils and calcareous algae nodules.

On Porto Santo highest occurrences of these Miocene Limestones are found on Pico Juliana at elevations of 340–350 m. In thickness these may attain 30 m. On this island dips are generally less than 30°, but at Ponta da Calheta, opposite Ilheu de Baixo, sedimentaries are dipping 60° to the SSE.

It is worth noting that the best description of the Ribeira S. Vicente, Madeira, sedimentary occurrences is to be found in the old work by HARTUNG (1864).

The Quaternary calcareous arenites and sands of the archipelago have long interested scholars. These are found at Ponta de S. Lourenço, Madeira and especially well developed in Porto Santo. The former occurrence, giving rise to a calcareous sandy beach, known as Prainha, is unique in being the only sandy beach in the island. From here, ALBERS (1854) studied 62 living species of *Helix* of which 10 were extinct, the sands being classified by him as of Diluvium age. These deposits occur as high as 100 m above the steep slopes down to the N side of the peninsula, as well as far up the slopes of Pico da Piedade, 108 m high, on the S side behind Prainha. Later studies have shown a great abundance of terrestrial gastropods, chiefly of the Helicidae family, present in these sands. These Prainha sands, whose faunal contents have been studied by LOWE (1851), ALBERS (1854), MAYER-EYMAR (1864), PAIVA (1867), WOLLASTON (1878), GIRARD (1892), NOBRE (1931), SILVA (1957), are classed as Quaternary. HARTUNG (1864) believed the fossils present were of marine origin, they were pulverized by the waves at a time prior to the progressive sinking of this part of the coast and the development of cliffing, and were later thrown up upon the strand as comminuted shell fragments, winds transporting the material up and inland to present heights. As per this explanation, therefore, these calcareous sands are naught else but indeterminate (because of degree of pulverization) fossil débris.

Such deposits have a much larger occurrence in Porto Santo. Throughout much of the SE exposed side of the island these are found, as far inland as around Pico do Castelo, Pico de Ana Ferreira and Fonte da Areia. The last-mentioned locality is only some 500 m from the NW coast, elevation 127 m, and here the sands attain their greatest thickness of 50 m. Such sands are also present throughout Campo de Baixo and Campo de Cima, along the SE coast for some 8–9 km from Ponta da Calheta to beyond the capital, Porto Santo. (Incidentally this beach is probably the cleanest, finest, most extensive in all of Macaronesia.) Similar calcareous sands are present as well in Ilheus Baixo and Cima.

D'ORCHYMONT (1936) stated that both at Ponta de Lourenço and in Porto Santo (especially between Picos Castelo and Ana Ferreira, on the NW slopes) these deposits form aeolian dunes, with stalagmatic calcareous concretions or then calcareous platy conconcretions, more or less horizontally banded. Cross-bedding is also present. All these calcareous deposits are very weakly cemented. Pluvial waters percolating through the sands become charged with dissolved lime, which is precipitated lower down in the amorphous state, thus binding together more securely the comminuted shell débris at depth. The concretions are in actuality formed in this way. Winds attack these formations, removing the grains one by one, and collecting them to still-humid stalagmitic masses, thus on occasion forming curious-shaped agglomerations. The calcareous sands are of yellowish, brownish or dirty white colour, grains being opaqaue and dark (often glassy green or glassy transparent) mixed at the base with basaltic and/or trachytic particles. Winds from the S and SE have transported the material up slopes towards the interior. The dominant winds, which come from the N and NW, have been able to blow the material up steeper NW slopes. Wave attack no less is more trenchant along the NW coasts, and this, plus stronger winds of the N-NW, transported the sands inland before the present steeper slopes were formed, as e. g. between Picos Castelo and Ana Ferreira. Within these dunal formations are found in great numbers terrestrial gastropods. It would thus appear that throughout the island, the role of wind transportation is paramount in accounting for the present calcareous sand localities removed from the coasts.

The granulometric features of these Porto Santo calcareous beach sands have been studied by PUREZA (1961), from which Table 25 is taken. The sands are of fine- to mediumgrain, very well calibrated, are essentially calcareous, comprising small shell fragments, of heavy minerals augite predominates. The sharp outlines, high densities and freshness of the heavy minerals indicates a near source. Both the heavy fraction and the calcareous material result from strong abrasive action causing intense fragmentation of the latter and subsequent deposition along the strand.

MOURA (1961) studied Foraminifera collected from beach localities along the SE coast and also from calcarenites of interior areas between Picos Castelo, Ana Ferreira and Serra da Feiteira referred to above by D'ORCHYMONT. MOURA believed that here there occurred a shallow platform where sublittoral deposits formed. Due to either isostatic or epeirogenic movements, the platform was raised above sea level, the deposits being then attacked by winds and the consequent fossilization of the numerous terrestrial gastropods. He noticed no essential difference between the foraminiferal forms of the beach and those of the interior, comprising chiefly genera of *Cibicides* and *Elphidium*. He supposed that the ecological conditions were not greatly different from today, sedimentation taking place in shallow depths. Upon emergence the sediments were acted upon by winds, giving rise to dunes and the colonization of terrestrial

Table 25    Characteristics of the Quaternary beach sands of the SE coast of Porto Santo (after PURE-ZA, 1961)

| Sample Number | Percentage Calcareous Material | % Mineral content (calibrated material) | | | | | | Granulometric parameters | | | |
|---|---|---|---|---|---|---|---|---|---|---|---|
| | | Augite | Hornblende | Zircon | Rutile | Opaques | Alterates | Median diam. (mm) (Md) | Index of asymmetry (As φ) | Index of heterometry (Qd φ) | Sorting coefficient (So) |
| 1 | 93.7 | 81 | 8 | – | – | 6 | 5 | 0.235 | 0.08 | 0.23 | 1.17 |
| 2 | 93.3 | 78 | 14 | – | 1 | 3 | 4 | 0.280 | 0.05 | 0.30 | 1.23 |
| 3 | 92.7 | 67 | 14 | – | – | 11 | 8 | 0.260 | 0.03 | 0.28 | 1.20 |
| 4 | 93.3 | 83 | 9 | – | – | 3 | 5 | 0.245 | −0.03 | 0.28 | 1.20 |
| 5 | 92.3 | 65 | 14 | – | – | 10 | 11 | 0.280 | 0.00 | 0.25 | 1.18 |
| 6 | 91.1 | 78 | 12 | – | – | 4 | 6 | 0.220 | −0.08 | 0.33 | 1.25 |
| 7 | 91.7 | 82 | 9 | – | – | 7 | 2 | 0.245 | 0.00 | 0.25 | 1.18 |
| 8 | 93.4 | 77 | 7 | – | – | 14 | 2 | 0.270 | −0.03 | 0.28 | 1.20 |
| 9 | 92.2 | 73 | 6 | – | – | 12 | 9 | 0.250 | 0.05 | 0.35 | 1.26 |
| 10 | 89.9 | 87 | 8 | – | – | 2 | 3 | 0.220 | −0.05 | 0.20 | 1.15 |
| 11 | 92.9 | 81 | 13 | – | – | 5 | 1 | 0.250 | 0.00 | 0.25 | 1.18 |
| 12 | 90.6 | 92 | 5 | – | – | 3 | – | 0.270 | 0.05 | 0.30 | 1.23 |
| 13 | 88.1 | 91 | 4 | – | – | 4 | 1 | 0.440 | −0.07 | 0.23 | 1.17 |
| 14 | 92.2 | 80 | 11 | – | – | 6 | 3 | 0.220 | −0.10 | 0.20 | 1.15 |
| 15 | 87.4 | 92 | 5 | – | – | 2 | 1 | 0.260 | 0.00 | 0.35 | 1.26 |
| 16 | 84.7 | 83 | 10 | – | – | 5 | 2 | 0.215 | 0.03 | 0.18 | 1.12 |
| 17 | 92.3 | 81 | 8 | – | – | 8 | 3 | 0.215 | −0.05 | 0.25 | 1.18 |
| 18 | 88.2 | 85 | 7 | – | – | 4 | 4 | 0.215 | −0.10 | 0.30 | 1.23 |
| 19 | 85.6 | 85 | 10 | – | – | 3 | 2 | 0.155 | −0.08 | 0.18 | 1.12 |
| 20 | 85.5 | 86 | 5 | – | – | 7 | 2 | 0.190 | 0.00 | 0.25 | 1.18 |
| 21 | 74.9 | 90 | 7 | – | – | 2 | 1 | 0.215 | −0.03 | 0.23 | 1.17 |
| 22 | 83.9 | 87 | 8 | – | – | 3 | 2 | 0.185 | 0.08 | 0.28 | 1.20 |
| 23 | 83.6 | 90 | 8 | 1 | – | 1 | – | 0.215 | −0.03 | 0.23 | 1.17 |
| 24 | 84.4 | 87 | 7 | – | – | 4 | 2 | 0.210 | −0.05 | 0.25 | 1.18 |
| 25 | 81.3 | 89 | 7 | – | – | 4 | – | 0.235 | −0.07 | 0.33 | 1.25 |

gastropods. Foraminifera indicate an age from Miocene to Present, the dunal formations, Plio-Pleistocene – as per HARTUNG – giving the date of the emergence as immediately prior to this. In summation, MOURA considered the fauna as representative of benthonic conditions, being a littoral development in warm, shallow waters.

MONTAGGIONI (1968) classified the SE strand of Porto Santo into: (i) emerged part, the strand, subdivided into: (a) lower strand, coast to edge of submarine beach, general slope 5°, with shell débris and basaltic gravels, zone wetted at low tide, hence salt-water incursions, but fresh-water percolates underground; (b) upper beach, difficult to determine upper limit against dunes but clearer lower limit, with no slope; (c) littoral dunes, 2–3 m in length, 1–1.5 m high, fixed by *Tamarix*, lying within 15–35 m from sea edge. Tubular limestones and vegetable fibres occur here. (ii) immerged part, up to ca. 1.2 km broad, extending to depths of 25 m, with a slope of 1–2°.

D'ORCHYMONT claimed that it could not be present molluscs which had formed this enormous calcareous accumulation along the SE coast, for today there are only a few and small occurrences of organisms thrown up by the seas. The formation of such calcareous sands, here and elsewhere in the world, has provoked much discussion in the past.

DALY (1924) and NESTEROFF (1955) envisaged the intervention of bacteria and organic matter in the induration, the latter provoking physico-chemical precipitation of amorphous limestone, which presumably is fragmented by wind and waves to form fine material. KUENEN (1933), EMERY & FOSTER (1948) and GINSBURG (1953) believed that evaporation took place in an inter-tidal zone, subsequent to solution by acidic waters. RUSSEL (1962), OTTMAN (1965), BLOCH & TRICHET (1966) believed that solution of limestone occurred through pluvial means and that phreatic nappes played a part.

For the Madeira-Porto Santo calcareous sands, HARTUNG (1864) thought that they were the result of trituration of fossil shells. On the other hand, MORAIS (1943) believed that purely physical means were more important than the intervention of life in the production of such. He remarked on the abundance of phosphate in all these weakly-cemented sands. In his view, submarine vulcanism, which initiated the islands, would raise the temperature of sea waters, thus provoking the precipitation of dissolved calcium carbonate. He referred to the paper by JOHNSON & WILLIAMSON (1916) wherein it was stated that sea water is saturated with calcium carbonate, that a variation in temperature or concentration of carbon dioxide in the adjacent air could cause the precipitation of carbonate. A change of 3 to 3.2 parts per 10,000 of carbon dioxide in the air would provoke the precipitation of 2 g of carbonate per cubic metre of saturated solution, whilst an increase in sea temperature of 2° C would yield the same result. Such a rise in temperature would result in a warmer current of sea water.

In the case of the Madeira archipelago, this raising of the sea temperature would arise above all from volcanic foci, thus supplying a steady implimentation of warmer water. It was presumed that bacterial products of ammonia would rob the carbon dioxide and oblige the carbonate to be precipitated.

MORAIS thus largely called upon physico-chemical processes. But MONTAGGIONI is more inclined to agree with the ideas of RUSSEL, BLOCH & TRICHET and OTTMAN. A tiny film is formed by precipitation of calcium carbonate in the contact zone of a phreatic nappe which is saturated with dissolved limestone, and the sea water. The fresh water, having percolated across carbonate rocks, is saturated in carbonates and bicarbonates. Its pH is basic, there is a high concentration of alkaline ions. By contrast, the sea water, which acts as the plugging or cushioning milieu, is almost neutral as regards pH. At the zone of contact, the abrupt fall in pH results in precipitation of calcium carbonate, such precipitation only being conceived as possible when fresh water is saturated in calcium salts after having percolated through carbonate layers. For the calcirudites of Ilheu de Cima, on the other hand, MONTAGGIONI would suggest rather physico-chemical plus biologic means – rapid evaporation of sea water in small pools inhabited by algae, diatoms, bacteria, as suggested by BLANC (1958).

Little chemical information, and such as it is very old, is available regarding calcareous deposits of the archipelago, either limestones or sands. MACAULAY (1840) and SCHWEIZER (1854) gave analyses of the Ponta D. Lourenço sands as follows:

| MACAULAY | % | SCHWEIZER | % |
|---|---|---|---|
| Calcium carbonate | 73.15 | Calcium carbonate | 84.29 |
| Diatomaceous earth | 11.90 | Magnesium carbonate | 5.48 |
| Calcium phosphate | 8.81 | Phosphate earth | 1.00 |
| Organic matter | 4.25 | Nitrogenous organic matter | 4.66 |
| | 98.11 | Water | 2.41 |
| | | Sand | 1.48 |
| | | | 99.32 |

SCHWEIZER (op. cit.) and HEER (1857) refer to lime masses in scoriaceous agglomerates in cliffs at Pico da Cruz, W of Funchal, and lime beds five feet thick associated with lavas, pyroclastics at Areeiro some 2 km W of the peak. From the latter area SCHWEIZER presented the following analysis of the limestone:

| | % |
|---|---|
| Silicic acid | 20.38 |
| Carbonic acid | 25.63 |
| Lime | 29.19 |
| Magnesia | 7.84 |
| Ferric oxide, phosphate, etc. | 0.36 |
| Organic matter | 4.76 |
| Water | 10.00 |
| Sand | 1.57 |
| | 99.73 |

He further commented that regarding the amount of oxygen, the quantity of carbonic acid is not sufficient to nourish the bases, lime and magnesia, so part of the latter have to be combined with silica. If we assume that all the lime combines with carbonic acid, then the rock contains 52.12% calcium carbonate, with 2.70% carbonic acid remaining for the magnesia. If further, magnesium carbonate is present as a neutral salt, $MgO, CO_2$, then 2.45% magnesia unites with carbonic acid. Under such assumptions then, the analysis would be:

| | % |
|---|---|
| Silicic acid | 20.38 |
| Magnesia bound to silica | 5.39 |
| Magnesium carbonate | 5.15 |
| Calcium carbonate | 52.12 |
| Ferric oxide, phosphate, etc. | 0.36 |
| Organic matter | 4.76 |
| Water | 10.00 |
| Sand | 1.57 |
| | 99.73 |

Rather low-grade lignite deposits, e. g. in Ribeira de S. Jorge, Paul da Serra, have long been known to scholars, much longer to the local inhabitants who used the material for fuel, but no explicit details are known of these occurrences. As mentioned further, in places plant remains have disintegrated into earthy ash material, seemingly on occasion measuring some tens of cms in thickness.

## Stratigraphy

As far as is known, the chronological succession and geographic distribution of sedimentary rocks within the archipelago are simple. MAYER-EYMAR (1864), from his studies of fossils occurring in the Ribeira S. Vicente, Madeira limestones and in similar rocks in Porto Santo and offshore islets, determined the age to be Vindobonian-Helvetian mostly. All later workers have confirmed a Vindobonian age, though some might be inclined to give equal prominence to the Tortonian.

The dune formations at Fonte da Areia (»Source of sands«), Porto Santo, were first determined by HARTUNG (1864) as being of Plio-Pleistocene age, because several terrestrial gastropod species were extinct and LYELL (1854) attributed such as always representing Tertiary. But when later most of these so-called ›extinct‹ forms were found to be living today, HARTUNG agreed to place these formations rather in the Quaternary, being chiefly so influenced by the studies of HEER (1857) on the dating of fossil plants in the Rib. S. Jorge, Madeira, which latter were placed in the Diluvium – i. e. Pleistocene.

Thus, as of the present, the only Tertiary in the archipelago is Middle Miocene.

The extensive calcareous sands, arenites, etc., all weakly-cemented sediments, are Quaternary in age. Further age refinement has not been attempted, but many fossils studied belong to the Holocene. MONTAGGIONI (1969) mentioned a radiocarbon dating of 14,000 years for Pelecypod shells (*Glycimeris pillosus*) dredged from a depth of 1,900 m off Madeira.

## Palaeontology

Palaeontological studies of the archipelago have been made by LOWE (1851, 1854), ALBERS (1854), HEER (1857), MAYER-EYMAR (1864), PAIVA (1867), WATSON (1873), WOLLASTON (1878), COTTER (1892), GIRARD (1892), JOKSIMOWITSCH (1911), COCKERELL (1922), NOBRE (1931), COX (in D'ORCHYMONT, 1936), MOURA (1961), LIETZ & SCHWARZBACH (1970) and the numerous papers of SILVA.

Though the initial stratigraphic dating of the archipelago was first obtained through the study of the Ribeira S. Vicente fossils, the greater numer of papers refer rather to fossil collections made in the Prainha area of Madeira and in Porto Santo.

As in other archipelagoes studied here, of significance is the great diversity of forms of the Helicidae family, many species of *Geomitra, Leptaxis* and *Helix* being represented amongst these terrestrial gastropods. These Helicidae all show affinities with European forms but are quite distinct from those of Equatorial Africa. MAYER-EYMAR considered the Prainha Quaternary gastropods to be marine, but all others have claimed they are of terrestrial origin. ALBERS described 10 species of Helicidae which are now extinct, from the Quaternary calcareous sands of Prainha, Madeira, and from the same region, WOLLASTON described 19 extinct species. SILVA commented that, judging from the fossil groups studied, especially the corals, echinoderms, *Spondylus, Lithothamnium* and *Amphistegina*, it was logical to assume that the Miocene deposits represented a reef formation formed under tropical conditions at depths not greater than 40 m. MOURA, from his study of the foraminifera, considered the fauna to be benthonic, representing a littoral aspect of shallow, warm waters. LIETZ & SCHWARZBACH stated that the marine Miocene fauna, especially the reef corals, indicated a somewhat warmer climate than today – on an average at least 2° C warmer than at present.

In the Ribeira S. Jorge, Madiera, HEER found fossil plants, later observed by HARTUNG, which differed little from modern plants on the island, which led him to consider them not older than Quaternary. Plant remains also occur at Paul da Serra, crumbling into ash. Those at the former locality have been transformed into low-grade lignite and evidently this lignite was exploited at one time.

The principal localities where fossils have been obtained include: Madeira: Rib. S. Vicente, Rib. S. Jorge, Prainha (Ponta de S. Lourenço), Caniçal, Paul da Serra; Ilheu de Baixo (behind Portinho, eastern slopes); Ilheu de Cima (Porto do Cais, Cabeço das Laranjas); Porto Santo: Rib. da Serra de Dentro, Pico Juliana, between Ribs. de Losna and da Quebrada, N of Pico dos Morenos, Ponta Calheta, Fonte da Areia, Ponta da Barbinha, in the small valleys flowing westwards opposite Ilheu de Ferro, the Quaternary littoral sands of the SE coast, etc. However, LIETZ & SCHWARZBACH indicate that fossil localities are more widespread in this island than hitherto believed. It is to be noted that to date no fossils have been reported from the steeper NW slopes of this island. In the Ribeira S. Vicente area of Madeira, corals occur at present elevations of 360-400 m, whilst on Porto Santo, highest occurrences of marine fauna lie at heights of 340-350 m on the slopes of Pico Juliana.

As the literature so often mentions the first dating of Madeira sedimentaries from the Rib. S. Vicente region from fossil studies made by MAYER-EYMAR (1864), but scarce ever mentions the particular fossils in question, we give a list here:

| | | | |
|---|---|---|---|
| 3 | *Clypeaster altus* LINN. | 1 | *P. multiformis* MAY. |
| 1 | *C. crassicostatus* AG. | 1 | *P. pilosus* LINN. (*Arca*) |
| 1 | *Cytherea madeirensis* MAY. | 2 | *Lima atlantica* MAY. |
| 1 | *Cardium comatulum* BR. | 3 | *Pecten nodusus*? LINN. (*Ostrea*) |
| 3 | *C. hartungi* BR. | 1? | *P. pesfelis* LINN. (*Ostrea*)? |
| 1 | *C. multicostatum* BROC. | 2 | *Spondylus inermis* BR. |
| 2 | *C. pectinatum* LINN. | 1 | *Monodonta aaronis* BAST. |
| 1 | *Chama gryphoides* LINN. | 1 | *Janthina hartungi* MAY. |
| 1 | *Lucina bellardiana* MAY. | 1 | *Turbinella paucinoda* MAY. |
| 1 | *L. interrupta* LAM. (*Cytherea*) | 1 | *Fasciolaria tulipiformis* MAY. |
| 1 | *L. lactea* LINN. (*Tellina*) | 3 | *Strombus italicus* DUCL. |
| 3 | *L. pagenstecheri* MAY. | 2 | *Cassis testiculus* LINN. (*Buscinum*) |
| 1 | *L. sinuosa* DON. (*Venus*) | 1 | *Conus puschi* MICHT. |
| 1 | *L. tigerina* (LINN.) (*Venus*) | 1 | *C. tarbellianus* GRAT. |
| 1 | *Pectunculus conjungens* MAY. | | |

1 = Very rare or one sample.
2 = Rare or two samples.
3 = From 3-10 samples.

From these he recognized 9 species as representing Mayencian (Pontian) or older, 12 of the Helvetian, 13 of the Tortonian and higher, 1, 2 and 1? representative of Mayencian, Helvetian and Tortonian only, respectively, and 10 of the Recent.

The fossil plant occurrence in the Ribeira do Meio, tributary of the Rib. S. Jorge, discovered by LYELL in 1854 (first fossil plant finds in Macaronesia) and studied by HEER, is likewise seldom itemized in the literature, and for general interest we list the findings here:

Pteris aquilina L.
P. cretica L.?
Trichomanes radicans Sw.
Woodwardia radicans Cav.?
Osmunda regalis L.
Asplenium marinum L?
A. bunburianum m.
Aspidium lyelli m.
Salix lowei m.
Myrica faya L. (Faya fragifera Webb)
Corylus australis m.
Ulmus suberosa Mönch.?
Oreodaphne foetens Ait. sp.

Clethra arborea L.
Erica arborea L.
Vaccinium maderense Link.
Vinca major L.
Myrtus communis L.
Ilex hartungi m.
Rhamnus latifolius Herit.
Pistacia phaeacum m.
Pittosporum?
Rosa canina L.?
Pesoralea dentata Dec.?
Phyllites (Rhus) ziegleri m.
Gramineen

Hartung (1864) also mentioned further collections made by a gentleman in 1859 from Ilheu da Vigia, in Porto da Cruz bay, where also fossilized wood occurs in tuffaceous beds with many pyrite nodules. Heer recognized Carex? and leaves of Rubus fruticosus L.

The Miocene strata of Porto Santo have yielded relatively rich fossil collections. The following have been reported by Mayer (1864), Cotter (1892a), Joksimowitsch (1911a), Silva (1956, 1959), and Lietz & Schwarzbach (1970).

Escharina biaperta Mich., E. incisa Milne-Edwards, Desmastraea mayeri From., D. orbignyana May., Phyllocaenia thyrsiformis? Mich., Astrocaenia fromenteli May., Heliastraea prevostana? M.-Edwards & Haime, H. reussana M.-Edwards & Haime, Danaia calcinata May., Rhabdocidaris sismondai May., Clypeaster altus Linné, C. crassicostatus Agassiz, Pericosmus latus Agassiz, Clavagella aperta Sowerby, Gastrochaena cuvieri May., G. gigantea Deshayes, Venus bronni May., Burdigalensis May., Cytherea madeirensis May., Cypricardia nucleus May., Cardium comatulum Brongn., C. hartungi Brongn., C. pectinatum Linné, Chama lazarus Linné, C. macerophylla Chemnitz, Diplodonta rotundata Montf., Lucina tigerina Linné, Cardita calyculata Linné, C. duboisi Deshayes, Pectunculus pilosus Linné, Arca lactea Linné, A. navicularis Brug., A. nivea Chemnitz, Lithodomus lyellanus May., L. moreleti May., Mytilus domengensis Lamarck, Pinna brocchi? d'Orbigny, Avicula crossei May., Perna soldanii Deshayes, Lima atlantica May., Spondylus delesserti Chenu., S. gaederopus Linné, Pecten burdigalensis Lamarck, P. latissimus Brocchi, P. reissi Brongn., Plicatula brownina May., Ostrea hyotis Linné, Hipponyx sulcatus Bors., Calyptraea porti-sancti May., Crepidula fornicata? Linné, Serpulorbis arenarius Linné, Vermetus intortus Lamarck, Vermiculus carinatus Hoern., Monodonta aaronis Bast., Neritopsis radula Linné, Natica redempta Micht., Cerithium nodolosum? Brug., Fasciolaria crassicauda May., F. nodifera Dujard., Tritonium costellatum May., Strombus italicus Ducl., Pseudoliva orbignyana May., Conus antiquus Lamarck, C. Borsoni May., C. calcinatus May., C. mercatii Brongn., C. reissi May., C. textile Linné, Cypraea argus Linné, C. brocchi Deshayes, C. pyrum Gmel., C. sanguinolenta Gmel., C. stenostoma May., C. stercoraria Linné, Serpula aulophora May., S. crenulosa May., S. elongata? Lamarck, Dendrophyllia ramea Blainv., D. cornigera Blainv., Heliastraea reussana? M.-Edwards & Haime, Danaia calcinata May., Venus cf. aglaurae Brongn., Venus multilamella

LAMARCK, *Chama gryphoides* LINNÉ, *Pectunculus multiformis* MAY., *Amphistegina haueri* D'ORBIGNY, *Clypeaster scilai* DESM., *Perna maxillata* var. *soldani* DESHAYES, *Radula lima* var. *dispar* MICHT., *Chlamys reissi* BRONN, *C. gloriamaris* var. *longolaevis*? SACCO, *C. noronhai* JOKSIM., *Aequipecten dentronensis* JOKSIM., *A. spinosovatus* SACCO, *A. tripartitus* JOKSIM., *Gigantopecten latissimus* BRONGN., *Amussiopecten burdigalensis* LAMARCK, *Parvochlamys* cf. *oolaevis* SACCO, *Spondylus brancai* JOKSIM., *S. baixonensis* JOKSIM., *S. noronhai* JOKSIM., *S. concentricus* BRONGN., *Alectryonia plicatula* var. *germanitala* DE GREY, *A. plicatula* var. *taurinensis* SACCO, *Pyncnodonta* cf. *brongniarti* BRN., *Septifer superbus* HÖRN., *S. oblitus* MICHT., *Lithophagus lyellianus* MAY., *L. papilliferus* JOKSIM., *L. moreleti*? MAY., *Arca tetragona* POLI, *A. tetragona* var. *perbrevis* SACCO, *A. clathrata* DEFRANCE, *Bathyarca pectuncoloides* var. cf. *septentrionalis* SARS., *Barbatia barbata* LINNÉ, *B. modioloides* CANTR., *Axinia pilosa* LINNÉ, *A. multiformis* MAY., *A. insubrinca* BROCCHI, *Codokia leonina* BAST., *Myrtea?* *(Lucina)* cf. *strigillata* REUSS, *Jagonia reticulata*? POLI, *Cerastoderma edule* var. *umbonata* WOOD, *Discor pectinatus* LINNÉ, *D. hartungi* MAY., *Callista madeirensis* MAY., *Omphaloclathrum miocenicum* MICHT., *O. aglaurae* BRONGN., *Ventricula multilamella* var. *taurominor* SACCO, *V. bronni* MAY., *Chamelaea gallina* var. *dertolaevissima* SACCO, *C. gallina* var. *janenschi* JOKSIM., *Psammophila oblonga* CHEMNITZ, *Tectura* cf. *taurinensis* SACCO, *Amalthea sulcata* var. *plioparva* SACCO, *Turitella bellardii* MAY., *Haustator tricinctus* BORD., *Cerithium vulgatum* var. *miospinosa* SACCO, *Zonaria pyrum* GMEL., *Z. sanguinolenta* GMEL., *Mandolina gibbosa* var. *mucronatoides* SACCO, *Oniscidia cythara* var. *postapenninica* SACCO, *Persona tortuosa* BORS., *Purpura rarisulcata* BELLARDI, *Murex borni*? HÖRNES, *Lyria magorum* BROCCHI, *Lamprodoma clavula* var. *subvittata* SACCO, *Sparella obsoleta* BROCCHI, *Lithoconus calcinatus* MAY., *L. antiquus* LAMARCK, *Conospirus dujardini* DESHAYES, *Chelyconus montisclavus* var. *mamillospira* SACCO, *Carcharodon megalodon*? AGASSIZ, *Amphistegina lessonii* D'ORBIGNY, *Ceratotrochus* cf. *duodecimcoctatus* GOLDFUSS, *Glycymeris multiformis* MAY., *Pedalion soldanii* DESHAYES, *Chlamys angelonii* DE STEF. & PANT., *C. costai*? FONTANNES, *Lima lima* LINNÉ, *Venus (Chione) multilamella* LAMARCK var. *taurorotunda* SACCO, *Olivella (Lamprodoma) cluvula* LAMARCK var. *subvittata* SACCO, *Lithothamnium* aff. *magnum* CAPEDER, *Dendrophyllia* cf. *amica* (MICHT.) *Caryophyllia* cf. *granulosa* DE ANG., *Palaeoplesiastraea* cf. *turonensis* (MICH.), *Lithophyllia* cf. *ampla* REUSS, *Ceratocyathus* sp., *Edwardsotrochus* sp., *Tarbellastraea* cf. *reussiana* M.-EDWARDS & HAIME., *Acanthocyatus* sp., *Balanus* sp.

## Geophysical Aspects

Some palaeomagnetic studies have been made of Madeira (WATKINS et al. 1966b; WATKINS & ABDEL-MONEM, 1971; WATKINS, 1973). Orientated samples of the extrusives largely in the eastern part of the island were studied. In Pliocene samples the average of the mean declination of remanent magnetism is 1.5° E of N, that of the mean inclination, –45° with respect to the horizontal. The average values for the latitude and longitude of the virtual magnetic poles resulting from declination-inclination figures are 84.5° N and 149° E of N, respectively. For Pleistocene samples, the average for the mean

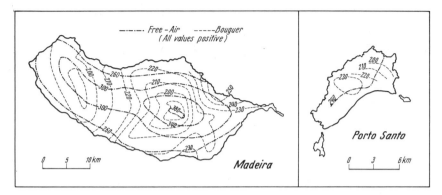

Fig. 51. Free-air and Bouguer anomalies, Madeira and Porto Santo. COELHO, 1968).

declination of remanent magnetism is 142° E of N, that of the mean inclination, –49° with respect to the horizontal. The latitude of the virtual magnetic pole is 82° N, the longitude, 150° E of N.

Madeira shows large areas of Upper MATUYAMA epoch (0.69–2.43 my). (Some K-Ar isotopic datings for Pleistocene samples give ages ranging from 0.74 to 1.64 my.) The GAUSS epoch (2.43 3.32 my) is substantiated by one isotopic date of 3.05 my.

Gravity surveys by COELHO (1968) are shown in Fig. 51. Free-air (FAYE) anomalies are less influenced by relief than BOUGUER anomalies, though of course both generally outline the broader aspect of the topography, to be expected as both are related to elevation above sea level. In areas of low relief the former anomalies are a direct measure of the degree of isostatic equilibrium; whilst in mountainous terrain they indicate a dependence upon relief which is related to regional compensation for the areal average elevation rather than the altitude of the observation site. On the other hand, BOUGUER anomalies throughout show an inverse dependence on regional elevation, and as the effects of surface masses are allowed for down to sea level, such anomalies then are chiefly related to deep compensating masses associated with changes in crustal structure and composition. In Madeira BOUGUER anomalies show lowest values where the highest terrain occurs (Pico Ruivo-Curral das Freiras region), high values trending N-S as a ›ridge‹ to the W of here, which includes Paul da Serra, and maximum values (more than + 260 mgals) in the Porto da Cruz area of the NE coast. In Porto Santo, maximum BOUGUER values are associated with a topographic ›saddle‹ extending NW-SE across the island and decreasing towards the NE where highest land lies. Hence BOUGUER anomalies do not reflect the topography-relief very closely whereas the Free-Air anomalies reflect this better, indicating that the former have a more intimate association with the nature of material at depth in portraying the gravitational effect of lateral density variations below sea level.

The interpretation of anomalies has no unique solution, for the anomalous property of the undetermined body is given by only certain limits, and further, for any specific property there are an infinite number of shapes and positions said body may take. The origin of gravity anomalies no less occur over a wide range of depths (not the case with magnetic anomalies), from near-surface to deep within basement rocks. This obviously means that before any quantitative study of gravity anomalies and a determined relation of such to geological disturbances can be undertaken it is necessary to isolate the anomaly from its background. Lacking such, as was also the case in the Azores (q. v.) we must therefore use all caution in correlating geological-geophysical cause and effect.

## Structure-Tectonics

As with other archipelagoes here, the literature makes frequent reference to fracturing, faulting, to account for the extensive cliffing, valley trends, scarps, etc., but as with other archipelagoes it is more likely that exogenic processes are more important. With a more pronounced relief than the Azores, greater rainfall than more southerly archipelagoes, the role of surficial agencies cannot be under-estimated, the more so when the rather spongy nature of the lavas and the copious development of pyroclastics is taken into consideration. From the high central topographic axis of the main island and the asymmetrically placed axis in Porto Santo, streams follow the direct, shortest paths down to the coasts, there are no valid reasons why they should do otherwise, and such linear paths are not to be thought of as fault controlled. Prominent scarps are erosional features, perhaps here and there fault-line scarps but proof is lacking that they represent fault scarps. Powerful marine erosion, loosening the ›toes‹ of slopes, promoting landslides, etc. more readily account for the pronounced cliffing. Mass gravitational movements result in very steep valley sides. Craters, calderas show plentiful evidences of the paramount importance of exogenic processes.

The many superb coastal and valley sections demonstrate the general horizontal nature of lava flows and pyroclastics, major foldings and faultings are not evident, which is not to say that more minor, superficial puckerings, wrinklings, slumpings, bendings, detaching of earth materials are lacking. The pronounced topographic features such as the craters-calderas of Curral de Freiras, Serra de Agua, Arco da Calheta, Arco S. Jorge, the Janela and Porto da Cruz valleys are the results of vulcanism and erosion rather than tectonic events. Calderas, especially that of Curral, have long been debated as to their origin, but the majority of workers favour a dominant role to erosion, though recognizing at least partial collapse due to magma withdrawal, and hence such are to be ascribed to volcano-erosive processes. Long ago DRUMONDO (1818) noticed that the Janela and Porto da Cruz streams were ›misfits‹, valleys too large to have been developed solely by running waters, that rather lava flows took advantage of minor depressions in the surface, to be followed by streams which excavated their beds in the lavas, so that such valleys are also of volcano-erosive origin. The valley of the Rib. Socorridos is considered as marking the site of fissuring associated with lava emissions, again not a fault valley. In toto then, the combined effects of vulcanism and exogenic processes are held responsible for structures, landforms within the archipelago.

However, the role of vertical movements is important, where we have Miocene limestones at elevations of 400 m, tilting of marine abrasion platforms, the separation of the Ilhas Desertas from the main island. But as per what is exposed and can be ascertained at shallower depths, such positive and negative movements have been en bloc, volcanic sequences show no great dislocations, deformations.

Whether Madeira-Porto Santo, Madeira archipelago-Iberia or then the archipelago with other Macaronesian archipelagoes were ever united has been much debated in the past, but we are no nearer solutions to these problems. The Madeira archipelago lies in the entrant between the Azores-Mediterranean seismic belt to the N and the Atlas seismic belt to the S, the islands lying about equidistant from the seismic foci of the 1755 Lisbon earthquake and the 1960 Agadir tremor. The archipelago also lies somewhat northward of the Alpine fold belt of the Atlas, but is a direct westward continuation of the great Guadalquiver trench of Spain (vd. Fig. 24). S of Madeira lies the Spanish Embayment, with waters over 4,000 m deep, trending NE-SW and heading into the Bay of Cadiz. South of this basin lie the Selvagen and Canary archipelagoes. To the NE of the Madeiras lie the seamounts of the Seine, Ampere, Josephina and Goringue banks on the northern edge of the Embayment, whilst to the S, aligned also NE-SW, are the Canary and Selvagens archipelgoes, the Dacia Banks or seamount. These seamounts are considered to represent guyots, truncated volcanic edifices built up on the sea floor. Thus N and S of the Spanish Embayment we have submarine features suggesting linkage of Madeira with Iberia, Canaries-Selvagens with Africa. The Canaries lie only some 100 km off the African coast at the nearest point, and likely this closer location to a mainland allows of more firm postulations (for the eastern Canary Islands at least) of continental affinities (vd. under Canary Islands). Porto Santo lies some 900 km distant from the nearest part of Iberia. For both the Canary and Madeira archipelagoes, biologists and palaeontologists repeatedly refer to mainland affinities of flora and fauna, migrations taking place along land bridges or intervening shallow seas, via current ›rafting‹ of various species, etc. To date, geological evidences other than palaeontological of a mainland (usually taken to be Iberia) linkage of Madeira are scant indeed, and such a concept is far from being accepted by all geologists cognizant with the general region in question. Strongly deformed strata in Fuerteventura, Canary Islands, may have resulted from more distant deformations associated with the Alpine orogeny of the Atlas, but no such similar powerful diastrophism is seen in Madeira, which may be due of course to greater distance, both longitudinally and transversely, from the belt of Alpine disturbance.

Instability characterizes the general Madeira-Canaries-mainlands area. Slopes down to the Spanish Embayment are steep, but whether these are fault scarps is not known, though such is the case for the Gloria Fault eastwards of the Azores somewhat to the N of Madeira (vd. Azores). We have drawn attention to the meeting, in this general area, of the American, Eurasian and African tectonic plates, the nudging, jostling, thrusting together of such engendering tectonic disturbance, with the postulating of lateral and vertical fault movements of large magnitude. Whether then the Madeira archipelago was once united with Iberia, the shallow banks representing all that suggests such linkage, or was once united with the Selvagens-Canary archipelagoes, now separated by the great subsidence block of the Spanish Embayment, such questions cannot be satisfactorily answered at this time. It will be noted from Fig. 24 that the magnetic quiet zone boundary follows offshore some 500 km or somewhat less the mainlands of

IberiaAfrica, lies E of Madeira and cuts about centrally through the Canary Islands. Such a boundary distinguishes disturbed (seaward) and more or less undisturbed (landward) magnetic fields, but at this time there are various interpretations as to what the relatively undistrubed magnetic field implies, and hence the tectonic significance of this feature remains open.

Eustatism, epeirogenic movements, isostatic adjustments, volcanic upbuilding have all certainly occurred in the Madeira arey, but within the islands themselves, there are scarce any evidences of faulting and folding, such en bloc movements as have occurred representing slow adjustments to stress fields or then if fracturing has occurred as sudden adjustments to stress fields, then such cannot be demonstrated in the field.

## Geologic Evolution

BOURCART (1946) and GRABHAM (1948) believed that the first generating submarine emissions in the Madeira area date from the beginning of the Cretaceous. In the Lower Cretaceous intense sedimentation took place on marginal oceanic plains and basins lying off the mainlands to the E. Geophysical studies in vicinal oceanic areas indicate the presence of three seismic reflecting horizons, at 570, 2,450 and 3,600 m below initial sea-bottom sediments. To MONTAGGIONI (1968), the lowest horizon possibly marks the boundary of the sima; the middle horizon marks the sial and the upper one, the sedimentaries. Sub-crustal currents caused magmas to ascend in regions of tension in the crust, and by the end of the Cretaceous, the arching of N. Africa-S. Iberia due to Alpine diastrophism, accentuated the marginal slopes of the socle, engendering stresses which gave rise to fractures, allowing further magma ascension. During the following thalassocratic stage further fissuring took place allowing magmas to break through the floor of the ocean and pour forth as submarine effusions, spilling over the Mesozoic sediments. Such conditions characterized the Palaeogene, and by the end of the Palaeogene, volcanics had built up to beyond sea level to create the primitive Madeira archipelago.

By early Miocene (perhaps even in later Oligocene times) the primeval islands were well established, in the case of Madeira proper froming a monogenic volcanic edifice now represented by the Pico Ruivo Complex. (This volcanic stage is presumed to occur at depth in Porto Santo.) Coral relief testifies to uplift, the building of a Miocene bioherm in a warm neritic environment. In deeper off-shore environments, below some 40 m in depth, *Globigerina* limestones of Vindobonian age were forming. Subsequent to the development of these biofacies, uplift of the islands occurred to varying elevations, with limestones now occurring as high as 400 m in Madeira, 350 m in Porto Santo. Contemporaneous with the formation of biogenic deposits there occurred diabasic, trachytic, doleritic intrusions, this volcanic phase representing the Vindobonian Volcanic Complex. In post-Vindobonian times effusions continued rather erratically, constituting the Paul da Serra Volcanic Complex. During this period also biodetritic limestones, lavas and pyroclastics were forming, a period of quiet emissions alternating with more violent episodes, development of reef organisms along coastal areas, erosion, transportation and deposition of biogenic deposits. The empiling up of

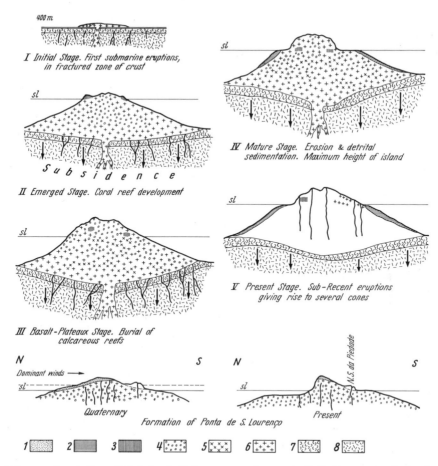

Fig. 52. Scheme of evolution of Madeira. 1: Calcareous marine sands. 2: Sedimentaries. 3: Reef limestones. 4: Pyroclastics. 5: Intrusives and extrusives. 6: Lavas. 7: Sial. 8: Sima. (Modified after MONTAGGIONI, 1968, based on GRABHAM, 1948).

these three Complexes during the Miocene (perhaps also into early Pliocene) put an extra stress on the crust, causing a downbuckling of the volcanic edifices which may have been of the order of two-three hundred metres. In post-Miocene times, trachytic lavas and tuffs some 600 m thick and plateau basalts some 400 m thick were developed. Of interest here is the occurrence in the Rib. S. Jorge (at 325 m elevation), also in the Paul da Serra, of horizontal fossilized plant beds and lignites, which are overlain by the above basalts, which latter occurred during the Pliocene but likely extend into the Quaternary, as the fossil flora is suggestive of the Quaternary. The pre-basalt surface was one of considerable relief, the lignites suggesting poorly-drained depressions, whilst coarse clastics – breccias, agglomerates, conglomerates – with a tendency towards angularity suggest scree or torrential deposition resulting from powerful erosion down steep slopes. Laterization is a common feature too of this pre-basalt surface. In

Quaternary times marine incursions of Sicilian and Tyrrhenian seas invaded the existing low, flat coastal areas, and in depressions here freshwater lakes formed which gradually dried out and furnished lacustrine deposits for aeolian re-working. The last transgression corresponds to the Flandrian cycle. These marine incursions left on the coasts biodetrital sands, these and the lacustrine deposits constituting important Quaternary deposits. Penecontemporaneous with these incursions the last vulcanicity was in progress, prolonged into sub-Recent times. The presence today of Quaternary marine terraces as high as 100 m result from a combination of both uplift and eustatic adjustments of sea associated with the Ice Ages.

Like all the archipelagoes, Madeira is essentially a product of Neogene times, the deciphering of earlier events being largely suppositional, and whether in truth we can hypothesize back to early Cretaceous times is highly questionable here in Madeira.

CHAPTER 6

# Geology of the Selvagens Archipelago

## General

The first geological information obtained of this tiny archipelago dates back some 80 years when COTTER (1892) described some fossils from here. GAGEL (1910, 1911) and FINCKH (1911) were the first to portray the general geology, especially igneous aspects.

To GAGEL the geology of the major island, Selvagem Grande, involved an older basement of phonolites, nephelinites and volcanic breccias, cut by basaltic dykes. Also present were projections or protuberances of fossiliferous limestones of marine detrital origin which he claimed were submarine ›veins‹ formed when the basement lay some 100 m below present sea level. The subsequent uplift and erosion of the basement gave rise to the Miocene sediments. When renewed vulcanism occurred, volcanic ash, lapilli and thick columnar basalts covered much of the sedimentaries, with here and there small lava excresences, small scoria and bomb cones.

FINCKH reported the occurrence and gave petrographic descriptions of phonolites, nephelinites, feldspathic basalts, limburgites and basaltic tuffs.

As per these authors, at least two volcanic phases could be determined: (a) an older, pre-Middle Miocene one, comprising phonolites and nephelinites, (b) a newer basaltic phase after the abrasion of the former.

Later studies show certain amendments, more refinement, but in essence the picture presented by GAGEL and FINCKH holds true today.

The early palaeontological studies and stratigraphic assignments of COTTER (op. cit.), BÖHM (1898) and JOKSIMOWITSCH (1911a) are accepted as of the present, though in this case almost no later work along these lines has been done.

## Igneous Rocks

As in all the archipelagoes discussed here, volcanics have overwhelming importance in the Selvagens. We may treat of our knowledge of such in chronological sequence, subsequent to the initial studies of GAGEL and FINCKH.

JÉRÉMINE (1939) published a short note on igneous samples which will be mentioned along with her later publications in due course. MORAIS (1940, 1948) studied some 150 rock samples from the archipelago from which he recognized phonolites, nephelinephonolites, nephelinites, tinguaitic-nephelinites, hornblende-nephelinites, melteigites, tauites of urtite-ijolite type, olivine-basalts, nepheline-basalts, devitrified basaltic lavas, peridotites, tuffs, palagonite tuffs, scoria, calcareous dyke rocks, marmorized limestones, calcitic limestones. He distinguished the following formations: (1) In Selvagem Grande, the basement is formed of nepheline-phonolites, well observed in southern coastal areas, and in the SE nephelinites occur. These are the oldest rocks present. (2) On these rocks are thick – some more than 10 m – calcareous sands, many of which penetrate fractures caused by vulcanism, so forming calcareous dykes. Basalts in contact with these are often spongy, much tuffaceous material and pumice, cinders, lapilli yield tuffaceous-argillaceous rocks up to 8 m thick. (3) Overlying these arenites, tuffs and pyroclastics are highly altered phonolites, ca. 50 m thick in the midst of which occur Miocene fossils. MORAIS thought that the arenites, fragmented pyroclastics were formed below sea level and later upraised when the island rose some 70 m. (4) The last eruptive episode gave rise to basaltic scoria forming such peaks as Atalaia. There also occurred numerous basaltic and peridotitic dyke injections. This basaltic episode more or less covered Selvagem Grande, except in S and SE coastal regions. (5) On these basalts are found calcareous sands and sandy soils, alteration products of basaltic scoria. These uppermost sands MORAIS thought were formed by aeolian action, winds coming from the N, when the coasts lacked their present pronounced cliffing. Selvagem Pequena and Fora are primarily constituted of a host of dykes both above and below sea level, aligned mostly NE-SW and NNW-SSE. The constituent rocks are similar to those in Selvagem Grande, but plutonics are absent except as small blocks pried loose by fluid dyke masses. At Pico do Veado and in Fora the rocks belong to the urtite-ijolite group. Basic rocks occur only as dykes in these two islets, there being no upper basaltic covering as in Selvagem Grande, and hence the last eruptive phase of the latter is lacking in Selvagem Pequena and Fora.

JÉRÉMINE (1939, 1950, 1951) recognized phonolites of two distinct groups: (i) abundant phenocrysts of nepheline, also haüyne, anorthose and many prisms of aegerineaugite, groundmass rich in nepheline, acicular aegerine and tiny microlites of feldspar, (ii) many very regular phenocrysts of nepheline, anorthose and haüyne less common, no augite, extremely fine matrix rich in nepheline and acicular aegerine, poor in feldspars. Typical phonolites are leucocratic, very feldspathic, though the trachytic and fluidal structure noted by FINCKH was not seen in the JÉRÉMINE samples. FINCKH also described amphibole-nephelinites not noted by JÉRÉMINE. The basalts in general have dark colours, compact and porous. The richness in augite and the association of nepheline, analcime and plagioclases caused JÉRÉMINE to name these rocks basanitic-nephelinitic-ankaramites. Within the basalts of Selvagem Grande are inclusions, not larger than some 5 cm, which are identical to the ›olivine nodules‹ mentioned by Lacroix (1907) in lavas of the 1906 Vesuvian outburst. In composition these Selvagens inclusions are lherzolites. Jérémine agreed with Lacroix in considering these as homogeneous inclusions or xenoliths, originating from deep zones where the magma is more basic than the basalt which pours out at the surface. But Jérémine did not believe that we could therefore postulate a crystalline basement in Selvagem Grande.

Barros (1961) has written of the petrography and petrochemistry of a small collection of ankaramites and phonolites from Selvagem Grande in the Geological Museum, Instituto Superior Tecnico, Lisbon. Chemical analyses, norms and Niggli parameters of three specimens are given in Table 26. Barros attempted some petrochemical correlations between the Selvagens, Canarias and Madeira, from which he postulated a closer link between the Selvagens-Canarias than with Madeira. In assessing such correlations, we must note that Barros gives data on only three Selvagens rocks, that he placed most emphasis for the Canarias on data furnished by Bourcart and Jérémine in 1937, since which time we have a vastly greater number of rock analyses for the Canarias.

A more recent study of the geology and petrography of the archipelago is that of Honnorez (1966) (Figs. 53, 54). For the major island, he describes in detail three sections (Table 27) at Enseada das Pedreiras (136 m section from sea level to summit of Pico dos Tornozelos), Enseada das Cagarras (from sea level to the astronomical marker at 104 m on the plateau) and at Enseada da Atalaia (183 m section from sea level to summit of Pico da Atalaia). For Selvagem Grande he postulated two volcanic episodes: (i) Green volcanics, occasionally tuffs, blackish dykes present, represented by his Formation A; (ii) Blackish tuffs (C2), pyroclastics (D1, D3) along with xenoliths and black lavas (D2). The lower ensemble comprises three types of volcanics: (a) Porphyritic green rocks, e. g. Cisterna Nova, Pta. da Atalaia, Pta. da Sepultura, Pta. de Leste. These rocks show many xenomorphic phenocrysts and hyaline automorphic phenocrysts scattered within a greenish matrix. When altered, the hyaline phenocrysts acquire a yellow-orange colour and the matrix changes to black. Within this type are to be placed the porphyritic nephelinitic phonolites. (b) Aphyric green rocks, e. g. Enseada das Cagarras, Enseada das Galinhas, Baixa da Pta. do Risco. These rocks show rare xenomorphic phenocrysts and some phenocrysts with hexagonal or rectangular shapes in a greygreen groundmass. When altered there occur small green colourings darker than the background which show a fluidal structure. Within this type are placed the aphyric nephelinitic tinguaites. (c) Intrusions of black volcanics, e. g. at Enseada das Cagarras. Rocks contain rare and small olivine phenocrysts in a highly vesiculated matrix, vacuoles filled with secondary white mineral matter. Here are placed porphyritic ankaramites.

The upper ensemble also comprises three groups: (a) Hyalotuffs (Formation C), massive, non-stratified accumulations of mostly non-coherent vitreous lapilli. On occasion the lapilli are cemented by secondary mineral encrustations and thus take on the appearance of tuffs. At Enseada das Pedreiras, formation C3 is entirely of submarine character. Honnorez, rather than employing the terms hyaloclastite, aquagene tuff, vitric tuff, subaqueous tuff, tuffite, preferred to coin the name hyalotuff for a rock,

Table 26    Petrographic data on rocks from Selvagen Grande (BARROS, 1962)

| | 1. | 2. | 3. |
|---|---|---|---|
| $SiO_2$ | 40.27 | 51.68 | 53.55 |
| $Al_2O_3$ | 13,73 | 20.66 | 20.80 |
| $Fe_2O_3$ | 9.03 | 3.14 | 3.11 |
| FeO | 3.12 | 1.64 | 0.74 |
| MnO | 0.12 | 0.08 | 0.22 |
| MgO | 7.92 | 1.88 | 0.61 |
| CaO | 11.91 | 2.99 | 1.42 |
| $Na_2O$ | 3.23 | 9.74 | 9.83 |
| $K_2O$ | 1.54 | 3.81 | 3.98 |
| $TiO_2$ | 3.60 | 0.86 | 0.58 |
| $P_2O_5$ | 1.16 | 0.07 | 0.10 |
| $CO_2$ | | | 2.04 |
| Cl | | | 0.14 |
| $H_2O+$ | 2.99 | 2.93 | 1.47 |
| $H_2O-$ | 1.47 | 0.55 | 1.18 |
| Total | 100.09 | 100.03 | 99.77 |

| | 1. | 2. | 3. |
|---|---|---|---|
| Or | 8.90 | 22.24 | 23.35 |
| Ab | 2.60 | 26.20 | 47.16 |
| An | 18.35 | 1.95 | 6.95 |
| Ne | 13.50 | 30.10 | 5.40 |
| $SiO_2CaO$ | 14.04 | 5.45 | |
| $SiO_2MgO$ | 19.80 | 4.70 | |
| Mt | | 2.55 | 1.39 |
| Il | 6.54 | 1.67 | 1.06 |
| Hm | 8.96 | 1.28 | 2.08 |
| Ap | 2.69 | | |
| Nc | | | 4.88 |
| Hl | | | 0.23 |
| En | | | 1.50 |
| Tn | 0.39 | | |
| C | | | 2.85 |
| Trit. $H_2O$ | 4.46 | 3.48 | 2.65 |
| Total | 100.23 | 99.62 | 99.50 |

| | 1. | 2. | 3. |
|---|---|---|---|
| k | 0.23 | 0.20 | 0.21 |
| mg | 0.56 | 0.43 | 0.22 |
| Q | 17.4 | 21.3 | 25.0 |
| L | 35.5 | 65.5 | 67.5 |
| M | 47.1 | 13.2 | 7.5 |

1. Basanitic Ankaramite; 2. Muritic Phonolite; 3. Muniongitic Phonolite.

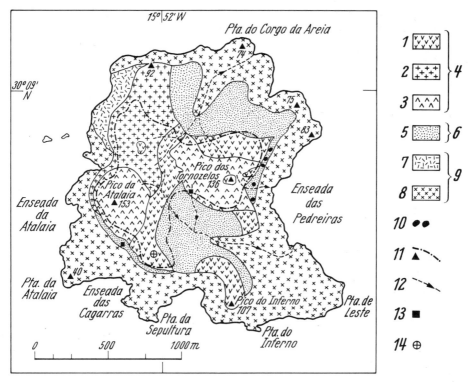

Fig. 53. Geological map of Selvagem Grande. 1: Basaltic lavas. 2: Consolidated basaltic pyroclastics. 3: Loose basaltic pyroclastics. 4: Upper volcanics. 5: Conglomerates, tuffs, limestones.
6: Intermediary sediments. 7: Phonolitic tuffs. 8: Phonolitic lavas. 9: Lower volcanics. 10: Fossil
localities. 11: 100 m contour (heights in m). 12: Valleys. 13: Cisterns. 14: Astronomical marker.
(Geology after HONNOREZ, 1966, and based on enlargement of Topographic Map 1 : 50,000 of
Inst. Geogr. e Cad., Lisbon, 1970).

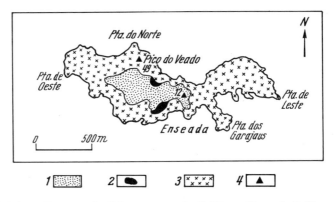

Fig. 54. Geological map of Selvagem Pequena. 1: Calcareous sands. 2: Tinguaitic-nephelinitic
phonolite dykes. 3: Pyroclastic agglomerate, dykes of ankaratite and nephelinitic tinguaite.
4: Heights in m. (HONNOREZ, 1966).

Table 27

Stratigraphic sections, Selvagem Grande (adopted from HONNOREZ, 1968)

| Formations | | Enseada das Pedreiras (136 m) | Enseada das Cagarros (104 m) | Enseada da Atalaia (183 m) |
|---|---|---|---|---|
| Formation D | D3 | Basalt lava flow. 30 m (90–136 m) | | Scoria, lapilli, bombs. Rich in xenoliths. Dips 27–30° to S & W (85–183 m) |
| Formation D | D2 / D2b | Basic lava. 7 m (95–104 m) | Basic vesicular lava. 5 m | Thin lava flows and lapilli. 5–10 m |
| Formation D | D2 / D2a | | | Olivine-rich basalt, at base scoriaceous. 1,5 m |
| Formation D | D1 | Scoria, lapilli, bombs. up to 10 m | | Scoria and lapilli. 0,5–1 m |
| | | Coarse lapilli. 10–15 cm | | |
| | | White limestone. 2–3 m | | |
| Formation C | C3 | Coarse, highly porous tuff. 1 m (80–90 m) | Coarse tuff. 5 m (90–95 m) | Stratified tuff. 0,5 m (ca. 80–85 m) |
| Formation C | C2 | Orange tuffite. 0,5 m | | Coarse orange tuff. 5 m |
| Formation C | C1 | White tuffite. Up to 10 cm | | |
| Formation B | B2 | Calcareous tuff. 10 m (75–80 m) | Stratified calcareous tuff. ±10–12 m (80–90 m) | Conglomerate-elements from A. 0,5 m |
| Formation B | B1 | Conglomerate-elements from A and dykes. ±0,5 m | Conglomerate-elements from A. ±0,5 m | |
| Formation A | | Green volcanics, altered rocks of phonolitic type. ±75 m (0–75 m) | Ditto, cut by calcareous dykes. ±80 m (0–80 m) | Green volcanics, altered rocks of phonolitic type. 80 m (0–80 m) |

consolidated or in the process of such, formed by the accumulation of basic vitreous lapilli resulting from subaquatic volcanic explosions. (b) Lavas and basic necks (Formation D2), e. g. at Pico dos Tornozelos. The rocks are jointed lavas, with many nodular crystals of olivine dispersed in an aphyric black matrix. This group includes porphyritic nepheline-basalts, aphyric basalts and porphyritic ankaramites. (c) Inclusions in Formation D3. Here occur peridotites, jacupirangites, also diopsidic augites, magnetites and titano-magnetites, also tuffaceous blocks.

In Selvagem Pequena occur basal pyroclastic agglomerates of vesicular lapilli. Mesocratic inclusions are common and may attain sizes of 20 cm diameter. These agglomerates are cut by vertical dykes, but as distinct from MORAIS, HONNOREZ informs us that the latter have N-S and E-W trends. So numerous are these dykes that they all but defy counting. In thickness they vary from a metre to several decimetres and include porphyritic and aphyric feldspathoidal ankaratrites, porphyritic-nephelinitic tinguaites, porphyritic-nephelinitic-tinguaitic-phonolites and shonkinites.

In Selvagem Pequena only two geological units are evident, a lower volcanic series represented by pyroclastic agglomerates and the network of dykes, and an upper sedimentary formation represented by calcareous sands. The lower units of both islands are taken to be correlatives, i. e. the agglomerates and the 50 m thick nephelinitic-tinguaitic-phonolite dykes of Selvagem Pequena and the phonolitic lavas of Selvagem Grande. On the other hand, the upper basaltic formation of Selvagem Grande is absent in the smaller island.

Igneous phenomena in the archipelago can be summarized thus: (1) The eruptives of the two islets belong to the same petrologic family, derived from the same sodic magma. (2) The oldest eruptives are represented by phaneritic xenoliths – jacupirangites and shonkinites. (3) Magmatic evolution involved first the development of sodic lavas poor in calcium and deficient in silica, the episode ending with alkcalcic lavas tending towards silica saturation. (4) The Atlantic character of the lavas has a tendency to diminish with time.

From the scarce data available regarding the igneous rocks of the archipelago, one can only attempt one or two petrochemical observations.

The K-mg diagrams would show a quasi-constancy in the K parameter whilst the mg parameter varies some 45 units.

The QLM diagram shows a grouping of points within the FRL triangle, i. e. subsaturated alkaline, though the trend is towards the supersaturated tephriticphonolites, present in other Macaronesian archipelagoes. This trend approximates after the fashion of that for the Canary Islands and is quite distinct from that for Madeira which latter shows a grouping along the RF line, i. e. $\alpha = 0$. On this basis one is inclined to associate the Selvagens with the Canaries rather than Madeira, but such can only be considered as very tentative, further studies are needed for the Selvagens.

## Sedimentary Rocks

These include calcareous sands, limestones and such hybrid material as tuffs, conglomerates and lapilli with calcareous cementation. The relative wide distribution within Macaronesia of extensive and at times thick accumulations of calcareous sands, arenites, etc. is a notable feature, especially in the Canarias and Madeira as also in the Selvagens, and more will be said on this topic later. For the last-named archipelago it is to be noted that calcareous arenaceous material may occur either as dykes and veinlets or then as deposits of considerable areal extents. On occasion the veined and dyked deposits acquire a relatively hard, compact appearance and the distinction between such, sandy limestones and limestones is often far from clear. As already noted, it was the opinion of MORAIS that these calcareous sands had a subaquatic origin, that uplift of the basement combined with aeolian action is likely responsible for their areal occurrences, the veined and dyked occurrences perhaps being due to infilling of cracks in the volcanics maybe even before the latter had completely cooled thus resulting in a ›metamorphism‹ of these calcareous sands and acquiring of more limestone features. Some dykes of these sands are more than a metre thick, and bedded occurrences are as much as + 10 m thick. Many of these calcareous sands show abundant kaolin, clays, and post-basalt material is often copiously mixed with *Helix* shells.

Some limestones are distinctly crystalline, may be moderately coarsely grained, finegrained, or then sandy and friable. GAGEL mentioned that at the sharp boundary of fine-grained white limestone and greyish-yellow disintegrated dolomite there is always a multiple deposit of beautifully crystallized calcite precipitated. Both the dykes and veins of calcareous sands and limestones may on occasion protrude so as to give the appearance of ruined walls of some ancient town or village. On occasion the limestones may show various degrees of marmorization. MORAIS contended that some dykes are dolomitic and also siliceous, that not always were the dykes and veins the result of infilling from the top but that in some instances calcareous material was injected from a volcanic focus.

Calcareous cementation of pyroclastics, conglomerates and breccias is a very common feature – indeed one might say this is the normal situation. The rudaceous deposits may be up to 7 m thick.

## Palaeontology

COTTER recognized the following fossils: *Nerita connectens* FONTANNES, *N.* aff. *galloprovincialis* MATHERON, *N. plutonis*? BAST., *N.* sp., *Lucina bellardiana* MAYER. BÖHM identified: *Nerita martiniana* MATHERON, *N. selvagensis* n. sp., *Ormastralium* aff. *carinatus* BORS. sp. var. *prohenica* SACCO, *Oxystele* aff. *amedei* BRONGN. sp. var. *magnoelata* SACCO, *Cabralia schmitzi* n. gen. n. sp. and *Rissoa* sp. In neither case are exact localities given, but we presume the faunal finds were from Selvagem Grande.

JOKSIMOWITSCH studied faunal remains from ›fossilführenden Sande‹ in the larger island. His sketsch-map shows localities where obtained – on the cliff-face fronting on to Enseada das Pedreiras – but in a postscript (1911b) to this paper, he remarked that

GAGEL had told him that the southern coastal sites shown by JOKSIMOWITSCH (in the bay E of Pta. da Sepultura) represent actually marine terraces. JOKSIMOWITSCH listed thirteen species: 65 of *Cabralia schmitzi* J. BÖHM, 30 of *Nerita martiniana* MATHERON, 30 of: *N. selvagensis* J. BÖHM, 12 of *Littorina neritoides* LINNÉ, 4 of *Oxystele böhmi* JOK., 2 of *Gibbula* sp. one each of *Gastrana mayeri* JOK., *Gibbula schmitzi* JOK., *Janthina hartungi* MAYER, *Tectarius nodulosus*? GMELIN, *Cerithium rugosum* WOOD, *Purpura sismondae* MICHT., *Fasciolaria* sp. Gastropodes greatly predominate over Bivalves. The *Tectarius* and *Cerithium* specimens came from Recent material in the N of the island.

JÉRÉMINE mentioned limestones rich in Foraminifera and Melobesiae. Rotalidae, Amphisteginidae and Textularidae can be recognized. Larger foraminifera are visible to the naked eye – *Robulus* and *Lepidocyclina*.

SILVA believed that the Quaternary calcareous sands were more likely of dune origin, and in these occur a great quantity of shells and shell fragments of a Helicidae, which he identified as *Theba pisana* MÜLLER 1774. *Euparypha macandrewiana* PFEIFFER is also noted (MORAIS). Such terrestrial gastropods supported SILVA's contention of a terrestrial origin for the calcareous sands, etc.

## Stratigraphy

BÖHM, on the basis of correlations with data of MAYER-EYMAR (1864) for the Azores, Madeira and Porto Santo, and ROTHPLETZ & SIMONELLI (1890) for Gran Canaria, took the age of the fossiliferous sediments to be Miocene. JOKSIMOWITSCH likewise postulated a Miocene age, by analogy with Gran Canaria – the Second Mediterranean Stage of SUESS, the beds being likely transgressive Tortonian. JÉRÉMINE, on the basis of the foraminiferal content, would suggest either Oligocene or then Lower Miocene. GAGEL, MORAIS, SILVA and HONNOREZ all accepted a Miocene age for the sediments of the Selvagens, presumably Vindobonian.

## Economic Geology

There is no record of any economic exploitation of mineral resources within the archipelago. However, JÉRÉMINE mentioned in the samples she studied specimens of phosphate and gypsum.

Under the microscope the former showed a concretionary structure, with large isotropic spherulites surrounded by a fibrous mineral or then finely laminated matter. A chemical analysis (reduced to 100) showed the following: $P_2O_5$ 33.39; CaO 1.54; $Al_2O_3$ 13.61; $Fe_2O_3$ 18.49; ignition loss 32.97, without taking into account some 40% $SiO_2$. The CaO is due to calcite. The specimen then is a phosphate of alumina and iron. The ferroaluminous phosphate barrandite is the only phosphate which closely approaches this specimen. JÉRÉMINE had no indications as to how the phosphate was formed, but doubtless this is a guano deposit, for many birds nest on the islets.

An earthy block was also examined, yellowish in colour, soft to the touch, adhering to the fingers slightly, easily reduced to powder, recalling closely randannite, a diatomaceous deposit. A chemical analysis showed: $SO_3$ 46.04; CaO 31.40, plus ignition losses of 1.80 (100° C) and 10.40 (1,000° C). The specimen is thus a sulphate of lime, with traces of phosphate, etc. The formation of such is likely due to evaporation of sea water in lagoons either in Recent or then Tertiary times. Well-crystallized gypsum crusts are known from the plentiful natural and artificial caves within the islets.


## Geological Evolution

In Selvagem Grande we can recognize four important geological events. The first episode involved phonolitic-type vulcanism, forming the basement of the island. These were viscous lavas, forming blisters, large dykes and sills, more rarely lava flows. With such material the construction of the island began, and there is no evidence to date of a crystalline socle. These phonolitic-type rocks are found today up to 80 m above sea level. Subsequent to the formation of such rocks there occurred dyke intrusions of feldspathoidal rocks with very large phenocrysts of hornblende. What might have been the volcano-tectonic and/or isostatic movements of the island at this time cannot be deciphered, but evidently this first event resulted in emergence long enough for an elevated abrasion surface to develop and coastal sedimentation to occur, forming the conglomerates at the base of the other sedimentaries, these conglomerates comprising phonolitic-type rocks having calcareous cementation.

The second episode was the formation of marine sediments during a period of volcanic quiescence. These strata are of Oligocene or Lower-Middle Miocene age.

The third event was renewed vulcanism, this time of basic character, represented by basaltic tuffites and basalts. This phase began with a brief period of submarine explosive activity, as evidenced by the quasi-continuous hyalotuffs. There followed a mixed monogenetic type of vulcanism, with the formation of volcanic cones formed of tuffs, loose and welded ejectamenta, basanitic basalts, ankaramites, etc. Alternating with this explosive activity were brief periods of quiet effusions, represented by flows of basalt and nephelinitic-basalt. As calcareous tuffs, hyalotuffs and limestones are now found at elevations up to some 90 m, uplift of the island to this amount is postulated.

The fourth and last period is concerned with the formation of Quaternary calcareous sands, sandy soils, found in the tableland interior and some lower coastal areas. For Selvagem Grande, opinion seems to favour an aeolian origin for such at a time when present pronounced cliffing was absent or nearly so, in order that material could be upswept to higher interior locations. If indeed such be the origin of these Quaternary deposits, and if the present cliffing was all-but non-existent during time of formation, then Quaternary times must have witnessed a second uprise after that responsible for the upraised marine Tertiary sediments. Marine terraces with a marine molluscan fauna of Quaternary age are now found 7 m above present sea level and the highest subRecent fossils occur some 3–4 m higher. Whether or not this second uplift was purely of isostatic origin cannot be determined. MORAIS favoured eustatic movements to explain the 70 m-raised-to–20 m deep submarine platform in Pliocene-Quaternary times, that such movements ended before the second eruptive phase, that the upraised fossil Tertiary beds occurred during or after the Miocene.

CHAPTER 7

# Geology of the Canary Archipelago

## General

Of all the Middle Atlantic archipelagos none has been studied, visited by more scholars than the Canary Islands. It follows therefore that the bibliography relating to these islands is much more extensive, and at the present time it also seems that more work is being done here than elsewhere within Macaronesia. Differing again from the other archipelagoes is the relatively wide international interest shown. German scholars in particular have been drawn to these islands, beginning with von Humboldt and continuing down to the present, including such names as von Buch, Hartung, von Fritsch, Reiss, Sauer, Rothpletz, Sapper, Knebel, Finckh, Gagel, von Wolff, Rothe, Schmincke, Klug, to mention the chief personalities. We no less find American, British, Portuguese, French, Belgian, Italian, Swiss, Austrian, Polish and Finnish scholars, not to mention a large number of Spanish scientists.

Not all islands have been studied to the same extent, Hierro and Gomera, for example, have been given much less attention than say Gran Canaria or Fuerteventura. The four eastern islands have acted more as magnets than the three western islands, though many scholars have taken extra time to visit, if not study, the truly spectacular Caldera de Taburienta in la Palma.

Over the years the Finnish geologist, Prof. Hans Hausen has carried out surveys of all the islands, publishing his monographs between 1955 and 1973. This laborious undertaking, carried out mostly alone, has yielded a most worthy and valuable contribution to our knowledge of the archipelago. His maps, however, are all of very small scale, some of rather indifferent quality, and generally of limited value in trying to follow the many detailed traverses he describes.

In 1961 Blumenthal presented a useful synthesis along with an interesting chart showing stratigraphic correlations of the various volcanic series of the various islands.

In 1968 there appeared a welcome change, a study by Klug treating rather of the morphology of the different islands, considerable attention being given to palaeontologic matters.

For the Symposium of the International Association of Volcanology held in the Canary Islands in 1968, Fuster et al. (1968) prepared up-to-date accounts and large-scale geological maps for Lanzarote, Fuerteventura, Gran Canaria and Tenerife. These monographs are almost entirely related to igneous matters, very little indeed being said on any other phases of Geology. One useful feature adopted here is the naming of volcanic formations by Roman numerals, Basaltic Series I, Basaltic Series II, etc. rather than the more cumbersome habit of using geographical-petrologic appellations. In perusing these monographs, however, one cannot avoid noticing the pedantic, didactic attitude adopted, the frequent censorious comments, the tendency to dogmatism, the depreciatory remarks made about the views of others. One would have preferred a somewhat more respectful vocabulary, the more so as these ›others‹ in turn have found plenty to critisize but in more temperate language.

During the past six-seven years, many more individual publications have appeared, mostly related to igneous geology, team efforts are underway, and all told, interest and work in this archipelago continues at a brisk pace.

## Geomorphology

Remarks bearing on the geomorphology of the archipelago have been made in the chapter on Geography, but we would make some further observations here.

The role of exogenic processes in moulding landscapes is usually dominant, but in the Canary Islands we must reckon not only with the agencies of marine and terrestrial erosion and deposition, aeolian transportation and deposition, differential weathering on various rypes of rocks, but also with vulcanism, often of violent explosive nature, the influence of deep fracturing, positive and negative movements of the islands, downward gravitational movement of earth materials. All such have been involved to varying degrees to yield the present landscapes and landforms.

In these volcanic islands, volcanic landforms dominate the scene, some of which we shall mention.

Cinder cones, whether adventitious or otherwise, dot the landscape in all islands, in places occurring so close together as to give a lunar appearance. Composed of ash and cinders, they are highly permeable and thus allow of the ready infiltration of meteoric waters thus tending to preserve their external appearance. But often atmospheric alteration of the surface has formed more compact clayey-calcareous carapaces which are much less permeable, here running water can etch out their courses, winds can transport loose, dry materials, so that their virginal state is seldom recognized. The smooth, less steep slopes present more aesthetically pleasing hills. In Fuerteventura and Lanzarote Quaternary and Recent cinder cones are very common. Cumulo-volcanoes result from the emissions of more viscous lavas whereby lateral spreading is reduced, instead flows pile up one on top of the other. Trachytic-syenitic vulcanism in particular results in notable examples of such, accompanied by pumaceous products forming lightcoloured aprons over the domes so created. Examples of such are to be seen e. g. by Pico Teide, Tenerife, Montana de Horno, Gran Canaria.

Strato-volcanoes show distinct interlayering of pyroclastics and flows. Cinder and scoria cones occur usually in the upper reaches of such structures, acting as ›safety valves‹ for the central emissions. Because it has been partially destroyed, leaving impressive interior cliffs, El Golfo, Hierro shows the remains of a large strato-volcanic structure.

Plugs, necks, spines, spatter cones are all arresting features by their sheer prominence, protruding markedly above the general surface to be visible far off. Plugs, necks, spines, formed by the more sluggish upward squeezing of lava through the conduit, their height being emphasized by differential erosion, attract attention by the precipitousness of their bare slopes, forming great monoliths or ›roques‹. In the islands of Gran Canaria (Roque Nublo stands 80 m high), Tenerife and Gomera especially these are outstanding. Less significant spatter cones (hornitos) of prominent irregular beehive shape frequently lend an almost eerie aspect to barren landscapes.

Although as will be mentioned later we subscribe to the view that exogenic rather than tectonic processes have been more active in creating the various landscapes, in certain islands, e. g. Gran Canaria, some massifs, such as Tamadaba and Guia, do have the characteristics of volcano-tectonic horsts, upraised volcanic blocks bounded by steep slopes, whose origin is conceived to have been the converse of collapse calderas. Such massifs have the characteristics of block mountains, a laccolithic-type of intrusion forcing its way upwards, uparching the roof and eventually being ›relieved‹ by faulting along its edges resulting in the marked abrupt change in elevation and the steep slopes.

The Spanish term ›malpais‹ refers to lava fields showing a chaotic surface appearance, with irregular blocks and slabs, sharp edges and corners, rounded and linear depressions, a hummocky, jagged terrain most difficult to traverse by any means. The meaning ›bad land‹ applies appropriately to such regions left in their natural state, but where Man has taken the effort to clear, break-up, level-off such land it can be useful agriculturally. Older and younger ›malpaises‹ can be found throughout the archipelago, showing varying degrees of natural and artificial alteration. In the vicinity of Chinyero volcano in Tenerife, Tinguaton, Lanzarote, and many other localities these inhospitable deserted areas can be seen.

Craters and calderas are well represented, especially the former. Craters, nested and otherwise, form the summits of many conical structures – in fact almost all cinder-scoria cones. The Spanish word ›caldera‹ (cauldron) is believed to have first entered the geological vocabulary when von Buch used the term during his visits to the islands in the early 19th century. In some languages, e. g. Portuguese, distinction is usually not made between craters and calderas, but in English calderas are always considered to have greater dimensions than craters. In the Canary Islands occur some calderas of world renown, e. g. those of Las Cañadas, Tenerife, Taburiente, La Palma, also lesser known ones of El Golfo, Hierro, Tirajana and Tejeda in Gran Canaria, Caldera Blanca, Lanzarote, Barranco Laja, Gomera and several in Fuerteventura. These tremendous scooped-out depressions with their towering curvilinear walls, ›holes in the ground‹ which allow one to peer deep into the interior of islands, have always drawn the attention of the layman and scientist alike. As we shall see, in these features also, exogenic processes are thought to have played a greater role than for example subsidence.

The above listing refers only to forms of volcanic origin, but note must be taken of other aspects and features of geomorphologic interest. ›Cuchillos‹ are long, narrow hill or mountain ranges with sharp crests. Outside of valley glaciated regions with their arêtes, the Canary Islands offer as good a region as any to observe the remarkable abruptness and narrow-pointed nature of ranges. Flanked on either side by deep gorges or then calderas and caldera-like depressions, the ›cuchillos‹ are striking landforms and offer great difficulties – at least as regards vehicles – in getting from one lower region to another. Most often such ranges are formed through the drastic erosion by running water of basaltic flows, very often intercalated with pyroclastics, such that slope profiles have a crude ›stepped‹ appearance, lavas forming steeper portions thereof. Rock composition and structure play very minor roles in the evolution of ›cuchillos‹; trenchant erosion by running water plus downhill gravitational movements are the real agents responsible.

Narrow-crested ridges, deep narrow valleys, gorges testify to the importance of fluvial erosion. During the greater part of the year valleys are dry or carry very little water and thus destruction by running water is distinctly limited on a time basis per annum, but smallness of area combined with relatively high average elevations for the islands means that at times of rain, running waters seek direct, short paths to the sea, they become torrential streams capable of eroding drastically, high velocities gave them great transporting abilities. Uprise of the islands and/or fresh outpourings of lavas have resulted in repeated rejuvenations of the landscape, re-invigorating the streams, maintaining them as powerful agents of erosion and transportation. Vertical corrasion takes command, swiftly streams hasten seaward, rejuvenations tending to maintain steep longitudinal profiles, transverse profiles are steep no less. Under such conditions then the effects of lateral corrasion are negligible, deposition is negligible, meandering rivers, flood plains are all but non-existent, narrow valleys are choked with transported material of all sizes awaiting the next onset of rains when fast-flowing streams will again nudge the heterogeneous mass further downstream and eventually out to sea. Lava flows, plugs, dykes, tors of Recent and Quaternary age show the ravages of erosion by running water to an almost alarming degree, yet further proof of the all-powerful role of stream erosion.

Due rather to erosive effects than tectonic causes, the steep slopes have acted as the ›triggers‹ for the downward gravitational motion of earth materials, with abundant landslides, rock falls, creep, flow, etc. (HAUSEN 1971). Such movements are of course aided by groundwaters acting as lubricants at depth, and no less by the extensive vulcanicity the islands have experienced when this was of explosive type. Such gravitational movements, along with stream erosion, are held as more likely agents forming the calderas, and even some valleys, e. g. Orotava and Guimar in Tenerife, are thought to have been chiefly formed as a result of such gravitational earth movements, streams transporting away dislodged materials.

Coastal scenery no less shows the importance of marine erosion, as well as landslide, etc. effects. Along many coastal sections in all islands great cliffs occur. Deep water lies in-shore, no reef barriers or off-shore islands-islets (except in the case of Lanzarote) and thus the main islands are open to the full force of the waves. Islands slope down generally steeply to the coast, marine action attacking the ›toes‹ of such slopes, promoting landslides, etc., waves transport away the loosened material, attack again.

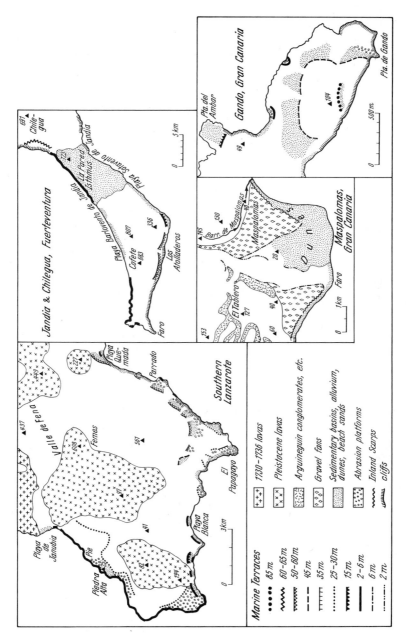

Fig. 55. Marine terraces and coastal features in some Canary Islands. (Modified after KLUG, 1968).

Sometimes there is a protecting barrier of talus between island slopes and the sea edge, slopes rising steeply upward further inland, in which case there occur somewhat broader, low regions, some of which are old marine terraces. The dominant winds come from the northern sector, storms originate westward out in the Atlantic. It follows then that these parts of the islands show more pronounced cliffed coasts, e. g. Famara in N. Lanzarote, eastern Anaga, Tenerife, NW and NE coastal parts of Hierro. By contrast, southern and southeastern exposures receive less rain, seas are somewhat quieter, here only are their possibilities for estuarine-delta type of low coasts, e. g. Maspalomas, Gran Canaria, Las Playas, Hierro, Sotavento de Jandia, Fuerteventura.

The action of winds in promoting deflation and abrasion are not significant within the archipelago, but wind transportation and deposition are notable. Long, warm, dry periods desiccate the surface materials – soils, loose rock material – and thus the everpresent winds can readily pick up the finer particles. Where strong on-shore winds occur, e. g. northern-eastern regions, such material can be carried quite far inland, as much as some 7–8 km in the case of Lanzarote. Though perhaps much transported material is deposited in the vicinal seas, some is deposited on the islands, to form dunes, sand sheets, etc. Thus we have the dunes of Lanzarote, so tediously pictured in travel brochures, of matronly ladies and paunchy gentlemen riding camels over the dunes into the setting sun. These ›jables‹ areas comprise both fossil and living dunes. The former occur at heights up to nearly 300 m, the ultimate source of these calcareous dune sands believed to be Quaternary marine shells and foraminiferal ooze. Active dunes tend rather nearer the coasts. Sand sheets are common on most islands; often in the quieter southern sections thereof.

These unstable islands have experienced repeated rejuvenations of the landscape, vigorous denudation has been maintained, weathering has chemically and physically broken down the rock material, making it more susceptible to erosion. Such instability of the islands has then allowed them to preserve their youthful character, and almost everywhere the geomorphological cycle is in a state of ›eternal youth‹. Yet, being relatively small islands, of volcanic composition, this youthful character is not identical with that associated with continental regions. Everything here in these islands seems to be condensed both in time and in space. Only in the eastern islands of Lanzarote and Fuerteventura does one find suggestions pointing rather to maturity. Stratigraphic and isotopic data indicate that geologically these islands are older than the others; the stage of geomorphological development confirms this.

## Igneous Rocks

The pioneer investigator of the Canary Islands rocks was VON BUCH (1825), a pupil of WERNER and hence a ›Neptunist‹. Though many of his concepts and conlusions regarding vulcanism and the volcanics may make rather curious reading today, he but reflected the ideas of his time and so cannot be censured on such scores. VON BUCH's studies related in particular to Lanzarote, Gran Canaria, Tenerife and La Palma, little attention was given to Fuerteventura and Hierro and scarce a mention of Gomera.

WEBB & BERTHOLET (1839) made a large collection of samples from various islands,

Table 28                      Chemical analyses of volcanic rocks, Canary Islands

|  | 1 | 2 | 3 | 4 | 5 | 6 | 7 | 8 | 9 | 10 |
|---|---|---|---|---|---|---|---|---|---|---|
| $SiO_2$ | 41.85 | 59.03 | 39.00 | 45.55 | 46.12 | 42.50 | 46.30 | 50.15 | 42.06 | 48.12 |
| $Al_2O_3$ | 12.24 | 18.20 | 12.74 | 13.13 | 12.28 | 12.03 | 13.70 | 13.76 | 1.00 | 19.12 |
| $Fe_2O_3$ | 5.20 | 0.54 | 3.42 | 3.48 | 1.94 | 2.90 | 2.70 | 1.54 | 0.81 | 1.93 |
| $FeO$ | 7.07 | 5.25 | 7.54 | 7.94 | 8.53 | 8.73 | 8.46 | 9.07 | 8.78 | 3.66 |
| $MnO$ | 0.20 | 0.14 | 0.19 | 0.17 | 0.16 | 0.18 | 0.18 | 0.12 | 0.17 | 0.13 |
| $MgO$ | 12.95 | 0.88 | 14.31 | 10.85 | 13.66 | 15.72 | 10.65 | 8.97 | 46.19 | 3.06 |
| $CaO$ | 11.75 | 2.60 | 14.02 | 10.71 | 10.43 | 10.51 | 10.20 | 10.09 | 0.82 | 6.31 |
| $Na_2O$ | 2.97 | 6.77 | 1.90 | 3.00 | 2.52 | 2.50 | 3.09 | 2.80 | 0.28 | 4.40 |
| $K_2O$ | 0.41 | 3.91 | 0.61 | 1.12 | 1.00 | 1.25 | 1.22 | 0.70 |  | 4.65 |
| $TiO_2$ | 3.21 | 0.68 | 2.32 | 2.35 | 2.07 | 2.77 | 2.78 | 1.98 | 0.13 | 2.03 |
| $P_2O_5$ | 0.82 | 0.41 | 1.16 | 0.60 | 0.77 | 0.77 | 0.70 | 0.30 | 0.08 | 0.88 |
| $CO_2$ |  | 0.52 |  |  |  |  |  |  |  |  |
| $H_2O+$ | 0.72 | 0.77 | 2.98 | 1.09 | 0.35 | 0.52 | 0.20 | 0.37 | 0.02 | 5.36 |
| $H_2O-$ | 0.27 | 0.16 |  |  |  |  | 0.10 |  |  |  |
| Total | 99.81(1) | 100.05(2) | 100.19 | 99.99 | 99.83 | 100.36 | 100.31(3) | 99.85 | 100.34(4) | 99.65 |

(1) Incl. 0.05 NiO; 0.09 $Cr_2O_3$; 0.01 $S_2$.             (4) Incl. 0.15 $Cl_2$.
(2) Incl. 0.19 $SO_3$.                               (5) Incl. 0.14 NiO; 0.05 $Cr_2O_3$.
(3) Incl. 0.01 NiO; 0.02 $Cr_2O_3$.

|  | 11 | 12 | 13 | 14 | 15 | 16 | 17 | 18 | 19 | 20 |
|---|---|---|---|---|---|---|---|---|---|---|
| $SiO_2$ | 43.90 | 41.98 | 43.00 | 41.10 | 43.20 | 44.15 | 59.80 | 68.35 | 47.60 | 35.66 |
| $Al_2O_3$ | 14.29 | 14.94 | 12.35 | 12.64 | 12.76 | 13.23 | 18.20 | 15.96 | 6.95 | 6.64 |
| $Fe_2O_3$ | 3.83 | 4.20 | 7.18 | 4.05 | 3.18 | 2.58 | 1.89 | 1.39 | 3.71 | 13.75 |
| $FeO$ | 8.90 | 9.12 | 6.07 | 8.42 | 8.87 | 10.10 | 1.56 | 0.29 | 5.71 | 11.31 |
| $MnO$ | 0.15 | 0.18 | 0.16 | 0.22 | 0.17 | 0.16 | 0.20 | 0.06 | 0.16 | 0.12 |
| $MgO$ | 8.38 | 7.13 | 10.09 | 12.37 | 12.22 | 11.19 | 1.29 | 0.52 | 12.59 | 10.10 |
| $CaO$ | 11.10 | 8.24 | 11.76 | 11.36 | 10.46 | 10.05 | 3.34 | 0.78 | 18.22 | 15.06 |
| $Na_2O$ | 2.56 | 2.40 | 3.16 | 3.14 | 3.10 | 3.29 | 7.44 | 6.20 | 1.30 | 0.49 |
| $K_2O$ | 1.08 | 1.42 | 1.30 | 1.58 | 1.46 | 1.27 | 4.32 | 5.12 | 0.62 | 0.20 |
| $TiO_2$ | 3.25 | 3.74 | 3.10 | 3.28 | 2.48 | 2.51 | 0.90 | 0.12 | 1.70 | 6.40 |
| $P_2O_5$ | 0.40 | 0.05 | 0.75 | 1.09 | 0.82 | 0.75 | 0.16 | 0.10 | 0.22 | Tr |
| $CO_2$ | 0.05 | 0.73 | 0.52 | 0.02 | 0.16 |  |  |  | 0.22 |  |
| $H_2O+$ | 1.09 | 3.87 | 0.63 | 0.43 | 0.58 | 0.43 | 0.87 | 1.08 | 0.22 | 0.47 |
| $H_2O-$ |  | 1.34 |  |  |  |  |  |  | 0.81 | 0.13 |
|  | 99.88 | 99.49 | 100.07 | 99.89(5) | 99.96 | 99.81 | 99.97 | 99.88 | 99.81 | 100.33 |

*Rock analyses from Canary Islands*

Lanzarote

1. Olivine-basalt (Series I). Penas del Chache. HAUSEN, 1959, p. 39.
2. Trachyandesite (Series I). Hacha Chica. HAUSEN, 1959, p. 50.
3. Oceanite (Series I). km 24, between Tegui- sa and Haria. IBARROLA, 1970. p. 355.
4. Olivine-basalt (Series II). Barr. de la Negra, lavas de La Atalaya de Haria. IBARROLA, 1970, p. 369.
5. Pyroxenitic olivine-basalt (Series II). Las Montanetas, lavas de Montana Bermeja. IBARROLA, 1970, p. 369.
6. Vitreous olivine-basalt (Series III). W slope of Montana Tinamala. IBARROLA, 1970, p. 369.
7. Olivine-basalt (Series IV). Sub-Recent. Valle Dorado, lavas de Montana la Corona. HAUSEN, 1959, p. 69.
8. Olivine-basalt (Series IV). Eruption of 1730– 36. IBARROLA, & LOPEZ 1967, p. 210.

Table 28 (continued)

| | 21 | 22 | 23 | 24 | 25 | 26 | 27 | 28 | 29 | 30 |
|---|---|---|---|---|---|---|---|---|---|---|
| $SiO_2$ | 48.90 | 41.10 | 38.00 | 43.10 | 42.10 | 67.30 | 68.4 | 59.69 | 43.57 | 48.63 |
| $Al_2O_3$ | 10.58 | 10.82 | 9.73 | 15.42 | 13.10 | 10.72 | 14.0 | 18.15 | 14.66 | 15.25 |
| $Fe_2O_3$ | 4.86 | 3.96 | 6.00 | 4.68 | 2.52 | 7.37 | 3.3 | 3.74 | 6.16 | 6.34 |
| FeO | 6.62 | 10.04 | 9.20 | 4.52 | 9.20 | 0.24 | 0.3 | 0.82 | 5.97 | 2.19 |
| MnO | 0.18 | 0.23 | 0.19 | 0.15 | 0.21 | 0.11 | 0.24 | 0.18 | 0.19 | 0.22 |
| MgO | 9.44 | 11.13 | 12.84 | 4.77 | 11.11 | 0.30 | 0.2 | 0.64 | 5.80 | 5.16 |
| CaO | 11.26 | 13.06 | 13.27 | 10.03 | 11.96 | 0.61 | 0.6 | 0.79 | 10.09 | 6.31 |
| $Na_2O$ | 2.01 | 2.88 | 2.90 | 4.80 | 3.81 | 5.54 | 6.4 | 8.05 | 4.24 | 4.96 |
| $K_2O$ | 0.99 | 1.00 | 0.60 | 3.80 | 2.00 | 5.24 | 4.9 | 5.18 | 2.54 | 2.76 |
| $TiO_2$ | 2.98 | 2.98 | 3.82 | 2.56 | 3.62 | 1.17 | 0.55 | 0.84 | 4.39 | 2.46 |
| $P_2O_5$ | 0.34 | 0.90 | 1.56 | 0.59 | 0.80 | 0.10 | 0.07 | 0.05 | 1.18 | 0.83 |
| $CO_2$ | | | | | | | | | | |
| $H_2O+$ | 1.03 | 1.63 | 2.09 | 4.98 | 0.39 | 1.37 | 0.5 | 1.00 | 1.56 | |
| $H_2O-$ | 0.65 | | | | | | | 0.80 | | 4.50 |
| Total | 100.01(6) | 99.73 | 100.20 | 99.75(7) | 99.82 | 100.07 | 99.4 | 99.93 | 100.35 | 99.61 |

(6) Incl. NiO; 0.01 $Cr_2O_3$; 0.02 BaO;          (8) Incl. 0.05 $Cr_2O_3$.
     0.04 $F_2$; 0.07 $V_2O_5$.                      (9) Incl. 0.12 BaO; 1.64 $SO_3$; 0.37 $Cl_2$.
(7) Incl. 0.28 $SO_3$; 0.07 Cl.               (10) Incl. 0.03 BaO.

| | 31 | 32 | 33 | 34 | 35 | 36 | 37 | 38 | 39 | 40 |
|---|---|---|---|---|---|---|---|---|---|---|
| $SiO_2$ | 43.51 | 51.11 | 43.23 | 55.08 | 55.85 | 60.78 | 59.60 | 60.35 | 61.30 | 45.25 |
| $Al_2O_3$ | 14.16 | 18.82 | 10.07 | 19.30 | 19.01 | 17.00 | 18.53 | 16.49 | 17.43 | 15.10 |
| $Fe_2O_3$ | 5.63 | 2.68 | 5.62 | 2.14 | 3.38 | 3.45 | 2.34 | 4.03 | 2.24 | 4.93 |
| FeO | 6.09 | 2.69 | 7.64 | 2.18 | 1.51 | 0.75 | 1.29 | 0.46 | 0.88 | 7.66 |
| MnO | 0.18 | 0.23 | 0.14 | 0.19 | 0.17 | 0.17 | 0.19 | 0.21 | 0.19 | 0.16 |
| MgO | 7.40 | 1.64 | 13.37 | 1.73 | 1.48 | 1.03 | 0.94 | 1.01 | 0.83 | 7.03 |
| CaO | 10.44 | 4.44 | 12.14 | 4.09 | 4.23 | 1.36 | 2.04 | 1.80 | 1.16 | 9.77 |
| $Na_2O$ | 3.44 | 8.72 | 2.16 | 6.51 | 5.80 | 7.20 | 7.75 | 7.43 | 7.79 | 3.50 |
| $K_2O$ | 1.06 | 4.60 | 0.78 | 3.94 | 4.09 | 5.28 | 4.97 | 4.97 | 5.46 | 1.82 |
| $TiO_2$ | 3.60 | 1.64 | 3.04 | 1.25 | 1.38 | 0.82 | 0.90 | 0.85 | 0.72 | 0.45 |
| $P_2O_5$ | 1.02 | 0.33 | 0.40 | 0.33 | 0.30 | 0.11 | 0.16 | 0.15 | 0.12 | |
| $CO_2$ | 0.42 | | | | | | | | | |
| $H_2O+$ | 2.06 | 1.07 | 0.78 | 2.59 | 2.49 | 1.98 | 1.13 | 1.98 | 1.68 | 0.27 |
| $H_2O-$ | 1.04 | 0.30 | | | | | | | | 0.18 |
| Total | 100.10(8) | 100.40(9) | 100.00 | 99.33 | 99.69 | 99.93 | 99.84 | 99.58 | 99.80 | 100.09 |

9. Dunite bomb. Locality not known. HAUSEN, 1959, p. 92.
10. Porphyritic essexitic-gabbro ("Pegmatoids" of Series I). Vega Nueva, Los Ajaches. FUSTER et al., 1968, p. 105.

Fuerteventura

11. Augitic olivine-basalt (Series I). Puerto de Cabras, S slope of Montana Rosa. FUATER et al., 1968, p. 149.
12. Olivine-basalt (Series I). Montana de la Go-

ma, between Valles Orteja and Pozo Negro. HAUSEN, 1958, p. 105.
13. Olivine-basalt (Series II). W of Ampuyenta FUSTER et al. 1968, p. 151.
14. Picrite-basalt lava (Series III). Caldera de Gairia. HAUSEN, 1958, p. 147.
15. Olivine-basalt (Series III). Barr. del Llano de Caima al Barr. del Cavadero, Montana Roja. FUSTER et al., 1968, p. 152.
16. Olivine-basalt (Series IV). Jacomar. CENDRERO, 1966, p. 220.
17. Alkali-syenite. Barr. de las Penitas. FUST? et al., 1968, p. 145.

Table 28 (continued)

| | 41 | 42 | 43 | 44 | 45 | 46 | 47 | 48 | 49 | 50 |
|---|---|---|---|---|---|---|---|---|---|---|
| $SiO_2$ | 48.00 | 44.73 | 59.70 | 59.36 | 41.90 | 46.40 | 42.35 | 44.40 | 50.30 | 42.55 |
| $Al_2O_3$ | 16.75 | 14.33 | 18.99 | 19.36 | 4.97 | 16.16 | 11.67 | 17.05 | 18.42 | 15.48 |
| $Fe_2O_3$ | 3.02 | 7.12 | 1.30 | 2.39 | 2.84 | 3.94 | 4.34 | 3.04 | 3.68 | 5.78 |
| $FeO$ | 6.61 | 4.90 | 2.02 | 0.74 | 10.08 | 4.85 | 9.15 | 7.71 | 4.88 | 6.59 |
| $MnO$ | 0.20 | 0.19 | 0.18 | 0.17 | 0.18 | 0.10 | 0.17 | 0.17 | 0.21 | 0.15 |
| $MgO$ | 5.45 | 8.84 | 1.21 | 0.73 | 23.53 | 8.48 | 12.05 | 5.36 | 3.15 | 5.65 |
| $CaO$ | 8.30 | 8.57 | 1.49 | 0.73 | 8.83 | 14.49 | 10.66 | 9.84 | 7.49 | 11.17 |
| $Na_2O$ | 4.91 | 4.15 | 8.10 | 8.88 | 0.60 | 1.80 | 2.62 | 3.96 | 4.70 | 2.94 |
| $K_2O$ | 2.02 | 1.96 | 5.52 | 5.97 | 1.14 | 0.52 | 1.14 | 1.90 | 2.20 | 1.70 |
| $TiO_2$ | 2.89 | 2.60 | 0.69 | 0.58 | 0.99 | 1.67 | 3.67 | 3.50 | 2.28 | 4.40 |
| $P_2O_5$ | 1.03 | 0.63 | 0.15 | 0.05 | 0.16 | 0.16 | 0.74 | 1.05 | 0.91 | 0.75 |
| $CO_2$ | | | | | | | 0.35 | 0.05 | | |
| $H_2O+$ | 0.61 | 1.71 | 0.63 | 1.08 | 4.23 | 1.79 | 1.01 | 1.75 | 1.86 | 2.29 |
| $H_2O-$ | | 0.11 | | | | | | | | |
| Total | 99.79 | 99.84 | 99.98 | 100.04 | 99.45 | 100.36 | 99.92 | 99.78 | 100.06 | 99.45 |

(11) Incl. 0.02 $Fe_2$; 0.08 $Cl_2$.     (13) Incl. 0.10 S.
(12) Incl. 0.06 $Fe_2$; 0.19 $Cl_2$.

| | 51 | 52 | 53 | 54 | 55 | 56 | 57 | 58 | 59 | 60 |
|---|---|---|---|---|---|---|---|---|---|---|
| $SiO_2$ | 43.10 | 46.05 | 48.85 | 51.20 | 55.80 | 56.08 | 49.35 | 42.96 | 43.64 | 44.50 |
| $Al_2O_3$ | 14.34 | 17.68 | 18.15 | 17.52 | 20.55 | 20.05 | 17.43 | 13.04 | 14.15 | 13.23 |
| $Fe_2O_3$ | 4.78 | 6.49 | 4.91 | 4.25 | 2.34 | 2.63 | 3.96 | 6.52 | 3.85 | 4.11 |
| $FeO$ | 7.84 | 4.29 | 4.76 | 4.14 | 0.05 | 1.41 | 5.65 | 8.49 | 7.62 | 7.76 |
| $MnO$ | 0.16 | 0.18 | 0.21 | 0.18 | 0.18 | 0.19 | 0.24 | 0.24 | 0.18 | Tr |
| $MgO$ | 9.45 | 4.05 | 3.11 | 3.45 | 0.37 | 1.12 | 3.07 | 8.42 | 7.64 | 13.19 |
| $CaO$ | 11.67 | 8.90 | 8.05 | 6.36 | 0.84 | 2.68 | 8.02 | 10.77 | 11.18 | 11.20 |
| $Na_2O$ | 2.46 | 3.12 | 4.64 | 4.70 | 7.65 | 9.31 | 5.60 | 3.60 | 4.15 | 1.69 |
| $K_2O$ | 1.14 | 1.70 | 2.10 | 2.48 | 5.50 | 5.02 | 2.20 | 1.43 | 1.79 | 0.74 |
| $TiO_2$ | 3.29 | 3.24 | 2.47 | 2.32 | 0.28 | 0.92 | 2.78 | 3.55 | 4.85 | 1.72 |
| $P_2O_5$ | 0.56 | 1.00 | 1.17 | 0.89 | 0.03 | 0.17 | 0.92 | 0.43 | 0.72 | 0.22 |
| $CO_2$ | | | 0.17 | | | | 0.05 | | | 0.36 |
| $H_2O+$ | 1.39 | 2.95 | 1.39 | 2.26 | 3.12 | 0.33 | 0.38 | 0.30 | 0.21 | 1.36 |
| $H_2O-$ | | | | | 0.69 | 0.05 | 0.20 | 0.08 | 0.08 | |
| Total | 100.17 | 99.95 | 99.88 | 99.75 | 100.50 (11) | 100.21 (12) | 99.85 | 99.83 | 100.06 | 100.18 (13) |

18. Quartz-trachyte. La Oliva. W side of Montana de Tindaya. MUNOZ, 1969, p. 303.
19. Pyroxenite. Barr. de Machin. FUSTER et al., 1968, p. 143.
20. Pyroxenolite. Angostura de la Penita. BOURCART & JEREMINE, 1938.

Gran Canaria

21. Plagioclase-basalt (Series I). Barr. de Tasartico. HAUSEN, 1962, p. 191.
22. Augitic olivine-basalt (Series I). Tejada-Cruz de Tejada road. FUSTER et al., 1968, 147.

23. Ankaramite (Series II). Barr. de Simon. FUSTER et al., 1968, p. 154.
24. Tephrite (Series III). S side of Cardones volcano. FUSTER et al., 1968, p. 155.
25. Ankaramite (Series IV). Cruz del Ingles. FUSTER et al., 1968, p. 156.
26. Ignimbritic trachyte. (Syenite-Trachyte Complex.) Lomo de la Montana de Ojeda. FUSTER et al., 1968, p. 149.
27. Ash-flow tuff (Syenite-Trachyte Complex.) Barr. del Taurito. SCHMINCKE & SWANSON, 1967, p. 659.

Table 28 (continued)

|                | 61 | 62 | 63 | 64 | 65 | 66 | 67 | 68 | 69 |
|----------------|------|------|------|------|------|------|------|------|------|
| $SiO_2$        | 48.23 | 51.02 | 68.54 | 37.46 | 44.55 | 43.26 | 38.12 | 40.73 | 41.53 |
| $Al_2O_3$      | 18.41 | 19.67 | 15.96 | 10.03 | 13.00 | 13.68 | 9.71 | 13.37 | 12.20 |
| $Fe_2O_3$      | 3.27 | 3.72 | 1.33 | 8,47 | 3.95 | 3.92 | 7.27 | 5.95 | 5.90 |
| $FeO$          | 5.00 | 3.65 | 1.63 | 6.41 | 9.20 | 9.39 | 6.32 | 8.94 | 7.44 |
| $MnO$          | Tr | 0.18 | Tr | 0.14 | 0.16 | 0.22 | 0.07 | 0.18 | 0.21 |
| $MgO$          | 1.92 | 1.70 | 0.24 | 13.93 | 8.27 | 9.22 | 12.16 | 9.11 | 11.12 |
| $CaO$          | 6.43 | 6.66 | 0.65 | 14.78 | 10.60 | 10.28 | 15.42 | 10.65 | 11.18 |
| $Na_2O$        | 7.77 | 7.00 | 6.25 | 2.00 | 3.09 | 3.60 | 3.27 | 2.98 | 2.20 |
| $K_2O$         | 3.16 | 3.51 | 4.90 | 0.76 | 1.90 | 1.47 | 1.21 | 1.24 | 1.60 |
| $TiO_2$        | 1.90 | 2.12 | 0.13 | 5.22 | 4.67 | 3.71 | 3.80 | 4.75 | 3.46 |
| $P_2O_5$       | 0.47 | 0.29 | 0.13 | 0.66 | 0.04 | 0.88 | 1.77 | 1.06 | 0.78 |
| $CO_2$         | 0.41 |      |      |      |      |      |      |      | 0.25 |
| $H_2O+$        | 3.05 | 0.41 | 0.42 | 0.28 | 0.10 | 0.18 | 0.72 | 0.62 | 1.51 |
| $H_2O-$        |      | 0.07 |      |      | 0.10 |      | 0.43 | 0.24 | 0.48 |
| Total          | 100.04 | 100.32 | 100.36 | 100.20 | 99.63 | 99.81 | 100.27 | 99.82 | 99.86 |
|                | (14) | (15) | (16) | (17) |      |      |      |      |      |

(14) Incl. 0.12 S.                                      (16) Incl. 0.7 S; 0.11 $ZrO_2$.
(15) Incl. 0.24 $SO_3$; 0.08 $Cl_2$.                    (17) Incl. 0.06 $Cl_2$.

|                | 70 | 71 | 72 | 73 | 74 | 75 | 76 | 77 | 78 |
|----------------|------|------|------|------|------|------|------|------|------|
| $SiO_2$        | 43.71 | 43.73 | 45.21 | 45.21 | 45.59 | 45.83 | 45.95 | 48.28 | 49.25 |
| $Al_2O_3$      | 14.55 | 12.55 | 16.79 | 14.20 | 13.53 | 16.04 | 15.90 | 16.30 | 17.10 |
| $Fe_2O_3$      | 4.96 | 4.13 | 3.07 | 4.50 | 8.83 | 5.51 | 3.02 | 4.44 | 2.54 |
| $FeO$          | 7.62 | 9.11 | 7.88 | 8.31 | 4.08 | 6.31 | 9.66 | 6.83 | 8.27 |
| $MnO$          | 0.18 | 0.21 | 0.18 | 0.21 | 0.20 | 0.19 | 0.23 | 0.24 | 0.24 |
| $MgO$          | 8.14 | 11.51 | 4.67 | 6.19 | 8.71 | 5.18 | 5.51 | 4.99 | 4.29 |
| $CaO$          | 9.90 | 10.85 | 9.80 | 10.19 | 10.20 | 9.60 | 9.62 | 8.22 | 7.87 |
| $Na_2O$        | 3.62 | 2.50 | 4.18 | 3.45 | 2.96 | 4.38 | 4.15 | 4.58 | 4.90 |
| $K_2O$         | 1.70 | 0.80 | 1.70 | 1.14 | 0.80 | 1.67 | 0.92 | 1.50 | 1.62 |
| $TiO_2$        | 3.90 | 3.33 | 4.45 | 4.38 | 3.06 | 3.60 | 3.90 | 2.70 | 2.67 |
| $P_2O_5$       | 1.06 | 0.52 | 1.19 | 0.84 | 0.53 | 1.49 | 0.76 | 1.19 | 1.21 |
| $CO_2$         | 0.28 | 0.14 | 0.12 | 0.31 | 0.21 |      | 0.02 | 0.27 | 0.01 |
| $H_2O+$        | 0.02 | 0.77 | 0.07 | 1.30 | 0.98 | 0.35 | 0.00 | 0.05 | 0.05 |
| $H_2O-$        |      | 0.19 | 0.02 | 0.26 | 0.43 | 0.05 | 0.10 | 0.77 | 0.14 |
| Total          | 99.91 | 100.34 | 99.57 | 100.49 | 100.11 | 100.20 | 99.74 | 100.36 | 100.16 |
|                |      |      | (18) |      |      |      |      |      |      |

(18) Incl. 0.01 $ZrO_2$; 0.13 $SO_3$; 0.10 $Cl_2$.

28.  Nepheline-phonolite (Phonolite Series). Montana del Horno. HAUSEN, 1962, p. 179.
29.  Pyroxene-basalt (Pre-Roque Nublo Series). Tejada. Mesa del Junquillo. ÁNGUITA, 1972, p. 403.
30.  Agglomerate (Roque Nublo Series). Tejeda. Mesa del Junquillo. ANGUITA, 1972, p.406.
31.  Basaltic lava associated with agglomerate (Roque Nublo Series). N side of Caldera de Tejeda. HAUSEN, 1962, p. 312.

32.  Haüyne-phonolite (Ordanchite Series). N wall of caldera La Caldereta. HAUSEN, 1962, p. 279.

Tenerife

33.  Average of two basalts (Old Basaltic Series). BRÄNDLE, 1973, p. 26.
34.  Average of four mafic phonolites (Old Basaltic Series). BRÄNDLE, 1973, p. 26.

35. Average of four mafic trachytes (Lower Canadas Series). BRÄNDLE, 1973, p. 26.
36. Average of nine peralkaline trachyte (Lower Canadas Series). BRÄNDLE, 1973, p. 26.
37. Average of eight phonolites (Upper Canadas Series). BRÄNDLE, 1973, p. 26.
38. Average of twnty-two eutaxites (Upper Canadas Series). BRÄNDLE, 1973, p. 26.
39. Average of seven peralkaline phonolites. Aventive cones. (Trachytic-Trachybasaltic Series). BRÄNDLE, 1973, p. 26.
40. Tephritoid (Series III). Suburbs of Villa de Orotava. SMULIKOWSKI et al., 1946, p. 103.
41. Amphibole-basalt (Series III). San Juan-Garachico road. IBARROLA, 1970, p. 378.
42. Alkali olivine-basalt (Series IV). Cone N of Arafo, Valle de Guimar. HAUSEN, 1955, p. 184.
43. Phonolite (Teide-Viejo Complex). BRÄNDLE, 1973, p. 24.
44. Average of six syenites. BRÄNDLE, 1973, p. 26.

Gomera

45. Wehrlite (Basal Complex). Barr. de la Rosa. BRAVA, 1964.
46. Olivine-gabbro (Basal Complex). Espina. CENDRERO, 1971, p. 62.
47. Olivine-augite basalt (Old Basalts). Hermigua-El Molinito. IBARROLA, 1969, p. 755.
48. Olivine-augite-basalt (Old Basalts). Montana de Igualero. IBARROLA, 1969, p. 755.
49. Basalt (Old Basalts). Quemado. IBARROLA, 1969, p. 755.
50. Basalt (Sub-Recent Basalts). Angulo, alt. 625 m. IBARROLA, 1969, p. 755.
51. Olivine-augite-basalt (Sub-Recent Basalts). Angulo, alt. 460 m. IBARROLA, 1969, p. 755.
52. Olivine-basalt (Sub-Recent-Basalts). Cumbre del Cepo, alt. 625 m. IBARROLA, 1969, p. 755.
53. Basalt (Sub-Recent Basalts). Cumbre del Chiguaré. IBARROLA, 1969, p. 755.
54. Basalt (Sub-Recent Basalts). Barr. de la Villa. IBARROLA, 1969, p. 755.

La Palma

55. Alkali trachyte. Montana Enrique. El Paso. HAUSEN, 1969, p.115.

56. Phonolite. Roque de Tenguia. San Antonio. HAUSEN, 1969, p. 115.
57. Trachybasalt. E of Faro de Barlvento. HAUSEN, 1969, p. 115.
58. Basanitoid. Tigalate. SMULIKOWSKI et al., 1946, p. 112.
59. Tephritoid. Volcano S. Antonio, Fuencaliente. SMULIKOWSKI et al., 1946, p. 116.
60. Essexite. Caldera, Barr. del Almendrero Amargo. GAGEL, 1915.
61. Sodalitic Gauteite. Caldera, Barr. del Almenderero Amargo. GAGEL, 1912.
62. Ordanchite. Malpais, N of Fuencaliente. JEREMINE, 1933, p. 256.
63. Alkali granite. Caldera. GAGEL, 1915.
64. Xenolith in S. Antonio lavas, Fuencaliente. JEREMINE, 1933, p. 256.
65. Basalt, 1949 eruption, Hoyo Negro crater. CAMARA et al., 1952., pp. 161–163.
66. Average of thirteen lavas with olivine, 1971 eruption of Teneguia. CHAIGNEAU & FUSTER, 1972, p. 2949.

Hierro

67. Ankaratrite. Valverde-La Estaca road. JEREMINE, 1935.
68. Olivine-basalt. Upper crater, volcano Tesoro. HAUSEN, 1973, p. 117.
69. Trachydolerite. Tesoro lava, coast at Tamaduste. HAUSEN, 1973, p. 117.
70. Olivine-basalt. Lava from volcano Tanganasoga, El Golfo. HAUSEN, 1973, p. 117.
71. Olivine-basalt. Lava of Tableland Series. S of La Estaca. HAUSEN, 1973, p. 118.
72. Trachydolerite. Profile above La Frontera, El Golfo. HAUSEN, 1973, p. 118.
73. Alkali basalt. Well in Pozo de la Salud. HAUSEN, 1973, p. 118.
74. Olivine-basalt. Lava of Tableland Series. S. of Punta La Estaca. HAUSEN, 1973, p. 118.
75. Olivine-basalt. Lava of Tableland Series. La Cuesta. HAUSEN, 1973, p. 118.
76. Alkali basalt. Boulder on slope NW of Orchilla. HAUSEN, 1973, p. 118.
77. Alkali basalt. Lava of Tableland Series. Above Tamaduste. HAUSEN, 1973, p. 118.
78. Trachydolerite. Lava of Tableland Series. Lava bank E of Tamaduste. HAUSEN, 1973, p. 118.

Table 29                    Molecular norms of volcanic rocks, Canary Islands

|     | 1 | 2 | 3 | 4 | 5 | 6 | 7 | 8 | 9 | 10 |
|-----|-----|-----|-----|-----|-----|-----|-----|-----|-----|-----|
| Or  | 2.4 | 23.1 | 3.7 | 6.5 | 5.8 | 7.1 | 7.2 | 4.2 |      | 28.8 |
| Ab  | 10.3 | 55.5 |      | 18.0 | 17.2 | 4.7 | 18.4 | 25.2 | 2.4 | 12.2 |
| An  | 18.8 | 6.9 | 24.7 | 19.2 | 18.9 | 17.4 | 19.8 | 23.2 | 1.5 | 19.5 |
| Ne  | 8.0 | 0.2 | 10.3 | 5.4 | 3.2 | 10.4 | 4.2 |      |      | 17.5 |
| Di  | 26.8 |      | 22.7 | 24.5 | 22.1 | 23.2 | 21.0 | 20.5 | 1.7 | 6.4 |
| Ol  | 16.5 | 8.0 | 29.5 | 18.2 | 26.5 | 29.0 | 18.3 | 9.1 | 89.2 |      |
| Mt  | 7.6 | 0.8 | 3.7 | 3.7 | 2.0 | 2.9 | 3.9 | 1.6 | 1.2 |      |
| Hm  |     |     |     |     |     |     |     |     |     |     |
| Il  | 6.1 | 1.3 | 3.2 | 3.4 | 2.8 | 3.8 | 5.3 | 2.8 | 0.2 |     |
| Ap  | 2.0 | 1.0 | 2.2 | 1.1 | 1.5 | 1.5 | 1.7 | 0.6 | 0.2 |     |
| Cal |     | 1.2 |     |     |     |     |     |     |     |     |
|     | (1) | (2) |     |     |     |     | (3) |     | (4) | (5) |

(1) Incl. 0.02 Pr; 0.1 Cm; 1.0 $H_2O$.        (4) Incl. 3.5 Hy; 0.02 $H_2O$.
(2) Incl. 0.3 Th; 0.5 C; 0.9 $H_2O$.        (5) Incl. 10.3 En+Hy; 1.7 Ap+Cc; 3.5 Acc.
(3) Incl. 0.02 Cm; 0.3 $H_2O$.

|     | 11 | 12 | 13 | 14 | 15 | 16 | 17 | 18 | 19 | 20 |
|-----|-----|-----|-----|-----|-----|-----|-----|-----|-----|-----|
| Or  | 6.5 | 8.4 | 7.8 | 9.3 | 8.6 | 7.2 | 24.2 | 30.0 | 3.7 | 1.2 |
| Ab  | 17.1 | 19.2 | 15.1 | 0.7 | 7.8 | 12.0 | 48.5 | 50.8 | 11.3 | 1.5 |
| An  | 25.2 | 26.3 | 15.8 | 15.7 | 16.4 | 17.7 | 8.6 | 1.8 | 6.3 | 16.3 |
| Ne  | 4.0 |      | 8.1 | 14.0 | 11.9 | 10.4 | 8.4 |      | 3.3 | 2.0 |
| Di  | 22.9 | 7.7 | 28.2 | 26.5 | 23.5 | 22.3 | 2.9 |      | 62.1 | 50.2 |
| Ol  | 14.6 | 11.0 | 10.7 | 18.2 | 23.4 | 22.8 |      |      |      | 14.2 |
| Mt  | 4.1 | 6.1 | 7.6 | 5.9 | 3.3 | 2.7 |      |      |      | 14.2 |
| Hm  |     |     |     |     |     |     |     |     |     | 0.8 |
| Il  | 4.6 | 7.1 | 4.4 | 6.2 | 3.4 | 3.4 |      |      | 2.4 | 9.6 |
| Ap  | 0.9 | 0.1 | 1.6 | 2.6 | 1.5 | 1.5 |      |      | 1.8 |     |
| Cal | 0.1 | 1.7 | 0.7 | 0.1 | 0.2 |     |     |     |     |     |
|     | (6) |     |     | (7) |     |     | (8) | (9) | (10) |     |

(6) Incl. 0.3 Hl; 6.1 Hy; 5.2 $H_2O$.       (9) Incl. 0.3 En+Hy; 10.3 Q; 1.3 Acc.
(7) Incl. 0.1 Cm; 0.4 $H_2O$.        (10) Incl. 6.5 Fo+Fa; 0.4 Cp; 0.3 Cc.
(8) Incl. 0.34 En+Hy; 4.0 Acc.

|     | 21 | 22 | 23 | 24 | 25 | 27 | 28 | 29 | 30 |
|-----|-----|-----|-----|-----|-----|-----|-----|-----|-----|
| Or  | 5.8 | 6.0 | 7.8 | 23.6 | 11.4 | 28.7 | 30.6 | 15.3 | 17.0 |
| Ab  | 17.0 | 1.1 |      | 1.1 |      | 45.8 | 47.0 | 14.1 | 30.8 |
| An  | 16.9 | 13.8 | 9.0 | 9.8 | 12.5 |      |      | 13.7 | 11.7 |
| Ne  |      | 15.0 | 16.8 | 24.2 | 20.2 |      | 9.4 | 14.8 | 9.4 |
| Di  | 28.9 | 37.3 | 15.9 | 29.0 | 28.2 | 1.1 | 2.8 | 24.2 | 5.6 |
| Ol  |      | 16.3 | 39.0 |      | 17.3 |      |      | 3.2 |     |
| Mt  | 7.1 | 4.5 | 3.2 | 5.2 | 4.1 | 0.01 | 0.8 | 5.2 | 5.8 |
| Hm  |     |     |     |     |     | 0.6 | 2.1 | 0.9 | 0.7 |
| Il  | 5.7 | 4.2 | 5.0 | 3.8 | 5.0 | 1.2 | 1.6 | 6.2 |     |
| Ap  | 0.8 | 1.8 | 3.3 | 1.2 | 1.5 | 0.2 | 0.1 | 2.4 | 1.7 |
| Cal |     |     |     |     |     |     |     |     |     |
|     | (11) |     |     | (12) |     | (13) | (14) |     | (15) |

(11) Incl. 2.3 Q; 13.4 Hy; 0.02 Cm; 0.02 Fr;      (13) Incl. 14.2 Q; 7.9 Ac.
      0.1 $V_2O_5$; 1.7 $H_2O$.              (14) Incl. 3.3 Ac; 0.2 Fo; 1.8 $H_2O$.
(12) Incl. 1.1 Hau; 1.0 Sod.            (15) Incl. 12.0 En+Hy; 5.3 Tit.

Table 29 (continued)

| | 31 | 32 | 33 | 34 | 35 | 36 | 37 | 38 | 39 | 40 |
|---|---|---|---|---|---|---|---|---|---|---|
| Or | 6.2 | 27.1 | 4.6 | 23.4 | 24.4 | 31.0 | 28.7 | 28.2 | 31.7 | 10.7 |
| Ab | 24.0 | 24.7 | 10.6 | 40.2 | 46.0 | 53.4 | 49.2 | 51.1 | 47.3 | 18.2 |
| An | 20.0 | 5.7 | 17.3 | 11.9 | 13.9 | | 1.1 | 1.4 | | 20.0 |
| Ne | 2.8 | 19.3 | 5.3 | 11.2 | 4.0 | 4.6 | 11.3 | 4.5 | 8.7 | 6.2 |
| Di | 17.6 | 9.6 | 24.2 | 1.8 | 0.5 | 2.6 | 3.9 | 2.9 | 2.0 | 20.2 |
| Ol | 7.8 | | 24.9 | | | | | | | 8.3 |
| Mt | 8.2 | 3.9 | 5.9 | 2.3 | 3.6 | 2.7 | 2.4 | 0.6 | | 7.2 |
| Hm | | | | | | 0.4 | | 0.8 | 0.2 | |
| Il | 6.8 | 3.1 | | | | | | | | 7.5 |
| Ap | 2.4 | 0.8 | 0.8 | 0.6 | 0.6 | 0.2 | 0.3 | 0.3 | | 1.1 |
| Cal | | | | | | | | | | |
| | (16) | (17) | (18) | (19) | (20) | (21) | (22) | (23) | (24) | (25) |

(16) Incl. 0.1 Cm; 1.0 $CaCO_3$; 3.1 $H_2O$.
(17) Incl. 0.6 Hl; 2.9 Th; 0.9 Wo; 1.0 $H_2O$.
(18) Incl. 6.4 Tit.
(19) Incl. 6.1 En+Hy; 2.6 Tit.
(20) Incl. 4.0 En+Hy; 2.9 Tit.

(21) Incl. 1.5 En+Hy; 1.7 Tit.
(22) Incl. 1.2 En+Hy; 1.8 Tit.
(23) Incl. 6.3 Eg; 2.0 En+Hy; 1.8 Tit.
(24) Incl. 5.5 Eg; 2.7 En+Hy; 1.4 Tit.
(25) Incl. 0.5 $H_2O$.

| | 41 | 42 | 43 | 44 | 45 | 46 | 47 | 48 | 49 | 50 |
|---|---|---|---|---|---|---|---|---|---|---|
| Or | 11.9 | 11.6 | 31.5 | 34.0 | 6.80 | 3.10 | 6.6 | 11.3 | 13.3 | 10.5 |
| Ab | 28.6 | 18.3 | 40.1 | 33.8 | 7.60 | 35.00 | 12.9 | 19.2 | 40.3 | 17.2 |
| An | 17.7 | 14.6 | | | 2.45 | 16.39 | 16.8 | 23.7 | 22.9 | 25.2 |
| Ne | 9.3 | 9.1 | 17.1 | 20.5 | 1.80 | | 6.5 | 10.3 | 1.6 | 6.2 |
| Di | 14.0 | 18.5 | 3.2 | 1.1 | | | 24.3 | 15.5 | 7.5 | 22.7 |
| Ol | 9.3 | | | | | | 20.8 | 9.5 | 5.4 | 3.9 |
| Mt | 3.2 | 8.9 | 0.8 | | 3.00 | 4.17 | 4.6 | 3.2 | 3.9 | 6.4 |
| Hm | | 1.0 | | | | | | | | |
| Il | 4.0 | 4.9 | | | 0.69 | | 5.2 | 5.0 | 3.2 | 6.4 |
| Ap | 2.0 | 1.5 | 0.3 | 0.1 | 0.30 | 0.30 | 1.4 | 2.2 | 1.9 | 1.5 |
| Cal | | | | | | | 0.9 | 0.1 | | |
| | (26) | (27) | (28) | (29) | (30) | | | | | |

(26) Incl. 9.4 Fo; 1.8 $H_2O$.
(27) Incl. 1.3 Eg; 4.3 En+Hy; 1.4 Tit.
(28) Incl. 6.8 Eg; 2.8 En+Hy; 1.1 Tit.

(29) Incl. 12.97 Wo; 12.95 En+Hy; 49.70 Fo+Fa; 2.07 Tit.
(30) Incl. 12.47 Wo; 13.79 En+Hy; 11.21 Fo+Fa; 3.54 Tit.

| | 51 | 52 | 53 | 54 | 55 | 56 | 57 | 58 | 59 | 60 |
|---|---|---|---|---|---|---|---|---|---|---|
| Or | 6.8 | 10.5 | 12.6 | 15.1 | 36.32 | 25.66 | 13.10 | 8.3 | 10.6 | 4.4 |
| Ab | 13.1 | 29.4 | 38.9 | 43.2 | 47.66 | 30.73 | 32.03 | 11.0 | 8.9 | 14.1 |
| An | 25.4 | 30.5 | 22.8 | 19.6 | 3.99 | | 16.32 | 15.3 | 14.7 | 26.4 |
| Ne | 5.5 | | 2.2 | | 10.07 | 31.02 | 8.15 | 10.5 | 14.2 | |
| Di | 24.0 | 7.7 | 8.0 | 5.6 | | 5.17 | 14.21 | 58.5 | 29.0 | 21.6 |
| Ol | 14.4 | | 4.2 | 1.8 | 0.69 | | 2.78 | 8.7 | 6.1 | 21.6 |
| Mt | 5.1 | 4.1 | 5.1 | 4.6 | | 2.15 | 5.79 | 9.5 | 5.6 | 6.0 |
| Hm | | 2.2 | | | | | | | | |
| Il | 4.6 | 4.6 | 3.4 | 3.2 | 0.50 | 1.49 | 5.33 | 6.8 | 9.3 | 3.3 |
| Ap | 1.1 | 2.0 | 2.3 | 1.9 | 0.06 | 0.33 | 2.14 | 1.0 | 1.7 | 0.7 |
| Cal | | | 0.5 | | | | | | | |
| | | (31) | | (32) | (33) | (34) | (35) | | | |

(31) Incl. 1.1 Q; 7.8 En+Hy.
(32) Incl. 5.0 En+Hy.
(33) Incl. 0.13 Hl; 2.42 He.

(34) Incl. 0.27 Hl; 1.70 Ac; 1.51 Wo; 0.18 He.
(35) Incl. 0.15 Th.

Table 29 (continued)

|      | 61   | 62   | 63   | 64   | 65    | 66   | 67    | 68    | 69    |
|------|------|------|------|------|-------|------|-------|-------|-------|
| Or   | 18.3 | 20.6 | 28.9 |      | 11.12 | 8.9  |       | 7.40  | 9.70  |
| Ab   | 20.4 | 26.6 | 52.9 |      | 11.00 | 11.5 |       | 13.46 | 10.28 |
| An   | 5.6  | 13.1 | 1.1  | 16.4 | 15.58 | 16.7 | 8.06  | 19.98 | 19.15 |
| Ne   | 24.7 | 16.5 |      | 9.1  | 8.24  | 10.2 | 15.05 | 8.37  | 6.01  |
| Di   | 15.6 | 12.5 | 1.2  | 31.7 | 29.29 | 23.0 | 16.60 | 21.60 | 24.60 |
| Ol   |      |      |      | 17.5 | 9.20  | 14.7 |       | 13.82 | 16.63 |
| Mt   | 4.6  | 5.3  | 1.9  | 6.0  | 5.57  | 5.6  | 9.51  | 6.33  | 6.35  |
| Hm   |      |      |      |      |       |      |       |       |       |
| Il   | 4.3  | 3.9  | 0.3  | 9.9  | 8.97  | 7.0  | 7.30  | 6.74  | 4.92  |
| Ap   | 1.0  | 0.7  | 0.3  | 1.7  |       | 1.9  | 4.37  | 2.30  | 1.68  |
| Cal  |      |      |      |      |       |      | 3.18  |       |       |
|      | (36) | (37) | (38) | (39) | (40)  |      | (41)  |       |       |

(36) Incl. 1.7 Wo.  
(37) Incl. 0.1 NaCl; 0.4 $Na_2SO_4$.  
(38) Incl. 11.6 Q; 0.2 Zr; 1.5 Hy; 0.2 Pyr.

(39) Incl. 0.1 NaCl; 4.3 He.  
(40) Incl. 0.28 $H_2O$.  
(41) Incl. 5.67 Le; 19.26 Wo; 9.66 Fo; 0.80 He.

|      | 70    | 71    | 72    | 73    | 74    | 75    | 76    | 77    | 78    |
|------|-------|-------|-------|-------|-------|-------|-------|-------|-------|
| Or   | 10.10 | 4.75  | 10.15 | 6.85  | 4.85  | 9.85  | 5.35  | 9.00  | 9.50  |
| Ab   | 17.38 | 16.53 | 25.38 | 29.53 | 27.05 | 29.30 | 28.58 | 37.40 | 37.56 |
| An   | 18.50 | 20.75 | 22.60 | 20.43 | 21.80 | 19.55 | 22.43 | 19.68 | 19.93 |
| Ne   | 9.25  | 3.70  | 7.27  | 1.33  |       | 6.18  | 5.53  | 2.52  | 3.90  |
| Di   | 19.04 | 23.40 | 14.32 | 19.08 | 20.24 | 14.92 | 16.44 | 10.92 | 8.92  |
| Ol   | 12.78 | 20.42 | 7.50  | 9.06  |       | 6.17  | 11.28 | 9.38  | 11.30 |
| Mt   | 5.21  | 4.37  | 3.21  | 4.80  | 3.75  | 5.82  | 3.21  | 4.73  | 2.67  |
| Hm   |       |       |       |       | 3.82  |       |       |       |       |
| Il   | 5.50  | 4.70  | 6.32  | 6.28  | 4.34  | 5.06  | 5.52  | 3.82  | 3.68  |
| Ap   | 2.24  | 1.04  | 2.56  | 1.84  | 1.07  | 3.15  | 1.66  | 2.54  | 2.54  |
| Cal  |       | 0.34  | 0.34  | 0.80  | 0.56  |       |       |       |       |
|      |       |       | (42)  |       | (43)  |       |       |       |       |

(42) Incl. 0.17 Pr; 0.18 Ha.

(43) Incl. 6.58 En; 5.94 Fo.

but these had to wait for about a hundred years before subjected to careful petrographic examinations.

LYELL & HARTUNG visited the archipelago during 1853–1854, special attention being given to Gran Canaria, Tenerife and La Palma. LYELL presented some of his results in his classic »Manual of Elementary Geology« (1855) and HARTUNG in 1857 and 1862.

With the introduction of thin-sections by SORBY and the refinement of petrographic microscopic techniques, especially by ZIRKEL and ROSENBUSCH along about the middle of the 19th century, an infinitely more minute and careful study could be made of rock samples, and hence it is only publications appearing since this time that give us adequate petrographic details considered necessary today. It follows then that although HARTUNG's publications, those of VON FRITSCH (1867) and VON FRITSCH & REISS (1868) are of distinct interest, yet details of the volcanics lack precision, concepts regarding vulcanology are often vague and not in accord with more modern views.

Table 30                                              Niggli parameters of volcanic rocks, Canary Islands

|     | 1 | 2 | 3 | 4 | 5 | 6 | 7 | 8 | 9 | 11 |
|-----|-----|-----|------|------|------|------|------|------|------|------|
| si  | 79.5 | 20.5 | | | | | 96 | | 53.5 | |
| ti  | 4.6 | 1.9 | | | | | 4.4 | | 0.2 | |
| p   | 0.7 | 0.6 | | | | | 0.6 | | 0.1 | |
| al  | 14 | 37.5 | | | | | 16.5 | | 1 | |
| fm  | 56 | 21.5 | | | | | 52.5 | | 97.5 | |
| c   | 24 | 9.5 | | | | | 23 | | 1 | |
| alk | 6 | 31.5 | | | | | 8 | | 0.5 | |
| k   | 0.08 | 0.28 | | | | | 0.21 | | 0.0 | |
| mg  | 0.66 | 0.21 | | | | | 0.63 | | 0.9 | |
| qz  | −44.5 | −21 | | | | | −36 | | −48.5 | |
| h+  | 4.6 | 9.0 | | | | | 1.4 | | | |
| Q   | | | 14.3 | 20.8 | 20.5 | 15.0 | | 27.9 | | 22.0 |
| L   | | | 27.4 | 31.7 | 28.4 | 28.0 | | 31.5 | | 33.3 |
| M   | | | 58.3 | 47.5 | 51.1 | 57.0 | | 40.6 | | 44.7 |
| F   | | | 38.7 | 42.5 | 37.4 | 36.8 | | 45.6 | | 50.7 |
| M   | | | 52.2 | 41.7 | 49.8 | 51.0 | | 39.1 | | 34.4 |
| A   | | | 9.1 | 15.8 | 12.8 | 12.2 | | 15.3 | | 14.9 |
| SI  | | | 51.5 | 41.1 | 49.4 | 50.5 | | 38.9 | | 33.9 |
|     | (1) | (2) | | | | | | | | |

(1) Incl. 0.02 $s_2$.                                              (2) Incl. 0.4 $so_3$; 2.5 $co_2$.

|     | 12 | 13 | 14 | 15 | 16 | 17 | 18 | 21 | 22 | 23 |
|-----|-----|------|------|------|------|------|------|------|------|------|
| si  | 98.5 | | 78 | | | 197.2 | 315.2 | 110 | | |
| ti  | 6.7 | | 4.7 | | | | | 5.0 | | |
| p   | 0.04 | | 0.9 | | | | | 0.3 | | |
| al  | 20.5 | | 14 | | | 39.2 | 43.5 | 14 | | |
| fm  | 51 | | 55 | | | 16.0 | 10.0 | 53 | | |
| c   | 21 | | 23 | | | 11.9 | 3.9 | 27 | | |
| alk | 7.5 | | 8 | | | 32.9 | 42.6 | 6 | | |
| k   | 0.28 | | 0.25 | | | 0.27 | 0.35 | 0.26 | | |
| mg  | 0.49 | | 0.64 | | | 0.39 | 0.36 | 0.60 | | |
| qz  | −31.5 | | −54 | | | | | −14 | | |
| h+  | 30.5 | | 2.7 | | | | | 7.7 | | |
| Q   | | 17.5 | | 16.4 | 18.1 | | | | 14.4 | 7.1 |
| L   | | 31.5 | | 31.7 | 32.6 | | | | 27.7 | 26.9 |
| M   | | 51.1 | | 51.9 | 49.3 | | | | 58.1 | 66.0 |
| F   | | 46.3 | | 40.4 | 44.1 | | | | 47.5 | 27.3 |
| M   | | 37.2 | | 43.8 | 39.7 | | | | 38.9 | 49.0 |
| A   | | 16.5 | | 15.8 | 16.2 | | | | 13.6 | 13.7 |
| SI  | | 36.3 | | 43.4 | 39.4 | | | | 38.4 | 48.6 |
|     | | (3) | (4) | | | | | (5) | | |

(3) Incl. 0.3 $cl_2$; 2.4 $co_2$.                                              (5) Incl. 0.1 $f_2$.
(4) Incl. 0.05 $co_2$.

Table 30 (continued)

|     | 24 | 25 | 28 | 31 | 32 | 33 | 34 | 35 | 36 | 37 |
|-----|-----|-----|-----|-----|-----|-----|-----|-----|-----|-----|
| si  |    |    | 218.5 | 98.5 | 149 |    |    |    |    |    |
| ti  |    |    | 2.4 | 6.1 | 3.7 |    |    |    |    |    |
| p   |    |    | 0.1 | 1.0 | 0.4 |    |    |    |    |    |
| al  |    |    | 39.5 | 19 | 32.5 |    |    |    |    |    |
| fm  |    |    | 16.5 | 46.5 | 20.0 |    |    |    |    |    |
| c   |    |    | 3 | 25.5 | 14.0 |    |    |    |    |    |
| alk |    |    | 41 | 9 | 33.5 |    |    |    |    |    |
| k   |    |    | 0.30 | 0.16 | 0.26 |    |    |    |    |    |
| mg  |    |    | 0.21 | 0.54 | 0.36 |    |    |    |    |    |
| qz  |    |    | -41 | -37.5 | -82 |    |    |    |    |    |
| h+  |    |    | 12.4 | 15.5 | 10.4 |    |    |    |    |    |
| Q   | 17.0 | 13.2 |    |    |    | 17.2 | 31.4 | 33.6 | 34.5 | 32.0 |
| L   | 47.0 | 34.6 |    |    |    | 24.8 | 56.5 | 54.6 | 55.3 | 58.8 |
| M   | 36.0 | 52.2 |    |    |    | 58.0 | 12.1 | 11.2 | 10.2 | 9.3 |
| F   | 39.5 | 40.4 |    |    |    | 43.7 | 25.2 | 28.6 | 22.2 | 19.9 |
| M   | 21.6 | 39.1 |    |    |    | 46.1 | 10.6 | 9.3 | 5.9 | 5.5 |
| A   | 38.9 | 20.5 |    |    |    | 10.1 | 64.2 | 62.1 | 71.9 | 74.6 |
| SI  | 21.1 | 38.8 |    |    |    |    |    |    |    |    |
|     |    |    |    | (6) | (7) |    |    |    |    |    |

(6) Incl. 1.4 $co_2$.                    (7) Incl. 0.9 $cl_2$; 3.7 $so_3$.

|     | 38 | 39 | 40 | 41 | 42 | 44 | 45 | 46 | 47 | 48 |
|-----|-----|-----|-----|-----|-----|-----|-----|-----|-----|-----|
| si  |    |    | 101 |    | 98 |    | 70 | 99.07 |    |    |
| ti  |    |    | 6.6 |    | 4.3 |    |    |    |    |    |
| p   |    |    | 0.4 |    | 0.5 |    |    |    |    |    |
| al  |    |    | 20 |    | 18.5 |    | 5.0 | 20.31 |    |    |
| fm  |    |    | 46.5 |    | 50 |    | 76.5 | 42.12 |    |    |
| c   |    |    | 23.5 |    | 20 |    | 16.0 | 33.12 |    |    |
| alk |    |    | 10 |    | 11.5 |    | 2.0 | 4.42 |    |    |
| k   |    |    | 0.25 |    | 0.24 |    | 0.56 | 0.15 |    |    |
| mg  |    |    | 0.50 |    | 0.58 |    | 0.77 | 0.64 |    |    |
| qz  |    |    | -39 |    | -48 |    |    |    |    |    |
| h+  |    |    | 2.0 |    | 12.5 |    |    |    |    |    |
| Q   | 34.7 | 34.34 |    | 24.2 |    | 29.9 | 11.9 | 26.85 | 16.9 | 22.6 |
| L   | 53.0 | 56.19 |    | 44.2 |    | 61.1 | 11.9 | 32.71 | 28.4 | 42.9 |
| M   | 12.3 | 9.47 |    | 31.6 |    | 9.0 | 76.2 | 40.44 | 54.7 | 34.5 |
| F   | 23.5 | 17.0 |    | 42.9 |    | 15.6 |    |    | 45.2 | 48.2 |
| M   | 5.9 | 4.9 |    | 25.1 |    | 4.0 |    |    | 41.8 | 24.7 |
| A   | 70.6 | 78.1 |    | 32.0 |    | 80.5 |    |    | 13.0 | 27.1 |
| SI  |    |    |    | 24.8 |    |    |    |    | 41.1 | 24.4 |

Table 30 (continued)

|      | 49 | 50 | 51 | 52 | 53 | 54 | 55 | 56 | 57 | 58 |
|------|----|----|----|----|----|----|----|----|----|----|
| si   |    |    |    |    |    |    | 222.46 | 175.96 | 128.98 | 89 |
| ti   |    |    |    |    |    |    | 0.80 | 2.16 | 5.47 |    |
| p    |    |    |    |    |    |    | 0.05 | 2.67 | 1.02 |    |
| al   |    |    |    |    |    |    | 45.78 | 37.02 | 26.87 | 16 |
| fm   |    |    |    |    |    |    | 9.48 | 15.64 | 32.74 | 51 |
| c    |    |    |    |    |    |    | 3.41 | 9.02 | 22.51 | 24 |
| alk  |    |    |    |    |    |    | 41.33 | 38.34 | 17.87 | 9 |
| k    |    |    |    |    |    |    | 0.32 | 0.26 | 0.21 | 0.21 |
| mg   |    |    |    |    |    |    | 0.22 | 0.33 | 0.37 | 0.51 |
| qz   |    |    |    |    |    |    | −42.86 | −73.44 | −42.50 | −47 |
| h+   |    |    |    |    |    |    |    |    |    |    |
| Q    | 29.6 | 21.9 | 20.3 | 28.6 | 28.2 | 30.5 |    |    |    |    |
| L    | 47.6 | 38.1 | 32.8 | 42.4 | 46.8 | 46.9 |    |    |    |    |
| M    | 22.8 | 40.0 | 46.9 | 29.0 | 25.0 | 22.6 |    |    |    |    |
| F    | 44.9 | 53.4 | 48.2 | 54.0 | 48.2 | 42.8 |    |    |    |    |
| M    | 17.3 | 25.6 | 37.5 | 21.0 | 16.4 | 18.6 |    |    |    |    |
| A    | 37.8 | 21.0 | 14.3 | 25.0 | 35.4 | 38.6 |    |    |    |    |
| SI   | 16.9 | 25.0 | 36.8 | 20.3 | 15.9 | 18.1 |    |    |    |    |
|      |    |    |    |    |    |    | (8) | (9) |    |    |

(8) Incl. 0.11 $f_2$; 0.25 $cl_2$.          (9) Incl. 0.30 $f_2$; 0.51 $cl_2$.

|      | 59 | 60 | 61 | 62 | 63 | 64 | 65 | 67 | 68 | 69 |
|------|----|----|----|----|----|----|----|----|----|----|
| si   | 94 | 87 | 131 | 140.5 | 311 | 66 | 96.1 | 69 | 83 | 83 |
| ti   |    |    |    |    |    |    | 7.63 | 5.2 | 7.3 | 5.2 |
| p    |    |    |    |    |    |    |    |    |    |    |
| al   | 18 | 15 | 29 | 32 | 43.5 | 10.5 | 16.4 | 10 | 16 | 14 |
| fm   | 45 | 57.5 | 26 | 23.5 | 12 | 57.5 | 50.0 | 53 | 53 | 56 |
| c    | 26 | 23.5 | 19 | 19.5 | 3 | 28 | 24.5 | 30 | 23 | 24 |
| alk  | 11 | 4 | 26 | 25 | 41.5 | 4 | 9.1 | 7 | 7 | 6 |
| k    | 0.22 | 0.23 | 0.21 | 0.25 | 0.33 | 0.38 | 0.29 | 0.20 | 0.21 | 0.32 |
| mg   | 0.55 | 0.67 | 0.30 | 0.30 | 0.13 | 0.67 | 0.53 | 0.63 | 0.52 | 0.59 |
| qz   | −50 | −29 | −73 | −59.5 | +45 | −50 | −40.3 | −59.7 | −47.2 | −42.5 |
| h+   |    |    |    |    |    |    |    |    |    |    |
| Q    |    |    |    |    |    |    |    | 3.7 | 16.9 | 17.1 |
| L    |    |    |    |    |    |    |    | 27.0 | 32.0 | 28.7 |
| M    |    |    |    |    |    |    |    | 64.3 | 51.1 | 54.2 |
| F    |    |    |    |    |    |    |    |    |    |    |
| M    |    |    |    |    |    |    |    |    |    |    |
| A    |    |    |    |    |    |    |    |    |    |    |
| SI   |    |    |    |    |    |    |    |    |    |    |

Table 30 (continued)

|     | 70    | 71    | 72    | 73    | 74    | 75    | 76    | 77    | 78    |
|-----|-------|-------|-------|-------|-------|-------|-------|-------|-------|
| si  | 93    | 87    | 108   | 104   | 99    | 107   | 106   | 118   | 123   |
| ti  | 6.3   | 5.0   | 8.1   | 7.7   | 5.0   | 6.4   | 6.9   | 5.0   | 5.0   |
| p   |       |       |       |       |       |       |       |       |       |
| al  | 18    | 15    | 24    | 19    | 17    | 22    | 22    | 23    | 25    |
| fm  | 49    | 56    | 39    | 46    | 44    | 42    | 44    | 42    | 39    |
| c   | 23    | 23    | 25    | 25    | 24    | 24    | 24    | 22    | 21    |
| alk | 10    | 6     | 12    | 9     | 7     | 12    | 11    | 13    | 14    |
| k   | 0.24  | 0.17  | 0.21  | 0.18  | 0.15  | 0.20  | 0.13  | 0.18  | 0.18  |
| mg  | 0.54  | 0.60  | 0.43  | 0.46  | 0.54  | 0.43  | 0.43  | 0.45  | 0.41  |
| qz  | −46.2 | −36.6 | −41.1 | −33.6 | −30.7 | −42.7 | −36.6 | −34.4 | −34.7 |
| h+  |       |       |       |       |       |       |       |       |       |
| Q   | 18.5  | 19.1  | 23.5  | 23.3  | 23.1  | 22.8  | 23.0  | 25.6  | 26.6  |
| L   | 36.7  | 29.4  | 42.4  | 34.8  | 31.4  | 40.8  | 40.1  | 41.3  | 43.5  |
| M   | 44.8  | 51.5  | 34.1  | 41.9  | 45.5  | 36.4  | 36.9  | 33.1  | 29.9  |

The first of what may be termed more modern treatments were those of SAUER (1876) and COHEN (1876) studying material collected by VON FRITSCH and REISS, and sometime later the paper by WALTER (1894).

The first significant contributions to the petrography of the volcanics are those of FINCKH (1908) regarding Fuerteventura and GAGEL regarding La Palma (1908).

Of earlier Spanish works, the only significant ones are those of CALDERON Y ARANA (1876, 1879, 1880) dealing principally with Gran Canaria.

All told, compared to the other archipelagoes described here, the bibliography relating to igneous petrology of the Canary Islands is an extensive one, and is increasing yearly.

## Lanzarote

HARTUNG (1857) classified the volcanics into three units: Youngest, Younger and Oldest Formations thus recognizing temporal distinctions. The first significant paper was that of HERNANDEZ-PACHECO (1910) who distinguished five principal groupings of the volcanics: Lavas of historical times; Recent lavas slightly altered; Old, much altered lavas; Basalts of homogeneous eruptions; Acidic volcanics. After a long interval there appeared the monograph of HAUSEN (1959) who grouped the rocks into: Historic, SubRecent, Quaternary volcanics and Basaltic Tableland Series. He regarded the Tableland Series as forming the exposed basement of the island, but this is to be interpreted as younger than the basement occurring in Fuerteventura (vd. below). Rock types recognized are shown as per Table 32. He stressed the overwhelming basaltic nature of the island and islets, typical of all formations. The basalts are generally olivine-bearing, with salic (trachytic) derivatives essentially lacking. Plutonic xenoliths occur in lavas and dyke rocks, also as volcanic bombs, such types as peridotites, gabbroidal rocks, anorthosites, olivinites (dunites) being recognized. To him, Lanzarote and the islets represented a sub-province of alkali-poor, olivine-rich basalts, grading into picrites, of hornblenditic-kaulaitic or essexitic-gabbroidal magma types. HAUSEN also

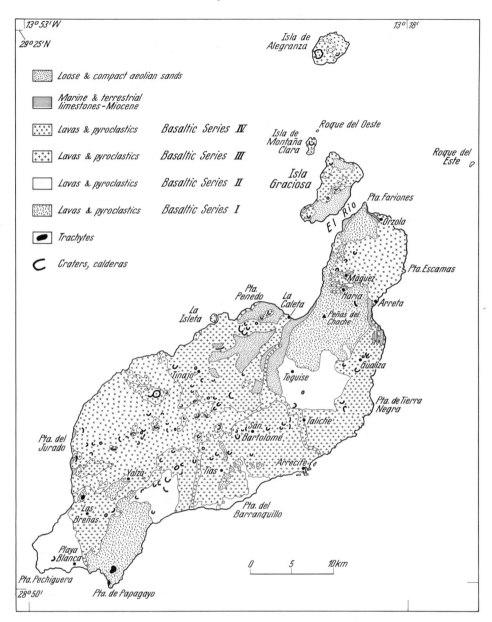

Fig. 56. Geological map of Lanzarote. (Modified after Inst. Geol. y Min. de Espana, 1968).

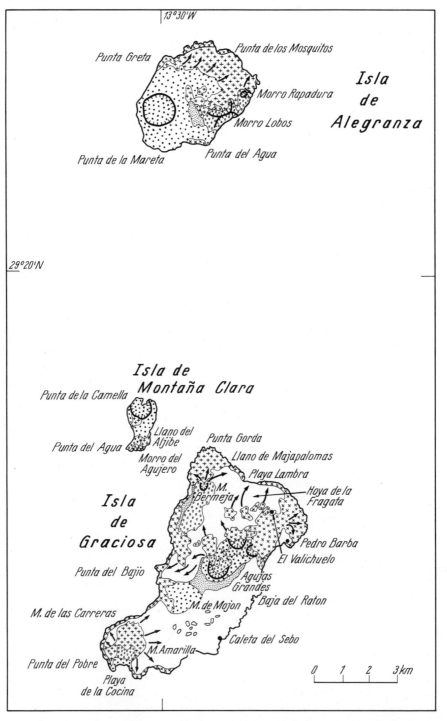

13°30'W

Punta Greta

Punta de los Mosquitos

Isla
de
Alegranza

Morro Rapadura

Morro Lobos

Punta de la Mareta

Punta del Agua

29°20'N

Isla de
Montaña Clara

Punta de la Camella

Llano del
Aljibe

Punta Gorda

Punta del Agua

Morro del
Agujero

Llano de Majapalomas

Playa Lambra

Isla
de
Graciosa

M.
Bermeja

Hoya de la
Fragata

Pedro Barba

El Valichuelo

Punta del Bajio

Agujas
Grandes

Baja del Raton

M. de las Carreras

M. de Mojon

Caleta del Sebo

M. Amarilla

Punta del Pobre

Playa
de la Cocina

0　1　2　3km

1　2　3　4　5　6　7　8

Table 31      Stratigraphic sequences proposed for Lanzarote (modified after FUSTER et al., 1968)

| Hartung (1857) | Hernandez-Pacheco (1910) | Hausen (1959) | Fuster et al. (1968) | |
|---|---|---|---|---|
| Jüngste Basaltformation | Lavas historicas | Historic volcanoes | Basaltic | Post-Sicilian |
| Jüngere | Lavas modernas poco alteradas | Sub-recent volcanoes | Series IV | |
| Basaltformation | Lavas viejas muy alteradas | Quaternary volcaneos | Basaltic Series III Basaltic Series II | |
| Älteste Basaltformation | Basaltos de erupcion homo génea | Basaltic tableland series | Basaltic Series I | Early Miocene |
| | Rocas volcanicas acidas | | Trachytes & trachytic tuffs | |

Table 32                    Principal rock types of the basaltic series of FUSTER et al. (1968)

| Unit | Lanzarote | Fuerteventura | Gran Canaria | Tenerife |
|---|---|---|---|---|
| Series IV | porphyritic & holocrystalline ol-basalts; ol.-aug.-basalts; vesicular basalts | ol-aug.-basalts; oceanitic basalts; doleritic basalts | porphyritic ankaramites; ordanichites; tephrites | ol-aug.-basalts; trachybasalts; trachydolerites; melano-trachytes; alk.-basalts |
| Series III | ol.-basalts; oceanites; scoriaceous & vitreous basalts | ol.-basalts; doleritic basalts; oceanites | alk.-basic-basalts; basanites; tephrites; ankaramites; scoriaceous & vitreous basalts | ol.-aug.-basalts; pyrox.-basalts tephritoids; trachybasalts; trachytes |
| Series II | ol.-basalts; ankaramites; ol.-plag.-basalts; granular basalts; scoriaceous & vitreous basalts | ol.-basalts; doleritic basalts; oceanites | ol.-pyrox.-basalts; amph.-basalts; nebasanites; ankaramites; oceanites | ol.-aug.-plag.-basalts; aug.-basalts; ol.-basalts; amp-basalts; hypocrystalline basalts; tephirites; trachytephrites |
| Series I | ol.-basalts; doleritic ol.-basalts; oceanites; trachytes; trachyandesites; "pegmatoids" | ol.-basalts; plag.-basalts; aug.-basalts; ol.-plag.-basalts; ol.--plag.-aug.-basalts; microcrystalline plag.-basalts; trachybasalts; oceanites | ol.-basalts; plag.-basalts; ol.-aug.-basalts; aug.-basalts; sakalavites | similar in general to II |

Fig. 57. Geological map of Las Isletas of Lanzarote. 1: Enclosed basins. 2: Sands. 3: Series IV, pyroclastics. 4: Series IV, lavas, scoria. 5: Series III, pyroclastics. 6: Series III, lavas, scoria. 7: Lava flow directions. 8: Crater, caldera borders. (Modified after FUSTER, IBARROLA & LOPEZ, 1966).

pointed out that on a temporal basis, the lavas showed little change in compostion from oldest to those of historic times.

FUSTER et al. (1968) stated that the only acidic rocks occurring – trachytes and trachytic tuffs at Punta Papagayo (ROTHE, 1967a, mentioned trachy-andesites in the general area) – could be correlated with formations of similar composition found at the base of their Basaltic Series I in Fuerteventura, and thus for Lanzarote these acidics would represent the oldest formation. In lavas of their Basaltic Series IV, III and II, »xenoliths coming from the substratum« are quite common in Lanzarote, including such types as dunites, peridotites, olivine-gabbros, olivine-hyperites, gabbros, norites, anorthositic-gabbros and anorthosites. HARTUNG and HERNANDEZ-PACHECO believed that such enclaves argued for a plutonic basement here, whilst HAUSEN took the view that if this represented basement material, then it was younger than that of Fuerteventura.

Table 33    Average compositions of basaltic rocks of Basalt Series II, III, IV, from
            Lanzarote and Fuerteventura (ÍBARROLA, 1970)

|  | 1 | 2 | 3 | 4 |
|---|---|---|---|---|
| No. Anal. | 40 | 25 | 13 | 11 |
| $SiO_2$ | 43.36 | 44.69 | 46.76 | 49.33 |
| $Al_2O_3$ | 12.73 | 12.98 | 13.53 | 13,70 |
| $Fe_2O_3$ | 4.01 | 4.73 | 4.16 | 2.38 |
| FeO | 8.11 | 7.56 | 7.70 | 8.28 |
| MnO | 0.16 | 0.16 | 0.15 | 0.14 |
| MgO | 12.19 | 11.73 | 10.28 | 9.77 |
| CaO | 11.33 | 10.67 | 10.46 | 9.67 |
| $Na_2O$ | 3.29 | 2.93 | 3.03 | 2.98 |
| $K_2O$ | 1.28 | 1.27 | 0.97 | 0.83 |
| $TiO_2$ | 2.65 | 2.62 | 2.40 | 2.13 |
| $P_2O_5$ | 0.89 | 0.66 | 0.56 | 0.39 |
| Or | 7.5 | 7.5 | 5.9 | 5.0 |
| Ab | 7.1 | 14.3 | 22.8 | 26.6 |
| An | 16.0 | 18,2 | 20.5 | 21.5 |
| Ne | 13.2 | 7.2 | 2.6 | |
| Di | 27.2 | 24.2 | 22.1 | 19.2 |
| En+Hy | | | | 7.7 |
| Ol | 19.5 | 18.8 | 17.3 | 13.8 |
| Mt | 4.1 | 4.9 | 4.3 | 2.6 |
| Il | 3.6 | 3.6 | 3.4 | 2.8 |
| Ap | 1.8 | 1.3 | 1.1 | 0.8 |
| Q | 16.1 | 18.7 | 22.2 | 25.9 |
| L | 31.6 | 31.2 | 32.1 | 31.9 |
| M | 52.3 | 50.1 | 45.7 | 42.2 |
| F | 41.1 | 42.6 | 44.5 | 44.3 |
| M | 42.8 | 42.3 | 40.0 | 40.1 |
| A | 16.1 | 15.1 | 15.5 | 15.6 |
| SI | 42.2 | 4I.6 | 39.3 | 39.6 |

1. Basanitoids              3. Alkaline olivine-basalts
2. Ankaramites              4. Tholeitic basalts

Fuster et al. pointed out that the basic-ultrabasic complex of Fuerteventura (vd. below) differed in degree of alkalinity from the plutonic xenoliths found in Lanzarote, and favoured as an explanation thereof the idea that the gabbro enclaves of Lanzarote came from deeper levels – perhaps high levels in the Upper Mantle – whereas in Fuerteventura the basement represented higher levels. However, at this time we must admit that correlations as regards basement material between these two islands are far from clear, in spite of only some 20 odd km separating them and basement strikes in Fuerteventura heading towards Lanzarote.

Finally we would mention the occurrence of »pegmatitoides« in the lavas of Basaltic Series I, as veins, veinlets, irregular masses and dykes, which petrologically range from theralitic gabbros to nepheline-monzonites. These are considerd to have formed as a result of direct crystallization from a residual magma via differentation of a parent basaltic magma (FERNANDEZ, 1969b).

## Fuerteventura

HARTUNG (1857) recognized the same three formations as in Lanzarote but added a fourth basal unit, »Sienit und Trapp Formation«, considered »alien to the archipelago in general« by HAUSEN (1958). This basal unit, comprising basanites, picrites, trachy-basalts but no pyroclastics was considered younger than the syenites, this latter term being used in an extremely loose manner. FINCKH (1908) who studied collections made by VON FRITSCH, determined that HARTUNG's ›Sienit Complex‹ comprised nordmarkites, pulaskites, akerites, essexites and such dyke rocks as bostonites, gauteites, camptonites, etc. All of these were intrusive into the Trapp Formation, a view opposed by earlier workers but since then generally agreed upon, though HAUSEN was somewhat sceptical about this. FERNANDEZ (1926) determined: (a) a basal holocrystalline series – syenites, diorites, granites, cut by kersantite and lamprophyre dykes, (b) old eruptive series, correlated with HARTUNG's ›Trapp‹ formation, (c) modern eruptive series, comprising poorly-preserved cones, with extensive pyroclastics, little lava, ropy lava flows and recent volcanoes. BOURCART & JÉRÉMINE (1938) believed that HARTUNG's ›Trapp‹ formation was the oldest in the island, formed of spilites, pyroclastics, dykes of syenite, trachyte and basalt, all intruded by syenites, diorites, gabbros and pyroxenites. Their stratigraphic grouping included: (a) Plateau basalts; (b) Plains basalts; (c) pre-historic basalts; (d) historic basalts. HAUSEN (1958a) grouped the igneous sequence as per Table 34. Following BOURCART & JÉRÉMINE, he preferred the term Spilite Complex for HARTUNG's ›Trapp‹ formation. As per HAUSEN the dykes, sills, lenticular bodies here include spilites (he used this term with considerable reservation) and keratophyre lava flows, these being disturbed into highly-inclined positions as a result of movements associated with the Hercynian orogenic cycle. This indeed implies a very old age which finds no substantiation anywhere else in the Canaries, or Macaronesia.

BLUMENTHAL (1961) thought HARTUNG's term ›Trapp‹ not too well chosen both from a structural and areal point of view. He accepted the name spilites but also with some reservation.

FUSTER et al. (1968) presented a stratigraphic sequence as shown in Table 34, showing correlations with divisions adopted by BOURCART & JÉRÉMINE and HAUSEN. References were made not only to those mentioned above but also those of FUSTER & AGUILAR

Table 34    Stratigraphic sequences proposed for Fuerteventura (modified after FUSTER et al., 1968)

| Hartung (1857) | Bourcart & Jérémine (1938) | Hausen (1958) | Fuster et al. (1968) | |
|---|---|---|---|---|
| Jüngste Basaltformation | Basaltes historiques | Recent volcanoes | Basaltic Series IV (Cinder volcanoes) | Post-Sicilian |
| Jüngere Basaltformation | Basaltes antéhistoriques | Sub-recent & late quaternary volcanoes | Basaltic Series III (Cinder volcanoes) | Post-Sicilian |
| | | | Basaltic Series II (Cinder volcanoes) | Post-Sicilian |
| | Basaltes des planes | Shield volcanoes | Shield volcanoes | |
| Älteste Basaltformation | Basaltes des plateaux | Basaltic Tableland Formation | Basaltic Series I (Fissural basalts) | M. Mio. |
| Sienit- and Trapp- Formation | Roches grenues | Ophiolites | Syenitic Ring Complexes | Pre – M. Miocene |
| | | | Subaerial tuffs & agglomerates | Pre – M. Miocene |
| | | | Submarine volcanics | Pre – M. Miocene |
| | Trapps | Spilite Complex | Detrital sedments | Pre – M. Miocene |
| | | | Basic Stratiform Complex | Pre – M. Miocene |

(1965), FUSTER & SANCHEZ (1967e), CENDRERO et al. (1967, 1968), ALONSO et al. (1968), FUSTER, GASTESI et al. (1968), FUSTER, HERNANDEZ-PACHECO et al. (1968). As per FUSTER and colleagues in their Fuerteventura monograph, considerable confusion has been perpetrated by previous workers especially as regards the ›Trapp‹ formation and associated plutonics. HARTUNG had already pointed out the high ratio of dykes to hostrocks, but this is even higher than he imagined, for the latter may represent as little as 5–10% of the ensemble. Zones with ca. 50% dykes are little disturbed. To these authors, the dyke complex is neither a stratigraphic, time nor lithological unit but rather a structural unit. They disagreed with BOURCART & JÉRÉMINE and HAUSEN regarding the relation of the plutonics to the ›Trapp‹ formation, claiming that the basics and ultrabasics were not intruded into the sedimentary-volcanic ›Trapp‹ sequence, that a non-conformity lay between the two, that the plutonics represented the oldest visible part of the basement, as in Gomera and La Palma. Syenitic-trachytic outcrops in the centre of the plutonic basement in the west-central part of the island were later than the basic representatives and formed ring-complexes at various levels. These syenitic complexes likely indicate an end phase of consolidation of the stratiform basic complex, with some trachytes penetrating into the base of Basaltic Series I. This stratiform complex, comprising largely rocks ranging from peridotites to gabbros is the visible foundation of the island, and into this, as in Gomera and La Palma, have been intruded

Table 35    Average composition of 26 Ultramafic Rocks of the Betancuria Massif, Fuerteventura.
1: Average of gabbros. 2: Average of alkalinized gabbros (reduced to 100 without $H_2O$).
(GASTESI, 1969)

|         | 1     | 2     |       | 1     | 2     |
|---------|-------|-------|-------|-------|-------|
| $SiO_2$    | 44.33 | 47.24 | Or    | 2.8   | 10.8  |
| $Al_2O_3$  | 16.37 | 17.15 | Ab    | 17.5  | 19.5  |
| $Fe_2O_3$  | 6.17  | 4.62  | An    | 34.6  | 22.5  |
| FeO     | 5.85  | 5.36  | Ne    | 1.4   | 11.1  |
| MnO     | 0.12  | 0.18  | Di    | 28.0  | 23.7  |
| MgO     | 7.19  | 5.48  | Fo+Fa | 5.1   | 3.4   |
| CaO     | 14.05 | 10.72 | Mt    | 6.2   | 4.9   |
| $Na_2O$    | 2.16  | 4.24  | Il    | 4.2   | 4.0   |
| $K_2O$     | 0.49  | 1.86  | Cp    | 0.4   | 0.3   |
| $TiO_2$    | 3.00  | 2.88  | Ce    | 0.1   | 0.1   |
| $P_2O_5$   | 0.21  | 0.15  |       |       |       |
| $CO_2$     | 0.05  | 0.07  |       |       |       |

Table 36    Average composition of 19 syenitic rocks from Fuerteventura (Adapted from MUNOZ, 1969)

|         |       |       |      |
|---------|-------|-------|------|
| $SiO_2$    | 62.85 | Or    | 29.7 |
| $Al_2O_3$  | 18.09 | Ab    | 53.7 |
| $Fe_2O_3$  | 2.12  | An    | 5.8  |
| FeO     | 1.10  | Ne    | 4.7  |
| MnO     | 0.16  | Di    | 2.1  |
| MgO     | 0.89  | En+Hy | 2.4  |
| CaO     | 1.78  | Acc   | 3.7  |
| $Na_2O$    | 6.91  |       |      |
| $K_2O$     | 5.05  |       |      |
| $TiO_2$    | 0.69  |       |      |
| $P_2O_5$   | 0.15  |       |      |
| $CO_2$     | 0.10  |       |      |

dykes and ring-complexes, the former only in these latter islands. This stratiform complex probably is either part of a unit in extent as great as that of the archipelago or then one of several island complexes where found outcropping or then represented by xenoliths in other islands, testifying to its occurrence there at depth, this basic-ultrabasic substratum being part of the ocean floor – Upper Mantle? Further references to this basal complex are to be found in the publications of GASTESI (1969), FERNANDEZ (1969) and MUNOZ (1969).

The dyke network of western Fuerteventura is a striking feature (FUSTER et al., 1968b; LOPEZ, 1969, 1970). The average strike is N 15 E, the rocks being principally of basaltic composition. Intense albitization and amphibolitization have all but destroyed primary minerals. The former process has also affected host rocks so that one can speak in terms of a regional metamorphism of intensity comparbale to that of Green Schists. These NNE-SSW striking dense dyke swarms would suggest tensional stresses acting more or less normal to this trend. Of various hypotheses proposed in explantion of

Table 37    Average composition of (A) 19 basaltic rocks of Recent vulcanism in Lanzarote, and (B) 23 basaltic rocks of Recent vulcanism in Fuerteventura (A. IBARROLA & LOPEZ, 1967; B. CENDRERO, 1966)

| | A | B | | A | B |
|---|---|---|---|---|---|
| $SiO_2$ | 46.38 | 43.90 | Or | 6.7 | 7.5 |
| $Al_2O_3$ | 12.76 | 13.22 | Ab | 18.5 | 18.5 |
| $Fe_2O_3$ | 3.44 | 3.50 | An | 17.7 | 10.5 |
| FeO | 7.98 | 8.38 | Ne | 5.4 | 10.3 |
| MnO | 0.13 | 0.16 | Di | 25.3 | 24.3 |
| MgO | 11.23 | 11.63 | Ol | 18.8 | 20.2 |
| CaO | 10.29 | 10.74 | Mt | 3.6 | 3.7 |
| $Na_2O$ | 3.09 | 3.11 | Il | 3.4 | 3.6 |
| $K_2O$ | 1.13 | 1.27 | Ap | 0.6 | |
| $TiO_2$ | 2.45 | 2.61 | Cp | | 1.4 |
| $P_2O_5$ | 0.56 | 2.61 | | | |
| $CO_2$ | 0.02 | | si | 96 | 87 |
| $H_2O$ | 0.34 | 0.53 | al | 15.5 | 15.5 |
| | | | fm | 54 | 54 |
| Total | 99.78 | 99.85 | c | 23 | 23 |
| | | | alk | 7.5 | 7.5 |
| | | | k | 0.19 | 0.21 |
| | | | mg | 0.64 | 0.63 |
| | | | Q | 20.8 | 17.9 |
| | | | L | 31.1 | 33.2 |
| | | | M | 48.1 | 49.9 |

these swarms, FUSTER et al. favoured the concept of displacement of the Atlantic rim sector leading to opening of abyssal fractures utilized by magmas to attain the surface. The dyke rocks – host rocks volume ratio would indicate that widening by dykes has at least tripled the initial extent of the formations. There is also a less well developed dyke network in the Jandia peninsula and also in the central eastern region, a much more sparse distribution of dykes in the northern part of the island. Those of Jandia show a rough diagonal pattern, those of the east a NW-SE trend, those of the north, diagonal, all these dykes being intrusive into Basaltic Series I. The rocks in question are again chiefly of basaltic type, but trachytic, phonolitic and camptonite dykes also occur. There appear to be three main generations of dyke development: (a) the oldest are the NNE multiple injection dykes, (b) dykes genetically related to Basaltic Series I, (c) salic dykes in intimate association with syenites and trachytes.

## Gran Canaria

CALDERON Y ARANA's publications of 1876, 1879, 1880 are the first to give more precise information on the volcanics of this island. He placed the rocks into three major groups: (a) those with sanidine as the prominent feldspar, (b) those with plagioclase as dominant feldspar, (c) those having no feldspar. In the first group he recognized sanidinites, liparites, phonolites and trachytes; in the second group, andesites, feldspar-basalts, dolerites, basanites and tephrites; in the third group, nepheline-basalts, limburgites and pyroxenites.

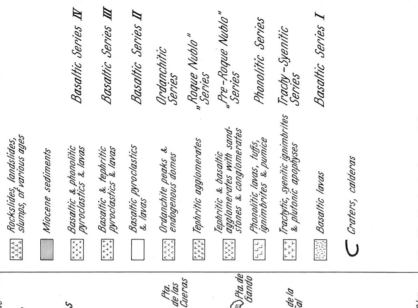

Alluvium

Rockslides, landslides, slumps, of various ages

Miocene sediments

Basaltic & phonolitic pyroclastics & lavas

Basaltic & tephritic pyroclastics & lavas

Basaltic pyroclastics & lavas

Ordanchite peaks & endogenous domes

Tephritic agglomerates

Tephritic & basaltic agglomerates with sand- stones & conglomerates

Phonolitic lavas, tuffs, ignimbrites & pumice

Trachytic, syenitic ignimbrites & plutonic apophyses

Basaltic lavas

Craters, calderas

Basaltic Series IV

Basaltic Series III

Basaltic Series II

Ordanchitic Series

"Roque Nublo" Series

"Pre-Roque Nublo" Series

Phonolitic Series

Trachy-Syenitic Series

Basaltic Series I

Fig. 59. Geological map of Gran Canaria. (Modified after Inst. Geol. y Minero de España, 1968).

Of more modern treatments, the first significant ones are those of JÉRÉMINE (1933), BOURCART (1935) and BOURCART & JÉRÉMINE (1937). Mme. JÉRÉMINE studied collections made almost a century before by WEBB & BERTHOLET, by RIPOCHE and her own collections. She found no evidence of an outcropping plutonic basement but recognized granular enclaves in tuffs. Her reporting of types of rhyolites, presumably in situ have been treated with some scepticism. Haüyne- and nepheline-bearing phonolites (including tahitites, ordanchites), basanites, tephrites, ankaramites, limburgites, ankaratrites are mentioned. BOURCART & JÉRÉMINE (1937) presented a stratigraphic sequence for Gran Canaria (Table 38) as follows: I. Old basalts; Old (II) and young (III) rhyolites; Old (II) and young (III) phonolites; Trachytes and micro-syenites (II and III); Basaltic rocks (IV); Plateaux basalts, valley basalts (V); Young basalts (VI); Granular rocks – syenites, sanidinites, gabbros, pyroxenolites and amphiboliticmonzonite-nephelinites. (Agreed, their tabulation can be interpreted in somewhat different ways.)

VUAGNAT (1960) described olivine-basalt pillow lavas in the Basaltic Series III of FUSTER et al. to be seen along the Puerto de la Luz-Tamaraceite road, in which there is »une sorte de passage entre des laves à coussins et les laves cordées«.

HAUSEN (1962) presented a stratigraphic sequence as per Table 38. He recognized two principal rock types, salic and basic, with intermediate types few in occurrence. He commented upon the relatively high ratio of salic to basic types, in this respect making the island unique in the archipelago. Using the rock nomenclature proposed by RITTMANN (1952, 1960) he recognized a large number of rocks – ca. 40 in number, exclusive of pyroclastics – being impressed by this »astonishly large« variety.

FUSTER et al. (1968) were not satisfied with the stratigraphic sequences of either BOURCART & JÉRÉMINE or HAUSEN and devised their own (Table 38). The FUSTER and BOURCART & JÉRÉMINE tabulations show considerably more agreement, the chief difference in the FUSTER and HAUSEN charts being that the latter separated his syenitic-trachytic complex into two units of different ages, his oldest basalts being intermediary, whereas FUSTER et al. claimed that HAUSEN's dislocated and young trachytes belong to the same unit and are of post-Basaltic Series I age. As per these authors, their Series I tabular formation is the oldest in the island, overlying material of unknown age and character. BOURCART & JÉRÉMINE believed that the island plutonics, present as ejectamenta or as veins in trachytes, were more or less contemporaneous in age with surface volcanics.

Along with syenites syngenetically related to trachytes, occur some small plutonic outcrops, e. g. near Las Lagunetas, whose relationships to the volcanics cannot be clearly determined.

In the Roque Nublo Formation and in Quaternary basalt formations are many basic-ultrabasic rocks which, as per FUSTER et al., are to be interpreted as enclaves rather than subvolcanic facies of the host rocks. To these writers, here in Gran Canaria there was present a basal complex similar to those of Fuerteventura, Gomera and La Palma, a statement not easy to reconcile with their comment: »En la parte emergida de la isla no se han encontrado, ni es facil que aparezcan, formaciones mas antiguas que la Serie I«.

Dyke occurrences are less spectacular here than in Fuerteventura, though FUSTER et al. remarked, including also the dyke systems of Gomera and La Palma that: »Las Islas

Table 38        Stratigraphic sequences proposed for Gran Canaria (modified after FUSTER et al., 1968)

| | Bourcart & Jérémine (1937) | Hausen (1962) | Fuster et al. (1968) | |
|---|---|---|---|---|
| VI | Arucas Tahitite / very recent Basalts | Recent & Quaternary vulcanism | Basaltic Series IV | Post-Vindobonian – late Quaternary |
| V | Valley Basalts | | Basaltic Series III | |
| | Plateau Basalts | Late-Tertiary vulcanism | Basaltic Series II | |
| IV | Vindobonian Ordanchites | Highly-Na-alkaline Phonolitic lavas | Ordanchitic Series | |
| | Nublo, Dehesa, etc. Breccias | Roque Nublo Agglomerates | Roque Nublo Series | |
| | Vindobonian Basànite | and inter-fingering tephritic lava effusions | Pre-Roque Nublo Series | |
| III | Gray Rhyolites, Merdejo Cinerites (Canto Blanco) White Phonolites & Trachytes | Pozzolane (Canto Blanco) Phonolite lavas | Phonolitic Series | pre-Vindobonian but Miocene |
| II | Syenites Rhyolites & Trachytes Phonolites | Syenitic Plutonic Bosses Young Trachytes | Syenitic-Trachytic Complex | |
| I | Old basalts | Tableland Basaltic Formation | Basaltic Series I | |
| | | Dislocated old trachytes | | |

Canarias son, sin duda, una de las zonas del mundo donde las inyecciones filonianas alcanzan mayor desarrollo y espectacularidad«. In some areas of Gran Canaria, e. g. the Caldera de Tejeda, the dyke network is imposing. HAUSEN believed the salic dykes to be older than the basic ones, with the latter occupying a greater time range. As in Fuerteventura, the ratio of dykes to host rocks can be remarkably high, 9:1 on occasion. Dykes are found transecting Series I, Phonolitic Series, Pre-Roque Nublo Series and Roque Nublo Series in particular, being especially well developed in the middle of the Syenitic-Trachytic Complex. To SCHMINCKE (1967c) and SCHMINCKE & SWANSON (1966, 1967), phonolitic-trachytic dykes in the last-mentioned represented an immense conesheet swarm intruding a hypothetical volcanic edifice erected in the centre of an old caldera. In this presumed old caldera area dykes appear to show no preferred orientation(s).

Further more recent papers dealing with igneous matters in Gran Canaria include those of SCHMINCKE (1969), FUSTER et al. (1969), HERNANDEZ-PACHECO (1969), LOTZE (1970), IBARROLA (1970), ANGUITA (1972) and ARANA et al. (1973).

| Table 39 | Average chemical composition of 31 rocks of the Ignimbritic Sequence, including trachytic rhyolites, comendites, pantellerites, trachytic and phonolitic ignimbrites, of Gran Canaria (adapted from SCHMINCKE, 1969) | | |
|---|---|---|---|
| | | $SiO_2$ | 67.33 |
| | | $Al_2O_3$ | 14.15 |
| | | Total Fe as FeO | 4.71 |
| | | MnO | 0.26 |
| | | MgO | 0.55 |
| | | CaO | 0.86 |
| | | $Na_2O$ | 6.49 |
| | | $K_2O$ | 4.47 |
| | | $TiO_2$ | 1.04 |
| | | $P_2O_5$ | 0.10 |

## Tenerife

WEBB & BERTHOLET (1839) were the first to distinguish various volcanic formations, and VON FRITSCH & REISS (1868) were the first to enter into some detail regarding such material. They recognized five major groupings: 1. Fine-grained rocks of trachytic type – trachytes, andesites, phonolites, feldspar-phonolites, nepheline-, nosean- and haüyne-phonolites. 2. Fine-grained rocks of basaltic type – basanites, tephrites. 3. Basalts with labradorite and nepheline as leucocrats, olivine, augite and magnetite as melanocrats. 4. Rare plutonics but represented by sanidinites and gabbros. 5. Vitreous rocks – pumice, ›eutaxites‹ and reference to palagonite-type rocks. CALDERON Y ARANA (1880) and VON WOLFF (1931) further extended our knowledge of Tenerife rocks and magmatic differentiations. JÉRÉMINE (1930, 1933) noted the presence of phonolites, ordanchites, tephroids, tephrites, basanites and plutonic xenoliths, whilst SMULIKOWSKI et al. (1946) (JÉRÉMINE and SMULIKOWSKI both made field trips during the International Geological Congress in Spain in 1926) noted that here, as also in Gran Canaria and La Palma there were two distinct rock groupings – trachy-tephrites and trachy-basanites with transitions to trachytes and basanites, and phonolites relatively poor in plagioclase and feldspathoids. Rare ordanchites and tahitites formed a connecting link. These authors, also JÉRÉMINE, adopted the nomenclature of LACROIX.

Table 40            Stratigraphic sequences proposed for Tenerife (partly after FUSTER et al., 1968)

| Hausen (1955) | Fuster et al. (1968) | | |
|---|---|---|---|
| Basaltic Adventive Volcanoes | Recent (acidic & basic) Series IV | | Pliocene-Quaternary |
| Pyroclastic Formation | Teide-Viejo trachybasalts & phonolites | | |
| | Basaltic Series III | | |
| Phonolitic-Trachyphonolitic-Trachytic Formation | Trachytic-Trachybasaltic Series | | |
| | Cañadas Series | Upper | |
| | | Lower | |
| Ancient Basaltic Formation | Old Series II & I | | between 2 & 12 M.Y. |
| Granular rocks of basement (?) | Plutonic Basement ? | | |

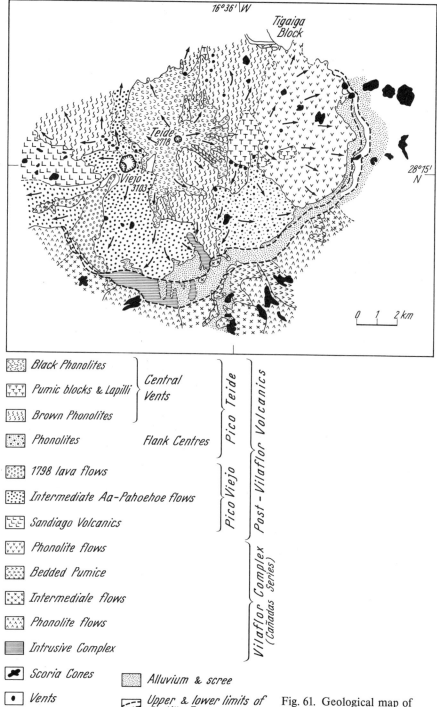

Black Phonolites
Pumic blocks & Lapilli — Central Vents
Brown Phonolites
Phonolites — Flank Centres
1798 lava flows
Intermediate Aa-Pahoehoe flows
Sandiago Volcanics
Phonolite flows
Bedded Pumice
Intermediale flows
Phonolite flows
Intrusive Complex
Scoria Cones
Vents
Flow directions
Alluvium & scree
Upper & lower limits of Portillo-Tauce scarps

Pico Teide
Pico Viejo — Post-Vilaflor Volcanics
Vilaflor Complex (Cañadas Series)

Fig. 61. Geological map of Las Cañadas, Tenerife. (Modified after RIDLEY, 1972).

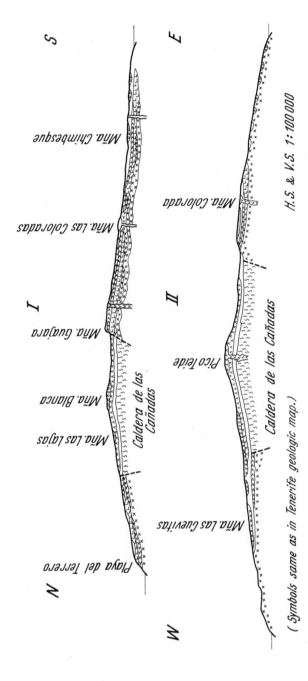

Fig. 62. Geological profiles, Tenerife. (Modified after FUSTER et al., 1968).

( Symbols same as in Tenerife geologic map.)

H.S. & V.S. 1:100 000

HAUSEN's monograph (1955b) was the first lengthy report on all aspects of the geology of Tenerife. He grouped the volcanics into five chief units (Table 40) and recognized some 23 types of lava rocks, 6 types of dyke rocks and 3 types of plutonics, as well as such pyroclastics as pozzuolanes, pumice, lapilli, agglomerates, tuffs, ashes and bombs. Basaltic lavas form thick series of individual thin concordant beds. Older

Table 41      Average composition of alkaline salic rocks of Tenerife (ARANA & BRÄNDLE, 1969)

|             | 1     | 2     | 3     | 4     | 5     | 6     |
|-------------|-------|-------|-------|-------|-------|-------|
| $SiO_2$     | 56.41 | 59.51 | 61.07 | 61.85 | 62.78 | 58.69 |
| $Al_2O_3$   | 19.79 | 19.85 | 17.67 | 15.57 | 17.78 | 19.97 |
| $Fe_2O_3$   | 3.06  | 2.69  | 3.53  | 4.59  | 2.68  | 1.66  |
| $FeO$       | 2.05  | 1.06  | 0.80  | 0.73  | 0.66  | 2.23  |
| $MnO$       | 0.20  | 0.13  | 0.25  | 0.26  | 0.19  | 0.16  |
| $MgO$       | 1.76  | 0.81  | 0.77  | 0.94  | 0.62  | 0.65  |
| $CaO$       | 4.27  | 2.09  | 1.28  | 1.79  | 1.35  | 1.59  |
| $Na_2O$     | 6.54  | 8.00  | 8.16  | 7.90  | 7.67  | 8.83  |
| $K_2O$      | 3.86  | 4.66  | 5.49  | 5.19  | 5.35  | 5.24  |
| $TiO_2$     | 1.41  | 0.88  | 0.86  | 0.94  | 0.72  | 0.71  |
| $P_2O_5$    | 0.34  | 0.32  | 0.08  | 0.11  | 0.11  | 0.15  |
| Or          | 22.5  | 26.7  | 31.5  | 29.8  | 30.8  | 29.7  |
| Ab          | 43.9  | 49.4  | 43.4  | 44.2  | 54.5  | 38.5  |
| An          | 13.0  | 4.3   |       |       |       |       |
| Ne          | 8.4   | 12.0  | 11.0  | 5.3   | 5.4   | 21.7  |
| Eg          |       | 7.2   | 12.8  | 2.7   | 1.1   |       |
| Di          |       | 0.8   | 2.1   | 2.8   | 2.8   | 3.3   |
| En+Hy       | 6.1   | 1.7   | 1.9   | 2.6   | 0.4   | 2.7   |
| Mt          | 3.2   | 2.8   | 0.9   |       | 1.7   | 1.2   |
| Ap          | 0.7   | 0.5   | 0.2   | 0.2   | 0.2   | 0.3   |
| Ti          | 1.8   | 1.8   | 1.8   | 2.1   | 1.5   | 1.5   |
| Ru          | 0.4   |       |       |       |       |       |
| si          | 177.1 | 206.4 | 219.1 | 223.9 | 238.3 | 199.0 |
| al          | 36.6  | 40.4  | 37.3  | 33.0  | 39.6  | 39.7  |
| fm          | 21.5  | 14.8  | 16.8  | 20.4  | 13.9  | 14.3  |
| c           | 14.3  | 7.7   | 5.0   | 7.0   | 5.5   | 5.7   |
| alk         | 27.6  | 37.0  | 40.9  | 39.6  | 41.0  | 40.3  |
| k           | 0.28  | 0.28  | 0.31  | 0.30  | 0.32  | 0.28  |
| mg          | 0.38  | 0.28  | 0.24  | 0.24  | 0.39  | 0.22  |
| Q           | 32.0  | 31.7  | 32.6  | 34.5  | 35.0  | 28.7  |
| L           | 56.0  | 60.2  | 55.9  | 49.7  | 56.6  | 62.6  |
| M           | 12.0  | 8.1   | 11.5  | 15.8  | 8.4   | 8.7   |

1. Average of   4 L. Canadas Series – nephelinitic latite-andesites.
2. Average of   6 U. Canadas Series – lava flow phonolites, no aegerine.
3. Average of 11 U. Canadas Series – lava flow phonolites with aegerine.
4. Average of 11 U. Canadas Series – "eutaxites" soda trachytes.
5. Average of   5 Trach.-Trachybasalt Series – soda trachytes.
6. Average of 14 Teide-Pico Viejo Comples rocks.

lavas are holocrystalline, dense or then porphyritic, often rich in cavities completely filled with secondary minerals, whereas young lavas are vitrophyric, porous and slaggy. Salic lavas show much thicker individual flows, often columnar jointed. No in situ plutonics were noted, such occurring only as isolated blocks, boulders of various dimensions.

FÚSTER et al. (1968) correlated their stratigraphic units with those of HAUSEN as per Table 40. The Old Basaltic Series are of exclusive basaltic type, aphyric and porphyritic, including such rocks as shown in Table 40. Their Cañadas Series is not entirely coincident with this term as used by others which latter restricted the unit to the central acidic structure here. FUSTER et al. divided the Series into an Upper division – largely comprising trachytes, mafic phonolites and trachy-basalts – and a Lower division of phonolites, peralkaline trachytes with some intercalated trachy-basalts. The Trachytic-Trachy-basaltic Series is distinguished from the phonolites of the Upper Cañadas not only on the basis of different composition but also by the distribution of vents and significant disconformities. Basaltic Series III is a homogeneous unit including mostly olivine-augite-basalts of porphyritic texture. Basaltic Series IV, though involving both acidic and basic rock types, is considered to represent the same and last eruptivity of the island, such a conclusion being reached chiefly by the state of preservation of these rocks. They recognized two distinct types of plutonic xenoliths – nepheline-syenites and gabbroidic fragments, with perhaps also dunites and pyroxenite enclaves. These authors, as distinct from say VON FRITSCH & REISS (1868), HAUSEN (op. cit.), BRAVO (1962a), GASTESI (1967), are somewhat more sceptical about postulating a plutonic basement underlying the entire archipelago. However, subsequently BORLEY et al. (1971) claimed that such plutonic xenoliths are in agreement with geophysical data in suggesting a sub-crustal structure of plutonics not only in Tenerife but for other Canary islands also.

ARANA & BRÄNDLE (1969) pointed out that the ratio of salics to basalts is higher in Tenerife than elsewhere within the Atlantic islands. (Vd. HAUSEN's statement regarding Gran Canaria above.) Salic rocks occur as two large ensembles, one the Cañadas structure and the other the Picos Teide-Viejo structure, both of which belong to the Middle Atlantic series, with marked alkalinization developing during the evolution thereof.

RIDLEY (1970b) argued that if only chemical analyses were considered for the island, the frequency distribution would show a marked bimodal character – excess of salic over intermediate types – but if we concentrate rather on areal and volume distribution, then this distinction becomes much less clear.

BRÄNDLE (1973) has remarked that trachytic-phonolitic rock types show a greater preponderance over basic types here in Tenerife than elsewhere throughout the Atlantic region. He surmizes various magmatic cycles corresponding to the major units of FUSTER et al. (1968), in which an increase in alkali content and a decrease in saturation takes place during the sequence, and hence a transition from trachytes to phonolites. To him, the gradual inclination seen in the oxide variation diagrams, along with absence of any »DALY Gap«, indicated that the end-terms trachyte-phonolite arose by fractional crystallization from basaltic magmas, though he did not rule out the influence of other processes, such as gaseous transfer.

Table 42 Average compositions of (a) Basaltic Canadas Series (Tenerife); (b) Basaltic Series III (Tenerife) and (c) Quaternary Basalts of Gran Canaria (IBARROLA, 1970)

|  | 1 | 2 | 3 | 4 | 5 | 6 | 7 | 8 | 9 | 10 |
|---|---|---|---|---|---|---|---|---|---|---|
| No. Anal. | 4 | 14 | 4 | 11 | 2 | 5 | 7 | 4 | 10 | 5 |
| $SiO_2$ | 44.18 | 48.55 | 51.27 | 43.53 | 48.60 | 47.21 | 51.57 | 38.44 | 44.77 | 42.35 |
| $Al_2O_3$ | 16.50 | 17.61 | 18.71 | 15.18 | 14.49 | 16.93 | 18.84 | 10.13 | 14.61 | 12.11 |
| $Fe_2O_3$ | 6.08 | 3.95 | 4.66 | 4.16 | 3.32 | 2.99 | 3.21 | 4.34 | 4.19 | 3.00 |
| FeO | 6.21 | 5.75 | 3.56 | 8.53 | 7.65 | 6.81 | 4.78 | 9.60 | 6.46 | 8.91 |
| MnO | 0.17 | 0.19 | 0.18 | 0.17 | 0.15 | 0.19 | 0.19 | 0.21 | 0.18 | 0.19 |
| MgO | 5.78 | 4.25 | 3.57 | 7.34 | 8.59 | 4.65 | 3.27 | 14.87 | 7.83 | 12.30 |
| CaO | 10.88 | 8.27 | 6.82 | 11.02 | 9.26 | 9.16 | 6.46 | 13.06 | 10.68 | 11.70 |
| $Na_2O$ | 3.31 | 4.93 | 5.31 | 3.61 | 3.64 | 4.68 | 5.54 | 2.87 | 4.70 | 3.42 |
| $K_2O$ | 1.95 | 2.73 | 2.82 | 1.72 | 1.50 | 2.25 | 2.89 | 0.99 | 2.56 | 1.64 |
| $TiO_2$ | 3.78 | 2.78 | 2.22 | 3.74 | 2.36 | 3.00 | 2.35 | 3.89 | 2.94 | 3.48 |
| $P_2O_5$ | 1.12 | 1.00 | 0.87 | 0.94 | 0.44 | 1.07 | 0.87 | 1.57 | 0.71 | 0.85 |
| $CO_2$ | 0.07 |  |  |  |  |  |  |  |  |  |
| Or | 11.6 | 16.0 | 16.5 | 10.2 | 8.8 | 13.3 | 16.8 | 5.7 | 14.9 | 9.5 |
| Ab | 18.8 | 26.4 | 37.4 | 11.8 | 27.0 | 24.0 | 37.1 |  | 5.2 |  |
| An | 24.7 | 17.8 | 18.7 | 20.2 | 18.7 | 18.7 | 17.8 | 11.7 | 11.1 | 12.7 |
| Ne | 6.8 | 10.6 | 5.9 | 12.4 | 3.3 | 11.0 | 7.2 | 15.3 | 22.0 | 18.1 |
| Di | 18.6 | 13.7 | 7.8 | 23.3 | 19.5 | 16.6 | 7.1 | 23.8 | 29.8 | 31.3 |
| Ol | 5.4 | 5.5 | 4.4 | 10.6 | 15.2 | 6.9 | 5.7 | 30.6 | 7.3 | 18.9 |
| Mt | 6.4 | 4.1 | 4.0 | 4.4 | 3.5 | 3.2 | 3.3 | 4.5 | 4.3 | 3.1 |
| Hm |  |  | 0.5 |  |  |  |  |  |  |  |
| Il | 5.3 | 3.8 | 3.1 | 5.2 | 3.3 | 4.2 | 3.2 | 5.4 | 4.0 | 4.8 |
| Ap | 2.2 | 2.0 | 1.7 | 1.8 | 0.9 | 2.1 | 1.7 | 3.0 | 1.4 | 1.6 |
| Q | 22.2 | 24.5 | 27.9 | 19.2 | 24.1 | 23.9 | 28.0 | 9.3 | 16.7 | 13.9 |
| L | 39.9 | 46.7 | 49.5 | 37.8 | 36.0 | 44.6 | 50.4 | 25.8 | 40.7 | 31.5 |
| M | 37.9 | 28.8 | 22.6 | 43.0 | 39.9 | 31.5 | 21.6 | 64.9 | 42.6 | 54.6 |
| F | 51.4 | 43.9 | 39.8 | 49.2 | 43.6 | 45.1 | 39.6 | 41.9 | 40.4 | 40.1 |
| M | 25.4 | 20.0 | 18.4 | 29.4 | 35.3 | 22.0 | 16.9 | 46.1 | 30.9 | 42.2 |
| A | 23.2 | 36.1 | 41.8 | 21.4 | 21.1 | 32.9 | 43.5 | 12.0 | 28.7 | 17.5 |
| SI | 24.8 | 19.7 | 17.9 | 28.9 | 34.8 | 21.7 | 16.6 | 45.5 | 30.9 | 42.0 |
|  | | a | | | | b | | | c | |

1. Ankaramitic basalts. 2. Tephoridic basalts. 3. Trachyandesites.
4. Basanitoids. 5. Olivine-basalts. 6. Tephritic trachybasalts.
7. Trachyandesites. 8. Basanites. 9. Tephrites.
10. Basanitoids.

## Gomera

VON FRITSCH (1867) mentioned the presence in the island of basalts, phonolites and andesites – the first petrological comments made. The first significant papers are those of FERNANDEZ (1907, 1918) who established two principal units: (a) phonolitic rocks overlying trachytic ones which in turn rest on a ›diabase‹ basement, the last-mentioned found only as boulders deep within valleys and considered of pre-Tertiary age. (b) around this nucleus are younger basaltic type rocks.

GAGEL (1926) likewise recognized two major units: (a) ›Grundgebirge‹ along with a lower ›Ältere Plateau-Basalte‹ formation. This was metamorphosed, tectonized and greatly altered, considering this to be the substratum. (FERNANDEZ (op. cit.) as seen above, recognized only loose plutonic boulders.) (b) ›Phonolithe‹ formation. Between the two was an unconformity, a clearly marked boundary distinguishing, as per GAGEL, a Palaeozoic basement complex and a very much younger series of volcanics. MÜLLER (1930) who carried out petrochemical investigations on GAGEL's samples, could see no valid reason for these unit distinctions.

BLUMENTHAL (1961) recognized a basal complex, comprising spilites of microdioritic and andesitic type, forming originally thick horizontal layers but disarranged (›trastrocados‹) into inclinations varying from 45° to vertical. There also occur here peridotitic-type rocks interstratified with basalts, all transected by holocrystalline dykes and off-shoots.

BRAVO (1964b) determined a basal complex with dyke networks, separated by a disconformity from agglomerates of nuée ardente origin, in which occur three basaltic series, again separated by disconformities. Phonolitic and trachy-phonolitic emissions took place after the complex was formed and continued during all the time that basaltic eruptions were active. His basal complex comprised chiefly gabbros and peridotites in which are seen »una serie de nebulosas«, with irregularly dispersed veins and diffuse transitions from one type of material to the other, suggesting a process of metasomatism or anataxis.

CENDRERO (1967a, 1970a, 1971) has done considerable work on this smaller island, but unfortunately his 1:50,000 maps cover only about one-third of the island, the northern part. His units, from top to base are:

Sub-Recent basalts
Roques Series
Discordance
Old Basaltic Series, divided into:
    upper old basalts
    polygenetic agglomerates
    discordance
    lower old basalts
Discordance
Trachytic-Phonolitic Series
Discordance
Basal Complex, with dyke networks

The Basal Complex includes wehrlites, pyroxenites, gabbros, olivine-gabbros, alkaline-gabbros, syenites and dunites, and what he terms a Submarine Series, comprising (a) highly altered basic volcanics of pillow structure, submarine agglomerates with abundant enclaves of both plutonic and volcanic material; (b) sedimentary rocks – limestones, shales, silts and cherts. He attached great importance to his Submarine Series, already described from Fuerteventura (FUSTER & AGUILAR, 1965; FUSTER et al., 1968) and in La Palma (GASTESI et al., 1966), whilst he recognized a large degree of similarity between the sedimentaries of Gomera, Fuerteventura and

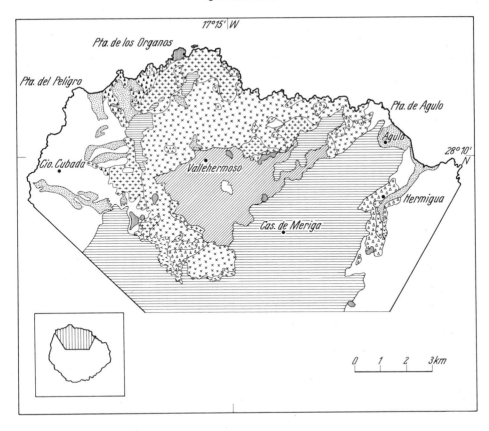

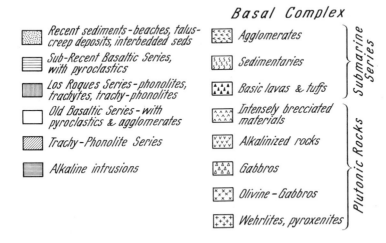

Fig. 63. Geological map of part of Northern Gomera. (Modified after CENDRERO, 1971).

Geology of the Canary Archipelago

Table 43   Chemical analyses, molecular norms and NIGGLI parameters of plutonic rocks, Gomera (CENDRERO, 1971)

| | 1 | 2 | 3 | 4 | 5 | 6 | 7 |
|---|---|---|---|---|---|---|---|
| $SiO_2$ | 43.65 | 45.45 | 45.40 | 42.80 | 43.20 | 44.15 | 40.90 |
| $Al_2O_3$ | 9.20 | 14.00 | 17.56 | 10.00 | 8.00 | 8.36 | 7.10 |
| $Fe_2O_3$ | 3.43 | 3.46 | 2.83 | 3.23 | 3.94 | 2.47 | 5.37 |
| FeO | 9.06 | 6.42 | 4.76 | 8.42 | 9.19 | 7.82 | 9.84 |
| MnO | 0.16 | 0.12 | 0.10 | 0.14 | 0.16 | 0.13 | 0.16 |
| MgO | 19.14 | 11.01 | 12.14 | 14.16 | 18.38 | 16.77 | 16.16 |
| CaO | 10.69 | 13.77 | 13.65 | 15.76 | 9.27 | 16.01 | 13.09 |
| $Na_2O$ | 0.96 | 1.64 | 1.10 | 0.88 | 1.34 | 0.78 | 0.52 |
| $K_2O$ | 0.40 | 0.50 | 0.34 | 0.22 | 0.86 | 0.50 | 0.22 |
| $TiO_2$ | 1.05 | 1.67 | 0.73 | 3.52 | 2.19 | 1.09 | 4.93 |
| $P_2O_5$ | 0.13 | 0.08 | 0.04 | 0.06 | 0.34 | 0.06 | 0.07 |
| $H_2O$ | 2.14 | 1.70 | 1.59 | 1.14 | 3.23 | 1.66 | 1.66 |
| Total | 100.01 | 99.82 | 100.24 | 100.33 | 100.09 | 99.80 | 100.02 |
| Or | 2.35 | 2.95 | 2.00 | 1.30 | 5.15 | 2.95 | 1.30 |
| An | 19.59 | 29.84 | 41.85 | 22.91 | 13.46 | 17.86 | 16.86 |
| Ab | 8.60 | 13.40 | 9.85 | 1.17 | 12.20 | 4.20 | 4.80 |
| Ne | | 0.90 | | 4.07 | | | |
| Wo | 11.58 | 13.24 | 9.19 | 17.36 | 9.39 | 23.03 | 12.78 |
| En+Hy | 13.52 | 13.22 | 13.48 | 17.34 | 11.22 | 16.97 | 17.08 |
| Fo+Fa | 38.32 | 19.07 | 19.10 | 24.90 | 39.10 | 30.03 | 30.67 |
| Ti | 2.19 | 3.54 | 1.50 | 7.41 | 4.62 | 2.28 | 10.59 |
| Il | | | | | | | |
| Mt | 3.57 | 3.66 | 2.94 | 3.40 | 4.17 | 2.58 | 5.77 |
| Ap | 0.25 | 0.15 | 0.07 | 0.10 | 0.67 | 0.10 | 0.12 |
| si | 76.79 | 92.07 | 89.88 | 78.63 | 79.07 | 77.97 | 73.95 |
| al | 9.53 | 16.70 | 20.47 | 10.81 | 8.62 | 8.69 | 7.55 |
| fm | 68.24 | 49.56 | 48.05 | 56.35 | 69.82 | 59.12 | 65.93 |
| c | 20.13 | 29.87 | 28.93 | 31.00 | 18.16 | 30.28 | 25.34 |
| alk | 2.08 | 3.86 | 2.53 | 1.82 | 3.37 | 1.89 | 1.16 |
| k | 0.21 | 0.16 | 0.16 | 0.14 | 0.29 | 0.29 | 0.21 |
| mg | 0.73 | 0.67 | 0.74 | 0.68 | 0.71 | 0.74 | 0.66 |
| Q | 17.06 | 23.84 | 25.91 | 18.35 | 16.15 | 17.39 | 15.52 |
| L | 18.33 | 28.62 | 32.23 | 19.30 | 18.49 | 16.69 | 13.78 |
| M | 64.61 | 47.54 | 41.86 | 62.35 | 65.36 | 65.92 | 70.70 |

1. Olivine-gabbro, Bllo. Canada Las Pilancas.
2. Olivine-gabbro, Ditto.
3. Olivine-gabbro, Montana de La Hoya.
4. Olivine-gabbro, Canda de Luchon.
5. Wehrlite, N coast E of Los Organos.
6. Olivine-gabbro, N of Vallehermoso.
7. Olivine-gabbro, Ca. a la Playa de Nallehermoso.

Lanzarote. He presumed that a submarine episode of regional extent occurred within the Canary Islands which, along with the presence of detritals containing rounded grains of quartz and quartzite (not endemic to the islands), suggested an African source for these sedimentaries.

The dyke network is again a notable feature as in Fuerteventura. At times these total 90% of the host rocks, and probably account for some 60% of the basal complex. These show no preferred orientation, are up to 20 m thick, some injected at deep levels in

earlier times, others of more surficial nature. Dyke rocks include syenites, trachytes,
basalts, phonolites and andesites chiefly.

   The overlying volcanic series are in unconformable relation to each other and lie
unconfromably upon the basement. The Old Basaltic Series is only found in contact
with the Trachytic-Phonolitic Series. The polygenetic agglomerates were considered
by GAGEL as part of his substratum and by BRAVO as being the oldest series in the island.
The Roques Series – chiefly phonolites, trachytes and trachy-phonolites – is admittedly
not well defined. BRAVO, as mentioned above, thought that his trachytes and
trachy-phonolites were being expelled all during the period of basaltic emissions, a view
more or less agreed upon by CENDRERO, and hence the stratigraphic positioning of this
Series is not to be rigorously interpreted. The numerous plugs or necks (›roques‹)
seemingly do not intrude into the Sub-Recent basalts, here and there do cut through the
Basal Complex and Trachytic-Phonolitic Series on occasion. The youngest recognized
unit comprises porphyritic basalts, flows very compact, usually horizontal, rocks have
a fresh appearance, and only a few dykes transect them.

   HAUSEN (1971b) wrote a relatively short monograph on Gomera, and unfortunately
his very small sketch map is poorly produced, difficult to decipher, lacking all detail.
Three units are described, a Basement, Younger Volcanic Formation and Phonolite
Intrusions. The deeply truncated Basement is unconformably overlain by somewhat
flat-lying basaltic lavas, tuffs and agglomerates, salic lavas playing a minor role. The

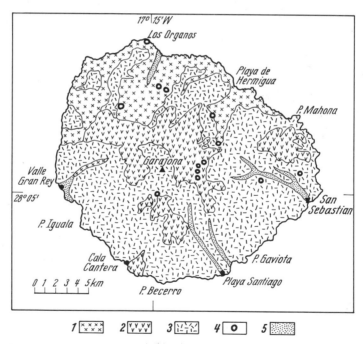

Fig. 64. Geological map of Gomera. 1: Dyke-dissected basement. 2: Phonolites and trachytes.
3: Basalt formation of insular basaltic shield. 4: Prominent phonolite necks. 5: Alluvium.
(Modified after HAUSEN, 1971).

basic volcanics are remnants of a large shield. The ›roques‹ (CENDRERO's Roques Series) are remarkable features, »standing hundreds of metres above the surrounding eroded terrain«, these plugs covering large areas but almost non-existent in the southern half of the island. He in general agreed with BRAVO in maintaining that salic magmas showed no tendency to show transitions into basic ones, that the two magmas have no common origin, that the salics are not late differentiates of the basics. On the other hand, to CENDRERO (1971), whilst there exists a spatial relation between the syenites and salic volcanics, there seems to be genetic relationship. His Trachytic-Phonolitic Series arose through the contamination of a phonolitic magma which latter was probably formed by differentiation in the upper part of a basaltic magma chamber. (It should be remarked that this more detailed 1971 report by CENDRERO was not available to HAUSEN when compiling his monograph).

## La Palma

LYELL (1855) and HARTUNG (1862) were the first to give more concrete information on igneous matters here. HARTUNG's . collection of rocks were reported upon by REISS (1861), the latter recognizing: (a) an older basement (›Die Diabasformation‹) and (b) an upper unit (›Die Lavenformation‹) the latter also including tuffs, agglomerates. In the deepest part of the Caldera de Taburiente REISS referred to dark, granular rocks which he termed ›Hypersthenites‹, forming a basement to the ›Diabasformation‹.

VON FRITSCH (1867) had little to say petrologically, but part of his rock collection was studied by SAUER (1876), remarking on phonolitic rocks, also diabases of the dyke system within the Caldera. COHEN (1876) disagreed with REISS in referring to the Caldera plutonics as ›hypersthenites‹, preferring to describe the rocks as essexites, diorites and syenites.

VAN WERWERKE (1879) mentioned nepheline-bearing limburgites in the Caldera and treated more comprehensively of the diabases.

GAGEL (1908, 1910, 1913, 1915) recognized many variations of plutonics within the Caldera, ranging from alkali-granites to ultrabasics, all stemming from the differentiation of an essexitic parental magma. Specifically he mentioned nepheline-syenites, monzonites, essexites, gabbro-essexites, olivine-free and olivine-bearing gabbros, trachy-dolerites, diabases, pyroxenites, madeirites, Ca-bostonite and camptonite dyke rocks and greenstones, as well as effusives, breccias and tuffs. His noting of alkali-granites, highly salic quartz- and alkali-feldspar granular rocks quite unaltered, was of special interest, and later ROVERTO (1927) described granite enclaves at S. Antonio volcano, Fuencalientes, well removed from the Caldera. However, HERNANDEZ-PACHECO & IBARROLA (1973a) considered GAGEL's data as unreliable, ROVERTO gave no detailed petrochemical information, and they dismissed this very unlikely occurrence of granites in La Palma.

SAN MIGUEL DE LA CAMARA et al. (1952) have described the alkaline-basaltic lavas and ashes emitted during the 1949 eruptions along Cumbre Vieja, the central southern spine of the island.

BLUMENTHAL (1961) visited the Caldera and from his rock collection Mme. JÉRÉMINE determined spilites, which she also recognized in Fuerteventura. He mentioned that gabbros, for example, occurred as blocks and masses within the spilites but was not in favour of a plutonic basement.

VUAGNAT (1961) discussed the occurrence of pillow lavas (spilitic-type basalts) in the deeper parts of the Caldera, also mentioned by BLUMENTHAL whilst GAGEL (1908b) had mentioned spheroidal trachy-dolerites in the same area. Pending more detailed studies, VUAGNAT could offer no hytpothesis to account for the occurrence of such lavas.

GASTESI et al. (1966) identified the following units for the Caldera: (a) The Wall Series – basaltic lavas and pyroclastics outwardly inclined at rather gentle dips. The dense dyke network which cuts the basal complex also penetrates into these surficial volcanics. (b) Post-Caldera formations, occurring throughout the central depths of the Caldera, forming isolated or aligned hillocks, with both volcanics and sedimentaries involved. GAGEL (1908b) was the first to suggest that these formations formed an extensive covering over the entire basal complex. (c) Basal Complex, here described in detail. Pillow lavas occur at altitudes varying from 150–600 m. Many dykes cut these lavas resulting in strong epidotization. The plutonics form enclaves of varying dimensions within a dense dyke network – the normal condition – but where dykes are less profuse, plutonics may have dimensions of several tens of m². Plutonics also occur as dykes (BLUMENTHAL recognized this also) – troctolites and gabbroidal rocks. The

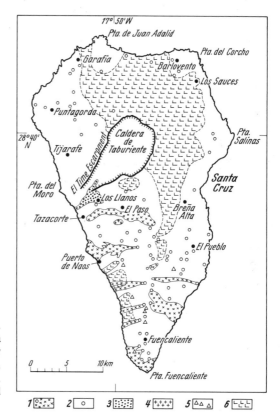

Fig. 65. Geological map of La Palma. 1: Recent and sub-Recent basalt lava flows. 2: Adventive basalts of Quaternary age. 3: Pre-Quaternary (?) fanglomerate. 4: Alkaline-trachytes. 5: Phonolite necks. 6: Trachybasalts ("cobertera"). (Modified after HAUSEN, 1969).

Basal Complex comprises dunites, wehrlites, pyroxenites, olivine-gabbros, olivine-diabases, gabbros, alkaline-gabbros (theralites, essexites, ijolites). There was a unique magmatic intrusion whose composition gave rise by assimilation to the various rocks encountered. Between the acidic and basic extremes, the intermediaries (gabbros and olivine-gabbros) are predominant, suggesting a gabbroidal or basaltic primitive magma, or rather alkali-basaltic.

HAUSEN (1969) has given the only modern, more extensive treatment of the whole island. His stratigraphic sequence, top to base, is:

Adventive alkali-basalt vulcanism – lavas, tuffs of Sub-
    Recent and Recent age
Ditto, of Quaternary age
Fanglomerates of Barr. de las Angustias
Phonolitic-trachytic vulcanism – widespread trachy-
    andesitic and trachy-basaltic
    effusions, essexitic magmas at
    depths, glowing avalanches of pyro-
    clastics forming core of northern
    dome
Effusions of ultrabasic picritic and oceanitic lavas.
Pronounced unconformity
Basement Complex – dyke systems, spilitic pillow lavas, tuffs, breccias, intercalated detritals

Xenoliths in the S. Antonio, Fuencalientes area include perkinites (pyroxenites and hornblendites) and olivine-rich rocks largely as bombs. Amongst the island igneous rocks, some 11 varieties of plutonics, 6 hypabyssal varieties and 14 volcanic varieties of rocks are present. The original source of the igneous rocks might be the Mantle, magmas welling-up through the sialic crust. Most rocks are thought belong to an essexitic magma sequence.

MIDDLEMOST (1970) spoke of: (a) Caldera Floor Formations = Basal Complex; (b) the El Time Formation = Wall Series of GASTESI et al., = ›Jungvulkanische Formation‹ of GAGEL. The latter unit outcrops in almost vertical walls up to 1,000 m high, forming the NW rim of the Caldera (El Time escarpment). The majority of the rocks here are thought to be eruptive products of the old Taburiente volcano, the Caldera being considered a cauldron collapse structure, later extensively eroded. MIDDLEMOST agreed with HAUSEN in regarding La Palma as an edifice begun under submarine conditions, from an initial alkali-basaltic parent magma.

HERNANDEZ-PACHECO (1971) presented the following sequence, top to base:

Post-Basal Complex Series
    Recent and Sub-Recent Series
    Cumbre Vieja Series
    Basaltic Series of the Caldera walls
    Old Basaltic Series of Cumbre Vieja
Unconformity
Basal Complex Units

Table 44    Chemical analyses (means) of some phonolites and basanites from La Palma (MIDDLE-
            MOST, 1972)

|          | 1     | 2     | 3     | 4    |
|----------|-------|-------|-------|------|
| $SiO_2$  | 51.9  | 46.5  | 48.7  | 47.9 |
| $TiO_2$  | 1.46  | 3.00  | 2.57  | 3.4  |
| $Al_2O_3$| 19.5  | 16.4  | 17.1  | 15.9 |
| $Fe_2O_3$| §     | §     | 3.94  | 4.9  |
| FeO      | 5.95  | 10.83 | 5.23  | 7.6  |
| MnO      | 0.18  | 0.20  | 0.12  | 0.2  |
| MgO      | 1.49  | 4.61  | 3.81  | 4.8  |
| CaO      | 4.57  | 8.49  | 6.03  | 8.0  |
| $Na_2O$  | 8.11  | 6.17  | 5.77  | 4.2  |
| $K_2O$   | 3.93  | 2.77  | 3.91  | 1.5  |
| $P_2O_5$ | 0.33  | 0.85  | 1.26  | 0.7  |
| $H_2O+$  | n.d.  | n.d.  | 0.70  |      |
| $H_2O-$  | n.d.  | n.d.  | 0.27  |      |

§ Total iron calculated as FeO.

1. Mean of 7 hauyne-phonolites.
2. Mean of 4 basanites.
3. Average tahitite (MCBIRNEY & AOKI, 1968).
4. Average hawaiite (MACDONALD, 1968).

Polygenetic agglomerates
Recent submarine emissions
Unconformity
Alkali-gabbros
Old Submarine Series
Metamorphosed salic rocks
Peridotites, olivine-gabbros, gabbros.

The Basal Complex unit is cut by dyke complexes, the oldest of which intrude only the four oldest members; next came dykes cutting the whole Complex, with the youngest system transecting the entire stratigraphic sequence. Granular rocks, and especially the alkali-gabbros, formed the ›roots‹ of deeply-eroded volcanic structures forming the primitive island. Submarine emissions represent early volcanic episodes and later ones are probably related to events leading to the formation of the Caldera. The Basal Complexes of La Palma, Gomera and Fuerteventura all display gabboidal rocks and submarine emissions as the oldest igneous manifestations, with later subaerial agglomerate formations and extensive dyke development. But La Palma does show some differences from the other two, e. g. the granular rocks here are of essentially olivine-gabbroic, salic and alkali-gabbroic types, the submarine emissions are more complex, of varying composition, extruded at different times. On the other hand the Basal Complex of La Palma does show some close similarities with those of Brava, Fogo in the Cape Verde Islands (ASSUNÇAO et al., 1968), possibly also S. Tiago.

MIDDLEMOST (1972) has criticized the use of the term normal basalts for many rocks, here in La Palma but also in Hierro, Gomera and Tenerife, believing that very few rocks

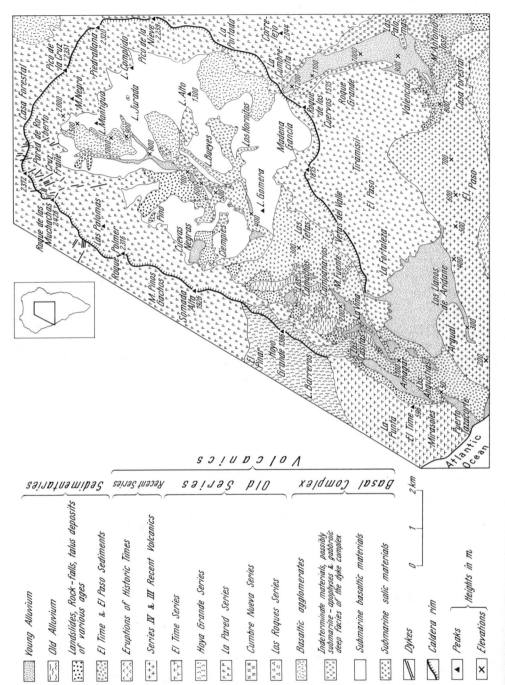

Fig. 66. Geological map of Caldera de Taburiente, La Palma. (Modified after HERNANDEZ-PACHECO & AFONSO, Direcc. Gen. de Obras Hidraulicas Map, 1974).

(sensu stricto) belong to this category. In La Palma and Tenerife the rocks differ from normal basalts in that they show a sodium-potassium enrichment over silica, and further, sodium predominates over potassium. The stronly alkalic nature of La Palma rocks can also be observed in the alkali-lime index of PEACOCK (1931), where the value is 47 and 49 for Tenerife. The La Palma value is very close to that of Tahiti, 46, and it is of interest to note several petrological analogies between these two remote islands, the La Palma rocks associating themselves with the ›Tahitian magmatic suite‹ of McBIRNEY & WILLIAMS (1970).

Finally we would note that the Teneguia eruption in La Palma of 1971 yielded highly alkaline-basalts (CHAIGNEAU & FUSTER, 1972).

## Hierro

Less has been written about this island than any other in the archipelago, and in almost all respects, scientific and otherwise, Hierro has been the neglected island.

Collections made by VON FRITSCH in 1863 were petrographically studied by WALTER (1894), the latter mentioning the occurrence of olivine-basalts, plagioclase-rich olivine-basalts, nepheline-tephrites, basanites, hornblende-andesites, xenolithic limburgites, palagonites and mixed tuffs. VON FRITSCH added a descriptive chapter to this dissertation, in which he mentioned the presence in Hierro of sanidinites, andesites and gabbroic xenoliths in the vicinity of the volcano Tenerife – typical basement material of other islands.

FERNANDEZ (1908) wrote of the island but made no mention of WALTER's publication. Neither WALTER nor FERNANDEZ gave chemical analyses, optical details of minerals, nor was any attempt made to devise a stratigraphic sequence.

JÉRÉMINE (1935) studied collections made by DENIZOT in 1930, commenting upon ankaratrites, amongst others, giving a chemical analysis thereof, the first available of Hierro rocks!

The last of the series of monographs on the Canary Islands by HAUSEN appeared in 1973 dealing with Hierro. Though having the word »Outlines« in the title, this is by far the best and most comprehensive geological account available of the island. The following sequence is given: (a) Tableland Series – the insular volcanic shield, and (b), Adventive Volcanic Formation – cinder cones, lavas, tuffs. The former comprises flatlying basaltic type rocks produced by an individual emission centre so that they represent a shield, the present remains of a circular volcanic shield whose central focus locality cannot be clearly defined. Two rock types are dominant, olivine-basalts and olivine-free-tephritic-basalts, the former occupying a lower position in the Series. The upper plagioclase-rich-basalts (trachy-basalts or trachy-dolerites) give rise to the tableland character of the formation. Between these two basaltic-type units there occur tuffs, cut by many dykes of olivine-basalt and bostonitic types. The Tableland Series is transected by dykes throughout, in type varying from plagioclase-rich porphyrites to lamprophyres and olivine-basalts. The minuscule islets of Roques de Salmor, off the NW coast, comprise porphyritic trachytes, presumed to represent the last visible vestiges of a larger trachytic body in the interior of the island whose factual presence is wanting. Trachyte chunks found at Valverde (NE interior location) by FERNANDEZ may represent

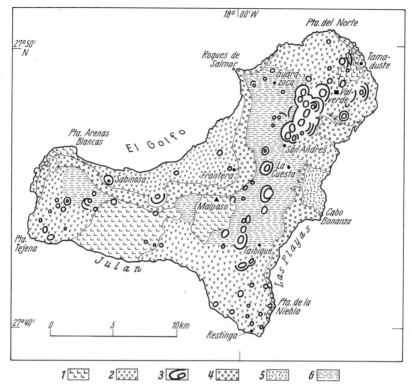

Fig. 67. Geological sketch map of Hierro. 1: Ash and lapilli, sub-Recent. 2: Lavas, pyroclastics, chiefly basaltic, Late Quaternary. 3: Cinder cones belonging to above. 4: Tableland series of alkali basalts – remnants of primative insular volcanic shield. 5: Boulder deposits. 6: Upland soils masking bedrock. (Modified after HAUSEN, 1973).

xenoliths or they may have been manually transported there for some purpose or other. Plugs intruded into the lower Series are few indeed, in marked contrast to La Palma, Gomera, Tenerife and Gran Canaria, but such as occur are intermediate in composition between phonolites and trachytes.

The Adventive Volcanic Formation dates back to late Quaternary and includes vulcanism likely just prior to Spanish settlement. The lavas are usually basic – ankaratrites, olivine-basalts, plagioclase-rich basalts, olivine-free-basalts, with basanites commonest. The youngest dissemination of black sands associated with vulcanism are rich in magnetite or Ti-magnetite.

The Hierro volcanics are typical alkali-basalts of the Atlantic suite, with younger lavas being more basic than older ones. Noteworthy is the relatively high iron content of the youngest volcanic manifestations. Dyke rocks tend to show a greater compositional variation, but salic varieties are rare. Hierro differs from its neighbours La Palma and Gomera in the almost total absence of salic derivatives, trachytes and phonolites showing far less dyke development. Also here in Hierro no basal complex is visible.

## Syntheses

Possibly well over a thousand analyses have been made of rocks from the archipelago. From such a vast array we can give here but a very small sampling of such in the accompanying tables and in so doing the author can always be attacked in that he has not been representative enough. So be it, but those seeking further details can always refer to the original publications, the great majority of those dealing with petrology having been referred to above. Specific reference may be made here to the publications of FUSTER et al. (1954). IBARROLA (1970) listed many analyses published in the interim, except for La Palma and Hierro.

Three publications have appeared, IBARROLA (1969, 1970), HERNANDEZ-PACHECO & IBARROLA (1973b) which attempt to summarize our present knowledge of igneous data on the archipelago. Below we shall outline the respective conclusions drawn therefrom.

In her earlier publication, Srta. IBARROLA (actually the wife of Prof. J. M. FUSTER) is primarily concerned with the Basaltic Series I-IV of FUSTER et al. (1968) as found in the four eastern islands, as well as what she termed Basaltic Series I of Gomera – the Old Basaltic Series and Sub-Recent Basalts of CENDRERO- The main points are:

Table 45    Average composition of Series I basaltic rocks from the Canary Islands (IBARROLA, 1969)

|  | 1 | 2 | 3 | 4 | 5 | 6 | 7 | 8 |
|---|---|---|---|---|---|---|---|---|
| No. Anal. | 10 | 13 | 7 | 6 | 11 | 28 | 19 | 33 |
| $SiO_2$ | 41.83 | 43.96 | 44.10 | 44.21 | 44.60 | 46.46 | 48.72 | 48.60 |
| $Al_2O_3$ | 12.25 | 11.32 | 11.20 | 15.65 | 14.44 | 14.64 | 16.90 | 16.49 |
| $Fe_2O_3$ | 4.57 | 4.38 | 2.84 | 6.65 | 4.71 | 3.27 | 5.30 | 4.19 |
| FeO | 8.20 | 8.33 | 9.91 | 6.55 | 7.99 | 9.11 | 5.70 | 7.40 |
| MnO | 0.17 | 0.16 | 0.16 | 0.16 | 0.17 | 0.14 | 0.18 | 0.18 |
| MgO | 12.75 | 14.73 | 15.13 | 6.17 | 9.36 | 8.19 | 4.86 | 4.70 |
| CaO | 12.45 | 10.92 | 10.69 | 11.42 | 10.41 | 10.33 | 8.70 | 7.79 |
| $Na_2O$ | 3.00 | 2.22 | 1.66 | 3.16 | 2.91 | 2.92 | 4.21 | 4.43 |
| $K_2O$ | 1.06 | 0.88 | 0.54 | 1.36 | 1.31 | 0.84 | 1.80 | 1.60 |
| $TiO_2$ | 2.79 | 2.56 | 2.74 | 3.85 | 3.22 | 3.01 | 2.74 | 3.16 |
| $P_2O_5$ | 0.91 | 0.52 | 0.30 | 0.78 | 0.66 | 0.37 | 0.87 | 0.69 |
| $CO_2$ | 0.02 | 0.02 | -- | 0.04 | 0.20 | -- | 0.02 | -- |
| Or | 6.0 | 5.2 | 3.3 | 8.2 | 7.8 | 5.0 | 10.7 | 9.7 |
| Ab | 2.2 | 11.4 | 13.0 | 20.9 | 19.1 | 25.3 | 34.6 | 37.1 |
| An | 16.6 | 18.8 | 21.3 | 25.0 | 22.7 | 24.5 | 22.2 | 20.7 |
| Ne | 14.7 | 5.1 | 1.2 | 4.8 | 4.3 | 0.9 | 1.8 | 1.9 |
| Di | 31.5 | 26.1 | 24.0 | 22.1 | 19.2 | 20.3 | 13.1 | 11.2 |
| Ol | 18.7 | 25.2 | 29.9 | 4.7 | 16.0 | 15.5 | 6.4 | 9.2 |
| Mt | 4.7 | 4.5 | 3.0 | 7.1 | 4.9 | 3.4 | 5.5 | 4.4 |
| Il | 3.8 | 3.6 | 3.8 | 5.6 | 4.4 | 4.4 | 4.0 | 4.4 |
| Ap | 1.8 | 0.9 | 0.5 | 1.5 | 1.3 | 0.7 | 1.7 | 1.4 |
| Cal | -- | -- | -- | 0.1 | 0.3 | -- | -- | -- |

1. Basanitoid
2. Ankaramite
3. Picrite-basalt of ankaramite type
4. Ankaramitic-basalt
5. Olivine-basalt
6. Alkalic Olivine-basalt
7. Hawaiite
8. Hawaiite

(a) Magmatic evolution in Upper Tertiary times within the archipelago was of a homogeneous nature, the products being of alkali type, ranging from ankaramites-basanitoids to hawaiitic types, the generating magmas being of olivine-alkali composition.

(b) In Gran Canaria and Tenerife during the Quaternary there was a transition to alkali-basic types (basanites, tephrites) with a gradual transition over to trachy-basalts; i. e. more alkaline.

Table 46          Tentative groupings of volcanic series of the Canary Archipelago

| Age | | | Hierro | La Palma | Gomera |
|---|---|---|---|---|---|
| Quaternary | Post-Sicilian | Recent Sub-Recent | Adventive volcanoes | Recent/Sub-Recent Adventive alk-basalt vulcanism | |
| | | | | Quaternary adventive alk-basalt vulcanism | |
| | | | Tableland Series | Phonolite and trachyte vulcanism | |
| Miocene–Pliocene | Post-Vindobonian | | | Trachyandesite and trachybasalt effusions essexitic magma at depth. | |
| | | | | Agglomerates | Polygenetic Agglomerates |
| | | | | Ultrabasic Effusions | |
| | Pre-Vindobonian | | | | Sub-Recent basalts Las Roques Series Old Basaltic Series |
| | | | | Basal Complex: Polygenetic agglomerates | Trachy-Phonolite Series |
| | | | | Basal Complex: Submarine emissions | Basal Complex: Submarine Series |
| | | | | Basal Complex: Alkaline gabbros, Old Submarine Series | |
| | | | Plutonic xenoliths in basement (?) | Basal Complex: Meta-salic rocks, spilites, gabbros, peridotites | Basic Plutonic Complex |

(c) During this same period in Lanzarote and Fuerteventura, less alkali types were evolved, of tholeiitic type.

(d) Complete transition between tholeiitic-type rocks and alkali-olivine-basalts occurs, the assumption being that the basalts showing affinities with tholeiites develope from alkali-basalts.

(e) Basalts are strongly alkaline in nature, with very high titanium and phosphorous contents in all rocks, basalts displaying distinct intra-oceanic characteristics.

(Note: The apparent parallelism of the units does not necessarily imply rigorous synchrony)

| Tenerife | Gran Canaria | Fuerteventura | Lanzarote |
|---|---|---|---|
| Recent Series IV | Basaltic Series IV | Basaltic Series IV | Basaltic Series IV |
| Teide–P. Viejo Volcanics | | | |
| Basaltic Series III | Basaltic Series III | Basaltic Series III | Basaltic Series III |
| Trachytic – Trachybasaltic Series | | | |
| Cañadas Series | | | |
| Basaltic Series II | Basaltic Series II | Basaltic Series II | Basaltic Series II |
| | Ordanchitic Series | | |
| | Roque Nublo Series | | |
| Polygenetic | Pre-Roque Nublo Series | | |
| | Phonolitic Series | | |
| sediments | Syenitic-Trachytic Series | | |
| Old Basalt Series | Basaltic Series I | Basaltic Series I | Basaltic Series I |
| | | Subaerial tuffs and agglomerates | Syenitic Ring Complex |
| | | Submarine volcanoes | |
| Plutonic xenoliths in basement (?) | Salic lavas of basement (?) | Basic Stratiform Complex | |

In the 1970 publication, IBARROLA treats of the same islands in somewhat greater detail, and may be summarized thus:

(a) Trachy- and ankaramitic-basalts are formed through the removal of Fe-Mg minerals during continuous fractionation.

(b) Serialization is well displayed in the archipelago rocks, and perhaps here we find the best examples in the world of variation features of alkali-olivine magmas.

(c) Differentiation is presumed to have occurred within deep levels of the Mantle.

(d) In post-Miocene times magmatic products of Lanzarote – Fuerteventura differ from those of Gran Canaria-Tenerife-Gomera, resurgence of vulcanism taking place during the Quaternary in the former islands, whereas this began in the Pliocene in the other islands.

(e) In this part of the Atlantic, since the Miocene volcanic materials originated from the Mantle via stress fissures, perhaps related to ocean-floor spreading.

(f) The divergence of products in the central islands appears to be due principally to the emplacement of deep magmas into shallower levels in the substratum, which latter was volumetrically increased by Miocene emissions.

HERNANDEZ-PACHECO & IBAROLLA based their conclusions on over 700 chemical analyses, only those analyzed by Spanish petrographers and in Spanish institutions, and thus HAUSEN's valuable information regarding Hierro is ignored. One rather questions this extremely nationalistic bias in spite of the reasons offered. Little new information is presented. They stress the fact that although La Palma, Tenerife and Gran Canaria rocks show alkaline-oceanic associations, those of the other islands, though also alkaline, are less typically oceanic. In all the Canary Islands successive magmatic cycles showed an increasing trend towards alkalinity, with the exception of recent eruptions in Lanzarote and Fuerteventura. On a petreological basis the archipelago can be grouped into four entities: Lanzarote-Fuerteventura-Gomera, Gran Canaria-La Palma, Tenerife and Hierro.

## Age of the Volcanic Materials

### Stratigraphic datings

Many scholars who have worked in the islands have stated the stratigraphic ages of various formations they recognized. Some have recognized a Palaeozoic age, e. g. GAGEL (1908), a possible Devonian or at least Palaeozoic age for the diabases of the Caldera in La Palma, basement material in Gomera (1926). HAUSEN (1958) has spoken of Hercynian disturbances in Fuerteventura as responsible for the tilting of his spilites. Vulcanism Jurassic or older has been postulated for the rocks in Fuerteventura, Gran Canaria, Gomera and La Palma by BLUMENTHAL (1961), pre-Palaeogene by the same writer for Tenerife; pre-Cretaceous for Gomera by CENDRERO (1971). FUSTER et al. (1968) for the eastern islands, on the other hand, did not recognize vulcanism here as earlier than Miocene. In almost all instances, there was very little to go upon in arriving at these conclusions. A Palaeozoic age for some of the islands has never been seriously considered by scholars in toto, even a Mesozoic age for some islands has been held in

Table 47    Presumed ages of the earliest vulcanism in the Canary Archipelago according to HAUSEN
            (1955–1973), BLUMENTHAL (1961), FUSTER et al. (1968) CENDRERO (1971), and
            HERNANDEZ-PACHECO (1971)

|  |  |
|---|---|
| Lanzarote | Eocene (HAUSEN)<br>Early Miocene (FUSTER et al.)<br>Pre-Miocene (BLUMENTHAL) |
| Fuerteventura | Palaeozoic (pre-Hercynian) (HAUSEN)<br>Helvetian or Burdigalian (FUSTER et al.)<br>Jurassic or older (BLUMENTHAL) |
| Gran Canaria | Eocene (? ) (HAUSEN)<br>Pre-Vindobonian but Miocene (FUSTER et al.)<br>Jurassic or older (BLUMENTHAL) |
| Tenerife | Eocene (HAUSEN)<br>Between 2 and 12 m.y. (FUSTER et al.)<br>Pre-Palaeogene (BLUMENTHAL) |
| Gomera | Early Tertiary (HAUSEN)<br>Pre-Cretaceous (CENDRERO)<br>Jurassic or older (BLUMENTHAL) |
| La Palma | Pre-Miocene (? ) (HAUSEN)<br>Pre-Miocene (HERNANDEZ-PACHECO)<br>Jurassic or older (BLUMENTHAL) |
| Hierro | Less than 3 m.y. (HAUSEN)<br>Pre-Vindobonian (BLUMENTHAL) |

doubt, and as per radioactive datings, the archipelago is a product of Kainozoic times.

Table 47 indicates some opinions of more recent workers regarding the ages of the oldest volcanics present.

### Isotopic datings

We have available a very short paper by ABDEL-MONEM et al. (1967), two more comprehensive publications by the same authors (1971, 1972) and some data concerning Fuerteventura by RONA & NALWALK (1970), all of which treat of radioactive geochronology. The following conclusions can be made:

(a) Lanzarote.    The oldest age (19 my) applies to trachy-basalts in the Punta Papagayo region. (Vd. Lanzarote above). Two other age values, averaging ca. 7 my in the same general area would agree with the view of FUSTER et al. that there is an important gap within Series I, and pre-trachyte basalts are clearly distinct from Series I basalts, as DRISCOLL et al. (1965) had suggested. The 500 m thick basalts in the N of the island range between 12 and 6 my, of Middle Tortonian age.

(b) Fuerteventura.    Values for a greenstone and alkali-syenite from the west-central Basement Complex have an average age of 37 my, whilst mineral ages in a hornblende-gabbro from here yield an average of 19.6 my. Mesozoic sediments in this part of the island are thought to be not younger than the Complex, which, however, could still place them in the Upper Palaeogene. ABDEL-MONEM et al. and RONA & NALWALK give averages ages of ca. 18 my for the Submarine Volcanics in the NW part of the island, whereas ABDEL-MONEM et al. quote an age of 11.8 my for a Series I sample in eastcentral Fuerteventura and 14.6 my for this Series elsewhere.

(c) Gran Canaria.    Oldest values for Series I gave an average value of 14 my, but because of limited sampling here, it was thought that the period of volcanic activity extended back to 17–18 my. The Syenitic-Trachytic Complex showed an average age of 13.2 my. FUSTER et al. disagreed with K-Ar datings for the Phonolite Series given in the very abbreviated paper by ABDEL-MONEM et al. of 1967 (vd. under Stratigraphy, Gran Canaria), the argument hinging largely on where the Miocene-Pliocene boundary is to be placed.

(d) Tenerife.    In the Anaga peninsula in the NE, rocks of the N slope yield an age of 15.7 my whilst those of the S slope give 4.65 my, suggesting a significant hiatus within Series I-II. Rocks of these Series in the NW Teno peninsula give an average of 6.6 my, and so it may be concluded that the Series I-II volcanic period extended from at least 16 my to 4.5 my. The Lower Cañadas yields an age of 1.54 my for lower sections, and the Upper Cañadas an age ranging from 1.27 to 0.67 my, the Cañadas Series being taken to represent the period between 2.0 and 0.6 my.

(e) Gomera.    The Basement Complex has a minimum age of ca. 15 my. The Old Basalts show two age clusters, one of ca. 11.6 my and the other 8.6 my, suggesting a hiatus within the series. As the Tableland Basalts yield an average age of 5 my, it is presumed that uplift and tilting of older basement material took place some 8–5 my ago, i. e. in uppermost Miocene times.

(f) La Palma.    Datings here refer only to lavas lying unconformably above the Basement Complex in the Caldera. The lowest flows give an average age of 1.57 my, the highest, 1.02 my. It is believed that such lavas draping the Complex are at least 1.6 my old, thus indicating a minimum age for the Caldera itself.

(g) Hierro.    Samplings were only done on the Tableland Series of HAUSEN. From the base of the El Golfo scarp the indicated age is 0.19 my, from which it can be concluded that the scarp was formed ca. 0.2 my ago, the same time as these authors would vavour for the initiation of the Cañadas Caldera of Tenerife. It is clear that the Tableland Series of Lanzarote, Fuerteventura, Gran Canaria, Tenerife, Gomera and Hierro are not correlative.

ABDEL-MONEM et al. claimed that their isotopic data are consistent with the timescale determined from geomagnetic polarity studies. Finally they point out that interisland correlations and stratigraphic age determinations presented by other workers, which were based chiefly on petrographic-structural considerations, result in an oversimplified picture of actual volcanic conditions.

Fig. 68 and Table 48 summarize isotopic data given.

We must realize that this is only the beginning of isotopic studies in the archipelago, that the sampling is very uneven, small in number (ca. 90), that those engaging in such work stayed only a very short time in each island, that they had no intimate knowledge of the geological environments. Hence, at this time it would be imprudent to place too much emphasis on these preliminary findings, there are still problems aplenty regarding temporal aspects of the vulcanisms of these islands.

Table 48    Isotopic age determinations of some volcanics from the Canary Islands (ABDEL-MONEM et al., 1971, 1972)

| Island | Volcanic Series | K–Ar age (m.y.) | No. samples analysed |
|---|---|---|---|
| Lanzarote | Basalt Series II, III, IV | 0.034 ∓ 0.03 to 0.96 ∓ 0.10 | 2 |
| | Basalt Series I | 5.30 ∓ 0.19 to 10.60 ∓ 1.12 | 8 |
| | Pre-Basalt Series I | 19.00 ∓ 0.68 | 1 |
| Fuerteventura | Shield Volcanics | 1.83 ∓ 0.24 to 4.25 ∓ 0.44 | 2 |
| | Basalt Series I | 11.80 ∓ 0.33 to 16.55 ∓ 0.61 | 4 |
| | Basalt Series IVa | 20.60 ∓ 0.94 | 1 |
| | Basement Complex and Submarine Volcanics | 18.40 ∓ 0.32 to 35.30 ∓ 0.92 | 3 |
| Gran Canaria | Basalt Series II (Post-Miocene) | 1.96 ∓ 0.10 to 2.80 ∓ 0.08 | 4 |
| | Roque Nublo Fm. | 3.50 ∓ 0.09 to 3.75 ∓ 0.12 | 2 |
| | Phonolite Series | 9.60 ∓ 0.11 to 10.90 ∓ 0.22 | 5 |
| | Ignimbritic-Trachyte Complex | 12.20 ∓ 0.22 to 15.00 ∓ 0.38 | 6 |
| | Basalt Series I Tableland Series | 10.20 ∓ 0.68 to 16.12 ∓ 0.40 | 5 |
| Gomera | Horizontal Basalts | 4.69 ∓ 0.12 to 5.23 ∓ 2.13 | 2 |
| | Old Basalts | 8.42 ∓ 0.29 to 12.00 ∓ 0.39 | 6 |
| | Basement Complex Intrusives | 14.60 ∓ 0.67 to 19.30 ∓ 1.58 | 2 |
| Tenerife | Trachy-basalt Series and Basalt Series III | < 0.20 to 0.67 ∓ 0.01 | 5 |
| | Canadas Series | 0.67 ∓ 0.01 to 1.54 ∓ 0.17 | 7 |
| | Basalt Series I, II | 0.84 ∓ 0.05 to 15.68 ∓ 1.60 | 13 |
| La Palma | Recent Alkaline Basalts | 0.60 ∓ 0.30 to 0.81 ∓ 0.09 | 3 |
| | Adventive Basaltic Quat. Volcanoes | 1.02 ∓ 0.03 to 1.57 ∓ 0.09 | 2 |
| Hierro | Tableland Basalt Series | 0.19 ∓ 0.01 to 3.05 ∓ 3.00 | 5 |

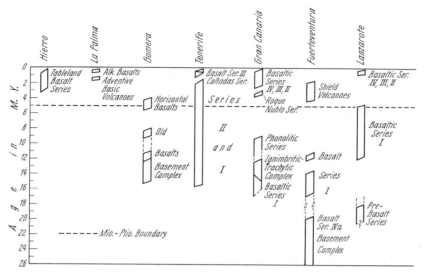

Fig. 68. Time-scale of vulcanism in the Canary Islands, based on isotopic datings. (Modified after ABDEL-MONEM et al., 1971, 1972).

## Sedimentary Rocks

Pre-Quaternary sedimentaries may be present throughout the archipelago but this is not certain as of now. They are indeed present in Lanzarote, Fuerteventura, Gran Canaria, highly probable in Tenerife, Gomera and La Palma, very doubtful in Hierro.

In Gran Canaria is an interesting occurrence, also the longest known in all Macaronesia. This is found in the NE, forming the so-called ›Las Palmas terrace‹, the capital being built on the lower slopes thereof.

Behind the capital is a steeper rise up to 80–100 m, then a more level tableland rises gradually inland to elevations of some 350 m, covering an area of some 25–30 km². In the scarp edge behind Las Palmas are coarse terrestrial conglomerates and marine limestones, the latter first drawing the attention of VON BUCH (1825). Numerous ravines radiate outwards to the E, NE and N from the higher terrain. The general appearance of the more level upland is that of a delta, where marine activity in Quaternary times attacked the scarp, it being assumed that formerly this upland area was of greater extent than now. Much of this ›apron‹ is formed of phonolite-type gravels and conglomerates – the ›Boulder Top Conglomerate‹ of HAUSEN (1962). Elsewhere this upland surface comprises post-Miocene olivine-basalts, Na-alkaline-lavas and nepheline-phonolites. A very generalized section of the scarp is thus:

Top    Very coarse conglomerates, in places post-Miocene and Quaternary/Sub-Recent basalts
       overlying these
       Fossiliferous beds, including sandstones, limestones and calcareous algal concretions,
       capped by littoral sandstones
       Conglomerates and sandstones showing littoral features
       Phonolites, overlain by thick occurrences of caliche – ›canto blanco‹

Two recent studies of these sedimentaries are those of KLUG (1968) and NAVARRO, APARICIO & GARCIA (1969). The former divided the rocks into three groups: (1) Lower Horizon, of gravels, pebbles, conglomerates, fluvially transported and built-out in delta fashion. Contemporaneous with this development the land was being slowly lowered – or then sea level was rising, for today we find pozzulana beds 10 m below sea level. Rock constituents are of phonolitic type, indicating that young eruptives had not yet formed. (2) Middle Horizon, including, base to top: fossiliferous sandstones, sandstones with *Lithothamnium*, limestones with Middle-Upper Miocene fauna, sandstones with *Lithothamnium*, and finally, fossiliverous sandstones, all of which suggests fluctuations of sea level. (3) Upper Horizon, a rather problematic unit, with extensive gravel-conglomerate fans which probably were formed after the Miocene beds underwent erosion.

The constituent phonolite material originated from the large central island volcano. As per FUSTER et al. (1968), these detrials extend upwards to hights of 300 m, forming an erosion platform varying in height from 60–80 to 300 m, although the total thickness of the sediments is not greater than 100 m. The fossiliferous horizons occur from 30–50 m above sea level. The strata dip 10–15° towards the ENE. These sedimentaries, described by HAUSEN as »one of the very rare occurrences of fossil beds in the Canaries«, have been repeatedly commented upon in the literature.

NAVARRO et al. also divide the beds into three groups: (1) Lower ›Piedmont‹ Horizon, the correlative of FUSTER et al.'s Phonolite Series, varies in thickness between 30 and 40 m, occurring at elevations up to 80–100 m. Much of the constituent material of the conglomerates comes from the Phonolite Series, lesser so from pre-Phonolite Series. Rocks include conglomerates, with clayey-sandy matrix, lenses of microconglomerates, sands and sandstones. BOURCART & JÉRÉMINE (1937) claimed these beds were of marine origin, HAUSEN thought they were of deltaic origin, whilst NAVARRO et al. considered them continental. Because the general character of this and the Upper Horizon are similar to that of material formed on lower mountain slopes, the term ›Piedmont‹ was coined for these Horizons. (2) Marine Horizon, correlative of FUSTER et al.'s Pre-Roque Nublo Series, lies at elevations varying between 60 and 80 m. Thickness ranges from a few decimetres to ca. 8 m. The unit shows well-graded stratification, coarsest at the base, of conglomerates, of phonolite fragments cemented with calcium carbonate, incorporating nodular-shaped organisms. Some tephritic, basaltic and agglomeratic material belonging to the Roque Nublo Series is also present. In the upper zones are sands of various dimensions. As per these authors, the significance of this Horizon is that the rocks indicate that as marine transgression was taking place, there began the emission of volcanics of the Pre-Roque Nublo Series. This is the Horizon which has aroused most palaeontological interest because of its fossil contents. (3) Upper ›Piedmont‹ Horizon, correlative of FUSTER et al.'s Ordanchite and Roque Nublo Series, occurs at elevations above 80–100 m, and is about 100 m thick. There is great variation in size of the detritals, little re-working is evident, the unit shows a chaotic appearance, comprising fragments of basalts, tephrites, agglomerates and some ordanchites. Various hypotheses have been put forward to account for this unit, the authors favouring the concept of a large sub-horizontal area left emergent after marine regression, an abrupt relief in the centre of the island formed by emissions of the

PreRoque Nublo and Roque Nublo volcanics which latter slowly spread in area during the emergence. Under a climate similar to the present, viz. infrequent but torrential rainfalls, material was easily fluvially moved but transported no great distance and abandoned on the peripheral zones of the upland area.

Fig. 69 shows various profiles of these Horizons, taken from NAVARRO et al.

Along the S coast, in the vicinity of Arguineguin, are found coarse conglomerates, agglomerates, limestones and pozzulana deposits, but so far no fossils have been obtained from here. HAUSEN and FUSTER et al. have remarked upon the likeness of these beds to those of the Las Palmas area. These southern occurrences were also thought to be of Miocene age by FUSTER et al., but HAUSEN favoured a Pliocene (?) age. HAUSEN described in some detail similar sedimentaries scattered in higher, interior parts of the island. FUSTER et al.'s Pre-Roque Nublo Series (Nuée ardente agglomerates of earlier writers, Roque Nublo Agglomerates of HAUSEN) is usually thought to represent the first post-Miocene volcanic phase. The Pre-Roque Nublo Series extends NNE-SSW across the island, and HAUSEN's sedimentaries have a similar trend. FUSTER et al. believed that these volcano-rudaceous deposits were contemporaneous with the Las Palmas sedimentaries. HAUSEN thought that the sandstones and conglomerates were deposited via running water within closed basins, whereas FUSTER et al. were inclined rather to conceiving of the original deposition of these rudites, arenites and calcareous rocks along an axis extending from Las Palmas to Arguineguin.

In Lanzarote HAUSEN (1959) classified the sedimentaries thus:

(1) Limestones of lacustrine and marine origin, best exemplified by occurrences in the Orzola-Punta Fariones region in the extreme N, where they underlie old basaltic flows several hundreds of metres thick. The uppermost sedimentary formation comprises pure, fine-grained, almost marmorized cream-coloured limestones, showing a remarkybly sharp contact with overlaing volcanics. Going down the sequence the limestones become less pure, admixed with volcanic material, and at the sea edge lava flows are again seen. The sedimentary series is ca. 30 m thick. In the uppermost pure layers are very well-preserved shells of *Helix*, indicating that when the oldest lava extrusions of the island were taking place, terra firma was present, where calcium carbonate (in ponds or lagoons?) was being formed as chemical precipitates. These limestones are then considered relatively old, perhaps early Tertiary.

In the semi-caldera of Cuchillo, near Soo, NW part of the island, are limestones with shell fragments. HAUSEN thought that these rocks originated from the substratum forming the low land in this region, punctuated by volcanic cones.

Along the S-SE coastal areas of Graciosa island occur yellowish calcareous sandstones which also cover considerable areas inland. These overlie a N-dipping limestone containing many rounded pebbles of various calcareous sandstones. HAUSEN thought this disturbed limestone was part of a sedimentary cover which once capped the old basement, the limestones being relatively young. As seen along the shore cliffs in the S of the island, the calcareous sandstones are well stratified, slightly inclined seawards, of »imposing thickness«. Close to the edge of the sea are many nests of *Antophora*. The whole calcareous sandstone complex is considered of terrestrial origin.

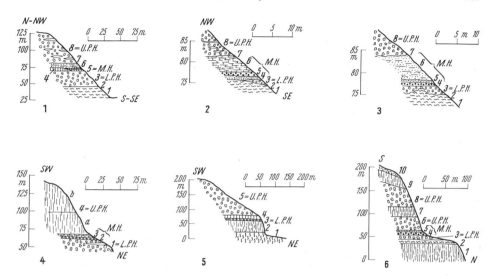

Fig. 69. Geological profiles of the "Las Palmas Terrace" sedimentaries in Gran Canaria. (Modified after NAVARRO, APARICIO & GARCIA, 1969).

1: Barranco de Guiniguada, near Castillo de San Francisco.

    1. Pumaceous ash-flows, 2. Erosive discordance, 3. Lower "Piedmont" horizon, 4. Flows of hauynitic phonolite, 5. Conglomerate, phonolite fragments, fossil. carbonate cemented, 6. Littoral sands, 7. Erosive discordance, 8. Upper "Pidemont" horizon.

2: Excavation at km 1.9, route Las Palmas – Tafira.

    1. Pumaceous ash-flows, 2. Erosive discordance, 3. Lower "Piedmont" horizon, 4. Conglomerate of rounded phonolite fragments, 5. Sandy pebbles developed from tephritic material, 6. Sands developed from sandy worm remains, 7. Erosive discordance, 8. Upper "Piedmont" horizon.

3: Autopista de Sur, deviation to Jinamar.

    1. Pumaceous ash-flows, 2. Erosive discordance, 3. Conglomerate of pebbles, etc. of phonolites, sandy-clayey matrix, 4. Conglomerates of tephritic pebbles, etc., 5. Sandy pebbles developed from tephritic material, 6. Well-stratified sands and micro-conglomerates, 7. Erosive discordance, 8. Conglomerates, sands, chiefly of tephritic and basaltic fragments.

4: Quarry in Barr. de las Majadillas to NW of El Cardon.

    1. Pebbles, etc. of phonolites, coarsely stratified, 2. 20–30 cm conglomerates of phonolitic type, calcareous cemented, 3. 30–50 cm finely-stratified whitish clays, 4. Basaltic conglomerate with two distinct structures: (a) pillow-structures, (b) pa-hoe-hoe structures.

5: Scarp above Autopista de Sur between Playas Laja and Marfea.

    1. Ignimbrites of phonolitic type, 2. Nepheline-phonolites flows, 3. 2 m conglomerate, essentially phonolitic fragments, sandy-clay matrix, 4. Pa-hoe-hoe basaltic flows, 5. Conglomerates, chiefly basaltic, tephritic and ordancitic material, with sandy lenses.

6: Small ravine from M. La Costa, km 3, Bahia Confital road.

    1. Phonolites flows, 2. Pumaceous ash-flows, 3. Phonolitic conglomerate, 4. 4 m white sands, 5. 2 m fine, grey sands, 6. 40 m phonolitic and basaltic conglomerate, 7. 30 m Pre-Roque Nublo Series, involving pillow and pa-hoe-hoe structures, 8. Conglomerates with sandy horizons, 9. Basaltic flows of Series II, 10. Lapilli of Series II.

(U.P.H. = Upper "Piedmont" horizon; M.H. = Marine horizon; L.P.H. = Lower "Piedmont" horizon).

Table 49                    Quaternary raised beaches (in m) in the Canary Islands (KLUG, 1968)

| | Holocene | Tyrr. IIb | Tyrr. IIa | Tyrr. I | Sicilian II |
|---|---|---|---|---|---|
| *Lanzarote* | | | | | |
| Playa de Calheta | 3.9 | –– | –– | –– | –– |
| Castillo Don Carlos | 3.6 | –– | –– | –– | –– |
| Playa Blanca | 3.6 | 4.9 | –– | –– | –– |
| S of Tias | –– | ––. | –– | –– | 60 |
| Playa Quemada | –– | 6 | –– | –– | –– |
| SE of Los Ajaches | –– | 6 | 15–18 | 25–30/35 | 55–60 |
| Rubicon Los Ajaches | 3–4 | 6–7 | 15–18 | 40–45 | 55–60 |
| Salinas de Janubio | –– | 6–7 | –– | –– | –– |
| | | | | | |
| *Fuerteventura* | | | | | |
| Gran Tarajal | –– | ca. 7 | 18 | –– | –– |
| Playa Blanca | 4 | –– | 17 | –– | –– |
| W coast | –– | 7 | 15 | 23–25/35 | 55 |
| Chilegua | –– | –– | –– | –– | 65 |
| Jandia | 3 – 15 | – 35 | | | |
| | | | | | |
| *Gran Canaria* | | | | | |
| Las Palmas | 4 | 7–8 | 18 | –– | –– |
| Rincon | –– | 13 | 22 | –– | –– |
| Ayala | –– | 6 | 15 | 35 | –– |
| Punta de Arucas | –– | –– | 15 | 35 | 55 |
| Punta Cebolla | –– | –– | 15 | 35 | –– |
| Banaderos Salinas | –– | 7.1 | –– | –– | –– |
| Banaderos | –– | 8.2 | 15.4 | 35–40 | –– |
| Banaderos Friedhof | –– | –– | –– | –– | 65 |
| Quintanillo | –– | –– | –– | –– | 90 |
| La Puntilla | 3.75 | –– | –– | –– | –– |
| San Andres | –– | 6–7 | 16 | 40 | –– |
| Pagador | 4.5 | –– | –– | –– | –– |
| Agaete N | –– | –– | –– | –– | 78–85 |
| Agaete E | –– | –– | –– | –– | 78–85 |
| Agaete S | –– | –– | –– | –– | 78–85 |
| Guayera | –– | –– | –– | 55 | –– |
| Punta Gondora | –– | –– | –– | ca. 100 | –– |
| Arguineguin | 4 | –– | –– | –– | –– |
| Arguineguin | 4.8 | –– | –– | –– | –– |
| Maspalomas W | ˙–– | 6 | –– | –– | –– |
| Juan Grande | –– | –– | –– | –– | 60–70 (?), 90–100 (?) |
| Arinaga | 4 | –– | 18 | –– | –– |
| Gando | –– | –– | 16 | –– | –– |
| Gando peninsula | 4 | –– | –– | 45 | 85 |
| La Laja | 3.5 | 8 | –– | –– | –– |
| Agua Dulce | 4 | 7 | –– | –– | –– |
| | | | | | |
| *Tenerife* | | | | | |
| S. Juan de la Rambla | –– | 8.2 | –– | –– | –– |
| La Roqueta | 4.8 | –– | ca. 15 | –– | –– |
| Punta Hidalgo | 3.5 | 7.6 | –– | –– | –– |
| Bajamar | 3.6 | –– | –– | –– | –– |
| Martianez | –– | 8 | –– | –– | –– |

Table 49 (continued)

| | Holocene | Tyrr. IIb | Tyrr. IIa | Tyrr. I | Sicilian II |
|---|---|---|---|---|---|
| Tegina | -- | -- | -- | -- | 60* |
| Teno | -- | 8 ? | -- | -- | -- |
| | | | | | |
| *Gomera* | | | | | |
| Punta Llana | ca. 4 | -- | 18 | -- | -- |
| Arguamul | 4 | -- | -- | -- | -- |
| Punta Delgada | 4 ? | -- | -- | -- | -- |
| Gran Rey | 3.5 | -- | 18 | 35 | -- |
| | | | | | |
| *La Palma* | | | | | |
| Punta Salinas | 4 | -- | -- | -- | -- |
| Puntallana | -- | -- | ca. 25 | -- | -- |
| Lomo Machin | -- | -- | ca. 25 | -- | -- |
| Charco Verde | -- | 6−13 | -- | -- | -- |
| | | | | | |
| *Hierro* | | | | | |
| Arenas Blancas | ca. 4 | -- | -- | -- | -- |
| Playas Cardones | ca. 4 | -- | -- | -- | -- |
| Hoya Tamaduste | -- | -- | ca. 18 | -- | -- |
| Playas Largas | 4 | -- | -- | 30 ? | -- |

* Pliocene? = Stratigr. classification questionable. (?) Presence not clearly detected. N.B. Oldest beaches in Gran Canaria pre-Tyrrhenian.

On the tiny islet of Roque del Oeste, N of Graciosa, bombs of marmorized limestone are mixed with tuffaceous rocks cut by basaltic dykes.

(2) Terrestrial calcareous sandstones.    Much of these are covered by alluvium. The sandstones are actually brittle oolitic limestones of clastic texture, somewhat equigranular, show poor stratification. The material looks like an aeolian deposit, but running water has been at least partially at work. The terrestrial origin is witnessed by such gastropod shells as *Helix* and *Stenogyra*. Maximum thickness seems to be ca. 10 m, occurring an elevations up to 50 m. As the rocks are friable they are readily destroyed by weathering agents, and hence occurrences are preserved only in sheltered localities or then when capped by lime-cemented material. It may be that much lies hidden beneath rudites, drifting sands, they may have been covered by lava flows, cinders.

(3) Terrestrial sands, gravels, drifting sands.    These comprise fluvial sands, gravels, piedmont gravels, creep débris, representing smaller areas of erosion and deposition. The drifted calcareous matter presumably being Quaternary marine shells and foraminiferal oozes. Such sands are well observed along the leeward (SE) slopes.

(4) Littoral sands and gravels, forming marine beaches along the SE coasts, also in extreme S forming Playa Blanca. In the Los Ajaches region (also in extreme S) are found some thick, quite extensive gravel accumulations along the coast.

(5) Superficial terrestrial travertine incrustations.    These, known locally as ›tosca

blanca‹ or ›canto blanco‹ are dense, fine-grained, concretionary limestones which may be of great purity in more superficial parts. Such rocks are to be found in Lanzarote in all parts which have not been affected by vulcanism in Historic Times. These represent chemical precipitates which have been concentrated from lime bicarbonate solutions in the substratum and drawn upwards by evaporation to the surface. The large quantities of lime needed for the process has been derived from the lime content of the minerals in the basalts, especially the plagioclases and pyroxenes. The entire process of formation presupposes a climate of alternating wet and dry seasons, perhaps somewhat more rainfall than today, but similar long, dry, warm periods.

In Fuerteventura occur sedimentaries of two types, distinct as regards lithology and age.

HAUSEN (1958, 1967), in discussing the Quaternary and Sub-Recent rocks which are more extensively distributed, divided these into two groups, viz. weathered products; transported and assorted deposits. He further distinguished the lime-carbonate sediments from the polymict gravel-sand-silt sediments. His classification is thus:

1. Limestones of various origin:
   a) Marine littoral limestones containing foraminifera
   b) Soft, arenaceous terrestrial limestones with macrofossils
   c) Travertine limestones
2. Fossiliferous littoral conglomerates and dark-coloured calcareous sandstones
3. Fanglomerates
4. Alluvial deposits:
   a) Talus deposits
   b) Piedmont gravels and sands
   c) Valley gravels and sands
   d) Sands, clays, muds of depressions
   e) Soil material decomposed by atmospheric action, e. g. lateritic clays, etc.
   f) Pebbly, sandy marine beaches
5. Workable soils

None of the above are terrestrial, sensu stricto. Group 1a is a littoral product, of calcareous dune sands indurated into calcareous sandstone-limestone. Further, the pebbly, etc. beaches include much reworked fluvial material. Though in toto all these rocks are thought to be young, it may be that some at least of the fanglomerates are Tertiary.

Marine limestones are chiefly limited to the NW coastal regions, lying on a terrace, maximum height above sea level, 15 m. This well-stratified ›terrace limestone‹ is relatively pure, and microscopically is seen to be filled with poorly-preserved foraminiferal shells. HAUSEN (1958a) gives a chemical analysis of limestone (1a) thus:

| | |
|---|---|
| Insolubles (in HCl) | 2.30 % |
| Sesquioxides | 0.64 % |
| $MgO$ | 1.20 % |
| $CaO$ | 53.06 % |
| $CO_2$ | 42.25 % |
| $H_2O$ | 0.59 % |
| | 100.04 % |

Of wider distribution are brittle, arenaceous limestones showing poor stratification, containing many shells of *Helix* and *Stenogyra*. Much of this material has been wind eroded, forming very fine-grained drifting calcareous sands. These limestones may attain thickness of 10 m.

The travertine limestones are hard, compact, fine-grained, rather like the Lithographic Stone of Solnhofen, Germany. They are weakly stratified, are pure only at the surface, passing down into brecciate material, on into rotten rock soaked with lime carbonate and so to unaffected igneous rock. A chemical analysis by HAUSEN of this travertine limestone shows:

| | |
|---|---|
| $SiO_2$ | 2.80 % |
| $Al_2O_3$ | 1.28 % |
| $Fe_2O_3$ | 0.84 % |
| CaO | 48.38 % |
| MgO | 3.20 % |
| $SO_2$ | 0.45 % |
| $Na_2O + K_2O$ | 0.10 % |
| $CO_2 + H_2O$ | 43.05 % |
| | 100.10 % |

Rudites and arenites occur chiefly along the E-SE coasts, lying on a quasi-horizontal marine abrasion platform of bedrock. Present are some very coarse conglomerates with sub-angular basalt ingredients in a sandy-clayey matrix. Beds, lenses, stringers of sandstone and calcareous sandstone are often studded with marine mollusc shells, mostly of the genus *Patella*. On the NW windward coast littoral conglomerates occur at higher elevations, e. g. the basal conglomerates covering the 15 m terrace mentioned above. The conglomerate here comprises well-rounded cobbles, pebbles of all types of rocks found in the hinterland. Here the rounding has been caused by fluvial action. Again the matrix is calcareous, with many mollusc shell fragments.

The fanglomerates are ancient piedmont indurated gravels, most extensively developed along the central sector of the leeward coast, where they attain thicknesses of 10 m.

Some other sedimentary occurrences in Fuerteventura are of much greater stratigraphic interest, being much older. These are found in the region between Puerto de la Peña and Caleta de la Peña Vieja and inland thereof, in the central part of the W coast, being exposed in coastal sections and in the deep valleys heading inland. ROTHE (1968a) has grouped the rocks into five units: (a) dark shales, marls, with sandy layers, in general finely bedded or laminated; (b) limestones, marlstones, both platy structure and thick bedded; (c) dark shales with layers of red and grey fine-grained platy limestones; (d) siltstones, sandstones, with clayey partings; (e) platy, thick bedded, very fine-grained limestones, with quartz-silt, pebbles, nodules and lenses of flints.

FUSTER et al. (1968) stated that the seeming macroscopic high degree of homogeneity and rhythmic character of the sedimentaries is not duplicated microscopically. The chief rock types are quartzites and quartzitic breccias, fine-grained detrital siliceous rocks showing graded rhythmic stratification. These gradually change into very finegrained rocks – stratified phtanites – of the original silica-gel composition. Calcareous shales usually alternate throughout, with unusually sharp transitions against quartzites. The limestones of Peña Vieja are rich in foraminifera and shells, also good traces of worm trails. Referring to the detritals here, FUSTER et al. claimed that the source region lay in the Africa mainland which is today some 100 km distant and separated by waters down to 2,000 m in depth, that similar detritals occurred in Lanzarote and in Gomera, the latter much further westward. Both ROTHE and these authors are inclined to interpret the sedimentaries as flysch deposits, the latter suggesting deposition via turbidity currents in a submarine environment.

Dips are variable, but 80–90° to the S or sometimes ca. 30° to the SW are commonest, and scarce ever are rocks dipping N. It appears that folding, with axes trending NW-SE, has taken place here, forming between Barrancos Peña and Ajuy a syncline with its NE side overturned to the N-NW. Some NE-SW striking faults have caused offsetting of the strata. Jointing is common, dyke-networks no less.

These W-C Fuerteventura occurrences were known to VON FRITSCH (1867) and GAGEL (1910), but seemingly ›disappeared‹ from the literature until ›re-discovered‹ by FUSTER & AGUILAR (1965), later by ROTHE. It is interesting that both BOURCART & JÉRÉMINE (1938) and HAUSEN (1958) make no mention thereof.

Units (a-c) of ROTHE are quoted by him as being some 500–700 m thick; unit (d) some 400–600 m. Thus a thickness of 900–1,300 m, exclusive of the youngest fine-grained limestones, is presumed here. This is very much in excess of the 435 + m (even taking account of the + sign) for the sedimentaries of Maio, Cape Verde Islands, and if substantiated, would constitute by far the thickest sedimentary occurrence in Macaronesia. On a thickness basis, therefore, these sedimentaries draw one's attention, but likewise stratigraphic information (see later) makes these occurrences of Fuerteventura of great interest.

In Tenerife, HAUSEN (1955) noted cross-bedded, highly friable sandstones at El Medano, extreme S coastal location. These are ca. 10 m thick and lie a few metres above high tide. Because of the softness, much of the sandstone has been eroded by wind and spray, forming an extensive beach between El Medano and Punta Roja. In a small ravine at El Medano the sandstones rest on agglomerates. HAUSEN thought this was a delta formation deposit, the ingredients being obtained through the disintegration of pozzulana deposits further inland, sand layers being formed at the same time as pozzulana mudflows spread over this southern lowland. FUSTER et al. (1968) disagree on this point, stating that pozzulana occurs throughout almost the entire volcanic sequence of the island, yet similar sands-sandstones are not prevalent everywhere, and further, pozzulana formation occurred at various times, not just once as HAUSEN believed. These authors also mentioned fossil finds in non-stratified pumaceous deposits, but gave no further specific information.

In Gomera, between Los Organos and Playa de Arguamul, in the extreme N, occur fine-grained detritals, often cross-bedded, comprising chiefly limestones, shales, silts and cherts. Argillaceous material and its structure would indicate sometimes quiet deposition, at other times deposition in a highly-aggitated environment, perhaps via turbidity currents. The beds are vertical or nearly so, striking NNE. A relatively rich microfauna is present, especially Radiolaria. So far almost no studies have been made of these Gomera sedimentaries.

In La Palma, in the lower part of the Barrancos de las Angustias and Hermosillo (former draining the stupendous Caldera de Taburiente), are found old conglomerates forming gravel fans – fanglomerates. In these ravines and along vicinal coastal sections such rocks are exposed. Crude stratification is sometimes present, with angular fragments in gravelly conglomerates. At the mouth of the Barr. Hermosillo almost perfect stratification of sandstones in seen. HAUSEN (1969) thought the conglomerates looked like torrential deposits of river gravels, etc. with rock fragments rolling down the steep lateral slopes and being mixed with sands, gravels, etc. and then consolidated. Going downstream in both of the Barrancos the stratification becomes better. Some earlier workers, e. g. LYELL (1855), HARTUNG (1862) thought that the conglomerates represented a type of marine gravel laid down at the foot of the El Time escarpment which bounds the Angustias valley to the W. VON FRITSCH (in GAGEL, 1908) is said to have found marine Miocene fossils at the base of the conglomerates, but repeated enquiries by the writer of various scholars on this point has elicited no further information. HAUSEN mentions »some hundreds of metres of thickness« for this fanglomeratic material.

Hierro, the smallest and least studied geologically of all the Canarian islands, has so far yielded no proven pre-Quaternary sedimentaries. The topography and the relief of the island militate against sedimentation, and only boulder avalanches, rock falls and other gravitational movements of rock material have furnished uncolidated material found in valley bottoms and along coastal stretches. Powerful wave attack along some sectors of the coasts has pulverized fallen débris into gravel and sand sizes.

## Stratigraphy

Though the earliest stratigraphic determinations were made in Gran Canaria, where the Neogene was recognized, we shall record the stratigraphy in chronological sequence.

Only in Fuerteventura, Hierro have Mesozoic rocks been postulated. the sedimentary occurrences in West-Central Fuerteventura (q. v. supra) were already known to GAGEL (1910) who thought they were Palaeozoic, though without presenting concrete evidence. Such an age is not considered present anywhere within Macaronesia, but at least GAGEL did recognize the relative greater age of these sedimentaries compared with others in the Canary archipelago.

ROTHE's (1968) paper gives what present stratigraphic-palaeontologic knowledge is available for these sedimentary occurrences, believed by him to be pre-volcanic. Dr. ROTHE has most kindly entered into lengthy correspondence regarding these rocks (as also other Canary matters) which amplifies what he has written.

His Peña Vieja limestones are rich in Foraminifera and other shells. ROTHE was in correspondence with Dr. R. LEHMANN of Bègles, France, regarding fossil material he had sent. LEHMANN reported that perhaps *Globigerina*, *Hedbergella* and *Pithonella* were present but no *Nannoconidae* or *Tintinnidae* were found, and that an Albian age for the material was possible. In the lower part of the Barranco de Ajuy ROTHE found »prints‹ of *Posidonia*-like lammellibranchs in the limestone-shale series and thin sections of carbonates from a relative younger part of the series revealed foraminifera, some of them with a double keel which is specific for *Globotruncana*......... *Globotruncana* appears first in the Cretaceous«. In his publication he specified the lamellibranch as *Posidonia bronni*. Trace fossils shown to a specialist only elicited the information »..... that they are at least not Palaeozoic. Thus, the possible *Posidonia* could not be a Palaeozoic species and there was a little more evidence for the Liassic species«. ROTHE searched the literature for geological sections similar to what he had found here in Fuerteventura, rivetting his attention on those of Tarfaya, in neighbouring Rio de Oro, coastal region of Africa, as reported in REYRE (1966). He then attempted to correlate his sequences in Fuerteventura with those of Tarfaya, and thus the picture is as per the table below:

| Fuerteventura | Tarfaya |
|---|---|
| Series e | Cenomanian-Turonian limestonds, 250–600 m thick |
| Series d<br>400–600 m thick | Lower Cretaceous 'Sables de Tantan'<br>– quartz sands, sandstones, shales, sandy marls, 700–1300 m thick |
| Series c–a<br>500–700 m thick | Malm sandstones and limestones, 1500 m thick, passing eastward into 'Sables de Tantan'. Below occur Lias and Dogger limestones, dolomites & sandstones, 650 m thick |

(For Series a-e vd. under Sedimentary Rocks.)

In his paper, ROTHE further attempts comparisons with lithologies-stratigraphy in Maio, Cape Verde Islands (q. v.), specifically of those towards the mouth of the Barranco de Ajuy, Fuerteventura, and the Ribeiro Barreiro, Maio. The writer has not seen the Canary occurrences, but from descriptions furnished in print and letters from ROTHE of the lithological aspects of these Fuerteventura rocks, it seems highly questionable how far one can push an analogy with those of Maio, except perhaps the common occurrence of flints. In making reference to Maio, the writer feels that ROTHE tends to accept the stratigraphy of this island, as presented in his paper by reference only to original work by STAHLECKER (1934) and TORRES & SOARES (1946), as being established without taking due recognition of the various debatable points about Maio stratigraphy.

Isotopic datings for Fuerteventura were not available to ROTHE when he published his paper, but now these have been published (ABDEL-MONEM et al., 1971). FUSTER et al. (1968) claimed that the Basement Plutonics were pre-M. Miocene and older than these sedimentary rocks, whereas ROTHE believed the sedimentaries to be pre-volcanic. Isotopic datings of the plutonics would indicate an age in excess of 35 m. y. ABDEL-MONEM et al. added: »These data at least show that the Mesozoic sediments exposed in the west-central coast of Fuerteventura are unlikely to be younger than the intrusive complex«. This would favour ROTHE's contention but would only indicate a pre-Oligocene age.

We must recognize the tenuous nature of the Fuerteventura-Tarfaya-Maio correlations, but in fairness to ROTHE, he freely admits that his correlations are speculative only at this time. We would further add that although some scholars would recognize Malm (Portlandian) in Maio, no suggestion has ever been made of Lias here, and Dogger very timorously as tentatively proposed for Fuerteventura.

COTTREAU & LEMOINE (1910) claimed that an echinoid found in some limestones associated with volcanics at La Caleta, NE coast of Hierro, indicated a Lower Cretaceous age. FERNANDEZ (1917) refuted this assertion, believing that if such a fossilized rock occurred, it represented ship-ballast. BLUMENTHAL (1961) and HAUSEN (1973), the latter engaging in extensive recent studies in the island, are both in agreement with FERNANDEZ – no Mesozoic is present, Tertiary very unlikely.

The longest known sedimentaries of the archipelago, those in the vicinity of Las Palmas, Gran Canaria, were early dated as Miocene, and all further work has substantiated the presence of the Vindobonian here. But in more recent times, isotopic datings of volcanics of the island rocks, plus a further detailed study of these sedimentaries by NAVARRO et al. (1969) and volcanic studies by ANGUITA (1972) allow further comment to be made.

The ›Pre-Roque Nublo Series‹ of FUSTER et al. (1968) ( = Roque Nublo Agglomerates of HAUSEN, 1962) is generally thought to represent the first volcanic phase after Miocene sedimentation. BOURCART & JÉRÉMINE (1937) claimed that the sandstones and conglomerates, plus the agglomerates of this Pre-Roque Nublo Series (which to date has yielded no fossils) represented Vindobonian. On the other hand, SCHMINCKE (1968a) termed these rocks as being Pliocene. ABDEL-MONEM et al. (1971), as per K-Ar isotopic datings, assigned an age of 3.75–3.50 my to the Roque Nublo Series, which they labelled Pliocene. Both FUSTER et al. and ANGUITA (1972) have questioned the isotopic datings, as they conflict with the palaeontological placing of the overlying sedimentaries. ABDELMONEM et al. pointed out that DYMOND (1966) and BERGGREN (1969) claimed that the Miocene-Pliocene boundary should be placed at 5 to 4.5 my rather than 13–12 my as hitherto believed, such a new time placing having isotopic, palaeomagnetic and faunal zone substantiation. To FUSTER et al. their Pre-Roque Nublo Series is Vindobonian, and at least the upper part of the Roque Nublo Series is Pliocene. ABDEL-MONEM et al. quote: »The age determinations reported here indicate that the limestone carrying the fossils is younger than 9.0 my. Using the inverse of the arguments used by FUSTER and others (1968) we suggest that our results place an upper limit on the absolute age of this palaeontological horizon«. ABDEL-MONEM et al. claimed there was a hiatus of at least 5 my between the emission of the Phonolite Series of FUSTER et al. (older than Pre-Roque Nublo) and the Roque Nublo Series, and it was in this time-interval that these Las Palmas sedimentaries were deposited. ANGUITA, on the other hand, accepts the time-equivalence of these fossil beds with the basal Roque Nublo Series. He argues that the first sentence of the above quote from ABDEL-MONEM et al. is lacking in precision, that they were not well enough acquaint with the available literature and by claiming that the age of these fossil beds is around 3.75 my is to make them contemporaneous with the Roque Nublo Series! ANGUITA thought that ABDEL-MONEM et al. were influenced in claiming a Pliocene age by SCHMINCKE's (1967a, 1968b) placing the age of his fossil plants in the Pliocene (probably Middle), which fossils were found at the base of his Roque Nublo volcanics. ANGUITA claims that this age assignment is not certain because of the slow evolution of the floral species found. (Correspondence with Prof. SCHMINCKE indicates that no further work has been done on the fossil plants of Gran Canaria, and hence admittedly the whole question of these remains somewhat vague as for the present.) In   these circumstances then, as per ANGUITA, one cannot correlate the isotopic and palaeontological datings, given that the end of the Vindobonian occurred some 11 my ago, and the precise delimitation of the Miocene-Pliocene boundary makes no sense in this context. It was his view that new laboratory and field studies (but the writer has been unable to pindown just exactly what were these studies, what were the findings) led to the conclusion that the time interval between the Phonolite and Roque Nublo Series is definitely less than 5 my. It requires to be stressed that during the past 7–8 years or so, a considerable literature has developed concerning the duration of the Miocene and Pliocene, no less the placing of the respective boundaries. BERGGREN especially has gone into these matters in considerable detail, and in his most recent paper (1973) the Pliocene is taken to span the interval between 5 and 1.8 my. In correspondence with the writer he has stated: »The age of the Miocene/Pliocene boundary as typified in the Mediterranean marine rocks is ca. 5 my and this is quite unambivalent. Vertebrate palaeontologists will have to adjust their thinking in this regard  and most  of them  already have  in actual fact«. Whilst vertebrate palaeontologists admittedly represent but one group of geologists, yet consensus of opinion is swinging in their direction, and due note needs to be taken of this regarding the vexed question of the age of these Las Palmas sedimentaries. It was the view of ROTHPLETZ & SIMONELLI (1890) that the majority of the fossils in these Las Palmas sedimentaries showed no change over an interval ranging from Aquitanian – perhaps even Tongrian – to Pliocene.

As of the present then, the view is that these Las Palmas sedimentary rocks rage through Miocene and Pliocene, but NAVARRO et al. stated that the stratigraphic position of the sedimentaries within the Pre-Roque Nublo Series is difficult to decipher, and their opinion is that these sedimentaries certainly are Vindobonian, but do range up into the Pliocene.

The calcareous sediments of the extreme N of Lanzarote, by analogy with those of Las Palmas, Gran Canaria (vd. supra) were inferred by ROTHE (1964, 1966) to be young Miocene, perhaps Vindobonian (Tortonian). FUSTER et al. (1968) referred to conglomerate horizons within palaeo-channels in their Basaltic Series I (Late MiocenePliocene?), as well as ›Miocene‹ calcareous strata at the base of this Series. No fossils have been found here, but forms shaped like birds' eggs occur in clayey-limy red soils. Without further elaboration, these authors likewise mention detritals in more evolved river valleys as being Pre-Quaternary. It was the view of ABDEL-MONEM et al. (1967) that, based on isotopic datings, Basaltic Series I was at least 12 my in age; but writing in 1971 they mention a possible argon loss in their samplings here, hence some uncertainty about this age assignment, but did believe the Series ranged from 10 to 6.4 my. They therefore claimed this supported the contention of FUSTER et al. that there was a significant gap within this Series.

As remarked above re. Gran Canaria, if we accept the Miocene-Pliocene boundary as being  younger  than  formerly believed (BERGGREN, 1973, adopts the  interval

Table 50      Elevations (in m) of marine terraces in the Canary Islands (after KLUG, 1968)

| Island | Flandrian | Neo-Tyrrhenian | Eu-Tyrrhenian | Palaeo-Tyrrhenian | Sicilian | Pliocene ? |
|---|---|---|---|---|---|---|
| Lanzarote | 3–4 | 4.9–7.0 | 15–18 | 25–45 | 55–60 | |
| Fuerteventura | 4 | 7 | 15–18 | 25–35 | 55–65 | |
| Gran Canaria | 3.5–4.8 | 6–13 | 15–22 | 35–ca. 100 | 55–100 ? | |
| Tenerife | 3.5–4.8 | 7.6–8.2 | ca. 15 | | | 60 |
| Gomera | 3.5–4.0 | | 18 | | | |
| La Palma | 4 | 6–13 | ca. 25 | | | |
| Hierro | 4 | | ca. 18 | 30 ? | | |

5.1–4.9 my) then indeed the sedimentaries in the extreme N of Lanzarote are Miocene, perhaps also ranging up into the Pliocene. The conglomerates and calcareous beds associated with Basaltic Series I, which latter is claimed by ABDEL-MONEM et al. to range from 10 to 6.4 my, would therefore place these sedimentaries within the Tortonian-Messinian of the Upper Miocene, which, as per BERGGREN (1972) cover the time range 10.5 to 5 my. If of course we were to show scepticism regarding the newer dating for the Miocene-Pliocene boundary, then the sedimentaries of Lanzarote may extend as far down as the Aquitanian.

Unfortunately almost no work has been done on the sedimentaries of Gomera and hence next to nothing is known stratigraphically here. CENDRERO (1971), by analogy with what he considered similar rocks in Fuerteventura, claimed that the Gomera sedimentaries spanned the range Cretaceous-Miocene, and placed them within his Submarine Series of the Basal Complex. ABDEL-MONEM et al. (1971), as per isotopic datings, assigned an age of ca. 15 my to this Basal Complex, i. e. Miocene, probably Vindobonian, and thus at this time, we may tentatively assign such an age to these Gomera sedimentaries.

The conglomerates, sandstones and gravels occurring in the floor of the Caldera de Taburiente, La Palma have yielded some marine fossils. These occur within clays formed in crevices and also on the rock floor at La Vina, at altitudes varying between 200 and 250 m above sea level. VON FRITSCH (1867) assigned a Helvetian age to these La Vina deposits. ABDEL-MONEM et al., on the basis of isotopic datings, claimed an age of 1.57 to 1.02 my to lavas on the NW wall above the Angustias valley, lying above a major unconformity above the Basement Complex of the Caldera. The sedimentaries within the Caldera lie at least 1,000 m below the summit of the NW wall, but this fact alone is not enough to postulate a pre-Quaternary age for the sedimentaries, for here rockfalls, landslides have been common in the past. It is indeed a pity that no further work on the lithology, stratigraphy and palaeontology of these La Palma sedimentaries has been done to date. It may well be that the Tertiary is present here, but whether this is Helvetian is uncertain, and a Quaternary age cannot be ruled out, as per our present knowledge.

Considerable areas of younger, generally less lithified sediments occur in Fuerteventura, in the N, the central-northern western coast, in smaller scattered localities along the eastern coast, in the El Jable peninsula and the extreme southern tip of the island. The rocks in question include marine limestones, polymictic silts and sands, gravels, conglomerates. In limestones occurring along the NW coast – the well-stratified, pure lime carbonate rock named the ›terrace limestone‹ by HAUSEN (1958a), COLOM (in HAUSEN 1958b) had assigned a Vindobonian age to the Foraminifera found therein. HAUSEN (1958a) on the other hand, considered all these younger sedimentaries as being Quaternary, actually formed during the last Inter-glacial Stage, some 200,000–100,000 years ago. In a personal communication, ROTHE has informed the writer that C–14 dating of these biocalcarenites suggested an age between 40,000 and 20,000 years ago. On informing Dr. COLOM of this, he agreed that such would favour a Quaternary age, remarking that his palaeontological studies were made not on the best of preserved foraminiferal species, and that the separation of Vindobonian, Pliocene, Quaternary foraminiferal species is often difficult. In HAUSEN's 1958b publication, he believed that the fanglomerates were older than the other Quaternary material, that likely the rudaceous and arenaceous constituents were Pliocene. Thus these younger Fuerteventura sedimentaries can be considered as ranging from Pliocene to Recent.

The sands, cross-bedded sandstones and pozzualane deposits of southern Tenerife, have yielded giant lizard and turtle fossil remains from the last-mentioned deposits. On the assumption that the sands and sandstones are pene-contemporaneous with the pozzualane deposits, HAUSEN (1955) claimed the rocks were Late or Terminal Tertiary, perhaps Pliocene or Villafranchian. However, as already pointed out, FUSTER et al. believed that the pozzualane deposits were present throughout most of the volcanic sequences of the island, and not restricted to one period of formation as HAUSEN would postulate. It is undeniable that pozzualane deposits are both geographically and temporally scattered, and hence as of this time, we must place little importance on HAUSEN's stratigraphic dating.

In Hierro, HAUSEN (1964) had considered the island as being relatively old, as distinct from FERNANDEZ (1908) who thought the island young indeed. ABDEL-MONEM et al. (1972), as per isotopic datings, claimed that the oldest rocks of Hierro were ca. 3 my old. HAUSEN (1973) now accepts this younger age, and hence the relatively few coarse sedimentaries would, in general, appear to be of Late Pleistocene-Holocene age, and none would appear to be older than Astian. (HAUSEN, 1973, mentions a carbonized wood embedded in a lava flow which gave an age of 2900 +/- 130 years. The lava thus belongs to the most recent vulcanism of the island, marking the end of vulcanicity in Hierro.) HAUSEN (1973) believes Hierro is the youngest of all the Canary Islands, formed essentially during the Pliocene.

## Palaeontology

It is clear from what has been said of the Canary Islands, and indeed all the Macaronesian archipelagoes, that the lithology, stratigraphy and palaeontology of the sedimentaries have been given relatively little attention. From the literature and from personal correspondence with many workers, one realizes that here and there fossils have been noted, perhaps collected, but too frequently collections have been laid aside for some future time, collections already studied have not been gone over again carefully, findings made a hundred years ago have not been given further taxonomic treatment nor stratigraphical appraisal. Realizing the relative paucity of palaeontological studies within the Canaries, we nevertheless present pertinent known information.

At the ›Las Palmas Terrace‹ in Gran Canaria, where the first stratigraphic dating in the archipelago was made, LYELL (1855) determined the following fauna: *Strombus bubonius, Cerithium procerum, Pecten jacobaeus, P. polymorphus, Cardita squamosa*. A more complete listing is given by ROTHPLETZ & SIMONELLI (1890): *Toxopneustes lividus* LAMARCK, *Mytilicardia calculata* LINNÉ, *Venus verrucosa* LINNÉ, *Patella lowei* D'ORBIGNY, *P. guttata* D'ORBIGNY, *Fissurella gibba* PHIL., *Phasianella pulla* PAYR., *Trochus turbinatus* BORN, *Monodonta richardii* PAYR., *Vermetus glomeratus* BIV., *V. subcancellatus* BIV., *Littorina affinis* D'ORB., *Cyclostoma canariense* D'ORB., *Cerithium lacteum* PHIL., *Columbella rustica* LAM., *Purpura (Polytropa) lapillus* LIN., *P. (Stramonita) haemastoma* LAM., *Marginella miliacea* LAM., *Mitra debrina* D'ORB., *Marinula firminii* (PAYR.), *Helix (Hemicyclus) malleata* FÉR.

Further determinations of specimens from the Sta. Catalina district of Las Palmas made by LECOINTRE, and now in the Museo Canario at Las Palmas, include the following: *Patella caerula mabillei* LOC., *P. gomesi* DROUET, *P. longicosta* LAM., *P. lowei* D'ORB., *P. cf. lugubris* GMEL., *Mesalia mesal* ADAN., *M. sagittifera* BORN, *Turritella meta* REEVE, *T. bicingulata* LAM., *Cymatium corrugatum* LAM., *Strombus bubonius* LAM., *Charonia nodifera* LIN., *C. nodiferum* LIN., *Murex hoplites* FISCHER, *M. tumulosus* SOW., *Cantharus assimilis* REEVE, *C. viverratus* KIEN., *Conus mediterraneus* HWASS, *C. prometheus* HWASS, *Arca barbata* LIN., *Chlamys corallinoides* LAM., *Jagonia eburnea* GMEL., *Cardium papillosum* POLI, *C. tuberculatum* LIN., *Meretrix tumens* POLI, *Venus casina* LIN., *V. multilamella* LAM., *Eastonia rugosa* LIN.

As remarked earlier, the great interest of the Las Palmas area is that here the first stratigraphic dating of Canarian sediments was made as early as 1825 by VON BUCH, viz. Neogene, greater refinement being made by LYELL (op. cit.) as Upper Miocene, and by ROTHPLETZ & SIMONELLI (1890) as Middle Miocene but ranging down also to the Aquitanian and up to the Pliocene.

DENIZOT (1934), ZEUNER (1958) and KLUG (1963, 1968) reported on the following, occurring at elevations of 78–85 m at Agaete: *Chlamys amphicyrta* LOC., *C. pes-felis* LIN., *Serpula* sp., *Flabellipecten* sp., *Anomia ephippium* LOC., *Chama gryphoides* LOC., *Cardiumpapillosum* POLI, *Cardium edule* LIN., *Ervilia* sp., *Tellina* sp., *Cardita antiquata* LIN., *Pectunculus bimaculatus* POLI, *P. violascens* LAM., *Trochus granulatus* BORN, *T. opistostewus* FONT., *T. magnus* LIN., *Turritella terebra* LIN., *T. subangulata* BROCCHI, *Natica catena* DA COSTA, *Murex aciculatus* LAM., *M. imbricatus* BROCCHI, *Meretrix chione* Lin., *Mitra cornicula* Lin., *Conus mediterraneus* Brug., *C. striatulus* Brocchi, *Vermetus intortus* Lam., *Venus verrucosa* Lin., *V. fasciata* Da Costa, *V. multilamella* Lam., *V. gallina* Lin., *V.* sp. *(ovata* Penn.?), *Marginella ambigua* Bav., *Columbella rustica* Lin., *Ostrea lamellosa* Brocchi, *Dentalium vulgara* Da Costa, *Turbo rugosus* Lin., *Lutraria oblonga* Omel., *Diva* sp., *Lima squamosa, Ranella laevigata, Fissurella graeca* Lin., *F. italica* Defrance, *Astarte castanea, Patella intermedia* Jeff., *Pecten jacobaens* Lin. From Banaderos, altitude 65 m, Klug (1968) reported the following: *Placopsilina* sp., *Serpula* sp., *Ostrea stentina* Payr., *Pecten* sp., *Chlamys varia* Lin., *Anomia* sp., *Modiola* cf. *barbata* Lin., *Arca* sp., *Pectunculus* sp., *Tapes aureus* Gmel., *Patella* sp., *Turritella* sp., *Mesalia brevialis* Lam., *Xenophora* sp., *Strombus bubonius* Lam., *Natica* sp., *Cypraea lurida* Lin., *Purpura* sp., *Nasa mutabilis* Lin., *Yetus gracilis* Brod., *Marginella amygdala* Kien., *Conus mediterraneus* Brug., *Ringicula* sp., *Dentalium* cf. *vulgare* Da Costa, *Balanus* sp., *Spondylus* sp. From Punta de Arucas, altitude 35 m, Klug (1968) reported: *Pholas parva* Mont., *Trochus turbinatus* Born, *T. labio* Lin., *T. lineatus* Da Costa, *Phasianella* sp., *Serpula* sp., *Murex* sp., *Bittium resticulatum* Da Costa, *Fossarus sulcatus* S. Wood, *Columbella rustica* Lin., *Patella intermedia* Jeff., *P. vulgata* Lin. From Guayera, altitude 55 m, Klug (1968) reported: *Cibicides lobatulus* (Walker & Jacob), *C. refulgens* Monf., *Elphidium crispens* (Lin.), *Eponides repandus* (Fichtel & Moll). From Punta Gondora, altitude 100 m, Klug (op. cit.) reported likewise on the following microfauna: *Quinqueloculina badenensis* d'Orb., *Q. dutemplei* d'Orb., *Q. triangularis* D'Orb., *Robulus* sp., *Discorbis globularis* (d'Orb.), *D. patelliformis* (Brady), *Gyroidinoides* sp., *Cibicides lobatulus* (Walker & Jacob), *C.* cf. *pseudoungerianus* (Cush.), *C. refulgens* Mont., *Planulina ariminensis* d'Orb., *Asterigerina planorbis* d'Orb., *Amphistegina* sp., *Elphidium crispum* (Lin.), *Eponides* sp.

From Lanzarote, Klug (1968) reported the following from a marine terrace varying between 55 and 60 m: (a) At the foot of Los Ajaches: *Arca (Fossularca) lactea* Lin., *Conus mediterraneus* Brug., *Cerithium atratum* Born, *Purpura* sp., *Patella safiana* Lam., *Helcion pellucidus* Lin. (b) At the southern base of Los Morros de Hacha Chica: *Arca noe* Lin., *Chama gryphoides* Lin., *Conus mediterraneus* Brug., *Cerithium atratum* Born, *Bittium reticulatum* Da Costa, *Nassa* sp., *Patella safiana* Lam. (c) Near Punta La Torreta, SW base of Los Ajaches: *Pectumculus* sp., *Tapes* sp., *Conus* sp., *Cerithium* sp. *?Nassa* sp. (d) Mouth of the small valley by El Cohon: *Serpula* sp., *Spondylus* sp., *Chama gryphina* Lam., *Cardita calyculata* Lin., *Tapes pullastra* Mont., *Conus mediterraneus* Brug., *?Fusus* sp., *Triton* sp., *Murex hoplites* P. Fischer, *Rapana* sp. cf. *coronata* Lam., *Clathurella purpurea* Mont., *Cerithium atratum* Born, *Columbella rustica* Lin., *Vermetus lumbricalis* Lin., *Neritina glabrata* Sow., *Patella safiana* Lam., *P. granularis* Lin., *Helcion pellucides* Lin. (e) From the Rubicon plain: *Elphidium crispum* Lin., *Amphistegina lessonii* d'Orb., also species of *Robulus, Cibides* and *Eponides*. At an elevation of 4 m at Montana Roja, Klug (op. cit.) mentions: *Serpula* sp., *Cardita calyculata* Lin., *Patella vulgata* Lin., *P. safiana* Lam., *P. granularis* Lin., *Trochus turbinatus* Born, *Purpura haemastoma* Lin., and the Recent land snails *Stenogyra decollata* Lin. and *Cepaea* sp.

In the terrestrial calcareous sandstones of Lanzarote, Hausen (1959) found fossil nests of *Antophora, Helix* and *Stenogyra* shells. Rothe (1964b, 1966) has referred to ostrich eggs, belonging probably to the species *Struthio camelus* LINNÉ in the Orzola limestones, land snails, *Monilearia* MOUSSON 1872, *Zootecus insularis* EHR. var. *subdiaphanus* KING, several genera of Foraminifera, of which *Globigerina* and *Globigerinoides* are the commonest, also some undetermined ostracods, bryozoa, echinoids and sponge spicules.

From Fuerteventura, KLUG (1968) reported the following from Los Molinos at an elevation of 4 m: *Patella intermedia* JEFF., *Cassius* sp., ?*Pyrula* sp.; from Los Atolladeros, elevation 55 m, in the Jandia peninsula: *Ostrea* cf. *edulis* LIN., *Spondylus* sp., *Lucina* sp., *Meretrix tumens* GMEL., *Dosinia isocardia* DUNK., *Venus* sp., *Patella intermedia* JEFF., *P. granularis* LIN., *P.* cf. *oculus* BRON, *Helcion* sp. (*pellucidus* LIN.), *Vermetus* sp., *Strombus bubonius* LAM., *Natica* sp., *Cassidaria* sp., *Purpura* sp. From NW of El Morro, KLUG (op. cit.) mentioned *Ostrea* cf. *edulis* LIN., *Purpura* sp. *Balanus* sp.     HAUSEN (1958b) referred to the following Foraminifera occurring in limestones throughout the island: (a) Toston: *Elphidium* sp., *Quinqueloculina* sp., *Amphiroa*. (b) Corralejos: *Amphiroa, Cibicides* cf. *lobatulus* WALKER & JACOB, *Textularia* cf. *sagittula* DEFR., *Elphidium complanatum* D'ORB., *Tricolulina* sp., *Quinqueloculina* sp. (c) Bahia de las Gaviotas: *Cibicides* cf. *lobatulus* WALKER & *Jacob*, *Textularia* cf. *sagittula* DEFR., *Elphidium complanatum* D'ORB., *Miliolas, Melobesias* and echinoid spines also. (d) Puerto de la Penita: As in (c), plus *Anomalina*, rare fragments of molluscs, echinoderms. (e) N of Jable de las Salinas: *Miliolas* and *Melobesias*, echinoid spines. (f) Playa de Urgan: *Cibicides* cf. *lobatulus, Textularia* cf. *sagittula, Triloculinas, Quinqueloculinas,* echinoid spines. (g) Between Terife and Chilegua: *Textularia* cf. *sagittula* DEFR., *Elphidium* cf. *complanatum* D'ORB., *Amphistegina* sp., *Quinqueloculina* sp., *Triloculina* sp. *Anomalina* sp. (??). (h) Gran Tarajal: *Cibicides* cf. *lobatulus* WALKER & JACOB, *Textularia* cf. *sagittula* DEFR., *Amphistegina* cf. *lessonii* D'ORB., *Amphiroa* sp., *Triloculinas, Quinqueloculinas, Elphidium* sp., echinoid spines and shell fragments of molluscs. (j) Barranco de las Pilas: *Melobesias* and mollusc shells. These Foraminifera of the younger sedimentaries of Fuerteventura were studied by COLOM, as referred to under the section on Stratigraphy. The older sedimentaries of West-Central Fuerteventura, reported on by ROTHE (1968), have so far yielded only one determined fossil, *Posidonia bronni*.

In Tenerife fossil bones have been reported by BRAVO (1953) belonging to the giant turtle *Testudo burchardi* E. ABEL and the giant lizard *Lacerta goliath* MERTENS. The latter became extinct towards the end of Tertiary, but rather similar degenerate forms, *Lacerta simonyi* and *Lacerta stehleni* have continued to present times.

In Hierro, the French botanist J. PITARD found an echinoid in limestones occurring within volcanics. COTTREAU & LEMOINE (1910) claimed that this specimen was *Discoidea pulvinata* var. *major*, and was taken to indicate Lower Cretaceous. As previously remarked under Stratigraphy, both fossil and limestones are now refuted.

From Gran Canaria, SCHMINCKE (1967a, 1968b) reported the first fossil plants, not only from this island but from the entire archipelago. Very well-preserved stems, branches and leaves of trees were found, some trunks measuring up to 10 m in length, 2 m in diameter, occurring at the base of his Roque Nublo Agglomerates. Carbonized plant fragments in fluviatile volcano-clastic sandstones in the same formation were also discovered. The occurrences are given as near Barrazalas, Pajonales and the E side of

Barranco de Hoya. Fossils determined as belonging largely to laurel trees. The finding of bamboo-like plants and palms (?) at elevations of 1,200 m at Pajonales is of interest, where today pines (*Pinus canariensis*) and briers (*Erica arborea*) are growing, would testify surely to subtropical conditions when these Middle Pliocene laurels, palms (?) and bamboo-like plants were thriving at this altitude. NOGALES & SCHMINCKE (1969) also mentioned finding at an altitude of 1,600 m on the road from Pinos de Galdar to Cruz de Tejeda, within a thick accumulation of lapilli, a 5.50 m high, 40 cm diameter trunk of *Pinus canariensis*. A C–14 dating of the trunk gave a date of 3,075±50 years, ca. 1,100 B. C. The lapilli are thought to be not older than 5,000 years. In a recent letter, Professor SCHMINCKE has informed the writer that unfortunately no further work has been done on the fossil plants of Gran Canaria.

Data regarding VON FRITSCH's supposedly Miocene fossils within the Caldera de Taburiente, La Palma, are vague in the extreme. There is reported (in GAGEL, 1908d) »Reste von Korallen und Balanen, dem Landhause La Vina ungefähr gegenüber, bis in Höhen von 200 bis 250 Meter über der See«. Later VON WOLFF (1931) claimed these fossils to be Helvetic, but apparently this is all we know, tantalizingly little.

HAUSEN (1969) mentioned an interesting find in La Palma of a »bomb composed of calcareous matter intermingled with microfossils, apparently of marine origin«, on the E side of Cumbre Vieja in the vicinity of the Sub-Recent volcano, Bidigoyo. The material – a slide and microphotographs – was sent to Dr. G. COLOM of Mallorca for study. COLOM recognized Echinoidea, Melobesiae, Foraminifera, probably Gastropoda. Of Foraminifera, he thought *Amphistegina* (Miocene) and Cretaceous species might be present, also a species of Miocene *Amphiora*, *Operculina* (?) and a Rotalidae. He was of the opinion the material indicated a Miocene age.

## Historic Vulcanicity

Table 10 indicates known vulcanicity within historic times in the Canary Islands, perhaps 12 occurrences as compared with perhaps 19 in the Azores.

Maybe as early as 1393 or 1399 there was eruptivity in Tenerife, though reports of such cannot be authenticated. Though the aboriginal Guanche population and various Mediterranean peoples knew the archipelago long before this, no verbal or written reports of vulcanicity have been handed down, and thus nothing is known of such between 2500–2000 B. C. and the 15th century A. D.

There is somewhat more substantiation for the 1430 eruptivity in Tenerife, WEBB & BERTHOLET (1839) referring to Guanche tales of three outbursts in the lower Orotava valley, at Mont. de la Horca, Mont. de los Frailes and Mont. Gananias. The occurrences of this presumed date were studied by older scholars, e. g. VON BUCH (1825), VON FRITSCH & REISS (1868), ROTHPLETZ (1889), KÜNZLI (1911). ROTHPLETZ described the rocks as enstatite-bearing andesites and augite-amphibole andesites, and HAUSEN (1955) mentioned a barkevite-bearing alkali-basalt from Mont. de la Horca.

The 1585 eruptivity is that at Mont. Quemada, La Palma, the first to be authentically dated. A lengthy lava stream flowed down the western slopes to reach near sea level at Tazacorte, midway up the western coast. Along with lava expulsions, ashes and lapilli were scattered over the southern slopes. The blistery, slaggy lavas show phenocrysts of augite, sometimes also olivine and magnetite, microlites of plagioclase and small grains of pyroxene and ore, within a vitreous matrix (HAUSEN, 1969). As this part of the island was then well populated, there were many eye-witnesses and great damage to structure of all kinds was caused.

In La Palma in 1646, San Martin in the Cumbre Viaja ridge erupted, sending lava streams down the eastern slopes and forming a large area of blistery and blocky lavas extending down to the coast. SMULIKOWSKI et al. (1946) analyzed a sample of this lava, calling the rock basanitoid with phenocrysts of olivine and augite, microlites of basaltic augite, slivers of twinned labradorite also anorthite, all cemented in a vitreous matrix, along with occult apatite and iron oxides (vd. No. 58, Tables 28, 29, 30).

During 1677–1678 eruptivity occurred in La Palma at the southern end of Cumbre Vieja at San Antonio, in the vicinity of Fuencalientes. Here we have what HAUSEN (op. cit.) termed »a model of an explosion crater«, completely enclosed, 50 m deep, crater walls 700 m above sea level. A great volume of black cinders were ejected, along with many varisized bombs. The lavas have been described by JÉRÉMINE (1933) and SMULIKOWSKI et al. (op. cit.), the former recognizing ordanchites whilst the latter describe a sample from here as tephrite (vd. No. 59, Tables 28, 29, 30).

Between 1704 and 1706 four distinct outbursts occurred in Tenerife, in the Fasnia region, Afaro in the Guimar valley and at Mont. Negra, when the port of Garachico on the NW coast was completely destroyed. The Fasnia lavas are oceanites; those of Arafo, ›porphyritic basalts‹ as per VON FRITSCH & REISS, basanites as per JÉRÉMINE, hyaline basanites and tephrites as per HAUSEN; those of Mont. Negra, ›tephratoidal‹ as per JÉRÉMINE, hornblende-bearing nepheline-basalts as per HAUSEN.

During 1730–1736 the earliest historic vulcanicity occurred in Lanzarote. Almost a quarter of the island was affected (Fig. 70). According to HAUSEN (1959) »The magnitude of outbursts and the quantity of erupted material . . . . . . . . surpassed all the events of that kind in the Canaries in Sub-Recent and Recent times«. During a period lasting from Sept. 1, 1730 to April 16, 1736, activity took place from many centres, outlining the trends of volcano-tectonic ENE-WSW fissures. Detailed descriptions are to be found in the works of E. HERNANDEZ-PACHECO (1910, 1960), FERNANDEZ (1919a), HAUSEN (1959), detailed descriptions of events being recorded by the priest CURBELO and reprinted in VON BUCH's work of 1825. Gigantic streams of lava flowed in general westward directions, enormous showers of bombs, lapilli and ashes were strewn over a wide area, with powerful eruptivity emanating from at least 25 volcanic centres, according to SAPPER (1906). The lavas are largely vesicular olivine-augite-basalts and olivine-basalts, with phenocrysts of olivine and pyroxene, sometimes also plagioclase, in a holocrystalline matrix largely comrising plagioclase and augite, fluidal texture quite common. Some impressive volcanic tubes or ›tunnels‹ are found in these eruptives, one several km in length, with laval stalagtites and stalagmites and also gypsum deposits (MONTORIOL, 1965).

The 1824 eruptivity in Lanzarote was much more restricted in area, covering only some 3 km$^2$. An eye-witness account was given by the priest PERDOMO, and accounts are to be found in HARTUNG (1857), VON FRITSCH (1867), SAPPER (1906), HERNANDEZ-PACHECO (1910) and HAUSEN (1959). Events took place in the same general area of the island but

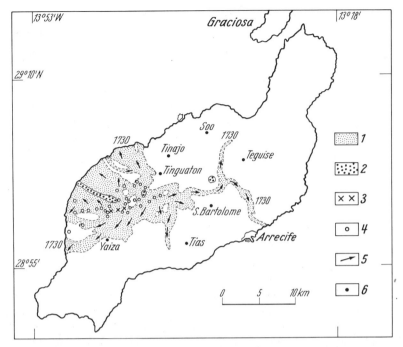

Fig. 70. Historic eruptivity in Lanzarote. 1: 1730–1736 eruptions. 2: 1824 eruptions. 3: Fumaroles of 1730–1736. 4: Emission centres. 5: Lava flow directions. 6: Towns. (Based on HERNANDEZ-PACHECO, 1910, HAUSEN, 1959, FUSTER et al., 1968).

restricted to three distinct localities aligned along an ENE-WSW trend – tectonic fissure? – the centres being Mont. Clerigo Duarte, Tinguaton and Volcan Nuevo del Fuego. Vulcanism this time lasted only ca. 3 months. Tinguaton, the last to be operative, expelled boiling waters along with lavas, HERNANDEZ-PACHECO claiming that these saline waters were of marine origin, the site being neither high nor far from the sea. Vesicular, porphyritic olivine-augite basalts and picrite-basalts, with magnetite inclusions, basaltic rock fragments of the earlier episode, typify the lavas.

Three periods of vulcanicity have occurred during this century. The first was that of Mont. Chinyero, NW Tenerife; in 1909, described by COLLET & MONTEGNIER (1910), FERNANDEZ (1910, 1911, 1912, 1919a, 1925), PERRET (1914) and HAUSEN (1955). Lava flows, up to 3.5 km in length coursed W-SW down the slopes towards the Santiago valley. Chinyero lies 11.5 km NW of Pico Viejo, outside the reconstructed perimeter of the immense Canadas caldera, and 12 km from Pico de Teide. Hence HAUSEN thought it unlikely that there was any immediate relation between the Picos and Chinyero in vulcanicity. PERRET believed that Chinyero was not a parasitic episode – as with other cinder cones of the island – but rather a renewal of activity of the central edifice of the two Picos. The very moderate eruptions of Chinyero he explained as due to a deep release of pressure into fissures opened by tremors, where much of the liquid-gaseous phases were contained, surplus material being very suddenly expelled to the surface so that fractionation had no time to take place, with the result that superficial effects were evident only in the slaggy ejections, blocky and glassy lavas, of insignificant volume. HAUSEN disagreed with PERRET, claiming that Chinyero, in both its morphological features and lava composition, is the same as in other smaller volcanoes in the same general region, that it was independent from the Picos volcanic centre. The Chineyero lavas are of aa type, vitreous in appearance, with phenocrysts of olivine, augite and plagioclase in a glassy groundmass, the rocks being termed vitreous alkali-basalts.

The second 20th century eruption took place in 1949 in La Palma (ORTIZ, 1951; BENITEZ, 1952; SAN MIGUEL DE LA CAMARA ET AL., 1952; MARTEL, 1960; HAUSEN, 1969). This occurred on the same central spine, Cumbre Vieja, as where the earlier eruptions had taken place. After more than 200 years of quietude, tremors began in 1936 and continued intermittently during the succeeding years. A violent shock occurred in March, 1949, seriously damaging the lighthouse at Fuencalientes in the extreme S part of the island. On June 23, strong tremors were felt all day, during the night, and by next day volcanic explosions burst forth. The first vent in action was Duraznero, when large falls of ashes, copious gas emanations and hot water expulsions, followed by a lava stream, resulted. Action here continued until July 8, and then, some distance to the N, on the western flank of the old volcano of Nambroque, a vent opened in the form of an adventive cone, creating a large crater, Hoyo Negro. Here no lavas were emitted but only ashes and boiling waters, accompanied by strong tremors. As this activity was in progress, a third vent developed, Llano del Banco, where a large hole opened on the western slope of the Sub-Recent volcano of Bidigoyo, and from this, great quantities of lava poured westwards down to the coasts. By July 30 vulcanism had ceased. ORTIZ estimated that the total volume of lavas produced from Duraznero and LLano del Banco was of the order of 55 million m³. SAN MIGUEL DE LA CAMARA et al. have given analyses of the lavas and cinders – vd. No. 65, Tables 28, 29, 30 – the rocks being classed as alkali- and plagioclase-basalts.

The 1971 eruptivity of La Palma is reported by CHAIGNEAU & FUSTER (1972, 1973), ARANA & IBARROLA (1973), FUSTER et al. (1973), IBARROLA, (1973), and also the special ›Teneguia‹ volume of the Instituto »Lucas Mallada«, C.S.I.C., Madrid (1974), unfortunately not available at the time of writing. The volcano Teneguia, again on the central spine, near to Fuencalientes, was in operation from Oct. 26 to Nov. 18. Warning earth tremors occurred for several days, then on Oct. 26 a 200 m long fissure, trending N10W, opened, with lavas and ejectamenta issuing along the entire length. In the next few days activity became concentrated at the extreme N end (Teneguia I) where a cinder cone developed, and at the southern extremity (Teneguia II) where lavas, scoria and bombs were expelled, creating an exogenous dome. Teneguia I remained the chief centre throughout the eruptive period, but the structure underwent some subsidence on Nov. 6, triggering some spectacular rocks falls down the western slopes. Other centres became active but were of ephemeral existence, e. g. Teneguia III, Nov. 1–3, Teneguia IV and Teneguia V, during period Nov. 7–18. The chief cone created by the coalescence of centres I, IV and V reached an altitude of ca. 130 m above the pre-existing topography. Lava expulsions covered an area of some 4 km², pyroclastics, ca. 10 km². At the beginning the lavas showed high viscosity, but after centres IV and V became active, much greater fluidity of lavas was notable, forming real flows of aa type.

Table 51                 Chemical analyses and CIPW norms of rhyolitic pumice of the 1971 eruption of Teneguia, La Palma, and comparisons with basalts, phonolite, nordmarkite (ARANA & IBARROLA 1973)

|                    | 1     | 2     | 3     | 4     | 5     | 6     | 7     | 8     |
|--------------------|-------|-------|-------|-------|-------|-------|-------|-------|
| $SiO_2$            | 66.7  | 70.7  | 72.0  | 74.2  | 44.49 | 43.27 | 54.8  | 66.25 |
| $Al_2O_3$          | 15.98 | 16.22 | 15.68 | 14.40 | 15.44 | 13.68 | 20.52 | 15.91 |
| $Fe_2O_3$          | 2.42  | 0.36  | 0.28  | 0.43  | 4.38  | 3.92  | 2.84  | 2.90  |
| FeO                | 0.72  | 0.63  | 0.77  | 0.35  | 7.96  | 9.39  | 1.35  | 0.54  |
| MnO                | 0.22  | 0.03  | 0.01  | 0.02  | 0.22  | 0.22  | 0.15  | 0.13  |
| MgO                | 0.61  | 0.46  | 0.45  | 0.91  | 7.18  | 9.22  | 1.27  | 0.70  |
| CaO                | 0.17  | 0.31  | 0.26  | 1.04  | 9.19  | 10.28 | 3.28  | 0.73  |
| $Na_2O$            | 7.55  | 6.10  | 5.26  | 5.53  | 4.33  | 3.60  | 8.62  | 6.56  |
| $K_2O$             | 4.46  | 4.20  | 4.34  | 2.02  | 1.80  | 1.47  | 4.80  | 4.72  |
| $TiO_2$            | 0.19  | 0.39  | 0.27  | 0.25  | 3.61  | 3.71  | 0.86  | 0.68  |
| $P_2O_5$           | 0.06  | 0.08  | 0.04  | 0.03  | 0.98  | 0.88  | 0.25  | 0.11  |
| $H_2O$             | 0.55  | 0.27  | 0.33  | 0.26  | 0.25  | 0.18  | 0.58  | 0.73  |
| Total              | 99.63 | 99.75 | 99.69 | 99.44 | 99.83 | 99.82 | 99.82 | 99.96 |
| Q                  | 5.9   | 18.0  | 23.2  | 30.5  |       |       |       |       |
| Or                 | 26.1  | 25.0  | 25.6  | 11.7  | 10.6  | 8.7   |       |       |
| Ab                 | 57.6  | 51.4  | 44.5  | 46.6  | 17.6  | 11.8  |       |       |
| An                 |       | 0.8   | 1.4   | 5.3   | 17.4  | 16.8  |       |       |
| C                  |       | 1.3   | 2.5   | 1.2   |       |       |       |       |
| Ne                 |       |       |       |       | 10.3  | 10.1  |       |       |
| Ac                 | 5.5   |       |       |       |       |       |       |       |
| Hy                 | 1.1   | 0.3   | 0.8   | 0.7   |       |       |       |       |
| En                 | 1.5   | 1.1   | 1.1   | 2.3   |       |       |       |       |
| Dy (Fe)            |       |       |       |       | 3.7   | 5.5   |       |       |
| Dy (Mg)            |       |       |       |       | 13.8  | 17.4  |       |       |
| Ol (Fe)            |       |       |       |       | 2.7   | 4.1   |       |       |
| Ol (Mg)            |       |       |       |       | 8.0   | 10.4  |       |       |
| Mt                 | 0.7   | 0.5   | 0.5   | 0.0   | 6.4   | 5.7   |       |       |
| Il                 | 0.3   | 0.8   | 0.5   | 0.5   | 6.9   | 7.1   |       |       |
| Ap                 | 0.3   | 0.3   | 0.0   | 0.0   | 2.3   | 2.0   |       |       |

1. Greyish pumice.
2. White pumice.
3. White pumice.
4. White pumice.

5. Aver. of 15 pyroxene-amphibole basalts, Teneguia.
6. Aver. of 13 pyroxene-olivine basalts, Teneguia.
7. Phonolite from neighbouring plug, Teneguia.
8. Nordmarkite, Pajara, Fuerteventura.

Concomitant with this variation in viscosity there was a composition change also. Earlier lavas contain phenocrysts of augite and basaltic hornblende within a microcrystalline or hypocrystalline matrix composed of opaque minerals. After centres IV and V were in action, lavas showed phenocrysts of olivine and augite, with or without amphibole – vd. No. 66, Tables 28–30, of Teneguia I olivinebasalts. The rocks in general can be described as highly alkaline-basalts. During Nov. 13-14, gases were escaping from Tenequia III at the rate of 25–32 km³ per hour at a velocity of 340-430 km per hour. Occluded gases determined from lavas and bombs are similar to those exhaled from fumaroles – HCl, $CO_2$, CO, $CS_2$, SCO, $H_2$, $N_2$, hydrocarbons, rare gases – though the proportions of the principal gases are different.

Of interest in this eruptivity was the development of acid pumice fragments along with large volumes of basic lapilli ejections. ARANA & IBARROLA discuss two possibilities of origin of the acidics. The pumice fragments may indicate a late differentiation phase of normal basaltic Teneguia products which would not accord with current concepts and experimental data on magmatic evolution. On the other hand, two cases of anatexis are examined, involving partial melting and total melting of pre-existing matter of composition very similar to that of the pumice fragments. Such a hypothesis would then recognize a substratum in La Palma of acid alkaline rocks, extreme members of a differentiated complex, which are not unknown in the Canary Islands, e. g. in Fuerteventura (vd. Table 51, No. 8). By the same token, such a possible basement complex would thus be larger in area in La Palma than that occurring in the base of Caldera de Taburiente.

## Geophysical Aspects

To date we have more published information regarding geophysical aspects of the Canary Islands and marine vicinity than for other archipelagoes. Gravity surveys were made of Tenerife and Lanzarote (MACFARLANE & RIDLEY, 1968, 1969), the western-central marine area has been covered by seismic refraction and gravity surveys (DASH & BOSSHARD, 1968, 1969), articles on the crustal structure (DASH & BOSSHARD, 1969; BOSSHARD & MACFARLANE, 1970). ABDEL-MONEM et al. (1971, 1972), along with their geochronological investigations of the archipelago also studied natural remanent magnetism, and WATKINS (1973) has also written of palaeomagnetism of the islands. ARANA & PALOMO (1973) carried out some reflection seismic studies off the W coast of Fuerteventura.

We may discuss the geophysics under the headings of Gravity, Seismic and Palaeomagnetic.

### Gravity

For his doctoreal thesis of 1968 MACFARLANE made gravity studies of Hierro, Tenerife, Gran Canaria and Lanzarote, but published information is only available for Tenerife and Lanzarote by him and RIDLEY. For the latter island, situated on the upper part of the continental slope the principal regional gravity trend shows an increase in BOUGUER anomalies towards the W, related to the transition from continental to oceanic crust. HAUSEN (1959) was of the opinion that the central part of the island, with horst mountains to N and S, was a tectonic graben. BOUGUER values show a marked decrease which coincides with a slope reversal in the gravity field for the island (Fig.71). Possibly the steep slope in the marine gravity anomalies indicate the N edge of a seaward extension of this structure. On the other hand, no sharp increase in anomalies occurs on the S margin of the presumed graben, but instead a gravity minimum. This minimum may be due to lateral displacement along the edge of the graben where increase in gravity is cancelled at the edge of the horst block. The BOUGUER map shows a marked ›high‹ in the SE part of the island which is aligned with the NNE-trending escarpment of the northern highlands. This ›high‹ is taken to represent a very high-density anomalous mass extending from near the surface to a depth comparable to that of the Moho. Gravity data then would tend to confirm the view of FUSTER et al. (1968) that a large gabbroic mass occurs at depth, as represented by xenoliths of gabbro, norite, etc. – fragments from deeper levels within the complex than those found in Fuerteventura. MACFARLANE and RIDLEY, however, believed that this mass is intimately related to surface volcanics, that material in deeper regions of the high-level magma chamber is accumulative. The Recent volcanics in the W of the island show no significant anomalies, which would suggest that the magma reservoir is located in the S-Central part of the main volcanic mass and moves into a peripheral position before eruption takes place along NW-SE weakness zones, which latter are associated with transverse faulting, suggested, e. g. by a westward shift of some 15–20 km of the NNE-trending scarp in the southern part of the island. To these authors the volcanic focus which the BOUGUER ›high‹ is taken to represent, constructed a large subaerial cone with ridges along a NNE-SSW rift zone, later deformed by earth movements so that today only the ridges remain as horsts.

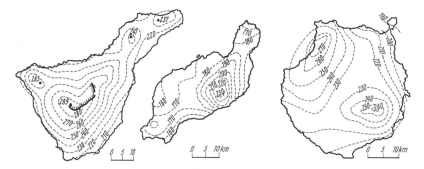

Fig. 71. Bouguer anomalies (in mgals), Tenerife, Lanzarote, Gran Canaria. (Modified after MACFARLANE & RIDLEY, 1968, 1969, BOSSHARD & MACFARLANE, 1970).

In Tenerife the Free-Air anomalies are typical for a regionally compensated island. Local BOUGUER anomalies (Fig. 71) show a prominent gravity ridge extending from Las Canadas towards the Anaga peninsula and less well-defined extending NW into the Teno peninsula and southwards into the Bandas del Sur region. A pronounced gravity ›high‹ of ca. 100 mgl lies somewhat W of the Tauce scarp. In the Anaga, Teno and La Laguna plain areas, gravity closure is less marked. The NE-trending gravity ridge also outlines the Pedro Gil topographic ridge, where extensive trachytic, trachy-basaltic and basaltic flows dip to the NW and SE. In the Teno peninsula occur dyke swarms of general NW orientation, and it would appear that here the gravity ridge reflects this concentration of dykes within fissures rather than elongate magma bodies below, the assumption being that the growth of the island was chiefly controlled by extrusions along three principal fissures zones. The Canadas and Basaltic III Series show greater rock varieties than occur in the basement, with a distinct low-pressure mineralogy, suggesting an origin in a magma chamber of shallow depth. Within the Las Canadas area is the highest BOUGUER anomaly in the island, which presupposes a large high-density body here, perhaps the locus of the magma chamber. The maximum possible depth to the upper surface of this body is 23 km, the total anomalous mass being 9.18 g. This body is thought to be an intrusion of mantle-like material into the crust, extending from the Moho to within ca. 4 km of the surface, 1.5 km of the upper part with lesser density representing rocks resulting from fractionation. With the exception of the Canadas and Basaltic III Series, the subaerial volcanics with their high-pressure minerals are opposed to the concept of a shallow magma chamber, which instead was probably developed deeper than 35 km. MACFARLANE and RIDLEY were inclined to think that the huge Canadas caldera was the result of landsliding, not a collapse structure, and that the role of mass gravitational movements in the Canaries has been underestimated in the past.

## Seismic

Refraction seismic investigations in the Canary marine environment show that P-wave velocities can be placed into five groups: (a) a surface layer with a velocity range of 2.85–3.56 km/sec. can be correlated with a tuff-clastic zone. (b) Velocities of 3.90–4.75 km/sec. are likely associated with pillow basalts. It could be that this layer represents the fractured and vesiculated surface of basalts, but it is unlikely that consolidated sediments can be correlated with this layer. (c) The upper layer of crustal rocks show a velocity range from 5.6–6.0–km/sec., typical of the oceanic layer, and probably represents massive basalts under the islands, the depth of the refractor being of the order of 7.8 km. (d) W of the islands velocities of 6.60–6.72 km/sec. were recorded, typical for oceanic layer 3, and velocities of 7.05–7.50 km/sec. were recorded to the N, S and W of Gran Canaria-Tenerife-Gomera, which may represent magma intruded into the oceanic layer. These velocities could correlate with alkaline gabbros and peridotites which are presumed to constitute a common basement for the archipelago. (e) The deepest zone gives velocities of 7.65–8.12 km/sec., in agreement with Upper Mantle velocities.

Reflection seismic profiles mostly parallel to the W coast of Fuerteventura, some 10 km offshore and opposite the outcropping basal complex of the Betancuria Massif, showed only one reflecting horizon. The upper layers of this significant horizon are some 100 m thick and are taken to represent material which can be correlated with that of the basal complex. Plutonics of the basal complex thus continue westward as an accidented submarine platform, with narrow deep valleys and pronounced submarine cliffing. The significant dyke intrusions seen in the Massif can also be detected in these profiles. Hence this complex can be taken as extending some 10 km W of the island where the platform is abruptly terminated by submarine cliffs.

From gravity and seismic studies, some statements can be made about crustal conditions in the general archipelago region. The islands lie on a transition zone between truly oceanic and truly continental crust. This transition zone is marked by strong faulting. Lanzarote-Fuerteventura, on the basis of BOUGUER anomalies values, do not seem to represent a continental raft separated from Africa, for such would imply

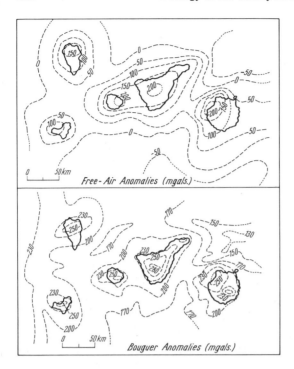

Fig. 72. Free-air and Bouguer anomalies, Central and Western Canary Islands. (Modified after DASH & BOSSHARD, 1969).

a crustal thickness of ca. 19 km here which is not typical continental crust. Under Tenerife the depth to the Moho is calculated as 16 km, which is greater by 1.5 km than calculations made from seismic data to N and S of the island. The Mantle depth W of the islands is ca. 11 km, reaching a depth of ca. 14 km S of Gomera-Tenerife and 15 km to the N of Tenerife-Gran Canaria (Fig.73). The latter depths are considerably greater than the standard 11.5 km of the Moho in oceanic areas. The two faults detected between Gran Canaria and Tenerife show a downthrow on the SE side of ca. 500 m for each interface. As noted above the basement is upwarped ca. 1 km under Tenerife with respect to the surrounding basement, this high basement being held responsible for the Tenerife-Gomera structural block. N and NE of Gran Canaria negative Free-Air anomalies occur in nearby deep sea basins, a common occurrence beyond depths of 2,000 m on continental margins. It might be that the Mantle is lowered under the continental block prior to attaining the edge of this margin, due to regional compensation for the continental extension. It is thus possible that these negative values in the Gran Canaria area represent parts of the negative zone of the continental extension (no correlation is possible with a submarine depression), in which case the anomalies imply increase in the degree of downwarping of the Mantle between Gran Canaria and the African mainland. From the Free-Air and BOUGUER values and patterns, Hierro, La Palma and Gran Canaria seem to be independent islands, whereas Tenerife and Gomera form a structural block, but it should be noted that such a grouping is not borne out by petrochemical considerations, as noted earlier. N of Gran Canaria the BOUGUER anomaly gradient is 6 mgl/km, taken as evidence of faulting perpendicular to

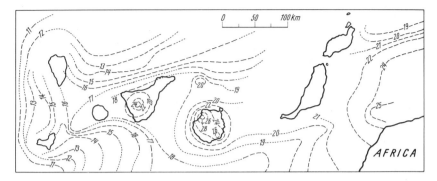

Fig. 73. Depth of the Mohorovicic discontinuity (in km) around Canary Islands. (After Boss-HARD & MacFarlane, 1970).

the gradient, i. e. NE-SW. Between La Palma and Tenerife-Gomera anomalies drop to 170 mgl which likely indicates a local crustal thickening. The regional BOUGUER change from W of La Palma to Gran Canaria approximates 60 mgl and if we assume the regional field to result from thickness variations only of the basement, then this would imply that the Moho is downwarped by ca. 3 km towards the mainland. As per crustal studies then, the western islands are underlain by crust of oceanic type; Tenerife and Gran Canaria represent transitional areas, and Fuerteventure and Lanzarote are characterized by continental type crust, the five western-central islands being independent volcanic edifices.

## Palaeomagnetic

ABDEL-MONEM et al. defined polarities as normal for virtual geomagnetic latitudes of more than 30°; intermediate for latitudes lower than this, and reversed for latitudes higher than 30° S.

Fig. 74 shows comparisons of K-Ar ages and palaeomagnetic polarities in the range Present to 17 my. Either because of lack of well-defined directions of remanent magnetism or then because of the limited exactitude of K-Ar values when correlated with the predicted polarity scale, not all the magnetic data could be used. It appears that the earliest reversed lavas occur in Gran Canaria, with an age between 12 and 14.5 my. As was noted in discussing isotopic age determinations no data are available as regards either K-Ar or magnetic polarities for the basal complex material of La Palma, which complex is probably comparable in age to those determined in Fuerteventura and Gomera. An encouraging feature of these studies is the large degree of similarity between values of the independently-defined polarity and the K-Ar determinations (cf. Fig. 74 and Table 48).

WATKINS gives palaeomagnetic data for Pleistocene samples from Lanzarote, Tenerife, La Palma and Hierro; Pliocene samples for Gran Canaria and Tenerife; Miocene samples for Lanzarote, Fuerteventura, Gran Canaria, Tenerife and Gomera, stratigraphic control being provided by the geochronology of ABDEL-MONEM et al. Analysed data were restricted to bodies having a virtual geomagnetic pole latitude higher than 45°. Tenerife has the greatest volume of Matuyama epoch material (0.69–2.43 my), but La Palma also shows large areas of Upper Matuyama material. The Gauss epoch (2.43–3.32 my) is best developed in Gran Canaria, but the Gilbert (3.32–ca. 5.1 my) is not well represented on any Canary island. It is only in the Anaga peninsula especially of Tenerife and in Lanzarote that there are likely lava sequences recording geomagnetic polarities of the immediate Gilbert epoch of 5.1–7.0 my. The virtual geomagnetic poles of each island are close to those from the Middle and Upper Tertiary of the Cape Verde Islands (q. v.). The mean virtual geomagnetic pole shows

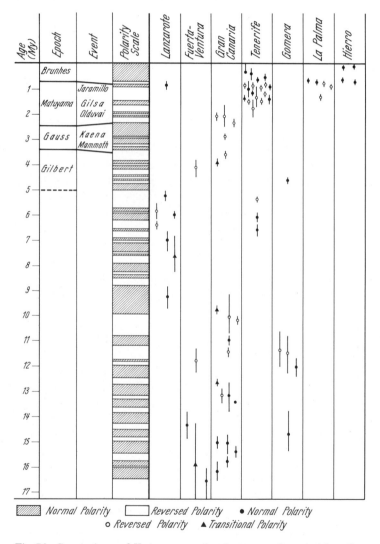

Fig. 74. Comparison of K-Ar ages and palaeomagnetic polarities, Canary Islands. (Modified after Abdel-Monem et al., 1971, 1972).

values in the range 90° to 180° E longitude quadrant, obviousuly different from the geographic poles. These VGPs for the Pleistocene, Pliocene and Miocene are all but identical. The interpretation favoured by WATKINS for this is the systematic long-period distortion of the geomagnetic field rather than simple polar wandering. No conclusions can be reached as to the rate of polar wandering during the Pleistocene-Miocene, but a rate of 0.45°/million years directly away from the geographic poles seems applicable. If there has been any distinct change in this rate during the Mid-Tertiary, it is more likely to have slowed rather than increased. The mechanism responsible for distorting the geomagnetic field away from that of an axial dipole during Pleistocene-Miocene seems not to have been operative for the remaining Tertiary.

## Structure-Tectonics

No detailed structural-tectonic studies or syntheses have been made of the archipelago. This is to be regretted, but one so frequently finds that dominantly igneous terrains are but meagerly described in such terms, petrographic interests seem to overwhelm scholars to the exclusion of all else.

For the archipelago there are two dominant ›schools‹ of thought, one emphasizing the role of tectonics, the other stressing rather the place of erosion as chief agents responsible. Such ›schools‹ crystallize around the modern workers of FUSTER et al. and HAUSEN, the former advocating erosion, the latter, tectonics. In many instances we find opposition between these two regarding the origin of various features. To take but a few examples: (a) the high cliffs of northern Lanzarote are of fault origin, various scarps outline faults as per HAUSEN whereas FUSTER et al. ascribe the cliffing to marine erosion, scarps outline old coastlines. (b) The Tableland Series of Lanzarote-Fuerteventura formed one large unit covering all of what is now the two islands, which later underwent strong tectonism with sinking of blocks, according to HAUSEN, whereas FUSTER et al. point to lack of fracturing and vertical displacements in their Series I, that erosion rather delineates the various ›blocks‹ or stratigraphic units. (c) In Gran Canaria HAUSEN postulated many faults, horst and graben blocks, whereas almost one by one FUSTER et al. seek to show faulting is not present, that in coastal areas once again it is erosion that must be stressed. (d) In Tenerife HAUSEN believed in one continuous structural block uniting the older units of Anaga, Teno and other outcrops of the Old Series which were later broken up, jostled about, some sinking, to result in the present distribution of these ›island cordilleras‹. FUSTER et al. argue that these ›islands‹ were of very limited extent, that powerful marine erosion attacking coastal sectors resulted in the pronounced cliffing we see today.

No less for Gomera, La Palma and Hierro, HAUSEN advances tectonism. The radial drainage network of Gomera is largely controlled by faulting, the El Time escarpment in La Palma is a great fault, the eastern part of the El Golfo scarp in Hierro is of fault origin. For Gomera BRAVO and CENDRERO stress more the role of erosion; in La Palma, GASTESI et al. seemed more in favour of erosion, though MIDDLEMOST favoured tectonism.

We might mention one or two features of special interest.

The most ›famous‹ fault within the archipelago is in Gran Canaria, first postulated by BOURCART (1935) and BOURCART & JÉRÉMINE (1937). This NW-SE trending feature, with displacement of the order of 700–800 m, presumed to have developed in Late Miocene times, divides the island into a western Palaeocanaria and an eastern Neocanaria. The former part underwent strong erosion whilst the eastern, downfaulted block was later covered with younger material. Four chief reasons were offered for postulating this fault: (a) ›Old‹ basalts (i. e. Series II) in contact with post-Roque Nublo basalts. (b) in places, e. g. between Berrazales and Barr. de Hondo, multiple dykes occur along the fault. (c) the abundance of post-Vindobonian materials in the eastern sector of the island. (d) presence of thermal springs at Berrazalas. This fault had been accepted by many later workers, e. g. BRAVO (1954a), MACAU (1957a), KLUG (1963, 1968), ROTHE (1964a, 1966), BOSSHARD & MACFARLANE (1970), as also HAUSEN (1962). On the other hand, the presence of such a fault has been challenged by FUSTER et al. (1968) and SCHMINCKE (1968a). The former remarked that »BOURCART pointed out an abnormal contact between Basaltic Series II and older formations which would mean that the fault is later than Series II. On the other hand (1937, p. 12) he assigns to that series an age immediately before the Vindobonian sediments and states that it is later than the fault«. The disparity in occurrences of post-Vindobonian in the eastern and western sectors can be explained, as per these authors, in that the vents from which the eruptives were emitted in Neocanaria migrated with time, but there is no genetic relationship with a presumed fault, which latter is supposed to be older, and further, post-Vindobonian basalts are much thinner than BOURCART imagined. To SCHMINCKE the Miocene basalts are n o t in direct contact with the fault, but continue to the N across the Barr. de Agaete, and further, these almost horizontal basalts are disconformably overlain by post-Roque Nublo basalts. These and other arguments of SCHMINCKE are convincing indeed, and inspection of the terrain leads one to agree in dismissing the reality of this fault.

The question of the origin(s) of the larger calderas, those of Canadas in Tenerife, Caldera de Taburiente in La Palma and El Golfo in Hierro in particular, have, in the past and present, lent themselves to much discussion. For these three instances, we tabulate (Table 52) the various theories or opinions expressed regarding the origin of such. Whether these calderas are due essentially to exogenic or tectonic processes is admittedly not convincingly proven either way at this time. Undeniably the majority of opinions favour erosional processes, but as we have already remarked above, in no instance have detailed structural studies been carried out, in not a few cases opinions have been stated without any vestiges of proof.

It is agreed that these great caldera depressions with curving rims, the many deep rectilinear valleys and also scarps, the pronounced high, steep cliffs of many coastal regions, abrupt slopes up to higher mountainous terrains, similar abrupt, steep slopes down to flat-floored sections of some valleys – all these do indeed suggest faulting as the likely agent of origin, that fault scarps, horsts and graben, fault-controlled valleys and coastal cliff areas are the explanations of many geomorphological features in the archipelago. Yet the predilection of so many scholars to see rather the significance of exogenic processes has a solid element of truth. Repeatedly workers have made reference to ›violent‹, ›strong‹, ›powerful‹, ›tremendous‹ erosive activity, whether

Table 52    Theories and opinions proposed regarding the origin of three major calderas in the Canary
            Islands

| Las Canadas<br>Tenerife | Caldera de Taburiente<br>La Palma | El Golfo<br>Hierro |
| --- | --- | --- |
| VON BUCH (1825) –<br>"crater of elevation" | VON BUCH – "crater of<br>elevation" | |
| WEBB & BERTHOLET (1839)<br>– origin same as Kilauea. | LYELL – erosion. | |
| SAINT-CLAIRE DEVILLE<br>(1846) – "crater of elevation". | HARTUNG (1862) –<br>erosion. | |
| LYELL (1855) – erosion. | SAPPER (1906) – erosion. | |
| HARTUNG – erosion. | VON KNEBEL (1906) –<br>"crater of elevation". | VON KNEBEL – sinking. |
| VON FRITSCH & REISS<br>(1868) – great explosion<br>plus exogenic processes. | GAGEL (1908) – erosion. | FERNANDEZ (1908) – sinking. |
| GAGEL (1910) – great<br>explosion like Krakatoa. | RECK (1928) – erosion. | |
| FRIEDLÄNDER (1915–1916)<br>– collapse like "Somma",<br>Vesuvius. | VON WOLFF (1931) –<br>erosion. | |
| HAUSEN (1955) – true col-<br>lapse caldera. | BLUMENTHAL – erosion. | BLUMENTHAL – sinking. |
| BLUMENTHAL (1961) –<br>"central type" of collapse<br>caldera. | GASTESI et al. (1966) –<br>erosion? | |
| BRAVO (1962) – exogenic<br>processes. | HAUSEN (1969) – land-<br>slides and erosion. | HAUSEN (1973) – landslides<br>and erosion. |
| MACAU (1963) – sinking. | RIDLEY (1971) – collapse<br>structure. | |
| MINGARRO (1963) –<br>collapse caldera. | HERNANDEZ-PACHECO<br>(1971) – erosion. | |
| BORLEY (1966) – collapse | MIDDLEMOST (1972) –<br>collapse structure. | |
| FUSTER et al. (1968) –<br>favour collapse? | | |
| RIDLEY (1971) – collapse | | |

terrestrial or marine. If one is fortunate enough – or unfortunate enough, depending upon the play of ›mind over matter‹ – to have been in the Canary Islands, tramping along impressive cliffed coastal regions or then trekking up tortuous steep valleys in the high interiors when stormy seas pound the coasts, when lashing winds and rains descend upon the islands, then even the novice must be impressed, even appalled, at the astonishing work of erosion as an agent in carving out the landscape. On such occasions streams come literally roaring down very steep slopes, materials ranging in size from clay particles to boulders can be observed actively being transported down slope, the abrasive action of wild waves armed with pebbles, cobbles, etc. being hurled relentlessly against the coasts, such phenomena must surely impress layman and geologist alike. Here in the Canary Islands we should consider the role of erosion but on a somewhat unusual scale of severity, along with the concomitant promotion of landslides, rockfalls, creep, etc. Undoubtedly many coastal cliffed sectors have been caused primarily by marine erosion, many scarp features are fault-line scarps rather than fault scarps, so-called ›horsts‹ are the result of intensive differential weathering on rocks of differing

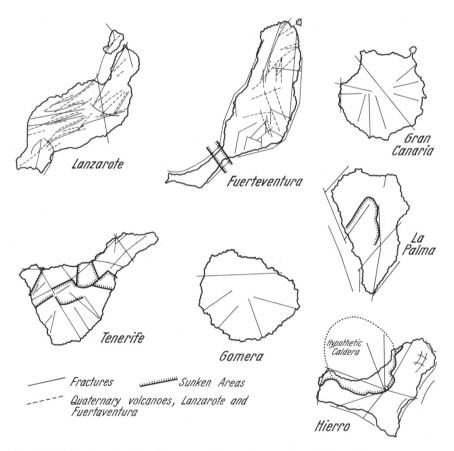

Fig. 75. Major structural trends proposed by various authors, Canary Islands.

physico-chemical constitution, ›grabens‹ result from intensive erosion of valley slopes and rapid infilling of the valley floors in many instances. Here in this archipelago we believe that exogenic agencies have had and still have a more profound effect than tectonic ones, that although faulting is present, this is on a much reduced, more localized scale, plays a minor role.

Fig. 75 shows the major structural trends proposed by various authors for individual islands.

Tectonic considerations are concerned with two topics: (a) tectonic alignments, and (b) relation of the archipelago to the African mainland and the nature of the insular crusts.

In the past, the delineation of tectonic trends represent purely subjective approaches based upon the scantiest of evidence. As the islands are aligned E-W, and as some islands show meridional relations to each other, it was perhaps natural to surmise fractures along these directions, it being assumed that such basal fractures offered the means for magmatic emanations to reach the surface, build up the respective islands.

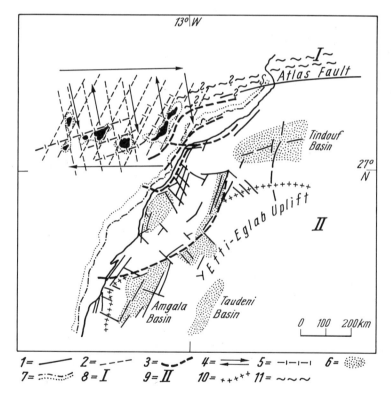

Fig. 76. Tectonic setting of Canaries Archipelago and relation to African mainland. 1: Faults. 2: Fractures. 3: Arcs of subsidence. 4: Major tectonic tensions. 5: Bouguer anomaly axes outlining fractures. 6: Tectonic basins. 7: 100 m and 600 m isobaths. 8: Folded Atlas domain. 9: Sahara shield. 10: Boundary between Precambrian and younger. 11: Atlas foldings. (Based on BRAVO 1954a, ALIA, 1960, BLUMENTHAL, 1961, SOUGY, 1962, DASH & BOSSHARD, 1968).

With perhaps a degree of more refinement, fractures were also assumed to take on diagonal directions, paying attention to the bathymetry, structural and topographic ›grain‹ of the islands. Earlier schemes, e. g. that of BRAVO (1954), were proposed before geophysical studies of the general area had been done, but from seismic and gravity studies, such as those of DASH & BOSSHARD (1968, 1969), MACFARLANE & RIDLEY (1968, 1969), we note similar WSW-ENE trends passing through the islands but S of and excluding La Palma. Others, e. g. BLUMENTHAL (1961) wished to link-up fold trends of the Atlas and the prominent South Atlas Fault with these Canarian alignments as they occur in the eastern islands. As we have seen, as far as the islands themselves are concerned, scholars have leaned rather towards the role of exogenic processes than tectonic processes as being responsible for the evolution thereof, though the concept of important deep fissures being responsible for island trends and also eruptive centres within the islands, especially those of Quaternary times, has usually been implied if not stated.

Whether we call these features fractures, faults, tectonic trends, lineaments, alignments, we must stress the personal, subjective interpretations in question, that factual evidence is all but non-existent, that such features should rather be described as vincula, as per the author (MITCHELL-THOMÉ, 1961).

E-W stretching of the Atlantic floor could be a factor responsible for dislocations more or less normal to this direction, whilst rotational or differential lateral displacements of plates could account for more latitudinally orientated features. But such is supposition only, and as has been truthfully and sadly remarked: »Of the drawing of alignments, there is no end«. Hence, at this time, we must admit that all such lengthy linear features and their trends stem from speculation rather than evidence. It is perhaps apposite to quote some unknown scholar: »This is, it seems to me, to be the thing I see – if I see what I think I see«.

The possible relation of the archipelago to mainlands – chiefly Africa – is a very old idea, and indeed may be said to date back to the Dialogues of PLATO and the ›Lost Atlantis Continent‹ legend. Possibly the first to postulate a linkage with Africa specifically was made in 1630 by ALONSO DE ESPINOSA in his ›Historia de la aparicion y de los milagros de la imagen de Nuestra Senora de Candelaria‹. As of all the archipelagoes studied here, the Canary Islands lie closest to a mainland – a mere 100 km separates Fuerteventura from the coast of Spanish Sahara – it is but natural that speculation should early have arisen amongst scholars regarding this topic.

Ideas on this matter group themselves into three categories: (a) no relationship with Africa, (b) connected to Africa, (c) each island an independent structure.

VON BUCH, LYELL, VON FRITSCH of earlier workers adopted the first view, the islands being volcanic cones or raised craters built up from the ocean floor by having some kind of linkage via fissuration used as means of egress for magmas. On the other hand, of older scholars, CUVIER, WEBB & BERTHOLET, GENTIL, SUESS, GAGEL did see a continental linkage, though the degree and type of connexion varied. And in this context, we would note that almost unanimously older naturalists and more recent biologists and palaeontologists, e. g. BUFFON, VON HUMBOLDT, GERMAIN, LUNDBLAD, JEANNEL, EVERS, have looked with favour upon a mainland connexion, either directly united, by land-bridges or by banks and shallow waterways. To some, e. g. HAUSEN, as the archipelago lies within the 4,000 m isobath, this makes it continental, though not real shelf islands as they lie beyond the continental slope, but situated on a common submarine platform. Thus the actual border of the African sialic block lies W of La Palma, the islands lying at the transition from stable continental block to unstable Atlantic basin. BRAVO also envisaged a common basal complex substratum linking the archipelago with Africa. MINGARRO (1963) stressed the structural relations between the archipelago and Africa, noting the fracture trends of both regions which not only caused eventual separation but also broke up the individual islands into their present distributions. He also saw possible relations with Spain, claiming that the latitudinally-oriented fractures converge eastwards towards the Guadalquiver fault of southern Spain, whilst ROTHE (1966) suggested possible landbridge linkage with Spain, but entered into no details. ROTHE & SCHMINCKE (1968) have no hestiation about attaching Lanzarote and Fuerteventura to Africa, pointing out that the quartz-sandstone xenoliths in younger basalts originate from pre-volcanic sandstones which are not of local origin but had a source in neighbouring Africa. The islands were not united in a block during the Tertiary as the crustal nature below the islands varies. Tensional fractures parallel to the African coast were opened during the dyke-formation episodes thereby separating the eastern islands from Africa. Lanzarote-Fuerteventure-Gran Canaria-Gomera, with their submarine platforms, represent an older nucleus than western Tenerife-La Palma-Hierro. (Though La Palma is linked to Gomera and Fuerteventura in the presence of a basal complex, the age of this in La Palma is uncertain at this time.) To these authors, Gran Canaria is neither part of a basaltic plateau linking together the islands, an uplifted block of continental crust nor yet an uplifted block of oceanic crust – though earlier ROTHE (1964, 1966) had postulated the last-mentioned – but rather a separate volcanic centre at least since post-Miocene times.

RONA & NALWALK (1970) appealed to ›down-to-basement‹ fractures as causing the separation of the archipelago from Africa and forming individual islands and islandgroups, N-S ›African‹ fractures and the extension westward of the S Atlas fault and splinters. This breaking up is supposed to have happened in early Cretaceous times, with further faulting-vulcanism in the Eocene related to Alpine tectonic activity.

HERNANDEZ-PACHECO & IBARROLA (1973b) comment that the more recent tendency has been to establish African relations on the basis of geophysical studies whereas they believe more stress should be placed on fundamental geochemical trends shown by the volcanics of the islands. Relying on the latter then, Lanzarote-Fuerteventura-Gomera show marked similarity, as also Gran Canaria-Tenerife-La Palma. Hierro shows variation trends more akin to the former group, but the alkalinity is higher, and thus perhaps represent a third group. The chemistry and petrology of the archipelago is not related in any way to distance from the African mainland, nor is the spatial distribution of the islands in direct relation to type of crust. The three typical oceanic islands of Gran Canaria-Tenerife-La Palma lie on a NW-SE tectonic trend (the ›Atlantic‹ trend) and in Tenerife the ›African‹ NE-SW trend is noticeable. The island thus lies on the crossing of two major tectonic alignments, and no less has this island a distinctive chemical character, and thus, as per these writers, Tenerife »holds the key to our understanding of the origin and evolution of the Canarian Archipelago«.

FUSTER et al. (1968) adopted a very sceptical view regarding relations with Africa, especially with reference to Lanzarote, with Africa on the one hand and the western islands on the other. They do, however, recognize characteristic ›African‹ trends (N70-75E) in the alignment of Quaternary vulcanism in the eastern islands. All hypotheses linking the archipelago with Africa are premature at this time, so they claim.

ABDEL-MONEM et al., on the basis of isotopic age studies, considered the islands to be separate volcanic structures, evolving separately from each other and presumably independent of African connexions. The crust underlying the archipelago shows a transition from continental-type for the eastern islands to oceanic-type for the western ones (ROTHE & SCHMINCKE, 1968; MACFARLANE & RIDLEY, 1968; DASH & BOSSHARD, 1968; BOSSHARD & MACFARLANE, 1970). Marked transition is evident in Gran Canaria, and so the eastern islands are certainly to be considered as part of Africa.

Related to more recent ocean-floor spreading ideas, it has been noted (WATKINS et al., 1966; WATKINS, 1973) from palaeomagnetic studies that there is a westward decrease in the age of the islands. The isotopic results of ABDEL-MONEM et al. give values of 20–37 my for the oldest volcanics of Lanzarote-Fuerteventura, 15 my in Gomera, 3 my for Hierro. This suggests ocean-floor spreading towards the E, newer vulcanism welling-up from depth and displacing eastwards already – formed islands-structures, evolved independently one of the other over at least the last 20 my. However, we should note that the peralkaline acid tendencies evident in Gran Canaria, far from the Mid-Atlantic Ridge, which are not associated to transitional basalts does not support the view put forth by McBIRNEY & GASS (1967) and BASS (1972) that the NIGGLI quartz number (QZ) is greatest on islands lying on or near the Mid-Atlantic Ridge, that such silicics occur preferentially in association with transitional mildly alkali-basalts in volcanic islands located near active crests of spreading oceanic ridges. FUSTER & CENDRERO (1973b) have postulated a ›ridge‹ where the Canary Islands now stand, not necessarily the same one as developed into the Mid-Atlantic Ridge, which could have acted as a ›trigger‹ for vulcanism in the general area.

Ocean-floor spreading ideas here postulate eastward movement: Wegenerian ›drift‹ conceives westward motion of the Americas from Europe-Africa, in which these archipelagoes represent scraped-off, detached pieces of Africa, initially dragged westward then left behind as African ›outposts‹ in the Atlantic. In both hypotheses there is the common presumption of E-W tensional forces operative.

So, as with tectonic alignments, so also with Canary-mainland relations, at this stage all is most vague, speculations pile up but factual evidences remain scarce in the extreme, and we must confess that both topics escape our ken.

## Economic Geology

As in all these archipelagoes, the metallics are of no significance. Basic and ultrabasic rocks of some islands have been unsuccessfully investigated for copper content. In Hierro, HAUSEN (1973) has spoken of Recent black sands which form a natural ore dressing over some 10 km² which »could lead to a certain commercial content of iron as they are rich in magnetite or Ti-magnetite«.

Various rocks are quarried for building purposes. Clays are used in pottery and tile manufacture, pozzulana, foraminiferal sands and clays in cement manufacture, limestones for production of lime. Lapilli are spread over fields, particularly in the drier islands of Lanzarote and Fuerteventura, to lower evaporation and promote water condensation. In these two islands again especially, salt is evaporated from sea waters. With the tremendous increase in tourism in the post-war years, building of villas, hotels, airports, roads, harbour extensions, etc. all geological material which enters into the building trades have shown a phenomenal boom, but in no sense are there any largescale industries utilizing earth materials.

The question of using geothermal energy, with special reference to Lanzarote, is under study at present (CALAMAI & CERON, 1970; Caja Insular de Ahorros, 1971; ARANA et al., 1973d, 1973e). Preliminary investigations began in 1969 and it is intended to engage in geologic, thermal geophysic and geochemical studies as well as carrying out borehole surveying. The region of most intense study is Montanas de Fuego-Timanfaya, N of Yaiza in western Lanzarote in an area of Basaltic Series IV lava flows of both aa and pahoehoe type. Here, at a few metres depth, temperatures of between 16° and 350° C are encountered over an area of some 200 km², with an anomaly gradient of 0.2° C/m, which corresponds to a thermal flux of 10 HFU. There are hopes of utilizing this geothermal energy after the manner of that at Lardello, Italy, where 10 kg of steam produce 1 kw. It is supposed that the heat here in Lanzarote is not transmitted by direct conduction from a superficial thermal focus, nor has the heat an exogenic origin – chemical reaction. It rather seems as if fluids are aerated, which activates transport of heat, the fluids which transport the heat being of magmatic type, which presumes that the superficial thermal anomalies are related to the emission of vapours across volcano-tectonic fractures. The great depth of these fluids likely forms a convection system below impermeable strata, the reservoir being supplied by sea water, the heat focus being a magmatic chamber near at hand (Fig. 77).

In Gran Canaria (Fuente La Ideal, Firgas, San Roque, Valsequillo, Manantial El Pastor, Moya, Fuente Agria, Teror, Los Berrazales, Sta. Catalina) are thermal springs varying in temperatures from 21° to 26° and yielding 0.5 to 2.0 decimetres/sec. In Tenerife are the thermal springs of El Pinalito and Agua Agria with temperatures of 20.8° C.

Climatically this more southern archipelago partakes more after the Cape Verde Islands in water shortages and problems, especially in the eastern islands. Though the climate is less arid than in the Cape Verde archipelago (the Canaries have no perennial streams whilst in Cape Verde are only two very minor ones), in the Canaries the great influx of tourists aggravates conditions to almost the same degree.

Gran Canaria uses some 198 million m³ water annually. With an average annual rainfall of 400 mm (ranging from 130 mm in low leeward sites to 800 mm in exposed areas above 1,500 m) and an area of 1,532 km² yields an average volume annually of ca. 612 million m³. The combined coefficients of runoff and evapotranspiration are of the order of 0.60, which means that only ca. 245 million m³ water annually infiltrates into the ground. All of this does not recharge the groundwater, and the annual groundwater recharge would appear to be little different from the annual consumption. When to this alarming condition it is added that water tables are being lowered in places as much

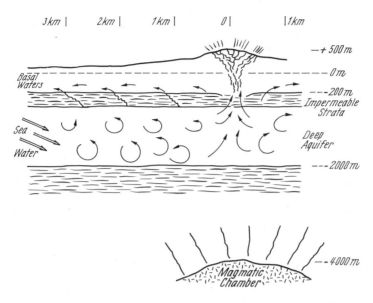

Fig. 77. Theoretical geothermal system under Montañas del Fuego, Lanzarote. (ARANA & FUSTER, 1973).

as 10 m per year, that pumping levels on the island are in places as low as 325 m, the critical nature of the situation becomes apparent.

DINGMAN & NUNES (1969) calculated that 34% of the annual precipitation was used in Gran Canaria, 29% in Tenerife, 18% in La Palma, 3.7% in Fuerteventura and 0.22% in Lanzarote. Tourists naturally demand all modern sanitary conveniences, which make extra heavy demands apart from irrigation and domestic water consumption. During the height of the tourist season in Gran Canaria perhaps some quarter of a million extra heavy consumers require water. (Native country people here can do very well with 50 litres/day/capita, whereas tourists need ca. 450 litres/day/capita for multifarious purposes!) An alarming and little short of criminal situation exists in Gran Canaria, for example, where daily golf courses are liberally watered with hundreds of thousands of litres and yet crops are allowed to wither away, banana exports having declined 40% in 1974 in this island (vd. »Notstand auf Gran Canaria«, STERN, Nr. 9, 44–50, 1975).

It can probably be accepted that within the archipelago, water for agricultural purposes represents ca. 85–92% of the total annual consumption. Agriculture, along with tourism, form the economic mainstay of the islands. The above authors, in this context, have stated: »The seriousness of the situation is extreme. If new sources of water cannot be found, the economy faces a complete collapse . . . . . . . . . . Water in the upper part of the cost range (5–17 cents American per m³ for irrigation water) is completely uneconomical for irrigation. As a result the banana plantations that were formerly irrigated every 20 days are now irrigated every 60 days. Irrigation at 60-dy intervals is sufficient to keep plants alive but is not adequate to produce crops«.

In line with this grave warning, UNESCO is in the last stages of completion of a water resources study of the archipelago. Admittedly then that common asset, water, presents most difficult economic problems, and as in the Cape Verde Islands, though for different reasons, annually the problems are intensified.

(In March, 1974 an International Symposium on Hydrology of Volcanic Rocks took place in Lanzarote, but at the time of going to press, papers presented at the Congress have not been published.)

## Geologic Evolution

To some, the origins of certain islands, e. g. Fuerteventura, go back to the Upper Palaeozoic, but such is a very minority view. To the great majority of scholars who have worked in these islands, a pre-Miocene date of origin was postulated but no thought of a Palaeozoic origin, and now that we have isotopic datings to aid us, there seems no doubt that the islands (except Hierro) date back to Early Tertiary or then Upper Mesozoic in some instances.

The eastern islands are believed to show continental affinities, both in the nature of crustal type and in the source of their Mesozoic sedimentaries. The western islands show a crust of oceanic type, pre-Quaternary sedimentaries are lacking or then doubtful, vulcanism completely dominates the scene, here are oceanic volcanic islands. The central islands then are transitional and in this context it is worth noting that diastrophism seems to have played a greater role here than elsewhere, a critical zone where stresses have tectonic significance. To a degree, the islands represent independent volcanic edifices, yet as they all lie within the 3,000 m isobath, as all magmatism is associated with basal fracturings, there is some common linkage between them all.

The oldest stratigraphically dated rocks occur in Fuerteventura, Cretaceous no doubt being represented here but whether Jurassic occurs is an open matter at this time. On this island also we have the oldest isotopic datings so far, ca. 35 my for the basement complex, or Oligocene. The Mesozoics have been folded and faulted, HAUSEN claiming that such indicated Hercynian distrubances. The deformation undergone by these strata could either have been related to emplacement of the basal complex or then more distant echoes of Alpine orogeny in the Moroccan Atlas, those favouring continental linkage naturally preferring to subscribe to the latter. Separation from Africa is presumed to have occurred early in the Tertiary, and hence one envisages great disturbanes here in the eastern Canaries, with foldings, faultings, major fracturings, subsidences, African ›drifting‹ northwards and these eastern islands moving westwards. (Such a concept of course of Wegenerian westward ›drift‹ is opposed to eastward movement through ocean-floor spreading away from the Central Atlantic Rift.)

The pre-Miocene history of most islands cannot as yet be too clearly deciphered, basement complexes are not evident in all islands, pre-Quaternary stratigraphy has not been carefully worked on, isotopic datings are too few, sedimentary-volcanic contacts are often very unclear, structural studies sadly lacking, sedimentology investigations all but non-existent, little palaeontological work has been done, geophysical investigations sparse. Unravelling the pre-Miocene evolution of the archipelago allows ample room for speculation but one is sorely cramped when it comes to factual data.

With the exception of Hierro, a product of Pliocene times, all islands appear to date from Early Tertiary, perhaps back to Middle Mesozoic for Fuerteventura and Lanzarote (?). Over a period of some 20 my events can be traced, vulcanism, submarine, subaerial effusions, explosive episodes, marine and terrestrial sedimentation, extensive periods of denudation, positive and negative movements of the islands of volcano-tectonic and isostatic origins, eustatic fluctuations. From E to W the evidence indicates older to younger islands – Mesozoic sediments in Fuerteventura whilst Hierro is only some 3 my in age. (The so-called Miocene beds in La Palma are doubtful at this time, and further we lack isotopic datings of the basement in the Caldera de Taburiente, but a minium age of 15 my years is proposed for that of Gomera.) This age trend E and W of the islands conforms to the concept here of ocean-floor spreading, younger eruptivity upwelling successivly and partially overlapping, pushing aside older eruptive episodes.

Interspersed with the constructive phases there have been repeated periods of denudation, some of relatively long duration, stripping away volcanics and sedimentaries and upon these planed-off areas fresh vulcanism has formed, thus creating many unconformable relationships within the sequences. The petrologic succession shows, according to different islands, detrital sedimention, from an African source (?), marine sedimentation with limestones chiefly, terrestrial deposition of fluvial and aeolian origin, submarine and subaerial vulcanism of lavas and pyroclastics, plutonic intrusions as dykes, sills, irregular bodies, quiet effusions and explosive outbursts causing interlayering, vulcanism from central vents, from fissures, adventitious cones. Interrupting these volcanic-sedimentary developments have been movements mentioned above, plus denudation, downward gravitational movements. Well into Recent times we note positive and negative movements of the islands, vulcanism extends into historic times, indeed as recently as 1971 in La Palma.

Here indeed then over a period of perhaps some 40 my these islands have gone through a ›lively‹ history, instability characterizes their geological development, they bear testimony to a vibrant, vigorous earth, and indeed in the proper perspective of geological time, we are impressed how remarkably active this part of our globe has been. As ARISTOTLE discerningly commented long ago: »All change their condition in the course of time«.

CHAPTER 8


# Geology of the Cape Verde Archipelago

## General

During the voyage of the »Beagle«, Darwin (1844) called at S. Tiago and his notes represent the first geological gleanings of the archipelago. Scattered writings followed – mostly referring to the vulcanism of Fogo or then palaeontological descriptions of fossils collected by others – and it was not until 1882 that Doelter's important contribution appeared. Friedländer (1912, 1913) was the next, treating mostly of matters vulcanological. With the appearance of Bebiano's monograph in 1932 there was now available a general account of the geology of the archipelago. Bebiano spent some five years engaging in reconnaissance surveys of all the islands except Fogo, and his report and maps have formed the basis of all later publications. Important though this contribution is, yet we must note the heavy emphasis placed upon igneous petrology, there is little reference made to sedimentaries, no stratigraphical information, merely names of a few fossils determined, in other words, an unbalanced contribution. Beginning in the 1940's and with increasing tempo, there have appeared more geological publications. However, most of these are of a piece-meal nature, particular topics pertaining to a particular island, and once again, most emphasis on igneous petrology. Only one island (Maio) has received a modern general treatment.

Although the Azores and Madeira have adequate modern geological maps, such cannot be said for the Cape Verde Islands, most available maps being slight amendments of originals of Bebiano or then maps referring only to smaller sections of certain islands.

It follows then that the literature and geological mapping of the archipelago is much less impressive than those relating to the Azores and Madeira. We would further remark that it is chiefly the Portuguese geologists who have interested themselves in these islands, a very different case from the Canaries, which have attracted an international group of workers.

## Geomorphology

The striking contrasts in topography and relief are less a reflexion of rock constitution and climatic conditions than the results of age. The truisms long ago formulated by a HUTTON and a LYELL are clearly evidenced in these islands: with the Earth, as with all living things, the ravages of Time cannot be concealed.

It has been remarked that on a topographic-relief basis, the archipelago can be divided intow two major groups: high islands with strong relief and low islands with mild relief, which reflect relative youth and old age respectively.

On first appraisal, one might be inclined to assign to marine and aeolian action the dominant roles in moulding the landscapes, but this is deceptive. The general barrenness, lack of surface waters, scant rainfall initially may incline one to think that running water has had little chance to show itself here, but such is not so. Deep, narrow gorges, waterfalls, steep stream longitudinal profiles, extensive ›aprons‹ or pediments, wide, smooth extents of gently-sloping plains all bear witness to the potency of streams

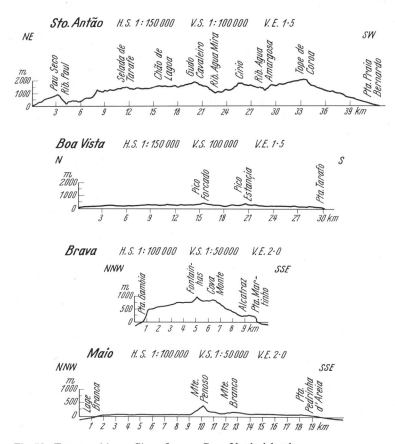

Fig. 78. Topographic profiles of some Cape Verde islands.

as major agents in the sculpture of the landscape. When it is further realized that many valleys have been carved out of tough, hard igneous rocks, that, geologically speaking, most of the erosion has occurred in a relatively short period, that all stream basins and streams are small, recognizing the infrequency of the rains, their erratic quantitative and temporal character, the very high evaporation, then by taking these facts into consideration, it is truly amazing how significant are streams as erosional-depositional agencies.

Valley characteristics in the younger islands (Sto. Antao, S. Tiago, Brava, e. g.) have youthful features; those valleys in the older islands (Sal, Boa Vista, Maio, e. g.) are

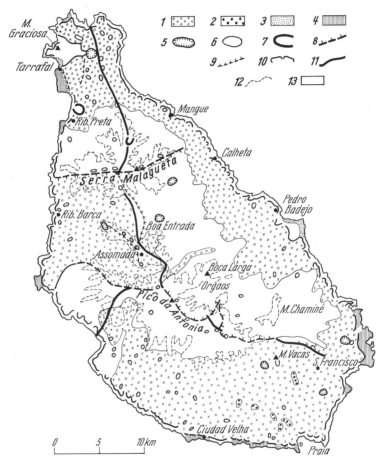

Fig. 79. Geomorphologic map of Ilha de S. Tiago. 1: "Achadas" – structural levels formed on lava beds having features of marine terraces. 2: Tabular topography simulating "achadas". 3: Beaches of sand. 4: Littoral deposits. 5: Cupulas and pinnacles. 6: Semi-destroyed cones. 7: Eroded craters. 8: Pronounced scarps. 9: Pronounced slopes. 10: Cliffs and ridge slopes. 11: Drainage divides. 12: 500 m contour. 13: Mountains and strong relief. (Modified after AMARAL, 1964).

synonymous with maturity-old age. Extremes in character and age are well represented, for example, by the Ribeira do Monte Trigo, in western Sto. Antao, descending 1,600 m in a distance of 4.4 km, much of it in a narrow, steep-walled gorge, flowing straight down to the sea, and the Ribeira Rabil in Boa Vista, falling 350 m in 24 km, a broad, sediment-choked, braided stream incised but a few metres below the general surrounding terrain, indecisively meandering towards the sea.

The role of running water as a transporting agent meets with difficulties in these islands. In the younger valleys, the steep lateral and longitudinal slopes allow loosened rock material to move downwards under gravity into the valley bottoms, there to present a most chaotic appearance of rock débris of all sizes. In the older valleys we find instead accumulations of material of gravel size and smaller which tend to choke the valley. The small size of the basins and streams, combined with the infrequent rains and small annual amounts means that when the valleys do carry running water, the volume and velocity of said streams, along with the gentle longitudinal profiles in the old valleys, such find difficulty of moving the débris littering the valleys. Such conditions are duplicated neither in small islands in temperate or arctic climes nor in continental deserts: they are peculiar to small islands experiencing arid conditions. And yet, in the long run, these infrequent streams eventually do manage to break-down the rock débris, difficult though it may be, the material is slowly transported downwards and out to sea, as the older valleys testify. This is all the more wondrous in that, as per the inhabitants, flash-floods such as happen in desert wadis, scarce ever occur in the islands.

Aridity is concomitant with aeolian activity, and thus the effects of wind as a geomorphologic agent are to be expected in the archipelago. As a means of erosion, deflation is more obvious than abrasion with the result that excavated hollows are frequent, whereas abrasion features such as pedestal and mushroom rocks are rare. It has been commented that throughout the year winds are generally quite strong, mostly from the NE, although SW winds very often have greater velocities. The scooping-out of depressions in loosely consolidated material is hence a relatively easy matter especially in the relatively thin alluvial coverings in valleys and plains. Desert pavements are to be found along windward coastal plains, but such features as desert varnish and dreikanters are not conspicuous, nor, as indicated above, unusually carved erosional remnants.

Alluvial fans and pediments constitute the intervening ground between steeper slopes and valleys or then plains. Whilst recognizing that once again such features are largely the result of fluvial processes, the role of aeolian agencies in this arid environment no less ply their part in the creation of such depositional and erosional features.

Dunes and sand sheets are common features, in some islands, e. g. Boa Vista, where dunes alone occupy some 15% of the island area. Because of the constancy and strength of the winds affecting the archipelago, fine particles are easily moved in exposed locations, the dunes tending to ›march‹ towards the SW. In Boa Vista, drifting sand sheets and dunes pose problems for roads, the airfield, small gardens around houses. Nowhere are dunes towering, majestic features and nowhere do they create typical desert landscape, complete with camels, such as is found in Lanzarote. The Cape Verde dunes tend to be amorphous in shape, thicker sand accumulations trailing off into

Table 53    Well-established old beaches in some Cape Verde Islands (after LECOINTRE, 1963; SERRALHEIRO, 1967, 1968)

| Islands | Levels (m) | Stratigraphic classification | Moroccan equivalents |
|---|---|---|---|
| S. Vicente Maio S. Tiago | 2– 6 | Flandrian | Mellahian |
| Maio S. Tiago | 8–12 | Neo-Tyrrhenian | Ouljian |
| Maio S. Tiago | 15–20 | Eu-Tyrrhenian | Harurian |
| Maio S. Tiago | 30–40 | Palaeo-Tyrrhenian | Anfatian |
| Maio S. Tiago | 50–60 | Sicilian II | Maarifian |
| Maio | 80–100 | Sicilian I | Messodian |

extensive sand plains. The potentialities of these dunes are sources of underground water in these parched islands is worthy of note.

The immensely powerful destructive effect of the waves is everywhere apparent along the coasts. In general, relatively deep water extends in-shore, seas are nearly always agitated by persistant winds, with the result that there is very little marine progradation but instead, the ceaseless eating-away of the islands characterizes the role of the seas. Strong cliffing typifies many areas of the more rugged islands, e. g. the N and NE coasts of Sto. Antao where fallen rock débris creates dangerous off-shore rocky areas. During a severe storm, by sheer luck the writer witnessed the detaching of a mass of cliff, estimated to be of the order of 80,000 m³, the loosened material hurtling down to the wild seas below, proof of the enormous destructive activity of the waves.

Islands have gained upon the seas by means of vertical movement. This is evidenced by raised marine abrasion platforms (e. g. at Ponta do Sol, Sto. Antao) but more spectacularly by marine terraces. Those occurring in S. Tiago, Sal and Maio have been given most attention. LECOINTRE (1963) and SERRALHEIRO (1968, 1970) have distinguished six levels in Maio, ranging from 2 to 100 m in altitude above present SL, five levels in S. Tiago, ranging from 2 to 60 m and three levels in Sal, ranging from 2 to 55 m. In the case of Maio, for example, land above 100 m represents only some 18% of its area, and thus some 82% of the island area has been acquired through vertical movements, all seemingly dating from the Quaternary, and in Sal some 55% land has been gained in a similar fashion. River terraces, well displayed in northern Sto. Antao, as also abandoned sea caves, and the marine terraces are all presumably due to eustatism essentially rather than isostatic adjustments, as first postulated by BEBIANO, i. e. vertical movements of the seas rather than the lands. But eustatism alone can scarce account

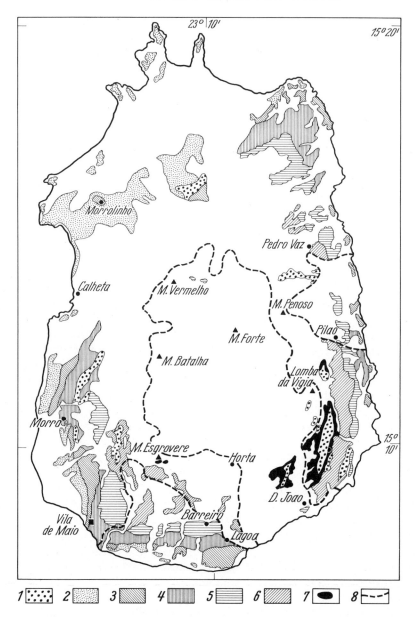

Fig. 80. Map showing extent of old marine terraces, Maio. 1: Fossil dunes. 2: 2–6 m terrace. 3: 8–12 m terrace. 4: 15–20 m terrace. 5: 30–40 m terrace. 6: 50–60 m terrace. 7: 80–100 m terrace. 8: Approximate extent of exposed igneous rocks. (Modified after SERRALHEIRO, 1967).

for marine terraces 100 m above present SL, and thus isostatism and epeirogenic movements must also be considered.

The islands of the archipelago are of volcanic origin, vulcanism is active today, and hence volcanic landforms are abundant. The most outstanding feature of course is the immense active cone of Pico in Fogo, and because vulcanism is still witnessed here, certain volcanic forms are much better preserved. Innumerable cinder cones dot the steep island slopes, almost all remarkably fresh in appearance – DA COSTA (1956–58) mentioned 86 adventitious cones scattered throughout the island. (It is of interest to note that during the last eruption in 1951, ashes were spread on all the outer slopes of the volcano, as much as 20 cm thick, but these were rapidly reworked by the soil and vegetation and nine years were later indistinguishable.)

The caldera of Pico measures some 9 km N-S and 7.5 km E-W. The caldera floor lies at an elevation of some 1,600 m, above which rises the crescent-shaped wall to a hight of 2,700 m. This wall (Bordeira) is breached on the eastern side where rises the internal cone of Pico to a hight of 2,829 m. The steep eastern slopes from Pico down to SL are mantled with an amazingly chaotic mass of blocky lavas and scoria devoid of all living forms. Elsewhere in the archipelago, e. g. at Cova, NE Sto. Antao, there occur small, beautifully preserved craters which long have been quiescent so that here the crater floors are carpeted with lush grasses and form excellent grazing areas for cattle. Here and there volcanic necks thrust upward, e. g. S. Joao and Orgaos in S. Tiago, dykes protrude prominently on occasion, e. g. in western S. Nicolau, impressive sharp, narrow mountain walls are present, e. g. Pico da Antonia, S. Tiago, calderas breached by the sea, e. g. the port of Mindelo, S. Vicente, or then by large valleys, e. g. Cha de Morte and the Ribeiras das Patas, Sto. Antao, mesa, lava-capped summits, e. g. Sal, spines (S. Tiago), impressive adventitious cones (Brava) – all such volcanic forms are to be met with in the archipelago. However nowhere, with the exception of Pico and its caldera, are the forms as impressive as in other Middle or South Atlantic Islands, and nowhere are there beautiful crater lakes such as occur, for example, in the Azores.

## Igneous Rocks

BEBIANO (1932) believed that some 83% of the total area of the archipelago comprised basaltic-type volcanics and pyroclastics, some 9% phonolites and kindred rocks. Though not accepting the figures literally, they do give a rough idea as to rock constitution of the islands. All later work has shown that the plutonics and volcanics tend towards under-saturated types, over-saturated types are all but absent, and saturated varieties are distinctly minor in occurrence. Present knowledge leads us to believe that basaltic-type volcanics and pyroclastics are present in all islands, phonolitic types in all except Ilheus Secos, and that diorites, limburgites, nephelinites and syenites are well represented.

DOELTER (1882), FRIEDLÄNDER (1912, 1913), BERGT (1913), PART (1930, 1946, 1950), BEBIANO (1932), JESUS (1932), ERMENT (1936), NEIVA (1940), ASSUNCAO (1954, 1955, 1968), ASSUNCAO et al. (1965, 1967, 1968), BURRI (1960) MACHADO et al. (1965, 1967, 1968), BARROS (1968), MITCHELL-THOMÉ (1972) have all published information regarding the

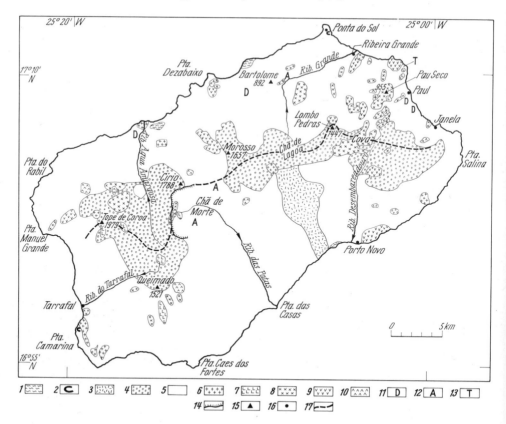

Fig. 81. Geological map of Sto. Antao. 1: Dunes. 2: Tertiary limestones. 3: Recent lavas. 4: Scoria, lapilli, tuffs. 5: Basalts, basaltic lavas alternating with lapilli, tuffs. 6: Limburgites. 7: Nephelinites, leucitites. 8: Phonolites, phonolitic lavas. 9: Basalts with feldspathoids. 10: Andesites with feldspathoids. 11: Dolerites. 12: Andesites. 13: Trachytes. 14: Bordeira – caldera rim. 15: Peaks. 16: Villages. 17: Topographic crest. (Modified after BEBIANO, 1932).

igneous rocks of the archipelago. Whilst field studies of these rocks is still in a somewhat preliminary stage, laboratory investigations on samples collected are sufficient to allow us to arrive at general assessments. The tables given here illustrate how uneven is our knowledge petrographically of the igneous rocks, and only for S. Vicente, Fogo, Ilheu Grande (Ilheus Secos) have we, at this time, a reasonably adequate compilation. One must be careful, therefore, in drawing too many conclusions for the archipelago as a whole, and we are scarce in a position as yet to say how typical these three islands are for the region as a whole.

It can be noted from the chemical analyses (135 in number) that only five have a silica content higher than 55%, a monzonite-syenite from Boa Vista having the highest value of 59.16%; that twenty seven have silica contents lower than 40%, a lherzite from Ilheu Grande having the lowest recorded value of 30.15% $SiO_2$.

As S. Vicente, Fogo and Ilheu Grande have been given more petrographic attention, we shall say some words on these islands.

The publication on S. Vicente by ASSUNCAO & CANILHO (1965) (vd. Tables 54–57, Nos. 5–17) is based upon a study of 112 samples. The rocks were divided into: (1) lavas with feldspars and feldspathoids – phonolites (and analcitites), basanites, basanitoids (and limburgites), (2) lavas without feldspars – nephelinites, etindites, ankaratrites, sometimes with melilite. Of the first group, phonolites are the most typical rocks, the basaltic facies types being not quite so abundant. The latter group includes equivalents of the ijolitic family, with clinopyroxenes and nephelines characteristic, and classed, as per LACROIX, as being nephelinites (sensu stricto), etindites and ankaratrites. Plutonics had been known since the days of JESUS (1932) and BEBIANO (1932), who referred in general terms to syenites and diorites, but the studies of ASSUNCAO & CANILHO and SERRALHEIRO (1966) showed a greater variety than had hitherto been suspected. The former authors did not consider the plutonics as belonging to a sialic crystalline

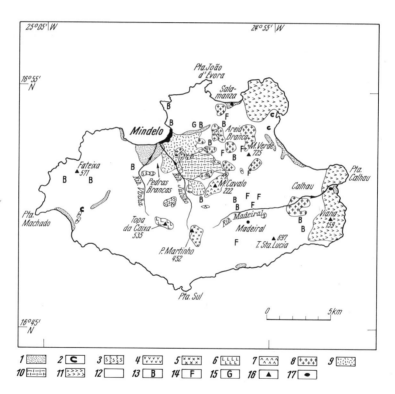

Fig. 82. Geological map of S. Vicente. 1: Dunes. 2: Tertiary limestones. 3: Syenites. 4: Diorites (monzonites). 5: Dolerites. 6: Lamprophyres. 7: Phonolites. 8: Limburgites, augitites. 9: Mindelo Series – basalts with many dykes. 10: Saladinha Series – basalts and diabases with calcareous dykes. 11: Basic Recent lavas. 12: Basaltic Series – basalts with breccias, lapilli, tuffs. 13: Olivine-basalts. 14: Basalts with feldspathoids. 15: Gabbros. 16: Peaks. 17: Villages. (Modified after BEBIANO, 1932).

Geology of the Cape Verde Archipelago

Table 54    Chemical analyses, Cape Verde rocks (PART, 1950a; ASSUNCAO & CANILHO, 1965; BARROS, 1968)

| | 1 | 2 | 3 | 4 | 5 | 6 | 7 | 8 | 9 |
|---|---|---|---|---|---|---|---|---|---|
| $SiO_2$ | 56.22 | 47.63 | 43.67 | 37.38 | 54.44 | 42.31 | 43.05 | 47.47 | 49.24 |
| $Al_2O_3$ | 22.74 | 18.94 | 17.58 | 18.03 | 18.54 | 13.15 | 14.26 | 18.01 | 18.48 |
| $Fe_2O_3$ | 0.84 | 1.47 | 4.91 | 8.61 | 2.62 | 4.70 | 5.29 | 3.46 | 3.41 |
| $FeO$ | 2.71 | 8.12 | 7.08 | 3.22 | 2.97 | 8.42 | 6.11 | 4.98 | 3.67 |
| $MnO$ | 0.26 | 0.28 | 0.27 | 0.26 | 0.19 | 0.19 | 0.17 | 0.14 | 0.15 |
| $MgO$ | 0.76 | 3.52 | 5.77 | 8.04 | 1.00 | 5.69 | 6.30 | 3.84 | 2.77 |
| $CaO$ | 1.94 | 6.94 | 10.58 | 12.42 | 2.81 | 12.03 | 13.09 | 9.14 | 7.15 |
| $Na_2O$ | 6.07 | 5.85 | 4.62 | 3.68 | 7.27 | 5.26 | 4.81 | 5.76 | 6.20 |
| $K_2O$ | 3.13 | 3.71 | 1.14 | 1.51 | 5.90 | 1.40 | 2.04 | 2.98 | 4.32 |
| $TiO_2$ | 0.56 | 2.56 | 2.56 | 2.57 | 0.84 | 4.18 | 3.59 | 2.53 | 2.62 |
| $P_2O_5$ | 0.04 | 0.64 | 0.69 | 1.49 | 0.12 | 0.41 | 0.77 | 1.19 | 0.60 |
| $CO_2$ | Tr. | 0.15 | Tr. | Tr. | 1.01 | 0.33 | -- | -- | -- |
| $Cl$ | 0.09 | 0.18 | -- | n.d. | -- | -- | -- | -- | -- |
| $SO_3$ | 0.26 | 0.27 | -- | n.d. | -- | -- | -- | -- | -- |
| $H_2O+$ | 3.34 | 0.13 | 0.84 | 1.34 | 2.76 | 2.67 | 1.11 | 0.88 | 1.81 |
| $H_2O-$ | 1.16 | 0.04 | 0.16 | 1.19 | | | | | |
| Total | 100.12 | 100.33 | 99.87 | 99.74 | 100.47 | 100.74 | 100.59 | 100.38 | 100.42 |

| | 10 | 11 | 12 | 13 | 14 | 15 | 16 | 17 | 18 |
|---|---|---|---|---|---|---|---|---|---|
| $SiO_2$ | 52.48 | 41.13 | 43.56 | 50.22 | 43.79 | 43.44 | 37.28 | 39.04 | 43.58 |
| $Al_2O_3$ | 19.27 | 12.33 | 18.42 | 20.12 | 19.60 | 12.14 | 12.36 | 10.34 | 9.99 |
| $Fe_2O_3$ | 4.27 | 6.59 | 3.06 | 2.77 | 3.50 | 2.89 | 5.75 | 4.83 | 2.56 |
| $FeO$ | 3.17 | 6.31 | 6.09 | 1.66 | 2.18 | 8.26 | 6.52 | 6.97 | 8;78 |
| $MnO$ | 0.22 | 0.19 | 0.21 | 0.21 | 0.24 | 0.23 | 0.33 | 0.19 | 0.13 |
| $MgO$ | 0.93 | 6;34 | 5;20 | 0.38 | 1.08 | 10.84 | 6.98 | 13.58 | 11.50 |
| $CaO$ | 1.25 | 12.07 | 14.14 | 3.09 | 6.07 | 13.35 | 14.06 | 13.53 | 13.36 |
| $Na_2O$ | 8.68 | 3.78 | 3.92 | 10.54 | 11.76 | 3.13 | 6.76 | 4.09 | 2.28 |
| $K_2O$ | 5.19 | 2.00 | 1.34 | 5.56 | 4.39 | 1.23 | 2.09 | 1.75 | 1.71 |
| $TiO_2$ | 1.82 | 4.09 | 2.53 | 0.68 | 1.38 | 2.91 | 5.24 | 3.45 | 3.97 |
| $P_2O_5$ | 0.42 | 0.48 | 0.34 | 0.04 | 0.24 | 0.35 | 0.66 | 0.71 | 1.33 |
| $CO_2$ | -- | 2.37 | -- | 0.46 | 2.01 | -- | 0.81 | 0.13 | -- |
| $Cl$ | -- | -- | -- | -- | -- | -- | -- | -- | 0.06 |
| $SO_3$ | -- | -- | -- | -- | -- | -- | -- | -- | -- |
| $H_2O+$ | 2.18 | 2.88 | 1.55 | 4.72 | 4.35 | 1.49 | 1.73 | 1.80 | 1.14 |
| $H_2O-$ | -- | -- | -- | | | | | | |
| Total | 99.88 | 100.56 | 100.36 | 100.45 | 100.59 | 100.26 | 100.57 | 100.41 | 100.73 |

*Rock and Localities, Cape Verde Islands*

(PART, 1950a; ASSUNCAO & CANILHO, 1965; BARROS, 1968)

*Santo Antao*

1. Hornblende-trachyte, Rib. da Torre.
2. Tahitite, E cliff, 600–800 ft., Tarrafal.
3. Hornblende-tephrite, E cliff, Tarrafal.
4. Melilite-nephelinite, E cliff, Tarrafal.

*Sao Vicente*

5. Feldspathoidal syenite, Pedras Brancas, W of Morro Juliao.
6. Augitite, dyke cutting above rock.
7. Theralitoid, between Pedras Brancas and Morro Juliao.

Table 54 (continued)

|  | 19 | 20 | 21 | 22 | 23 | 24 | 25 | 26 | 27 |
|---|---|---|---|---|---|---|---|---|---|
| $SiO_2$ | 39.13 | 36.77 | 42.89 | 38.60 | 56.26 | 54.97 | 54.53 | 52.18 | 55.11 |
| $Al_2O_3$ | 10.20 | 9.80 | 11.58 | 11.64 | 11.68 | 20.06 | 18.90 | 19.07 | 19.27 |
| $Fe_2O_3$ | 4.40 | 3.79 | 2.13 | 9.44 | 3.61 | 3.43 | 5.01 | 3.36 | 2.67 |
| FeO | 8.93 | 7.89 | 12.78 | 5.33 | 1.87 | 1.25 | 1.74 | 1.30 | 1.41 |
| MnO | 0.15 | 0.14 | 0.19 | 0.71 | 0.81 | 0.21 | 0.18 | 0.07 | 0.08 |
| MgO | 12.72 | 14.94 | 10.00 | 6.23 | 0.22 | 0.43 | 3.57 | 1.58 | 0.05 |
| CaO | 13.03 | 15.67 | 11.22 | 14.43 | 2.36 | 2.60 | 3.43 | 4.56 | 1.33 |
| $Na_2O$ | 3.32 | 2.49 | 1.92 | 5.43 | 7.19 | 8.27 | 5.29 | 4.06 | 9.11 |
| $K_2O$ | 0.61 | 0.97 | 1.11 | 2.49 | 5.21 | 5.14 | 3.48 | 5.51 | 6.54 |
| $TiO_2$ | 4.98 | 4.07 | 4.52 | 4.23 | 0.60 | 0.64 | 1.54 | 1.24 | 0.17 |
| $P_2O_5$ | 0.77 | 1.40 | 0.26 | 0.80 | 0.31 | 0.20 | 0.24 | 0.38 | 0.08 |
| $CO_2$ | 0.52 | –– | 0.20 | –– | 1.49 | 0.99 | –– | –– | 2.00 |
| Cl | 0.02 | 0.06 | n.d. | 0.05 | 0.11 | –– | –– | 0.06 | 0.64 |
| $SO_3$ | –– | –– | n.d. | –– | –– | –– | –– | –– | –– |
| $H_2O+$ | 1.10 | 1.87 | 0.82 | 0.40 | 0.99 | 2.17 | 2.66 | 5.30 | 1.59 |
| $H_2O-$ | 0.26 | 0.39 | 0.58 | 0.78 | 0.31 | –– | 0.85 | 1.92 | 0.29 |
| Total | 100.14 | 100.25 | 100.21 | 100.56 | 100.02 | 100.36 | 101.42 | 100.59 | 100.26 |

|  | 28 | 29 | 30 | 31 | 32 | 33 | 34 | 35 | 36 |
|---|---|---|---|---|---|---|---|---|---|
| $SiO_2$ | 51.59 | 48.71 | 54.18 | 37.86 | 55.50 | 48.96 | 53.18 | 54.66 | 49.27 |
| $Al_2O_3$ | 18.90 | 19.62 | 21.52 | 4.37 | 20.52 | 18.24 | 19.62 | 21.96 | 22.69 |
| $Fe_2O_3$ | 4.61 | 4.18 | 1.93 | 5.14 | 1.62 | 3.57 | 3.39 | 1.10 | 0.74 |
| FeO | 6.10 | 7.37 | 1.74 | 9.00 | 1.38 | 4.48 | 3.57 | 2.19 | 2.73 |
| MnO | –– | –– | 0.08 | n.d. | 0.43 | 0.25 | 0.04 | 0.21 | 0.13 |
| MgO | 3.20 | 4.71 | 0.76 | 22.78 | 0.18 | 1.49 | 1.40 | 0.35 | 3.12 |
| CaO | 7.23 | 8.36 | 2.61 | 13.62 | 0.92 | 6.12 | 4.84 | 3.02 | 5.99 |
| $Na_2O$ | 3.81 | 3.07 | 4.14 | 1.53 | 10.37 | 6.48 | 7.45 | 8.91 | 5.97 |
| $K_2O$ | 2.33 | 1.90 | 4.27 | 1.02 | 4.63 | 3.99 | 3.84 | 5.55 | 4.02 |
| $TiO_2$ | 1.03 | 1.21 | 0.68 | 3.38 | 0.40 | 1.96 | 1.80 | 0.81 | 3.24 |
| $P_2O_5$ | 0.36 | 0.42 | 0.08 | 0.29 | Tr. | 0.42 | 0.42 | 0.18 | 0.33 |
| $CO_2$ | –– | –– | –– | –– | –– | 1.88 | Tr. | –– | 0.54 |
| Cl | –– | –– | 0.15 | –– | –– | 0.05 | 0.09 | –– | –– |
| $SO_3$ | –– | –– | 0.06 | –– | –– | Tr. | Tr. | –– | –– |
| $H_2O+$ | 1.36 | 1.22 | 4.36 | 1.19 | 3.89 | 2.17 | 0.67 | 0.74 | 1.68 |
| $H_2O-$ | –– | –– | 3.30 | –– | 0.44 | 0.30 | 0.20 | 0.28 | –– |
| Total | 100.52 | 100.67 | 99.86 | 100.18 | 100.28 | 100.36 | 100.51 | 99.96 | 100.45 |

8. Essexitoid, between Pedras Brancas and Morro Juliao.
9. Essexitoid, small valley S of small Juliao peak, 1.7 km from top.
10. Analcitic syenite, ca. 1.5 km W of Morro Juliao.
11. Doleritic Basanitoid, 150 m SW of M. de Joao.
12. Theralite, 100 m WNW of M. de S. Joao.
13. Phonolite, scarp of Rib. Flo. de Pedra, E of Morro do Cavalo.

14. Nephelinite, SE of Monte da Fonte Nova, a little S of Craquinha and Passarao, by Rib. Lameira.
15. Ankaratritic basanitoid, 800 m SW of Areia Branco houses.
16. Etindite, 1170 m SE of Rib. Flo de Pedra.
17. Ankaratrite, summit of hill, left side, where Rib. Madeiral ends.
18. "Basanitoid", 2 km N40W from Monte Madeiral.
19. Nepheline-ankaratrite, 1 km S30W of Monte Amargoso.

Table 54 (continued)

| | 37 | 38 | 39 | 40 | 41 | 42 | 43 | 44 | 45 |
|---|---|---|---|---|---|---|---|---|---|
| $SiO_2$ | 43.56 | 38.03 | 37.18 | 43.46 | 59.16 | 46.40 | 35.76 | 36.16 | 41.60 |
| $Al_2O_3$ | 16.17 | 13.63 | 10.37 | 14.13 | 18.46 | 12.93 | 9.76 | 6.85 | 11.88 |
| $Fe_2O_3$ | 5.61 | 9.07 | 5.64 | 6.81 | 2.04 | 5.69 | 4.70 | 6.27 | 5.07 |
| $FeO$ | 8.59 | 3.45 | 7.53 | 7.00 | 1.99 | 6.18 | 6.48 | 6.94 | 7.24 |
| $MnO$ | 0.15 | 0.16 | 0.26 | n.d. | 0.34 | 0.11 | 0.21 | n.d. | 0.12 |
| $MgO$ | 6.09 | 8.55 | 12.52 | 5.18 | 0.74 | 7.50 | 16.97 | 13.88 | 7.22 |
| $CaO$ | 8.22 | 15.42 | 15.08 | 12.56 | 1.38 | 12.02 | 15.28 | 18.88 | 13.42 |
| $Na_2O$ | 4.47 | 1.88 | 2.87 | 2.96 | 7.50 | 2.67 | 3.46 | 2.45 | 3.39 |
| $K_2O$ | 1.76 | 0.76 | 0.93 | 1.39 | 4.99 | 1.10 | 1.38 | 1.00 | 0.51 |
| $TiO_2$ | 3.80 | 5.06 | 4.60 | 4.23 | 1.39 | 3.62 | 3.48 | 4.61 | 4.98 |
| $P_2O_5$ | 0.55 | 0.89 | 0.82 | 0.59 | 0.06 | 0.60 | 1.37 | 0.79 | 0.71 |
| $CO_2$ | -- | Tr. | 0.14 | -- | -- | -- | 0.25 | -- | 0.17 |
| $Cl$ | -- | -- | -- | 0.15 | -- | -- | 0.05 | -- | -- |
| $SO_3$ | -- | -- | -- | -- | -- | -- | Tr. | -- | -- |
| $H_2O+$ | 0.94 | 3.22 | 1.58 | 1.81 | 1.76 | 0.84 | 0.76 | 2.07 | 3.44 |
| $H_2O-$ | -- | -- | 0.89 | 0.13 | 0.49 | 0.69 | 0.13 | 0.36 | 0.46 |
| Total | 99.91 | 100.12 | 100.41 | 100.40 | 100.30 | 100.35 | 100.04 | 100.46 | 100.11 |

| | 46 | 47 | 48 | 49 | 50 | 51 | 52 | 53 | 54 |
|---|---|---|---|---|---|---|---|---|---|
| $SiO_2$ | 44.38 | 44.00 | 41.94 | 36.24 | 53.76 | 40.16 | 43.12 | 53.65 | 44.55 |
| $Al_2O_3$ | 16.84 | 14.54 | 12.91 | 8.22 | 22.18 | 10.34 | 12.94 | 20.56 | 11.62 |
| $Fe_2O_3$ | 3.34 | 6.51 | 4.24 | 5.45 | 1.33 | 5.18 | 1.98 | 1.00 | 5.53 |
| $FeO$ | 5.00 | 4.29 | 8.28 | 6.32 | 2.53 | 8.44 | 9.52 | 1.36 | 5.20 |
| $MnO$ | 0.17 | 0.13 | 0.08 | 0.13 | 0.09 | 0.15 | 0.26 | 0.08 | 0.18 |
| $MgO$ | 2.70 | 3.85 | 8.15 | 16.66 | 0.15 | 11.58 | 8.09 | 1.28 | 9.40 |
| $CaO$ | 9.12 | 11.22 | 12.78 | 17.18 | 2.10 | 13.20 | 12.62 | 4.50 | 13.16 |
| $Na_2O$ | 7.17 | 4.79 | 2.64 | 2.67 | 8.74 | 2.37 | 2.65 | 6.34 | 2.19 |
| $K_2O$ | 3.15 | 1.39 | 1.28 | 1.11 | 5.96 | 0.66 | 1.42 | 5.08 | 1.86 |
| $TiO_2$ | 3.36 | 4.42 | 5.24 | 3.20 | 0.39 | 4.56 | 3.45 | 1.30 | 3.24 |
| $P_2O_5$ | 0.77 | 1.11 | 0.65 | 1.14 | Tr. | 0.38 | 0.44 | 0.30 | 0.48 |
| $CO_2$ | 0.11 | Tr. | -- | Tr. | Tr. | Nil | 1.60 | 0.24 | 0.08 |
| $Cl$ | 0.13 | -- | -- | -- | 0.37 | 0.38 | -- | -- | n.d. |
| $SO_3$ | 0.12 | -- | -- | -- | 0.18 | Nil | -- | -- | n.d. |
| $H_2O+$ | 3.34 | 2.87 | 1.74 | 1.61 | 2.01 | 2.12 | 1.36 | 3.30 | 1.31 |
| $H_2O-$ | 0.63 | 0.98 | 0.33 | 0.32 | 0.24 | 0.32 | 0.32 | 0.27 | 0.15 |
| Total | 100.33 | 100.10 | 100.26 | 100.25 | 100.03 | 99.84 | 99.77 | 99.26 | 98.95 |

20. Melilitic ankaratrite, 1 km N15W from survey mark, Monte Verde.
21. Olivine-basalt, near lighthouse, S. Pedro.
22. Nepheline-ankaratrite, 200 m N of Casa de Nha Claudia.
23. Nepheline-syenite, Pedras Brancas.
24. Nepheline-syenite, Pedras Brancas.
25. Trachy-andesite, between Pedras Brancas and Bahia S. Pedro.
26. Trachyte, 1.3 km N15W of Monte Fateixa.
27. Sodalite-phonolite, Monte Cavalo.

28. Trachy-dolerite, Salamanza.
29. Trachy-dolerite, N of pier, Mindelo.

*S. Nicolau*

30. Hornblende-trachyte, Rib. Brava valley, Vila.

*Sal*

31. Ankaratrite, very peridotitic and melilitic.
32. Nepheline-syenite (monzonitic), 1.2 km N13W of Morro de Carvao.

Table 54  (continued)

| | 55 | 56 | 57 | 58 | 59 | 60 | 61 | 62 | 63 |
|---|---|---|---|---|---|---|---|---|---|
| $SiO_2$ | 49.81 | 42.53 | 42.18 | 42.08 | 41.52 | 51.16 | 46.95 | 38.94 | 49.07 |
| $Al_2O_3$ | 20.76 | 9.48 | 14.01 | 15.03 | 15.24 | 21.53 | 18.98 | 13.64 | 13.57 |
| $Fe_2O_3$ | 2.92 | 3.22 | 4.58 | 3.25 | 3.99 | 2.64 | 3.64 | 6.44 | 6.87 |
| FeO | 1.80 | 10.66 | 8.28 | 8.68 | 6.27 | 1.86 | 1.47 | 4.81 | 1.46 |
| MnO | 0.13 | 0.24 | 0.13 | 0.33 | 0.21 | 0.07 | 0.15 | 0.34 | 0.30 |
| MgO | 0.99 | 11.56 | 5.90 | 5.52 | 5.07 | 0.68 | 0.79 | 3.88 | 0.97 |
| CaO | 4.65 | 14.83 | 13.16 | 12.74 | 11.17 | 1.92 | 5.34 | 15.79 | 8.69 |
| $Na_2O$ | 8.95 | 2.22 | 3.69 | 4.16 | 5.68 | 10.53 | 9.39 | 1.98 | 5.19 |
| $K_2O$ | 6.19 | 1.02 | 2.26 | 2.84 | 3.73 | 5.69 | 5.93 | 1.69 | 6.63 |
| $TiO_2$ | 1.10 | 4.02 | 5.06 | 4.24 | 3.89 | 0.49 | 0.63 | 3.95 | 0.45 |
| $P_2O_5$ | 0.23 | 0.21 | 0.82 | 0.77 | 1.20 | 0.05 | 0.14 | 1.23 | 0.49 |
| $CO_2$ | 0.21 | 0.15 | -- | Nil | Nil | Tr. | 1.66 | Tr. | 4.28 |
| Cl | n.d. | -- | -- | -- | n.d. | 0.34 | 0.31 | 0.07 | -- |
| $SO_3$ | 0.35 | -- | -- | -- | n.d. | 1.14 | 0.19 | 0.24 | -- |
| $H_2O+$ | 0.76 | Tr. | 0.21 | 0.08 | 0.56 | 1.72 | 2.89 | 4.51 | 1.98 |
| $H_2O-$ | 0.23 | 0.13 | 0.10 | 0.16 | 0.26 | 0.45 | 1.69 | 3.00 | 0.14 |
| Total | 99.08 | 100.27 | 100.38 | 99.88 | 99.79 | 100.27 | 100.15 | 100.51 | 100.09 |

| | 64 | 65 | 66 | 67 | 68 | 69 | 70 | 71 | 72 |
|---|---|---|---|---|---|---|---|---|---|
| $SiO_2$ | 53.91 | 45.37 | 51.78 | 40.52 | 39.36 | 35.67 | 35.72 | 30.15 | 31.64 |
| $Al_2O_3$ | 18.61 | 12.34 | 18.96 | 15.18 | 23.94 | 7.55 | 7.78 | 10.36 | 6.65 |
| $Fe_2O_3$ | 2.69 | 8.12 | 5.46 | 2.70 | 2.15 | 14.57 | 14.68 | 11.67 | 15.29 |
| FeO | 0.40 | 1.29 | 0.86 | 3.00 | 1.29 | 5.12 | 4.86 | 7.17 | 8.60 |
| MnO | 0.09 | 0.27 | 0.14 | 0.10 | 0.07 | 0.12 | 0.10 | 0.14 | 0.17 |
| MgO | 0.84 | 1.35 | 0.50 | 5.48 | 1.52 | 10.78 | 9.80 | 9.54 | 10.14 |
| CaO | 3.08 | 11.77 | 2.66 | 14.30 | 7.43 | 17.10 | 19.06 | 15.14 | 16.26 |
| $Na_2O$ | 4.23 | 5.92 | 10.08 | 7.85 | 11.26 | 0.96 | 0.72 | 2.12 | 1.53 |
| $K_2O$ | 9.68 | 4.60 | 6.63 | 1.80 | 3.26 | 0.28 | 0.16 | 1.61 | 0.55 |
| $TiO_2$ | 0.34 | 0.29 | 0.75 | 0.55 | 3.27 | 7.00 | 6.63 | 5.80 | 7.51 |
| $P_2O_5$ | 0.13 | 1.96 | 0.07 | 1.58 | 0.28 | 0.23 | 0.07 | 4.26 | 0.34 |
| $CO_2$ | 2.47 | 4.82 | 0.10 | 1.69 | 2.53 | < 0.10 | < 0.10 | 0.71 | < 0.10 |
| Cl | -- | -- | -- | -- | -- | -- | -- | -- | -- |
| $SO_3$ | -- | -- | -- | -- | -- | -- | -- | -- | -- |
| $H_2O+$ | 2.97 | 2.17 | 1.64 | 3.89 | 3.29 | 0.69 | 0.83 | 0.82 | 0.76 |
| $H_2O-$ | 0.37 | 0.09 | 0.04 | 1.07 | 0.18 | 0.31 | 0.28 | 0.10 | 0.12 |
| Total | 99.81 | 100.36 | 99.57 | 99.71 | 99.83 | 100.38 | 100.69 | 99.59 | 99.56 |

33. Nepheline-monzonite, 1.5 km N of Casa de Soldado.
34. Nepheline-monzonite, 2 km S25E of Palmeira village.
35. Nepheline-phonolite, 300 m E of Curralona.
36. Dioritic esseyite, 500 m NW of Morro das Pedras.
37. Essexite-gabbroid-dolerite, between Morro das Pedras and M. Carvao.
38. Augitite, Pedra Lume.
39. Ankaratrite, Porto de Santa Maria.
40. Luscladite.

*Boa Vista*

41. Monzonite-syenite, Cabeço de Tarrafes.
42. Dolerite, Morro Negro.
43. Melilitic basalt (ankaratrite), Monte Abrohal.

*Maio*

44. Ankaratrite, very peridotitic and melilitic.
45. Olivine-basalt (ankaramite), 1 km SE of Morro.
46. Monchiquite, Morro D'Agua.
47. Nepheline-basanite, Ponta Pedrenau.

Table 55

NIGGLI and RITTMANN parameters, S. Vicente (ASSUNCAO & CANILHO, 1965)

| | 5 | 6 | 7 | 8 | 9 | 10 | 11 | 12 | 13 | 14 | 15 | 16 | 17 |
|---|---|---|---|---|---|---|---|---|---|---|---|---|---|
| si | 182.5 | 96.5 | 95.6 | 121.1 | 137.2 | 173.8 | 96.7 | 100.4 | 137.2 | 118.2 | 87.3 | 76.8 | 72.5 |
| al | 36.5 | 17.5 | 18.6 | 26.9 | 30.2 | 37.5 | 17.0 | 24.8 | 30.2 | 31.1 | 14.3 | 14.9 | 11.3 |
| fm | 17.1 | 39.5 | 37.0 | 28.9 | 23.9 | 19.2 | 40.9 | 32.7 | 23.9 | 13.1 | 49.0 | 37.7 | 52.2 |
| c | 10.0 | 29.3 | 31.1 | 24.9 | 21.3 | 4.3 | 30.4 | 31.5 | 21.3 | 17.5 | 28.8 | 31.0 | 26.9 |
| alk | 36.2 | 13.6 | 13.2 | 19.1 | 24.3 | 38.7 | 11.5 | 10.7 | 24.3 | 38.1 | 7.7 | 16.2 | 9.3 |
| k | 0.34 | 0.14 | 0.21 | 0.25 | 0.31 | 0.28 | 0.25 | 0.18 | 0.31 | 0.19 | 0.20 | 0.16 | 0.22 |
| mg | 0.29 | 0.49 | 0.56 | 0.50 | 0.48 | 0.23 | 0.54 | 0.54 | 0.48 | 0.33 | 0.66 | 0.57 | 0.72 |
| ti | 2.1 | 7.1 | 5.97 | 4.8 | 5.4 | 4.5 | 7.2 | 4.4 | 5.4 | 2.7 | 4.3 | 8.1 | 4.8 |
| p | 0.16 | 0.38 | 0.71 | 1.2 | 0.70 | 0.57 | 0.4 | 0.27 | 0.70 | 0.22 | 0.36 | 0.56 | 0.55 |
| qz | -62.3 | -57.9 | 57.2 | -55.3 | -60.0 | -77.4 | -49.3 | -42.2 | -60.0 | -113.2 | -43.5 | -84.1 | -64.7 |
| | | | | | | | | | | | | | |
| Si° | 0.74 | 0.62 | 0.62 | 0.68 | 0.60 | 0.69 | 0.66 | 0.70 | 0.60 | 0.55 | 0.66 | 0.47 | 0.52 |
| Az° | 0.64 | 0.49 | 0.48 | 0.54 | 0.57 | 0.63 | 0.40 | 0.50 | 0.57 | 0.54 | 0.46 | 0.43 | 0.42 |

basement but rather they represent intra-volcanics, such as are found, for example, at M. Somma, Vesuvius. The S. Vicente plutonics have similar compositions to corresponding lavas, with slight textural differences. They occur as small dyke-type intrusions in the floor of a caldera, chiefly between Topo da Caixa and Monte Sossego. Syenites, with and without feldspathoids, gabbros with and without the same minerals, ijolites and melteigites are recognized, the syenites being later than the gabbros. The unsaturated gabbroic rocks appear to correspond to essexites or then mafraites. The non-feldspathoidal ijolites and melteigites likely correspond to melanocratic magmatic segreagations very poor in silica. The authors contend that the process of differentiation has led to the development of alkaline rocks with a remarkable deficiency in silica, and thus the strongly Atlantic nature of the rocks is established. Also present are dykes of dolerites, teschenites and lamprophyres, and volcanic breccias are very common. Many dykes are extremely rich in carbonates, at times accompanied by silicate oxides of iron, etc., which are probably carbonatites, known in Fogo, Brava and Ilheus Secos. Of distinct interest is the almost total absence of rocks of the calc-alkaline series. The rocks have not undergone assimilation of sialic matter, a condition believed

Table 56                         NIGGLI parameters, Ilheu Grandes (Ilheus Secos) (BARROS, 1968)

|     | 63    | 64    | 65    | 66    | 67   | 68   | 69   | 70   | 71   | 72    |
|-----|-------|-------|-------|-------|------|------|------|------|------|-------|
| Q   | 22.5  | 29.1  | 17.0  | 20.1  | 9.6  | 6.9  | 10.0 | 11.0 | 5.6  | 22.5  |
| L   | 46.9  | 61.4  | 43.0  | 60.2  | 50.1 | 74.3 | 16.7 | 14.0 | 27.1 | 46.9  |
| M   | 30.6  | 9.5   | 40.0  | 19.7  | 40.3 | 18.8 | 73.3 | 75.0 | 67.3 | 30.6  |
| si  | 142.0 | 191.0 | 119.4 | 153.6 | 88.5 | 98.3 | 64.4 | 64.9 | 55.4 | 142.0 |
| al  | 23.0  | 39.0  | 19.1  | 33.3  | 19.5 | 35.1 | 8.1  | 8.0  | 11.3 | 233.0 |
| fm  | 23.4  | 13.2  | 25.0  | 16.6  | 28.1 | 12.6 | 56.7 | 54.0 | 53.3 | 23.4  |
| c   | 26.9  | 11.7  | 33.2  | 8.4   | 33.4 | 19.8 | 33.1 | 37.0 | 29.8 | 26.9  |
| alk | 26.7  | 36.1  | 22.7  | 41.7  | 19.0 | 32.5 | 2.1  | 1.0  | 5.6  | 26.7  |
| k   | 0.50  | 0.60  | 0.30  | 0.30  | 0.13 | 0.20 | 0.15 | 0.15 | 0.30 | 0.50  |
| mg  | 0.20  | 0.34  | 0.20  | 0.13  | 0.60 | 0.50 | 0.50 | 0.50 | 0.50 | 0.20  |
| ti  | 0.90  | 0.85  | 0.60  | 1.67  | 0.90 | 6.10 | 9.54 | 9.06 | 8.04 | 0.90  |
| p   | 0.70  | 0.19  | 2.18  | 0.08  | 1.44 | 0.30 | 0.11 | 0.05 | 3.30 | 0.70  |

48.  Ankaratrite, Ponte de Osso de Baleia.
49.  Melilitic ankaratrite, Monte Batalha.

*S. Tiago*

50.  Hornblende-phonolite, 5 km N of Praia.
51.  Olivine-nephelinite, Monte S. Pedro, 5 km N of Praia.
52.  Olivine-basalt, entrance to Porto Praia.
53.  Monzonitic nepheline-syenite, Rib. S. Jorge, 5 km N of Praia.
54.  Essexite, Rib. S. Jorge, 5 km N of Praia.

*Fogo*

55.  Haüyne-phonolite, 5 km up Rib. Trindade.
56.  Nepheline-basanite, Rib. Joao Pinto.
57.  Nepheline-basanite, Patim.
58.  Tephrite, Rib. Trindade.
59.  Leucite-nephelinite, 3 km up Rib. Trindade.

*Brava*

60.  Haüyne-phonolite, 1.5 km S of Furna.
61.  Leucite-phonolite, above Fonte Vinagre.
62.  Melanite-haüynite, mouth of Rib. "Lacacan".

*Ilheu Grande* (Ilheus Secos)

63.  Feldspathoidal syenite, E of Baia da Cagarra.
64.  Feldspathoidal syenite, Monte Gordo.
65.  Feldspathoidal syenite, Monte Gordo.
66.  Feldspathoidal syenite, between Ponta Ribeirinho and Porto Grande.
67.  Ijolite, Porto Grande.
68.  Ijolite, Porto Grande.
69.  Jacupirangite, Monte Gordo.
70.  Jacupirangite, Monte Grande.
71.  Lherzite, Porto Grande.
72.  Biotitite, Monte Grande.

Table 57    Molecular norms, Cape Verde rocks (PART, 1950a; ASSUNCAO & CANILHO 1965; BARROS, 1968)

|        | 1     | 2     | 3    | 4    | 5     | 6     | 7     | 8     | 9     |
|--------|-------|-------|------|------|-------|-------|-------|-------|-------|
| or     | 18.35 | 21.68 | 6.7  | 3.9  | 35.03 | 8.34  | 11.68 | 17.79 | 25.58 |
| ab     | 48.73 | 14.67 | 14.3 |      | 31.05 | 5.69  | 1.98  | 16.44 | 16.50 |
| an     | 9.45  | 17.09 | 23.9 | 27.8 | 0.28  | 7.78  | 11.68 | 14.18 | 9.73  |
| ne     |       | 16.04 | 13.4 | 17.0 | 16.40 | 21.06 | 20.80 | 17.50 | 19.46 |
| lc     |       |       |      | 3.9  |       |       |       |       |       |
| hl     | 0.15  | 0.29  |      |      |       |       |       |       |       |
| th     | 0.57  | 0.57  |      |      |       |       |       |       |       |
| nc     |       | 0.37  |      |      |       |       |       |       |       |
| ac     |       |       |      |      |       |       |       |       |       |
| wo     |       |       |      |      | 2.67  | 19.72 | 19.95 | 9.86  | 9.28  |
| di     |       | 11.43 | 19.4 | 18.4 |       |       |       |       |       |
| en     |       |       |      |      | 1.30  | 13.30 | 15.70 | 7.30  | 6.90  |
| hy     | 5.73  |       |      |      |       |       |       |       |       |
| fs     |       |       |      |      | 1.32  | 4.88  | 0.90  | 1.58  |       |
| fo     |       |       |      |      | 0.56  | 0.63  |       | 1.51  |       |
| fa     |       |       |      |      | 1.22  | 0.20  |       | 0.82  |       |
| shan   |       |       |      |      |       |       |       |       |       |
| cs     |       |       |      |      |       |       |       |       |       |
| cc     |       |       |      |      | 2.30  | 0.80  |       |       |       |
| ol     |       | 9.74  | 7.4  | 8.1  |       |       |       |       |       |
| mt     | 1.16  | 2.09  | 7.2  | 3.5  | 3.71  | 6.73  | 7.66  | 5.34  | 4.64  |
| il     | 1.06  | 4.86  | 4.9  | 5.0  | 1.52  | 7.90  | 6.84  | 4.86  | 5.02  |
| hm     |       |       |      | 6.2  |       |       |       |       | 0.16  |
| ap     |       | 1.34  | 1.7  | 3.7  | 0.34  | 1.01  | 2.02  | 2.69  | 1.34  |
| kp     |       |       |      |      |       |       |       |       |       |
| ns     |       |       |      |      |       |       |       |       |       |
| pf     |       |       |      |      |       |       |       |       |       |
| C      | 6.43  |       |      |      |       |       |       |       |       |
| Q      | 3.84  |       |      |      |       |       |       |       |       |
| $H_2O$ |       |       |      |      |       |       |       |       |       |

necessary in the course of calc-alkaline differentiation process. The carbonatites are thought to represent an extreme differentiate of an alkaline magma, the observed calcite in feldspathoidal rocks only very rarely being due to alteration of primary minerals, and then only to a very small degree. As the initial phases of eruptivity likely date from the Late Tertiary, perhaps even in the Cretaceous, it is unlikely that limestones here in S. Vicente are responsible for calcitic minerals in the igneous rocks, limestones of earlier date not been known here at present.

The NIGGLI isofal value for the island is quoted as 132.

As regards Fogo, MACHADO & ASSUNCAO (1965) and ASSUNCAO, MACHADO & SILVA (1967) furnish us with petrologic details on collections made (Table 58). On a time basis the volcanics can be divided into: those expelled before the creation of the caldera, and those posterior to its formation. The former include nephelinites, basanites and other unsaturated rocks such as etindites, but ankaratrites are rare. The later eruptives include basanites, limburgites and related rocks. In both cases, the extreme deficiency in silica is a most notable point. In the 43 samples chemically analyzed $SiO_2$ ranged from 30.36% to 47.06%, or 49.81% in PART's (1950) sample (No. 55, Table 54). Carbonatites

Table 57 (continued)

|  | 10 | 11 | 12 | 13 | 14 | 15 | 16 | 17 | 18 |
|---|---|---|---|---|---|---|---|---|---|
| or | 30.58 | 11.68 | 7.78 | 33.36 | 10.84 | 7.23 |  |  | 10.0 |
| ab | 29.68 | 14.80 | 6.29 | 6.16 |  | 0.73 |  |  | 4.7 |
| an |  | 10.84 | 28.36 |  |  | 15.29 |  | 4.73 | 11.9 |
| ne | 22.29 | 9.30 | 14.46 | 35.57 | 41.18 | 14.09 | 28.40 | 18.74 | 7.9 |
| lc |  |  |  |  | 12.04 |  | 9.59 | 7.85 |  |
| hl |  |  |  |  |  |  |  |  |  |
| th |  |  |  |  |  |  |  |  |  |
| nc |  |  |  |  |  |  |  |  |  |
| ac | 2.77 |  |  | 8.32 | 10.16 |  | 4.16 |  |  |
| wo | 1.39 | 12.99 | 15.71 | 4.99 | 6.96 | 20.18 | 11.72 | 14.79 |  |
| di |  |  |  |  |  |  |  |  | 36.3 |
| en | 1.06 | 11.20 | 9.30 | 0.90 | 2.70 | 14.10 | 9.90 | 11.85 |  |
| hy |  |  |  |  |  |  |  |  |  |
| fs | 0.18 |  | 3.43 | 3.24 | 2.11 | 4.36 | 0.26 | 1.19 |  |
| fo | 0.87 | 3.22 | 2.59 |  |  | 9.10 | 5.25 | 15.44 |  |
| fa | 0.16 |  | 1.12 |  |  | 3.16 | 0.10 | 1.73 |  |
| shan |  |  |  | 1.83 | 2.68 |  | 9.87 | 6.75 |  |
| cs |  |  |  |  |  |  |  |  |  |
| cc |  | 5.30 |  | 1.00 | 4.50 |  | 1.80 | 0.30 |  |
| ol |  |  |  |  |  |  |  |  | 13.6 |
| mt | 4.87 | 9.28 | 4.41 |  |  | 4.18 | 6.26 | 6.96 | 3.5 |
| il | 3.50 | 7.75 | 4.86 | 1.37 | 2.74 | 5.47 | 9.88 | 6.69 | 7.6 |
| hm |  | 0.16 |  |  |  |  |  |  |  |
| ap | 0.10 | 1.34 | 0.67 | 0.10 | 0.34 | 1.01 | 1.68 | 1.68 | 3.1 |
| kp |  |  |  |  |  |  |  |  |  |
| ns |  |  |  |  |  |  |  |  |  |
| pf |  |  |  |  |  |  |  |  |  |
| C |  |  |  |  |  |  |  |  |  |
| Q |  |  |  |  |  |  |  |  |  |
| $H_2O$ |  |  |  |  |  |  |  |  |  |

have small outcrops in the vicinity of S. Felipe, where they are cut by veinlets of both alkaline eruptives and ijolitic-type rocks. The carbonatites are taken to represent an old (pre-Tertiary?) basement complex. Assuncao et al. treat of the petrology of the various lava outpourings of the 18th, 19th and 20th centuries. They consider that the weight relations of $K_2O + Na_2O/SiO_2$, $Al_2O_3/SiO_2$ and $MgO/0.9\ Fe_2O_3 + FeO + MgO$ to be of the greatest significance here. As one would expect, silica increases with degree of differentiation (Fig. 83), though this is all but unnoticable except in basement rocks and old lavas. The more recent lavas tend to be richer in $SiO_2$ and MgO, show less alkalis and alumina. The undersaturated nature of all these rocks is evident in the QLM diagram. It was the belief of Assuncao et al. that the phonolites, melilites and associated rocks recorded by Part (Table 54 Nos. 55, 58, 59) from the Ribeira Trindade represent loose blocks of the carbonatitic basement.

Ilheu Grande, lying 6.4 km N of Brava, has been investigated by Barros (1968). (Vd. Table 54 Nos. 63–72, Table 59.) Here the rocks can be grouped into: (i) feldspathoidal syenites and associated types – lujavrites, shonkinites, (ii) ijolites, (iii) perkinites – jacupirangites, lherzites, biotitites, (iv) carbonatites. A sample of carbonatite, when

Table 57 (continued)

|      | 19      | 20     | 21    | 30     | 31    | 44    | 50     | 51    | 52     |
|------|---------|--------|-------|--------|-------|-------|--------|-------|--------|
| or   | 3.3     |        | 6.1   | 25.58  |       |       | 35.58  | 3.9   | 8.34   |
| ab   | 1.0     |        | 11.5  | 33.01  |       |       | 21.48  | 4.2   | 13.10  |
| an   | 11.4    | 12.8   | 19.7  | 11.95  | 2.2   | 3.6   | 5.84   | 16.7  | 18.90  |
| ne   | 14.5    | 11.1   | 2.6   |        | 6.8   | 12.2  | 26.13  |       | 5.11   |
| lc   |         | 4.8    |       |        | 4.8   | 4.8   |        |       |        |
| hl   |         | 0.1    |       | 0.23   |       |       | 0.59   | 0.6   |        |
| th   |         |        |       | 0.14   |       |       | 0.43   |       |        |
| nc   |         |        |       |        |       |       |        |       |        |
| ac   |         |        |       |        |       |       |        |       |        |
| wo   |         |        |       |        |       |       |        |       |        |
| di   | 35.3    | 19.9   | 26.5  |        | 21.9  | 26.1  | 4.14   | 36.3  | 25.00  |
| en   |         |        |       |        |       |       |        |       |        |
| hy   |         |        |       | 2.43   |       |       |        |       |        |
| fs   |         |        |       |        |       |       |        |       |        |
| fo   |         |        |       |        |       |       |        |       |        |
| fa   |         |        |       |        |       |       |        |       |        |
| shan |         |        |       |        |       |       |        |       |        |
| cs   |         | 9.5    |       |        | 11.0  | 15.8  |        |       |        |
| cc   | (1.20)  |        |       |        |       |       |        |       | 3.60   |
| ol   | 14.5    | 23.5   | 19.6  |        | 37.7  | 15.8  | 0.97   | 11.1  | 13.51  |
| mt   | 6.5     | 5.6    | 3.0   | 2.78   | 7.4   | 8.8   | 1.86   | 7.7   | 3.02   |
| il   | 9.6     | 7.7    | 8.5   | 1.37   | 6.5   | 8.8   | 0.76   | 8.7   | 6.54   |
| hm   |         |        |       |        |       | 0.2   |        |       |        |
| ap   | 2.0     | 3.4    | 0.7   | 0.34   | 0.7   | 2.0   |        | 1.0   | 1.01   |
| kp   |         |        |       |        |       |       |        |       |        |
| ns   |         |        |       |        |       |       |        |       |        |
| pf   |         |        |       |        |       |       |        |       |        |
| C    |         |        |       | 6.22   |       |       |        |       |        |
| Q    |         |        |       | 8.40   |       |       |        |       |        |
| $H_2O$ |       |        |       |        |       |       |        |       |        |

spectrographically examined, showed 4,200 ppm Ba, 3,200 ppm Sr, the presence of La, Ti, Y and Zr. The Sr value is much lower than in specimens analyzed from Fogo and Brava; Brava samples have much lower Ba values, Fogo specimens a wide range above and below that of Ilheu Grande. Again we would note the alkaline, undersaturated nature of the plutonics occurring along with volcanics of similar nature and carbonatites.

To date we have 135 igneous rock analyses for the archipelago, divided thus: Fogo 48, S. Vicente 27, Sal 14, Ilheu Grande 10, Maio 20, S. Tiago 5, Sto. Antao 4, Brava 3, Boa Vista 3, S. Nicolau 1. The extreme unevenness of sampling is evident, indicating the caution necessary in assessing matters petrological for the archipelago. Be this as it may, it appears that certain conclusions can be tentatively made.

PART's (1950a) tables of 49 analyses, including published data of BEBIANO (1932), ERMERT (1936) and LACROIX (1934), as well as analyses on DARWIN and CHILD samples, were realized as being insufficient by him, and he felt constrained merely to point out a few matters. Topics which he mentioned included: (a) absence of acidic-type rocks; (b) relative scarcity of intermediate-type rocks; (c) in the basaltic-type rocks, the

Table 57 (continued)

| | 55 | 56 | 57 | 58 | 59 | 60 | 61 | 63 | 64 |
|---|---|---|---|---|---|---|---|---|---|
| or | 36.70 | 0.5 | 13.3 | 3.89 | 3.9 | 33.92 | 31.14 | 38.92 | 57.27 |
| ab | 7.34 | | | | | 16.77 | | 15.72 | 16.77 |
| an | | 12.5 | 14.7 | 13.62 | 5.0 | 0.28 | | | |
| ne | 35.22 | 10.2 | 17.0 | 19.31 | 26.1 | 33.23 | 34.93 | 9.37 | 9.66 |
| lc | | 4;8 | | 10.03 | 13.9 | | 3.05 | | |
| hl | | | | | | 0.59 | 0.59 | | |
| th | 0.57 | | | | | 1.99 | 0.43 | | |
| nc | | | | | | | | | 0.21 |
| ac | 0.92 | | | | | | 9.70 | 9.70 | |
| wo | 5.34 | | | | 0.9 | 1.28 | 2.44 | 2.43 | 2.10 |
| di | 5.40 | 46.8 | 36.0 | 35.75 | 32.4 | 4.91 | 7.41 | 5.19 | |
| en | | | | | | | | | |
| hy | | | | | | | | | |
| fs | | | | | | | | | |
| fo | | | | | | | | | |
| fa | | | | | | | | | |
| shan | | | | | | | | | |
| cs | | | | | | | | | |
| cc | | (0.3) | | | | | | 9.80 | 5.50 |
| ol | | 12.2 | 0.7 | 2.42 | | | | 0.76 | 0.61 |
| mt | 3.02 | 4.7 | 6.7 | 4.64 | 4.9 | 3.71 | 0.46 | 4.64 | 0.70 |
| il | 2.13 | 7.6 | 9.7 | 8.06 | 7.6 | 0.91 | 1.22 | 0.32 | 2.24 |
| hm | 0.48 | | | | | | | | |
| ap | 0.67 | 0.5 | 2.0 | 2.02 | 2.7 | | 0.34 | 1.34 | |
| kp | | | | | | | | | |
| ns | | | | | | | | | |
| pf | | | | | | | | | |
| C | | | | | | | | | 1.33 |
| Q | | | | | | | | | |
| $H_2O$ | | | | | | | | 2.12 | 3.34 |

principal minerals – anorthite, nepheline, magnesium olivine, pyroxene – all have a silica percentage ranging from 43 to 45, almost the same or somewhat higher than that of the rocks containing them; (d) richness in lime, which enters very largely into the abundance of pyroxene and early-formed calcic feldspar when present. This lime-rich feature is thought to be a primitive character, perhaps suggesting some degree of contamination from Mesozoic sediments; (e) adopting a time-sequence of vulcanism, based on BEBIANO, PART remarked on the widespread and fairly uniform nature of the Stage II or ›Main basalts‹ (Early M. Tertiary, as per BEBIANO) whereas the later phase (Stage III, Late Tertiary) is highly localized in type, followed by Stage IV (Recent and Quaternary) where again lavas are widespread and fairly uniform in type.

The Cape Verde archipelago is distinguished from other Macaronesian islands by the total absence of oversaturated rocks, by the paucity in saturated rocks, by the overwhelming role of the undersaturated types. (All writers have stressed these points. However, BEBIANO referred to obsidian exposures at Monte Abrolhal, Boa Vista. Some 2 km distant, near Rocha Preta, the writer (1972) found tonalites and obsidians outcropping. Chemical analyses of two obsidian samples showed water content by

Table 57 (continued)

|      | 65    | 66    | 67    | 68    | 69    | 70    | 71    | 72    |
|------|-------|-------|-------|-------|-------|-------|-------|-------|
| or   | 27.24 | 38.13 | 2.35  | 13.99 |       |       |       | 1.63  |
| ab   | 17.82 | 0.50  | 4.12  | 3.09  |       |       | 4.57  |       |
| an   |       |       | 0.91  | 5.50  | 15.47 | 17.52 | 14.27 | 9.65  |
| ne   | 10.79 | 32.57 | 35.31 | 53.40 | 4.40  | 3.30  | 7.44  | 7.01  |
| lc   |       |       |       |       | 1.30  | 0.74  |       |       |
| hl   |       |       |       |       |       |       |       |       |
| th   |       |       |       |       |       |       |       |       |
| nc   |       |       |       |       |       |       |       |       |
| ac   | 10.63 | 15.80 |       |       |       |       |       |       |
| wo   | 2.37  | 3.77  | 2.73  |       |       |       |       |       |
| di   | 7.29  | 3.33  | 35.36 | 7.74  | 41.42 | 40.34 | 20.83 | 29.25 |
| en   |       |       |       |       |       |       |       |       |
| hy   |       |       |       |       |       |       |       |       |
| fs   |       |       |       |       |       |       |       |       |
| fo   |       |       |       |       |       |       |       |       |
| fa   |       |       |       |       |       |       |       |       |
| shan |       |       |       |       |       |       |       |       |
| cs   |       |       |       |       | 3.27  | 6.46  | 0.81  | 9.66  |
| cc   | 11.40 |       |       |       |       |       |       |       |
| ol   |       |       |       | 0.31  | 5.36  | 4.00  | 10.21 | 8.19  |
| mt   | 4.18  |       |       | 4.08  |       |       | 6.42  | 6.51  |
| il   | 0.61  | 1.42  | 1.09  | 2.91  | 11.07 | 10.48 | 11.23 | 14.26 |
| hm   | 1.60  |       |       | 2.29  | 14.57 | 14.68 | 7.47  | 10.80 |
| ap   | 4.70  |       | 3.90  |       | 0.54  | 0.17  | 10.29 | 0.81  |
| kp   |       | 0.60  | 4.97  | 3.73  |       |       | 5.51  | 0.92  |
| ns   |       | 1.57  |       |       |       |       |       |       |
| pf   |       |       |       | 3.33  | 1.99  | 1.89  |       |       |
| C    |       |       |       |       |       |       |       |       |
| Q    |       |       |       |       |       |       |       |       |
| $H_2O$ | 2.26 | 1.68 | 4.96  | 3.47  | 1.00  | 1.11  | 0.92  | 0.88  |

weight averaging 8.56%, average $SiO_2$ content 54.40%, norm calculations showed a rather low average excess of albite over orthoclase of 4.85, and hence one would perhaps be inclined to refer to the specimens as hydrotachylyte. But even so, this is of interest, for no other glasses have been recorded from the archipelago. The samples may be basaltic glasses, though the low average specific gravity of 2.34 is more in keeping with obsidian.) This is clearly indicated in the isofal indices for Macaronesia, as follows: Cape Verde 130 (Fogo 108), Azores 158, Madeira 143, Canaries 133. (We would further mention that the Cape Verde value is more extreme than that of any of the South Atlantic Islands; MITCHELL-THOMÉ, 1970). There is then a distinct petrologic individuality of the Cape Verde archipelago, and in the entire Atlantic and bordering areas, the only place showing petrographic identity with the Cape Verde islands is the Los archipelago, off the coast of Conakry, République Guinée (LACROIX, 1911). BURRI (1960) also drew some affinities of the Cape Verde rocks with those occurring in coastal Sénégal, and ASSUNCAO (1970) claimed that it is in the Rift area of East Africa that closest petrologic analogies are to be found, and BURRI (op. cit.) also mentioned similarities with the Young Tertiary-Quaternary vulcanism of the Rhenish Highlands.

Table 58                        Chemical analyses, Fogo rocks (ASSUNCAO, MACHADO & SILVA, 1967)

|                    | 1      | 2     | 3      | 4     | 5      | 6     | 7      | 8     | 9     |
|--------------------|--------|-------|--------|-------|--------|-------|--------|-------|-------|
| $SiO_2$            | 41.41  | 42.89 | 41.34  | 41.45 | 41.41  | 41.04 | 41.08  | 42.72 | 41.12 |
| $Al_2O_3$          | 14.67  | 13.30 | 14.58  | 14.23 | 14.05  | 13.73 | 15.31  | 15.69 | 15.68 |
| $Fe_2O_3$          | 6.39   | 5.49  | 5.70   | 5.37  | 6.58   | 5.66  | 5.28   | 5.18  | 6.62  |
| FeO                | 7.06   | 6.80  | 7.20   | 7.55  | 6.76   | 7.64  | 8.28   | 7.13  | 7.05  |
| MnO                | 0.17   | 0.14  | 0.14   | 0.15  | 0.09   | 0.16  | 0.13   | 0.12  | 0.14  |
| MgO                | 8.02   | 7.72  | 7.41   | 7.86  | 9.69   | 8.08  | 7.69   | 6.76  | 6.39  |
| CaO                | 12.92  | 12.55 | 13.03  | 12.67 | 12.75  | 13.32 | 13.18  | 10.53 | 12.92 |
| $Na_2O$            | 3.13   | 3.74  | 3.35   | 3.30  | 2.89   | 3.11  | 2.94   | 3.72  | 3.15  |
| $K_2O$             | 1.83   | 2.24  | 2.05   | 2.07  | 1.75   | 1.79  | 1.85   | 2.42  | 2.05  |
| $TiO_2$            | 3.79   | 3.65  | 4.04   | 3.91  | 3.66   | 4.09  | 3.98   | 3.79  | 4.07  |
| $P_2O_5$           | 0.79   | 0.69  | 0.87   | 0.87  | 0.75   | 0.86  | 0.74   | 0.93  | 0.87  |
| $CO_2$             | --     | --    | --     | --    | --     | --    | --     | --    | --    |
| $H_2O+$            | 0.21   | 0.19  | 0.21   | 0.29  | 0.20   | 0.25  | 0.13   | 0.47  | 0.18  |
| $H_2O-$            | 0.10   | 0.16  | 0.08   | 0.08  | 0.09   | 0.07  | --     | 0.07  | 0.05  |
| Total              | 100.49 | 99.56 | 100.00 | 99.80 | 100.67 | 99.80 | 100.59 | 99.53 | 99.99 |

|                    | 10     | 11    | 12     | 13    | 14     | 15    | 16     | 17    | 18    |
|--------------------|--------|-------|--------|-------|--------|-------|--------|-------|-------|
| $SiO_2$            | 41.93  | 44.30 | 42.37  | 42.64 | 43.16  | 41.67 | 42.21  | 41.89 | 41.37 |
| $Al_2O_3$          | 15.88  | 16.27 | 14.75  | 15.10 | 16.17  | 13.87 | 17.36  | 16.99 | 14.73 |
| $Fe_2O_3$          | 4.05   | 3.25  | 4.33   | 6.95  | 5.51   | 6.10  | 5.08   | 4.77  | 4.74  |
| FeO                | 8.49   | 7.35  | 8.33   | 5.47  | 6.12   | 6.91  | 6.30   | 6.94  | 7.78  |
| MnO                | 0.21   | 0.24  | 0.16   | 0.14  | 0.21   | 0.11  | 0.19   | 0.14  | 0.18  |
| MgO                | 7.11   | 5.49  | 5.74   | 5.84  | 5.27   | 7.66  | 7.33   | 5.74  | 6.02  |
| CaO                | 12.08  | 10.85 | 11.97  | 11.98 | 11.01  | 12.87 | 9.18   | 10.37 | 11.63 |
| $Na_2O$            | 3.41   | 4.27  | 3.93   | 3.76  | 4.74   | 3.51  | 4.83   | 5.00  | 4.42  |
| $K_2O$             | 2.26   | 2.95  | 3.59   | 2.54  | 3.12   | 1.92  | 2.71   | 2.92  | 2.78  |
| $TiO_2$            | 3.95   | 3.41  | 3.86   | 3.78  | 3.56   | 3.93  | 3.62   | 3.79  | 3.87  |
| $P_2O_5$           | 0.88   | 0.86  | 1.09   | 0.88  | 0.96   | 0.60  | 0.86   | 1.15  | 1.65  |
| $CO_2$             | --     | --    | --     | --    | --     | --    | --     | --    | --    |
| $H_2O+$            | 0.16   | 0.24  | 0.16   | 0.31  | 0.19   | 0.23  | 0.37   | 0.02  | 0.26  |
| $H_2O-$            | 0.06   | 0.05  | 0.06   | 0.12  | 0.05   | 0.24  | 0.30   | 0.19  | 0.25  |
| Total              | 100.47 | 99.53 | 100.65 | 99.51 | 100.07 | 99.62 | 100.24 | 99.91 | 99.68 |

*Rocks and Localities of Fogo*
(ASSUNCAO, MACHADO & SILVA, 1967)

(a) Lavas of historical eruptions:

1. Basanite, near Tinteiro, 1769 (?) lava.
2. Basanite, S of Relva, 1785 lava.
3. Basanitoid, S of Relva, 1785 lava.
4. Basanite, lagoa Atras, 1785 lava.
5. Basanitoid, N of Relva, 1799 lava.
6. Ankaramitic basanite, S of Relva, 1847 lava.
7. Basanite, W of Corvo, 1852 lava.
8. Basanitoid, Caldeira da Cha, 1857, lava.
9. Basanite, Cova Matinho, 1857 lava.
10. Basanitoid, Cova Matinho, 1951 lava.
11. Basanitoid, Cha, S side, 1951 lava.

12 Limburgite, Cha, N side, 1951 lava.

(b) Lavas later than caldeira − not historical:

13. Basanitoid, principal crater, N edge.
14. Basanite, lava to SW of Caldeira da Cha.
15. Augitite, Relva lava.
16. Augitite, lagoa Atras lava.
17. Augitite, heteromorph furchitic, Faja dos Mosteiros, scoria.
18. Augitite, heteromorph furchitic, Faja dos Mosteiros, ropy lava.
19. Limburgite, S. Jorge, recent lava.

Table 58 (continued)

| | 19 | 20 | 21 | 22 | 23 | 24 | 25 | 26 | 27 |
|---|---|---|---|---|---|---|---|---|---|
| $SiO_2$ | 41.79 | 41.80 | 43.05 | 42.41 | 41.75 | 41.71 | 42.46 | 42.43 | 37.54 |
| $Al_2O_3$ | 15.21 | 14.92 | 14.72 | 16.57 | 16.55 | 14.42 | 15.77 | 16.42 | 15.33 |
| $Fe_2O_3$ | 3.33 | 5.74 | 6.19 | 5.97 | 5.10 | 4.69 | 6.07 | 5.18 | 11.28 |
| FeO | 7.42 | 7.34 | 5.91 | 5.40 | 7.05 | 7.85 | 5.26 | 7.48 | 0.98 |
| MnO | 0.12 | 0.14 | 0.17 | 0.16 | 0.12 | 0.12 | 0.18 | 0.14 | 0.14 |
| MgO | 12.02 | 6.97 | 8.05 | 5.13 | 6.99 | 7.02 | 6.99 | 8.85 | 5.41 |
| CaO | 10.88 | 10.76 | 12.34 | 11.52 | 10.60 | 11.95 | 11.40 | 9.80 | 14.24 |
| $Na_2O$ | 3.00 | 4.38 | 3.31 | 4.58 | 4.00 | 3.96 | 4.24 | 3.59 | 5.50 |
| $K_2O$ | 1.94 | 2.45 | 1.64 | 2.80 | 2.66 | 2.63 | 2.43 | 2.14 | 1.90 |
| $TiO_2$ | 3.06 | 3.92 | 2.79 | 3.71 | 4.04 | 4.20 | 3.55 | 3.62 | 3.86 |
| $P_2O_5$ | 0.53 | 1.16 | 0.60 | 1.59 | 0.88 | 1.03 | 0.89 | 0.74 | 1.21 |
| $CO_2$ | -- | -- | -- | -- | -- | -- | -- | -- | 0.27 |
| $H_2O+$ | 0.26 | 0.10 | 1.26 | 0.12 | 0.12 | 0.03 | 0.35 | 0.12 | 1.60 |
| $H_2O-$ | 0.06 | 0.08 | 0.34 | 0.13 | 0.21 | 0.13 | 0.21 | 0.19 | 0.94 |
| Total | 99.62 | 99.76 | 100.37 | 100.09 | 100.07 | 99.74 | 99.80 | 100.70 | 100.20 |

| | 28 | 29 | 30 | 31 | 32 | 33 | 34 | 35 | 36 |
|---|---|---|---|---|---|---|---|---|---|
| $SiO_2$ | 41.94 | 42.55 | 38.25 | 46.25 | 42.72 | 43.57 | 42.72 | 43.32 | 42.03 |
| $Al_2O_3$ | 16.67 | 17.95 | 14.82 | 19.03 | 16.64 | 16.43 | 16.43 | 17.18 | 15.36 |
| $Fe_2O_3$ | 4.01 | 5.27 | 7.13 | 4.81 | 5.86 | 4.17 | 7.35 | 4.58 | 6.88 |
| FeO | 6.38 | 3.67 | 4.39 | 3.24 | 5.80 | 7.38 | 4.46 | 7.77 | 5.65 |
| MnO | 0.15 | 0.21 | 0.20 | 0.21 | 0.23 | 0.11 | 0.19 | 0.20 | 0.12 |
| MgO | 4.46 | 2.90 | 4.43 | 2.09 | 5.15 | 5.18 | 6.72 | 6.19 | 6.01 |
| CaO | 10.56 | 9.56 | 11.76 | 8.15 | 10.63 | 11.44 | 9.97 | 10.28 | 12.08 |
| $Na_2O$ | 6.00 | 7.60 | 5.14 | 6.47 | 4.47 | 4.88 | 4.33 | 3.54 | 4.03 |
| $K_2O$ | 0.87 | 4.54 | 3.98 | 3.71 | 3.07 | 2.14 | 2.49 | 2.56 | 2.49 |
| $TiO_2$ | 3.50 | 2.73 | 3.25 | 2.49 | 3.80 | 3.22 | 2.58 | 3.43 | 3.87 |
| $P_2O_5$ | 1.41 | 0.86 | 1.60 | 0.79 | 1.15 | 0.56 | 0.77 | 0.66 | 0.84 |
| $CO_2$ | 0.31 | 0.32 | 0.40 | -- | -- | -- | -- | -- | -- |
| $H_2O+$ | 2.45 | 0.91 | 2.89 | 1.69 | 0.06 | 0.39 | 1.43 | 0.20 | 0.09 |
| $H_2O-$ | 0.92 | 0.46 | 1.73 | 1.00 | 0.29 | 0.30 | 0.11 | 0.21 | 0.10 |
| Total | 99.63 | 99.53 (a) | 99.97 (b) | 99.93 | 99.57 | 99.77 | 100.55 | 100.12 | 99.55 |

(a) 0.54 $SO_3$, Total 100.07.            (b) 0.54 $SO_3$, Total 100.51.

20. Limburgite, Achada Furna, W branch, recent lava.
21. Limburgite, lava from "chimney", Achada Furna.
22. Manchurite, Dacabalaio, W branch, recent lava.
23. Augitite, Decabalaio, E branch, recent lava.
24. Limburgite, Figueira Pavao, W branch, recent lava.
25. Basanite, Figueira Pavao, E branch, recent lava.
26. Basanitoid, N of Cova Figueira, recent lava.

(c) Lavas and hypabyssals prior to caldeira:

27. Haüynitic nephelinite, caldeira edge, N side.
28. Manchurite, Bordeira, S side.
29. Nephelinite, Bordeira, S side.
30. Haüynitic nephelinite, Bordeira, S side.
31. Micro-essexite (intra-vulcanic? ), Rib. Ilheu, near Monte Portel.
32. Basanitoid (dyke? ), beach escarpment, S. Felipe.
33. Basanitoid, lava by road, Fonte Aleixo.
34. Basanite, lava, S of Monte Paragem.

Table 58 (continued)

|                  | 37    | 38    | 39    | 40    | 41     | 42    | 43    |
|------------------|-------|-------|-------|-------|--------|-------|-------|
| $SiO_2$          | 41.49 | 35.53 | 36.30 | 35.75 | 31.67  | 47.06 | 30.36 |
| $Al_2O_3$        | 15.45 | 13.39 | 14.46 | 10.43 | 12.69  | 15.90 | 8.76  |
| $Fe_2O_3$        | 5.26  | 6.92  | 7.21  | 10.49 | 10.37  | 5.65  | 12.00 |
| FeO              | 1.87  | 3.60  | 4.54  | 3.36  | 1.21   | 4.14  | 1.00  |
| MnO              | 0.13  | 0.17  | 0.18  | 0.16  | 0.22   | 0.19  | 0.23  |
| MgO              | 3.91  | 4.98  | 4.96  | 6.05  | 5.63   | 6.26  | 7.20  |
| CaO              | 12.15 | 17.00 | 12.47 | 16.26 | 15.13  | 10.87 | 15.00 |
| $Na_2O$          | 3.72  | 2.49  | 2.82  | 2.38  | 0.60   | 3.82  | 1.00  |
| $K_2O$           | 6.19  | 1.70  | 2.50  | 1.17  | 2.66   | 1.01  | 1.61  |
| $TiO_2$          | 1.56  | 3.86  | 4.55  | 3.94  | 4.12   | 1.22  | 3.64  |
| $P_2O_5$         | 0.78  | 1.19  | 1.20  | 0.48  | 1.77   | 0.08  | 0.72  |
| $CO_2$           | --    | 2.40  | 3.64  | 4.74  | 6.17   | --    | 10.08 |
| $H_2O+$          | 6.40  | 4.88  | 2.98  | 2.67  | 3.86   | 2.88  | 3.34  |
| $H_2O-$          | 0.80  | 1.62  | 1.97  | 1.69  | 4.06   | 0.61  | 4.21  |
| Total            | 99.71 | 99.73 | 99.78 | 99.57 | 100.16 | 99.69 | 99.35 |
|                  |       |       |       |       |        |       | (c)   |

(c) 0.24 $SO_3$, Total 99.59.

35. Doleritic basanitoid, lava, N of Monte Paragem.
36. Limburgite, augititic tendency, lava, S of Cova Figueira.

(d) Siliceous basement rocks:

37. Melteigite, ijolitic tendency, carbonatite veinlets, Rib. Pico.
38. Ijolite, heteromorph mafraite, carbonatite vein, Rib. Pico.

39. Basanitic lava, veinlets in basement, R. Trindade.
40. Basanitic lava, non-basement vein, R. Trindade.
41. Silico-carbonatite lava, non-basement vein, R. Trindade.
42. Rock showing micro-theralitic tendency, R. Trindade.
43. Silico-carbonatitic rock, R. Trindade.

Table 59    Spectrographic analyses, carbonatite samples from Ilheu Grande, Fogo and Brava, Cape Verde Islands (BARROS, 1968)

|                           | Ba (ppm)          | Sr (ppm)             | La, Ti, Y       | Zr              |
|---------------------------|-------------------|----------------------|-----------------|-----------------|
| Ilheu Grande              | 4200 (a)          | 3200 (b)             | Present (c)     | Present (c)     |
| Fogo (various samples)    | 520 to > 6000     | 4700 to 13,400       | Present         | ------          |
| Brava (various sample)    | 490 to 1470       | 4400 to 11,200       | Present         | ------          |

(a) Semi-quantitative spectrographic doseage with Hilger spectograph of wide dispersion.
(b) Doseage with atomic absorption spectograph, Perkin-Elmer 290 B.
(c) Qualitative spectrograph investigation with Hilger spectrograph of wide dispersion.

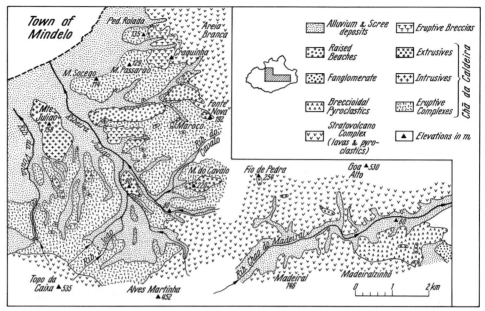

Fig. 83. Geology of Ribeira Juliao – Ribeira Madeiral region, S. Vicente, Cape Verde Islands. (Modified after SERRALHEIRO, 1966).

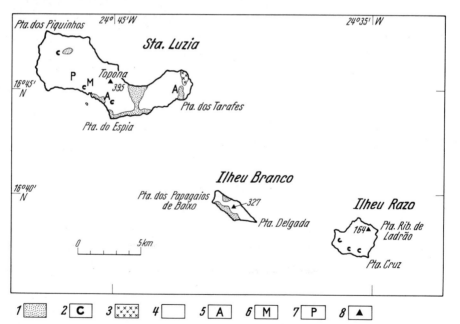

Fig. 84. Geological map of Sta. Luzia and Ilhaus Branco and Razo. 1: Dunes. 2: Tertiary sediments. 3: Dolerites. 4: Basalts, with breccias, lapilli, tuffs. 5: Andesites. 6: Nepheline-monozites, tinguaites. 7: Phonolites. 8: Peaks. (Modified after BEBIANO, 1932).

BURRI (1960) made a petrochemical study on the basis of 64 chemical analyses available to him then. Since that time we have published data on NIGGLI parameters of 23 further samples by ASSUNCAO & CANILHO (1968) and BARROS (1968) relating to S. Vicente and Ilheu Grande respectively, RITTMANN values for 13 samples from S. Vicente. BURRI grouped the Cape Verde rocks into four divisions, as follows:

| | |
|---|---|
| Series Ia | »Basaltic-trachytic«.<br>$Si^{\circ} > 0.79$<br>al = fm 32<br>si 154 |
| Series Ib | »Basaltic-Phonolitic«<br>$0.76 > Si^{\circ} > 0.65$<br>al = fm 29<br>si 126 |
| Series II | Foidreich (Feldspathoidal)<br>$0.63 > Si^{\circ} > 0.52$<br>al = fm 27<br>si 112 |
| Series III | Lowest-silicified Melilite Rocks.<br>$0.52 > Si^{\circ}$<br>al = fm ca. 25 (extrapolated)<br>si ca. 100 (extrapolated) |

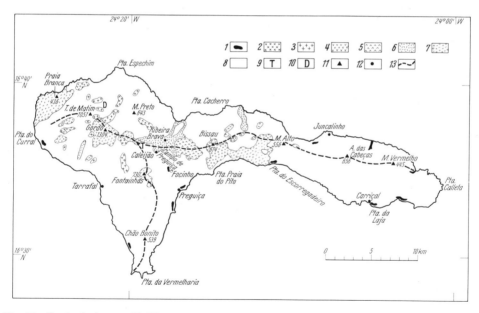

Fig. 85. Geological map of S. Nicolau. 1: Fossiliferous Tertiary sediments. 2: Trachytes. 3: Andesites. 4: Essexites. 5: Phonolites, tinguaites. 6: Vila Complex – lavas with many trachyte and phonolite dykes. 7: Scoria, lapilli, tuffs. 8: Basalts, with agglomerates, breccias, lapilli, tuffs. 9: Tephrites. 10: Diorites. 11: Peaks. 12: Villages. 13: Topographic axes. (Modified after BEBIANO, 1932).

Tables 54–57 show how the S. Vicente and Ilheu Grande newer analyses fit into this classification.

ASSUNÇAO (1968) remarked that the quasi-total absence of calc-alk rocks in the islands indicated that assimilation could not have occurred from sialic magmatic material, whereas, on the other hand, such assimilation is indeed responsible in other Atlantic island rocks, e. g. Ascension (MITCHELL-THOMÉ, 1970).

Of interest is the palagonite/submarine lavas-nephelinitic syenites and associated

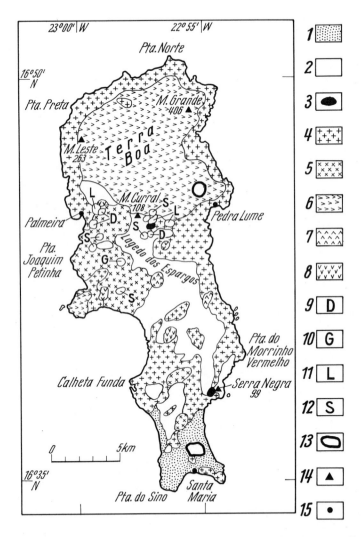

Fig. 86. Geological map of Sal. 1: Dunes. 2: Tertiary-Quaternary sediments. 3: Metamorphosed limestones. 4: Basalts, with limburgites. 5: Doleritic basalts. 6: Basaltic lavas and tuffs. 7: Tinguaites. 8: Phonolites. 9: Diorites. 10: Gabbros. 11: Dolerites. 12: Syenites, monzonites. 13: Salinas. 14: Peaks. 15: Villages. (Modified after BEBIANO, 1932).

rocks – carbonatite distribution within Fogo, Brava, Ilheus Secos and S. Tiago (ASSUNÇAO, MACHADO & GOMES, 1965; MACHADO & ASSUNÇAO, 1965; MACHADO, LEME & MONJARDINO 1967; ALVES et al., 1972). In the three first-mentioned islands these display a roughly concentric pattern, such association being absent elsewhere in the archipelago. Seas between Brava-Secos and Fogo exceed 1,000 m in depth, and if these rock associations were once all united, as seems probable, then vertical movements of this order are postulate, indeed a most significant amount. (On the basis of gravimetric

Table **60**      Spectrographic analyses of carbonatites from S. Tiago (in ppm.) (ALVES et al., 1972)

| Sample No. | | Ba | Sr | Y | Nb | Observation |
|---|---|---|---|---|---|---|
| S 586 | A | 150 | 9600 | < 100 | 410 | Essential calcite; biotite, dolomite, pyro- |
|  | B | 190 | 11000 | < 100 | 300 | chlore. Late silicification. |
|  | Aver. | 170 | 10300 | < 100 | 355 | |
| S 593 | A | 120 | 4300 | < 100 | < 300 | Breccioidal carbonatites, essentially of |
|  | B | 100 | 2400 | < 100 | 450 | calcite. |
|  | Aver. | 100 | 3385 | < 100 | ~ 375 | |
| S 594 | A | 240 | 16800 | 180 | 630 | Essential calcite; dolomite accessory, |
|  | B | 250 | 15200 | 210 | 520 | abundant apatite. |
|  | Aver. | 245 | 16000 | 195 | 575 | |
| S 688 | A1 + A2 | 310 | 11800 | 110 | 480 | Calcite, apatite essential; biotite, clino- |
|  | B1+B2 | 350 | 11800 | 400 | < 300 | amphibole and pyroxene, as accessories. |
|  | Aver. | 330 | 11800 | ~ 100 | ~ 390 | |
| S 691 | A | 480 | 3030 | < 100 | < 300 | Apatitic sovite, with anquerite and dolo- |
|  | B | 250 | 2970 | < 100 | < 300 | mite. Calcite much scarcer than in above |
|  | Aver. | 365 | 3000 | < 100 | < 300 | samples. |
| S 692 | A | 1120 | 10200 | < 100 | 550 | Essential calcite; apatite, biotite, opaque |
|  | B | 980 | 12100 | < 100 | < 300 | minerals, pyrochlore and secondary quartz. |
|  | Aver. | 1050 | 11150 | < 100 | ~ 425 | |
| S 694 | A | 700 | 19700 | < 100 | < 300 | Essential calcite; much apatite and mica, |
|  | B | 620 | 18000 | < 100 | < 300 | lesser amounts of amphiboles, pyroxenes, |
|  | Aver. | 660 | 18850 | < 100 | < 300 | as little barytes. |
| S 695 | A | 1120 | 2830 | 170 | < 300 | |
|  | B | 1220 | 3630 | 230 | < 300 | Identical to S 692. |
|  | Aver. | 1170 | 3230 | 200 | < 300 | |
| S 867 | A | 450 | 20300 | 110 | < 300 | |
|  | B | 390 | 27300 | 140 | 330 | Essential calcite and apatite. |
|  | Aver. | 420 | 23800 | 125 | ~ 315 | |
| S 869 | A1 + A2 | 750 | 11000 | < 100 | < 300 | Essential calcite and apatite; abundant bio- |
|  | B | 1050 | 15700 | 150 | < 300 | tite; pyroxene partially, substituted by |
|  | Aver. | 900 | 13350 | ~ 125 | < 300 | calcite. |
| S 870 | A | 730 | 9300 | 100 | < 300 | Calcite, apatite, biotite essential; dolomite, |
|  | B | 1870 | 10000 | 130 | 590 | anquerite scarce; quartz and clino-amphibole |
|  | Aver. | 1300 | 9650 | 115 | ~ 445 | interstitial. |

Table 61     Chemical analyses and spectrographic trace elements (in ppm.) of carbonatites from Fogo (ASSUNCAO, MACHADO & GOMES, 1965)

|         |     | 1 | 2 | 3 |
|---------|-----|------|------|------|
| $SiO_2$   |     | 0.04 | 3.36 | 3.27 |
| $Al_2O_3$ |     | 0.04 | 0.15 | 0.09 |
| $Fe_2O_3$ |     | 0.83 | 2.15 | 2.37 |
| FeO     |     | 0.50 | 0.21 | 0.64 |
| MnO     |     | 0.46 | 0.40 | 0.13 |
| MgO     |     | 1.44 | 0.56 | 0.98 |
| CaO     | (a) | 52.85 | 50.53 | 50.88 |
| $Na_2O$   |     | 0.43 | 0.38 | 0.51 |
| $K_2O$    |     | 0.07 | 0.05 | 0.27 |
| $TiO_2$   |     | 0.12 | 0.04 | 0.30 |
| $P_2O_5$  |     | 0.93 | 1.77 | 3.19 |
| $CO_2$    |     | 41.49 | 39.42 | 36.34 |
| $H_2O+$   |     | 0.19 | 0.43 | 0.44 |
| $H_2O-$   |     | 0.15 | 0.18 | 0.17 |
| Total   |     | 99.56 | 99.63 | 99.58 |
| Ba      |     | 1.800 | 2.000 | 520 |
| Sr      |     | 13.400 | 9.600 | 9.500 |
| Nb      | (b) |       |       |       |
| La      | (c) | 1.300 | 600? | 600? |
| Y       | (d) | 200? | 200? | 200? |

(a) Incl. BaO and SrO
(b) Value below limit of sensitivity – ca. 600 ppm.
(c) Limit of sensitivity ca. 600 ppm.
(d) Limit of sensitivity ca. 200 ppm.

1. Ribeira da Trindade, near Monte Barro.
2. Ditto.
3. Ribeira do Pico, near Monte Almada.

studies, MENDES-VICTOR (1970) believed there was »une structure cachée« between Fogo-Brava, and his maps of the Bouguer, regional and residual anomalies of these two islands lend strong support to the concept of a major disturbance here.) We would also mention that carbonatites are strongly suspected in S. Vicente and Sal. Table 60 shows spectrographic analyses of some S. Tiago carbonatites, Table 61 for Fogo carbonatites.

In recent times, the Belgians (KLERKX et al, 1974; PAEPE et al., 1974) have shown interest in the Cape Verde Islands, especially Maio. In the first paper, analyses were made of Sr isotopic compositions and concentrations in K, Rb and Sr. The $Sr^{87}/Sr^{86}$ ratios, ranging from 0.7029 to 0.7033 (Table 62) signify a comagnatic origin for the Kainozoic volcanics. As there is lacking a correlation between the Sr isotopic composition and K-content of the lavas, this would imply that those lavas having a high $K_2O/K_2O + Na_2O$ ratio are developed via differentiation at shallow depth from a primary magma. The authors point out that the majority of values determined for other oceanic islands show values of Sr isotopic composition which are definitely higher than those obtained from Cape Verde Islands. It was their view that this primary magma for the archipelago was of nephelinitic type formed as a result of partial melting of only a small fraction of undepleted Mantle peridotite under hydrous conditions; phlogopite

Table 62        Chemical analyses, norms and Rb, Sr and K contents of some Cape Verde rocks (KLERKX, DEUTSCH & PAEPE, 1974)

| | 1 | 2 | 3 | 4 | 5 | 6 | 7 | 8 | 9 | 10 |
|---|---|---|---|---|---|---|---|---|---|---|
| $SiO_2$ | 38.86 | 37.11 | 37.20 | 43.50 | 45.24 | 46.18 | 54.09 | 42.69 | 44.42 | 54.17 |
| $Al_2O_3$ | 8.98 | 9.91 | 11.24 | 12.63 | 16.56 | 16.90 | 21.92 | 14.76 | 13.23 | 22.30 |
| $Fe_2O_3$ | 4.92 | 4.89 | 5.03 | 2.23 | 3.80 | 5.19 | 2.25 | 3.54 | 3.43 | 0.58 |
| FeO | 6.28 | 6.35 | 6.72 | 9.92 | 7.33 | 4.95 | 0.84 | 7.47 | 7.57 | 1.62 |
| MnO | 0.19 | 0.20 | 0.20 | 0.18 | 0.23 | 0.22 | 0.14 | 0.20 | 0.12 | 0.06 |
| MgO | 14.25 | 14.01 | 11.90 | 9.33 | 4.12 | 4.12 | 0.45 | 5.51 | 7.59 | 0.32 |
| CaO | 17.20 | 15.44 | 15.04 | 11.67 | 9.40 | 8.42 | 2.62 | 11.54 | 11.97 | 1.44 |
| $Na_2O$ | 2.85 | 3.24 | 3.03 | 2.46 | 4.55 | 3.94 | 9.39 | 5.34 | 3.02 | 7.63 |
| $K_2O$ | 1.12 | 0.72 | 1.32 | 1.58 | 1.87 | 2.23 | 6.27 | 2.21 | 2.44 | 8.62 |
| $TiO_2$ | 3.30 | 2.64 | 3.50 | 3.67 | 3.20 | 3.23 | 0.69 | 4.24 | 3.52 | 0.62 |
| $P_2O_5$ | 1.29 | 1.33 | 1.41 | 0.56 | 1.41 | 1.33 | 0.05 | 1.01 | 0.24 | 0.05 |
| $H_2O+$ | 1.60 | 2.45 | 2.20 | 1.20 | 1.30 | 1.75 | 0.75 | 1.15 | 1.65 | 1.80 |
| $H_2O-$ | 0.32 | 0.96 | 0.60 | 0.70 | 0.20 | 1.00 | 0.10 | 0.10 | 0.10 | 0.80 |
| Total | 99.16 | 99.25 | 99.29 | 99.63 | 99.21 | 99.46 | 99.56 | 99.76 | 99.26 | 100.01 |
| Q | | | | | | | | | | |
| Or | | | | 9.34 | 11.05 | 13.18 | 37.05 | 13.06 | 14.42 | 50.94 |
| Ab | | | | 8.09 | 23.44 | 30.23 | 17.69 | 2.96 | 4.17 | 7.56 |
| An | 8.40 | 10.37 | 13.17 | 18.75 | 19.24 | 21.84 | | 9.78 | 15.34 | 1.14 |
| Lc | 5.19 | 3.34 | 6.12 | | | | | | | |
| Ne | 13.06 | 14.85 | 13.89 | 6.89 | 8.16 | 1.68 | 32.59 | 22.88 | 11.59 | 30.88 |
| Ac | | | | | | | 1.42 | | | |
| Di | 22.83 | 25.60 | 25.93 | 28.66 | 14.76 | 8.76 | 2.42 | 32.69 | 33.95 | 4.70 |
| Hy | | | | | | | | | | |
| Ol | 19.18 | 18.75 | 14.32 | 14.49 | 6.21 | 4.35 | | 1.62 | 5.93 | |
| Ln | 12.19 | 7.74 | 5.96 | | | | | | | |
| He | | | | | | 0.15 | 0.96 | | | |
| Mt | 7.13 | 7.09 | 7.29 | 3.23 | 5.51 | 7.31 | 1.16 | 5.13 | 4.97 | 0.84 |
| Il | 6.27 | 5.01 | 6.65 | 6.97 | 6.08 | 6.13 | 1.31 | 8.05 | 6.69 | 1.18 |
| Ap | 2.99 | 3.08 | 3.27 | 1.30 | 3.27 | 3.08 | 0.12 | 2.34 | 0.56 | 0.12 |
| Rb ppm | 29 | 19 | 38 | 34 | 54 | 56 | 191 | 53 | 54 | 181 |
| Sr ppm | 1265 | 1342 | 1457 | 714 | 1364 | 1252 | 1166 | 1167 | 1159 | 705 |
| $Sr_{87}/Sr_{86}$ | 0.7031 | 0.7032 | 0.7032 | 0.7029 | 0.7030 | 0.7033 | 0.7032 | 0.7031 | 0.7033 | 0.7029 |
| $Rb/Sr.10^{-2}$ | 2.3 | 1.4 | 2.6 | 4.8 | 4.0 | 4.5 | 16.4 | 4.5 | 4.7 | 25.7 |
| %K | 0.46 | 0.30 | 0.55 | 0.65 | 0.77 | 0.92 | 2.59 | 0.91 | 1.01 | 3.56 |
| K/Rb | 159 | 158 | 145 | 191 | 143 | 164 | 136 | 172 | 187 | 197 |

*Rocks and Localities*

1. Porphyritic melilite-olivine-nephelinite, flow. Monte Batalha, Maio.
2. Ditto, Ponta Preta, Maio.
3. Porphyritic olivine-nephelinite, flow. Pedra Lume, Sal.
4. Porphyritic mela-olivine-nepheline-phonotephrite, dyke. Road from Mindelo to Viana, N of Madeiral, S. Vicente.
5. Nepheline-phonotephrite, dyke. N of Sta. Maria, Sal.
6. Olivine-nepheline-mugearite, dyke. N of Sta, Maria, Sal.
7. Highly porphyritic nepheline-phonolite, small intrusion. W of Morro das Pedras, Sal.
8. Theralite, small intrusion. S of Monte Juliao, S. Vicente.
9. Essexite, dyke. N of Figueira Seca, Maio.
10. Nepheline-syenite, small intrusion. Monte Vermelho, Maio.

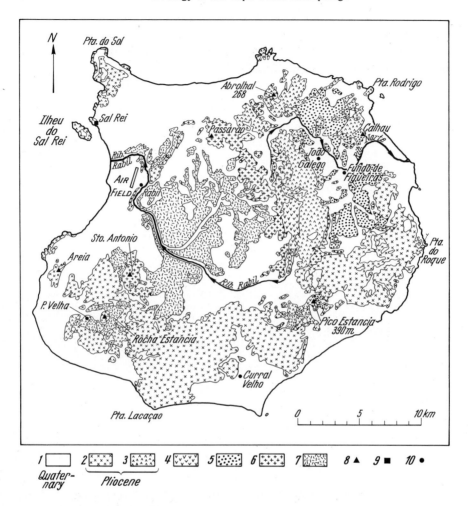

Fig. 87. Geological map of Boa Vista. 1: Alluvium, beach and dune sands, marine terrace deposits, pyroclastic cones, of Pleistocene and Holocene age. 2: Lava flows, pillow lavas, of basaltic type, Chao de Calheta Formation. Also calcarenites and fossiliferous limestones. 3: "Chimneys", craters, breccioidal flows, tuffs, ignimbrites, of phonolitic type, also conglomerates, Pico Forcado Formation. 4: Lava flows with breccias and ignimbrites, of phonolitic type, M. Cacador Formation. 5: Pyroclastics, dykes, flows with inclusions of carbonatite and fluorite, of basaltic type, Fundo de Figueiras Formation. 6: Dykes, flows, breccias and ignimbrites, of phonolitic type, M. Passarao Formation. 7: Conglomerates, syenites, nepheline-syenites, phonolites, as "chimneys", dykes, breccias, Old Internal Complex. 8: Peaks. 9: Capital. 10: Villages. (Modified after SERRALHEIRO et al., 1974).

representing this hydrous phase. The low Rb/Sr ratio of such a magma, resulting from the high Sr content, implies that in the deeper regions of the Mantle where the nephelinitic magma develops, the Rb/Sr ratio is lower than in the upper zones thereof.

In Maio, the authors of the second paper have concentrated on the submarine volcanics – pillow lavas, pillow breccias, hyaloclastites, specific samples being collected from the S of the island. The rocks studied included both basalts and greenstones (Table 63), the latter showing a greenschist facies character. In the basalts the olivine is entirely replaced by such alteration products as chlorites, calcite, serpentines, hematite,

Table 63    Chemical composition of basalts from the oldest pillow formation of Maio (Nos. 4−7, greenstones) and trace element contents (in ppm.) of same samples (PAEPE, KLERKX, HERTOGEN & PLINKE, 1974)

|  | 1 | 2 | 3 | 4 | 5 | 6 | 7 |
|---|---|---|---|---|---|---|---|
| $SiO_2$ | 48.32 | 48.76 | 48.21 | 49.79 | 45.22 | 49.73 | 52.34 |
| $TiO_2$ | 1.28 | 1.21 | 1.18 | 1.47 | 1.47 | 1.38 | 1.30 |
| $Al_2O_3$ | 13.90 | 14.02 | 14.75 | 14.69 | 13.15 | 13.66 | 13.52 |
| $Fe_2O_3$ | 4.18 | 3.97 | 1.48 | 3.92 | 7.00 | 4.59 | 3.79 |
| FeO | 6.60 | 7.28 | 7.83 | 7.11 | 5.28 | 6.30 | 4.84 |
| MnO | 0.17 | 0.19 | 0.15 | 0.12 | 0.17 | 0.19 | 0.15 |
| MgO | 7.64 | 7.91 | 6.69 | 5.33 | 5.18 | 4.68 | 4.06 |
| CaO | 11.66 | 10.49 | 11.51 | 10.81 | 11.26 | 12.48 | 9.93 |
| $Na_2O$ | 2.40 | 3.05 | 3.17 | 3.88 | 4.52 | 4.09 | 5.13 |
| $K_2O$ | 0.09 | 0.15 | 0.54 | 0.50 | 0.50 | 0.48 | 0.26 |
| $H_2O+$ | 1.32 | 2.55 | 2.91 | 1.58 | 5.18 | 2.13 | 3.23 |
| $H_2O-$ | 1.46 | 0.85 | 0.65 | 0.35 | 0.70 | 0.35 | 0.70 |
| $P_2O_5$ | 0.12 | 0.10 | 0.08 | 0.12 | 0.16 | 0.15 | 0.12 |
| Total | 99.14 | 100.53 | 99.15 | 99.67 | 99.79 | 100.21 | 99.37 |
| La | 2.2 | 2.0 | 1.9 | 2.5 |  | 2.6 |  |
| Ce | 5.9 | 7.0 | 5.7 | 8.1 |  | 7.5 |  |
| Nd | 7.8 | 8.0 | 6.2 | 9.0 |  | 9.0 |  |
| Sm | 2.8 | 2.7 | 2.6 | 3.3 |  | 3.1 |  |
| Eu | 1.05 | 1.02 | 1.01 | 1.24 |  | 1.18 |  |
| Tb | 0.77 | 0.75 | 0.67 | 0.81 |  | 0.82 |  |
| Tm | 0.45 | 0.47 | 0.40 | 0.50 |  | 0.43 |  |
| Yb | 3.2 | 3.2 | 3.0 | 3.6 |  | 3.4 |  |
| Lu | 0.54 | 0.55 | 0.49 | 0.56 |  | 0.54 |  |
| Sc | 47.4 | 47.2 | 46.0 | 46.3 |  | 43.7 |  |
| Co | 48.2 | 48.6 | 46.4 | 35.5 |  | 35.7 |  |
| Hf | 1.96 | 1.88 | 1.80 | 2.25 |  | 2.09 |  |
| Cr | 213 | 207 | 235 | 229 |  | 222 |  |
| Sr |  | 400 | 309 | 216 |  | 449 |  |
| Cu |  | 147 | 137 | 113 |  | 154 |  |

1. Exposures in valley-heads of two easterly ephemeral tributaries located along middle course of Rib. do Morro.
2. Ditto.
3. Cliff-face S of D. Joao, ca. 500 m E of mouth of Rib. D. Joao.
4. Cliff-face, 300 m W of mouth of Rib. D. Joao.
5, 6, 7. Cliff-face ca. 500 m W of mouth of Rib. D. Joao.

opaque iron ore. The greenstones show a thin glassy crust, interior to which is a variolitic zone and a massive core forming the bulk of the pillows (Table 64). The prevalence of abundant calcic plagioclase phenocrysts and the presence of a Ti-poor subcalcic augite has not previously been remarked upon samples studied from the island. $P_2O_5$ and $TiO_2$ values show scarce any effects of low-grade metamorphism or incipient weathering, and further these samples show considerably lower $TiO_2$ and $P_2O_5$ contents than in any previously determined Maio samples. These writers note expecially the constancy of $TiO_2$ and $P_2O_5$ contents from the cores and chilled margins of the pillows (Table 64), which confirms that these two major ingredients are throughout the most diagnostic features for distinguishing those basalts with tholeiitic affinities and those with alkaline tendencies, as varying cooling conditions are not related to considerable concentration gradients as solidification of the pillows takes place. These chemical data for the old (L. Cretaceous and perhaps older) pillow lavas then indicate the olivine-tholeiite composition of these Maio rocks, and also indicate a similarity to oceanic tholeiitic basalts.

Much more work has been done on the igneous rocks of the Canary Islands than those of Cape Verde, and hence in the former the appreciation of various units, compositions and structures take a more prominent place in geological thinking. This applies especially to a basal complex, much written about and discussed for the former archipelago, but treated rather ›en passant‹ for the Cape Verde Islands.

Table 64      Chemical composition of the core (1), the variolitic zone (2) and the glassy crust (3) of basaltic pillow lavas belonging to the oldest pillow formation of Maio, and trace element contents (in ppm.) (PAEPE, KLERKX, HERTOGEN % PLINKE, 1974)

| | 1 | 2 | 3 | | 1 | 2 | 3 |
|---|---|---|---|---|---|---|---|
| $SiO_2$ | 49.73 | 50.32 | 40.11 | La | 2.6 | 2.8 | 3.1 |
| $TiO_2$ | 1.38 | 1.53 | 1.53 | Ce | 7.5 | 8.8 | 9.0 |
| $Al_2O_3$ | 13.66 | 15.51 | 13.91 | Nd | 9.0 | 10.5 | 9.6 |
| $Fe_2O_3$ | 4.59 | 3.52 | 5.09 | Sm | 3.1 | 3.4 | 3.6 |
| FeO | 6.30 | 5.64 | 10.08 | Eu | 1.18 | 1.26 | 1.33 |
| MnO | 0.19 | 0.15 | 0.20 | Tb | 0.83 | 0.85 | 0.93 |
| MgO | 4.68 | 4.53 | 11.59 | Tm | 0.43 | 0.47 | 0.50 |
| CaO | 12.48 | 9.67 | 5.21 | Yb | 3.4 | 3.7 | 3.5 |
| $Na_2O$ | 4.09 | 4.63 | 1.51 | Lu | 0.54 | 0.60 | 0.52 |
| $K_2O$ | 0.48 | 1.19 | 6.49 | Sc | 43.7 | 47.6 | 47.9 |
| $H_2O+$ | 2.13 | 2.42 | 3.77 | Co | 35.7 | 51.9 | 46.8 |
| $H_2O-$ | 0.35 | 0.40 | 1.05 | Hf | 2.09 | 2.35 | 2.46 |
| $P_2O_5$ | 0.15 | 0.15 | 0.17 | Cr | 222 | 233 | 233 |
| | | | | Sr | 449 | 494 | 287 |
| Total | 100.21 | 99.66 | 100.70 | Cu | 154 | 137 | 28 |

Fig. 88. Geological map of Ilha de Maio. 1: Holocene – Alluvium beach sands, dunes, pebbles, etc. 2: Pleistocene - old beaches, fossil, dunes. 3: Neogene (Miocene?) – conglomerates and breccias. 4: Palaeogene – Pedro Vaz conglomerate. 5: U.–M. Cretaceous – shales, clays, shaley limestones. 6: L. Cretaceous – compact fossiliferous limestones, with silex layers, passing shaley limestones at top. 7: U. Jurassic? – compact limestones with silex layers. 8: U. Jurassic? – shale-limestone-eruptives complex and crystallized limestones. 9: Undiff. Mesozoic (U. Juras.? and

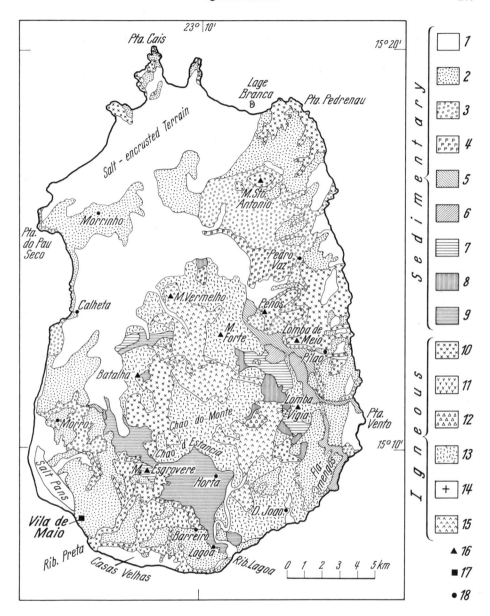

L. Cret.) – shale-limestone-eruptives complex, compact limestones with shale and silex. 10: Anka-ratrites, basanites, nephelinites, etc. of 4 th lava phase, Pliocene, 11: Subaerial and submarine volcanics – nephelinites, limburgites, augitites of 3 rd lava phase, Palaeogene. 12: Eruptive breccias, U. and L. Cret. ?. 13: Submarine lavas – basanites, etindites, basanitoids of 2 nd and 1 st lava phase, U. and L. Cret. ?. 14: Feldspathoidal syenites and fine-grained intrusives, U. Cret. ?. 15: Essexite, M. Cret. 16: Peaks. 17: Capital. 18: Villages. (Modified after SERRALHEIRO, 1970).

The concept of a plutonic basement had been recognized by earlier scholars such as DOELTER (1882), GAGEL (1910), BERGT (1913) – the ›Tiefengesteine‹ concept – but to these men and some others later, this basement was thought to represent Precambrian and/or Palaeozoic. BEBIANO challenged this age concept though not the concept of a basement; and this view has prevailed.

Plutonics, as outcrops, dykes, plugs, xenoliths have been recognized in much of the Cape Verde archipelago. In S. Vicente the floor of Cha da Caldeira, nepheline-syenites, analcitic-syenites, gabbroic diorites, olivine-gabbros, theralites, ijolites, etc. are outcropping. Intruded into such are many dykes, veins, plugs, in composition forming lavas with and without feldspars, all of which have orientations difficult to decipher. In Maio, the central eruptive complex comprises breccias and lavas intersected by many dykes and smaller intrusive bodies of plutonic type – essexites, syenites, ijolites, etc., the dykes being chiefly ultrabasics. In Fogo and Brava, especially the latter, we have ring complexes in the basement formed of nepheline-syenites and associated under-saturated rocks surrounding a central carbonatite plug. In northern S. Tiago plutonics – mostly of syenitic and dioritic type – are found deep within valleys, carbonatite dykes occur especially in western parts, plutonic enclaves are known here and there.

Hence the question of plutonics, as smaller intrusive bodies, dykes, ring structures, enclaves, is not in doubt, but do such represent the actual fundament of the archipelago?

In S. Vicente the essential volcanic structure is a large strato-cone comprising basaltic-type rocks with and without feldspars, pyroclastic and dykes (SERRALHEIRO, 1966). As we have seen, Cha da Caldeira is associated with plutonics. The caldera is primarily due to collapse (though erosion also has been responsible in sculpturing the feature), this concept receiving added confirmation from the gravity studies of MENDES VICTOR (1970). Thus initially we had the erection of a stratiform volcanic feature into which plutonics were intruded, subsidence occurred at the caldera, brought down to a lower level and now visible within the floor of the caldera.

In Maio the oldest Mesozoic strata (Portlandian?) are believed to occur at Monte Branco. Here we have the ›complexo argilo-calco-eruptivo‹ of SERRALHEIRO (1970), along with layers of flint nodules. The igneous ingredients comprise basaltic-type rocks. On what this ›complex‹ or indeed other younger Mesozoics rests, cannot be determined, but the presence of volcanics in this ensemble must testify to a previous occurrence of volcanic emissions, a basement of volcanics. In Brava the oldest stratigraphic unit comprises submarine lavas largely palagonized, into which were intruded nepheline-syenites, etc. In Sal nepheline-syenite dykes intrude basaltics, small sill-like intrusions of doleritic-type rocks can be seen in the S of the island penetrating ankaramites occurrences.

Thus one concludes that within the archipelago in general, eruptives preceded intrusives, that the former were submarine emissions. Plutonic basal complexes are recognized in the Canary Islands – Fuerteventura, La Palma, Gomera – and very likely Mesozoics occur in the first mentioned. ROTHE (1968a) suggested here that the sediments might range from Turonian down to Liassic and referred to analogies with Maio rocks. Upper Cretaceous is quite possible in Fuerteventura, but at this time we view most sceptically strata as old as Lias. In Maio Portlandian might be present but

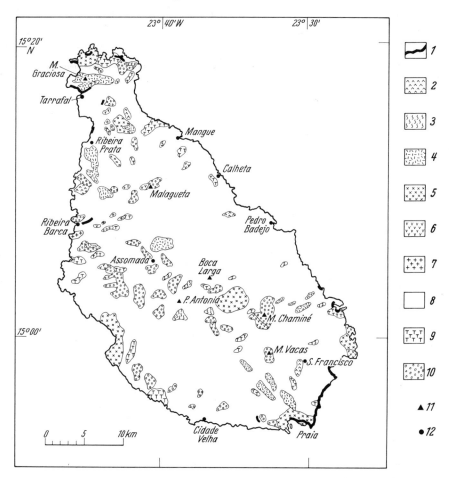

Fig. 89. Geological map of Ilha de S. Tiago. 1: Sedimentaries, including fossiliferous limestones, intercalated with eruptives, Recent-Neogene. 2: Andesitic rocks. 3: Trachytic and trachy-andesitic rocks. 4: Phonolitic rocks. 5: Limburgitic rocks. 6: Augititic rocks. 7: Syenitic rocks. 8: Basaltic rocks. 9: Alkaline-basalts. 10: Tephra cones. 11: Peaks. 12: Villages. (Modified after BEBIANO, 1932, MITCHELL-THOMÉ, 1960).

nothing older has been suggested; Neocomian-Aptian is well established, possibly Albian-Cenomanian, maybe also Senonian, but Palaeogene is an open question. These Maio sedimentaries have been intruded by plutonics as ring complexes, dykes, small irregular bodies, certainly within Lower Cretaceous strata, doubtful whether such attain Senonian-Palaeogene rocks. Presumed Miocene is in unconformable relation with plutonic dykes.

For the Canary Islands, the basal complex would appear to be of pre-Miocene age. FUSTER et al. (1968) claimed that contacts of the Fuerteventura sedimentaries with near formations cannot be clearly distinguished, but: »In any case, they are later than the

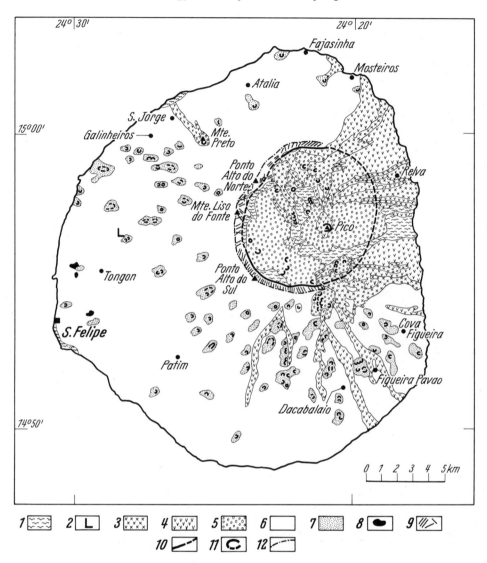

Fig. 90. Geological map of Ilha do Fogo. 1: Beach and talus deposits, Recent. 2: Micaceous and siliceous limestones, M. Miocene. 3: Basanites, limburgites and kindred lavas from 18 th, 19 th, 20 th century eruptions. 4: Basanites, limburgites and kindred lavas of recent eruptives – later than formation of caldera. 5: Cinder cones and scoria accumulations – later than formation of caldera. 6: Nephelinites and similar lavas, alternating with tuff or scoria beds, from eruptive activity prior to formation of caldera. 7: Principal tuff or scoria cones, prior to formation of caldera. 8: Old Complex – carbonatites and various alkaline rocks, with associated dykes. 9: Principal dykes – nephelinites or similar rocks, including intrusive types. 10: Faults. 11: Craters. 12: "Bordeira" – caldera scarp. ▲: Peaks. ■: Capital. ●: Villages. (Modified after MACHADO & ASSUNÇAO, 1965).

plutonic massif and earlier than, or simultaneous with, the submarine volcanic formations«. From isotopic datings (ABDEL-MONEM et al, 1971) we can give general ages of 37 my for the basement rocks, ca. 20 my for the submarine volcanics, which would indicate a maximal Upper Palaeogene age for these sediments. Thus here the basal complex may be of Oligocene age.

In composition and structures, the basal complexes recognized in the Canary Islands show much in common with plutonic occurrences in the Cape Verde Islands, especially in Maio and S. Vicente. But as we have seen, these plutonics in the latter do not constitute the fundament: this is formed of volcanics. Hence here in Cape Verde we recognize a pre-Cretaceous ›basal complex‹ formed of submarine lava expulsions and, by analogy with the Canary Islands (though it might be risky to push this analogy too far), the Cape Verde plutonic episode would relate to Late Palaeogene times.

A petrochemical summation, based largely on the work of ASSUNÇAO & CANILHO (1969–70), brings forth the following features.

The archipelago rocks are markedly subsaturated, with phonolites as the final differentiation products, i. e. strongly ›Atlantic‹ character.

In the QLM diagram, the analyses are grouped essentially below the MF axis. No tholeiitic tendency is shown.

Silica-total alkalis diagrams indicate a spread of $SiO_2$ from 36 to 60, $Na_2O + K_2O$ from 3 to 18, with a distinct grouping between 40 and 45% silica and alkali values between 4 and 10, indicative of the pronounced alkaline character of the rocks. We should note, however, that many more analyses are available for Fogo and Brava, lesser so for S. Vicente and Maio. We must also take note that the carbonatites of S. Vicente, S. Tiago, Fogo, Brava and quite possible in other islands, integrate as extreme terms in the alkaline differentiation series. One notes a certain mineralogical continuity between the silicate rocks and the carbonatites, for we have predominantly silicate rocks containing carbonates as essential minerals, on occasion up to more than 10% $CO_2$. The diagram for Fogo indicates a small number of dispersed points along the silica abscissa, showing nephelinites with phonolitic and tahitic tendencies though true phonolites are missing. The points with low silica values belong to the basement, to the same series whose extreme term is of carbonatitic composition. Analyses of lavas of historic eruptions of the 18th, 19th and 20th centuries in Fogo show an enrichment in time of total alkalis, and notably of potash compared to soda.

The $SiO_2$-($FeO + Fe_2O_3$/$FeO + Fe_2O_3 + MgO$) diagrams show ranges of between 40–45% $SiO_2$ and between 0.55 and 0.75 as the index of Fe enrichment. Differentiation here is more marked for S. Vicente and Maio than for Fogo, especially for the first-named.

$MgO$-($FeO + Fe_2O_3$) diagrams show a range of Fe between 3 and 15, magnesia between 0 and 19, defining a regular variation curve. But here the very low values, either in magnesia or iron, are due to phonolites or then intrusives of similar composition – chiefly feldspathoidal syenites – whereas in the Azores such represents trachytes. Differentiation in these diagrams is considerably more limited for Fogo than other islands.

Isofalic values confirm the ›Atlantic‹ character of strong degree. For Fogo, ASSUNÇAO & CANILHO give an isofal of 120, whereas ASSUNÇAO (1968) quoted a value of

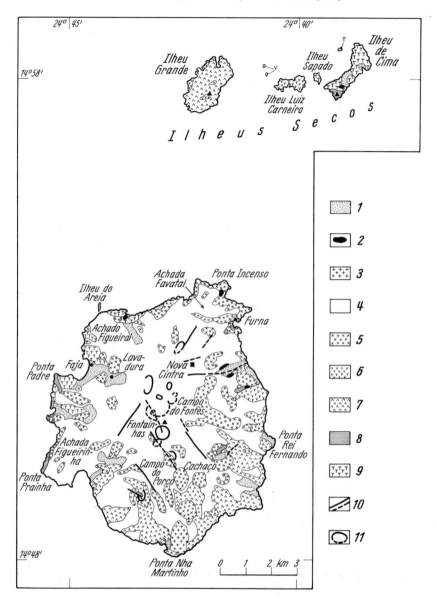

Fig. 91. Geological map of Brava and Ilheus Secos. 1: Beach and talus slope deposits. 2: Marine or terrestrial limestones. 3: Basanitic and kindred ankaratritic lavas and pyroclastics. 4: Phonolitic ash, sometimes intercalated with phonolitic lavas. 5: Extrusive or hypabyssal phonolites, sometimes passing into nephelinites. 6: Carbonatites, sometimes with nepheline-syenite inclusions. 7: Nephelinitic syenites, with pyroxenitic, carbonatitic, etc. segregates. 8: Ankaratrites and kindred lavas, associated with palagonites, including often a complex network of dykes. 10: Faults. 11: Craters. ▲: Peaks. ■: Capital. ●: Villages. (Modified after MACHADO, LEME, MONJARDINO & SEITA, 1968).

108, but the writer places more emphasis on the latter value. Maio has a value of 120, S. Vicente 132, for the archipelago, probably about 130, but this is not well established.


## Sedimentary Rocks

Sedimentary rocks, Pleistocene and older, appear to be present throughout the archipelago. Until such time as the sedimentaries of W-C Fuerteventura, Canary Islands (q. v.) receive more substantiation, those of the Cape Verde Islands have the greatest thicknesses, highest dips and the oldest determined strata in Macaronesia.

The literature dealing with sedimentary occurrences in the archipelago is few in number. The standard references treating of all the islands are those of BEBIANO (1932) and TORRES & SOARES (1946). To date the only island to be systematically studied in a more detailed fashion is Maio, and the work of SERRALHEIRO (1970) gives an adequate account of the sedimentaries. Further references to the archipelago sedimentaries are to be bound in STAHLECKER (1934), TRAUTH (1936, 1938), TORRES & SOARES (1950), BERTHOIS (1950c), LECOINTRE (1962, 1963), MITCHELL-THOMÉ (1960, 1964, 1972, 1974), ROMARIZ & SERRALHEIRO (1967), SERRALHEIRO (1967, 1968) and ROMARIZ (1970). Though this might seem a satisfactory compilation, the treatment given the sedimentaries varies widely.

The rocks of Maio unquestionably are the most interesting, have been given most attention. BEBIANO divided these into four lithological categories: (1) Compact, hard limestones of siliceous-calcareous type, whitish or greyish in colour, incorporate flint nodules, under the microscope have a sub-crystalline, dolomitic appearance, in places rocks are metamorphosed somewhat, often the beds are vertical. (2) Sandy limestones, on occasion molassic or marly, of average hardness, polygenetic in origin, whitish and yellowish in colour, very slightly inclined. (3) Conglomerates comprising limestones and basalts, bonded by calcareous sands. (4) Consolidated dunes and loose sands, containing fossilized vegetation remains. The first two types occupy about half the island, surrounding a central igneous nucleus. As per the above, BEBIANO, on the basis of types (1) and (2), classified the sedimentaries into: (a) Hard, compact, greyish, steeply dipping limestones, mostly isolated occurrence, of Mesozoic age. (b) Quasi horizontal whitish limestones occupying large areas and considered of Neogene age.

SERRALHEIRO (1970) classified the Maio rocks on a stratigraphic basis, with lithologic sub-divisions, thus:

I.  Mesozoics
    A. Upper Jurassic (Portlandian?)
        1.  Shale-Limestone-Eruptives Complex
        2.  Light-coloured compact limestones intercalated with flints

    B. Eocretaceous
        1.  Shales, marls and marly limestones
            a) Eastern occurrences
            b) Western occurrences
        2.  Light-coloured compact limestones intercalated with flints
            a) Eastern occurrences
            b) Western occurrences

C. Undifferentiated Mesozoics (U. Jurassic-L. Cretaceous?)
     1. Shale-Limestone-Eruptives Complex
     2. Light-coloured compact limestones intercalated with flints

II.   Palaeogene
     1. Pedro Vaz Conglomerate
       a) NE occurrences
       b) SW occurrences

III.   Neogene
     1. Conglomerate-breccia deposits
     2. Compact limestones and conglomerates

IV.   Quaternary
A. Pleistocene
     1. Old beaches, coarse conglomerates and white calcareous sands

B. Holocene
     2. Restricted essentially to the littoral, valleys
       a) Beach sands and dunes
       b) River alluvium
       c) Torrential deposits

Group I-A-2 shows flint intercalations about every 30–50 cm in the limestones, intercalations measuring from 1–15 cm thick. In toto, they comprise ca. 15% of the unit. Intercalated flints are less altered than when occurring isolated, the alteration, proceeding from exterior inwards, yielding a whitish surface layer much less resistant to erosion. Usually the flints disintegrate into small prisms, thus facilitating removal and yielding limestone layers free of flints, so that often one has the impression the limestones are more abundant than in reality. Strike of the beds from N-S to E-W, with dips ranging from 36–80° in a general NE direction. From group I-B-2-b, in the Ribeira Morro, FRIEDLÄNDER first collected fossils studied by HENNIG (1913). From here also STAHLECKER (1934) made important finds, dividing the rock sequence into his 14 horizons ranging from Hauterivian to Aptian. The rocks have N-NW strikes, dips of 60–70° to the E-NE. The group I-B-1 is strongly folded, measures up to 200 m in

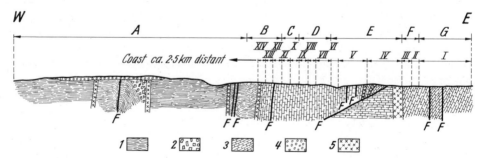

Fig. 92. Geological profile of Lower Cretaceous, Ribeira do Morro, Maio. 1: Clays and marls. 2: Rubble rocks. 3: Limestones, flint layers, marly and shaley limestones. 4: Old beach deposits, limestones, conglomerates. 5: Dykes. F: Faults. I–XIV: Fossiliferous "horizons" of STAHLECKER, 1934. A: Albian?. B: Aptian. C: Barremian-Aptian. D: U. Barremian. E: L. Barremian. F: Hauterivian-Barremian. G: Hauterivian. Length of section: ca. 630 m? (Modified after SERRALHEIRO, 1970).

thickness, with dips ranging from 55-80°, dipping to E and W. Group I-C, which SERRALHEIRO believed was essentially U. Jurassic, has strikes ranging from NW to NE with dips from 20-70° to NW, SW, but vertical strata also occur here. The Pedro Vaz Conglomerate is conglomeratic in lower parts, grading up to well-stratified sands, with the former adjacent to the central eruptives, the latter towards the coastal peripheries. Conglomerates comprise rounded, polished volcanic rocks with smaller quantities of hard limestone pebbles, all bonded by fine, altered sands. The upper part of the unit comprises both sands and clays-shales with poorly preserved foraminifera. The unit shows dips to the NE, S and SW at angles of 30-36°. Group III-1 comprises terrestrial detritals, with breccias inland gradually passing into conglomerates, formed from the former, towards peripheral areas. In general the rocks dip at ca. 20° to the WSW. In group III-2 occur within the limestones, fossils establishing a Miocene-Pliocene age. The Pleistocene occurs at various altitudes. In the Ribeira das Casas Velhas the following succession is seen: 2-6 m Flandrian; 8-12 m Neo-Tyrrhenian; 15-20 m EuTyrrhenian; 30-40 m Palaeo-Tyrrhenian; 50-60 m Neo-Sicilian; 80-100 m PalaeoSicilian, the stages being palaeontologically established. Here occur conglomerates at the base of volcanics, limestones and friable calcarenites, with white sands containing marine fossil shells, also black sands, the ilmenites, magnetites and pyroxenes derived from volcanics.

Probably after Maio, S. Tiago shows the most extensive development of sedimentaries. Here they generally occur near and parallel to the coasts or then along the sides of the lower end of valleys. In the region of Tarrafal Bay, in the N, sedimentaries are well exposed, where conglomerates and fossiliferous limestones occur. A section near the quay, for example, shows: (base) 2 m of coarse, rounded conglomerate comprising basalt, phonolite, cemented by calcareous sandstones; 2 m coarse fossiliferous calcareous sandstones; 2 m conglomerate like the lower but more phonolite ingredients; 2 m columnar basalt. In this general region, strata dip towards the S-SE at angles up to 20°. Along the NE coastal region many occurrences of sedimentaries are to be seen as well as in lower valleys draining to this coast, then again in the SE-S coastal sector. Praia, the capital, is built on a small plateau rising 40 m above sea level, formed essentially of basalts, limburgites and sedimentaries. Towards the quay the following succession is seen: (top) 10 m limburgitic rocks; 30 m basalts, scoria; 1 m ferruginous-siliceous sandstones, including fossils, rounded basalt fragments; 1 m similar sandstones with corals and large basaltic boulders; ca. 10 m ashy-grey calcareous sandstones, many fossils, also very large basalt boulders. A section from Praia across the Praia Negra to the Achada Grande (on which the landing field is built) is shown in Fig. 94.

The sedimentaries of S. Nicolau vie with those of Maio in the numbers of fossils they have yielded, although the rocks are far less developed than in the latter island. The rocks here can be grouped into: (1) Marly limestones, somewhat marmorized, of microcrystalline composition, rich in fossils, relatively steep dips. (2) Sandy limestones, of polygenetic origin, slightly marmorized, somewhat crystalline appearance, rich in fossils, also particles of volcanics and minerals therefrom. (3) Sandy limestones admixed with much tuffaceous material, very rich in fossils. (4) Sedimentaries formed as result of erosion-deposition of group (3), comprising arenaceous and calcareous material

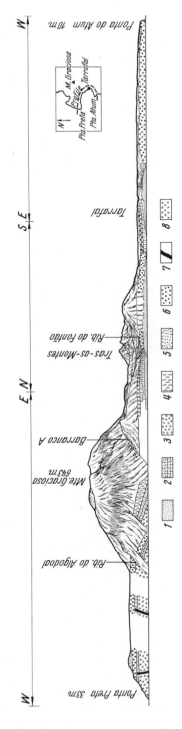

Fig. 93. Panorama and sketched geologic profiles, Tarrafal Bay, S. Tiago. 1: Beach sands. 2: Limestones and conglomerates. 3: Conglomerates. 4: Disintegration-alteration phonolites. 5: Explosive material. 6: Columnar basalts passing up to "laminar" basalts. 7: Dykes. 8: "Basal Series". (Modified after AMARAL, 1964).

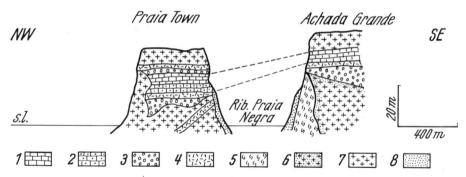

Fig. 94. Geological profile across Rib. Praia Negra at Praia, S. Tiago. 1: Limestone. 2: Sandy limestone. 3: Tuff. 4: Agglomerate. 5: Volcanic conglomerate. 6: Basalts and pyroclastics. 7: Basalt. 8: Scree.

including fossils associated therewith. It is assumed that the erosion, transportation and deposition of group (3) to form these deposits was accomplished by marine means. The first group has an interesting occurrence at Monte Focinho where, on the W slopes thereof, two layers of highly fossiliferous marly limestones, 3 m and 6 m thick, associated with basalts and tinguaites, are dipping at 49° to the W (Fig. 95). This occurrence, at an elevation of 250 m, represents the second highest occurrence of Tertiaries in the archipelago.

The sedimentaries of S. Vicente can be grouped into: (1) Sandy limestones at times like polygenetic arenites, of various facies: (a) includes rounded fragments of volcanics and shells in a crystalline limestone containing Foraminifera, a gravitationally formed deposit, in which wind, rivers and the sea have been active in its formation; (b) polygenetic calcareous sandstones, containing fossils, mineral and basaltic fragments; (c) calcareous-arenaceous material overlying fine conglomerates; (d) calciferous arenites, showing crude stratification. (2) Conglomerates comprising volcanics with a lime-sand cement containing marine mollusc fragments. Many dunes included in this category, of calcareous sands, and notable scarcity of limestones. At times, the calcareous sands are consolidated to form calcareous sandstones which are hard, compact, used in building houses, etc. Plant remains sometimes evident. (3) Limestones

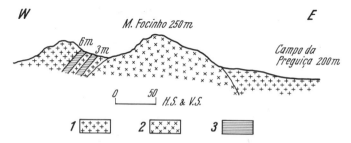

Fig. 95. Geological section through Monte Focinho, S. Nicolau, showing fossiliferous limestones. 1: Basalt. 2: Tinguaite. 3: Marly limestone. (Modified after BEBIANO, 1932).

19  Mitchell-Thomé, Middle Atlantic Islands

Table 65    Mineral and Granulometric Features of some sands from S. Vicente (ROMARIZ & SERRALHEIRO, 1967)

| Sample Nos. | Locality | Mineral Comp. | | | Granulometric Parameters | | | | | |
|---|---|---|---|---|---|---|---|---|---|---|
| | | $CaCO_3$ | Non-carbonate detritals | Clays | Md | $Q_1$ | $Q_3$ | Qd | Skq | K |
| V– 9 | Rib. S. Juliao, Golf course. | 7.5 | 91.7 | 0.8 | 1.80 | 1.30 | 2.25 | 0.48 | $\overline{0}$.025 | 0.237 |
| V–125 | Baia das Gates. Reddish sands. | 91.7 | 3.5 | 4.8 | 2.29 | 1.35 | 3.10 | 0.87 | $\overline{0}$.06 | 0.20 |
| V–126 | Ditto. Upper white sands. | 92.6 | 7.3 | 0.1 | 2.65 | 2.40 | 2.98 | 0.29 | 0.05 | 0.22 |
| V–133 | Casas do Calhau. Black sands. | 16.5 | 83.4 | 0.1 | 1.00 | 0.65 | 1.55 | 0.45 | $\overline{0}$.04 | 1.20 |
| V–134 | Calhau, near mouth Rib. de Mancanjes. | 93.2 | 5.5 | 1.3 | 1.32 | 0.65 | 2.01 | 0.68 | 0.01 | 0.24 |
| V–137 | Ditto. | 61.7 | 38.1 | 0.2 | 1.70 | 1.40 | 2.00 | 0.30 | $\overline{0}$.40 | 0.23 |

V–9, V–133 = Siliceous sands; others = calcareous sands.

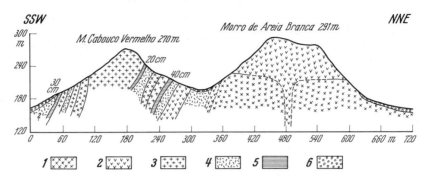

Fig. 96. Geological section through M. Cabuco Vermelho and M. de Areia Branco, S. Vicente, showing steep-dipping Mesozoic (?) limestones. 1: Basalts. 2: Phonolites. 3: Andesites. 4: Tuffs, lapilli. 5: Limestones. 6: Talus deposits. (Modified after Bebiano, 1932).

of micro- and macro-crystalline character, more or less dolomitized and ferriferous, which may have dips as high as 50°, intimately associated with volcanics (vide Fig. 96).

In Sto. Antao good exposures are seen in Tarrafal Bay, on the W coast. Where on raised beaches with basalt bedrock, sandy limestones of polygenetic origin up to 2.5 m thick occur, containing Foraminifera and other shell fragments. At Ponta dos Tarrafinhos, on the S coast near Porto Novo are dunes containing a great number of fossilized vegetal remains which litter the surface. These comprise mostly the stems and roots of the plant *Tamarix*, likely *T. gallica* Linn. The remains form calcareous nuclei of aggulinated sands, fragments of augite, magnetite, volcanics, shells of Molluscs, Echinoids, Foraminifera, *Lithothamnium*, etc., calcareously cemented together. Similar vegetal remains are seen in Boa Vista, Ilheu Branco, S. Vicente, Sal and Maio.

In Boa Vista, sediments and sedimentaries cover about one-third of the island, comprising limestones with many Molluscan shell fragments, sandy-silty limestones with Gastropods, Molluscs, Bivalves, Radiolaria, etc., calcareous sands and sandstones, silts and siltstones, some mudstones and clays. Loose sand sheets and dunes cover large areas of this island, as also caliche deposits. Many of the dunes are ›active‹, very often the routes and landing field at Sal Rei have to be cleared of drifting sands and moving dunes.

No less in Sal there are large areas occupied by various rocks of calcareous type, again often forming sand sheets, dunes to a lesser extent, except in the S. All limestones are of polygenetic origin. Calcarenites, limestones also occur in Brava and the Ilheus Secos lying N thereof. In the islets such rocks have dips as high as 40°, usually to the S.

Sandy limestones, micro-brecciated limestones and extensive calcareous dunes occur in Sta. Luzia and Ilheus Branco and Razo.

In Fogo, Bebiano referred to metamorphosed limestones of gneissic texture, holocrystalline, granular, marmorized, occurring in the Ribeira do Pico, ca. 3 km N of S. Felipe. This and some other occurrences in near-by valleys are now known to be carbonatites (Machado & Assunçao, 1965). However, the writer (Mitchell-Thomé, 1964) discovered a small outcrop in the Ribeira Sanha, some 2.5 km N of the Ribeira do Pico, of micaceous and siliceous fine-grained limestones containing fossils. The rocks are considered to be in situ, not boulders, seemingly enclosed in deeply-weathered nephelinites, but admittedly field relations are not easy to decipher.

In summation then, we can say that ca. 90% of the Cape Verde sedimentary rocks comprise limestones, marlstones, dolomites and transitions, with calcitic limestones, chiefly of fossil fragments, being the commonest. These clastic-biochemical rocks are primarily allochthonous. After the calcareous rocks, conglomerates, chiefly of oligomictic type, are the most frequent. Arenaceous pure rocks are relatively scarce, with tuffaceous sandstones predominating. Purer verieties of argillaceous rocks likewise are not common, they lack induration, fissility and lamination is poor.

Duricrusts (Krustenkalke, croûte calcaire, caliche) are present, especially prominent in Sal, Boa Vista and Maio. At Caldeira Pedra da Lume, Sal, KREJCI-GRAF (1960) reported a thickness of 3–5 m. Thicknesses of 60–100 cm are to be found in the archipelago, but in general these are only a few centimetres thick. Chemically these Cape Verde duricrusts have a higher $CaCO_3$ content, lower $MgCO_3$ content, as also $Fe_2O_3$, $Al_2O_3$ and $SiO_2$, than those in other Middle Atlantic Islands (vd. Table 8), a reflexion on the more extreme arid conditions pertaining in this archipelago. The economic significance of these duricrusts relates to their adverse effects in prohibiting the infiltration of rainfall downwards to the soils-rocks below. Sedimentaries are presumed to cover ca. 9% of the archipelago. The greatest development is in the coastal plains, usually not more than 2 km inland, and reaching a maximum elevation of 265 m in Maio. The Tertiaries have lower dips, although values of 49° and 50° are found in S. Nicolau and S. Vicente respectively. The Mesozoics have much higher dips, many being vertical. Younger rocks, on an average, show thicknesses of 2–3 m, though in S. Tiago we have rocks some 34 m thick, in Ilheus Secos, perhaps 24 m thick. In Maio we reckon on 435+ m of sedimentary rocks, the greatest thickness so far substantiated in all the Middle Atlantic Islands.

Disturbances seen in the sedimentaries are of pseudo- and/or volcano-tectonic origin, comprising slumpings, glidings, minor puckerings, resulting largely from gravitational movement or then the emplacement of igneous material. Structures acquired during the processes of lithification and diagenesis are common – cross bedding, wave- and rillmarks, nodules, concretions, septaria, current bedding all are plentiful. Intra-formational conglomerates seem always to be rather thin. Pronounced unconformities are rare, the most significant being in Maio where angular unconformities occur.

## Stratigraphy

DOELTER (1882, GAGEL (1910), BERGT (1913), CHEVALIER (1935) and D'ORCHYMONT (1936) believed that in the archipelago there was a ›basal complex‹ of Precambrian and/or Palaeozoic age. BEBIANO (1932) made no mention of pre-Mesozoic strata, held this view to the end of his days, and today all are agreed that the oldest sediments belong to the Upper Mesozoic.

Oldest rocks occur in Maio, and this lonesome little island has achieved a distinction of sorts in geological circles, firstly because it is doubtless here that the earliest age-identified strata in Macaronesia occur, and also because of the continued discussions, disagreements as to the exact age of the oldest beds and fossil identifications.

## Mesozoic

In 1912 FRIEDLÄNDER collected fractured aptychi from the Ribeira do Morro, Maio, which were reported upon by HENNIG (1913). Identical fossil fragments and more fossils were reported by STAHLECKER (1934), further study of the same specimens made by TRAUTH (1936, 1938) and SOARES (1944–47, 1952, 1953). (SOARES also studied collections made by SALDANHA (1946–48.) Actually HENNIG determined only one specimen *Aptychus atlanticus* n. sp., differing only slightly in sculpturing from *Aptychus angulocostatus*. He recognized a specimen which closely corresponded to *Aptychus* cf. *euglyptus* OPPEL, his others merely being labelled *Aptychus* sp. In a cautious summation, HENNIG suggested that this fauna was comparable in age to the Upper Jurassic as occurring, for example, at Solnhofen, Bavaria, although he noted that *Aptychus latus*, the commonest aptychus at Solnhofen, was not present in Maio. The matter rested thus, i. e. the possibility that the oldest Maio beds were Malm, until the appearance of STAHLECKER's paper in 1934.

STAHLECKER identified almost all his »very numerous« aptychi as *Aptychus angulocostatus*, only one specimen having a similarity to HENNIG's *Aptychus atlanticus* HENNIG. TRAUTH (1936, 1938) recognized the following species in the FRIEDLÄNDER collection: *Lamellaptychus angulocostatus* (PET.) var. *atlanticus* (STAHLECKER's *Lamellaptychus angulocostatus*), *Aptychus* cf. *euglyptus*, *Ammonites euglyptus* OPPEL and *Laevilamellaptychus hennigi* TRAUTH (HENNIG's *Aptychus* sp.). TRAUTH considered that all these forms indicated a Neocomian age, and STAHLECKER also had recognized a Neocomian age for his findings. SOARES (1944–47), however, argued that *Laevilamellaptychus hennigi* TRAUTH indicated the Malm (Portlandian?), and further, that all the other forms of this genus studied by TRAUTH are to be referred to the Dogger and Malm of Europe and the Tithonian of Argentina. From a further collection made by SALDANHA in 1945 at Morro, Maio, SOARES (1952) claimed that the determinations, as well as the facies characteristics of the rocks – limestones with flint nodules and showing styolites – referred such to the Portlandian. SOARES's publication of 1953 takes on the proportion of a monograph dealing with the Maio aptychi. Here and in his 1952 paper, he quotes extracts of letters received from TRAUTH, one of which says: »In stratigraphic regard I cannot contradict you and E. HENNIG's meaning that many of the Maio Aptychi are originated from U. Jurassic strata (Portland-Tithon): but the *Lamellaptychus angulocostatus* var. *atlanticus* I think indicates already transition from U. Jurassic to Neocom (ev. Berrias?) or Neocom, and STAHLECKER's *Lamellaptychus angulocostatus* and *Lamellaptychus seranonis* certainly, as also demonstrate the Ammonites L. Cretaceous (Neocom)«. SOARES was also in correspondence with STAHLECKER about this question of age.

Over the years a keen student of the Maio fauna has been Dr. KARL STAESCHE of Stuttgart who, as distinct from SOARES, has made field studies in the island. The lowest fossil horizon in the Ribeiro Morro, termed Horizon I by STAHLECKER and designated Neocomian, TRAUTH and STAESCHE agreed. In the lowest strata underneath this horizon, neither STAHLECKER nor STAESCHE found any recognizable fossils in this 50 m section. Even presuming that SOARES' collection came from this hitherto supposedly unfossiliferous section, STAESCHE believed that any of the arguments published by SOARES were not adequate for establishing an Upper Jurassic age for these strata. (SOARES, for example, determined only new species or varieties in the SALDANHA collection.) STAESCHE made a most diligent search, both in the field and in the laboratory in these lower beds for fossils and concluded that in this lowermost 50 m section there were no recognizable organic structures.

For Maio, STAHLECKER recognized the Neocomian (Valangian, Hauterivian, Barremian), and TRAUTH originally placed the FRIEDLÄNDER specimens also in the Neocomian. SOARES appears to prefer to place all the lower Neocomian of STAHLECKER in the upper Malm. HEINZ (1935), however, also recognized *Inoceramus* species in Maio which, according to him, proved the presence of Lower Cretaceous.

The most recent worker in Maio, SERRALHEIRO (1968, 1970) placed these Ribeira Morro beds in his »Undifferentiated Mesozoic (U. Juras? and L. Cret?)« category, whereas outcrops in the eastern part of the island were placed in the »U. Juras (Portlandian?)«. Both he and STAHLECKER commented upon the lithological and palaeontological similarities between these western and eastern occurrences in the island, but SERRALHEIRO refrains from making any further dogmatic remarks.

From some marmorized limestones at Ponta do Escorregadeiro, on the S coast of the E-W trending part of S. Nicolau, SOARES (TORRES & SOARES 1946) classified the many Foraminifera as *Peneropolis* aff. *planulatus* FICHTEL & MOLL var. *Assunçaoi*. These, along with some species of *Cardita, Cerithium, Columbella, Conus, Cypraea* and *Purpura*, he placed in the Plaisancian, whereas other species of *Cerithium, Euthria* and *Mitra* he classed as Vindobonian. But in 1959, MAYNC (vd. also 1949) re-identified the Foraminifera as *Iberina lusitanica* (EGGER) emend. MAYNC, a Portlandian species. SOARES has written the author that: ».....la présence d'*Iberina lusitanica* trouvée dans une pâte métamorphisée remplissant des exemplaires de *Cerithium (Conocerithium) tauroconicum* (SACCO) dont le test se montre métamorphisée en aragonite, récoltés à Ponta do Escorregadeiro....... on peut dire que ce sédiment de remplissage a été remanié (ou poussé) par des actions volcaniques les plus anciennes, qui l'auront arraché à des couches profondes vraisemblablement d'âge depuis Kimmeridgien jusqu'au Jurassique final«, an opinion confirmed by MAYNC. A switch from Upper Pliocene to Upper Jurassic is indeed a considerable time difference. So far, no further work has been done on these limestones; one wonders if further re-identifications are necessary, one questions whether the Malm is really represented here in S. Nicolau.

SOARES, SALDANHA and FURON (literature cited and personal letters) do believe that Upper Jurassic is present in Maio, and SERRALHEIRO seems not averse to this. STAHLECKER, TRAUTH and STAESCHE were of the view that the oldest Maio strata were Neocomian in age, and STAESCHE (personal communication) has written: ».....Jurassic, if at all, can be represented only by a small part of the lowermost beds«. As of now, the Jurassic is not firmly established in S. Nicolau. Some writers are inclined to consider the finding of salt diapirs off the African coasts (Senegal Basin, Aaium Basin, N-NW of Cape Verde Islands) as lending some substance to the presence of pre-Cretaceous strata in the Cape Verde archipelago. These submarine salt diapirs have been regarded as ›possibly Jurassic or Trias‹ by AYMÉ (1965), perhaps Late-Triassic-Middle Jurassic by RONA (1969, 1970), Trias-Lias by TEMPLETON (1971). The above ages of the diapirs are not certain, and further, as of the present, one cannot assess the significance thereof as such pertains to the Cape Verde Islands.

In summary, then, whether pre-Cretaceous rocks occur in the archipelago cannot be satisfactorily answered at present.

Whether or not post-Aptian Cretaceous occurs in the archipelago is also open to doubt. STAHLECKER thought this was absent; FURON (1935) believed it present, though up to that time not detected. TORRES & SOARES (1946) adopted a view that as regards Maio at least, the contention of STAHLECKER was correct.

The westward-dipping limestones at Monte Focinho, S. Nicolau (vd. Fig. 95) were thought by TORRES & SOARES to have been deposited during the time-interval Eocene-Vindobonian. In 1948 SOARES thought these Monte Focinho beds were either Senonian or Lutetian, and also suggested that the azoic and/or metamorphosed limestones occurring in S. Vicente, Sal, Maio, S. Tiago and Ilheus Secos were either Senonian or Nummulitic. From the 3 m thick limestone at Monte Focinho, S. Nicolau, BEBIANO & SOARES (1952) discovered a Pelecypod taken to be *Cardita (Venericardia)* aff. *libyca* ZITTEL, also eleven imperfect specimens of *Turritella*, identified by SOARES as *Turritella (Zaria) bonei* BAILY. The writers remark: »From the two molluscan species discussed above, we cannot be certain of the precise age of the bed in which they occur. Nevertheless they appear to offer the first suggestion of the presence of Senonian deposits in the Archipelago of Cape Verde (S. Nicolau Island); and this suggestion is strengthened by the fact that *Turritella (Zaria) bonei* BAILY has a world-wide distribution in the Upper Cretaceous«.

Again in 1958, SOARES remarked that the marly limestones of S. Nicolau bear close analogy with similar rocks found in S. Vicente, Sal, Maio, S. Tiago and Ilheus Secos, from which he again presumed the likely occurrence of Senonian in the archipelago.

SOARES & FURON (op. cit., 1968) refer specifically to Senonian in the Cape Verde Islands, but such has not been suggested by others, e. g. for Maio, SERRALHEIRO (1970) would only recognize possible Aptian-Albian. (BOURCART's suggestion (1946) of Senonian in Sal and S. Tiago represents but a notion.)

Concluding then we must say, as per the Scottish verdict, ›non-proven‹ for Albian-Upper Cretaceous in the archipelago. (SOARES has informed the writer (via letter) that he would prefer to restrict his Senonian to the Monte Focinho limestones, but even here, SERRALHEIRO (personal communication) would prefer to assign to the Tertiary.)

Yet another stratigraphic uncertainty refers to the Palaeogene. TORRES & SOARES (1946) claimed Eocene present in S. Nicolau, Sal, S. Vicente, S. Tiago and Brava; Oligocene in S. Nicolau, Maio and Boa Vista. In 1968 SERRALHEIRO termed his conglomerates and sands of his Pedro Vaz Conglomerate as ›Palaeogene (?)‹, but in 1970 removed the interrogation mark. In neither publication is any evidence presented for such an age designation. (His latter publication mentions some families of very poorly preserved Foraminifera found in clays here but such constitutes no proof, pro or con.) Both FURON (1935) and BOURCART (1946) believed that during Palaeogene times, or part thereof, all the archipelago was emergent, thus accounting for the absence of such strata. It is during this pre-Neogene emergent period that SERRALHEIRO (1968) postulated intense erosion to form his detritals during Palaeogene (?) times. As we have seen, SOARES now prefers to call his Monte Focinho, S. Nicolau limestones possible Senonian instead of Lutetian (?) as earlier believed, and as remarked, SERRALHEIRO would prefer a Tertiary age for these rocks, but as per fossil evidence so far obtained, this is of Vindobonian and Plaisancian age, not Palaeogene.

So again the matter of Palaeogene sedimentaries is left in doubt. TORRES & SOARES (1946) claimed that Neogene occurred in all islands except Fogo. The greatest number of fossil species at that time (and this is still true today) had been recorded for S. Nicolau, and hence the Neogene was better understood in that island, although the stratigraphic analysis is not of the clearest. In S. Nicolau the Vindobonian was recognized, both Helvetian and Tortonian. The very disproportionate numbers of fossils collected and studied for the various islands entails difficulties in deciphering the stratigraphy thereof, but these authors believed Vindobonian to be present in all islands, though SOARES (personal communication) would now omit Brava from the list. On the other hand, the determination of fossils in the micaceous-siliceous limestones of Fogo (vide supra) would add this island to the list of these authors.

That Neogene is present in the archipelago has been accepted by all workers, though perhaps not as widespread as TORRES & SOARES would have us believe. Then LECOINTRE (1962, 1963) presented some upsetting opinions. He was most critical of supposed Neocomian, Miocene and Pliocene in Sal, and, by inference, most of the Tertiary within the entire archipelago. He remarked that many Mediterranean Miocene molluscs emigrated progressively in time because of a gradual climatic cooling as the Quaternary approached, so that these molluscs now are found in sub-tropical eastern Atlantic regions. And so, according to LECOINTRE, generally strata in the Cape Verde archipelago which have been considered Miocene should rather be assigned to the Quaternary. He pointed out that the commonest fossil in Sal (and, we would add, quite plentiful in Boa Vista, Maio, S. Tiago, to mention some other islands) is *Arca senelis* LINNÉ, which is a tropical species not known before the Quaternary in Mauritania, where, significantly, it occurs endemically. Referring to Sal, LECOINTRE believed that even old Quaternary was absent, the sequence here being a Tyrrhenian I raised beach (30–55 m above present sea level), and Ouljian (Tyrrhenian III) 7 m level and a Flandrian 2 m beach-level. (LECOINTRE equates the Ouljian with Tyrrhenian II but it is usual to equate this with 5–10 m Tyrrhenian III raised beach level – vide, e. g. FURON, 1966.) In a letter to the writer soon after the appearance of his 1962 paper, LECOINTRE had written: »Altogether I believe that perhaps all the predecessors (of Cabo Verde) believed to be Miocene is Quaternary«.

To banish the Neogene from the archipelago seems a rather extreme position to take, and SERRALHEIRO, for example, the most recent worker in the islands, although recognizing the stratigraphic complexity of the archipelago, adheres to the Neogene, for certain islands at least.

No other later publications of LECOINTRE refer to this matter of the Cape Verde Tertiaries. Dr. LECOINTRE, a distinguished scholar of the Quaternary of NW Africa and of islands of interest here, regrettably died in 1972, and hence the writer was not able to probe further as to whether LECOINTRE may have made some private studies regarding the Cape Verde islands.

Sicilian, Tyrrhenian and Flandrian raised beaches have been determined for several islands (Table 53) whilst Holocene is represented by active dunes, marine terraces, coastal-river alluvium, scree deposits, etc.


## Palaeontology

Palaeontological collections and determinations are more extensive for the Cape Verde Islands than for any other archipelago. Beginning with DARWIN in 1832, further notable collections and/or studies were continued by MORELET (1873), FISCHER (1874), ROCHBRUNE (1881), NOBRE (1894), FRIEDLÄNDER (1912), HENNIG (1913), BEBIANO (1932), STAHLECKER (1934), TRAUTH (1936, 1938), SALDANHA (1946), TORRES & SOARES (1946), STAESCHE in the early 1960's, LECOINTRE (1963), SERRALHEIRO (1967, 1970). Up till the time of publication, the work of TORRES & SOARES gives the best overall account of the palaeontology of the archipelago, treating extensively of all earlier publications and including some useful syntheses. A most interesting section entitled »Bionomic, Palaeontologic and Biogeographic Factors« goes into considerable discussion regarding the tectonic nature of the archipelago, relations with other Middle Atlantic archipelagoes, Antillean and Mediterranean biogeographic similarities to faunal contents of Cape Verde. If we note that here and in so many earlier works that biogeographic associations and palaeogeographic descriptions are based simply upon distributions of faunal-floral species, without recourse to other considerations, especially tectonic and geophysical, then by the same token there is a tendency today for the pendulum to have swung to the other extreme, that biological considerations are pushed aside or then not given due attention. Whatever the modern views of tectonicians and geophysicists, we cannot lightly ignore the fact that there are close palaeontological associations between the Cape Verde Islands and other Middle Atlantic Islands, with SW Europe, the Mediterranean and the littoral coasts of NW Africa. This is well seen, e. g. in the distribution of fluviatile and terrestrial Mollusca, an essentially continental fauna, as first pointed out by GERMAIN (1926), the Cape Verde, Canary, Madeira and Azores archipelagoes having a particularly rich fauna in Helicidae, which show close affinities with those of Europe and Hispano-America, but are quite independent of those forms of Equatorial Africa.

To date, S. Nicolau has yielded the greatest number of species collected, though not the greatest number of fossils. Maio has naturally attracted great interest palaeontologically, but only here and only the Mesozoic fauna has been subjected to renewed studies by various scholars, as also the fauna of Sal by LECOINTRE. In 1946 TORRES & SOARES remarked – and the situation has not changed since – that the disparity in numbers of species collected and studied from the various islands created a serious disproportion when attempting to engage in palaeontologic-stratigraphic analyses.

In essence then our palaeontological knowledge to date is of reconnaissance nature, most collections have not been subjected to rigorous study, and from LECOINTRE & SERRALHEIRO (1966) we see the need for revisions, but such have scarce begun. We must also note that many of the palaeontologists who worked on Cape Verde collections had no personal knowledge of the islands, hence unaware of geological environments. Such applies, e. g. in the case of HENNIG, TRAUTH and SOARES. It is quite likely that this lack of field acquaintance on the part of the above three has contributed in some measure to the lengthy discussions regarding the Maio Mesozoic stratigraphy. The following are fossil determinations from the various islands.

### Sto. Antao

*Tamarix senegalensis* DE CANDOLLE, *T. canariensis* (WILD) PITARD, *T. gallica* (?) LINNÉ var?, *Lithothamnium* sp., *Lithophyllum* sp., *Miolina* sp., *Amphistegina haueri* D'ORBIGNY, *Elphidium crispus* (Linné), *Polymorphina variata* JONES, PARKER & BRADY, *Bigeneria* cf. *nodosaria* D'ORBIGNY.

### S. Vicente

*Arca plicata* CHEMNITZ, *Cardita aculeata* (POLI) *sulcidentata* ROCHBRUNE, *C. calyculata L. oblonga* REQUIEN, *C. calyculata* L. *obtusata* REQUIEN, *Lucina eburnea* (GMEL.), *Spondylus* cf. *concentricus* BRONN, *Venus ovata* PENNANT, *V. verrucosa* L. *simulans* SOWERBY, *Fissurella alabastrites* REEVE, *Gadinia afra* (GMEL.), *Glyphis gibberula* LAMARCK, *Patella guttata* D'ORBIGNY, *Purpura haemastoma* (LINNÉ), *P. nodosa* (LINNÉ), *Siphonaria pectinata* (LINNÉ) *lineolata* SOWERBY, *Elphidium crispus* (LINNÉ) = *Polystomellina discorbinoides* YABE & HANZAWA, *Miliolina trigonula* LAMARCK, *Cancris auricula* (FICHTEL & MOLL), *Lithothamnium isthmi* HOWE, *Lithophyllum decussatum* ELLIS & SOLANDER (?), *Faujasina carinata* D'ORBIGNY, *Amphistegina* sp., *Textularia* sp., *Biloculina* sp., *Epistomina regularis* TERQUEM, *Globigerina Linnaeana* d,ORBIGNY.

### Sta. Luzia

*Elphidium crispus* (LINNÉ), *Orbiculina* aff. *adunca* FICHTEL & MOLL var. VIANAI, *Lithophyllum decussatum* ELLIS & SOLANDER, *Lucina columbella* LAMARCK, *Venus multilamella* LAMARCK, *V. verrucosa* LINNÉ var. *simulans* SOWERBY, *Dosinia exoleta* LINNÉ ( = *Cytherea exoleta* LAMARCK), *Melania tamsii* DUNKER ( = *M. tuberculata* MULLER), *Trochamina nitida* (?) BRADY, *Discorbina opercularis?* D'ORBIGNY, *Quinqueloculina striata?* D'ORBIGNY, *Bolivina robusta?* BRADY (?), *Orbiculina compressa?* D'ORBIGNY, *Rotalia becarii* LINNÉ var. *soldanii* PARKER & JONES (?), *Anomalina amonoides?* (REUSS), *Planorbis* sp. (?), *Patellina* sp.

### Razo

*Lithophyllum decussatum* ELLIS & SOLANDER, *Bigenerina* aff. *nodosaria* (?) D'ORBIGNY, *Elphidium crispus* (LINNÉ).

### S. Nicolau

*Pectunculus* aff. *fichteli* DESHAYES ( = *P. pulvinatus* LAMARCK), *P. glycimeris* LINNÉ ( = *P. pilosus* LAMARCK) *P. glycimeris* LINNÉ var. *inflata* (BROCCHI), *P. siculus* REEVE ( = *P. bimaculatus* POLI), *Cardita* aff. *calyculata* LINNÉ var. *crassicosta* P. S., *C. trapezia* (LINNÉ) BRUG., *C. straeleni* CHAVAN, *?C.* aff. *pectuncularis* (?) LAMARCK, *C.* aff. *elongata*

Bronn, var. *semivarens* Fontannes, *Pecten* sp. (? = var. *P.* aff. *pesfelis* Linné), *P. corallinoides* d'Orbigny, *P.* cf. *scabrellus* Lamarck (= *P. dubius* Brocchi), *P.* aff. *opercularis* Linné var. *ignotus* Rochbrune, *Turritella fenauxi* Cossmann, *T. bicingulata* Lamarck, *Ranella marginata* Gmel., *R. scrobiculata* Klener, *Nassa costulata* Renier, *N. tritoniformis* Kienner, *Mitra fusiformis* Brocchi, *M.* cf. *operta* Bellardi, *M. cornicola* Linné, *Conus* aff. *Dujardini* Lamarck, *C.* aff. *venulatus* Hwass, *C. papilionaceous* Brug., *C. testudinarius* Martini, *C. guinaicus* Brug., *C. tamsianus* Dunker, *C. minutus* Reeve, *C. pigmaeus* Reeve, *Brizalina (Bolivina)* aff. *senariensis* (Costa), *Rotalia soldanii* d'Orbigny, *Textularia* sp., *Biloculina* sp., *Triloculina* sp., *Discorbina* sp., *Clypeaster martini* Desmoulins, *C. altus* Klein, *Spondylus gaderopus* Linné, *Cardita* aff. *senegalensis* Reeve (= *C. calyculata* Lamarck), *Cerithium submitratum* Cowper-Reed, *C. tauroconicum* (Sacco), *C. vulgatum* Brug. var. *tuberculata* Phillipi, *C. oemulum* Sowerby, *Columbella nobrei* P. S., *Purpura inconstans* Michelloti, *P. hemastoma* (Linné), *P. neritoides* Lamarck, *Euthria* cf. *subnosa* Hoernes & Awinger, *E. cornea* (Linné), *E.* aff. *intermedia* Michelloti, *Cypreae* cf. *picta* Gray, *C. spurca* Linné, *C. lurida* Linné, *C. pirum* Gmel., *C. zonata* Chemnitz, *Peneropolis* aff. *planulatus* Fichtel & Moll var. *assunçaoi*, *Lithothamnium isthmi* Howe (aff. *Nullipora ramosissima* Reuss), *L. vaughani* Howe, *Lithophyllum decussatum* Ellis & Solander, *Amphistegina mamillate* d'Orbigny, *A. haueri* d'Orbigny, *A. parisensis* Terquem, *Miliolina (Triloculina)* aff. *valvularis* Reuss, *Miliola (Quinqueloculina) seminulum* (Linné), *Elphidium crispus* (Linné), *Cypridina haueri* Romer, (?) *Lagena* aff. *ornata* (d'Orbigny), *Cibicides concentrica* Cushman, *C. lobatula* (Walker & Jacob), *Globigerina bulloides* d'Orbigny, *G. linnaeana* d'Orbigny, *Arca noe* Linné, *A. lactea* Linné, *A. imbricata* Brug., *A. gradata* Sowerby, *Chama gryphoides* Lamarck, *C. gryphina* Lamarck, *C.* aff. *calcarata* (?) Lamarck, *Lucina columbella* Lamarck (= *Linga columbella* Lamarck), *Venus bebianoi* P. S., *V. multilamella* Lamarck, *V. verrucosa* Linné var. *simulans* Sowerby, *V. squamosa* (Linné), *Fissurella benguellensis* Dunker, *F. humphreyi* Reeve, *F. alabastrites* Reeve, *F. phillippiana* Dunker (= *F. sterocrata* Quenstedt), *F. gibberula* Lamarck, *F. italica* Defrance, *Littorina* aff. *affinis(?)* d'Orbigny, *L.* aff. *sulcata* Pilkington var. *(?)* (= *L. striata* King), *L.* aff. *pulchella* Dunker, *Analthea* cf. *chamaeformis* Rochbrune, *Natica* aff. *lineolata* Deshayes (= ? var. *N.* aff. *porcellanea* d'Orbigny), *N.* aff. *collaria* (?) Lamarck, *Melania tamsi* Dunker, *Murex* aff. *fasciatus* Sowerby, *M.* aff. *labrosus* Michelloti, *Siphonaria algesira* Quoy & Gaimard, *Pleurostoma* aff. *spirata* Lamarck, *P. suessi* Hoernes, *Niso eburnea* Risso, *Patella adamsoni* Dunker, *Acmaea* aff. *rugosa(?)* Quoy & Gaimard, *A. fischeri* Rochbrune, *Harpa rosea* Lamarck, *Cancellaria cancellata* Linné var. *minor* Sacco, *Fusus syracusanus* Lamarck, *Latyrus filosus* Schubert & Wagner, *Oliva flammulata* Lamarck, *O. acuminata* Lamarck, *Strombus bubonis* Lamarck, *Terebra fuscata* Brocchi, *T. plicatula* Lamarck, *T. basteroti* Nyst, *T. corrugata* Lamarck, *Trochus (Gibbula) magus* Linné, *Capulus* aff. *elegans* Deshayes, *Vermetus selectus* Monterosato, *Cassis crumena* Brug., *Triton deshayesi* Michelloti, *Marginella quadripunctata* Locard, *Dendrophyllia* sp., *Columbella rustica* Linné, *Iberina lusitanica* (Egger) emend Maync.

## Sal

*Helix (Leptaxis) advena* WEBB & BERTHOLET, *H. primaeva, H. atlantica, H myristica, Lithothamnium isthmi* HOWE, *L. aninae, Lithophyllum aninae* FOSLIE, *Mesophyllum erubescens* FOSLIE, *Arca senelis* LINNÉ, *A. noe* LINNÉ, *Codokia orbicularis* LINNÉ, *Ostrea* sp. (*edulis?*), *O. (Pycnodonta) hyotis* LINNÉ, *O. (Gryphaea) cucullata* BRON, *O. stentina* PAYRAUDEAU, *Chama gryphina* LINNÉ, *Strombus bubobius* LK, *Chlamys flabellum* GMEL., *Modiola lutat* (AD.) DAUTZENBERG, *Lucina columbella* LK, *Capsa lacunosa* CHEMNITZ, *Tapes decussatus* LINNÉ, *Cardita calyculata* LINNÉ, *Jagonia eburnea* GMEL. (= *J. pecten* LK), *Patella intermedia* JEFFREYS, *P. teneriffae* MABILLE, *P.* cf. *safiana* LK, *Columbella rustica* LINNÉ, *Venus verrucosa* LINNÉ, *Vermetus masier* DESHAYES, *Cerithium guinaicum* PHILIPPI, *C. atratum* BORN, *Cantharus viverratus* KIENER, *Cassis testiculus* LINNÉ var. *senegalica* GMEL., *Conus* cf. *testudinarius* HWASS, *C.* aff. *mediterraneus* HWASS, *Siphonaria grisea* GMEL., *Echinometra lucunta* LINNÉ, *Spondylus gaederopus* LINNÉ, *Pectunculus* cf. *vovan* LAMY, *Fissurella verna* GOULD, *F. nubecula* LINNÉ, *F. coarctata* KING, *Nerita senegalensis* GMEL., *Murex hoplites* P. FISCHER, *Cypraea* cf. *lurida* LINNÉ, *Purpura neritoidea, P. haemastoma* LINNÉ, *P. neritoides* LINNÉ, *Harpa rosea* LK, *Psammobia intermedia* DESHAYES, *Cancellaria cancellata* LINNÉ, *Gadinia afra* GMEL., *Dosinia isocardia* DUNKER, *Gastrana matadoa* (ADAMSON) GMEL., *Lathyrus filosus* SOWERBY, *Glyphis gibberula* LINNÉ, *Orbicula* aff. *adunca* FICHTEL & MOLL var. VIANAI, *Cardisoma armatum* HERKL, *Testudo calcarata* SCHNEIDER (= *T. sulcata* GMEL. = *T. radiata* var. *senegalensis* GRAY), *Phragmites* sp.

## Boa Vista

*Arca (Senilia) senilis* LINNÉ, *Mitra* aff. *operta* BELLARDI, *Oliva flammulata* LAMARCK, *Conus* aff. *franciscanus* LAMARCK, *Bulla (Haminae) hydatis* LINNÉ, *Terebra fuscata* BROCCHI, *Cancellaria cancellat* LINNÉ, var. *similis* SOWERBY, *Amphistegina haueri* D'ORBIGNY, *A. lessonii* D'ORBIGNY, *Pecten corallinoides* D'ORBIGNY, *Bolivina robusta?* BRADY, *Textularia aglutinans* D'ORBIGNY, *Eponides* sp., *Planorbis* sp., *Nonion striolatum?* (COSTA) CUSHMAN, *Quinqueloculina striata?* D'ORBIGNY, *Orbiculina compressa?* D'ORBIGNY, *Anomalina* sp., *Trochamina nitida?* BRADY, *Patellina* sp., *Rotalia becarii* LINNÉ, *R. opercularis?* D'ORBIGNY, *Ostrocode (Cypris?)*.

## S. Tiago

*Arca decussata* SOWERBY, *A. noe* LINNÉ, *A. plicata* CHEMNITZ, *A. plicata* CHEMNITZ *acanthis* FONTANNES, *A. senilis* LINNÉ, *A. lactea* LINNÉ n. sp., *A. tenella* REEVE, *A. papillifera* HOERNES, *A. diluvii* LAMARCK var. *pertransversa* SACCO, *A. barbata* LINNÉ, *A. (Senilia) senilis* (LINNÉ) var. *Jorgei, Chama gryphina* LAMARCK, *C. gryphoides* LINNÉ, *Chlamys corallinoides* LINNÉ, *C. operculina* (LINNÉ), *C. operculina* (LINNÉ) *latecostatus* MONTEROSATO, *C. flabellum* (GMEL.), *C. scabrella* (LK) *sarmenticia* (GOLDFUSS), *C. pesfelis* LINNÉ, *C. crispa* (B) *subsqamea* (FONTANNES), *C. multistriata* (POLI), *Diplodonta circularis* DUNKER, *D. diaphana* (GMEL.), *Donax pulchellus* HANLEY, *D. trunculus* LINNÉ, *Dosinia isocardia* D. *blancheti* DOLLFUSS, *D. exoleta* (LINNÉ), *D. lupinus* POLI, *Gari incarnata* (LINNÉ), *Gastrana fragilis* LINNÉ, *Glycimeris bimaculatus* POLI, *Gryphae cuculata* (BORN), *G. gryphoides* (SCHLOTHEIM), *G. virleti* (DESHAYES), *Isognomon sulcata* LAMARCK, *Lucina columbella* LAMARCK, *L. eburnea* (GMEL.), *L. aurantia* (DESHAYES),

*Macorna tenuis* (Da costa), *Modiolus adriaticus* Lamarck, *Ostrea edulis* Linné, *O. squarrosa* Serres, *O. stentina* Payraudeau, *O. hyotis* (Linné), *O. navicularis* Brocchi, *O. cochlear* Poli, *O. (Alectryonia) cuculata* Born, *O. (A.) plicatula* (Linné) Gmel. var. *germanitala* Gray, *O. (A.) plicatula* (Linné) Gmel. var. *taurinensis* Sacco, *Pecten jacobeus* Linné, *P.* aff. *opercularis* Linné, var. *ignotus* Rochbrune, *P.* aff. *benedictus* Lamarck, *P.* aff. *sub-benedictus* Fontannes, *P.* aff. *tigris* (?) Lamarck, *P.* aff. *sub-malvinae* Blanckenhorn, *P.* aff. *scabrellus* Lamarck, *P.* aff. *zenonis* Cowper-Reed, *Pinna tetragona* Brongn., *P.* aff. *pectinata* Linné, *Semele modesta* Adams, *Solecurtas candidus* Bronn, *Tagelus caribaeus* (Lamarck), *Tellina planata* Linné, *Venerupis irus* Linné, *Venus casina* Linné, *V. foliaceo-lamellosa* (Schroeter), *V. verrucosa* Linné, *V. verrucosa* Linné, *simulans* Sowerby, *V. multilamelloides* Sacco, *V. pereffosa* Dautz & Fisch, *V. plicata* Gmel. var., *Bursa corrugata* Perry, *B. scrobiculator* (Linné) n. sp., *Cantharus sulcatus* (Gmel.), *Fissurella alabastrites* Reeve, *F. conioides* Reeve, *F. glaucopsis* Reeve, *F. nubecula* Linné *liliacina* (Costa), *Glyphis gibberula* Lamarck, *Hipponix antiquatus* (Linné), *H. pilosus* (Deshayes), *Patella guttata* d'Orbigny, *Purpura haemastoma* (Linné), *P. nodosa* (Linné), *Siphonaria pectinata* (Linné) *lineolata* Sowerby, *S. pectinata* (Linné) *palpebrum* Reeve, *Williamia gussoni* (Costa), *Arbacia lixula* (Linné), *Echinometra lucunter* (Linné), *Capsa lacunosa* (Chemnitz), *Cardita aculeata* (Poli), *C. trapezia* Brug., *Cardium edule* Linné, *C. fasciatum* Montagu, *C. paucicostatum* Sowerby var. *produca* B. D. D., *Cryptodon flexuosus* Michelotti *michelotti* Hörn, *Ervilia zibonica* Doderlein, *Limopsis minuta* (Philippi), *Lucinopsis undata* (Pennant), *Lutraria lutraria* Linné, *Spondylus concentricus* Bronn, *S. gaederopus* Linné, *Venericardia antiquata* Linné n. sp., *Argobucium reticularis* (Linné), *Drupa nodulosa* Adams, *Trochochlea turbinata* Born, *Monodonta tamsi* Dunker, *Tellina* aff. *serrata* Renier var., *Turritella bicingulata* Lamarck, *T. bicarinata* Eichwald var. *taurocrassula* Sacco ( = *T. subarchimedes* d'Orbigny), *Terebra gatunensis kugleri* Rutsch, *Capulus elegans* Deshayes ( = *Pileosis lamellosus* Chenu), *Vermetus selectus* Monterosato, *Fasciolaria coronata* Lamarck, *Murex branderis* Linné, *Cypraea spurca* Linné ( = *C. flaveola* Lamarck), *Clypeaster martini* Desmoulin, *Lithophyllum* cf. *retusum* Foslie, *L. africanum* Foslie var. *truncata* Foslie, *Tellina* aff. *serrata* Renier var., *Potamides (Tympanotomus) fuscata* Linné, *Cassis testiculus* Linné ( = *C. crumena* Brug. *testiculoides* Sacco), *Cancellaria cancellata* Linné var. *similis* Sowerby, *Natica collaria* Lamarck, *Lithophyllum decussatum* Ellis & Solander, *L. isthmi* Howe, *Amphistegina lessonii* d'Orbigny, *A. vulgaris* Parker, Jones & Brady, *Biloculina* sp., *Rotalia becarii* Linné, *Globigerina bulloides* d'Orbigny, *Elphidium crispus* (Linné), *Textularia* aff. *gibbosa* d'Orbigny, *Lithothamnium vaughani* Howe, *Turritella bicingulata* Lamarck, *Operculina complanata* Parker & Jones.

## Fogo

*Oliva flammulata* Lamarck, *Arca (Senilia) senilis* Linné, *Chama gryphina* Lamarck, *Cerithium oemulum* Sowerby.

## Brava

*Arca (Senilia) senilis* Linné, *Nerita strata* Chemnitz, *Patella lusitanica* Gmel. *P. vulgata* Linné, *P. guineensis* Dunker, *Rotalia becarii* d'Orbigny, *Amphistegina lessonii*

D'ORBIGNY, *A. hauerii* D'ORBIGNY, *A. parisensis* TERQUEM ( = var. *A. lessonii* D'ORBIGNY), *Lithothamnium isthmi* HOWE, *L. vaughani* HOWE, *Lithophyllum decussatum* ELLIS & SOLANDER, *Miliolina* sp., *Cypridina* aff. *similis* REUSS, *Cibicides* sp., *Globigerina bulloides* D'ORBIGNY, *Biloculina bulloides* D'ORBIGNY, *Bolivina aenariensis* COSTA, *Miliolina trigonula* LAMARCK, *Rotalia becarii* D'ORBIGNY var. *soldanii* (PARKER & JONES) ( = *R. soldanii* D'ORBIGNY.)

## Maio

*Aptychus atlanticos* HENNIG n. sp. ( = ( = *Lamellaptychus angulocostatus* PET. var. *atlantica*), *A.* cf. *euglyptus, A. angulocostatus* PICTET & DE LORIOL, *A.* cf. *seranonis* COQUAND, *Laevilamellaptychus hennigi* TRAUTH 1936, *L.* aff. *xestus* TRAUTH var. SOUSATORRESI, *Lamellaptychus saldanhai, L. saldanhai* var. *assunçaoi, Ammonites euglyptus* OPPEL, *Cornutella* sp., *Bathopyramis* sp., *Cenosphoera* sp., *Staurosphoera* sp., *Theocorys* sp., *Lytoceras* aff. *subfimbriatum* D'ORBIGNY, *L. sabaudianum* PICTET & DE LORIOL, *L.* aff. *anicoptychum* UHLIG, *L. phestus* MATHERON, *L.* sp. (aff. *L. subfimbricatum* D'ORBIGNY aff. *L. liebig* OPPEL), *Hamulina* sp., *H.* cf. *hamus* QUENSTEDT, *H. subcylindrica* D'ORBIGNY, *H. hamus* QUENSTEDT, *Crioceras duvali* LÉV., *C. emerici* LÉV., *C.* cf. *meyrati* PICTET, *Pulchellia* aff. *pulchella* D'ORBIGNY, *P. rhombocostata* STAHLECKER, *P. subcaicedi* SAYN, *P. hoplitiformis* SAYN, *P. (?) africana* STAHLECKER, *P.* aff. *compressissima* D'ORBIGNY, *Heteroceras giraudi* KILIAN, *H. multicostatum* STAHLECKER, *Phylloceras* cf. *guettardi* RASPAIL, *P.* aff. *infindibulum* D'ORBIGNY, *Parahoplites* cf. *hitzeli* JACOB, *Inoceramus* sp., *Desmoceras* sp., *Ptychoceras* aff. *morloti* OOSTER, *P. gaultinum* PICTET, *P. meyrati* OOSTER, *Costidiscus recticostatus* D'ORBIGNY, *Ancyloceras maioensis* STAHLECKER, *A. matheronianum* D'ORBIGNY, *Toxoceras filicostatum* STAHLECKER, *Douvilleiceras irregulare* STAHLECKER, *Leptoceras heeri* OOSTER, *L.* cf. *beyrichi* KARSTEN, *L. (?) spinosum* STAHLECKER, *Bochianites hennigi* STAHLECKER, *Psilotissotia favrei* OOSTER, *Puzosia* sp., *Akidocheilus* sp. TILL, *Arca (Senilia) senilis* LINNÉ, *A. plicata* CHEMNITZ, *A. noe* LINNÉ, *A. decussata* SOWERBY, *A.* cf. *tetragona* POLI, *Ostrea* aff. *lingula* SOWERBY ( = *O.* aff. *sub-lingua* D'ORBIGNY), *O. gryphoides?* SCHLOTHEIM, *O. cucullata* BORN var., *O. stentina* PAYRAUDEAU, *Eastonia rugosa* CHEMNITZ, *Mytilus charpenteri* DUNKER, *Strombus bubonius* LAMARCK, *Testudo calcarata* SCHNEIDER ( = *T. sulcata* GMEL.), *Lucina (Kodackia) pecten* LAMARCK ( = *L. reticulata* (POLI), *L. aurantia* DESHAYES, *L. columbella* LAMARCK, *L. eburnea* (GMEL.), *L. imbricatula* ADAMS, *L. imbricatula* ADAMS *filiata* DALL, *Hipponix (Amalthea)* aff. *chamaeiformis* ROCHEBRUNE, *H. antiquatus* (LINNÉ), *H. pilosus* (DESHAYES), *Fissurella humphreyi* REEVE, *F. benguellensis* DUNKER, *F.* aff. *alabastrites* REEVE, *F. philippiana* DUNKER, *F. angustata* (SOWERBY), *F. conioides* REEVE, *Patella plumbea* LAMARCK, *P. guttata* D'ORBIGNY, *Corax* sp., *Gymnodus heterodon* DELFORTRIE, *Amphistegina parisensis* TERQUEM, *Orbiculina* aff. *adunca* FICHTEL & MOLL var. VIANAI, *Elphidium crispus* (LINNÉ), *Lithothamnium vaughani* HOWE, *L. decussatum* ELLIS & SOLANDER, *L. isthmi* HOWE, *Globigerina bulloides* D'ORBIGNY, *Textularia* sp., *?Gyroidina (Rotalia) soldanii* D'ORBIGNY, *Rotalia becarii* LINNÉ, *Globorotalia* aff. *menardi* (D'ORBIGNY), *Biloculina depressa* D'ORBIGNY var. ( = *B.* aff. *elongata* D'ORBIGNY var. *ventruosa* REUSS) *Anomalinella* aff. *rostrata* BRADY, *Amphistegina mamillata* D'ORBIGNY, *A. haueri* D'ORBIGNY, *Triloculina (Miliolina)* *oblonga* MONTAGU, *Cardita aculeata* (POLI) *sulcidentata* ROCHEBRUNE, *Cardium fasciatum* MONTAGU, *Dosinia isocardia* DUNKER, *D. isocardia* DUNKER *blancheti* DOLLFUSS, *Glycimeris bimaculatus* POLI, *G. glycimeris* LINNÉ, *Gryphaea cuculata* (BORN), *Isognomon oerna* AUCTORUM, *Ungulina rubra* (DAUDIN), *Venus casina* LINNÉ, *V. verrucosa* LINNÉ *simulans* SOWERBY, *Cantharus sulcata* (GMEL.), *Crepidula aculeata* (GMEL.), *C. crepidula* (LINNÉ), *Purpura haemastoma* (LINNÉ), *P. nodosa* (LINNÉ), *Chama gryphina* LAMARCK, *Chlamys corallinoides* LAMARCK, *Semele modesta* ADAMS, *Spondylus* cf. *gaederopus* LINNÉ, *Argobucinum* cf. *cruenata* SOWERBY, *Cymatium parthenopaeum* var. SALIS, *C. parthenopaeum* var. SALIS *problematicum* DAUTZENBERG & FISCHER, *C. tranquebaricum* (LAMARCK), *C. trigonum* (GMEL.), *Avicula hirundo* (LINNÉ) *companyoi* FONTANNES, *Lima inflata* (LINNÉ), *L. lima* (LINNÉ), *Lucina orbicularis* (LINNÉ), *L. ornata* AGASSIZ, *Lutraria* aff. *lutraria* LINNÉ, *L.* aff. *oblonga* (CHEMNITZ), *Panopea faujasi* MENARD, *P. oligofaujasi* MENARD *proxima*? (MICHELOTTI), *Venus fasciata* (DA COSTA) *raricostata* JEFFREYS, *Calyptra trochiformis* GMEL., *Echinometra lucunter* (LINNÉ), *Donax rugosus* LINNÉ, *Lithophaga lithophaga* (LINNÉ), *Venus multilamella* LAMARCK, *Macoma translucida* (SOWERBY), *M. innominata* BERTIN, *Tagelus caribeus* LAMARCK, *Tellina* sp., Teleostei, Vermes, *Fucoidea*.

## Vulcanology

Active vulcanism within historic times is known only in Fogo. RIBEIRO (1960) has given a detailed account of the geography and an account of the various eruptions within historic times, along with excellent photographs of the island.

The central cone of Pico rises to an elevation of 2,829 m, and as this cone lies closer to the NE, eastern and northern slopes are steep. The summit, lying some 6.25 km due W of the eastern coast, slopes here are ca. 25°. The 500 m isobath hugs the island at an average distance of some 5 km, the 1,000 m isobath, some 10 km distant, and thus here in essence we have a most imposing volcanic structure rising some 4,000 m from the sea bed with a slope of ca. 13.5°, the pedestal having an area of some 640 km².

On the western, northern and southern sides of the island slopes range from 12° to 18°, rising to heights varying from 1,913 m to 2,700 m abruptly ending in a stupendous wall (Bordeira) with almost a vertical drop down to the inner level floor of the caldera (Cha das Caldeiras), lying at an elevation of ca. 1,625 m. Pico rises from the caldera floor slightly E of centre, there also being a small crater here, diameter 500 m, about 180 m in depth, from which rises the culminating point. The original caldera measured about 9 km N-S and 8 km E-W, but the eastern wall has been completely breached by lava flows of the ›Vesbio stage‹, so that here lava flows extend uninterrupted from sea level almost to the summit. Pico can be compared with Vesuvius and Etna thus:

|                       | Fogo      | Vesuvius   | Etna        |
|-----------------------|-----------|------------|-------------|
| Height                | 2829 m    | 1182 m     | 3279 m      |
| Height of caldera wall| 2700 m    | 1132 m     | 1000 m      |
| Diameter of caldera   | 8.5 km    | 3.75 km    | 5 km        |
| Area of volcano       | 476 km²   | 200 km²    | 1673 km²    |

According to Ribeiro (op. cit.) although volcanic forms had been recognized by voyagers to the Azores during 1454-55, seemingly such were not known then in the Cape Verde islands. Fogo (then known as Sao Felipe) is first mentioned in a document and depicted on a map dating from 1460, but it is in the first years of the 16th century that we first hear of vulcanism: »In the year 1500 there fell a huge piece from within this mountain when a fire (fogo) appeared at the same time at a place in the mountain where before there had been a summit« (Fernandes, 1940). Ribeiro thought that Fernandes did not base his description on actual observations, but nevertheless, this probably represents the first actual description of an explosive phase of vulcanism in the island. Other voyages and chronicles during the 16th and 17th centuries make repeated references to either the volcanic nature of the island or then vulcanism. It is reasonably well established that eruptions occurred in 1564, 1596, 1604, 1664, 1675, 1680, extensive expulsion of sulphurous gases in 1689, further activity in 1693, 1695, 1699, 1712, 1713, 1721-25. Seemingly there were three longer periods of eruptivity, from 1500-1564, 1604-1664 and from 1689-1725. Explosive action occurred in 1500, 1564, 1596, 1664, 1689 and during 1721-1725 (dates not too accurate). Beginning in 1785 we have more accurate and scientific descriptions, for by sheer good fortune, the naturalist Joao da Silva Feijo happened to be in Fogo when this event took place, excellently described and many sketches (1786). Further eruptions have been documented for 1799, 1816, 1847, 1852, 1857 and 1909, and of course the latest one of 1951 is well documented – vd. especially Ribeiro (op. cit.).

As remarked above, the eastern rim of the caldera has been completely breached, flows mantling the slopes down to the sea. Flows are much reduced in number, thickness and areal extent on southern slopes, and only two reach the coast. Both within the caldera floor and the nephelinitic scoriaceous outer slopes there occur about one hundred parasitic cones, most forming prominent small hills. The rectilinear arrangement of many of these suggests fissure control, the majority of these forms being cinder cones.

Two eruptive phases are recognized, taking their names from Vesuvius: (a) an earlier pre-caldera or ›Somma‹ stage, and (b) a post-caldera or ›Vesbio‹ stage. The former, which gives rise to the island proper, can be clearly observed in coastal cliff sections, where lava flows and pyroclastics are intercalated throughout heights of 100 m. Tephrites and nephelinites predominate, with basanites and augitites playing a minor role. Pyroclastics tend to be coarse, many having a brecchoidal appearance. From the ›Serra‹ (exterior scarps) and the crest of the ›Bordeira‹ (major wall), it is seen that the rocks are of two types: (i) highly feldspathoidal alkaline lavas, (ii) olivinitic lavas frequently devoid of feldspars. In the all-but perpendicular interior wall of the Bordeira occur great lava masses alternating with breccia, lapilli and tufa. A great number of quasi-vertical dykes, which may be up to 1,000 m thick, mostly comprising nephelinitic-type rocks, some ijolitic, are seen transecting the inner slopes, some extending outwards into the floor of the caldera, some tending to parallel the wall configuration. Immense dejection cones of coarse tufa, deeply ravined, are common features within the caldera. Some 80% of the ›Somma‹ rocks exposed comprise nephelinites, tephrites, basanites and augitites, along with pyroclastics.

The ›Vesbio‹ phase shows quite similar lava types, though there is less petrographic variation – nephelinites are much rarer, whilst basanites, olivine-basalts, ankaramites, limburgites and augitites more common. These younger lavas are usually poorer in alkalis and alumina, richer in magnesium than the previous lavas. All rocks of the ›Vesbio‹ stage show a fresher appearance, especially noticeable in lavas formed within historic times. Lava flows emanating from Pico (›Vulcao‹) on the caldera floor and those flowing down the eastern and southern slopes comprise chiefly limburgites, augitites and basanites. The 1951 eruption constructed two new peaks, Montes Orlando and Randall, in the SE section of the caldera, from which localities most of the flows sped forth downwards towards the sea. During the ›Somma‹ phase, lavas extruding from the central vent poured downwards and outwards in all directions, but with later foundering and creation of the caldera, lavas were directed towards the NE, E and SE.

The oldest rocks of Fogo, forming the basement, are carbonatites with associated alkaline dyke swarms. Such is to be seen in three small outcrops near S. Felipe, the basement being considered pre-Tertiary by workers. However, we should recall again the presence of probable Middle Miocene limestones occurring near these carbonatite exposures.

There appears to have been more or less continuous eruptivity from the earliest known times (1500) until about 1760, since when only short, flank eruptions have occurred. In general, these latter lasted only for one-two weeks, but the latest 1951 event continued for some two months.

MACHADO (1965b) presented his views as to the probable mechanism of Fogo. The present volume of the caldera is approx. 24 km³, and if such were caused by explosive action, then a vast quantity of ejectamenta should have littered the slopes, but in actuality it is doubtful if such explosive material accounts for 4 km³. (At Crater Lake, Oregon, 70 km³ of material was dislodged, but the volume of the remaining ejectamenta is placed at only 26.5 km³, of which a mere 6.1 km³ comprises rocks originating from the exploded material.) Because of this discrepancy, MACHADO favoured the idea of the sinking into the magma of a large cylindrical block, the ›Bordeira‹ representing then a circular fault – viz. cauldron subsidence, as first explained by CLOUGH, MAUFE & BAILEY (1909). The subsidence was likely due to simple isostatic adjustment of the central part of the cone and not to explosive drainage of the magma chamber, for acid pumice

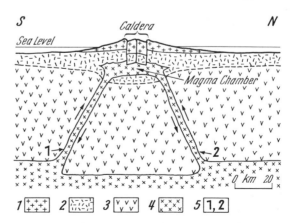

Fig. 97. Hypothetical profile to explain the mechanism of Fogo Volcano. 1: Lavas. 2: Sialic (?) crust. 3: Solid Upper Mantle (peridotite). 4: Plastic Upper Mantle – olivine crystal mush and interstitial molten basaltic magma. 5: Ring dykes. (Modified after MACHADO, 1965).

emissions are not present. On the assumption that the width of a caldera is an indication of the depth below of the magma chamber, then at Pico the latter would be about 8 km down. In substantiation of a shallow magma chamber, MACHADO remarked that Fogo eruptions tend to show coincidence with a minimal Earth tide period of 18.6 years, which would suggest an isolated chamber being expelled upwards due to tidal compression. Militating against such a view is the absence of differentiation, suggesting quasi-permanent re-feeding of the magma chamber, which could not then be isolated. He attempted to reconcile these seemingly conflicting views by assuming that such a type of chamber results from cauldron subsidence, the feeding being via ring fractures which pierce the plastic substratum, likely comprising an olivine crystal mush and interstitial molten basaltic magma. Release of pressure, consequent upon tidal periodicity, would allow this mush to be squeezed upwards, and at higher levels the basaltic magma could thus feed the eruptions. Such a mechanism implies a constant supply of magma, whilst the olivine crystal mush, filling the ring structures, could withstand the relatively quick tidal impulses, so creating the effect of a magma chamber isolated from the olivine crystal mush zone of the upper mantle.

The above hypothesis of MACHADO is lacking in all factual evidence. In considering the discrepancy between volume of exploded material and postulated present volume we must note that Fogo is not a large island, that much of the ejected material could have fallen in the neighbouring seas, especially if strong, persistent NE winds, then as now, were operative, that vertical oscillations of both land and sea have occurred. Then we must note in Fogo the total absence of any ring structures, either ring-dykes or cone-sheets, other than the caldera wall itself, but to date no evidences are seen along the wall of great vertical downdropping of a subsided block. Attempting to correlate times of eruptivity with tidal periods of 18.6 years is far-fetched indeed – of the twenty intervals of eruptivity, only six show a periodicity close to 18.6 years, varying from 18.6 years by periods as much as 7.6 years, in other words, how broad a latitude is one to accept? Even granting that Earth tides act as triggers, the direct cause(s) of eruptivity here still evades us.

**Geophysical Aspects**

WATKINS, RICHARDSON & MASON (1968) collected 500 rock samples from the islands, of which 157 were studied in detail as regards their magnetic properties. In summary, the separate island results showed the following:

Sto. Antao: Samples had a large range altitudinally but only one reversed polarity was found, taken to indicate a long reversed Miocene geomagnetic polarity epoch.

S. Vicente: Though topographically lower than Sto. Antao, S. Vicente showed more polarity variation; but at higher elevations only reversed polarities occur. Perhaps the period of reversed geomagnetic polarity in Sto. Antao coincided with a period of volcanic activity in S. Vicente, though the volcanics in question differ chiefly in being thinner in the latter island. The Piedras Blancas quartz-monzonite plug showed reversed polarity, the same for the limburgite dykes intruding it.

S. Nicolau: The N-S trending scarp behind the capital Brava shows reversed polarity throughout.

Sal: Columnar basalt plugs in the NE differ in emplacement from the normal polarity phonolite masses in the centre of the island and the lavas at Palmeira.

Maio: As in Sal, weathering has virtually eliminated all but a few suitable outcrops below the post-Upper Cretaceous unconformity, and hence no axial dipole is likely to result from the data.

S. Tiago: Here there is a suggestion of dominantly normal polarity in the central region and reversed polarity in the southern area.

Fogo: Normal polarity showed from one sample on the NE coast, the extrusive sampled being of Recent-Pleistocene age, and as the geomagnetic field is believed to have shown normal polarity since 700,000 years, this would be in keeping with its postulated age.

NE sto. Antao and S. Vicente comprise dominantly reversed magnetic lavas, probably caused by the relatively long-duration reversed geomagnetic polarity epoch during the Miocene. Perhaps the rapid accumulation of reversed magnetized laval sections in the two islands cannot positively be precluded. Except in NE Sto. Antao and S. Vicente, the authors believed that polarity variations would prove most useful in further stratigraphic work in the islands. S. Tiago is markedly different from islands to the N by the predominance of normal polarity. As the palaeomagnetic poles for Sto. Antao and S. Vicente are similar to those for S. Nicolau and S. Tiago (but see below), the sampled lavas being considered mostly Miocene, those of Sto. Antao and S. Vicente are similarly thought to represent Miocene.

From the palaeomagnetic pole positions of the islands (Fig. 98) the virtual geomagnetic pole position for the archipelago is in good agreement with the Miocene

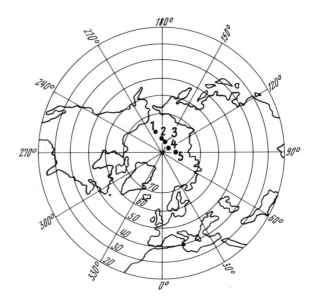

Fig. 98. Virtual geomagnetic poles. Cape Verde Islands. 1: Maio. 2: S. Tiago. 3: Sta. Antao. 4: S. Nicolau. 5: S. Vicente. (WATKINS, RICHARDSON & MASON, 1968).

Table 66                                                          Geomagnetic data regarding

|            | Magnetic data | | | | | |
|            | Mean Decl. | Mean Incl. | N | Fisher statistical values | | |
|            |            |            |   | R | K | A95 |
|------------|-----------|-----------|---|-------|----------|------|
| Sto. Antao | 16.9 | 28.3 | 34 | 33.97 | 979.48 | 0.79 |
| S. Vicente | 16.4 | 25.3 | 12 | 11.99 | 1059.65 | 1.33 |
| S. Nicolau | 17.0 | 27.0 | 15 | 14.99 | 1954.18 | 0.87 |
| Sal        | 16.6 | 25.3 | 13 | 12.99 | 1138.13 | 1.23 |
| Boa Vista  | 16.1 | 24.5 | 26 | 25.97 | 844.54 | 0.98 |
| Maio       | 17.0 | 22.3 | 11 | 11.00 | 3839.53 | 0.74 |
| S. Tiago   | 17.1 | 22.6 | 35 | 34.96 | 829.72 | 0.84 |
| Fogo       | 16.9 | 23.3 | 15 | 14.98 | 848.60 | 0.32 |
| Brava      | 17.2 | 22.6 | 5  | 5.00 | 54475.53 | 0.33 |

geomagnetic pole position for this part of the Atlantic and is very similar to those deduced for the Canary Islands and Madeira by these same authors (1966). It was also their view that the Cape Verde Islands had not been displaced relative to Africa since Miocene times.

Magnetic studies (MENDES-VICTOR, 1970) executed between October 1961 and July 1963, showed for May 1962 that mean declinations varies from -16.4 for S. Vicente to -17.2 for Brava, mean inclinations from 22.3 for Maio to 28.3 for Sto. Antao. The magnetic field direction showed in general a regular distribution, with mean inclination values increasing with latitude. Between Sto. Antao and S. Vicente, separated by only 12 km at the nearest points, there was an inclination difference of 3°. To account for this difference, reference is made to the single reverse polarity encountered in Sto. Antao by WATKINS et al. (op. cit.) whereas several such reversed polarities were met with in S. Vicente. WATKINS et al. claimed that as the geomagnetic poles for Sto. Antao and S. Tiago were very close, this could be taken to mean that the lavas in question were of the same age which were sampled, viz. Miocene. However, they expressed the same hypothesis for S. Vicente whose pole is azimuthally displaced almost 90° from that of Sto. Antao. MENDES-VICTOR also remarked that the mean directions for samples taken from S. Vicente and S. Nicolau scarce fit into the picture when gravimetric results are taken into consideration. As for Sal and Maio, the difficulties encountered with samples here is surely related to their age and structural deformation experienced. (As regards this tendency of both WATKINS et al. and MENDES-VICTOR to lump together on an age basis Sal and Maio, we must note what we have said earlier, where Mesozoic certainly has been proven in Maio but this cannot be said for Sal.) As regards S. Tiago, MENDESVICTOR noted the inclination difference between here and Sto. Antao cannot be readily interpreted because sampling in the former island was not done in the northern part by WATKINS et al.

From a gravimetric survey of the islands (Fig. 99) the following points can be made: (1) On S. Vicente, S. Nicolau, Sal, Maio, S. Tiago and Fogo eruptive centres are well outlined by gravimetric anomalies. (2) It appears that secondary eruptive centres occur

Cape Verde Islands (modified after WATKINS et al., 1968; MENDES-VICTOR, 1970)

| Palaeomagnetic data | | | | | | | |
|---|---|---|---|---|---|---|---|
| No. bodies sampled | Total No. cores from samples | Fisher angle of confidence | Fisher coeff. precesion | Declin. NRM | Inclin. NRM | Co-ords of virtual mag. poles. | |
| 40 | 120 | 6.5 | 12.9 | 358.7 | + 22.7 | 168.2 | 84.5 |
| 46 | 143 | 6.4 | 12.0 | 6.7 | + 26.8 | 87.1 | 83.0 |
| 12 | 36 | 7.2 | 37.3 | 1.7 | + 26.2 | 124.7 | 86.8 |
| 5 | 16 | 46.5 | 3.7 | 15.3 | − 00.7 | 114.1 | + 67.3 |
| – | – | – | – | – | – | – | – |
| 4 | 18 | 41.5 | 5.9 | 352.6 | + 12.8 | 197.2 | + 78.7 |
| 30 | 103 | 5.2 | 26.8 | 357.4 | + 17.1 | 178.9 | + 82.3 |
| 1 | 8 | 3.2 | 296.1 | 358.2 | + 00.8 | 161.7 | 75.2 |
| – | – | – | – | – | – | – | – |

in Maio, S. Tiago and Fogo. (3) Sto. Antao seems to have undergone a basculatory movement along a NW-SE axial trend which somewhat masks the gravimetric definitions corresponding to eruptive centres. (4) Boa Vista is exceptional in showing an important mass deficiency. (5) Regional gradients converge in general towards the interior sea perhaps thereby suggesting a common magnatic chamber for the archipelago. (6) Between Sto. Antao and S. Vicente the difference between BOUGUER maximums and minimums is 36 and 23 mgls respectively, whereas between Maio and S. Tiago these are 30 and 35 mgls respectively. As in both cases the island groups are close to each other, it is likely that some deep structure in responsible for the differences noted. (7) The negative residual anomalies are certainly due to the fact that MENDES-VICTOR used a mean density of 2.64 in his calculations for the socle, whilst phonolites, syenites, trachytes and pyroclastics can have lower densities. (8) Maximal residual and regional anomalies, minimal BOUGUER and Free-Air anomalies occur within the channel separating Sto. Antao and S. Vicente. (9) Qualitative studies of the gravity field show a large regional anomaly in the Cape Verde area, confirmed by aeromagnetic profiles.

MENDES-VICTOR believed that near Sto. Antao and S. Vicente, a marine profile showing a regional value of 210 mgls was related to a rising of the upper mantle at the time of formation of the islands, that this rising, which would cause an alteration of physical properties, would result in the anomaly picture determined. The differences of 67 mgls for the BOUGUER maximum in Sto. Antao and this 210 mgls regional value, that of 103 mgls for S. Vicente, are surely due to overloading related to principal eruptive centres. However, Boa Vista shows a maximum difference of 92 mgls with respect to the mean regional value of 195 mgls obtained from an E-W marine profile obtained here. The weak BOUGUER anomaly values noted here presumably resulted from local differentiations within the crust itself.

As regards other islands away from the N-S marine profile across the S. Vicente Canal and the E-W profile through the Boa Vista-Maio region, MENDES-VICTOR attempted to calculate the regional anomaly from the above results got from the

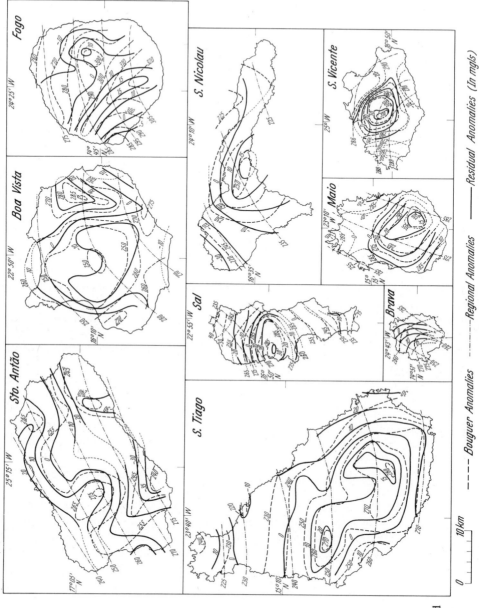

Fig. 99.
Gravity maps of
the Cape Verde
Islands. (Modified
after MENDES-
VICTOR, 1970).

Fig. 100. Positive and negative resi-
dual gravity anomalies, Cape Verde
Islands. (Modified after MENDES-
VICTOR, 1970).

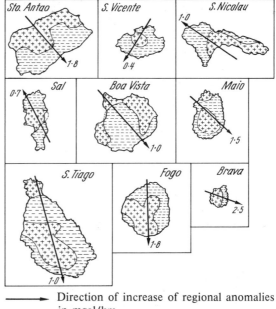

──────▶ Direction of increase of regional anomalies
in mgal/km.

profiles for the other islands of the archipelago. Taking the differences between the
BOUGUER anomaly minimums for each island and those for S. Vicente and Boa Vista, the
values obtained were: S. Nicolau, 165 mgls; Sal, 184 mgls; Maio, 206 mgls; S. Tiago,
171 mgls; Fogo, 209 mgls; Brava, 204 mgls. He also computed maximal crustal
anomalies and crustal thicknesses for the various islands, as shown in Table 67, as well
as calculated excess masses for some islands.

Table 67      Crustal features, Cape Verde Archipelago (MENDES-VICTOR, 1970)

| Island | Crustal anomaly mgls. | Crustal thickness km | Excess of mass tonnes |
|---|---|---|---|
| S. Vicente | 103 | 20 | $7.1 \times 10^7$ |
| Sto. Antao | 67 | 13 | |
| S. Nicolau | 87 | 17 | |
| Sal | 113 | 22 | $2.6 \times 10^8$ |
| Boa Vista | 92 | 18 | |
| Maio | 105 | 20 | $3.4 \times 10^8$ |
| S. Tiago | 110 | 21 | |
| Fogo | 116 | 22 | |
| Brava | 74 | 14 | |

## Structure-Tectonics

The great preponderance of structures shown are either of pseudo-tectonic or volcano-tectonic origin. In some islands the strong relief, combined with the nature of the rainfall, promote mass-wasting in the form of rockfalls, rockslides, slumping, debris flow. In this arid environment, the regolith is essentially a result of mechanical weathering and is relatively thin so that mechanical attack is easily accomplished. Sedimentaries and pyroclastics are characterized by structures chiefly imposed by such means. Crossbedding, of aeolian and wave origin, is well seen in several localities, e. g. the papery calcareous sandstones of Montinho de Lume, just outside Vila Maio, Maio.

Igneous emplacements, either massive or as dykes chiefly, have disturbed frequently the vicinal rocks and so created disturbance thereof, fracturing no less has developed.

In general we could say that in the sedimentary rocks, syngenetic structures are characterized by cross-bedding, wave- and rill-marks, concretions; accretionary epigenetic structures comprise nodules, septaria, clastic dykes. The role of running water is most prominently seen in current bedding, occasionally torrential bedding.

Sedimentaries show tilting rather than folding, throughout the archipelago jointing seems commoner than faulting, and in general we could say that pronounced folding, faulting are significantly lacking – but see Maio below.

Though diastems are common, significant unconformities are few in number. The most important one, an angular unconformity, occurs between the Mesozoics and Tertiaries in the vicinity of Barreiro, Maio. Here horizontal, friable sandy limestones, some 3 m thick, rest directly of volcanics and Cretaceous compact, hard limestones dipping NNE at angles of some 75° (Fig. 101). We have already remarked that nowhere else in the archipelago are dips as high as in these Maio Mesozoics, which in places are vertical, the highest Tertiary dips seemingly being those of 49° at Monte Focinho, S. Nicolau. In fact, other than with these Maio Mesozoics, one is impressed how gentle dips are throughout the archipelago.

SERRALHEIRO (1970) does stress the importance of faulting, development of complicated dyke patterns along fracture lines and a large anticline (ɔgrande pseudodobraɔ) in Maio, predominantly in the SE part. As per his map of faults, made from aerial photograph interpretations, these are aligned in four principal directions – N-S, E-W and the two diagonal directions, the majority tending to be diagonally

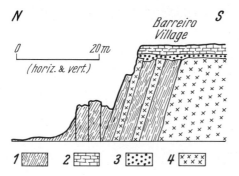

Fig. 101. Geologic section, Ribeira Barreiro, Maio. 1: Mesozoic limestones. 2: Tertiary limestones. 3: Tertiary conglomerates. 4: Basalts, lamprophyres. (After BEBIANO, 1932).

orientated. This extensive fracturing is restricted to Mesozoic terrain. We readily agree that from what is known at present, the geology of this island differs in several important respects from that of other islands, no less must we recognize that only Maio and S. Tiago have been given more than reconnaissance study, due to the later investigations of SERRALHEIRO, yet withall, the writer is sceptical of this proliferation of faulting in Maio. Aerial photographs were used in the delineation of such, but no indication is given as to what checking of faulting was done in the field. SERRALHEIRO definitely assumes that tectonism has played an important role in the development of

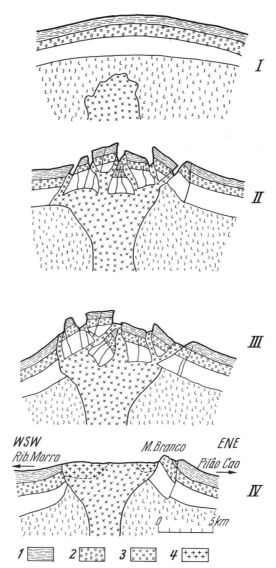

Fig. 102. Schematic outline of essexite "diapir" intrusion into the Mesozoics in Southern Maio. I: Initial stage. Arched Mesozoics. Ascendancy of essexite intrusion. II: Emplacement of essexite "diapir", fracturing, jostling of blocks, dyke formation. III: Further jostling of blocks and accentuations of dips. IV: Present state after intense erosion. 1: Cretaceous. 2: Jurassic. 3: Essexite. 4: Dyke complex. (Based on SERRALHEIRO, 1970).

the island, but to the writer such folding and fracturing as may be present is a response to volcanic emplacements, hence of volcano-tectonic origin. To account for these highly inclined Mesozoics of Maio, the writer (1964) envisaged a pushing aside of initially more horizontally inclined strata by later viscous lava intrusions, first bending the superimcumbent sedimentaries then more violently thrusting them aside, thus increasing their dips. SERRALHEIRO (op. cit.) develops this idea further, where a major fault, trending NNW-SSE, with a throw of 450 m, suggested to him a complex diapiric structure (Fig. 102) with a ›root‹ some 4,000 m in depth. Confirmation of such an idea is forthcoming from the gravimetric study of the island made by MENDES-VICTOR (1970) (Fig. 99) with high BOUGUER values and residual anomalies aligned NW-SE, with the alignment of the eruptive centre trending N-S. SERRALHEIRO also postulated the presence beneath Maio of a rift developed by essexite intrusions.

In S. Nicolau and Sto. Antao two important faults can be recognized. In the former island there is a curvilinear N-S fault on the western side of Campo de Preguiça, outlined as a prominent fault-scarp extending for some 10 km. This striking topographic feature was postulated first by BEBIANO (1932) to account for the M. Focinho marine limestones, now lying 250 m above sea level. The fault hades to the E, the limestones and the block W of the fault being upraised and tilted to the W, strata in both E and W blocks dipping to the W. On the basis of gravimetric studies, MENDES-VICTOR (op. cit.) believed that the root of the island lay E of Campo de Preguiça, i. e. E of the fault, this representing the depressed block.

In Sto. Antao a likely fault of reverse type, striking parallel to the northern coast, has resulted in an upraised block, tilted to the N, between the Ribeira Grande valley to the S and the seacoast to the N. The N wall of the valley looks very much like a fault-scarp, trending for some 10 km in a NE-SW direction. The studies of MENDES-VICTOR show no substantiation of this fault, but he does refer to »un accident tectonique« trending NW-SE in the western highest part of the island. Physiographic hints and studies of aerial photographs would suggest many more smaller faults in the islands but direct field evidence has pin-pointed only a few.

Jointing, especially in the volcanics, is a prominent feature, and most of such appear to result from tension rather than shear. Columnar jointing in the volcanics is not common, though some excellent examples occur in S. Nicolau. Limestones being the commonest sedimentary rocks and these being rocks susceptible to jointing, it follows that the limestones display extensive jointing – transverse, cross, longitudinal, flat-lying. To date no detailed studies have been made of fractures in general, and hence our knowledge about all aspects of such is rudimentary indeed.

In his reconnaissance studies, BEBIANO (1932) postulated large fracture systems which appear to link-up the islands into tectonic alignments or lineaments. In his day he had to base such linkages essentially upon the trends of bathymetric contours, and further at a time when bathymetric investigations of the Eastern Atlantic had not reached their present refinement. Thus BEBIANO showed a major fracture running WNW-ESE through Sto. Antao-S. Vicente-Sta. Luzia-S. Nicolau to Boa Vista and beyond, etc. The subjective approach of the author is ever so manifest in the drawing of linkages based primarily upon bathymetric contours, where geological knowledge is only of reconnaissance nature, where all geophysical data are lacking. Linkages of such a sort the writer preferred to name ›vincula‹, arbitrary delineations whose function is copulative rather than consanguineous (MITCHELL-THOME, 1961). Vincula lack the substance and control of lineaments which latter, as defined by BROCK (1957) are ›alignments of a precision which rules out fortuity‹. The writer (op. cit., 1966) has criticized these linkages made for the Cape Verde region, and the point need not be laboured here. However, it must be noted that since the time BEBIANO and the writer were writing, MENDES-VICTOR (1970) has published his gravimetric and magnetic studies of the archipelago. He is inclined to accept a major fracture which was made use of by the eruptives of Sto. Antao, S. Vicente, Sta. Luzia and S. Nicolau, agreeing in general trend with the transform fault postulated in this region by LE PICHON (1968) and with the above-mentioned trend of BEBIANO. But to date there is no further bathymetric or geophysical evidence in support of BEBIANO's other four major delineations, and all told, our present knowledge, geological, geophysical and oceanographic of this general area does not warrant the drawing of lineaments either inter-island or with the African mainland.

## Economic Geology

Salt, pozzulana are the sole mineral exploitations in the archipelago. In Sal salinas occur at Santa Maria in the extreme S of the island and at Pedra Lume, in the NE. At the former locality, sea water infiltrates the coastal sands into diked traps and allowed to evaporate under the strong sunlight and winds, readily promoting evaporation. According to the height of the area to assure depth consonant with sea level, ditches, varying from 1–3 m in depth, are dug in the littoral sands. Sea water is raised by means of wind-operated pumps. The crystallized salt is scraped into heaps and loaded directly on to ships.

The salina at Pedra Lume is of geological interest as it is a crater of an extinct volcano, some 800 m in diameter, distant from the sea one kilometre and in subterranean communication with the sea. Oceanic tides flush the sea water inwards to the crater and upon evaporation, salt pans are formed. Salt obtained here is usually placed in sacks and taken on small boats out to larger vessels anchored off-shore.

As far back as 1841, 11,500 tons were being exported annually of salt, the revenue being equal to that of total exports of S. Tiago, the most prosperous island then as now. In 1969 Sal exported 27,500 tons salt, being the main supplier for the archipelago.

Pozzulana exploitation from volcanic ashes in Sto. Antao for the production of Portland cement now amounts annually to ca. 18,500 tons. Crude kilns produce some lime in certain islands, there is also a rudimentary ceramic industry, but these are insignificant activities.

Some springs would qualify as of mineral type, but only one, that of Vinagre in Brava, is exploited commercially in a small way, these highly carbonated waters being quite the best tasting in all the archipelago.

The obtaining of adequate water supplies has long been a problem. As we have seen, the archipelago is arid to semi-arid at all times but when droughts occur for successive years, living conditions become almost catastrophic, in historic times there having been repeated economic crises. Since the archipelago was first known, the climate has not changed, areas have not changed, but most certainly the population has changed. During the period 1870–1970, this increased from 76,000 to 272,000 – 356% increase! Therein lies the major water problem. Water supplies solely for domestic needs are sufficient as of the present, but this ignores the large quantities used and needed further for agricultural purposes – the economic mainstay of the islanders. Increased irrigation is needed to feed the extra peoples, thus engendering domestic supplies. In some islands present water consumption for domestic purposes is as low as 7 litres per day per capita, and for the archipelago as a whole, this is 23 litres/day/capita. Even at present, water for irrigation needs represents 93% of total water consumption. Writing in 1960, when the archipelago population was some 200,000, the writer calculated total water consumption, all uses, as 84,000 m³ daily, total yields, 236,000 m³ daily, 35% and 54% respectively of available daily supplies. But consideration of non-recoverable water presents a much grimmer picture, for in some fifteen years the projected population will be needing some 76% of all available supplies.

Only the pyroclastics possess adequate hydrologic properties, and of these, lapilli and ash beds constitute excellent aquifers, as well as sand dunes, where thicker and more extensive. The abundant tuffs act more as aquicludes, and as regards alluvium, this is poorly developed in the small valleys, has a heavy admixture with clays, silts. Run-off plus evaporation account for 75–95% of water losses from the infrequent rainfalls. Of the rain that falls, only some 1–7% is utilizable as groundwater. Thus the hydrology, climate, burgeoning population all combine to make water an ever-present and increasing problem in the archipelago.

## Geologic Evolution

As of the present, and as per stratigraphic dating, the Cape Verde archipelago is the oldest in the Middle Atlantic region.

The crustal nature is oceanic, the archipelago is not of continental association. Events seemingly began with submarine emanations, the locus thereof being controlled by fissures which allowed lavas to rise up into the sea bed. These volcanics constitute the true fundament of the area in question, and very possibly date from the Jurassic. In Maio we have sedimentaries dating back to the Neocomian, perhaps even Portlandian. To some the Neocomian beds have been interpreted to indicate relatively deep environments of deposition – 2,000 m has been mentioned – others prefer to see majolica-type limestone without mentioning depths (COLOM, 1954 and personal comminications) whilst others again, e. g. SERRALHEIRO (1970) would claim that only the limestones represent deeper marine environments. The writer (MITCHELL-THOMÉ, 1964, 1972) has criticized these pelagic concepts, for pelagic sediments owe their characteristics to remoteness from sources of supply of terrigenous materials as much as to depth of marine environment. The famous chalk of the Dover cliffs and of much of NW Europe was once considered a deep-sea deposit, but today is regarded to represent maximum depths of 1,500 m and in many occurrences, far shallower, the pelagic aspect being due to lack of terrigenous ingredients. In a modified way such is presumed for these Maio Mesozoics, they represent neritic sedimentation in marginal seas.

The eastern islands of Sal, Boa Vista and Maio, chiefly on the basis of their more advanced geomorphological development, have been thought of as the older islands, but as the volcanic fundament also can be observed in western islands, e. g. S. Vicente, Brava, it could be that post-fundament unequal degree of uplift, perhaps more periodic in one area than another, could account for the differences in geomorphologic development. As of the present, only in Maio have we thick occurrences of Mesozoics, highly disturbed as a result of diapiric-type intrusions. KLERKX & DE PAEPE (1971) believed that deformation of these rocks was almost contemporaneous with their deposition and closely related to the growth of an eruptive ridge forming at the end of the Jurassic or beginning of the Cretaceous. This is a deep structure, with diapiric structural ›roots‹ some 4,000 m in depth, whilst MENDES-VICTOR (1970) envisaged a rift developed here by essexitic intrusions. The writer no less (MITCHELL-THOMÉ, 1964) believed that the up-ending and deformation of these Maio Mesozoics occurred soon after these rocks were formed. (Agreed that by analogy with the Canary Islands, we have suggested a Late Palaeogene age for the plutonics in Cape Verde, but we also implied that such analogy should be treated with reserve, and it might be that here in Cape Verde the plutonism was of earlier date – Lower Palaeogene. Much depends on clinching the argument as to whether or not Palaeogene occurs in Maio.) RONA et al. (1970c), on the basis of magnetic anomaly studies between Cape Verde and Canary Islands, suggested that this ›Mesozoic oceanic ridge‹ of KLERKX & DE PAEPE was an important oceanic feature. Accepting the Cretaceous-Jurassic boundary to occur at ca. 130–135 my, and accepting that the opening of the N. Atlantic began some 120 my ago, the concept of such a ›ridge‹ developing and disturbing the Lower Cretaceous strata of Maio, which latter were formed before the Atlantic spreading began and partially contemporaneous therewith, such a concept seems reasonable.

PAEPE et al. (1974) on the basis of their determination of Lower Cretaceous or older oceanic tholeiitic basalts in Maio, and as per the present known structure of the island believe that the former either belong to or are then closely related to an old abandoned oceanic ridge crest (KLERKX & PAEPE, 1971) which developed near the site of the archipelago soon after the opening of the N. Atlantic – taken by them to have been some 110–120 my ago. (As of the present there is no unanimity of opinion as to when the initiation of the N. Atlantic opening occurred, published data indicating ages ranging from 110 to 190 my ago.) The uniformity of the chondrite-normalized REE patterns of the archipelago tholeiites and of more recently formed tholeiites of midoceanic ridges would confirm the view that the Upper Mantle differentiation occurred before L. Cretaceous-U. Jurassic times. The tholeiitic magma phase was likely of relatively short duration in comparison to the strongly alkaline magmatic phase initiated during the M. Cretaceous. To these authors the fast period of ocean floor spreading ended by this time, when large-scale transverse faulting took place, resulting in volcanic cessation in the archipelago ridge of the tholeiitic phase and instead there welled-up through these deep-seated fractures the strongly under-saturated alkaline magmas from depths of more than 80 km which rocks formed a carapace over the islands during the Tertiary and Quaternary.

The initiation of the Atlantic Ocean was succeeded by marked transgressions in the Albian which continued through the Senonian and reached a maximum in the Maestrichtian, regression coming about during the Danian. During the late Senonian, due perhaps to localized magmatic pulsations of the archipelago region, there was emergence and consequent drastic denudation removing much of the Mesozoic sedimentary coverings of the islands. It might be, as FURON (1935) and BOURCART (1946) stated, because of the emergence of the archipelago during part or all of the Palaeogene that could account for the absence of such strata in the archipelago, for as we have seen, nowhere can they be substantiated, although the argument is firmer for Lutetian in Maio and S. Nicolau. By Burdigalian times, sedimentation was taking place at least in S. Nicolau and S. Tiago, and everywhere within the archipelago (Brava excepted) the Vindobonian is either present or then highly probable, marine transgressions having probably begun in the Helvetian. Transgressive conditions probably continued until Astian times, during which it was likely that vulcanism was in abeyance. Regressions set in during the Quaternary with the formation of littoral, estuarine and aeolian deposits. Fresh vulcanism began again and has continued down through historic times to the last outburst in Fogo in 1951.

Both PART (1950a) and ASSUNÇAO (1968) have attempted to portray the sequence of igneous events in the archipelago. PART recognized four stages thus: Stage I, earliest sills of Maio, of Eocene (?) age; Stage II, basalts and ashes of the ›Main basalt‹ series, Early-Middle Tertiary; Stage III, basalts, alkali-basalts, ashes, phonolites; intrusions of nepheline-syenites, nepheline-monzonites and essexites, of Late Tertiary age; Stage IV, basalts and ashes, Quaternary and Recent.

ASSUNÇAO also proposed four phses: Phase I includes the basaltic and lamprophyric dykes and sills cutting the Maio Mesozoics, hence later and thought to have occurred during Cretaceous-Lower Tertiary times. Phase II of basaltic outpourings cannot be well dated, but some time during the Palaeogene is suggested, as in Maio likely Vindobonian sediments overlie these volcanics. Phase III is characterized by alkaline-basaltic lavas, but of note in this phase is the variety of volcanics – phonolites, tahitites, melilites, ankaratrites, etc. as well as intrusions of ijolites, melteigites. What we term Phase III-a is represented by smaller extrusions and intrusions of phonolitic type, often of dyke structure, which are later than the Phase II basaltic episode, which occurred likely during the Neogene but are pre-Quaternary in age. Phase IV comprises Quaternary vulcanism and down to the present day. Like Phase II, basaltic lavas are involved especially limburgites.

It is obvious that in the present status of our imprecise stratigraphic information and in the absence of isotopic datings, the actual volcanic sequences and times of such are but very imperfectly known, and certainly as regards the temporal aspect of vulcanisms we know very little indeed.

The Quaternary was marked by significant oscillations of the strands, rudites occurring at various elevations above present sea level, often admixed with arenaceous material. Old marine beaches have been described by BERTHOIS (1950c), LECOINTRE (1963) and SERRALHEIRO (1967, 1968). Table 53 illustrates data better established in some islands, whilst Table 11 shows further data for the archipelago. Old beaches occur as high as 100 m in Maio, highest so far known in the archipelago, and here also, at Monte

Branco, at an elevation of 265 m are found the oldest recognized marine Mesozoic beds, also the highest known occurrence of pre-Quaternary sedimentaries within the islands. Such then indeed testify to the role of vertical movements.

Isostatic adjustments, eustatism, vulcanism and epeirogenesis have been involved in these positive and negative movements, but the distinguishing of these, their relative importance, their effects, cannot at this time at least be determined in these oceanic islands.

# CHAPTER 9

# Caetera desunt

The stimulus of scientific quest goes on, and it would be a sad day for mankind if there were no more knowledge to be sought. The ›excelsior‹ motive of the climber is echoed by the further probing needs of the scientist, in both instances this inner yearning driving them on to yet more accomplishments.

In finally reviewing the geology of these islands, we shall mention rather the unknowns, the uncertainities, the gaps needed to be filled.

Geomorphologic studies throughout the archipelagoes scarce exist. Volcanic landforms pass through a series of erosional stages as do other landforms, but there are differences. With the former, initial shapes are more varied, they tend to be less altered by destructive agencies, for these forms develop quickly so that erosion has little effect during growth processes. Landforms of volcanic origin differ also from other contructional types in that the forces of growth are paroxysmal, there are recurrent interruptions in the regulated progress of the erosional cycle. We note further that here in Macaronesia, geomorphological processes are taking place sometimes in warm, dry semi-arid environments, sometimes in cooler, moister environments such that the degree and type of volcanic erosional forms of Corvo, for example, differ from those of Sal.

In all these island groups exogenic agencies seem to have been more important in moulding landscapes than structure-tectonics, but this matter requires further probing. Distinctions between fault scarps and fault-line scarps, erosion versus structure in cliff formations, horsts and graben versus the role of differential weathering, the significance, if any, of fissures, faults in controlling certain valley trends, the relative importance of mass gravitational movements versus subsidence in caldera formations – these are some matters requiring further attention.

Igneous studies vary widely from one island group to another, from one island to another, from one part of an island to another part. Those islands or parts thereof which have received more attention – more available chemical analyses, etc. of more samples, have tended to be taken as representative of the particular island or archipelago, are more frequently referred to in the literature. Yet continued studies are yielding results which change the picture here and there. Carbonatites in Brava, Fogo, S. Tiago, tholeiitic pillow lavas in Maio, probably obsidian (or then hydrotachylyte) in Boa Vista, peralkaline acid rocks in Gran Canaria and S. Miguel, extremely high isofal values in Terceira and extremely low in Fogo, rhyolitic pumices in La Palma – such findings give new perspectives to the igneous geology.

Basal Complexes of basics-ultrabasics are recognized for some islands within the Cape Verde and Canary archipelagoes, suggestions have been made as to correlations between the archipelagoes, but neither on petrographic nor temporal bases can much be said as of the present. In the Azores basic-ultrabasic plutonics, either as enclaves or outcrops, appear to be negligible, why this should be so is not clear, nor is the nature of the fundament here known.

Then there is the ever-present difficulty with nomenclature, the confusions, contradictions, redundancies. There is great need of review here of all the determinations made, to weed-out, clear-up the uncertainties, ambiguities existing.

In view of the long and often convulsive volcanic activity within these small, exposed, drastically eroded islands, it is almost a wonder that any significant sedimentary remains are left to study. Yet thicknesses of several hundred metres of Mesozoics occur in Maio and Fuerteventura, elsewhere thicknesses of tens of metres of Neogene in many islands. With the exception of the Maio Mesozoics, the Neogene of Sta. Maria and the ›Las Palmas Terrace‹ deposits of Gran Canaria, little attention has been paid to the sedimentaries of these archipelagoes.

From what we know, the overwhelming importance of organic, biochemical and biomechanical deposits is of major significance, chiefly shallow marine facies, with limestones, calcareous sands, sandstones, shales and clays. The role of organisms then has been primarily responsible for sedimentary formation. By the same token, we notice the general paucity of other rock types, conglomerates and breccias excepted, which latter more usually occur through mass gravitational movements. The sediments, in toto, are authigenic, products formed in situ in a marine environment usually of shallow type. Yet here and there we do find indications of allogenic sedimentaries, presumably having an origin as continental products moved westward out across the continental shelves. Even flysch and molasse deposits have been postulated. Studies here are necessary in connexion with hypotheses of continental linkage, relations to Alpine orogeny, we look forward to more factual evidence.

Mesozoics occur in Maio and Fuerteventura, are suspected in some other islands, but further investigation, further refinement is needed. After more than 60 years, the question of Malm in Maio is still debated, and as regards Fuerteventura, our studies have just begun. With the Vindobonian, the stratigraphic record is well established, but as some islands date back to Mesozoic when sedimentaries were forming, one wonders if the Mesozoic might not be of wider distribution in Macaronesia.

Are Miocene strata present in La Palma, might there be Cretaceous in Hierro, is Palaeogene present in the Cape Verde group, is Upper Jurassic present in S. Nicolau, are pre-Malm strata present in Fuerteventura, is the Oligocene present in the Selvagens? These tantalizing questions cannot be answered today.

Often the sedimentaries of these archipelagoes have been taken to be younger or older merely by their general character, their ›appearance‹. This is indeed a dangerous and unscientific way of ascribing stratigraphic age, for sedimentaries on occasion can camouflage their age better than the theatrical make-up artist. We think of the

Torridonian Sandstones of NW Scotland, generally ›looking‹ remarkably young yet of Precambrian age, or then the Dibdibba formation of Iraq, a continental unit of younger Neogene-older Pleistocene, which in places has the ›appearance‹ of an old, weathered, compact grit. We have mentioned that it has been queried whether much of the Neogene in the Cape Verde Islands might not be Quaternary, not even old Quaternary, but this, other similar instances, other stratigraphic questions make it clear that much remains to be done.

Palaeontological studies in Maio have stablished the Mesozoic, but in the neighbouring islands of Sal and Boa Vista, though invariably referred to as older islands and by implication Mesozoic also, very little fossil work has been done, supposition, analogy alonge prompts us so to state.

That re-examination of collections is needed is forcibly demonstrated from S. Nicolau. Here foraminifera originally determined as *Peneropolis* aff. *planulatus* FICHTEL & MOLL, var. ASSUNÇAO indicating Neogene were later proven to be *Iberina lusitanica* (EGGER) emend MAYNC and assigned to the Malm. Such an instance certainly makes one somewhat doubtful about many stratigraphic datings based on palaeontological determinations. The supposedly ›Reste von Korallen und Balanen‹ in the detritals in the floor of the Caldera de Taburiente, La Palma, have never been determined, yet the literature repeatedly refers to Miocene here. On what evidence, in view of the fact that no isotopic datings are available?

Whilst fossil flora collections are meagre in comparison to the fauna, yet palaeobotanical studies are all but non-existent except for work done over a hundred years ago in Madeira.

Only recently have more detailed vulcanological investigations been made. Capelinhos (Azores), Teneguia (Canaries) and Pico (Cape Verde) have been given more attention, but in comparison to an Etna, Vesuvius, Hekla, Paricutin, our knowledge of the geological, chemical, mechanical aspects of Macaronesian vulcanicity is but imperfectly known.

Marine geophysical studies in this general area of the N. Atlantic date back some two decades or so, but only recently have the islands themselves been surveyed, and such is only a beginning. In view of the baffling tectonic problems associated with the area, information is keenly awaited.

Only for the Canary Islands (plus a few for the Azores) have we radiometric datings of the volcanics. The more precise narrowing of time sequences compared to those based on stratigraphy-palaeontology appears to have resolved some questions, but realizing that isotopic datings are not the ›open sesame‹ to all time problems, we must note that the advent of such in the Canaries on occasion have merely compounded the issues.

Within the islands foldings and proven faultings are singularly wanting. Tertiary strata show only rather gentle dips and tiltings, nowhere do there appear to be lengthy faults or significant displacements. Only the Mesozoics have undergone more intense deformation, for at this stage, Palaeogene cannot be proven within the region. Whether then we are to ascribe the strong disturbances in the Mesozoics as distantly related to Alpine orogeny or then to local causes resulting from volcanic emplacements is not certain. The receding effects of orogenies may spread outwards to impressive distances. Earth movements associated with the Alpine storm were felt in SE England some 700 km away from the Tethyan trough. Fuerteventura's strongly deformed Mesozoics lie much closer to Alpine orogenic areas of N. Africa, whilst those of Maio lie about the same distance away from the Hercynian West African Fold Belt. In the latter case of course we cannot ascribe the deformation to the late Palaeozoic, and here it is more probable that disturbances resulted from local igneous emplacement. In Fuerteventura it might be that the deformations represent fainter echoes of Alpine orogeny, but in Lanzarote no Mesozoic has been determined, and though some would postulate pronounced fracturing in the island, such is not proven and intense foldings seem to be totally absent. It may be that at depth in Lanzarote Mesozoic does occur, it too might be highly disturbed like that of Fuerteventura, but in the absence of proof thereof in the meantime, we are more inclined to believe that in the latter island also the phenomenon is a local event. However, this question of the origins, causes of the highly disturbed Mesozoics of Maio and Fuerteventura requires further study.

When it comes to tectonic fractures, great fissures, lineaments, transform and transcurrent faulting of imposing dimensions, we enter a domain where speculation takes precedence over fact. Admittedly such marine geophysical work as has been done delineates or postulates some major cracks which are presumed to have some role in the disposition of archipelagoes and/or islands, trends are pointed out, supposedly great fissures here and there are marked by volcanic outpourings, etc., but are these realities? We have an imposing array of hypotheses, much ingenuity has been shown in erecting theories, much freedom of the imagination has been exercised in applying the concepts of ocean-floor spreading, considerable attention has been devoted to ascertain the role and place of the general Macaronesian region within the framework of global tectonics, but factual evidence is pitifully small. We must steer a path between the two famous aphorisms of HUXLEY – »the slaying of a beautiful hypothesis by an ugly fact« and »those who refuse to go beyond fact, rarely get as far as fact«. Structural and tectonic studies of the general area as of the moment are only in the embryo stage.

For several islands, the sequence of volcanic events has been recorded, but in few instances have such been integrated into the overall geological evolution where known sedimentaries have been stratigraphically dated. As usually the latter are intercalated with the volcanics, as proven uplifts and subsidences are manifest in many areas, there is need of embodying the sum total of our known information into a coherent whole portraying the evolution of islands and archipelagoes. Questions of inter-island, interarchipelago, islands-archipelagoes-continents relations or connexions have long been debated, but still there is no unanimity of opinion. Before proceeeding with further speculations along these lines, we need a better understanding of island and archipelago evolution. Only when our comprehension of such is more on a par with that related to Iberia and N. Africa can we with more confidence consider continental correlations.

If we have emphasized the unevenness of our information of these islands, the strong bias towards but one aspect of the geology, the questions unanswered, the studies needed, we should not lose sight of what has been done, what information is available. In perusing a magnificent series of volumes recently published on the Geology of Poland, a long-peopled country, worked over by a long succession of international scholars, a country offering the amenities of travel, convenience for field work, a

Table 68

Principal geological features of the Middle Atlantic Archipelagos

| Archipelago | Physiographic characteristics | Principal igneous rocks | Sedimentaries | | |
|---|---|---|---|---|---|
| | | | Max. thick. | Max. elev. | Max. dips |
| Azores | Crater- and caldera lakes. Cliffs up to 150 m. Hill ranges. Relief, topography not spectacular. | Basalts, basanitoids, trachytes, andesites. | ca. 12 m | 400 m | 30° |
| Madeira | Strong cliffing-up to 580 m. Extensive beaches in P. Santo only. Madeira, massive compact. NW coeast of P. Santo strongly indented. Imminent river "captures". | Basanites, basalts, trachytes, trachydolerites, essexites. | ca. 30 m | 400 m | 60° |
| Selvagens | Tableland appearance. Cliffs up to 80 m. Few prominent peaks. | Phonolites, nephelinites, basalts. | ca 10 m | ca. 90 m | 25° |
| Canaries | In places strong cliffing-up to 400 m. Occasional low, sandy coasts. Strong relief, high elevations. Eastern islands more mature. | Basalts, trachybasalts, trachytes, tephrites, trachydolerites, oceanites, phonolites, gabbros, syenites, essexites. | +900 m? | 300 m | 85° (Meso.) 25° (Tert.) |
| Cape Verde | Craters but few calderas. Cliffing less pronounced. Eastern islands more mature, elsewhere strong relief. | Basalts, basanites, phonolites, trachytes, ankaratrites, limburgites. | +435 m | 265 m | 90° (Meso.) 49° (Tert.) |

Table 68 (continued)

| Archipelago | Age of oldest strate | Structural features | Inter-island relations | Inter-archipelago relations | Time of origin |
|---|---|---|---|---|---|
| Azores | Vindobonian | Some horsts, graben. Active faults. Surficial deformations. | S. Miguel–Sta. Maria–Formigas. Corvo–Flores. Faial–Pico–S. Jorge. | None? | Palaeogene–Early Miocene. |
| Madeira | Vindobonian | Surficial deformations through exogenic processes. | Madeira–Ilhas Desertas | Selvagens? ? | Cretaceous |
| Selvagens | Vindobonian | Mass gracitational movements. | All related | Madeira? ? Canaries? ? | Palaeogene? |
| Canaries | Dogger? Liassic?? | Mesozoics highly disturbed. Few significant faults. Collapse calderas? Mass gravitational movements. | Fuerteventura–Lanzarote–Gomera? Gran Canaria–La Palma–Tenerife–Hierro? Tenerife–Gomera? | Eastern islands and eastern Cape Verde islands. | Middle–Upper Mesozoic(?) to Pliocene |
| Cape Verde | Malm? | Mesozoics highly disturbed. Few significant faults. Surficial deformations via exogenic processes. | Sal–Boa Vista–Maio–S. Tiago. Fogo–Brava. Brava–Ilheus Secos. | Eastern islands and eastern Canary islands. | Jurassic |

progressive Geological Survey, eminent universities of long standing, the writer was impressed to learn how in the year 1972 there still was so much to do, how extensive were the problems, how vague the understandings of this or that geological matter, etc. If then we consider Macaronesia from this perspective, the sum total of our geological knowledge represents a most worthy contribution, great is our debt to the labours of the many men who have interested themselves in these lovely islands, we look forward with confidence that slowly we shall pry forth more of Nature's secrets.

The Latin heading of this chapter, which, in this day of the demoting of classical languages, the writer needs offer no apology in translating for the reader, can be taken to mean: »The remainder is wanting«.

# Abstract

The Portuguese and Spanish Middle Atlantic Islands, lying off the coasts of Europe and Africa, total some 15,000 km². Most were made known to Europeans in the 15th century, but in the Canary Islands an aboriginal population probably dated back to some 2,500 years B. C.

Climatic conditions are most pleasant, but the Canary and Cape Verde group, especially the latter, experience semi-aridity and aridity, except in the higher, more exposed interiors.

Agriculture forms the economic basis for all archipelagoes, but in the Canary Islands and Madeira particularly, increasing tourism forms an important source of revenue.

The archipelagoes have a total population of some two million, only the Selvagens having no permanent inhabitants.

As a generalization, the islands are high in comparison to their areas. In Pico de Teide, 3,718 m, Tenerife, and Pico, 2,829 m, Fogo, are the two highest summits to be found in the islands of the Atlantic. Strong relief typifies the region – deep, narrow valleys, sharp ridges, steep slopes down to coasts, pronounced high cliffing common, Cabo Girao in Madeira, 580 m, being one of the most stupendous cliffs in the world. In each archipelago, the eastern islands are more subdued, more level tracts of land, valleys more open, and on other geological grounds we have reasons for believing that such islands are older.

All are volcanic islands. Alkalic rocks predominate, typical of the ›Atlantic‹ suite. The calc-alkaline ›Pacific‹ suite, and lesser so, the potassic ›Mediterranean‹ series are also to be found. Strongly alkaline or Na-alkaline rocks are typical of the Canary and Cape Verde Islands, whilst in the Azores, the tendency is to weakly alkaline-acidic. Though oversaturated plutonics are most doubtful, acidic volcanics do occur. Of special interest is the very high isofal value determined for Terceira, 240, the extreme yet recorded for any Atlantic island.

On all archipelagoes, areal exposures of sedimentaries other than PleistoceneHolocene friable deposits, are of minor occurrence, yet of infinitely greater significance than those found in the South Atlantic Islands, Falklands excepted. Sedimentaries tend to be thin, of gentle dips, but in Maio and Fuerteventura occur thick, highly-disturbed strata of older age.

Malm might be present in Maio, Cretaceous certainly, and Cretaceous and questionable older beds in Fuerteventura. In all the island groups except the Azores, sedimentary Tertiary rocks are probable, and in these islands, sedimentaries occur only in Sta. Maria and the Formigas Banks.

Vulcanism is still active in the Azores, Canary and Cape Verde Islands. Since the archipelagoes were discovered by Europeans, some 57 known occurrences at least have taken place, the latest in 1971 in La Palma. In the Madeira and Selvagem archipelagoes no historic vulcanicity is known.

Of all the island groups, the Azores is the most active seismically.

It is highly questionable how significant structures of tectonic origin might be. Pronounced folded and faulting is rare, but on the other hand, more surficial distrubances, due to vulcanism and mass gravitational movements are notable features. Even the great calderas are not purely subsidence features, and throughout all the archipelagoes the role of exogenic processes cannot be underestimated.

There are no metallics of any commercial interest. Building stones, clays, sands, pumice, pozzulana, lime, salt are exploited. The question of utilizing geothermal energy in the Canary Islands is now being investigated. In the Canary and Cape Verde Islands especially, water shortage is an increasing problem, with human and agricultural needs rising alarmingly, comtounded by droughts, falling water tables, salt-water intrusion.

In more recent years, geochronological and geophysical studies have been prosecuted, but such represent only a beginning. The former, along with palaeontological-stratigraphic determinations, is enabling us to unravel the geological evolution of these island groups. Geophysical investigations both in and around the islands are yielding some further insights into the tectonic setting, oceanic and continental relations, crustal nature.

# General Bibliography

ALIA, M. (1960): La Tectonica del Sahara Espanol. - 2lst Internat. Geol. Congr., **18**: 193–202, Copenhagen.

AYMÉ, J.-M. (1965): The Senegal Salt Basin. - In: Salt Basins around Africa, 83–90. Coll. Inst. Petr., London. Elsevier, Amsterdam.

BASS, M. H. (1972): Occurrence of Transitional Abyssal Basalts. - Lithos, **5**: 57–67, Oslo.

BERGGREN, A. (1969): Rates of Evolution in some Cenozoic Planktonic Foraminifera. - Micropal., **15**: 351–365, New York.

- (1972): A Cenozoic Time-Scale - Some Implications for Regional Geology and Palaeobiogeography. - Lethaia, **5**: Oslo.

- (1973): The Pliocene Time Scale: Calibration of Planktonic Foraminiferal and Calcareous Nannoplankton Zones. - Nature, **243**: 391–397, London.

BLANC, J. J. (1958): Recherches géologiques et sédimentologiques en Méditerranée Nord-oriental. - Résult. Sci. Camp. »Calypso«. Fasc. 4: Masson, Paris.

BLOCH, J. P. & TRICHET, J. (1966): Un example de grès de plage. (Côte ligure italienne). - Marine Geol., **4**: 375–377, Amsterdam.

BORLEY, G. D. (1974): Oceanic Islands. - In: The Alkali Rocks. Ed. by H. SOERENSEN; 311–330. Interscience Inc., NewYork.

BOUVET, J. (1971): Anomalies de Bouguer. Europe-Afrique. - Bur. Grav. Intern., Assoc. Intern. Géodesia 3rd ed. 18pp., plus map, scale 1/10 M. Paris.

BROCK, B. B. (1957): World Patterns and Lineaments. - Trans. Geol. Soc. S. Africa, **60**: 127–160, Johannesburg.

CHAYES, F. (1970): Rhyolites of the Oceanic Islands. - Carnegia Inst. Year Book, **68**: 177, Washington.

CLOUGH, C. T.; MAUFE, H. B. & BAILEY, E. B. (1909): The Cauldron Subsidence of Glen Coe and the associated Igneous Phenomena. - Quart. J. Geol. Soc., **45**: 611–678, London.

DALY, R. A. (1924): Geology of American Samoa. - Carnegia Inst., **340**: 93–143, Washington.

DEWEY, J. F. & BIRD, J. M. (1970): Mountain Belts and the new Global Tectonics. - J. Geophy. Res., **75**: 2625–2647, Washington.

DIETRICH G. & ULRICH, J. (1967): Atlas zur Ozeanographie. - 1–77, Bibliogr. Inst., Mannheim.

DYMOND, J. R. (1966): Potassium-Argon Geochronology of Deep-Sea Sedimentary Materials. - Ph. D. Thesis, Univ. of California, San Diego.

EMERY, K. O. & FOSTER, J. F. (1948): Water tables in marine beaches. - J. Mar. Res., **7**: 644–654, New Haven, Conn.

FURON, R. (1966): Introduction à la stratigraphie de l'Afrique. - Lex. stratig. intern., 109pp., C.N.R.S., Paris.

GINSBURG, R. N. (1953): Beach-rocks in S. Florida. - J. Sed. petr., **25**: 85–92, Tulsa.

HOOKER, J. (1849): Journal of the Voyage to the Niger of Dr. J. R. T. VOGEL. Niger Flora, London.

HSÜ, K. J. & RYAN, W. B. F. (1971): Implications concerning ocean floor genesis and destruction from deep sea drilling in the Mediterranean Sea and eastern Atlantic Ocean. - Internat. Assoc. Seism. & Phys. Earth's Interior Congr., Abstracts, **44**: Moscow.

JOHNSTON, J. & WILLIAMSON, J. (1916): The role of inorganic agencies in the deposition of calcium carbonate. - J. Geol. **24**: Chicago.

KUENEN, P. H. (1933): Geology of Coral Reefs. - Snellius Exped., **5**, 2: 126 pp., Brill., Leiden.

LACROIX, A. (1893): Les enclaves des roches volcaniques. - 710 pp., Macon, Protat frères, Paris.

(1907): Etude minéralogique des produits silicates de l'éruption du Vesuv (Avril 1906). - Nouv. Arch. Mus. Hist. Nat., **9**: Paris.

(1911): Les syénites néphélinitiques de l'archipel de Los et leurs minéraux. - Nouv. Arch. Mus. Nat., **5**,3: 162 pp., Paris.

- (1934): Mission au Tibesti. - Mém. Acad. Sci., **61**: 169–369, Paris.

LE PICHON, X. (1968): Sea-Floor Spreading and Continental Drift. - J. Geophys. Res., **73**: 3661–3697, Washington.

LE PICHON, X. & FOX, P. J. (1971): Marginal offsets, fracture zones and the early opening of the N. Atlantic. - J. Geophys. Res., **76**:6294–6308, Washington.

McBIRNEY, A. R. & GASS, I. G. (1967): Relations of Oceanic Volcanic Rocks to Mid-Ocean Rises and Heat-Flow. - Earth Planet. Sci. Lett., **2**: 265–276, Amsterdam.

McBIRNEY, A. R. & WILLIAMS, H. (1970): Geology and Petrology of the Galapagos Islands. - Mem. Geol. Soc. Amer., **118**: 197 pp., Boulder, Colo.

MACHADO, F. (1965): Elementos de Vulcanologia. - Estud. Ens. e Docum., Junta Invest. Ultramar, **119**: 138 pp., Lisbon.

- (1969): Oceanic fissure eruptions, subvolcanic intrusions and volcanic magma chambers. - Bull. Volcan., **33**: 1229–1236, Naples.
- (1970): Curso de Sismologia. - Estud. Ens. e Docum., Junta Invest. Ultramar, **125**: 156 pp., Lisbon.
MAYNC, W. (1949): The foraminiferal genus *Choffatella* . . . . . - Ecl. Geol. Helv., **42**,2: 529–547, Berne.
- (1959): The foraminiferal genera *Spirocyclina* and *Iberina*. - Micropal., **5**,1: 33–68, New York.
MITCHELL-THOMÉ, R. C. (1961): Lineaments and Vincula. - Trans. Geol. Soc. S. Africa, **64**: 1–15, Johannesburg.
- (1962): Faulting and Orogeny. - Acta Geol, **7**,3/4: 415–425, Budapest.
- (1966): Wrench Faults and Lineaments. - J. Geol. U.A.R., **10**: 85–106, Cairo.
- (1970): Geology of the South Atlantic Islands. - Beitr. z. region. Geol. d. Erde, **10**: 367 pp., Gebr. Borntraeger, Stuttgart.
MORGAN, W. J. (1968): Rises, Trenches, Great Faults and Crustal Blocks. - J. Geophys. Res., **73**: 1959–1982, Washington.
- (1971): Convection plumes in the lower mantle. - Nature, **230**: 42–43, London.
NESTEROFF, W. (1955): Les récifs coralliens du banc Farsan Nord (Mer Rouge). - In: Result. Sci. Camp. »Calypso«. Ann. Inst. Océanogr., **30**: 2–53, Monaco.
OTTMAN, F. (1965): Introduction à la Géologie marine et littorale. - 260 pp., Masson, Paris.
PEACOCK, M. A. (1931): Classification of Igneous Rock Series. - J. Geol, **39**: 54–67, Chicago.
PITMAN, W. C. & TALWANI, M. (1972): Sea floor spreading in the North Atlantic. - Bull. Geol. Soc. Amer., **83**: 619–646, Boulder, Colo.
REYRE, D. (Ed.) (1966): Bassins sédimentaires du littoral africain. - Assoc. Serv. Géol. Afr., Symposium, Paris.
RITTMANN, A. (1952): Nomenclature of Volcanic Rocks. - Bull. Volcan., **12**: 75–102, Naples.
- (1960): Vulkane und ihre Tätigkeit. - 2nd ed., 188 pp., Ferd. Enke, Stuttgart.
RONA, P. A. (1969): Possible Salt Domes in the deep Atlantic off North-west Africa. - Nature, **224**, 5215: 141–143, London.
- (1970): Comparison of Continental Margins of Eastern North America at Cape Hatteras and North-western Africa at Cap Blanc. - Bull. Amer. Assoc. Petr. Geol., **54**: 129–157, Tulsa.
RUSSEL, R. (1962): Origin of beach rocks. - Geomorphology, **6**: 1–16.
SHAND, S. J. (1950): Eruptive Rocks. - 4th ed., 488 pp., Thos. Murby & Co., London.
SOUGY, J. (1962): West African Fold Belt. - Bull. Geol. Soc. Amer., **73**: 871–876, New York.
TEIXEIRA,-C. (1950): A propos d'une hypothèse sur la structure de l'Océan Atlantique. - Bol. Mus. Lab. Min. Geol., Fac. Cien., Univ. Lisboa, **18**: 13 pp., Lisbon.
TEMPLETON, R. S. M. (1971): The geology of the continental margin between Dakar and Cape Palmas. - Symposium: The Geology of the East Atlantic Continental Margin. Ed. by F. M. DELANY. Inst. Geol. Sci. Rept., **70/16**: 43–60, London.
TILLEY, C. E. (1950): Some aspects of magmatic evolution. - Quart. J. Geol. Soc., **106**: 37–61, London.
ZBYSZEWSKI, G. (1971): Carta Geologica do Quaternario de Portugal na escala de 1/1 M. Noticia Explicativa. - 39 pp., Lisbon.
ZEUNER, F. E. (1952): Pleistocene Shore Lines. - Geol. Rdsch., **40**: 39–50, Stuttgart.

# Bibliography relating to the Middle Atlantic Islands

(No claim is made that this is a definitive bibliography, but it is believed that herewith are presented all the significant and/or better known references treating of these archipelagoes.)

ABDEL-MONEM, A.; FERNANDEZ, L. A. & BOONE, G. A. (1968): Pliocene-Pleistocene minimum K-Ar ages of the older eruptive centres, Eastern Azores. - Amer. Geophys. Union, Trans., Abstracts, **49**: 363, Washington.
ABDEL-MONEM, A.; WATKINS, N. D. & GAST, P. W. (1967): Volcanic History of the Canary Islands. - Amer. Geophys. Union, Trans., **48**: 226–227, Washington.
- (1968): Volcanic Stratigraphy and Magnetic Polarity History of the Canary Islands and Madeira. - Internat. Symposium on Volcanology, Abstracts. Spain-Canary Islands.
- (1971): Potassium-Argon Ages. Volcanic Stratigraphy and Geomagnetic Polarity History of the Canary Islands: Lanzarote-Fuerteventura-Gran Canaria-Gomera. - Amer. J. Sci. **271**: 490–521, New Haven.
- (1972): Potassium-Argon Ages. Volcanic Stratigraphy and Geomagnetic Polarity History of the Canary Islands: Tencrife-La Palma-Hierro. - Amer. J. Sci., **272**: 805–825, New Haven.
ADE-HALL, J. M. & WATKINS, N. D. (1970): Absence of correlations between opaque petrology and natural remanence polarity in Canary Islands lavas. - Roy. Astr. Soc. Geophys. J., **19**: 351–360, London.

ALFONSO, L. (1953): Esquema de geografia fisica de las Canarias. - La Laguna, Tenerife.

AGOSTINHO, J. (1932): Vulcanismo dos Açores. Vista Geral. - Rev. A Terra, **4**: 32-36, Coimbra.

- (1934): Sinopse do estudo de P. ESENWEIN sobra a Petrografia dos Açores. - Açoreana, Bol. Soc. Af. Chaves **1**: 59-65, Angra.

- (1936): The Volcanoes of the Azores Islands. - Bull. Volcan., **8**: 123-138, Naples.

- (1937a): Tectonica, sismicidade e vulcanismo das ilhas dos Açores. - Açoreana, Bol. Soc. Af. Chaves, **1**: 85-98, Angra.

- (1937b): Sobre a tectonica da ilha de Santa Maria. - Açoreana, Bol. Soc. Af. Chaves, **1**: 281-285, Angra.

- (1937c): Volcanic Activity in the Azores for 1933-36. - Bull. Volcan., **2**: 183-192, Naples.

- (1938): Nomenclatura geografica das Ilhas doe Açores. - Rev. A Terra, **32**: 10 pp., Coimbra.

- (1941): A erupçao submarina de 1720 entre a Terceira e S. Miguel. - Açoreana, Bol. Soc. Af. Chaves, **2**: 268-270, Angra.

- (1950a): Clima dos Açores. - Açoreana, Bol. Soc. Af. Chaves, **4**: Angra.

- (1950b): O Monte Brasil. - Açoreana, Bol. Soc. Af. Chaves, **4**: 343-355, Angra.

- (1955a): Relato da sismicidade dos Açores e historia sismica do arquipelago . . . . . . . . - Bol. Ord. Eng., **4**, 21, 108: 4 pp., Lisbon.

- (1955b): Os abalos sismicos na ilha Terceira em Dezembro de 1950 e em Janeiro de 1951. - Bol. Ord. Eng., **4**, 22, Lisbon.

- (1960): Actividade vulcanica nos Açores. - Açoreana, Bol. Soc. Af. Chaves, **5**: 362-478, Angra.

- (1964): Seismic Activity in Sao Jorge Island, Azores, Feb.-May, 1964. - Açoreana, Bol. Soc. Af. Chaves, **6**: 99-102, Angra.

AGOSTINHO, J. & CHAVES, F. A. (1943): Caracteristicas do Magnetismo Terrestre nos Açores. - Serv. Meteor. Açores, 18 pp., Angra.

ALBERS, J. C. (1854): Malacographie Madeirensis. - Geogr. Reiner, Berlin.

ALBUQUERQUE, L. S. M. (1826): Observaçoes sobre a ilha de S. Miguel. - Lisbon.

ALBUQUERQUE, M. DE (1837): Observaçoes para servirem para a historia geologica das Ilhas da Madeira, Porto Santo e Desertas. - Mem. Acad. Real das Sci., **12**, Lisbon.

ALONSO, U.; CENDRERQ, A.; FUSTER, J. M.; GASTESI, P.; HERNANDEZ-PACHECO, A.; MUNOZ, M. & SANCHEZ-CELA, V. (1968a): Mapa geologico de Espana 1:50,000. La Oliva. - Inst. Geol. Min. Esp., **381**: 16pp., Madrid.

ALONSO, U.; FERNANDEZ, S.; FUSTER, J. M. & SANCHEZ-CELA, V. (1967): Mapa geologico de Espana 1:50,000. Teguise. - Inst. Geol. Min. Esp., *374*: 14 pp., Madrid.

- (1968b): Mapa geologico de Espana 1:50,000. Jandia. - Inst. Geol. Min. Esp., **386**: 9 pp., Madrid.

ALVES, C. A. M.; SERRALHEIRO, A.; MACEDO, J. R.; CRAMEZ, P.; SOUSA, A. A.; MENDES, F. & GOMES, R. A. D. (1972): Carbonatitos de Santiago, Cabo Verde. - I Congr. Hispano-Luso-Amer. de Geol. Econ., 563-576, Lisbon.

AMARAL, I. (1964): Santiago de Cabo Verde. A Terre e os Homens. - Mem. Junta Invest. Ultramar. **48**: 444 pp., Lisbon.

ANGUITA, F. (1972): La evolucion magmatica en el ciclo Roque Nublo (Gran Canaria). - Estud. Geol., **28**: 377-428, Madrid.

- (1973): Genesis of Roque Nublo Formation: A Special Kind of Ignimbritic Eruptions in Gran Canaria. - Bull. Volcan., **37**: 111-121, Naples.

ARANA, V. (1966): Estudio geologico y petrografico de los diques de la pared de Las Canadas del Teide. - Unpubl., Depto. de Petrologia, Univ. Madrid.

- (1971): Litologia y estructura del Edificio Canadas, Tenerife (Islas Canarias). - Estud. Geol. **27**: 95-135, Madrid.

ARANA, V.; BADIOLA, E. R. & HERNAN, F. (1973a): Peralkaline Acid Tendencies in Gran Canaria (Canary Islands). - Contr. Miner. Petr., **40**: 53-62, Heidelberg.

ARANA, V. & BRÄNDLE, J. L. (1969): Variation Trends in the Alkaline Salic Rocks of Tenerife. - Bull. Volcan., **33**: 1145-1165, Naples.

ARANA, V.; BRÄNDLE, J. L. & IBARROLA, E. (1971): Contribucion al quimismo de la Series Canadas. - Estud. Geol., **27**, Madrid.

ARANA, V. & FUSTER, J. M. (1973d): Estado de los estudios sobre los recursos geotermicos en el area de las Montanas de Fuego (Lanzarote, Islas Canarias). - Estud. Geol., **29**: 281-286, Madrid.

ARANA, V. & IBARROLA, E. (1973b): Rhyolitic pumice in the basaltic pyroclasts from the 1971 eruption of Teneguia volcano, Canary Islands. - Lithos, **6**: 273-278, Oslo.

ARANA, V.; ORTIZ, R. & YUGUERO, J. (1973e): Study of Thermal Anomalies in Lanzarote (Canary Islands). - Geothermics **2,2**: 73-75.

ARANA, V. & PALOMO, C. (1973c): Interpretacion de unos perfiles sismicos de reflexion en la costa occidental de Fuerteventura (Islas Canarias). - Estud. Geol., **29**: 287-292, Madrid.

Assunçao, C. F. T. (1954a): Expedicao Cientifica a Ilha do Fogo. Estudios Petrograficos (1952–53). - Mem. Sér. Petrog. I, Junta Invest. Ultramar., 156 pp., Lisbon.
- (1954b): Recensao do trabalho de Gerald M. Part: Volcanic Rocks from the Cape Verde Islands, London, 1950. - Garcia de Orta, 2: 93–96, Lisbon.
- (1955a): A permanencia da composicao das lavas na actividade eruptiva da Ilha do Fogo. - Garcia de Orta, 3: 199–204, Lisbon.
- (1955b): Sobre os Grandes Cristais de Hornblenda Kaeusutitica da Ilha do Fogo (Erupçao de 1951). - Garcia de Orta, 4: 71–79, Lisbon.
- (1959): Contribuçao para a petrografia dos produtos emitidos pelo vulcao dos Capelinhos (Faial). - Mem. Serv. Geol. Portugal, 4: 57–64, Lisbon.
- (1961): Estudo petrografico da ilha de S. Miguel (Açores). - Comun. Serv. Geol. Portugal, 45: 81–176, Lisbon.
- (1968a): Geologia da Provincia de Cabo Verde. - In: Curso de Geologia do Ultramar. Junta Invest. Ultramar, 1: 3–51, Lisbon.
Assunçao, C. F. T. & Canelhas, M. G. S. (1971): Sobre a utilizaçao do indice colorimetrico na petrografia dos vulcanitos. - Bol. Mus. Lab. Miner. Geol., Fac. Cien., Univ. Lisboa, 12,1: 3–20, Lisbon.
Assunçao, C. F. T. & Canilho, M. H. (1969–70): Notas sobre Petrografia comparada das ilhas Atlanticas. - Bol. Mus. Lab. Miner. Geol., Fac. Cien., Univ. Lisboa, 12,2: 305–342, Lisbon.
- (1965a): Petrografia da Ilha de S. Vicente. - Garcia de Orta, 13: 235–258, Lisbon.
Assunçao, C. F. T.; Machado, F. & Gomes, R. A. (1965b): On the occurrence of carbonatites in the Cape Verde Islands. - Bol. Soc. Geol. Portugal, 16: 179–188, Porto.
Assunçao, C. F. T.; Machado, F. & Serralheiro, A. (1968b): New Investigations on the Geology and Volcanism of the Cape Verde Islands. - 23rd Internat. Geol. Congr. 2: 9–16, Prague.
Assunçao, C. F. T.; Machado, F. & Silva, L. C. (1967): Petrologia e Vulcanismo da Ilha do Fogo (Cabo Verde). - Garcia de Orta, 15: 99–110, Lisbon.
Balachowsky, T. (1946): Etude biogéographique des Coccoides des îles Atlantides (Canaries et Madère). - Mém. Soc. Biogéogr., 8: 209–218, Paris.
Baonza del Prado, E. & Plata, A. B. (1969): Estudio preliminar sobre la edad de muestras de aguas subterraneas tomadas en la isla de Gran Canaria. - Docum. Invest. Hidrol. Supl. Cient. de la revista »Agua«, 5, Barcelona.
Barrois, C. (1898): Recherches sur la faune d'eau douce des Açores. - Mém. Soc. Sc. Agric., Sér. 5, 6: Lille.
Barros, L. A. (1961): Sobre e petrologia da Selvagem Grande (Arquipelago das Selvagens). - Bol. Mus. Lab. Miner. Geol., Fac. Cien., Univ. Lisboa, 9 (1): 43–51, Lisbon.
- (1968): Petrografia do ilheu Grande (Ilha Brava, Cabo Verde). - Garcia de Orta, 16: 249–258, Lisbon.
Barros, L. A. & Oliveira, M. A. F. T. (1969): Sobre a petrografia da ilha de Porto Santo (Arquipelago da Madeira). - Bol. Soc. Geol. Portugal, 17: 87–100, Porto.
Bebiano, J. B. (1927): Missao geografica de Cabo Verde (1927). Alguns trechos do »Relatorio sobre o reconhecimento geologico da ilha de Sant'Iago. - Bol. Ag. Ger. Colon., III, 25: 39–77, Lisbon.
- (1929): A situaçao scientifica do Arquipelago de Cabo Verde. O vulcao do Fogo - uma das maiores belezas geologicas do mundo. - Bol. Ag. Ger. Colon., V, 45: 3–13, Lisbon.
- (1930): Alguns trechos do »Relatorio sobre o reconhecimento geologico da Ilha do Maio«. - Bol. Ag. Ger. Colon., 80: 3–33 Lisbon.
- (1932): A Geologia da Arquipelago de Cabo Verde. - Comun. Serv. Geol. Portugal, 18: 275 pp., Lisbon.
- (1933): Breve noticia acerca do vulcao da Ilha do Fogo. - Bol. Mus. Lab. Miner. Geol, Fac. Cien., Univ. Lisboa, 2: 133–148, Lisbon.
Bebiano, J. B. & Soares, J. M. P. (1952): Note on some supposed Senonian fossils from Sao Nicolau Island (Cape Verde Islands). - 18th Internat. Geol. Congr., 14: 186–189, London.
Benitez, S. (1945): Ensayo de sintesis geologica del Archipelago Canario. - Publ. de »El Museo Canario«, Las Palmas de Gran Canaria.
- (1946): Sintesis geologica del Archipelago Canario. - Estud. Geol., 5: 3–19, Madrid.
- (1952): La erupcion de »Las Manchas« en la isla de La Palma y el vulcanismo canario. - Publ. de »El Museo Canario«, 13: 51–72, Las Palmas.
- (1959): Gran Canaria y sus Obras Hidraulicas. - Cab. Ins. de Gran Canaria, 224 pp., Las Palmas.
Bennet, M. G. (1811): A Sketch of the Geology of Madeira. - Trans. Geol. Soc., 1, London.
Bergt, A. (1913): Vd. Friedländer, 1913.
Berthois, L. (1950a): Sur une roche siliceuse de Biscoutos, Ile de Terceira, Açores. - Açoreana, Bol. Soc. Af. Chaves, 4: 246–262, Angra.

BERTHOIS, L. (1950b): Sur la présence d'une microfaune dans le calcaire de Santa Maria (Açores). - Açoreana, Bol. Soc. Af. Chaves, **4**: 277-285, Angra.
- (1950c): Contribution à la connaissance lithologique de l'Archipel du Cap-Vert. - Min. Colon., Junta Invest. Colon., Ensaios e Docum., **7**: 194 pp., Lisbon.
- (1951): Sur la présence de basses terrasses marines dans l'Archipel des Açores (Portugal). - C. R. 76ème Congr. Soc. Sav. à Rennes: 101-106, Rennes.
- (1953a): Terrasses marines d'altitude + 5 à + 8 m dans l'Archipel des Açores. - Açoreana, Bol. Soc. Af. Chaves, **5**: 64-70, Angra.
- (1953b): Contribution à l'étude lithologique de l'Archipel des Açores. - Comun. Serv. Geol. Portugal, **34**: 5-64, Lisbon.
BLUMENTHAL, M. (1960): Über vulkanische Bergpfade auf den Canaren. - Die Alpen, **2**: 81-100, Bern.
- (1961): Rasgos principales de la geologia de las Islas Canarias, con datos sobre Madeira. - Bol. Inst. Geol. Min. de Espana, **72**: 5-130, Madrid.
BOETTGER, O. (1908): Liste der Mollusken aus einem Sande im Barr. vom Tegina auf Tenerife (Canaren). - Z. dt. geol. Ges., **60**: 246-249, Berlin.
BÖHM, J. (1898): Fossilien von den Selvagens-Inseln. - Z. dt. geol. Ges., **50**: 33-39, Hannover.
BOOTH, B. (1973): The Granadilla Pumice Deposit of Southern Tenerife, Canary Islands. - Proc. Geol. Assoc., **84**,3: 353-370, London.
BORLEY, G. D. (1966): The Geology of Tenerife. - Proc. Geol. Soc., **1635**: 173-176, London.
BORLEY, G. D. & ABBOTT, M. J. (1968): Petrology of the Alkaline Volcanic Rocks of Tenerife. - 23rd Internat. Geol. Congr., Abstracts: 40, Prague.
BORLEY, G. D.; SUDDABY, P. & SCOTT, P. (1971): Some Xenoliths from the Alkalic Rocks of Tenerife, Canary Islands. - Contr. Miner. Petr., **31**: 102-114, Heidelberg.
BORY DE ST. VINCENT, G. M. (1803): Essais sur les Iles Fortunées et de l'antique Atlantide, ou Précis de l'histoire de l'Archipel des Canaries. - Paris.
BOSSHARD, E. & MACFARLANE, D. J. (1970): Crustal Structure of the Western Canary Islands from Seismic Refraction and Gravity Data. - J. Geophys. Res., **75**: 4901-4918, Washington.
- (1971): Reply to comments by H-U. SCHMINCKE (1971) on above paper. - J. Geophys. Res., **76**: 7306, Washington.
BOURCART, J. (1935): Géologie de la Grande Canarie. - C. R. somm., Soc. Géol. France, **5**: 124-125, Paris.
- (1946): Géologie des Iles Atlantides. Contribution à l'étude du peuplement des Iles Atlantides. - Soc. Biogéogr., Mém., **8**:9-40, Paris.
BOURCART, J. & JÉRÉMINE. E. (1937): La Grande Canarie. - Bull. Volcan., **2**: 1-77, Naples.
- (1938): Reconnaissance géologique dans l'île de Fuerteventura (Archipel Canarien). - Bull. Volcan., **4**: 51-109, Naples.
BOUVET, J. (1971): Anomalies de Bouguer. Europe-Afrique. - Bur. Grav. Internat., Assoc. Internat. Géodésie, 3rd ed., 18 pp., plus map, scale 1/10 M., Paris.
BRAGA, J. M. & GALHANO, M. H. (1965): Foraminiferos do arquipelago da Madeira. - Publ. Inst. Zool. »Dr. Nobra«, **94**, Lisbon.
BRANCO, A. C; ZBYSZEWSKI, G.; ALMEIDA, F. M. & FERREIRA, O.V. (1959): Le volcanisme de l'île de Faial. - Rapp. de la première miss. géol., Mem. Serv. Geol. Portugal, **4**: 9-27, Lisbon.
BRANCO, A. C.; ZBYSZEWSKI, G.; MEDEIROS, A. C. & ALMEIDA, F. M. (1957): Etude géologique de la région de Furnas dans l'île de S. Miguel (Açores). - Comun. Serv. Geol. Portugal, **38**: 5-64, Lisbon.
BRÄNDLE, J. L. (1973): Evolucion geoquimica de los materiales volcanicos salicos y alcalinos de la isla de Tenerife. - Estud. Geol., **29**: 5-51, Madrid.
BRAVO, T. (1952): Aportacion al estudio geomorfologico y geologico de la costa de la fossa tectonica del Valle de la Orotava. - Bol. R. Soc. Esp. Hist. Nat., **50**: 5-32, Madrid.
- (1953): *Lacerta maxima* n. sp. de la fauna continental extinguida en el Pleistoceno de las Islas Canarias. - Estud. Geol., **17**: 7-34, Madrid.
- (1954a): Geografia general de las Islas Canarias. - I: 410 pp., Goya Edic., Sta. Cruz de Tenerife.
- (1954b): Tubos en las coladas volcanicas del Teide. - Bol. R. Soc. Esp. Hist. Nat., Tomo homenaje: 105-115, Madrid.
- (1955): Algunos yacimientos de augita en Tenerife. - Estud. Geol., **12**: 27-36, Madrid.
- (1960): Formaciones Post-Miocenas de Gran Canaria. - Rev. Museo Canario, **21**: 405-411, Las Palmas.
- (1962a): El circo de »Las Canadas« y sus dependencias. - Bol. R. Soc. Esp. Hist. Nat., **60**: 93-108, Madrid.
- (1962b): Investigaciones geologicas de los emplazamientos de los embalses previstos en el plan

de J. Amigo para el aprovechamiento de las aguas superficiales de la Caldera de Taburiente (La Palma). – Sta. Cruz de La Palma.

Bravo, T. (1964a): Geografia general de las Islas Canarias. – II: 592 pp., Goya Edic., Sta. Cruz de Tenerife.

– (1964b): Estudio geologico y petrografico de la isla de Gomera. – Estud. Geol., 20: 1–56, Madrid.

– (1973): Geografia general de las Islas Canarias. – III, Goya Edic., Sta. Cruz de Tenerife.

Brito, R. S. (1955): A Ilha de S. Miguel. Estudo Geografico. – Publ. Cent. de Estud. Geogra., 214 pp., Lisbon.

Brochu, M. (1969): Existence d'une zone périglaciaire dans la région sommitale du Pic (ou Pico), dans l'île du Pic aux Açores. – Z. Geomorph., N. F. 13,1: 115–118, Berlin.

Bronn, H. G. (1860): Die fossilien Reste von Santa Maria, der südlichsten der Azorischen Inseln. – In: Hartung, 1860.

Brun, A. (1910b): Etude au Volcan de Chinyero. – Arch. Sc. Phys. Nat., 39: Geneva.

Brun, A. & Colet, L. (1910a): Etudes des materiaux récoltés par M. Henry F. Montaignier F. R. G. S. au Volcan de Chinyero (Tenerife, Canarias). Eruption de nov. 1909. – Arch. Sc. Phys. Nat., 39: Geneva.

Brun, A. & Montaignier, F. (1908): Quelques recherches sur le volcanisme du Pico de Teyde et au Timanfaya (troisième partie). – Arch. Sc. Phys. Nat., 25, Geneva.

Buch, L. von (1825): Physikalische Beschreibung der Canarischen Inseln. – 201 pp., Berlin. Also published in »Gesammelte Schriften«, 3, Berlin.

Bullar, J. & H. (1841): A Winter in the Azores and a Summer at the Baths of Furnas. – London.

Bunbury, C. J. F. (1858): On some Fossil Plants from Madeira. – Proc. Geol. Soc., 15, London.

Burchard, O. & Ahl, E. (1928): Neue Funde von Riesen-Landschildkröten auf Tenerife. – Z. dt. geol. Ges., 77: 439–447, 447, Berlin.

Burri, C. (1960): Petrochemie der Capverden und Vergleich des Capverdischen Vulkanismus mit demjenigen des Rheinlands. – Schweiz. Miner. Petr. Mitt., 40: 115–161, Zurich.

Cab. Ins. de Gran Canaria (1959): Gran Canaria y sus Obras Hidraulicas. – Las Palmas.

Cabral, F. M. (1873): Rapports des observations faites sur les eaux minérales de la Vallée de Furnas durant les années 1870, 1871, 1872. – In: Les Eaux Thermales de l'île de S. Miguel (Açores) Portugal: 79–150, Lisbon.

Caja Ins. de Ahorros (1971): Plan insular de ordenacion de la Isla de Lanzarote. – Bol. 11, Centro de Invest. Econ. y Social, Las Palmas.

Calamai, A. (1968): Rapporto sulla missione eseguita nell'isola di Lanzarote (Canarie). – E.N.E.I. (unedit.), Rome.

Calamai, A. & Ceron, P. (1970): Air convection within »Montana del Fuego« (Lanzarote Island, Canarian Archipelago. – U. N. Symp. on Development and Utilization of Geothermal Resources, Paper 5/8, Pisa.

Calderon, S. (1876): Resena de las Rocas de la isla volcanica de Gran Canaria. – An. Soc. Esp. Hist. Nat., 9, Madrid.

– (1879): la evolucion en las rocas volcanicas en general y en las de Canarias en particular. – An. Soc. Esp. Hist. Nat., 8: 265–333, Madrid.

– (1880): Nuevas observaciones sobre la litologia de Tenerife y Gran Canaria. – An. Soc. Esp. Hist. Nat., 9: 203–283, Madrid.

– (1884a): Areniscas y dunas de las Islas Canarias. – Act. R. Soc. Esp. Hist. Nat., 13, Madrid.

– (1884b): Edad geologica de las Islas Atlanticas y su relacion con los continentes. – Bol. Soc. Geogra., 9: 377–399, Madrid.

Calvo, L. L. (1960): Rapport sur les travaux géodésiques, Helsinki, 1960. – Inst. Geogr. y Cad., Madrid.

Campos, V.; Machado, F. & Garcia, J. A. (1962): Le volcanisme de l'île de Faial et l'éruption du Volcan de Capelinhos . . . . . – Serv. Geol. Portugal, Mem. 9, Lisbon.

Cann, J. R. (1967): A second occurence of dalyite and the petrology of some ejected syenite blocks from S. Miguel (Azores). – Miner. Mag., 36: 227–232, London.

Canto, E. P. (1879): Anno de 1562. Erupçao na ilha do Pico. – Arch. Açores, 1: 360–367, Ponta Delgada.

– (1880a): Anno de 1580. Erupçao na ilha de S. Jorge. – Arch. Açores, 2: 188–193, Ponta Delgada.

– (1880b): Anno de 1630. Erupçao na valle das Furnas, ilha de S. Miguel. – Arch. Açores, 2: 527–547, Ponta Delgada.

– (1881): Erupçao na ilha do Fayal (Anno de 1672). – Arch. Açores, 3: 344–351, 426–434, Ponta Delgada.

– (1882a): Anno de 1760–1761. Terremoto e erupçoes na ilha Terceira. – Arch. Açores, 4: 362–365, Ponta Delgada.

CANTO, E. P.  (1882b): Tremores de terra nos Açores (Anno de 1800). - Arch. Açores, **4**: 365-368, Ponta Delgada.
- (1882c): Anno de 1718. Erupçao na ilha do Pico. - Arch. Açores, **4**: 497-506, Ponta Delgada.
- (1883a): Anno de 1720. Erupçao na ilha do Pico. - Arch Açores, **4**: 343-345, Ponta Delgada.
- (1883b): Erupçao submarina junto da ilha Terceira (Anno de 1867). - Arch. Açores, **5**: 499-503, Ponta Delgada.
- (1884): Anno de 1808. Erupçao na ilha de S. Jorge. - Arch. Açores, **5**: 437-447, Ponta Delgada.
- (1887a): Erupçao no Capello, Ilha do Fayal (Anno de 1672). - Arch. Açores, **9**: 425-432, Ponta Delgada.
- (1887b): Note sur les propriétés optiques de quelques minéraux des roches de l'Archipel Açoréen. - Bull. Soc. Fr. de Minér., **10**: 7 pp., Paris.
- (1888): Recherches micrographiques sur quelques roches de l'île de S. Miguel. - 91 pp., Lisbon.
- (1891): Ensaio critico sobre a bibliografia geologica dos Açores e nomeadamente S. Miguel. - Arq. Açores, **10**: 268-303, Ponta Delgada.
CARDENES, D. (1940): Gran Canaria, Continente en miniatura. - Rev. Geogra. Esp., **8**, San Sebastian.
CASTELO BRANCO, H. C. L. (1938): The Climate of Madeira. - Deleg. do Turismo da Madeira. - 118 pp., Funchal.
CASTRO E SOLLA, L. (1940): Relatorio da visita de S. Miguel, em 1937, a fim de serem estudas ›in loco‹ as condiçoes de valorizaçao das nascentes de aguas mineromedicinais, que servirao de base para elaboraçao do programa de consurso para adjudicaçao da exploraçao das nascentes das aguas minerais das Furnas. - Publ. Dir. Ger. Minas e Serv. Geol. Portugal: 109-134, Lisbon.
CENDRERO, A. (1966): Los volcanes recientes de Fuerteventura (Islas Canarias). - Estud. Geol., **22**: 201-226, Madrid.
- (1967a): Nota previa sobre la geologia del complejo basal de la isla de La Gomera (Canarias). - Estud. Geol. **23**: 71-79, Madrid.
- (1970a): The Volcano-plutonic Complex of La Gomera. - Bull. Volcan., **34**: 537-561, Naples.
- (1970b): Report on the International Symposium on Volcanology held in Spain (Canary Islands) in Sept. 1968. - Earth and Extraterrestrial Sci., **1**: 79-88, Belfast.
- (1971): Estudio geologico y petrologico del Complejo basal de la isla de La Gomera (Canarias). - Estud. Geol., **27**: 3-74, Madrid.
CENDRERO, A. & FUSTER, J. M. (1968a): Mapa geologico de Espana. 1:50,000. Lobos. - Inst. Geol. Min. Esp., **380**: 8 pp., Madrid.
- (1968b): Mapa geologico de Espana 1:50,000. Istmo de la Pared. - Inst. Geol. Min. Esp., **384**: 7 pp., Madrid.
CENDRERO, A.; FUSTER, J. M. & SAGREDO, J. (1967b): Mapa geologico de Espana 1:50,000. Cotillo. - Inst. Geol. Min. Esp., **379**: 9 pp., Madrid.
CHAIGNEAU, M. & FUSTER, J. M. (1972): L'éruption du Teneguia (La Palma) et la composition des laves et gaz fumeroliens. - C. R. Acad. Sci., **274**: 2948-2951, Paris.
- (1973): Relations entre les gaz occlus et la composition des laves du Teneguia (La Palma), Iles Canaries. - C. R. Acad: Sci., **276**: 1405-1408, Paris.
CHAUTARD, J. (1907): Les roches éruptives de la presqu'île de Cap Vert. - Bull. Soc. Géol. France, **7**: 427-438, Paris.
CHAVES, F. A. (1906a): A temperatura das nascentes termais das Furnas na ilha de S. Miguel. - Lisbon.
- (1906b): Nascentes nas ilhas do Arquipelago dos Açores: Terceira, S. Jorge, Graciosa, Faial, Flores. - Arq. Açores, **13**, Ponta Delgada.
- (1908): Gisements de diatomées fossiles à Furnas (île de S. Miguel). - Bull. Soc. Port. Sci. Nat., **2**: 231-255, Lisbon.
- (1920): Erupçöes submarinas nos Açores ... - Arq. Açores **13**: 53-60, Ponta Delgada.
- (1924): As Formigas. Monographie sur les îlots qui se trouve au NE de Santa Maria. - Ponta Delgada.
- (1943): Caracteristicas do magnetismo terrestre nos Açores. - Serv. Meteor. dos Açores, 18 pp., Angra.
CHEVALIER, A. (1935a): Les îles du Cap-Vert. Flore de l'Archipel. - Rev. Bot. Appl. **15**: 733-1090, Paris.
CHEVALIER, A. & FURON, R. (1935c): Sur quelques dépôts tertiaires et quaternaires des îles du Cap Vert. - C. R. Acad. Sci., **201**: 226-227, Paris.
CHEVALIER, A.; JOLEAUD, L. & PETIT, G. (1935b): Les dépôts quaternaires de l'ancien cratère de Pedra de Lume (île de Sal, archipel du Cap Vert). - C. R. Acad. Sci., **200**: 1334-1335, Paris.
CLOOS, H. (1939): Zur Tektonik der Azoren. Ber. intern. Golfstrom-Expedition. - Abh. Preuss. Akad. Wiss., Phys.-Math. Kl., **5**: 59-64, Berlin.

COCHIUS, H. (1864): Untersuchungen über die chemische Zusammensetzung der wichtigsten vulkanischen Gesteine Madeiras und Porto Santo. - Z. f. prakt. Chemie, 93: 124–161.

COCKERELL, T. D. A. (1922): Land Snails of the Madeira Island. - Nature, 109: 446, London.

COELHO,-E. P. (1968a): Trabalhos gravimetricos no Arquipelago da Madeira. - Cad. Tec. Inf., 13: 14 pp., Inst. Geogr. e Cad., Lisbon.

– (1968b): Trabalhos gravimetricos no Arquipelago dos Açores. - Cad. Tec. Inf., 14: 44 pp., Inst. Geogr. e Cad., Lisbon.

COELLO, J. (1971): Contribucion a la tectonica de la Isla de Hierro (Canarias). - Estud. Geol., 27: 335–340, Madrid.

COHEN, E. (1876): Über die sogenannten Hypersthenite von Palma. - N. Jb. Miner. etc., 75, 747–752, Stuttgart.

COLLET, W. & MONTAIGNIER, F. (1910): Sur la récente éruption de Chinyero à Tenerife. - Arch. Sci. Phys. Nat., 29, Geneva.

COLOM, G. (1954): La Sedimentacion Pelagica de la Isla de Maio (Archipelago de Cabo Verde) y sus Equivalentes Mediterraneos (Malm-Neocomiense). - R. Soc. Esp. Hist. Nat., Vol. homen Prof. E. HERNANDEZ-PACHECO: 179–192, Madrid.

CORRENS, C. W. (1927): Geologische Beobachtungen auf der Insel Sal (Kapverdische Inseln). - Z. Ges. Erdk.: 376–398, Berlin.

COSTA, J. V. B. (1885): A Ilha do Fogo de Cab Verde e o Seu Vulcao. - Bol. Soc. Geogr., 5a: 376–398, Lisbon.

COSTA, M. A. (1956–58): Acerca do Reconhecimento Hidrogeologico do Arquipelago de Cabo Verde. - Three typed reports, Praia, S. Tiago.

COTTER, J. C. B. (1892a): Noticia de alguns fosseis terciarios do Arquipelago da Madeira. Fosseis das praias levantadas. - Comm. Com. Trab. Geol. Portugal, 2: 232–250, Lisbon.

– (1892b): Noticia de alguns fosseis terciarios da ilha de Santa Maria no Arquipelago dos Açores. - Comm. Com. Trab. Geol. Portugal, 2: 255–287, Lisbon.

– (1953): Noticia de alguns fosseis terciarios da ilha de Santa Maria. - Açoreana, Bol. Soc. Af. Chaves, 5: 71–75, Angra.

COTTREAU, J. & LEMOINE, P. (1910): Sur la présence du Crétacé aux Iles Canaries. - Bull. Soc. Géol. France, 4: 267–271, Paris.

CROFTS, R. A. (1965): The raised beaches of west Fuerteventura, Canary Islands. - B. A. thesis, Liverpool Univ.

DARWIN, C. (1844): Geological Observations on the Volcanic Islands. - 674 pp. (2nd ed. 1876), Smith, Elder & Co., London.

– (1877): Geologische Beobachtungen über die vulcanischen Inseln. Ges. Werke (Übers. CARUS), 11/2. - I-VIII, 176 pp., E. Schweizerbart'sche Verlagsbuchh., Stuttgart.

DASH, B. P. & BOSSHARD, E. (1968): Crustal studies around the Canary Islands. - 23rd Internat. Geol. Congr., 1: 249–260, Prague.

– (1969): Seismic and gravity investigations around the Western Canary Islands. - Earth Planet. Sci. Lett., 7: 169–177, Amsterdam.

DENAEYER, M.-E. (1968): Volcanologie de Fuerteventura et de Lanzarote. - Bull. Soc. belge de Géol., 77,2/3: 337–345, Bruxelles.

DENIZOT, G. (1934): Sur la structure des Iles Canaries, considerée dans ses rapport avec le problème de l'Atlantide. - C. R. Acad. Sci., 199: 372–373, Paris.

DE OSSUNA, M. (1897): El problema de la Atlantida y geologia de la region de Anaga (Islas Canarias). - Bol. Inst. Geogr. Argentino, 18, Buenos Aires.

DEUTSCH, S. & KLERKX, J. (1973): The Isotopic Composition of Strontium in Basic Volcanics of Central Chile, Cape Verde Islands and Mt. Etna. - Fortschr. Miner., 50,3: 66, Stuttgart.

DIETZ, R. S. & SPROLL, W. P. (1970): East Canary Islands as a microcontinent within the Africa-North America Continental Drift fit. - Nature, 226: 1043–1045, London.

DINGMAN, R. J. & NUNEZ, J. (1969): Hidrogeologic Reconnaissance of the Canary Islands, Spain. - U. S. Geol. Surv., Prof. Paper 650-C: 201–208, Washington.

DITTLER, E. & KÖHLER, A. (1927): Mineralogische-petrographische Notizen vom Pico de Teyde. - Cbl. Miner. Geol. Pal'ont., A, 1927,4: 134–143, Stuttgart.

DOELTER, C. (1882a): Die Vulkane der Kapverden und ihre Produkte. - 171 pp., Leuschner u. Lubensky, Graz.

– (1882b): Os volcoes das ilhas de Cabo Verde e os seus produtos. Translated by E. ACKERMANN. - Bol. Soc. Geogr., 1910, Sér. 27a: 49–64, 101–113, 137–151, 165–180, 210-222, 239–248, 278–287, 321–338, 365–376, 397–407, Lisbon.

D'ORCHYMONT, A. (1936): Porto Santo, ses sables calcaires. L'Atlantide. - Bull. Mus. roy. d'Hist. nat. Belge, 12,43: 1–24, Bruxelles.

DRESCHER, F. (1924): Eruptivgesteine der Insel Flores. - Diss. Univ. Basel.

DRISCOLL, E. M.; HENDRY, G. L. & TINKLER, K. J. (1965): The geology and geomorphology of Los Ajaches, Lanzarote. - Geol. J., **4** (2): 321-334, Liverpool.

DROUET (1861): Eléments de la Faune açoréenne. - Mém. Soc. Agr., Sci., Arts et Belles-Lett. du Dépt. de l'Aube, **12**: 297-298, Troyes.

DRUMONDO, J. P. F. P. (1818): Noticias mineralogicas e da Ilha da Madeira. - In: O Investigador Portugues em Inglaterra, **21**, Lisbon.

DUPUY DE LOME, E. & MARIN DE LA BARCENA, A. (1959): Estudio hidrogeologico de la Isla de Hierro (Canarias). - 61 pp., Madrid?


EIGEL, F. (1890): Über einige Eruptivgesteine der Kap Verden. - Tscherm. Miner. Petr. Mitt., **11**: 91-104, Vienna.

ERMERT, H. (1936): Beitrag zur Kenntnis der Gesteine der Capverdischen Inseln Sao Vicente und Sal, mit einem Überblick über die Kapverdischen Inseln als Gesteinsprovinz. - Chem. d. Erde, **10**: 155-187, Jena.

ESENWEIN, P. (1929): Zur Petrographie der Azoren. - Z. Vulk., 3,12: 128-227, Stuttgart.

EVERS, A. M. J. (1960): Die Malachiidae der Kanarischen Inseln. - Entomol., **55**/3: 219-247, Krefeld.

- (1963): Die Malachiidae von Madeira. - Comm. Biol., **25**,2, Helsinki.

- (1966): Probleme der geographischen Verbreitung und der Artbildung auf den atlantischen Inseln. - Dt. Entom. Z., **13**,4: 299-305, Berlin.

EVERS, A. M. J.: HOHENESTER, A.; KLEMER, K.; STRASSEN, R. & ROTHE, P. (1966): Sind die Kanarischen Inseln kontinentalen Ursprungs? - Umschau Wiss. Tech., **66**: 501-502, Frankfurt/Main.

EVERS, A. M. J.; KLEMMER, K.; MÜLLER-LIEBENAU, L.; OHM, P.; REMANE, R.; ROTHE, P. & STRASSEN, R. (1970): Erforschung der mittelatlantischen Inseln. - Umschau Wiss. Tech., **70**: 170-176, Frankfurt/Main.


FEIJO, J. S. (1786): Memoria sobre a nova volcanica do Pico da Ilha de Fogo... - Arq. Hist. Ultramarino, Lisbon.

FERNANDES, V. (1940): O Manuscripto »Valentin Fernandes«. - Ed. by Acad. Port. da Hist., Lisbon.

FERDANDEZ, E. & PEREZ, V. (1967): Las aguas subterraneas de Tenerife. - Anal. Edaf. y Agrobiol., **26**, Madrid.

- (1969): The subterranean waters of Tenerife. Origin and Chemical Characteristics. - Centro Edaf. y Biol. Appl. de Tenerife. Talanta, **16**: 1067-1078.

FERNANDEZ, M. L. (1907): Algunas rocas de las islas de La Palma y Gomera. - Mem. R. Soc. Esp. Hist. Nat., **5**, Madrid.

- (1908): Observaciones geologicas en la isla de Hierro (Canarias). - Mem. R. Soc. Esp. Hist. Nat., **5**: 49-92, Madrid.

- (1910): Sobre la erupcion volcanica del Chinyero (Tenerife). - Bol. R. Soc. Esp. Hist. Nat., **10**: 104-122, Madrid.

- (1911): Erupcion volcanica del Chinyero (Tenerife) en Nov. 1909. - Anal. Junta Ampl. Estud. Invest. Cien., **5**: 1-98, Madrid.

- (1912): Nuevos datos sobre el Volcan Chinyero (Tenerife). - Bol. R. Soc. Esp. Hist. Nat., **12**: 74-78, Madrid.

- (1916): Sobre el Teide y Las Canadas (Tenerife). - Conf. en la R. Soc. Esp. Hist. Nat., **16**: 437-438, Madrid.

- (1917a): Sur la structure et la composition pétrographique du Pic du Teyde. - C. R. Acad. Sci., **165**: 561-563, Paris.

- (1917b): Le Pic du Teyde et le Cirque de Las Canadas à Tenerife. - C. R. Acad. Sci., **165**: 471-473, Paris.

- (1917c): El Teide y la geologiy de Canarias. - Conf., Sta. Cruz de Tenerife, 27 pp.

- (1917d): Sur la non-existence du Crétacé dans l'île de Hierro. - C. R. Acad. Sci., **165**, Paris.

- (1918a): Sur la constitution de l'île de Gomera. - C. R. Hebd. des Séanc., Acad. Sci., **167**, Paris.

- (1918b): Observaciones geologicas en la isla de Gomera (Canarias). - Trab. Mus. Nac. Cien. Nat., Serv. Geol., **23**: 87 pp., Madrid.

- (1919a): Las erupciones de fecha historica en Canarias. - Mem. R. Soc. Esp. Hist. Nat., **11**, Madrid.

- (1919b): Algunas consideraciones sobre la constitucion geologica del Archipelago Canario. - Bol. R. Soc. Esp. Hist. Nat., **19**: 298-305, Madrid.

- (1924): Datos hidrogeologicos en el Valle de La Orotava. - Sta. Cruz de Tenerife, 95 pp.

- (1925): Datos sobre el volcanismo canario. - Bull. Volcan., **2**: 129-155, Naples.

- (1926): Iles Canaries. - 14th Internat. Geol. Congr., **A-7** Excursion, 122 pp., Madrid.

FERNANDEZ, S. (1969a): Pegmatitoides in the Horizontal Basalts (Series I) of Lanzarote and Fuerteventura Islands. - Bull. Volcan., **33**: 989-1007, Naples.
- (1969b): Pegmatitoides en la serie basaltica fisural de las islas de Lanzarote y Fuerteventura. - Estud. Geol., **25**: 53-100, Madrid.
FERREIRA, A. B. (1968): A Ilha Graciosa. - Inst. Alta Cultura, Centr. Estud. Geogra. Univ. Lisboa, 290 pp., Lisbon.
FERREIRA, M. R. P. V. (1969): As ocorrencias de rochas plutonicas na Ilha de Porto Santo. - Mem. e Not., Univ. Coimbra, **68**: 3-13, Coimbra.
FERREIRA, O. V. (1952): Os Pectinideos do Miocenico da ilha de Santa Marta (Açores). - Rev. Fac. Cien. Lisboa, **2 C**: 243-258, Lisbon.
- (1955): A fauna miocenica da ilha de Santa Maria. - Comun. Serv. Geol. Portugal, **36**: 9-44, Lisbon.
- (1957): A erupçao do vulcao dos Capelinhos (Faial-Açores). - Bol. Soc. Geogr., **75**: 355-359, Lisbon.
- (1961): Equinideos do Miocenico de Portugal Continental e Ilhas Adjacentes. - Comun. Serv. Geol. Portugal, **45**: 529-564, Lisbon.
FINCKH, L. (1908): Über Tiefen- und Ganggesteine von Fuerteventura. - Z. dt. geol. Ges., **60**: 76-80, Berlin.
- (1911): Die vulkanischen Gesteine der Insel Selvagem Grande. - N. Jb. Miner. Geol. Paläont., Beil.-Bd., **31**: 415-420, Stuttgart.
- (1913): Die Gesteine der Insel Madeira und Porto Santo. - Z. dt. geol. Ges., **65**: 453-517, Berlin.
FISCHER, P. (1874): Sur les fossiles des îles de Cap Vert, rapportés par M. COSSAC. - C. R. Acad. Sci., **73**: 11-13, Paris.
FISCHER, P. H. (1946): Sur les Mollusques littoraux des Iles Canaries. - Mém. Soc. Biogéogr., **8**: 279-294, Paris.
FORJAZ, V. H. (1963a): Resumo geologico das ilhas dos Açores. - Atlantide, 7,4/5: 243-245, Angra.
- (1963b): Topografia e temperaturas do vulcao dos Capelinhos (Setembro 1962). - Bol. Mus. Lab. Min. Geol., Fac. Cien., Univ. Lisboa, 9,2: 125-130, Lisbon.
- (1963c): Sobre as isotermicos e as temperaturas do vulcao dos Capelinhos (Açores) dos anos 1961, 1962 e 1963. Noticia preliminar. - Bol. Soc. Port. Cien. Nat., **10**: 46-51, Lisbon.
- (1965-66): Observaçoes realizadas no vulcao dos Capelinhos (Açores) em Agosto e Setembro de 1963. - Bol. Mus. Lab. Min. Geol., Fac. Cien. Porto, 10,2: 89-94, Porto.
FORJAZ, V. H. & MONJARDINO, J. L. (1964a): Noticia preliminar sobre os tufos vulcanicos fossiliferos de Sto. Antonio, ilha do Pico, Açores. - Atlantide, **8**: 179-184, Angra.
FORJAZ, V. H. & WESTON, F. S. (1964b): Actividade vulcanica dos Açores de 1959 a 1964. - Bol. Nuc. Cult. da Horta, 3,3: 339-408, Horta.
- (1965): Actividade vulcanica dos Açores de 1959 a 1964. - Atlantide, 9,6: 254-261, Angra.
- (1967): Volcanic Activity in the Azores. Report for 1959-64. - Bull. Volcan., **31**: 261-266, Naples.
FOUQUÉ, F. (1867a): Sur les gaz qui dégagent en mer du lieu de l'éruption qui c'est manifestée aux Açores le 1er Juin 1867. - C. R. Acad. Sci., **65**: 674-675, Paris.
- (1867b): Sur les phénomènes volcaniques observés à Terceira (îles Açores). Lettres de M. FOUQUÉ à M. Ch. SAINTE CLAIRE-DEVILLE. - C. R. Acad. Sci., **65**: 965-971, 1050-1053, 1153-1155, Paris.
- (1868a): Sur la composition des gaz dégagés dans la dernière éruption des Açores. - C. R. Acad. Sci., **66**: 915-917, Paris.
- (1868b): Eruptions sous-marines des Açores. - Rev. Cours Sci. France et de l'Etranger, **11**: 179-183, Paris.
- (1873a): Viagens geologicas os Açores. - Cultivador, **15/16**, Ponta Delgada.
- (1873b): Etude des eaux minérales de l'île S. Miguel et particulièrement des eaux geysériennes de Fornas et de Ribeira Grande. - Rapp. sur les eaux therm. de l'île de S. Miguel (Açores), Lisbon.
- (1873c): San Jorge et ses éruptions. - Rev. Cours Sci. France et l'Etranger, **48**: 1198-1201, Paris.
(1873d): Voyages géologiques aux Açores. - Rev. Deux Mondes, **103**: 40-65, Paris.
(1873e): Recherches micrographiques sur quelques roches de l'île Sao Miguel. - Imp. Nac., Lisbon.
FRIEDLÄNDER, I. (1912): Über das Vorkommen älterer Gesteine, darunter Kalkstein mit Aptychen auf den Kapverden. - Akad. Anz., **19**, Vienna.
- (1913): Beiträge zur Kenntnis der Kapverdischen Inseln. - 109 pp., Dietrich Reiner, Berlin.
- (1915-16): Über vulkanische Verwerfungstäler. - Z. Vulkan., **2**, Berlin.
- (1929): Die Azoren. - Z. Vulkan., **12**: 77-107, Berlin.

FRISCH, T. (1970): The detailed Mineralogy and Significance of an Olivine-Two Pyroxene Gabbro Nodule from Lanzarote, Canary Islands. - Contr. Min. Petrol, **28**: 31–41, Heidelberg.

FRISCH, T.; SCHMINCKE, H.-U. (1968): Petrology of clinopyroxene-amphibole inclusions from the Roque Nublo volcanics, Gran Canaria, Canary Islands. - Bull. Volcan., **33**: 1073–1088, Naples.

FRITSCH, K. VON (1862): Briefliche Mitt. an G. ROSE. - Z. dt. geol. Ges., **14**: 544–550, Berlin.

- (1867a): Reisebilder von den Kanarischen Inseln. - Pet. Mitt. Ergh., **5**,22: 1–44, Gotha.

- (1870): Über die ostatlantischen Inselgruppen. - Ber. Senck. Naturforsch. Ges.: 72–113, Frankfurt/Main.

- (1878): Hierro. - Leopoldina, **14**: 61–64, Dresden.

- (1894): Hierro. Geogn. Aufzeich. - In: WALTER, Petrographische Studien an Gesteinen der Insel Hierro. Diss. Halle (Faber), Magdeburg.

FRITSCH, K. VON; HARTUNG, G. & REISS, W. (1867b): Tenerife, geologisch-topographisch untersucht. Ein Beitrag zur Kenntnis vulkanischer Gebirge. - Winterthur.

FRITSCH, K. VON & REISS, W. (1868): Geologische Beschreibung der Insel Tenerife. - 496 pp., Wurster Verlag, Winterthur.

FRUTUOSO, G. (1591): Saudades da Terra. Introd. by D. PERES. - 3 vols., 1924–31, Porto.

FURON, R. (1935): Notes sur la paléogéographie de l'Océan Atlantique. I. La géologie des îles du Cap Vert. - Bull. Mus. Nat. d'Hist., **2**,7/4: 270–274, Paris.

- (1968): Géologie de l'Afrique. - 3rd ed., 400 pp., Payot et Cie., Paris.

FUSTER, J. M. & AGUILAR, M. J. (1965): Nota previa sobre la geologia del macizo de Betancuria, Fuerteventura (Islas Canarias). - Estud. Geol., **21**: 181–197, Madrid.

FUSTER, J. M.; APARICIO, A. & ARANA, V. (1973a): The Oct.-Nov. 1971 eruption of Teneguia volcano (La Palma, Canary Islands). - Estud. Geol., Vol. Teneguia, Madrid.

FUSTER, J. M.; ARANA, V.; BRANDLE, J. L.; NAVARRO, M.; ALONSO, U. & APARICIO, A. (1968d): Geologia y Volcanologia de las Islas Canarias. Tenerife. - 218 pp., Inst. ›Lucas Mallada‹, Madrid.

FUSTER, J. M. & CENDRERO, A. (1973b): Canary Islands: Evidence of origin on an oceanic ridge. Abstr. II. Bien. R. Soc. Esp. Hist. Nat., Sept. Santander.

FUSTER, J. M.; CENDRERO, A.; GASTESI, P.; IBARROLA, E. & LOPEZ, J. (1968b): Geologia y Volcanologia de las Islas Canarias. Fuerteventura. - 239 pp., Inst. ›Lucas Mallada‹, Madrid.

FUSTER, J. M.; FERNANDEZ, S. & SAGREDO, J. (1968c): Geologia y Volcanologia de las Islas Canarias. Lanzarote. - 177 pp., Inst. ›Lucas Mallada‹, Madrid.

FUSTER, J. M.; GARCIA, L.; HERNANDEZ-PACHECO, A.; MUNOZ, M. & RODRIGUEZ, A. (1968a): Geologia y Volcanologia de las Islas Canarias. Gran Canaria. - 243 pp., Inst. ›Lucas Mallada‹, Madrid.

FUSTER, J. M.; GASTESI, P. & MUNOZ, M. (1968e): Mapa geologico de Espana 1:50,000. Puerto de Cabras. - Inst. Geol. Min. Esp., **383**: 17 pp., Madrid.

FUSTER, J. M.; GASTESI, P.; LOPEZ, J. & MUNOZ, M. (1967c): Mapa geologico de Espana 1:50,000. Graciosa. - Inst. Geol. Min. Esp. **373**: 12 pp., Madrid.

FUSTER, J. M.; HERNANDEZ-PACHECO, A.; LOPEZ, J. & PAEZ, A. (1967a): Mapa geologico de Espana 1:50,000. Alegranza. - Inst. Geol. Min. Esp., **371**: 7 pp., Madrid.

- (1967b): Mapa geologico de Espana 1:50,000. Montana Clara. - Inst. Geol. Min. Esp., **372**: 8 pp., Madrid.

FUSTER, J. M.; HERNANDEZ-PACHECO, A. & PAEZ, A. (1967d): Mapa geologico de Espana 1:50,000. Haria. - Inst. Geol. Min. Esp., **375**: 13 pp., Madrid.

- (1968f): Mapa geologico de Espana 1:50,000. Tuineje. - Inst. Geol. Min. Esp., Madrid.

FUSTER, J. M.; IBARROLA, E. & LOBATO, M. P. (1954): Analises quimicos de rocas espanoles publicados hasta 1952. - Monogr. Inst. ›Lucas Mallada‹, **14**: 89 pp., Madrid.

FUSTER, J. M.; IBARROLA, E. & LOPEZ, J. (1966): Estudio volcanologico y petrologico de las Isletas de Lanzarote (Islas Canarias). - Estud. Geol., **22**: 185–200, Madrid.

FUSTER, J. M.; PAEZ, A. & SAGREDO, J. (1969): Significance of basic and ultramafic rock inclusions in the basalts of the Canary Islands. - Bull. Volcan., **33**: 665–693, Naples.

FUSTER, J. M. & SANCHEZ-CELA, V. (1967e): Mapa geologico de Espana 1:50,000. Puerto de Lajas. - Inst. Geol. Min. Esp., **382**: 7 pp., Madrid.

GAGEL, C. (1903): Geologische Beobachtungen auf Madeira. - Z. dt. geol. Ges., **55**: 117–121, Berlin.

- (1908a): Der Pic de Teyde auf Tenerife. - Himmel u. Erde, **20**: 320–328.

- (1908b): Die Caldera von La Palma. - Z. Ges. Erdk., **3**: 168–186, 222–250, Berlin.

- (1908c): Bezeichnung der vulkanischen Kesseltäler und Schluchten. - Z. Ges. Erdk., **4**: 481–484, Berlin.

- (1908d): Das Grundgebirge von La Palma. - Z. dt. geol. Ges., **60**: 25–31, Berlin.

- (1910): Die mittelatlantischen Vulkaninseln. - Hand. Reg. Geol., **7**,10: 1–32, Heidelberg.

- (1911): Beiträge zur Kenntnis der Insel Selvagem Grande. - N. Jb. Miner. Geol. Paläont., Beil.Bd., **31**: 386–412, Stuttgart.

GAGEL, C. (1913): Studien über den Aufbau und die Gesteine Madeiras. I. Teil. - Z. dt. geol. Ges., **64**: 344–491, Berlin.
- (1914): Vulkanische Erscheinungen der nord-westafrikanischen Inseln. - Geolog. Charakterbilder, **20**, Gebr. Borntraeger, Berlin.
- (1915a): Studien über den Aufbau und die Gesteine Madeiras. II. Teil. - Z. dt. geol. Ges., **66**: 449–481, Berlin.
- (1915b): Tiefengesteine von den Canarischen Inseln. - Cbl. Miner. Geol. Paläont., **1915**,12: 373–384, Stuttgart.
- (1926): Begleitworte zu der Karte von Gomera, mit einem Anhang über die Calderafrage. - Z. dt. geol. Ges., **77**: 551–580, Berlin.
GARCIA DEL CASTILLO (1880): Nota geologica referente a la isla de Tenerife. - Bol. Com. Mapa Geol. Esp., 7, Madrid.
GASTESI, P. (1967): Nota sobre unas rocas granudas basicas encontradas en Tenerife (Islas Canarias). - Estud. Geol., **23**: 81–84, Madrid.
- (1969a): Petrology of the Ultramafic and Basic Rocks of Betancuria Massif, Fuerteventura Island (Canarian Archipelago). - Bull. Volcan., **33**: 1008–1038, Naples.
- (1969b): El complejo plutonico basico y ultrabasico de Betancuria, Fuerteventura (Islas Canarias). - Estud. Geol., **25**: 1–51, Madrid.
GASTESI, P.; HERNANDEZ-PACHECO, A. & MUNOZ, M. (1966): Las rocas holocristalinas de la Caldera de Taburiente, Isla de La Palma (Canarias). - Estud. Geol., **22**: 113–134, Madrid.
GERMAIN, L. (1926): Faune malacologique terrestre et fluviatile des îles du Cap Vert. - C. R. Congr. Soc. Sav. Sci., Imp. Nat.: 376–405, Paris.
GIRARD, A. A. (1892): Noticia de alguns molluscos terrestres fosseis do Arquipelago da Madeira. - Com. Trab. Geol. Port., **2**, Lisbon.
GONZALEZ, J. (1910): Algunos datos geologicos de Gran Canaria. - Bol. R. Soc. Esp. Hist. Nat., **10**: 398–408, Madrid.
GRABHAM, C. W. (1948): Esboço da formaçao geologica da Madeira. - Bol. Mus. Mun. Funchal, **3**: 65–83, Funchal.
GUTZWILLER, A. (1909): Eine Studienreise nach den Kanarischen Inseln. - Ber. Realschule, Basel.
- (1910): Beitrag zur Kenntnis der Eruptivgesteine von Tenerife. - Verth. d. naturf. Ges., **21**, Basel.
HARTNACK, W. (1930): Landeskunde einer Insel (Madeira). - Jb. Pomm. Geogr. Ges., **47/48**: - 198 pp., Hamburg.
HARTUNG, G. (1857): Die geologischen Verhältnisse der Inseln Lanzarote und Fuerteventura. - N. Denkschr. allg. Schweiz Ges. Naturwiss., **15**,4: 1–168, Zurich.
- (1860): Die Azoren in ihrer äußeren Erscheinung und nach ihrer geognostischen Natur. - I-VIII, 350 pp., Engelman Verlag, Leipzig.
- (1862): Betrachtungen über Erhebungskrater, ältere und neuere Eruptivmassen, nebst einer Schilderung der geologischen Verhältnisse der Insel Gran Canaria. Also the paper: Über die Entstehung der Caldera von La Palma. - Engelman Verlag, Leipzig.
- (1864): Geologische Beschreibung der Inseln Madeira und Porto Santo. - 299 pp., Engelman Verlag, Leipzig.
HAUSEN, H. (1951): On the Ground Water Conditions in the Canary Islands and their Irrigation Cultures. - Acta Geogr., **12**,2: 1–45, Helsinki.
- (1954): Hidrografia de las Islas Canarias. Rasgos generales y riego de los cultivos subtropicales. - Inst. Estud. Canarios., Monogr., **4**,12: 1–84, Univ. La Laguna, Laguna, Tenerife.
- (1955a): Algunos aspectos geologicos y geomorphologicos de la mas antigua de las Islas Canarias. - El Museo Canario, Las Palmas.
- (1955b): Contributions to the Geology of Tenerife. - Soc. Sci. Fenn., Comm. Phys.-Math., **18**,1: 254 pp., Helsinki.
- (1956): Fuerteventura. Some Geological Aspects of the Oldland of the Canarian Archipelago. - Acta Geogr., **15**,2: 1–48, Helsinki.
- (1958a): On the Geology of Fuerteventura. - Soc. Sci. Fenn., Comm. Phys.-Math., **22**,1: 1–211, Helsinki.
- (1958b): Contribucion al conocimiento de las formaciones sedimentarias de Fuerteventura (Islas Canarias). - An. Estud. Atlant., **4**: 1–48, Madrid-Las Palmas.
- (1959): On the Geology of Lanzarote. - Soc. Sci. Fenn., Comm. Phys.-Math., **23**,4: 1–116, Helsinki.
- (1960): Las »Calderas Canarias«. - An. Estud. Atlant., **6**: 133–194, Madrid - Las Palmas.
- (1961): Canarian Calderas. A Short Review based on Personal Impressions, 1947-57. - Bull. Com. Geol. Finlande, **196**: 179–213, Helsinki.
- (1962): Contributions to the Geology of Gran Canaria. - Soc. Sci. Fenn., Comm. Phys.-Math., **27**,1: 1–418, Helsinki.

HAUSEN, H. (1964): Rasgos geologicos generales de la Isla de Hierro (Archipelago Canaria). – An. Estud. Atlant., **10**: 547–593, Madrid – Las Palmas.

– (1965): Some comments on the structural geology of Gomera. – Acta Geogr., **18**,7: 3–15, Helsinki.

– (1967): Sobre el desarrollo geologico de Fuerteventura (Islas Canarias). – An. Estud. Atlant., **13**: 11–27, Madrid – Las Palmas.

– (1968): Algunos aspectos geologicos de la Isla de La Gomera. Patronato de la »Casa de Colon«. – An. Estud. Atlant., **14**, Madrid – Las Palmas.

– (1969): Some Contributions to the Geology of La Palma. – Soc. Sci. Fenn., Comm. Phys.-Math., **35**: 1–140, Helsinki.

– (1970): Desprendimientos en las Islas Canarias. – An. Estud. Atlant., **16**: 1–29, Madrid – Las Palmas.

– (1971a): Rockfalls, Landslides and Creep in the Canaries. – Acta Geogr., **23**: 1–43, Helsinki.

– (1971b): Outlines of the Geology of Gomera. – Soc. Sci. Fenn., Comm. Phys.-Math., **41**,1: 1–53, Helsinki.

– (1973): Outlines of the Geology of Hierro (Canary Islands). – Soc. Sci. Fenn., Comm. Phys.-Math., **43**,1: 65–148, Helsinki.

HEER, O. (1857): Über die fossilen Pflanzen von St. Jorge in Madeira. – N. Denkschr. allg. Schweiz. Ges. Naturwiss. **15**, Zurich.

HEEZEN, B. C. & JOHNSON, G. L. (1963): A Moated Knoll in the Canary Passage. – Dt. Hydrogr. Zeit., **16**,6: 269–272, Hamburg.

HEEZEN, B. C.; THARP, M. & EWING, M. (1959): The floors of the ocean. I. The North Atlantic. – Bull. Geol. Soc. Amer., Spec. Paper **65**: 1–122, New York.

HEINZ, R. (1935): Unterkreide Inoceramus von der Kapverden Insel Maio. – N. Jb. Miner. Geol. Paläont., Beil.-Bd., Abt. B, **73**,2: 302–311, Stuttgart.

HENNIG, E. (1913): Aptychen von den Kapverdischen Inseln. – Z. dt. geol. Ges., **65**: 151–158, Hannover.

HERRERA, L. (1953): Historia general de las Islas Canarias. – Montevideo (Uruguay).

HERNANDEZ-PACHECO, A. (1969): The Tahitites of Gran Canaria and Hauynitization of their Inclusions. – Bull. Volcan., **33**: 701–728, Naples.

– (1971): Nota previa sobre el complejo basal de la isla de La Palma (Canarias). – Estud. Geol., **27**: 255–265, Madrid.

HERNANDEZ-PACHECO, A. & IBARROLA, E. (1973a): Sobre la supuesta existencia de unas »rocas graniticas« en la isla de La Palma (Canarias). – Estud. Geol., **29**: 107–109, Madrid.

– (1973b): Geochemical variation trends between the different Canary Islands in relation to their geological position. – Lithos, **6**: 389–402, Oslo.

HERNANDEZ-PACHECO, E. (1910): Estudio geologico de Lanzarote y de las Isletas Canarias. – Mem. R. Soc. Esp. Hist. Nat., **6**: 1–331, Madrid.

– (1960): En relacion con las grandes erupciones volcanicas de siglo XVIII y 1824 en Lanzarote. – El Museo Canario, Las Palmas.

HERNANDEZ-PACHECO, F.; ALIA, M.; VIDAL, C. & GUINEA, M. (1949): El Sahara Espanol. Estudio Geologico, Geografico y Botanico. – Inst. Estud. Africanos, 810 pp., Madrid.

HONNOREZ, J. (1966): Contribution à l'étude géologique et pétrographique de l'Archipel des Selvagens. – Bull. Acad. roy. Sci. d'Outre-Mer, Classe des Sci. Tech., N. S., **16**,4: 1–43, Bruxelles.

HUGHES, D. J. & BROWN, G. C. (1972): Basalts from Madeira Archipelago. A Petrochemical contribution on the Genesis of Oceanic Alkali Rocks Series. – Contr. Miner. Petr., **37**: 91–109, Heidelberg.

HUMBOLDT, A. VON (1814): Voyages aux régions équinoxiales du Nouveau Continent, 1799–1804. – Paris.

IBARROLA, E. (1969): Variation Trends in Basaltic Rocks of the Canary Islands. – Bull. Volcan., **33**: 729–777, Naples.

– (1970): Variabilidad de los magmas basalticos en las Canarias Orientales y Centrales. – Estud. Geol., **26**: 337–399, Madrid.

IBARROLA, E. & LOPEZ, J. (1967a): Estudio petrografico y quimico de las erupciones recientes (Series IV) de Lanzarote (Islas Canarias). – Estud. Geol., **23**: 203–213, Madrid.

IBARROLA, E. & VIRAMONTE, J. (1967b): Sobre el hallazgo de sienitas nefeliniticas en Tenerife (Islas Canarias). – Estud. Geol., **23**: 215–222, Madrid.

JAEGER, F. (1908): Bemerkungen z. d. Ausführungen von Dr. C. GAGEL (betr. GAGEL 1908b). – Z. Ges. Erdk., **3**: 483–484, Berlin.

JÉRÉMINE, E. (1930): Composition chimique et minéralogique de la roche du Pico de Teide. – Bull. Soc. Minér. France, **53**: 210–215, Paris.

JÉRÉMINE, E. (1933): Contribution à l'étude pétrographique de trois îles de l'archipel Canarien, Tenerife, La Palma, Gran canaria. - Bull. Soc. Minér. France, **56**,4/5: 189-261, Paris.
- (1935): Contribution à l'étude des îles Hierro et Gomera (Archipel Canarien). - Bull. Soc. Minér. France, **58**: 350-363, Paris.
- (1939): 72éme Congr. Soc. Sav., 167 pp.
- (1950): Contribution à la connaissance lithologique de la Grande Salvage. Bull. Inst. Océanogr., **969**: 10 pp., Monaco.
- (1951): Contribution à la connaissance lithologique de la Grande Selvagem. - Rev. Fac. Cien. Univ. Lisboa, **2**,1: 5-20, Lisbon.
- (1957): Etude microscopique des roches de la région de Furnas (S. Miguel, Açores). - Comun. Serv. Geol. Portugal, **38**: 65-90, Lisbon.
JESUS, A. M. (1932): Subsidos para a petrologia do Arquipelago de Cabo Verde (Ilha de S. Vicente). - Comin. Serv. Geol. Portugal, **17**: 86-103, Lisbon.
JOHN, J. VON (1896): Chemische Untersuchungen an Gesteinen von Angra Pequena, der Capverdischen Insel S. Vicente, von Cap Verde und von der Insel S. Miguel (Azoren). - Jb. k. k. geol. Reichsanst., **46**: 279-292, Vienna.
JOKSIMOWITSCH, Z. J. (1911a): Die zweite Mediterran-Stufe von Porto Santo und Selvagem. - Z. dt. geol. Ges., **62**: 43-96, Berlin.
- (1911b): Nachtrag zu meiner Arbeit: Die zweite Mediterran-Stufe von Porto Santo und Selvagem. - Z. dt. geol. Ges., **62**: 163, Berlin.
KABANA, M. C. (1952): Sobre el origin del Archipelago Canario. - Notas y Comm. Inst. Geol. Min. Esp., **25**: 155-160, Madrid.
KLERKX, J.; DEUTSCH, S. & PAEPE, P. (1974): Rubidium, Strontium content and Strontium Isotopic Composition of Strongly Alkalic Basaltic Rocks from the Cape Verde Islands. - Contr. Miner. Petr., **45**: 107-118, Heidelberg,.
KLERKX, J. & PAEPE, P. (1971): Cape Verde Islands: Evidence for a Mesozoic Oceanic Ridge. Nature Phys. Sci., **233**,41: 117-118, London.
KLUG, H. (1961): Oberflächengestaltung des nördlichen Lanzarote. - Mainzer Geogr. Stud. (Festschr. W. PANZER): 163-176, Braunschweig.
- (1963): Wissenschaftliche Ergebnisse meiner Kanarenreise 1962. - Jb. Vgg. »Freunde Univ. Mainz«, **12**: 39-65, Mainz.
- (1967): Die Talgenerationen der Kanarischen Inseln. - Dt. Geographentag Bad Godesberg: 369-381, Steiner Verlag, Wiesbaden.
- (1968): Morphologische Studien auf den Kanarischen Inseln. - Schr. Geogr. Inst. Univ. Kiel, **24**,3: 158 pp., Kiel.
KNEBEL, W. VON (1906): Studien zur Oberflächengestaltung der Inseln Palma und Hierro. - Globus, **90**,20/21, Braunschweig.
- (1907): Der vulkanische Aufbau der Insel Gran Canaria. - Globus, **92**,21/22, Braunschweig.
KNECHT, S. (1959): Der Vulkan von Capelinhos. - Kosmos, **55**,3: 93-98.
KRAUSE, D. C. & WATKINS, N. D. (1970): North Atlantic Crustal Genesis in the vicinity of the Azores. Geophy. Jour., **19**: 261-283, London.
KREJCI-GRAF, K. (1955): Vulkaninseln und Inselvulkane. 3. Madeira. - Natur u. Volk, **85**,2: 40-51, Frankfurt/Main.
- (1956a): Über Rutschfaltung auf den Azoren. - In: Geotekt. Symposium zu Ehren von HANS STILLE: 38-44, F. Enke Verlag, Stuttgart.
- (1956b): Vulkanologische Beobachtungen auf den Azoren. - Frankfurter Geogr., **30**: 5-30, Frankfurt.
- (1958a): Rätselhafte Inschriften auf den Atlantischen Inseln. I. Eine Neuentdeckung auf den Capverden. - Umschau, **58**,8/9: 229-231, Frankfurt/Main.
- (1960): Geologie der Makaronesen. 4. Krustenkalke. - Z. dt. geol. Ges., **112**: 30-61, Hannover.
- (1961a): Vulkaninseln und Inselvulkane. 5. Santa Maria (Azoren). - Natur u. Volk, **91**,10: 351-358, Frankfurt/Main.
- (1961b): Die Caldera von Graciosa, Azoren. - Z. dt. geol. Ges., **113**: 85-95, Hannover.
- (1961c): Vertikal-Bewegungen der Makaronesen. - Geol. Rdsch., **51**: 73-122, Stuttgart.
- (1961d): Versteinerte Büsche. - N. Jb. Geol. Paläont. Abh., **113**: 1-22, Stuttgart.
- (1961e): Vulkaninseln und Inselvulkane. 4. Porto Santo. - Natur u. Volk, **91**,2: 35-38, Frankfurt/Main.
- (1962): Vulkaninseln und Inselvulkane. 6. Sao Miguel (Azoren). - Natur u. Museum, **92**,3: 71-78, Frankfurt.
- (1965): Die mittelatlantischen Vulkaninseln. - Mitt. geol. Ges. Wien, **57**,2: 401-431, Vienna.
KREJCI-GRAF, K.; FRECHEN, J.; WETZEL, W. & COLOM, G. (1958b): Gesteine und Fossilien von den Azoren. - Senckenbergiana Lethaea, **39**: 303-351, Frankfurt/Main.

KUBIENA, W. L. (1956): Materialien zur Geschichte der Bodenbildung auf den Westkanaren. – 61ème Congr. Sci. du Sol, **38**: 241–246, Paris.

KUNZLI, D. E. (1911): Petrographische Resultate von einer Tenerifereise. – Mitt. Naturforsch. Ges., **4**,16, Solothurn.

LAUGHTON, A. S.; HILL, M. N. & ALLAN, T. D. (1960): Geophysical investigations of a seamount 150 miles north of Madeira. – Deep-Sea Res., **7**: 117–141, New York.

LAUGHTON, A. S.; WHITMARSH, R. B.; RUSBY, J. S. M.; SOMERS, M. L.; REVIE, J.; McCARTNEY, B. S. & NAFE, J. E. (1972): A Continuous East-West Fault on the Azores-Gibralter Ridge. – Nature, **237**,5352: 217–220, London.

LAUTENSACH, H. (1949): Madeira. – Erdkunde, **3**: 212–229, Bonn.

LECOINTRE, G. (1962): Le Quaternaire de l'Ile de Sal (Archipel du Cap Vert). – C. R. somm. Soc. Géol. France, **3**: 92–93, Paris.

– (1963): Sur les terrains sédimentaires de l'île de Sal, avec remarques sur les îles de Santiago et de Maio. – Garcia de Orta, **11**: 275–289, Lisbon.

– (1966): Quelques remarques sur le Quaternaire de l'île de Gran Canaria. – Actes Ve Congr. Panafr. de Préhist. et Etude du Quat., 165–177.

LECOINTRE, G. & SERRALHEIRO, A. (1966): Sur quelques coquilles vivantes et fossiles de l'Archipel du Cap-Vert. – J. Conchy., **105**: 216–220, Paris.

LECOINTRE, G.; TINKLER, K. J. & RICHARDS, H. G. (1967): The Marine Quaternary of the Canary Islands. – Acad. Nat. Sci., **119**,8: 325–344, Philadelphia.

LE DANOIS, E. (1938): L'Atlantique, histoire et vie d'un océan. – Albin Michel, Paris.

LEPIERRE, C. (1917): Analise das aguas minero-medicinais do Vale das Furnas, S. Miguel. – Lisbon.

– (1927): Composiçao quimica da agua do Carrapacho. A Uniao 9712/March 22. – Lisbon.

– (1929): Termas do Carrapacho, Ilha Graciosa, Açores. Estudo da radioactividade das aguas. – Publ. Com. Admin. da Junta Geral, 7 pp., Angra.

LIETZ, J. (1973): Fossile Piedmont-Schwemmfächer auf der Kanaren-Insel Gran Canaria und ihre Beziehung zur Lage des Meeresspiegels. – Z. Geomorph., N. F., **18**: 105–120, Berlin – Stuttgart.

LIETZ, J. & SCHWARZBACH, M. (1970): Neue Fundpunkte von marinem Tertiär auf der Atlantik-Insel Porto Santo (Madeira-Archipel). – N. Jb. Geol. Paläont. Mh., **1970**,5: 270–282, Stuttgart.

– (1971): Quartäre Sedimente auf der Atlantik-Insel Porto Santo (Madeira-Archipel) und ihre paläoklimatische Deutung. – Eiszeitalter u. Gegenwart, **22**: 89–109, Öhringen.

LOPEZ, J. (1968): The dyke swarm of Fuerteventura (Canary Islands). – Internat. Symp. Volcan., Abstracts. Spain – Canary Islands.

– (1969): Le complex filonien de Fuerteventura (Iles Canaries). – Bull. Volcan., **33**: 1166–1185, Naples.

– (1970): Estudio petrografico y geoquimico del complejo filoniano de Fuerteventura (Islas Canarias). – Estud. Geol., **26**: 173–208, Madrid.

LOTZE, F. (1970): Das Bauschema der Insel Gran Canaria (Kanarische Inseln). – N. Jb. Geol. Paläont. Mh., **1970**,12: 701–704, Stuttgart.

LOWE, R. T. (1851): Primitae et Novitiae Faunae et Florae Madeirae et Portus Sancti. – London.

– (1854): List of all the land and freshwater shells recent and fossil, of the Madeiran Islands. – Proc. Zool. Soc., London.

LUNDBLAD, O. (1947): Makaronesien und Atlantis. – Zool. Bidr., **25**: 201–323, Uppsala.

LYELL, C. (1854): On the Geology of some parts of Madeira. – Quart. J. Geol. Soc., **10**, London.

– (1855): Manual of Elementary Geology. – 498 pp., London.

– (1875): Principles of Geology. 2 vols. – London.

MACAU, F. (1957a): Los Volcanos del Cenozoico en Gran Canaria. – 20th Internat. Geol. Congr., **1**,2: 409–424, Mexico.

– (1957b): Los tubos volcanicos originarios de manantiales. – 20th Internat. Geol. Congr., **1**,2: 425–437, Mexico.

– (1957c): Estudio hidrologico de Gran Canaria. – An. Estud. Atlant., **3**: 9–46, Madrid – Las Palmas.

– (1958): Contribucion al estudio del Mioceno Canario. – Bol. R. Soc. Esp. Hist. Nat., **56**: 477–486, Madrid.

– (1959a): Aplicacion de la geologia al estudio de un presupuesto para la construccion de una carratera. – Rev. Obras Publ., **106**: 1–12, Madrid.

– (1959b): Las »Calderas« de Gran Canaria. – An. Estud. Atlant., **5**: 9–36, Madrid – Las Palmas.

– (1960a): El problema hidraulico canario. – El Museo Canario, Las Palmas.

– (1960b): Contribucion al estudio del Quaternario de Gran Canaria. – An. Estud. Atlant., **6**: 117–132, Madrid – Las Palmas.

– (1963): Sobre el origen y edad de las Islas Canarias. – An. Estud. Atlant., **9**: 467–518, Madrid – Las Palmas.

MACAULAY, J. (1840): Notes on the Physical Geography, Geology and Climate of the Island of Madeira. - Edin. New Phil. J., **24**, Edinburgh.

MACDONALD, G. A. (1953): Pahoehoe, Aa and Block Lava. - Amer. J. Sci., **251**: 169–191, New Haven.

MACFARLANE, D. J. & RIDLEY, W. I. (1968): An interpretation of gravity data for Tenerife, Canary Islands. - Earth Planet. Sci. Lett., **4**,6: 481–486, Amsterdam.

- (1969a): An interpretation of gravity data for Lanzarote, Canary Islands. - Earth Planet. Sci. Lett., **6**: 431–436, Amsterdam.

- (1969b): Gravity data for some Canary Islands. - Proc. Geol. Soc., London.

MACHADO, F. (1946): Genese de alguns solos dos Açores. - Bol. Com. Regul. Cereais de Arquipelago dos Açores, **3**, Ponta Delgada.

- (1948): Frequencia dos sismos sentidos nas Ilhas do Faial e do Pico. - Açoreana, Bol. Soc. Af. Chaves, **4**: 236–245, Angra.

- (1949): O terramoto de S. Jorge em 1757. Angra. 99- Bol. Soc. Af. Chaves, **4**: 311–324, Angra.

- (1953): Perda de calor em camaras magmaticas dos Açores. - Açoreana, Bol. Soc. Af. Chaves, **5**: 23–45, Angra.

- (1954): Earthquake intensity anomalies and magma chambers of Azorean volcanoes. - Trans. Amer. Geophys. Union, **35**: 833–837, Washington.

- (1955a): The fracture pattern of Azorean volcanoes. - Bull. Volcan., **17**: 119–125, Naples.

- (1955b): Alguns aspectos sismicidade dos Açores. - Bol. Ord. Engen., **4**,107: 6 pp., Lisbon.

- (1956): O Vulcao na Ilha do Pico. - Bol. Nuc. Cult. da Horta, **1**: 37–45, Horta.

- (1957): Caldeiras vulcanicas dos Açores. - Atlantida, **1**: 275–278, Angra.

- (1958a): Actividade vulcanica da ilha do Faial (1957–58). - Atlantida, **2**: 225–236, 305–315, Angra.

- (1958b): Variaçao secular do vulcanismo açoreano. - Bol. Nuc. Cult. da Horta, **1**: 225–235, Horta.

- (1959a): Actividade vulcanica da Ilha do Faial. Noticia preliminar. - Atlantida, **3**: 40–55, 153–159, Angra.

- (1959b): A erupçao do Faial em 1672. - Mem. Serv. Geol. Portugal, **4**: 89–99, Lisbon.

- (1959c): Submarine pits of the Azorean plateau. - Bull. Volcan. **21**: 109–116, Naples.

- (1960): A erupçao dos Capelinhos (Açores) e a energia das regioes vulcanicas. - Electricidade, **4**: 344–346, Lisbon.

- (1962a): Erupçoes historicas do sistema vulcanico Faial-Pico-S. Jorge. - Atlantida, **6**: 84–91, Angra.

- (1962b): Actividade do Vulcano do Fogo, Cabo Verde. - Atlantide, **6**: 183–191, Lisbon.

- (1962d): Sobre o mecanismo da erupçao dos Capelinhos. - Mem. Serv. Geol. Portugal, **9**: 9–19, Lisbon.

- (1963): Erupçoes da ilha de La Palma (Canarias). - Bol. Mus. Lab. Min. Geol., Fac. Cien., Univ. Lisboa, **9**,2: 143–156, Lisbon.

- (1964a): Alguns problemas do vulcanismo da Ilha de Tenerife. - Bol. Soc. Port. Cien. Nat., **10**: 26–45, Coimbra.

- (1964b): Formaçao de fracturas em regioes vulcanicas. - Bol. Soc. Geol. Portugal, **15**: 175–190, Lisbon.

- (1965a): Vulcanismo das ilhas de Cabo Verde e das otras ilhas atlantidas. - Junta Invest. Ultramar, Ens. e Docum., **117**: 83 pp., Lisbon.

- (1965b): Mechanism of Fogo Volcano, Cape Verde Islands. - Garcia de Orta, **13**: 51–56, Lisbon.

- (1965c): Sequencias eruptivas das Canarias, Cabo Verde e Açores. - Bol. Soc. Geol. Portugal, **16**: 11–18, Lisbon.

- (1965–66): Anomalias das intensidades do terramoto de S. Miguel (Açores) em 1522. - Bol. Mus. Lab. Min. Geol., Fac. Cien., Univ. Lisboa, **10**: 109–117, Lisbon.

- (1966): Contribuiçao para o estudo do terramoto de Nov. 1 de 1755. - Rev. Fac. Cien., **14**: 19–31, Lisbon.

- (1967a): Active volcanoes of the Azores. Catalogue of the Active Volcanoes of the World . . . . . **21**, Atlantic Ocean. - Internat. Assoc. Volcan., 9–52, Rome.

- (1969): Sobre a tectonica do Atlantico Norte a Oeste de Portugal. - Rev. Fac. Cien. Univ. Lisboa, **16**: 1–14, Lisbon.

- (1973): Estudo reologico de uma lava do vulcao do Fogo (Cabo Verde). - Garcia de Orta, Ser. Geol., **1**,1: 9–14, Lisbon.

MACHADO, F. & ASSUNÇAO, C. F. T. (1965d): Carta geologica de Cabo Verde. Noticia explicativa da folha da ilha do Fogo. Estudos petrograficos. - Garcia de Orta, **13**: 597–604, Lisbon.

MACHADO, F. & FORJAZ, V. H. (1965e): A crise sismica de S. Jorge de Fev. de 1964. - Bol. Soc. Geol. Portugal, **16**: 19–36, Porto.

MACHADO, F.; LEME, J. A. & MONJARDINO, J. (1967b): O Complexo Sienito-Carbonatitico da ilha Brava, Cabo Verde. - Garcia de Orta, **15**: 93–98, Lisbon.

MACHADO, F.; LEME, J. A.; MONJARDINO, J. & SEITA, M. F. (1968)): Carta geologica de Cabo Verde. Noticia explicativa da folha da ilha Brava e dos ilheus Secos. - Garcia de Orta, 16: 123-130, Lisbon.
MACHADO, F. & NASCIMENTO, J. M. (1965): Movimentos do solo na proximadade da chaminé dos Capelinhos. - Bol. Soc. Geol. Portugal, 26: 1-10, Lisbon.
MACHADO, F.; PARSONS, W. H.; RICHARDS, A. F. & MULFORD, J. W. (1962c): Capelinhos eruption of Fayal Volcano, Azores, 1957-1958. - J. Geophys., 67: 3519-3529, Washington.
MACHADO, F.; QUINTINO, J. & MONTEIRO, J. H. (1972): Geology of the Azores and the Mid-Atlantic Rift. - Proc. 24th Internat. Geol. Congr., 3: 134-142, Montreal.
MARTEL, M. (1951): Genesis del Archipelago Canario. - Estud. Geol., 13: 69-79, Madrid.
- (1952): Contribucion al estudio geologico y paleontologico de Gran Canaria. - Estud. Geol., 15: 109-135, Madrid.
- (1954): La peninsula de Anaga y estudio de algunos arenales del litoral de Tenerife. - An. Edafol. y Fisiol., 13, Madrid.
- (1960): El Volcan de San Juan, La Palma (Canarias). - Madrid.
MARTINEZ, F. (1965): Nueva campana paleomastologica en Tenerife. - Fossilia, 3/4: 9-12.
MASCART, J. (1910): Impressions et observations dans un voyage à Tenerife. - Paris.
- (1911): L'Archipel Canarien. - Rev. Scient., 8, Paris.
MATZNETTER, J. (1958a): Studienreise nach den Kapverdischen Inseln. - Wien. Mitt. d. Geogr. Ges., 100,3: 273-280, Vienna.
- (1958b): Die Kanarischen Inseln. - Pet. Mitt. Ergh., 266, Gotha.
- (1960): Die Kapverdischen Inseln. - Wien. Mitt. d. Geogr. Ges., 102: 40 pp., Vienna.
- (1968): Die Inseln der ostatlantischen Archipele als reliefbedingte Klimatypen. - Wetter u. Leben, Jh. 20,5/8: 93-109, Frankfurt/Main.
MAYER-EYMAR, K. (1864): Paläontologische Verhältnisse, systematisches Verzeichnis der FossilienReste von Madeira, Porto Santo und Santa Maria nebst Beschreibung der Inseln Madeira und Porto Santo. (Mit dem systematischen Verzeichnis der fossilen Reste dieser Inseln und der Azoren von KARL MAYER. - In: G. HARTUNG (1864).
McMASTER, R. L.; LACHANCE. G. & THOMAS, P. (1968): Seismic reflectivity studies on NW African Continental Shelf: Strait of Gibralter to Mauritania. - Amer. Assoc. Petr. Geol. 52: 2387-2395, Tulsa.
MEDEIROS, C. A. (1967): A Ilha do Corvo. - Inst. Alta Cultura, Centr. Estud. Geogr., Univ. Lisboa: 252 pp., Lisbon.
MELLA, A. (1958): Vergleichende Untersuchungen über eine wichtige chileanische Bodenform und ähnliche Bildungen in Spanisch-Guinea und auf den Kanarischen Inseln. - Z. Pflanzenernähr., Düng. u. Bodenkde., 83: 99-103, Weinheim.
MENANT, G. (1958): L'enfer des Açores. - Paris Match, 487: 32-37, 41-43, Paris.
MENDES-VICTOR, L. A. (1970): L'interprétation des mesures gravimétriques et magnétiques aux Iles du Cap Vert et la théorie de l'expansion des fonds océaniques. - Thesis, Fac. Sci., 198 pp. Univ. Strasbourg,
MENDONÇA, D. A. A. (1945): O sismo de 1522 em S. Miguel. - Insulana, 1,4: 19 pp., Ponta Delgada.
- (1947): Fisiografia e geotectonica da regiao de Vila Franca do Campo. - Insulana, 3: 15 pp., Ponta Delgada.
- (1953): Os sismos de 26 de Junho de 1592 e a sismicidade da ilha de S. Miguel. - Mem. Serv. Meteor. Nac., 18: 9 pp., Lisbon.
- (1955): Modelo hipotetico do mecanismo interessando a ilha de S. Miguel. - Bol. Ord. Engen., 4,116: 9 pp., Lisbon.
- (1956): Analysis and interpretation of a transitory geomagnetic anomaly in the secular variation in the Iberian Peninsula and N. Atlantic. - Serv. Meteor. Nac., 301,82, Lisbon.
- (1957): A convective system in the mantle between the NE of Africa and the Azores. - Comm. Assoc. I. U. G. G., Toronto.
- (1959): A crustal deforming agent and the mechanism of the volcanic activity in the Azores. - Bull. Volcan., 21: 95-102, Naples.
MENEZES, A. L. (1952-53): Le Portugal Hydromineral. - Dir. Gen. Minas e Serv. Geol., 2 vols., Lisbon.
MENEZES, A. L. & NARCISO, A. (1940): Relatorio da vista de inspecçao em 1938 as nascentes de aguas minero-medicinais da ilha de S. Miguel, Açores ... - Publ. Dir. Gen. Minas e Serv. Geol.: 135-162, Lisbon.
MENEZES, M. (1927): A agua do Carrapacho. - A Uniao, 9669, 9724, 9725, 9740.
MENSCHING, H. (1954): Eine geographische Forschungsreise nach Nordafrika und zu den Kanarischen Inseln. - Erdk., 8: 212-217, Bonn.

MERTENS, R. (1942): *Lacerta goliath* n. sp., eine ausgestorbene Rieseneidechse von den Kanaren. - Senchenbergiana, **24**: 330–339, Frankfurt/Main.
MEUSEL, H. (1954): Reliktvegetation der Kanarischen Inseln in ihren Beziehungen sur süd- und mitteleuropäischen Flora. - In:M. GERSCH, Gesammelte Vorträge über moderne Probleme der Abstammungslehre, **I**, Jena.
MEYER, H. (1896): Die Insel Tenerife. - Leipzig.
MIDDLEMOST, E. A. K. (1970): San Miguel de la Palma. A volcanic island in section. - Bull. Volcan., **34**: 216–239, Naples.
– (1972): Evolution of La Palma, Canary Archipelago. - Contr. Miner. Petr., **36**: 33–48, Heidelberg.
MIGUEL, S. (1961): Los volcanes de La Palma. - El Museo Canario, **21**, Las Palmas.
MINGARRO, F. (1963): Contribucion al estudio geologico de la isla de Tenerife (Islas Canarias). - Not. y Com. Inst. Geol. Min. de Esp., **71**: 179–212, Madrid.
MIRANDA, R. (1947): Cabo Verde. A sismicidade do arquipelago nos anos de 1944–1945. - Mem. Not. Coimbra, **20**: 17 pp., Coimbra.
MITCHELL-THOMÉ, R. C. (1960): Estudo hidrogeologico do Arquipelago de Cabo Verde. - C. O. M. A. P. R. O., 11 vols. (roneo), Lisbon.
– (1964): The Sediments of the Cape Verde Archipelago. - Publ. Serv. Géol. Luxembourg, **14**: 229–251, Luxembourg.
– (1969): Etudes sur le relief structural et le relief tectonique dans les archipels macaronésiens. - Unpubl. Rept., 65 pp.
– (1972): Outline of the Geology of the Cape Verde Archipelago. - Geol. Rdsch., **61**,3: 1087–1109, Stuttgart.
– (1974): The Sedimentary Rocks of Macaronesia. - Geol. Rdsch., **63**: 1179–1216, Stuttgart.
– (in press): Groundwater Resources in the Cape Verde Archipelago. - Simp. Intern. Hidrol. Terr. Volcan., Lanzarote, Canary Islands, March, 1974. **V**.
MONIZ, A. C. (1883): Ilha Graciosa (Açores). Descripçao Historica e Topografica. - Angra.
MONTAGGIONI, L. (1968a): Recherches de la géologie marine et littorale dans l'archipel de Madère (Océan Atlantique). - Thesis, Lab. de Géol., Fac. Sci., Univ. Aix-Marseille, 204 pp., Marseille.
– (1968b): Conditions de sédimentation et de différentiation des associations minérales dans l'Archipel de Madère (Océan Atlantique). - C. R. Acad. Sci., **267**: 1258–1261, Paris.
– (1969):Sur la présence de Coraux profonds et de thanatocoenoses quaternaires dans l'Archipel de Madère (Océan Atlantique). - C. R. Acad. Sci., **268**: 3160–3163, Paris.
MONTORIOL, P. J. (1965): Contribucion al conocimiento mineralogico y mineralogenico de un nuevo tipo de yacimiento de yeso descubierto en los »tubos de lava« de la isla de Lanzarote (Canarias). - Bol. R. Soc. Esp. Hist. Nat., **63**: 77–85, Madrid.
MORAIS, J. C. (1939): A Ilha da Madeira. A estructura da montanha vulcanica. - Bol. Soc. Geogr., **57a**: 227–253, Lisbon.
– (1940): Arquipelago das Selvagens. - Mem. Not. Publ. Mus. Min. Geol. Univ. Coimbra, **2**: 1–39, Coimbra.
– (1943): A Ilha de Porto Santo e as suas rochas. - Mem. Not. Publ. Mus. Min. Geol. Univ. Coimbra, **12**: 1–48, Coimbra.
– (1945): O Arquipelago da Madeira. - Mem. Not. Publ. Mus. Min. Geol. Univ. Coimbra, **15**: 1–61, Coimbra.
– (1948): Os Arquipelagos da Madeira e Selvagens. - Bol. Soc. Geol. Portugal, **7**: 1–32, Porto.
– (1953): Furnas das Açores. - Mem. Not. Publ. Mus. Min. Geol. Univ. Coimbra, **35**: 48–75, Coimbra.
MORELET, A. (1860): Notice sur l'historie naturelle des Açores suivie d'une description des Mollusques terrestres de cet archipel. - 214 pp., Paris.
– (1873): Notice sur les coquilles rapportées par MM. BOUVIER et DE CESSAC des Iles du Cap-Vert. - J. Conchy., **13**: 231–243, Paris.
MOTTET, G. (1972): Observations géomorphologiques à l'île volcanique de Terceira (Açores). - Rev. Port. de Géogr., **7**: 199–255, Lisbon.
MOURA, A. R. (1961): Foraminiferos das areias de praia e dos calcarenitos da Ilha de Porto Santo. - Mem. Not. Fac. Cien. Univ. Lisboa, **51**: 63–82, Lisbon.
MÜGGE, O. (1883): Petrographische Untersuchungen an Gesteinen von den Azoren. - N. Jb. Miner. Geol. Pal., **2**: 189–244, Stuttgart.
MÜLLER, G. (1964): Frühdiagenetische allochthone Zementation mariner Küsten-Sande durch evaporitische Calcit-Ausscheidung im Gebiet der Kanarischen Inseln. - Beitr. Miner. Petr., **10**: 125–131.
MÜLLER, G. & TIETZ, G. (1966): Recent dolomitization of Quaternary biocalcarenites from Fuerteventura (Canary Islands). - Contr. Miner. Petr., **13**: 89–96, Heidelberg.

MÜLLER, W. (1930): Untersuchungen über das Grundgebirge der Insel La Gomera (Canaren). - Chemie d. Erde, **4**,3: 369–394, Jena.

MUNOZ, M. (1969): Estudio petrologico de las formaciones alcalinas de Fuerteventura (Islas Canarias). - Estud. Geol., **25**: 257–310, Madrid.

- (1970): Ring Complexes of Pajara in Fuerteventura. - Bull. Volcan., **33**: 840–861, Naples.

- (1973): Inclusiones maficas y ultramaficas en las formaciones volcanicas de la isla de Gran Canaria. - Estud. Geol., **29**: 113–129, Madrid.

NAVARRO, J. M. (1967): Estudio geologico de la hoja de Fasnia (Tenerife). - Unpubl., Madrid.

NAVARRO, J. M.; APARICIO, A. & GARCIA, L. (1969): Estudio de los depositos sedimentarios de Tafira a Las Palmas. - Estud. Geol., **25**: 235–248, Madrid.

NEIVA, J. M. C. (1940): Consideraçoes sobre o quimismo das formaçoes eruptivas do Arquipelago de Cabo Verde. - Publ. Mus. Lab. Min. Geol., **17**: 54 pp., Porto.

- (1946): Afinidades provinciais petrograficas entre Ilhas do Atlantico. - Bol. Soc. Geol. Portugal, **5**: 159–164, Porto.

NOBRE, A. (1894): Subsidos para a fauna malacologica do arquipelago do Cabo Verde. - An. Sci. Nat., **1**: 168–172, Lisbon.

- (1931): Molluscos terrestres, fluviais e das aguas salobras do Arqipelago da Madeira. - Inst. Zool., Univ. Porto, Porto.

- (1941): Fauna malacologica de Portugal. Molluscos terrestres e fluviais. - Mem. Est. Mus. Zool., Univ. Coimbra, **124**, Coimbra.

NOGALES, J. & SCHMINCKE, H.-U. (1969): El Pino Enterrado de la Canada de las Arenas (Gran Canaria). - Cuad. Bot. Canar., **V**: 23–25.

NÖGGERATH, J. (1861): Das Gediegen-Blei von Madeira. - N. Jb. Miner. Geol. Petrofact., **1861**: 129–133, Stuttgart.

ORTI, C.; ROSSO DE LUNA, I. & DUPUY DE LOME, E. (1955): Estudio de la hidrogeologia subterranea de la Caldera de Taburiente en la isla de La Palma. - Com. Reg. Hac. Argual y Tazacorte: 15 pp., La Palma.

ORTIZ, J. R. (1951): La erupcion del Nambroque en la Isla de La Palma. - Bol. Inst. Geol. Min. Esp., **63**: 3–163, Madrid.

OSANN, A. (1888): Über Sanidinite von Sao Miguel. - N. Jb. Miner. Geol. Paläont., **1888**,I: 117–130, Stuttgart.

OSUNA, M. (1897): El problema de la Atlantida y geologia de la region de Anaga (Islas Canarias). - Bol. Inst. Geogr. Argentina, **18**, Buenos Aires.

OVERSBY, V. M.; LANCELOT, J. & GAST, P. W. (1971): Isotopic composition of lead in volcanic rocks from Tenerife, Canary Islands. - J. Geophys. Res., **76**: 3402–3413, Washington.

PAEPE, P. & KLERKX, J. (1971): Peridotite Nodules in Nephelinites from Sal (Cape Verde Islands). - Ann. Soc. Géol. Belg., **41**: 311–316, Bruxelles.

PAEPE, P.; KLERKX, J.; HERTOGEN, J. & PLINKE, P. (1974): Oceanic Tholeiites on the Cape Verde Islands: Petrographical and Geochemical Evidence. - Earth Planet. Sci. Lett., **22**: 347–354, Amsterdam.

PAIVA, B. C. (1867): Monographia Molluscorum Terrestreum, Fluvialum, Lacustrium Insularum Maderensium. - Olissipone.

PARSONS, W. H. & MULFORD, J. W. (1959): Capelinhos Volcano, Fayal Island, Azores. - Cranbrook Inst. Sci., News Lett., **28**,2: 10–21, Bloomfield Hills, Mich.

PART, G. M. (1930): Report on rocks collected from St. Vincent, Cape Verde Islands. Rept. Geol. Coll. made during voyage of »Quest«. - Brit. Nat. Hist. Mus., Chap. **11**: 117–125, London.

- (1946): An Augitite from S. Vicente, Cape Verde Islands. - Geol. Mag., **83**: 241–242, Hertford, Herts.

- (1950a): Volcanic Rocks from the Cape Verde Islands. - Bull. Brit. Mus. (Nat. Hist.). Mineralogy, **1**,2: 27–72, London.

- (1950b): Occurrence of Nepheline-Monzonite and allied types in the Cape Verde Archipelago. - Geol. Mag., **87**: 421–426, Hertford, Herts.

- (1951): Tertiary and Pleistocene Sediments from the Cape Verde Archipelago. - Geol. Mag., **87**, Hertford, Herts.

PEREIRA, E. C. N. (1956): Ilhas de Zargo. - Ed. Cam. Municipal, **1**: 1–618; **2**: 619–1400, Funchal.

PERRET, F. A. (1914): The volcanic eruption of Tenerife in the autumn 1909. - Z. Vulk., **1**: 20–31, Berlin.

PREISWERK, H. (1909): Sodalittrachyt von Pico de Teide. - Cbl. Miner. Geol. Pal., **13**: 393–396, Stuttgart.

PRIOR, G. T. (1903): Contributions to the petrology of British East Africa. Comparison of volcanic rocks from Pantelleria, the Canary Islands, Ascension, St. Helena, Aden, and Abyssinia. - Miner. Mag., **13**: 222–263, London.

PUREZA, F. G. (1961): The sands of the beach of the island of Porto Santo. - Mem. Not. Fac. Cien. Univ. Lisboa, **51**: 25–34, Lisbon.

QUINTINO, J. (1962a): Levantomento geomagnetico da ilha de S. Miguel (Açores). - Serv. Meteor. Nac., RT **638**, GEO **19**, Lisbon.

- (1962b): Levantomento geomagnetico da ilha Terceira (Açores). - Serv. Meteor. Nac., RT **688**, GEO **34**, Lisbon.

- (1962c): Levantomento geomagnetico da ilha do Faial (Açores). - Serv. Meteor. Nac., RT **689**, GEO **35**, Lisbon.

- (1970): O sismo de 28 de Fevereiro de 1969. - Bol. Mus. Lab. Min. Geol., Fac. Cien., **11**: 265–292, Lisbon.

QUINTINO, J. D. S. (1966): Necessidades crescentes no consumo de energia. A exploraçao de novas fontes e suas disponibilidades nos Açores. - Bol. Distrito, **25**,2: 7–15, Junta Ger. Dist. Aut. Ponta Delgada.

RAYNAL, R. (1950): Volcans du Maroc et des Canaries. - Hesperis: 134–135.

RECK, H. (1927): Zur Deutung der vulkanischen Geschichte und der Calderabildung auf der Insel La Palma. - Z. Vulkan., **11**: 217–243, Berlin.

REINISCH, R. (1906): Gesteine der atlantischen Inseln St. Helena, Ascension, Sao Vicente (Kapverden) und Sao Miguel (Azoren). - Deutsche Südpolarexped. 1901–1903. **2** (Geographie und Geologie): 643–662, Berlin.

REISS, W. (1861): Die Diabas- und Laven-Formation der Insel Palma. - Kreidel: 1–75, Wiesbaden.

- (1862): Mitteilungen über die tertiären Schichten von Sta. Maria, der südlichsten der Azoren, und ihre organischen Einschlüsse. - N. Jb. Miner. Geogn. Geol. Petrefakt., **1862**: 1–22, Stuttgart.

RENARD, A. (1888): Notes sur les roches de Pico de Teyde (Tenerife). - Mém. Soc. Belge Géol., **67**, Bruxelles.

- (1889): Rocks of the Cape Verde Islands. »Challenger« Reports, Physics and Chemistry. - Rep. Sci. Res. Voy. »Challenger«, **2**,7: 13–23, London.

RIBEIRO, O. (1948): Notulas de geomorfologia Madeirense. - Bol. Soc. Geol. Portugal, **7**: 113–118, Porto.

- (1949): L'île de Madère. Etude géographique. - Congr. internat. Géogr., **24**: 1–177, Lisbon.

- (1954): A Ilha do Fogo e as Suas Erupçoes. - Junta Invest. Ultramar., Mém., Sér. Géogr. (2nd ed. 1960), **1**: 319 pp., Lisbon.

RIBEIRO, O. & BRITO, R. S. (1957–58): Primeira noticia da erupçao dos Capelinhos na ilha do Faial. - Naturalia, **2**: 192–224, Lisbon.

RIDLEY, W. I. (1967): Volcanoclastic rocks in Tenerife, Canary Islands. - Nature, **213**: 55–56, London.

- (1970a): Morphology of Quaternary Phonolite Lavas from Tenerife, Canary Islands. - Geol. Mag., **107**: 559–560, Hertford, Herts.

- (1970b): The Abundance of Rock Types on Tenerife, Canary Islands, and its Petrogenetic Significance. - Bull. Volcan., **34**: 196–204, Naples.

- (1970c): The Petrology of the Las Canadas Volcanoes, Tenerife, Canary Islands. - Contr. Miner. Petr., **26**: 124–160, Heidelberg.

- (1971): The origin of some collapse structures in the Canary Islands. - Geol. Mag., **108**: 477–484, Hertford, Herts.

- (1972): The Field Relations of the Las Canadas Volcanoes, Tenerife, Canary Islands. - Bull. Volcan., **35**: 318–334, Naples.

ROCHBRUNE, A. T. (1881): Matériaux pour la faune de l'Archipel du Cap Vert. - Nouv. Arch. Mus., **2**,IV: 215–340, Paris.

ROESER, H. A.; HINZ, K. & PLAUMANN, S. (1971): Continental margin structure in the Canaries. - Inst. Geol. Sci. Rept. **70**/16: 27–36, ICSU/SCOR Work. Part. 31, Symp. Cambridge, 1971. The Geology of the East Atlantic Continental Margin. Ed. by F. DELANY.

ROMARIZ, C. (1970): Litofacies do Arquipelago de Cabo Verde. II. Calcaritos dos Ilheus Rombos. - Garcia de Orta, **18**: 247–252, Lisbon.

ROMARIZ, C. & SERRALHEIRO, A. (1967): Litofacies do Arquipelago de Cabo Verde. I. Ilha de S. Vicente. - Garcia de Orta, **15**: 535–544, Lisbon.

ROMERO, J. (1951): La erupcion del Nambroque en la isla de La Palma. - Bol. Inst. Geol. Min. Esp., **63**: 3–164, Madrid.

RONA, P. (1969): Possible Salt Domes in the Deep Atlantic off Northwest Africa. - Nature, **224**,5215: 141–143, London.

- (1970a): Comparison of continental margins of Eastern North America at Cape Hatteras and North-western Africa at Cap Blanc. - Bull. Amer. Assoc. Petr. Geol., **54**: 129–157, Tulsa.

RONA, P.; BRAKL, J. & HEIRTZLER, J. R. (1970c): Magnetic Anomalies in the Northeast Atlantic between the Canary and Cape Verde Islands. - J. Geophys. Res., **75**,35: 7412-7420, Washington.

RONA, P. & NALWALK, A. J. (1970b): Post-Early Pliocene Unconformity on Fuerteventura, Canary Islands. - Bull. Geol. Soc. Amer., **81**: 2117-2122, Boulder, Colo.

ROTHE, P. (1964a): Zur geologischen Geschichte der Insel Gran Canaria. - Natur u. Mus., **94**,1: 1-9, Frankfurt/M.

- (1964b): Fossile Strausseneier auf Lanzarote. - Natur u. Mus., **94**,5: 175-187, Frankfurt/Main.

- (1966): Zum Alter des Vulkanismus auf den östlichen Kanaren. - Soc. Sci. Fenn., Comm. Phys.Math., **31**,13: 1-80, Helsinki.

- (1967a): Petrographische Untersuchungen an Basalten und Trachyandesiten. Ein Beitrag zur Vulkano-Stratigraphie von Lanzarote (Kanarische Inseln, Spanien). - N. Jb. Miner. Mh., **1967**,2/3: 71-84, Stuttgart.

- (1967b): Prävulkanische Sedimentgesteine auf Fuerteventura (Kanarische Inseln). - D. Naturwiss., **54**,14: 366-367, Berlin.

- (1968a): Mesozoische Flysch-Ablagerungen auf der Kanareninsel Fuerteventura. - Geol. Rdsch., **58**,1: 314-332, Stuttgart.

- (1968b): Dolomitization of Biocalcarenites of Late-Tertiary Age from Northern Lanzarote (Canary Islands). - In: Recent Developments in Carbonate Sedimentology in Central Europe, ed. by G. MÜLLER & G. M. FRIEDMAN, 38-45. Springer-Verlag, Berlin - Heidelberg - New York.

- (1968c): Ostkanaren gehörten zum afrikanischen Kontinent. - Umschau Wiss. Tech., **4**: 116-117, Frankfurt/Main.

- (1970): Aragonitic ›Algal Lapilli‹ from Lagoonal Environment (Lobos, Canary Islands). - J. Sediment. Petr., March: 497-499, Tulsa.

ROTHE, P. & SCHMINCKE, H.-U. (1968d): Contrasting Origins of the Eastern and Western Islands of the Canarian Archipelago. - Nature, **218**,5147: 1152-1154, London.

ROTHÉ, J. P. (1968): Seismicité de l'Atlantique Oriental et de la Méditerranée Occidentale. - Coll. Internat. Géol. Géophys. Sous-Marine, Villefranche-sur-Mer.

ROTHPLETZ, A. (1889): Das Thal von Orotava auf Tenerife. - Pet. Mitt., **35**: 237-251, Gotha.

ROTHPLETZ, A. & SIMONELLI, V. (1890): Die marinen Ablagerungen auf Gran Canaria. - Z. dt. geol. Ges., **42**: 677-736, Berlin.

- (1898): Die marinen Ablagerungen auf Gran Canaria. - Bol. Com. Mapa Geol. Esp., **23**: 1-83, Madrid.

ROUCH, M. J. (1946): Océanographie et climatologie des Iles Atlantides. - Mém. Soc. Biogéogr., **8**: 41-57, Paris.

ROVERTO, G. (1927): Dal Pico del Teide alla Caldera die Taburiente. - L'Universo, **VIII**,1: 1-42.

RUTTE, E. (1958): Kalkkrusten in Spanien. - N. Jb. Geol. Paläont. Abh., **106**: 52-138, Stuttgart.

SAGREDO, J. (1969): Origen de las inclusiones de dunitas y otras rocas ultramaficas en las rocas volcanicas de Lanzarote y Fuerteventura. - Estud. Geol., **25**: 189-233, Madrid.

SAINTE CLAIRE DEVILLE, C. (1846a): Géologie de Tenerife et Fogo (Cap Vert.) J. Univ. Sci., **1**, Paris.

- (1846b): Observations sur l'Ile de Tenerife. - Bull. Soc. Géol. France, **2**,3, Paris.

- (1848a): Voyage géologique aux Antilles et aux Ténérife et Fogo. - Gide et Boudry, Paris.

- (1848b): Etude géologique sur les îles de Tenerife et de Fogo. - J. Univ. Sci., **1**, Paris.

- (1867): Récit de l'éruption sous-marine qui eut lieu Ier Juin 1867 entre les îles Terceira et Graciosa aux Açores. - C. R. Acad. Sci., **65**: 662-668, Paris.

SALDANHA, L. (1946-48): Cartas de Cabo Verde. - Rev. ›O Rosario‹: 81-91, Lisbon.

SAN MIGUEL DE LA CAMARA, M.; FUSTER, J. M. & MARTEL, M. (1952): Las erupciones y materiales arrojados por ellos en la Isla de La Palma, Junio-Julio de 1949. - Bull. Volcan. **12**: 145-163, Naples.

SANTIAGO, M. (1960): Los volcanes de La Palma. - El Museo Canario, **75-76**: 281-346, Las Palmas.

SAPPER, K. (1906a): Kanarische Inseln. - Geogr. Z., **12**: 481, Leipzig.

- (1906b): Beiträge zur Kenntnis von Palma und Lanzarote. - Pet. Mitt., **52**: 143-153, Gotha.

- (1927): Vulkankunde. - Stuttgart.

SARMENTO, A. A. (1903): As Desertas. - Typ. Camoes, Funchal.

- (1906): As Selvagens. - Heralde da Madeira, Funchal.

SAUCIER, H. (1964-65): A propos du problème des Caldeiras. Observations dans l'île Graciosa (Açores). - Comun. Serv. Geol. Portugal, **48**: 213-246, Lisbon.

SAUCIER, H. & ROCHE, A. (1965): Etude paléomagnetique des laves de Faial et de Graciosa. - Comm. Serv. Geol. Portugal, **48**: 255-263, Lisbon.

SAUER, E. G. F. & ROTHE, P. (1972): Ratite Eggshells from Lanzarote, Canary Islands. - Science, **176**: 43-45, Washington.

SAUER, G. A. (1876): Untersuchungen über phonolithische Gesteine der Kanarischen Inseln. - Z. ges. Naturwiss., **13**: Halle.

SCHMINCKE, H.-U. (1967a): Mid-Pliocene Fossil Wood from Gran Canaria. Preliminary Note. – Cuad. de Botan., **11**: 19–20.
- (1967c): Cone sheet swarm, resurgence of Tejeda Caldera and the early Geologic History of Gran Canaria. – Bull. Volcan., **31**: 153–162, Naples.
- (1968a): Faulting versus erosion and the reconstruction of the mid-miocene shield volcano of Gran Canaria, Canary Islands. – Geol. Mitt., **8**: 23–50, Aachen.
- (1968b): Pliozäne subtropische Vegetation auf Gran Canaria. – **55**,4: 185–186, Berlin.
- (1968c): The geologic framework and origin of alkali trachytic to alkali rhyolitic ignimbrites on Gran Canaria. – Internat. Symp. Volcan., Spain-Canary Islands. Abstracts.
- (1969): Ignimbrite sequence on Gran Canaria. – Bull. Volcan., **33**: 1199–1219, Naples.
- (1971a): Tektonische Elemente auf Gran Canaria. – N. Jb. Geol. Paläont. Mh., **1971**,11: 697–700, Stuttgart.
- (1971b): Comments on paper by E. BOSSHARD & D. J. MACFARLANE »Crustal Structure of the Western Canary Islands from Seismic Refraction and Gravity Data«. – J. Geophys. Res., **76**,29: 7304–7305, Washington.
- (1973): Magmatic Evolution and Tectonic Regime in the Canary, Madeira and Azores Island Groups. – Bull. Geol. Soc. Amer., **84**: 633–648, Boulder, Colo.
SCHMINCKE, H.-U. & SWANSON, D. A. (1966): Eine alte Caldera auf Gran Canaria? (Vorläufige Mitteilung). – N. Jb. Geol. Paläont. Mh., **1966**,5: 260–269, Stuttgart.
- (1967b): Laminar viscous flowage structures in ash-flow tuffs from Gran Canaria, Canary Islands. – J. Geol., **75**,6: 641–664, Chicago.
- (1967d): Ignimbrite Origin of Eutaxites from Tenerife, Canary Islands. – N. Jb. Geol. Paläont. Mh., **1967**,11: 700–703, Stuttgart.
SCHMINCKE, H.-U. & WEIBEL, M. (1972): Chemical study of rocks from Madeira, Porto Santo, and Sao Miguel, Terceira, (Azores). – N. Jb. Miner. Abh., **117**,3: 253–281, Stuttgart.
SCHMITZ, E. (1901): Les îles »Salvages«. – Le Cosmos, Rev. Sci. Appl., **45**: 741–745, Paris.
SCHOTT, G. (1942): Geographie des Atlantischen Ozean. – 438 pp., Boysen, Hamburg.
SCHULTZE, H. (1908): Über ein Sediment auf Tenerife (Canaren). – Z. dt. geol. Ges., **60**: 243–246, Berlin.
SCHWARZBACH, M. (1964): Edaphisch bedingte Wüsten. Mit Beispielen aus Island, Teneriffa und Hawaii. – Z. Geomorph., **8**,4: 440–452, Berlin.
SCHWEIZER, A. (1853–55): Über Kalke von Madeira. – Mitt. naturf. Ges., **3**: 421–430, Zurich.
SCOFIELD, J. (1958): A New Volcano bursts from the Atlantic. – Nat. Geogr. Mag., **113**,6: 735–757, Washington.
SENFT, F. (1872): Diabasartiges Gestein von der Ribeira de Maçampes auf Madeira. – N. Jb. Min. Geol. Pal., Stuttgart.
SERRALHEIRO, A. (1966): Contribuçao para o Conhecimento Geologico da Ilha de S. Vicente (Cabo Verde). – Garcia de Orta, **14**: 139–152, Lisbon.
- (1967): Sobre as praias antigas de alguns ilhas de Cabo Verde. – Garcia de Orta, **15**: 123–138, Lisbon.
- (1968): Formaçoes sedimentares do Arquipelago de Cabo Verde. – Junta Invest. Ultramar.: 7–22, Lisbon.
- (1970): Geologia da ilha de Maio (Cabo Verde). – Junta Invest. Ultramar.: 103 pp., Lisbon.
- (1971): A Achadinha da Praia (Cabo Verde). Um caso tipico de inversao de relevo vulcanico. – Garcia de Orta, **19**: 279–288, Lisbon.
SERUGHETTI, J. & ROCHE, A. (1968): Etude paléomagnetique des laves de l'île de Flores.
SILVA, G. H. (1956a): Contribution à la connaissance de la faune fossile de l'île de Porto Santo. – Rev. Fac. Cien. Univ. Coimbra, **25**: 5–7, Coimbra.
- (1956b): Gastropodes terrestres fosseis do Quaternario da Ilha de Porto Santo... – Mem. Not. Publ. Mus. Lab. Min. Geol., Univ. Coimbra, **41**: 40–43, Coimbra.
- (1957a): Descriçao de gastropodes terrestres fosseis do Quaternario da Ilha de Porto Santo. – Mem. Not. Publ. Mus. Lab. Min. Geol. Univ. Coimbra, **44**: 10–31, Coimbra.
- (1957b): Nota sobre alguns gastropodes terrestres fosseis das Ilhas da Madeira e Selvagens. – Mem. Not. Publ. Mus. Lab. Min. Geol. Univ. Coimbra, **44**: 33–43, Coimbra.
- (1959a): Elementos para o conhecimento da fauna fossil do Quaternario da Ilha de Porto Santo. – Mem. Not. Publ. Mus. Lab. Min. Geol. Univ. Coimbra, **46**: 1–9, Coimbra.
- (1959b): Fosseis do miocenico marinha da Ilha de Porto Santo. – Mem. Not. Publ. Mus. Lab. Min. Geol. Univ. Coimbra, **48**: 1–22, Coimbra.
SIMONY, O. (1892a): Über eine naturwissenschaftliche Reise nach der westlichen Gruppe der Canarischen Inseln. – Mitt. Geogr. Ges., **33**: 325, Vienna.
- (1892b): Canarische Inseln, insbesondere Lanzarote und die Isletas. – Schr. Ver. Verbreit. naturwiss. Kenntn., **32**: 325–398, Vienna.

SMITH, J. (1840): On the Geology of Madeira. – Proc. Geol. Soc., **3**, London.
SMULIKOWSKI, K. (1933): Sur quelques laves des îles Canaries. – Mém. XIVe Congr. Méd. Nat. Polon.: 233–236, Poznan.
– (1937): Sur l'anorthose de Pico de Teide. – Arch. Min. Soc. Sci. Let., **13**: 31–51, Warsaw.
SMULIKOWSKI, K.; POLANSKI, A. & TOMKIEWICZ, M. (1946): Contribution à la pétrographie des îles Canaries. – Arch. Min. Soc. Sci. Let., **15**: 57–145, Warsaw.
SOARES, J. M. P. (1944–47): A Proposito dos »Aptychi« da Ilha de Maio (Arquipelago de Cabo Verde). – Bol. Soc. Port. Cien. Nat., **15**,1–4: 101–108, Lisbon.
– (1948): Observations géologiques sur les îles du Cap Vert. – Bull. Soc. Géol. France, **18**: 383–389, Paris.
– (1950): Breve historia geologica do Arquipelago de Cabo Verde. – Conf. Internat. Afr. Ocid., Bissau, 1947, **1**: 79–84, Lisbon.
– (1951): »Aptychi« da Ilha de Maio (Arquipelago de Cabo Verde). – Conf. Internat. Afr. Ocid., Bissau, 1947, **3**: 134–138, Lisbon.
– (1952): A proposito da stratigrafia da Ilha de Maio. – An. Fac. Cien. Univ. Porto, **36**: 26–35, Porto.
– (1953): A proposito dos »Aptychi« da Ilha de Maio (Arquipelago de Cabo Verde). – Junta Miss. Geogr. e Invest. Ultramar.: 111 pp., Lisbon.
– (1958a): Description d'une faunule de Pectinidés des Iles de Santiago et de Sao Nicolau (Archipel du Cap Vert). – Conf. Internat. Afr. Ocid., S. Tomé, 1956, **2**: 271–303, Lisbon.
– (1958b): Sobre alguns exemplares de Turritelas fosseis da Ilha de Sao Nicolau (Arqhipelago de Cabo Verde). – Conf. Internat. Afr. Ocid., S. Tomé, 1956, **2**: 307–328, Lisbon.
STAHLECKER, R. (1934): Neocom auf der Kapverden-Insel Maio. – N. Jb. Miner. Geol. Paläont., Beil.Bd., Abt. B, **73**: 265–301, Stuttgart.
STÜBEL, A. (1865): Cabo Girao und Camara de Lobos auf Madeira. – Isis.
– (1910): Die Insel Madeira. – Leipzig.
TACQUIN, A. (1902–03): Les Pluies de Sable aux Canaries. – Bull. Soc. Géol. Belge, **16**: 540–541, Bruxelles.
TAUSCH, L. (1884): Die von Prof. DOELTER auf den Capverden gesammelten Conchylien. – Jhb. Mal. Ges., **11**: 181–198.
TAZIEFF, H. (1957): L'activité du volcanisme sous-marin: Quand une île surgit de la mer. – Sci. et Avenir, **130**: 618–622, Paris.
– (1958): L'Eruption 1957–58 et la Tectonique de Faial (Açores). – Bull. Soc. belge Géol., **67**: 13–49, Bruxelles.
– (1959): L'éruption sous-marin de Faial (1957–58). – Nature (France), **3288**: 145–151, Paris.
TEIXEIRA, C. (1950a): Notas sobre a Geologia das Ilhas Atlantidas. – An. Fac. Cien. Univ. Porto, **33**: 193–233, Porto.
– (1950b): A propos d'une hypothèse sur la structure de l'Océan Atlantique. – Mus. Lab. Min. Geol. Univ. Lisboa, **18**: 11 pp., Lisbon.
TERAN, M. (1963): Quelques aspects de la Géographie des Iles Canaries. – Rev. Géogr., **38**: 165–204, Lyon.
TINKLER, K. J. (1966): Volcanic Chronology of Lanzarote (Canary Islands). – Nature, **209**,5028: 1122–1123, London.
TORRES, A. S. (1927): Notas para o estudo da fauna fossil do Arquipelago de Cabo Verde. – Bol. Ag. Ger. Colon., **25**: 185–187, Lisbon.
– (1932): Notas para o estudo da fauna fossil do Arquipelago de Cabo Verde. – Comun. Serv. Geol. Portugal, **18**: 185, Lisbon.
TORRES, A. S. & SOARES, J. M. P. (1946): Formaçoes sedimentares do Arquipelago de Cabo Verde. I. Actualizaçao de conhecimentos. – Minist. Colon., Junta Miss. Geogr. Invest. Colon., Mém., Sér. Geol. **III**, 397 pp., Lisbon.
– (1950): A idade dos sedimentos do Arquipelago de Cabo Verde. – Conf. Internat. Afric. Occid., Bissau, 1947, **2**: 85–92, Lisbon.
TRAUTH, F. (1936): Die Laevilamellaptychi des Oberjura und der Unterkreide. – Ann. Natur. Hist. Mus., **47**: 127–145, Vienna.
– (1938): Die Lamellaptychen des Oberjura und der Unterkreide. – Palaeontographica, **88**: 115–229, Stuttgart.
TRICART, J. (1960): Observations géomorphologiques dans le Nord de l'île du Sal (Cap-Vert). – Bull. Inst. franç. Afr. Noire, **22**,4: 1127–1152.
VUAGNAT, M. (1960): Sur les laves en coussin des environs de Las Palmas, Grande Canarie. – Arch. Sci., **13**,1: 153–157, Geneva.
– (1961): Sur la présence de laves sous-marines dans le soubassement de la Caldera de Taburiente La Palma (Canaries). – Arch. Sci., **14**,1: 143–148, Geneva.

WALKER, G. P. L. & CROSSDALE, R. (1971): Two plinian-type eruptions in the Azores. – J. Geol. Soc., 127: 17–55, London.

WALTER, O. (1894): Petrographische Studien an Gesteinen der Insel Hierro. – Diss., Univ. Halle. Geognostische Aufzeichnungen über die Inseln von K. VON FRITSCH. 125 pp., Faber, Magdeburg.

WATKINS, N. D. (1973): Palaeomagnetism of the Canary Islands and Madeira. – Geophys. J., Roy. Astron. Soc., 32: 249–267, London.

WATKINS, N. D. & ABDEL-MONEM, A. (1971): Detection of the Gilsa geomagnetic polarity event on the Island of Madeira. – Bull. Geol. Soc. Amer., 82: 191–198, Boulder, Colo.

WATKINS, N. D.; ABDEL-MONEM, A. & GAST, P. W. (1968b): Magneto-stratigraphic mapping of Tenerife. – Internat. Symp. Volcan., Abstracts. Spain-Canary Islands.

WATKINS, N. D.; RICHARDSON, A. & MASON, R. G. (1966a): Palaeomagnetism of the Macaronesian Insular Region: The Canary Islands. – Earth Planet. Sci. Lett., 1: 225–231, Amsterdam.

– (1966b): Palaeomagnetism of the Macaronesian Insular Region: Madeira. – Earth Planet. Sci. Lett., 1: 471–475, Amsterdam.

– (1968a): Palaeomagnetism of the Macaronesian Insular Region: The Cape Verde Islands. – Geophys. J., Roy. Astron. Soc., 16: 119–140, London.

WATSON, B. B. (1878): On some Marine Mollusca from Madeira, including a new genus of the Muricidae, a new *Eulima* and the whole of the Rissoae of the Group of Islands. – Proc. Zool. Soc., London.

WEBB, P. B. & BERTHOLET, S. (1939): Histoire naturelle des Iles Canaries. 4 vols. Vol. 2, Géologie. – Béthune, Ed., Paris.

WEBSTER, J. W. (1821): A description of the Island of St. Michael. – Boston.

WENK, E. & TROMMSDORFF, V. (1965): Etude optique de quelques plagioclases dans les basaltes à olivine de la Caldeira de Graciosa. – Comun. Serv. Geol. Portugal, 48: 247–253, Lisbon.

WERWECKE, L. (1879a): Limburgit von La Palma. – N. Jb. Miner. Geol. Paläont., 1879: 481–485, Stuttgart.

– (1879b): Beitrag zur Kenntnis der Gesteine der Insel Palma. – N. Jb. Miner. Geol. Paläont., 1879: 815–831, Stuttgart.

WESTON, F. S. (1964): List of recorded volcanic eruptions in the Azores, with brief reports. – Bol. Mus. Lab. Geol. Fac. Cien. Univ. Lisboa, 10: 3–18, Lisbon.

WOLFF, F. VON (1914): Der Vulkanismus. I. Allgemeiner Teil. – 221 pp., Stuttgart.

– (1931): Der Vulkanismus. II. Spezieller Teil. 1. Lief., Der Atlantische Ozean. – 829–1111, Stuttgart.

WOLLASTON, T. V. (1878): *Testacea Atlantica*, or the land and freshwater shells of the Azores, Madeiras, Salvages, Canaries Cape Verdes and St. Helena. – London.

WUST, G. (1940a): Das Relief des Azorensockels und des Meeresbodens nördlich und nordwestlich der Azoren. – Am. d. Hydrog. Marit. Meteorol., 8, Berlin.

– (1940b): Das submarine Relief bei den Azoren. – In: DEFANT, Bericht über die ozeanographischen Untersuchungen. – Abh. Preuss. Akad. Wiss., Berlin.

ZBYSZEWSKI, G. (1954): Le volcan de Furnas dans l'île de S. Miguel (Açores). – C. R. 19th Congr. Internat. Géol., 15,17: 139–151, Algiers.

– (1957): Esboço Geologico da Ilha de S. Miguel. Exposiçao documental das actividades distritais Roteiro e notas explicativas. 4–9, Ponta Delgada.

– (1959a): Alguns casos practicos de utilidade da geologica no estudo da ilha de S. Miguel (Açores). – Mem. Acad. Cien., 8: 1–15, Lisbon.

– (1960): L'éruption du Volcan de Capelinhos (Ile de Faial, Açores). – Bull. Volcan., 23: 77–100, Naples.

– (1961a): Etude géologique de l'île de S. Miguel (Açores). – Comun. Serv. Geol. Portugal, 45: 5–79, Lisbon.

– (1961b): L'éruption du volcan des Capelinhos dans l'île de Faial (Açores). – 21st Internat. Geol. Congr., 26: 108–115, Copenhagen.

– (1962a): A erupçao do vulcao dos Capelinhos no quadro da estrutura da ilha do Faial (Açores). – Mem. Acad. Cien., 8: 3–17, Lisbon.

– (1962b): Contribution à la connaissance de la Géologie du District de Ponta Delgada (Açores). – Estud. Cien. Homen. ao Prof. Dr. J. CARRINGTON DA COSTA. Junta Invest. Ultramar.: 665–709, Lisbon.

– (1963a): Les phénomènes volcaniques modernes dans l'Archipel des Açores. – Comun. Serv. Geol. Portugal, 47: 231 pp., Lisbon.

– (1964): Contribuçao para o conhecimento da geologia da Ilha do Pico (Açores). – Mem. Acad. Cien., 9: 3–13, Lisbon.

ZBYSZEWSKI, G. (1966): Reconhecimento geologico da ilha das Flores (Açores). - Mem. Acad. Cien., 10: 171-188, Lisbon.
- (1966-67a): As observaçoes de F. FOUQUÉ sobre o vulcanismo dos Açores. - Bol. Nuc. Cult. da Horta, 4,2-3: 17-95, Horta, Faial.
- (1966-67b): Uma carta inedita de W. W. REISS a CARLOS RIBEIRO sobre os terrenos terciarios dos Açores e da Madeira. - Bol. Nuc. Cult. da Horta, 4,2-3: 43-53, Horta, Faial.
- (1968a): Levantamentos geologicos da ilha Terceira (Açores). - Mem. Acad. Cien., 12: 185-199, Lisbon.
- (1968b): Le volcanisme des îles de Flores et Corvo (Açores). - 23rd Internat. Geol. Congr., 2: 275-281, Prague.
- (1970a): Levantamentos geologicos da ilha Graciosa (Açores). - Mem. Acad. Cien., 14: 163-171, Lisbon.
- (1970b): As possibilidades de aproveitamento da energia geotermica nos Açores. - Bol. Minas, 7,3: 1-15, Lisbon.
- (1971a): Reconhecimento geologico da parte ocidental da ilha da Madeira. - Mem. Acad. Cien., 15: 7-23, Lisbon.
- (1972a): Levantamentos geologicos na parte oriental da ilha da Madeira e nas ilhas Desertas. - Mem. Acad. Cien., 16: 29-40, Lisbon.
ZBYSZEWSKI, G. & ALMEIDA, F. M. (1950): Os peixes miocenicos portugueses. - Com. Serv. Geol. Portugal, 31: 309-412, Lisbon.
ZBYSZEWSKI, G.; ALMEIDA, F. M.; FERREIRA, O. V. & ASSUNÇAO, C. F. T. (1958): Carta Geologica de Portugal na escale de 1:50,000. Noticia explicativa da folha B, S. Miguel (Açores). - Serv. Geol. Portugal, 37 pp., Lisbon.
- (1959d): Carta Geologica de Portugal na escala de 1:25,000. Noticia explicativa da folha Faial (Açores). - Serv. Geol. Portugal, 25 pp., Lisbon.
ZBYSZEWSKI, G.; FERREIRA, C. R. & FERREIRA, O. V. (1962c): Etude géologique de l'île de Pico (Açores). - Comun. Serv. Geol. Portugal, 46: 5-66, Lisbon.
ZBYSZEWSKI, G.; FERREIRA, C. R.; FERREIRA, O. V. & ASSUNÇAO, C. F. T. (1963b): Carta Geologica de Portugal na escale 1:50,000. Noticia explicativa da folha A, Ilha do Pico (Açores). - Serv. Geol. Portugal, 25 pp., Lisbon.
- (1963c): Carta Geologica de Portugal na escale 1:50,000. Noticia explicativa da folha B da Ilha do Pico (Açores). - Serv. Geol. Portugal, 21 pp., Lisbon.
ZBYSZEWSKI, G. & FERREIRA, O. V. (1959b): Le volcanisme de l'île de Faial. - Rapp. deuzième miss. géol., Mem. Serv. Geol. Portugal, 4: 29-55, Lisbon.
- (1961d): La faune marine des basses plages quaternaires de Praia et de Prainha dans l'île de Santa Maria (Açores). - Comun. Serv. Geol. Portugal, 45: 467-478, Lisbon.
- (1961e): A erupçao do Pico do Sapateiro e a Fonte do seculo XVI da Ribeira Seca (Ilha de S. Miguel, Açores). - Comun. Serv. Geol. Portugal, 45: 565-571, Lisbon.
- (1962d): La faune miocène de l'île de Santa Maria (Açores). - Comun. Serv. Geol. Portugal, 46: 247-289, Lisbon.
ZBYSZEWSKI, G.; FERREIRA, O. V. & ASSUNÇAO, C. F. T. (1959c): Carta Geologica da Portugal na escala de 1:50,000. Noticia explicativa da folha A, S. Miguel (Açores). - Serv. Geol. Portugal, 22 pp., Lisbon.
- (1961c): Carta Geologica de Portugal na escale 1:50,000. Noticia explicativa da folha de Ilha de Santa Maria (Açores). - Serv. Geol. Portugal, 28 pp., Lisbon.
ZBYSZEWSKI, G.; MEDIROS, A. C.; FERREIRA, O. V. & ASSUNÇAO, C. F. T. (1967): Carta Geologica de Portugal na escala 1:25,000. Noticia explicativa da folha Ilha do Corvo. - Serv. Geol. Portugal, 16 pp., Lisbon.
- (1968c): Carta Geologica de Portugal na escala de 1:25,000. Noticia explicativa da folha Ilha das Flores (Açores). - Serv. Geol. Portugal, 31 pp., Lisbon.
- (1971b): Carta Geologica de Portugal na escala de 1:50,000. Noticia explicativa da folha Ilha Terceira. - Serv. Geol. Portugal, 43 pp., Lisbon.
- (1972b): Carta Geologica de Portugal na escala de 1:25,000. Noticia explicativa da folha Ilha Graciosa (Açores). - Serv. Geol. Portugal, 31 pp., Lisbon.
- (1973): Carta Geologica de Portugal na escala de 1:50,000. Noticia explicativa da folha Ilhas Desertas. - Serv. Geol. Portugal, 19 pp., Lisbon.
ZEUNER, F. E. (1958): Lineas costeras del pleistoceno en las Islas Canarias. - An. Estud. Atlant., 4: 9-16, Madrid - Las Palmas.

# Addendum to Bibliography

Since the MS was sent to the press, the following publications have appeared corrected up until Juli, 1975:

AFONSO, A. (1974): Geological sketch and historic volcanoes in La Palma, Canary Islands. – Estud. Geol., Vol. Teneguia, 7–13, Madrid.

AMARAL, I. (1974): Alguns aspectos geomorfologicos do litoral da ilha de Santiago (Arquipelago de Cabo Verde). – Garcia de Orta, Ser. Geogr., 2, 1: 19–27, Lisbon.

ANGUITA, F. & APARICIO, A. (1973): Aglomerados tipo „Roque Nublo" en la isla de La Palma. – Estud. Geol., 29: 335–342, Madrid.

ANGUITA, F. & HERNAN, F. (1974): El modelo de fractura propagante comparado con el del punto caliente en las Islas Canarias. – Asam. Nac. Geod. y Geofis., Diciembre 1974, Madrid.
– (1975): A Propagating Fracture Model versus Hot Spot Origin for the Canary Islands. – Earth Planet. Sci. Lett., 27: 11–19, Amsterdam.

ANGUITA, F. & RAMIREZ DEL POZO, J. (1974): La datacion micropaleontologica de la Terraza de Las Palmas (Gran Canaria). – Estud. Geol., 30: 185–188, Madrid.

ARANA, V. & FUSTER, J. M. (1974): La erupcion del volcan Teneguia, La Palma, Islas Canarias. – Estud. Geol., Vol. Teneguia, 15–18, Madrid.

BARROS, L. A.; MATIAS, M. J. & MIRANDA, A. M. (1974): Preliminary note on the petrology of Madeira Island. – Bol. Mus. Lab. Min. Geol. Fac. Cien., Univ. Lisboa, 14 (1): 5–27, Lisbon.

BECK, R. H. & LEHNER, P. (1974): Oceans, new frontiers in exploration. – Bull. Amer. Assoc. petr. Geol., 58: 376–395, Tulsa.

BENNEL-BAKER, M.; SMEWING, J. D. & STILLMAN, C. J. (1974): The Basal Complex of Fuerteventura, Canary Islands. – Jour. Geol. Soc. (Abstr.), London.

BERNARD-GRIFFITH, J., CANTAGREL, J.-M., MATOS, C. A., MENDES, F., SERRALHEIRO, A. & MACEDO, J. R. (1975): Donnés radiométriques potassium-argon sur quelques formations magmatiques des îles du Cap Vert. – C. R. Acad. Sci., 280: 2429–2432, Paris.

BORLEY, G. D. (1974): Aspects of the Volcanic History and Petrology of the Island of Tenerife, Canary Islands. – Proc. Geol. Assoc., 85, 2: 259–279, London.

BRANDLE, J. L.; FERNANDEZ, S. & LOPEZ, J. (1974): Mineralgy of the materials from Teneguia volcano, La Palma, Canary Islands. – Estud. Geol., Vol. Teneguia, Madrid.

DILLON, W. P. & SOUGY, J. M. A. (1974): Geology of West Africa and Canary and Cape Verde Islands. – In: A. E. M. NAIRN & F. G. STEHLI (edit.), The Ocean Basins and Margins, 315–367. Plenum Press, New York.

FERNANDEZ, S.; HERNAN, F.; NAVARRO, L. F. & PLIEGO, D. (1974): Petrographic study of basaltic materials emitted by Teneguia volcano (La Palma, Canary Islands, Oct. 27 – Nov. 19, 1971). – Estud. geol., Vol. Teneguia, 27–33, Madrid.

GASTESI, P. (1973): Is the Betancuria Massif, Fuerteventura, Canary Islands, an uplifted piece of oceanic crust? – Nature Phys. Sci., 246: 102–104.

GRUNAU, H. R., LEHNER, P., CLEINTUAR, M. R., ALLENBACH, P. & BAKKER, G. (1975): New Radiometric Ages and Seismic Data from Fuerteventura (Canary Islands), Maio (Cape Verde Islands) and Sao Tome (Gulf of Guinea). – Progress in Geodynamics, Roy. Neth. Acad. Arts & Sci., 89–118, Amsterdam.

HERNANDEZ-PACHECO, A. (1973): Sobre el significado de las rocas granudas gaboides de los Complejos Basales de las islas de Fuerteventura, La Palma y La Gomera. – Estud. Geol., 29: 549–557, Madrid.

IBARROLA, E. (1974): Temporal modification of the basaltic materials from the 1971 eruption of the Teneguia volcano (La Palma, Canary Islands). – Estud. Geol., Vol. Teneguia, 49–58, Madrid.

IBARROLA, E. & MARTORELL, J. (1973): Melilitas olivinicas en Gran Canaria, derivadas de magmas basalticos alcalinos. – Estud. Geol., 29: 319–324, Madrid.

KLUG, H. (edit.) (1973): Beiträge zur Geographie der mittelatlantischen Inseln. – Schrift d. Geogr. Inst. d. Univ. Kiel, 39: 199 pp., Kiel.

LIETZ, J. (1975): Marines und terrestrisches Quartär auf Gran Canaria (Kanarische Inseln) und seine paläoklimatische Deutung. – N. Jb. Geol. Paläont. Abh., 150, H. 1: 73–91, Stuttgart.

LIETZ, J. & SCHMINCKE, H.-U. (1975): Miocene–Pliocene sea level changes and volcanic episodes on Gran Canaria (Canary Islands) in the light of new K-Ar ages. – Palaeogeol. Palaeoclim. Palaeoecol., **18**: 213–239, Amsterdam.

MACHADO, F. & PLIEGO, D. (1974): Rheology of the lava of Teneguia eruption (Island of La Palma, Canary Islands, 1971), – Estud. Geol., Vol. Teneguia, 35–40, Madrid.

MENDES, F. & VIALETTE, Y. (1974): Teneurs en K, Rb, Sr et composition isotopique du strontium d'échantillons provenant de l'éruption d'Octobre–Novembre 1971 aux Canaries. – Estud. Geol., Vol. Teneguia, 59–64, Madrid.

MÜLLER, C. & ROTHE, P. (1975): Nannoplankton contents in regard to Petrological Properties of Deep-Sea Sediments in the Canary and Cape Verde Areas. – Marine Geol., **19**: 259–273, Amsterdam.

MUNOZ, M. & SAGREDO, J. (1974): Clinopyroxenes as Geobarometric Indicators in Mafic and Ultramafic Rocks from Canary Islands. – Contr. Miner. & Petr., **44**: 139–147, Heidelberg.

MUNOZ, M.; SAGREDO, J. & AFONSO, A. (1974): Mafic and ultramafic inclusions in the eruption of Teneguia volcano (La Palma, Canary Islands). – Estud. Geol., Vol. Teneguia, 65–74, Madrid.

O'NION, R. K. & PANKHURST, R. J. (1974): Petrogenetic significance of isotope and trace element variations in volcanic rocks from the Mid-Atlantic. – Jour. Petrol., **15**: 603–634, London.

ROTHE, P. (1974): Canary Islands – Origin and Evolution. – Die Naturwiss., **61**, 12: 525–533, Heidelberg.

SCHMINCKE, H.-U. (1975): Volcanology of peralkaline silicic volcanic rocks. – Bull. Volcan., **38**, Naples.

– (1975): Geology of the Canary Islands. – In: G. KUNKEL (edit.), The Canary Islands. Monogr. Biol.

SCHMINCKE, H.-U.; BREY, G. & STAUDIGEL, H. (1974): Craters of phreatomagmatic origin on Gran Canaria, Canary Islands. – Naturwiss., **61**: 125, Heidelberg.

SCHMINCKE, H.-U. & FLOWER, M. J. F. (1974): Magmenevolution auf atlantischen Vulkaninseln? – Naturwiss. **61**: 288–297, Heidelberg.

SERRALHEIRO, A.; ALVES, C. A. M.; MACEDO, J. R. & SILVA, L. C. (1974): Note préliminaire sur la géologie de l'île de Boa Vista (Cap-Vert). – Garcia de Orta, Ser. Geol., **1**, 3: 53–60, Lisbon.

YOUNG, R. A. & HOLLISTER, C. D. (1974): Quaternary sedimentation on the Northwest African continental rise. – Jour. Geol., **82**: 675–689, Chicago.


Publications which came to the writer's attention after the completion of the MS include the following:

BENRELL, M. J. (1969): Ultrabasic and basic nodules from the Azores. – Proc. Geol. Soc., **1658**: 252–253, London.

BREY, G. (1973): Aufbau, Entstehung und Diagenese der Roque Nublo Brekzie, Gran Canaria. – Diplomarbeit, Ruhr-Univ., 70 pp., Bochum.

EGLOFF, J. (1972): Morphology of Ocean Basin seaward of NW Africa: Canary Islands to Monrovia, Liberia. – Bull. Amer. Assoc. Petr. Geol., **56**, 4: 694–706, Tulsa.

EVERS, A. M. J. (1964): Das Entstehungsproblem der makaronesischen Inseln und dessen Bedeutung für die Artentstehung; Entomol. Blätt., **60**: 81–87.

FRISCH, T. (1971): Alteration of chrome spinel in a dunite nodule from Lanzarote, Canary Islands. – Lithos, **4**: 83–91, Oslo.

GIERMANN, G. (1967): Vallées sous-marines sur la pente méridionale de l'île de Madère. – Bull. Inst. Océanogr. **67**, 1380, Monaco.

KRAUSE, D. C. (1965): East and West Azores Fracture Zones in the North Atlantic. – In: W. F. WHITTARD & R. BRADSHAW (edit.), Submarine Geology and Geophysics, 163–173. Butterworth, London.

LUYENDK, B. P. & BUNCE, E. T. (1973): Geophysical study of the northwest African margin off Morocco. – Deep Sea Res., **20**: 537–549, New York.

MÜLLER, J. (1969): Mineralogisch-sedimentpetrographische Untersuchungen an Karbonatsedimenten aus dem Schelfbereich um Fuerteventura und Lanzarote (Kanarische Inseln). – Diss., Univ. Heidelberg, 99 pp., Heidelberg.

356                           Addendum to Bibliography

ROMARIZ, C. (1971a): Notas petrograficas sobre rochas sedimentares portuguesas. XI. Os biocal-
caritos neriticos de S. Vicente (Ilha da Madeira). – Bol. Mus. Lab. Min. Geol., Fac. Cien., Univ.
Lisboa, **12**: 27–35, Lisbon.

– (1971b): Notes petrograficas sobre rochas sedimentares, portuguesas. XI. Calcaritos afanicos da
Ilha da Madeira. – Bol. Mus. Lab. Min. Geol., Fac. Cien., Univ. Lisboa, **12**: 55–65, Lisbon.

RONA, P. A. & FLEMING, H. S. (1973): Mesozoic plate motions in the eastern central North
Atlantic. – Marine Geol., **14**: 239–252, Amsterdam.

ROTHE, P. (1973): Sedimentation in the Deep-Sea areas adjacent to the Canary and Cape Verde
Islands. – Marine Geol., **14**: 191–206, Amsterdam.

SCHMINCKE, H.-U. (1969): Petrologie der phonolithischen bis rhyolithischen Vulkanite auf Gran
Canaria, Kanarische Inseln. – Habilitationsschr., Univ. Heidelberg, 151 pp., Heidelberg.

TIETZ, G. F. (1969): Mineralogische, sedimentpetrographische und chemische Untersuchungen an
quartären Kalkgesteinen Fuerteventuras (Kanarische Inseln). – Diss., Univ. Heidelberg,
150 pp., Heidelberg.

WIRTHMANN, A. (1970): Zur Klimageomorphologie von Madeira und anderen Atlantikinseln. –
Karlsruher Geogr., **2**: 56 pp., Karlsruhe.

# Subject Index

# Fossil and Biologic Index

# Locality Index

# Author Index